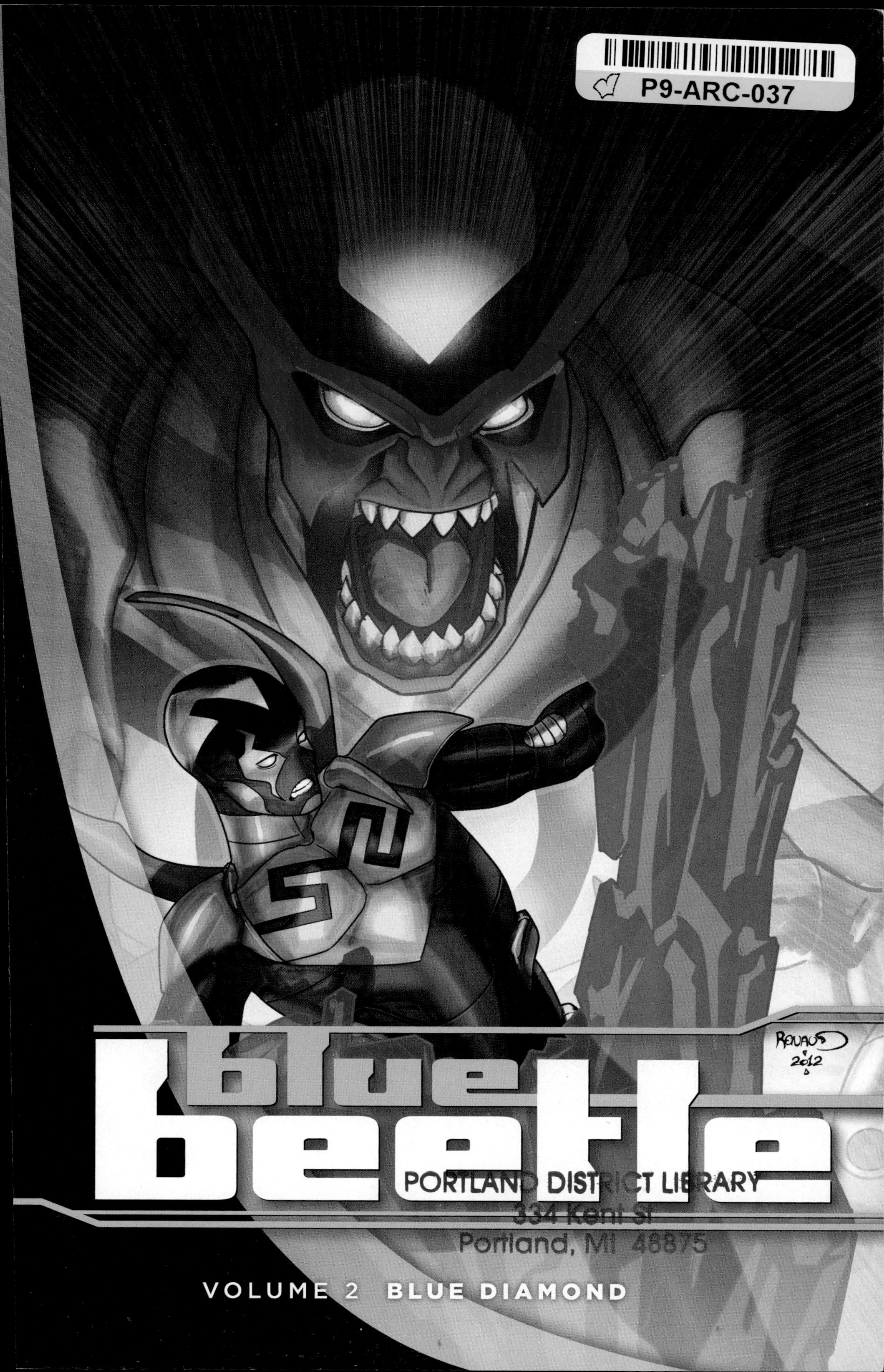

RENAUD 2012
blue beetle
VOLUME 2 BLUE DIAMOND

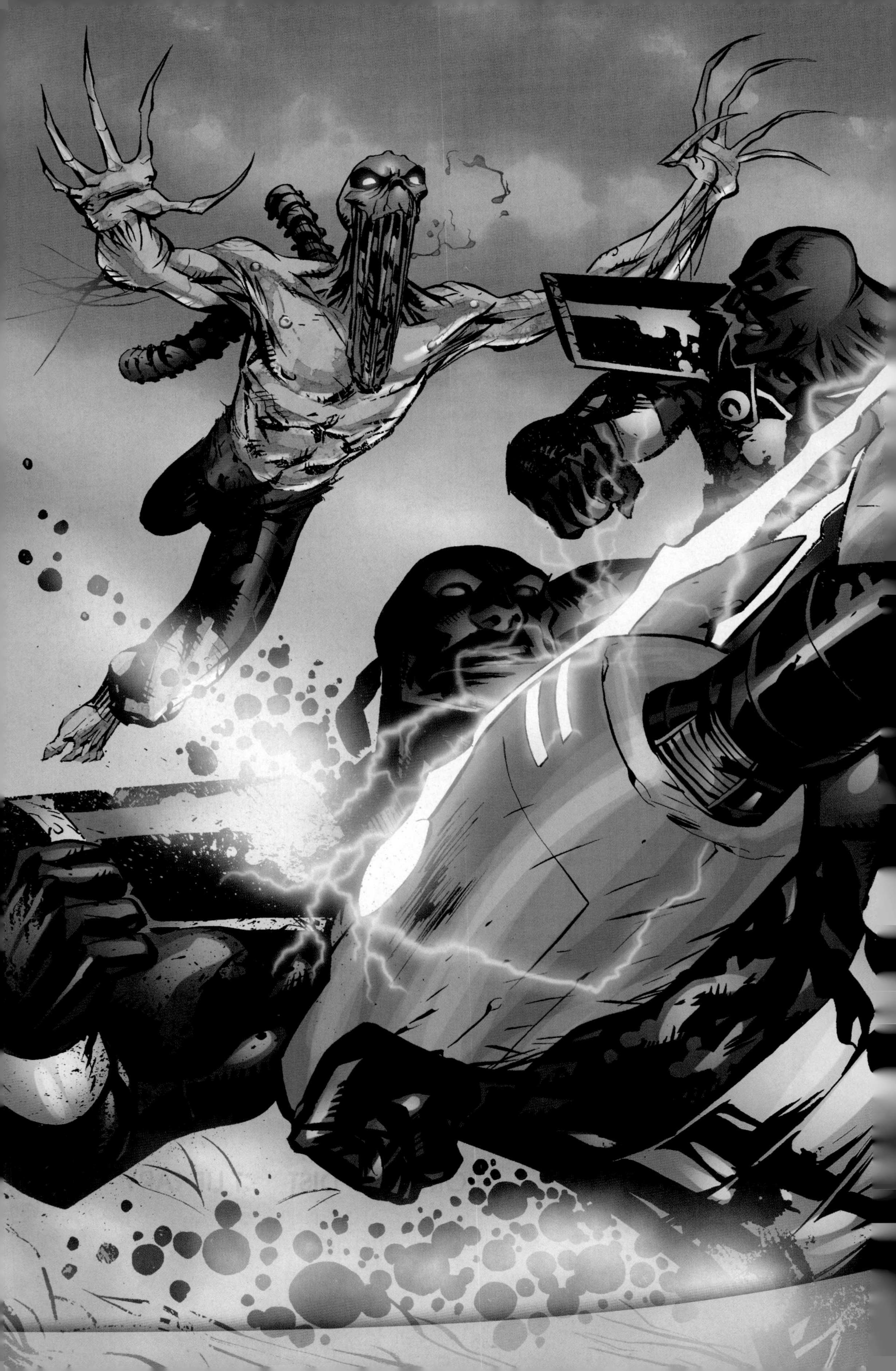

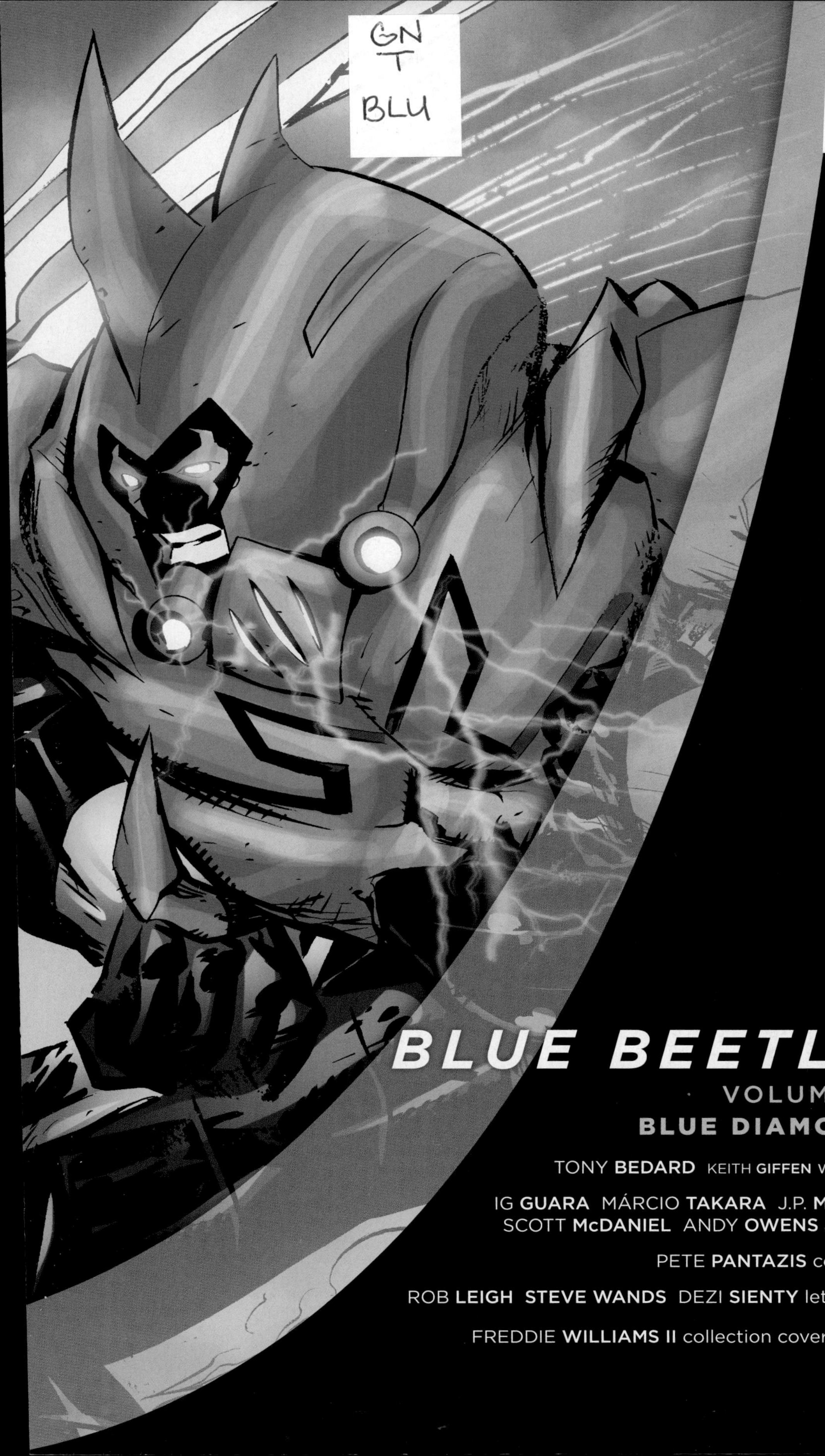

BLUE BEETLE

VOLUME 2
BLUE DIAMOND

TONY **BEDARD** KEITH **GIFFEN** writers

IG **GUARA** MÁRCIO **TAKARA** J.P. **MAYER**
SCOTT **McDANIEL** ANDY **OWENS** artists

PETE **PANTAZIS** colorist

ROB **LEIGH** **STEVE WANDS** DEZI **SIENTY** letterers

FREDDIE **WILLIAMS II** collection cover artist

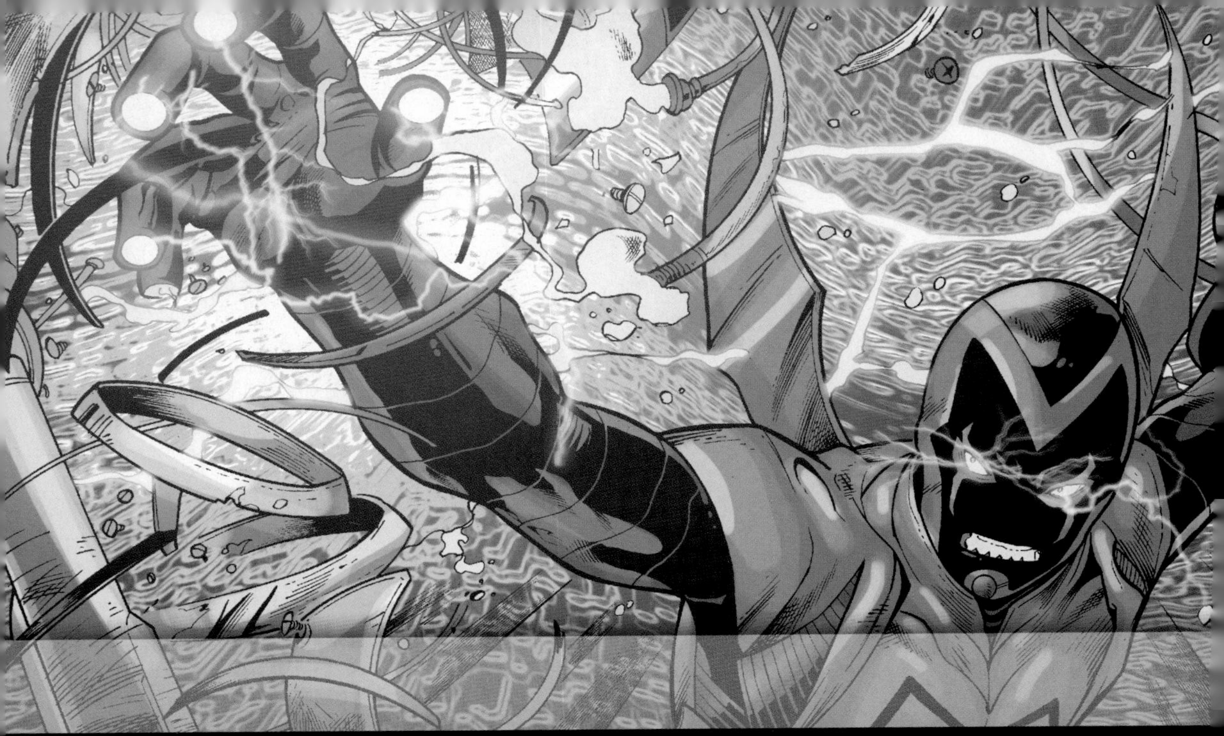

HARVEY RICHARDS PAT McCALLUM Editors – Original Series DARREN SHAN SEAN MACKIEWICZ Assistant Editors – Original Series
ROBIN WILDMAN Editor ROBBIN BROSTERMAN Design Director – Books
ROBBIE BIEDERMAN Publication Design

BOB HARRAS VP – Editor-in-Chief

DIANE NELSON President DAN DIDIO and JIM LEE Co-Publishers GEOFF JOHNS Chief Creative Officer
JOHN ROOD Executive VP – Sales, Marketing and Business Development AMY GENKINS Senior VP – Business and Legal Affairs
NAIRI GARDINER Senior VP – Finance JEFF BOISON VP – Publishing Operations MARK CHIARELLO VP – Art Direction and Design
JOHN CUNNINGHAM VP – Marketing TERRI CUNNINGHAM VP – Talent Relations and Services
ALISON GILL Senior VP – Manufacturing and Operations HANK KANALZ Senior VP – Digital
JAY KOGAN VP – Business and Legal Affairs, Publishing JACK MAHAN VP – Business Affairs, Talent
NICK NAPOLITANO VP – Manufacturing Administration SUE POHJA VP – Book Sales
COURTNEY SIMMONS Senior VP – Publicity BOB WAYNE Senior VP – Sales

BLUE BEETLE VOLUME 2: BLUE DIAMOND

DC Comics, 1700 Broadway, New York, NY 10019
A Warner Bros. Entertainment Company.
Printed by RR Donnelley, Salem, VA, USA. 3/22/13. First Printing.

ISBN: 978-1-4012-3850-6

Library of Congress Cataloging-in-Publication Data

Bedard, Tony.
Blue Beetle. Volume 2, Blue diamond / Tony Bedard, Ig Guara, Marcio Takara, J.P. Mayer.
p. cm.
"Originally published in single magazine form in Blue Beetle 0, 7-16."
ISBN 978-1-4012-3850-6
1. Graphic novels. I. Guara, Ig. II. Takara, Marcio. III. Mayer, J. P. IV. Title. V. Title: Blue diamond.
PN6728.B583B44 2012
741.5'973–dc23
2012040576

SUSTAINABLE FORESTRY INITIATIVE
Certified Chain of Custody
At Least 20% Certified Forest Content
www.sfiprogram.org
SFI-01042
APPLIES TO TEXT STOCK ONLY

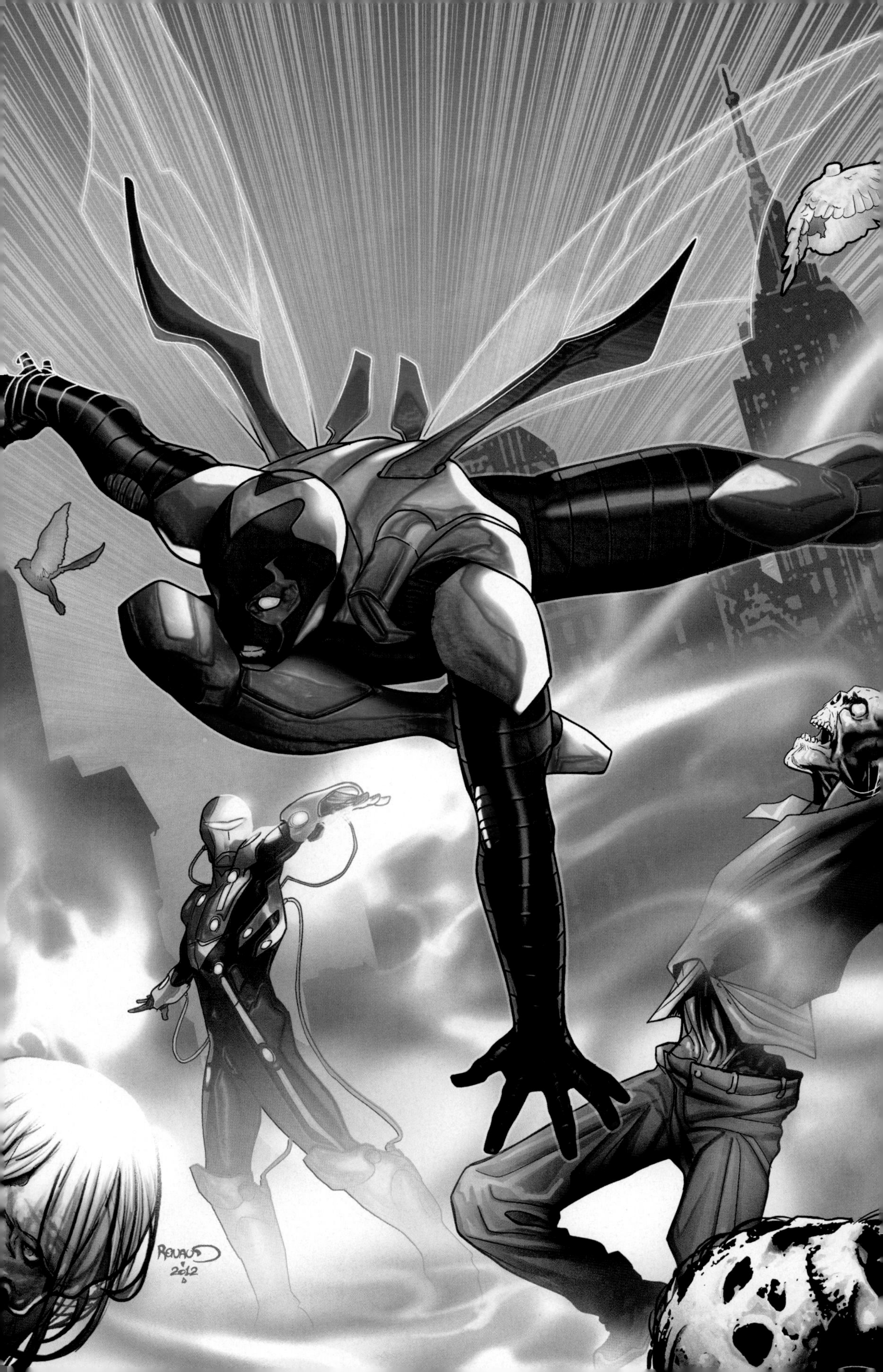
RENAUD
2012

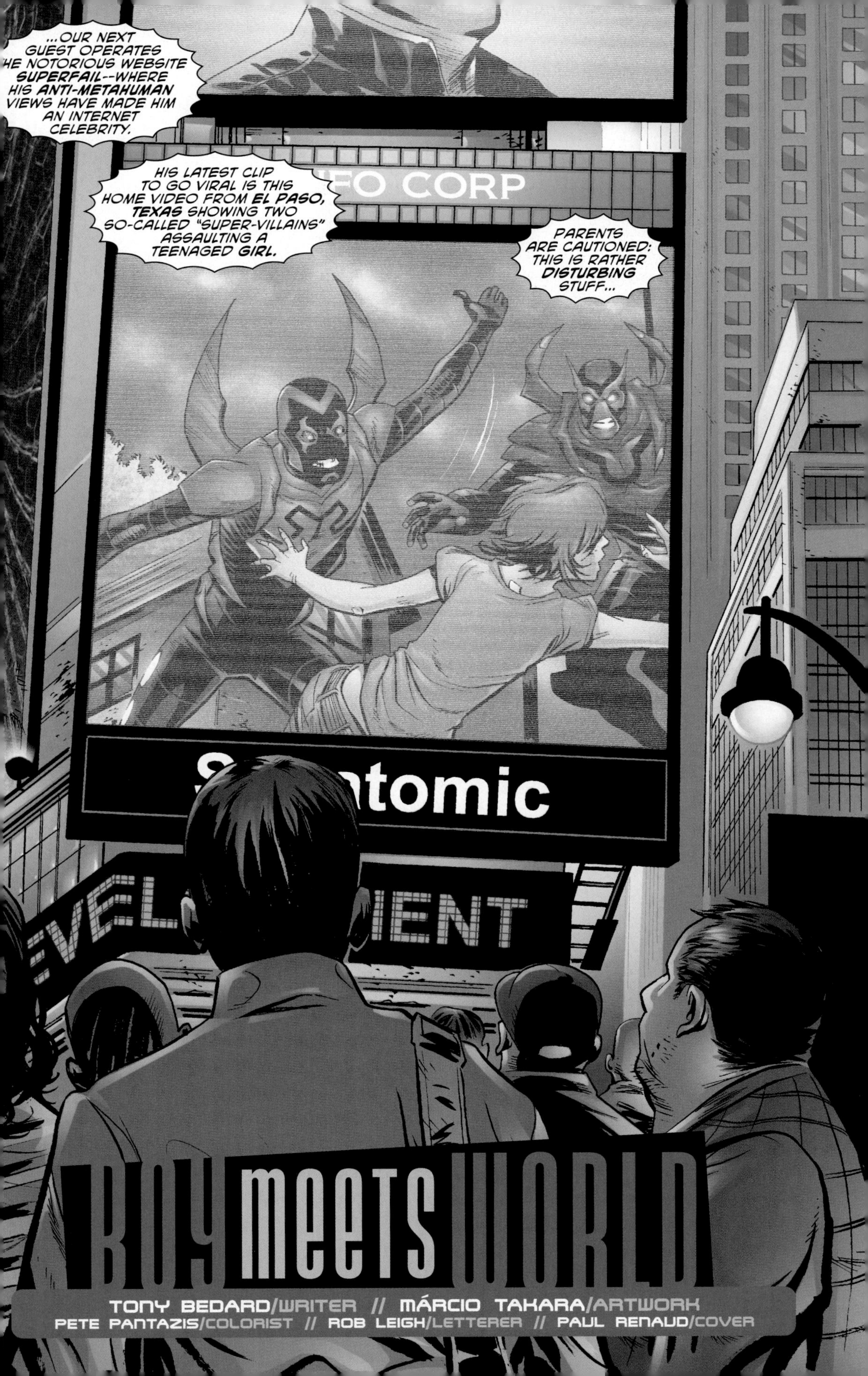
...OUR NEXT GUEST OPERATES HE NOTORIOUS WEBSITE SUPERFAIL--WHERE HIS ANTI-METAHUMAN VIEWS HAVE MADE HIM AN INTERNET CELEBRITY.
HIS LATEST CLIP TO GO VIRAL IS THIS HOME VIDEO FROM EL PASO, TEXAS SHOWING TWO SO-CALLED "SUPER-VILLAINS" ASSAULTING A TEENAGED GIRL.
PARENTS ARE CAUTIONED: THIS IS RATHER DISTURBING STUFF...
BOY meets WORLD
TONY BEDARD/WRITER // MÁRCIO TAKARA/ARTWORK
PETE PANTAZIS/COLORIST // ROB LEIGH/LETTERER // PAUL RENAUD/COVER

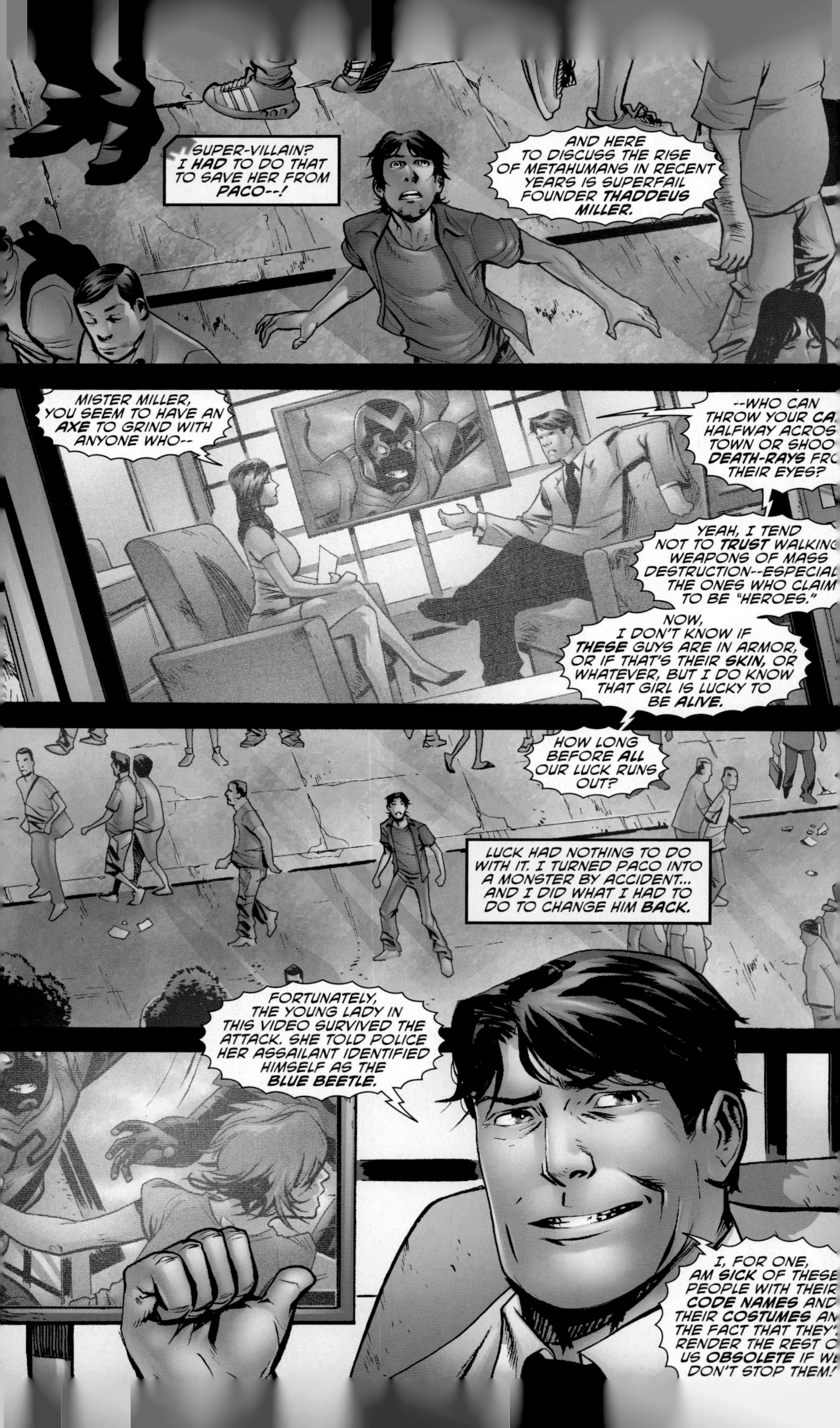
SUPER-VILLAIN? I HAD TO DO THAT TO SAVE HER FROM PACO--!
AND HERE TO DISCUSS THE RISE OF METAHUMANS IN RECENT YEARS IS SUPERFAIL FOUNDER THADDEUS MILLER.
MISTER MILLER, YOU SEEM TO HAVE AN AXE TO GRIND WITH ANYONE WHO--
--WHO CAN THROW YOUR CA HALFWAY ACROS TOWN OR SHOO DEATH-RAYS FRO THEIR EYES?
YEAH, I TEND NOT TO TRUST WALKING WEAPONS OF MASS DESTRUCTION--ESPECIAL THE ONES WHO CLAIM TO BE "HEROES."
NOW, I DON'T KNOW IF THESE GUYS ARE IN ARMOR, OR IF THAT'S THEIR SKIN, OR WHATEVER, BUT I DO KNOW THAT GIRL IS LUCKY TO BE ALIVE.
HOW LONG BEFORE ALL OUR LUCK RUNS OUT?
LUCK HAD NOTHING TO DO WITH IT. I TURNED PACO INTO A MONSTER BY ACCIDENT... AND I DID WHAT I HAD TO DO TO CHANGE HIM BACK.
FORTUNATELY, THE YOUNG LADY IN THIS VIDEO SURVIVED THE ATTACK. SHE TOLD POLICE HER ASSAILANT IDENTIFIED HIMSELF AS THE BLUE BEETLE.
I, FOR ONE, AM SICK OF THESE PEOPLE WITH THEIR CODE NAMES AND THEIR COSTUMES AN THE FACT THAT THEY' RENDER THE REST O US OBSOLETE IF WE DON'T STOP THEM!

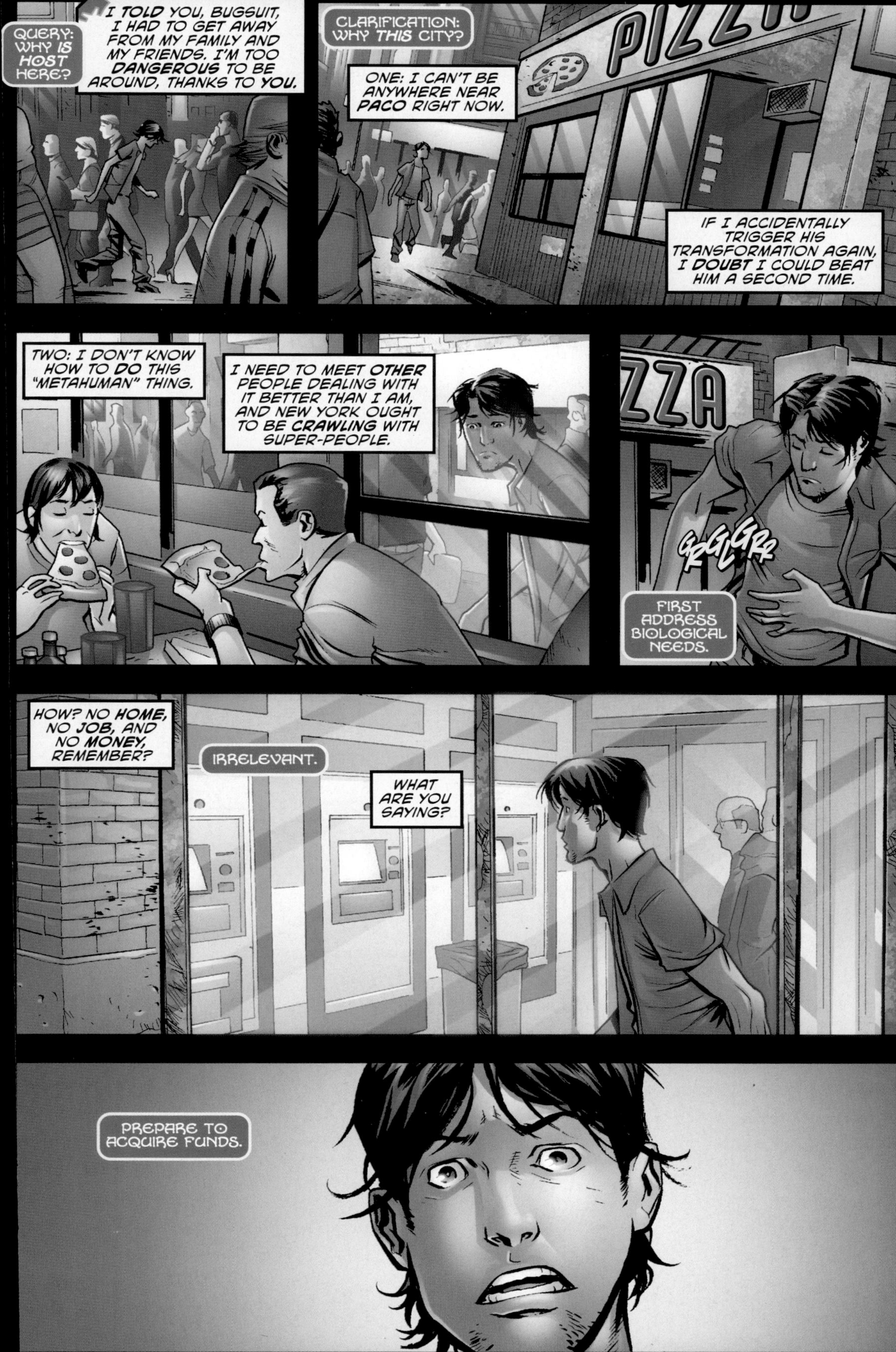
QUERY: WHY IS HOST HERE?
I TOLD YOU, BUGSUIT, I HAD TO GET AWAY FROM MY FAMILY AND MY FRIENDS. I'M TOO DANGEROUS TO BE AROUND, THANKS TO YOU.
CLARIFICATION: WHY THIS CITY?
ONE: I CAN'T BE ANYWHERE NEAR PACO RIGHT NOW.
PIZZA
IF I ACCIDENTALLY TRIGGER HIS TRANSFORMATION AGAIN, I DOUBT I COULD BEAT HIM A SECOND TIME.
TWO: I DON'T KNOW HOW TO DO THIS "METAHUMAN" THING.
I NEED TO MEET OTHER PEOPLE DEALING WITH IT BETTER THAN I AM, AND NEW YORK OUGHT TO BE CRAWLING WITH SUPER-PEOPLE.
ZZA
GRGLGRR
FIRST ADDRESS BIOLOGICAL NEEDS.
HOW? NO HOME, NO JOB, AND NO MONEY, REMEMBER?
IRRELEVANT.
WHAT ARE YOU SAYING?
PREPARE TO ACQUIRE FUNDS.

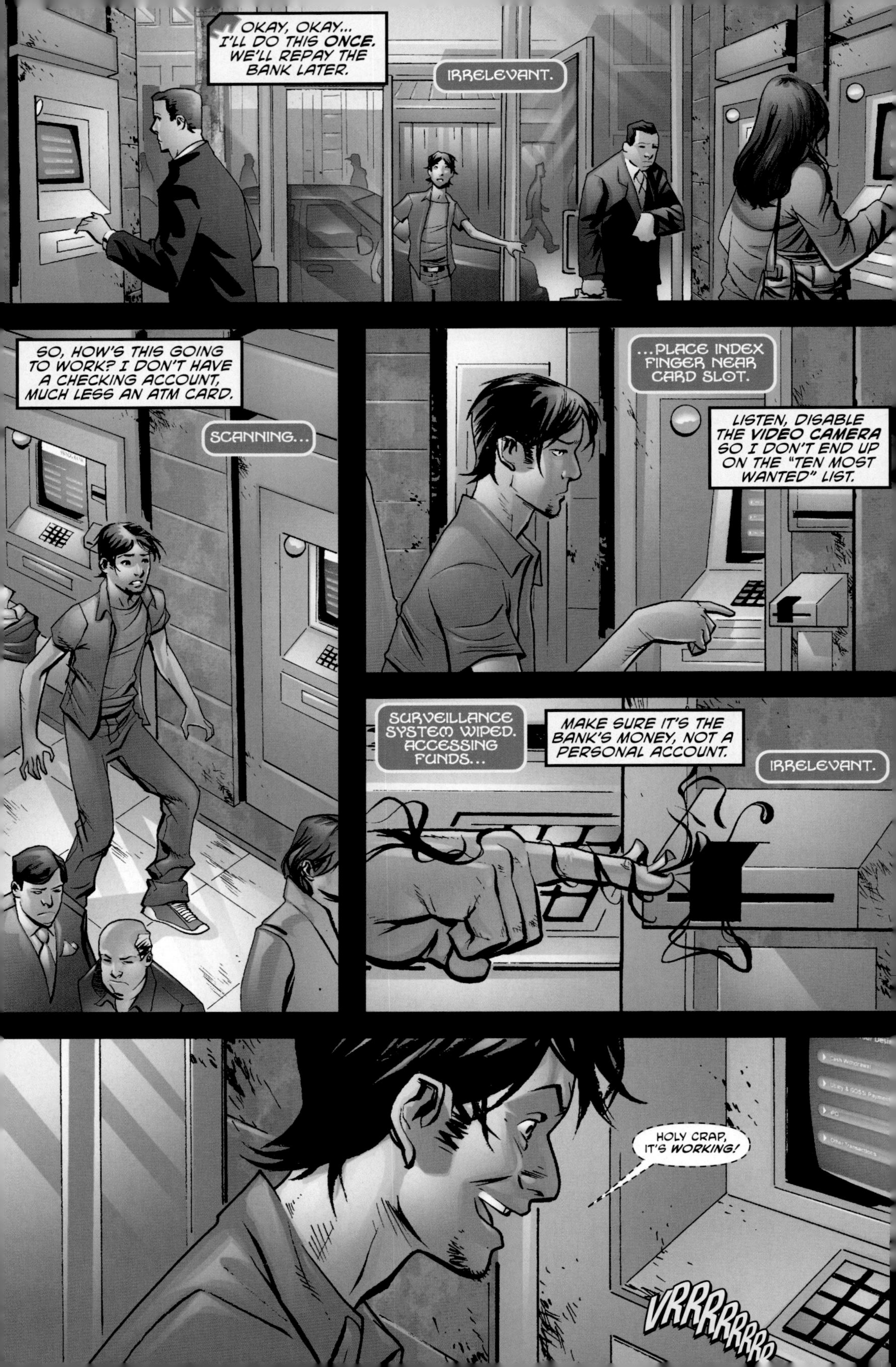
OKAY, OKAY... I'LL DO THIS ONCE. WE'LL REPAY THE BANK LATER.
IRRELEVANT.
SO, HOW'S THIS GOING TO WORK? I DON'T HAVE A CHECKING ACCOUNT, MUCH LESS AN ATM CARD.
SCANNING...
...PLACE INDEX FINGER NEAR CARD SLOT.
LISTEN, DISABLE THE VIDEO CAMERA SO I DON'T END UP ON THE "TEN MOST WANTED" LIST.
SURVEILLANCE SYSTEM WIPED. ACCESSING FUNDS...
MAKE SURE IT'S THE BANK'S MONEY, NOT A PERSONAL ACCOUNT.
IRRELEVANT.
HOLY CRAP, IT'S WORKING!
VRRRRRRRRD

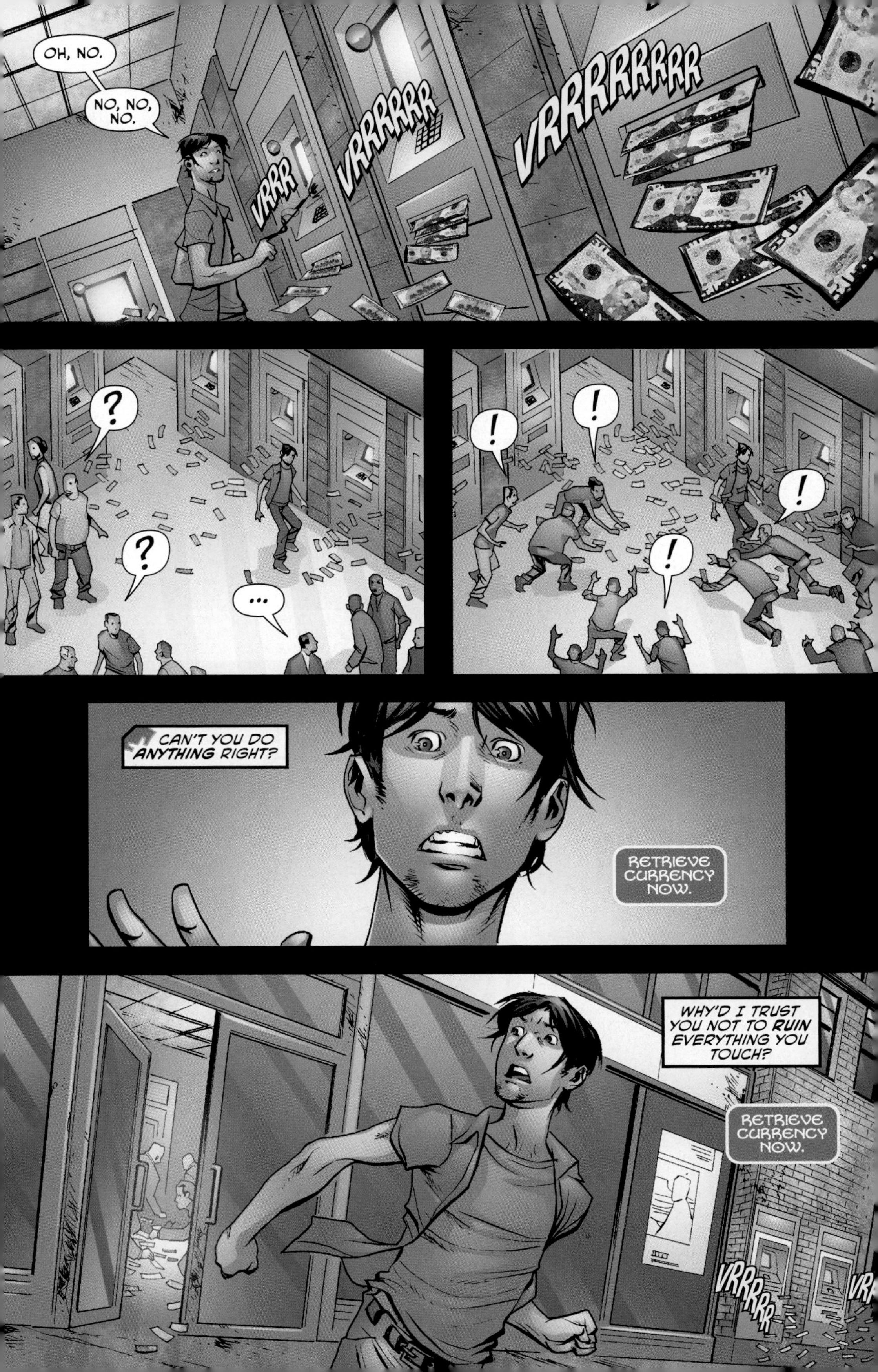
OH, NO.
NO, NO, NO.
VRRR
VRRRRRR
VRRRRRRRR
?
?
...
!
!
!
!
!
CAN'T YOU DO ANYTHING RIGHT?
RETRIEVE CURRENCY NOW.
WHY'D I TRUST YOU NOT TO RUIN EVERYTHING YOU TOUCH?
RETRIEVE CURRENCY NOW.
VRRRRR

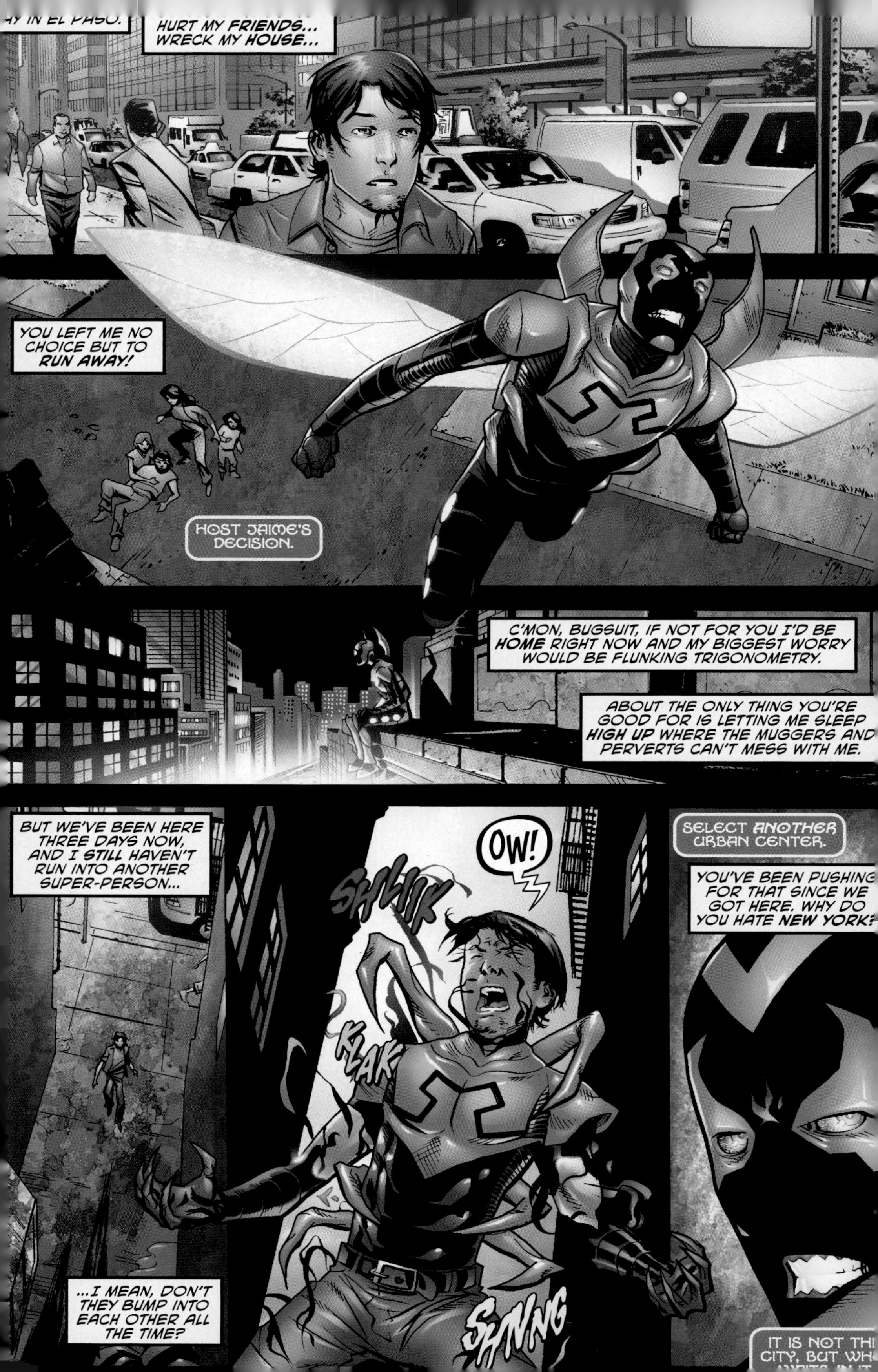

IN EL PASO.
HURT MY FRIENDS... WRECK MY HOUSE...
YOU LEFT ME NO CHOICE BUT TO RUN AWAY!
HOST JAIME'S DECISION.
C'MON, BUGSUIT, IF NOT FOR YOU I'D BE HOME RIGHT NOW AND MY BIGGEST WORRY WOULD BE FLUNKING TRIGONOMETRY.
ABOUT THE ONLY THING YOU'RE GOOD FOR IS LETTING ME SLEEP HIGH UP WHERE THE MUGGERS AND PERVERTS CAN'T MESS WITH ME.
BUT WE'VE BEEN HERE THREE DAYS NOW, AND I STILL HAVEN'T RUN INTO ANOTHER SUPER-PERSON...
...I MEAN, DON'T THEY BUMP INTO EACH OTHER ALL THE TIME?
OW!
SHLIIK
KLAK
SHNNG
SELECT ANOTHER URBAN CENTER.
YOU'VE BEEN PUSHING FOR THAT SINCE WE GOT HERE. WHY DO YOU HATE NEW YORK?
IT IS NOT THI
CITY, BUT WH

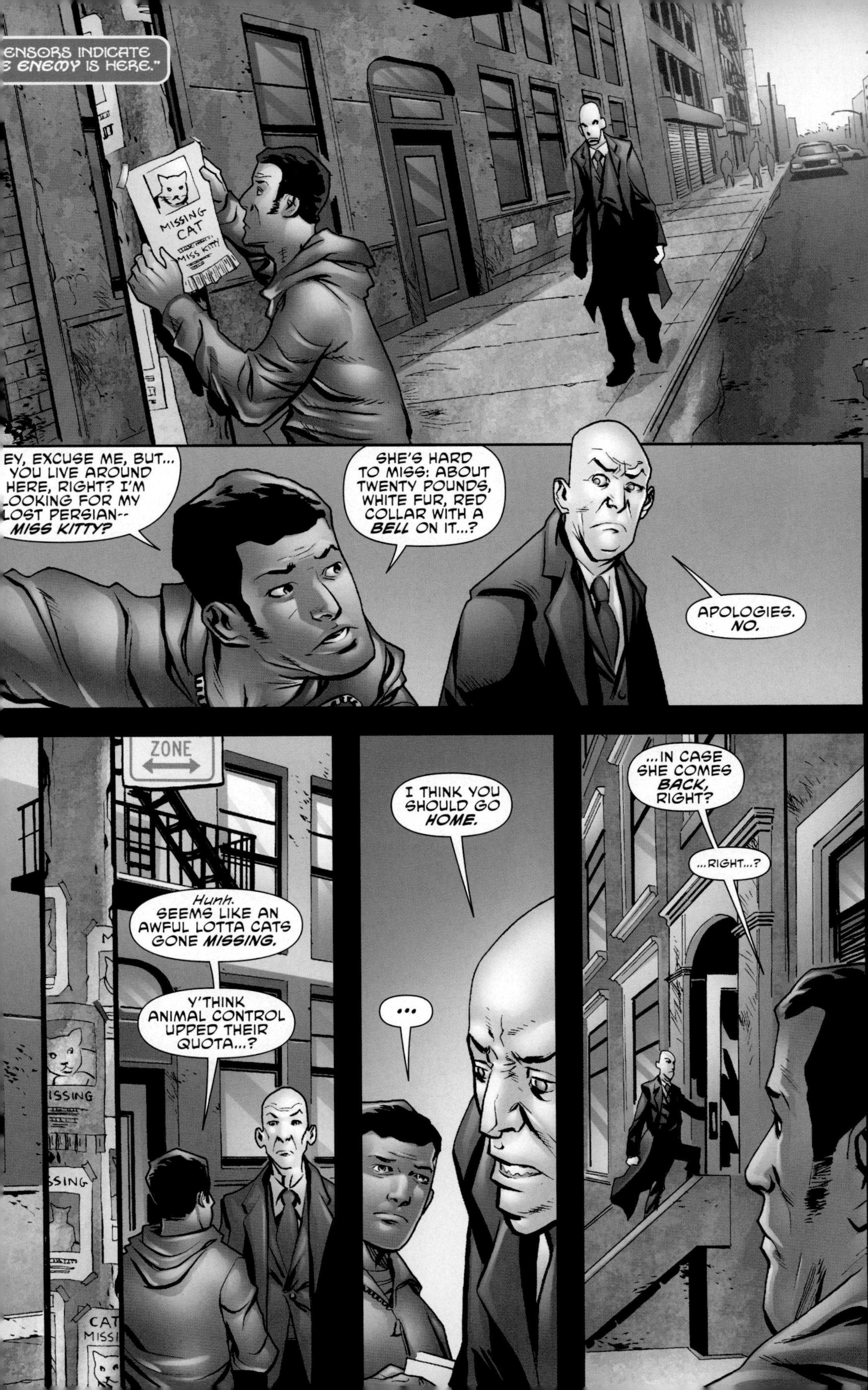
ENSORS INDICATE
E ENEMY IS HERE."
MISSING CAT
MISS KITTY
EY, EXCUSE ME, BUT... YOU LIVE AROUND HERE, RIGHT? I'M LOOKING FOR MY LOST PERSIAN-- MISS KITTY?
SHE'S HARD TO MISS: ABOUT TWENTY POUNDS, WHITE FUR, RED COLLAR WITH A BELL ON IT...?
APOLOGIES. NO.
ZONE
Hunh. SEEMS LIKE AN AWFUL LOTTA CATS GONE MISSING.
Y'THINK ANIMAL CONTROL UPPED THEIR QUOTA...?
I THINK YOU SHOULD GO HOME.
...
...IN CASE SHE COMES BACK, RIGHT?
...RIGHT...?

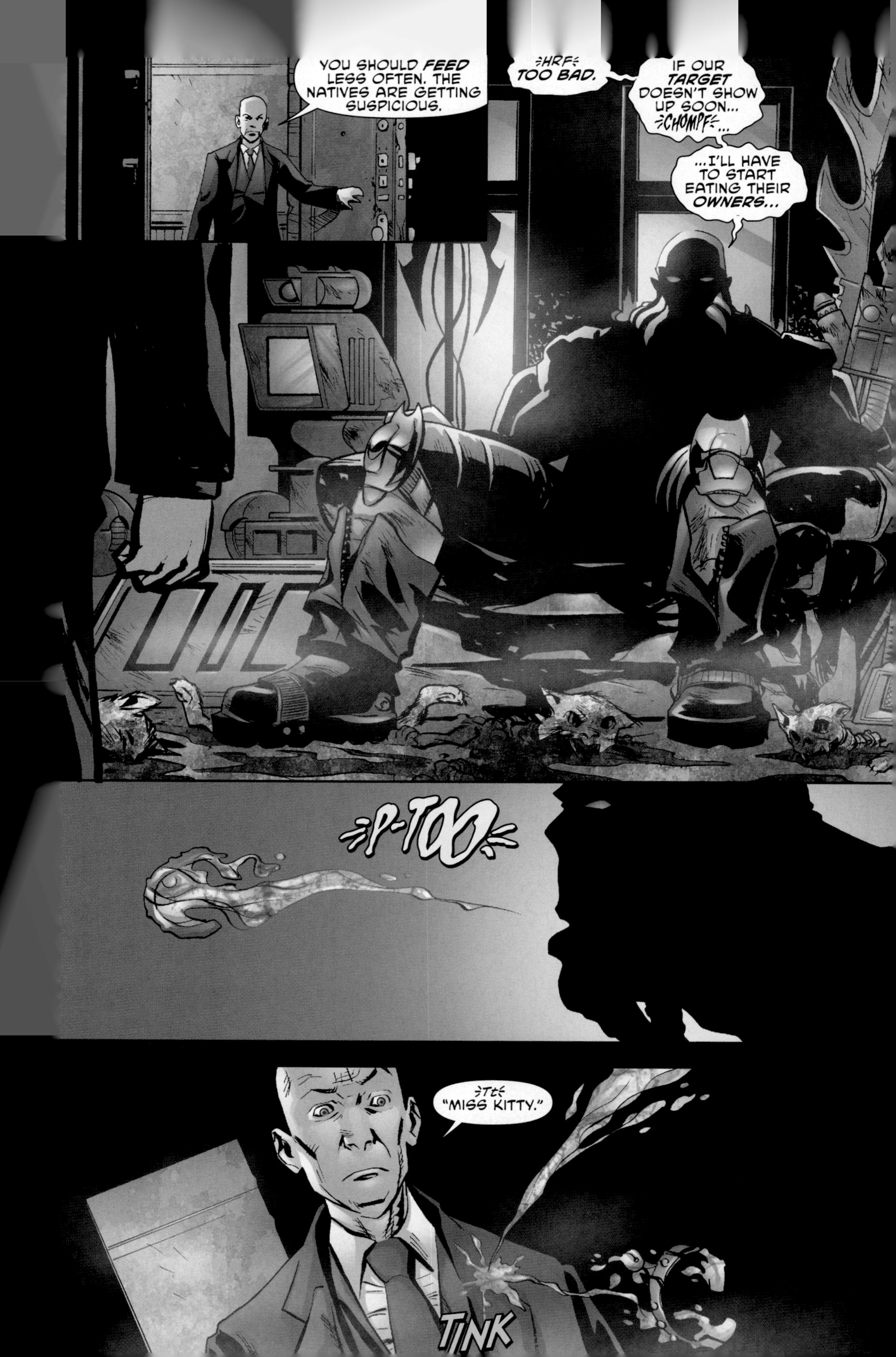
YOU SHOULD FEED LESS OFTEN. THE NATIVES ARE GETTING SUSPICIOUS.
HRF TOO BAD.
IF OUR TARGET DOESN'T SHOW UP SOON... CHOMPF...
...I'LL HAVE TO START EATING THEIR OWNERS...
P-TOO
Tt "MISS KITTY."
TINK

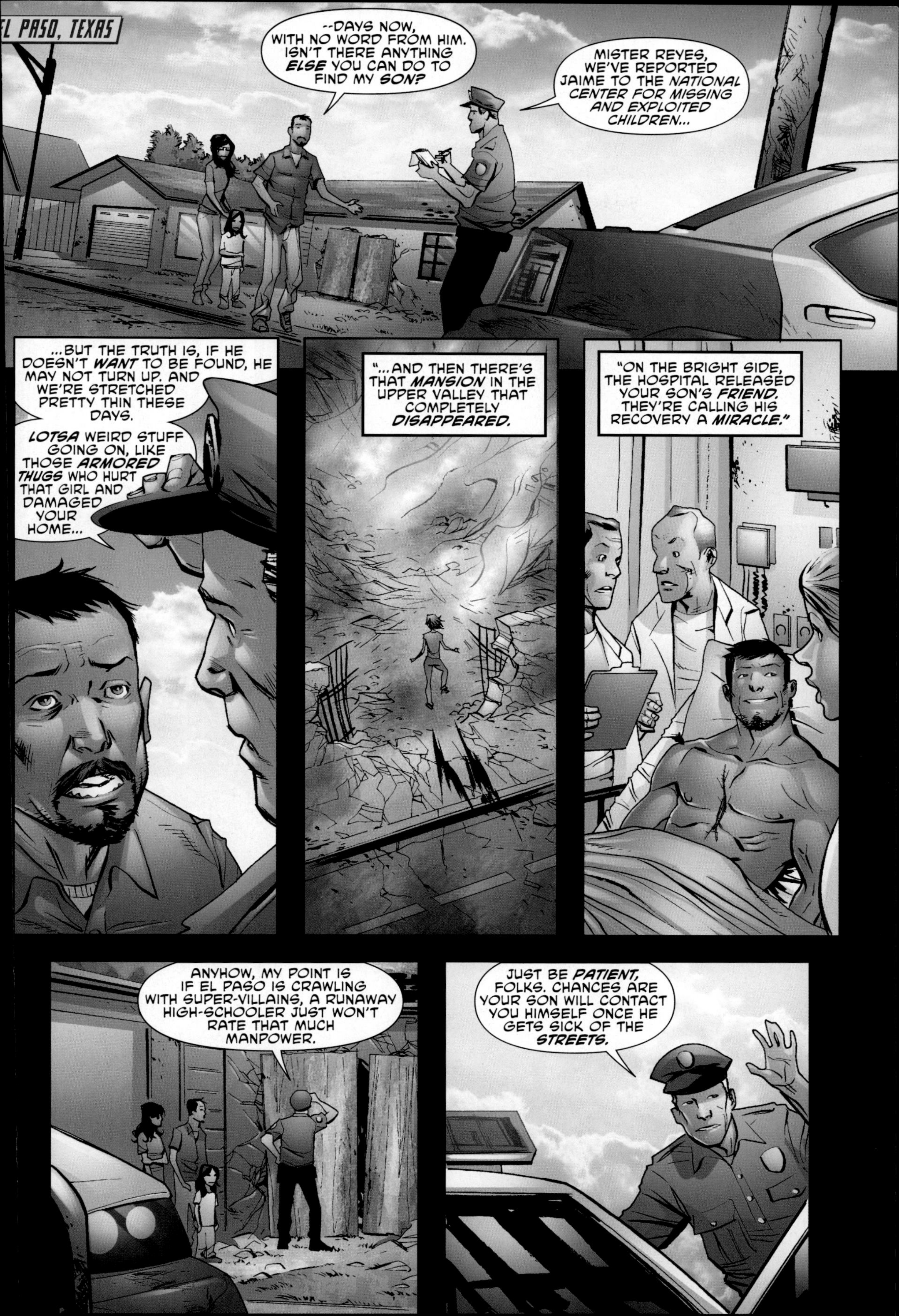
EL PASO, TEXAS
--DAYS NOW, WITH NO WORD FROM HIM. ISN'T THERE ANYTHING ELSE YOU CAN DO TO FIND MY SON?
MISTER REYES, WE'VE REPORTED JAIME TO THE NATIONAL CENTER FOR MISSING AND EXPLOITED CHILDREN...
...BUT THE TRUTH IS, IF HE DOESN'T WANT TO BE FOUND, HE MAY NOT TURN UP. AND WE'RE STRETCHED PRETTY THIN THESE DAYS.
LOTSA WEIRD STUFF GOING ON, LIKE THOSE ARMORED THUGS WHO HURT THAT GIRL AND DAMAGED YOUR HOME...
"...AND THEN THERE'S THAT MANSION IN THE UPPER VALLEY THAT COMPLETELY DISAPPEARED.
"ON THE BRIGHT SIDE, THE HOSPITAL RELEASED YOUR SON'S FRIEND. THEY'RE CALLING HIS RECOVERY A MIRACLE."
ANYHOW, MY POINT IS IF EL PASO IS CRAWLING WITH SUPER-VILLAINS, A RUNAWAY HIGH-SCHOOLER JUST WON'T RATE THAT MUCH MANPOWER.
JUST BE PATIENT, FOLKS. CHANCES ARE YOUR SON WILL CONTACT YOU HIMSELF ONCE HE GETS SICK OF THE STREETS.

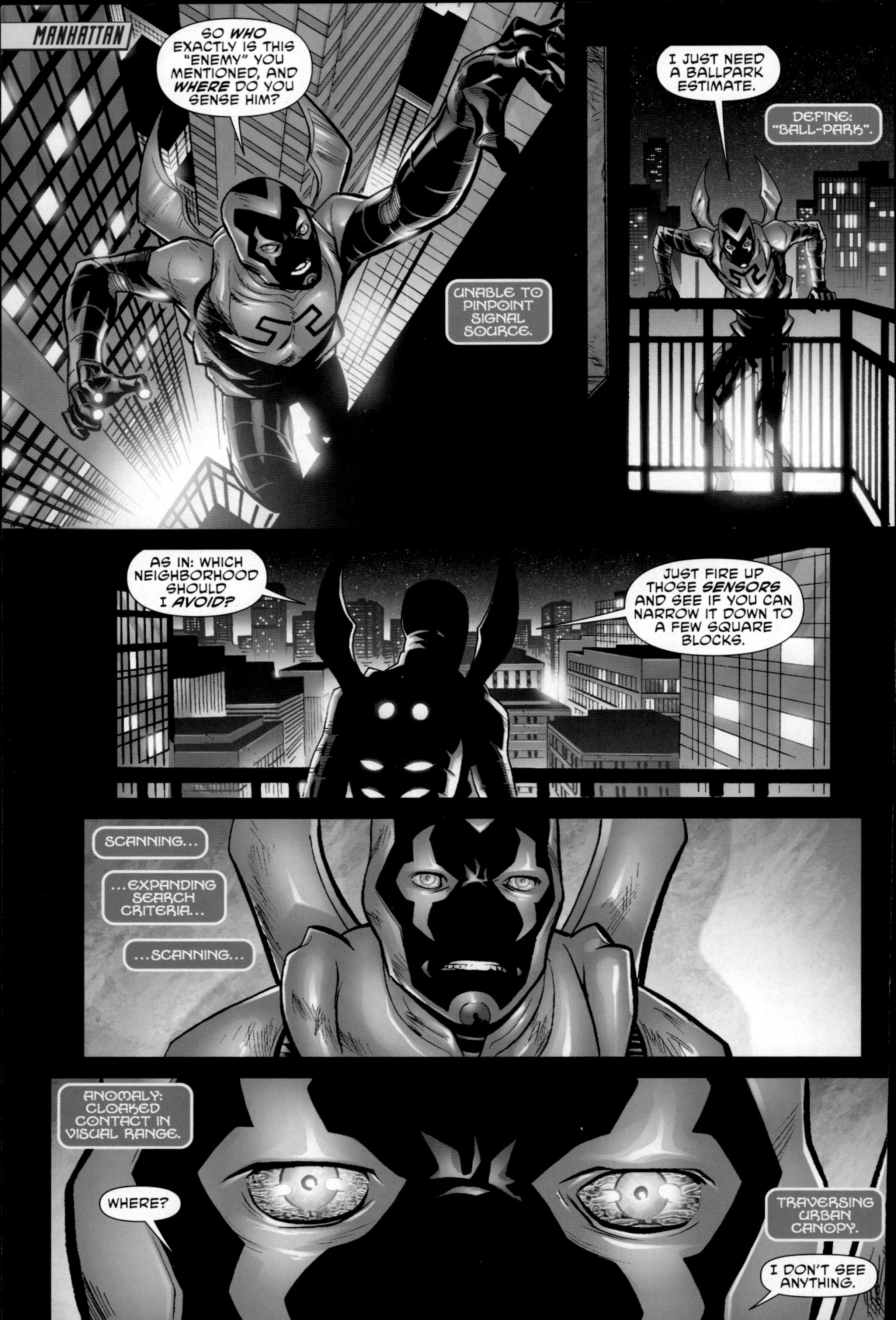
MANHATTAN
SO WHO EXACTLY IS THIS "ENEMY" YOU MENTIONED, AND WHERE DO YOU SENSE HIM?
UNABLE TO PINPOINT SIGNAL SOURCE.
I JUST NEED A BALLPARK ESTIMATE.
DEFINE: "BALL-PARK".
AS IN: WHICH NEIGHBORHOOD SHOULD I AVOID?
JUST FIRE UP THOSE SENSORS AND SEE IF YOU CAN NARROW IT DOWN TO A FEW SQUARE BLOCKS.
SCANNING...
...EXPANDING SEARCH CRITERIA...
...SCANNING...
ANOMALY: CLOAKED CONTACT IN VISUAL RANGE.
WHERE?
TRAVERSING URBAN CANOPY.
I DON'T SEE ANYTHING.

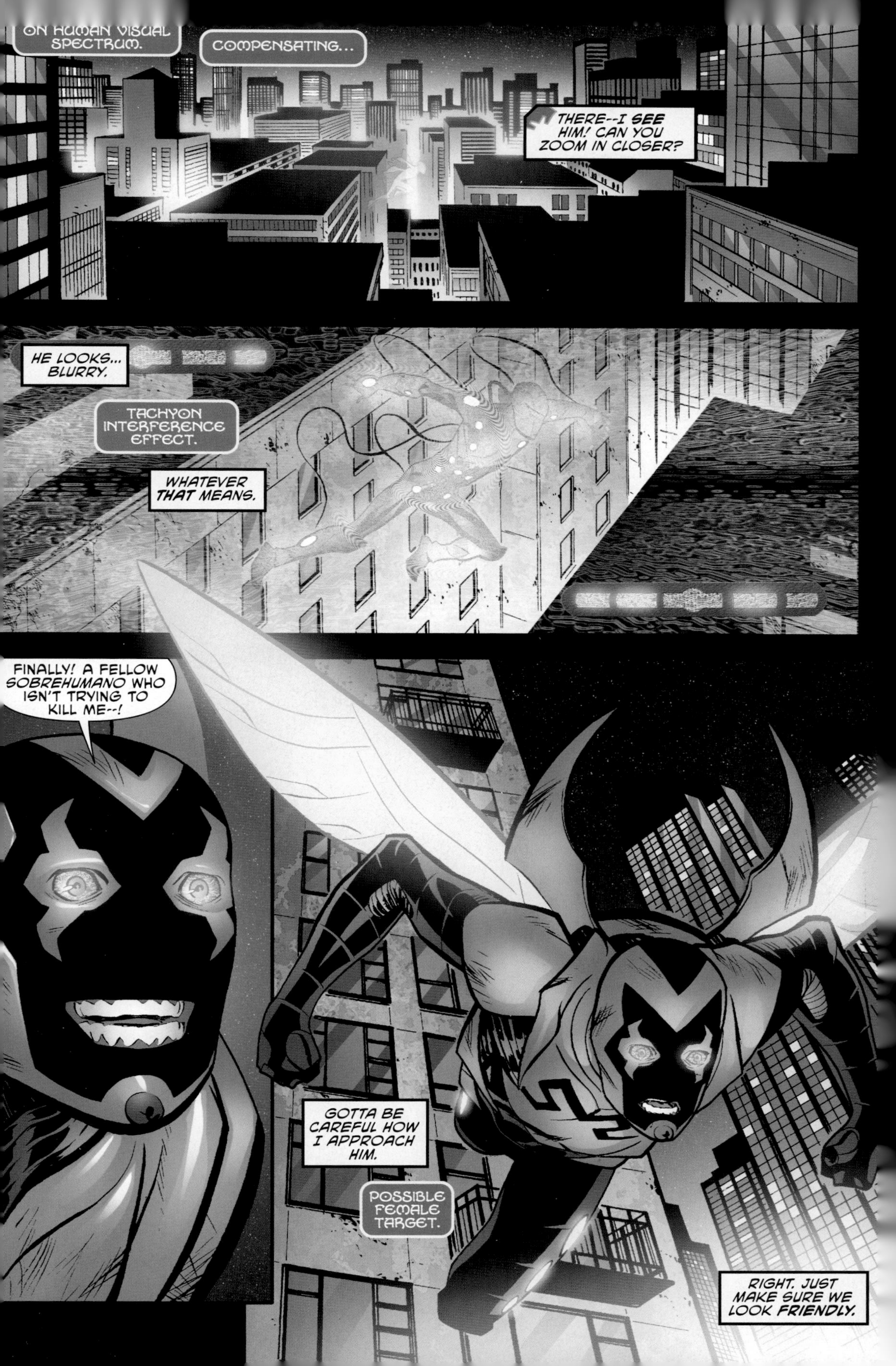

ON HUMAN VISUAL SPECTRUM.
COMPENSATING...
THERE--I SEE HIM! CAN YOU ZOOM IN CLOSER?
HE LOOKS... BLURRY.
TACHYON INTERFERENCE EFFECT.
WHATEVER THAT MEANS.
FINALLY! A FELLOW SOBREHUMANO WHO ISN'T TRYING TO KILL ME--!
GOTTA BE CAREFUL HOW I APPROACH HIM.
POSSIBLE FEMALE TARGET.
RIGHT. JUST MAKE SURE WE LOOK FRIENDLY.

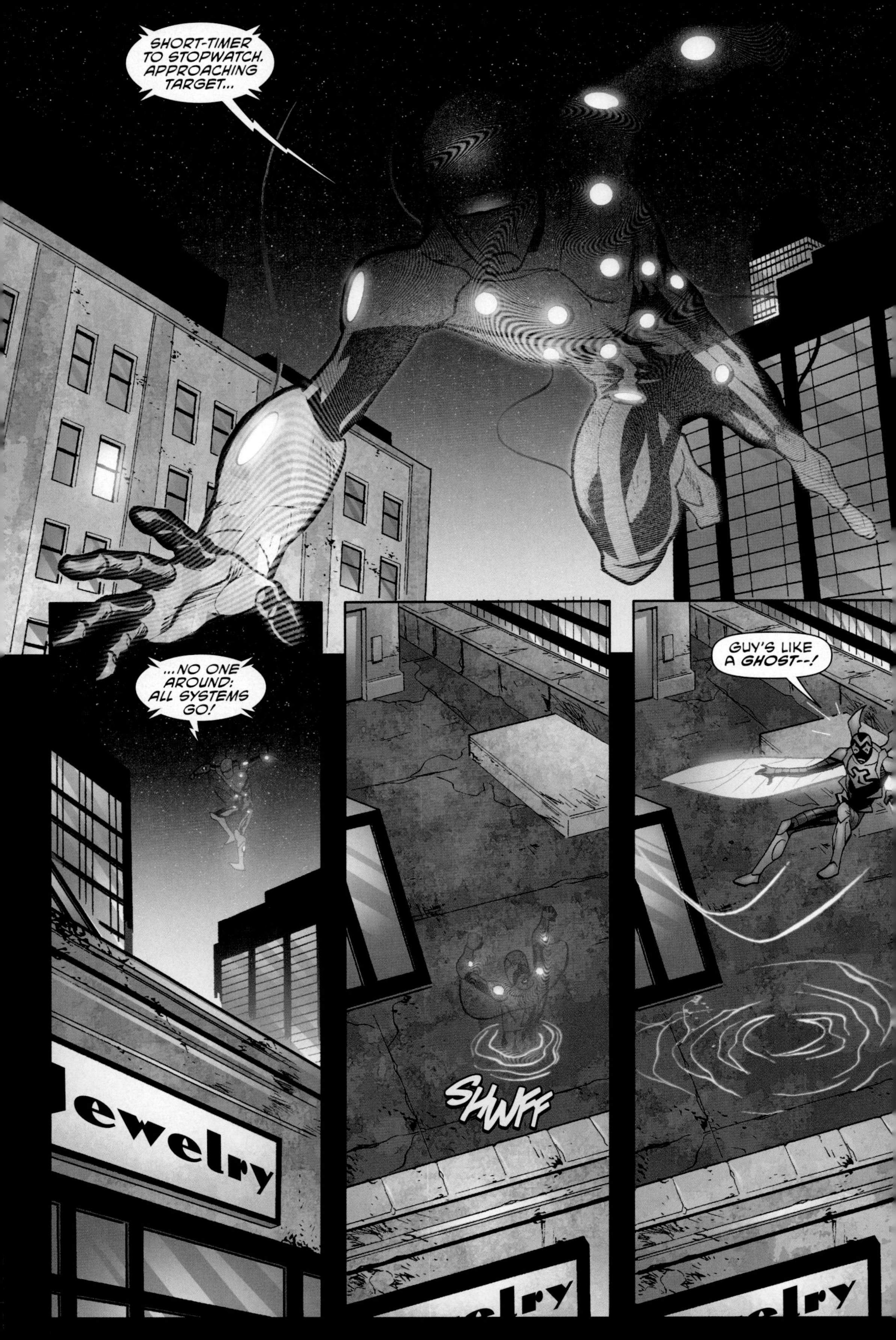
SHORT-TIMER TO STOPWATCH. APPROACHING TARGET...
...NO ONE AROUND: ALL SYSTEMS GO!
ewelry
SHWFF
ewelry
GUY'S LIKE A GHOST--!
ewelry

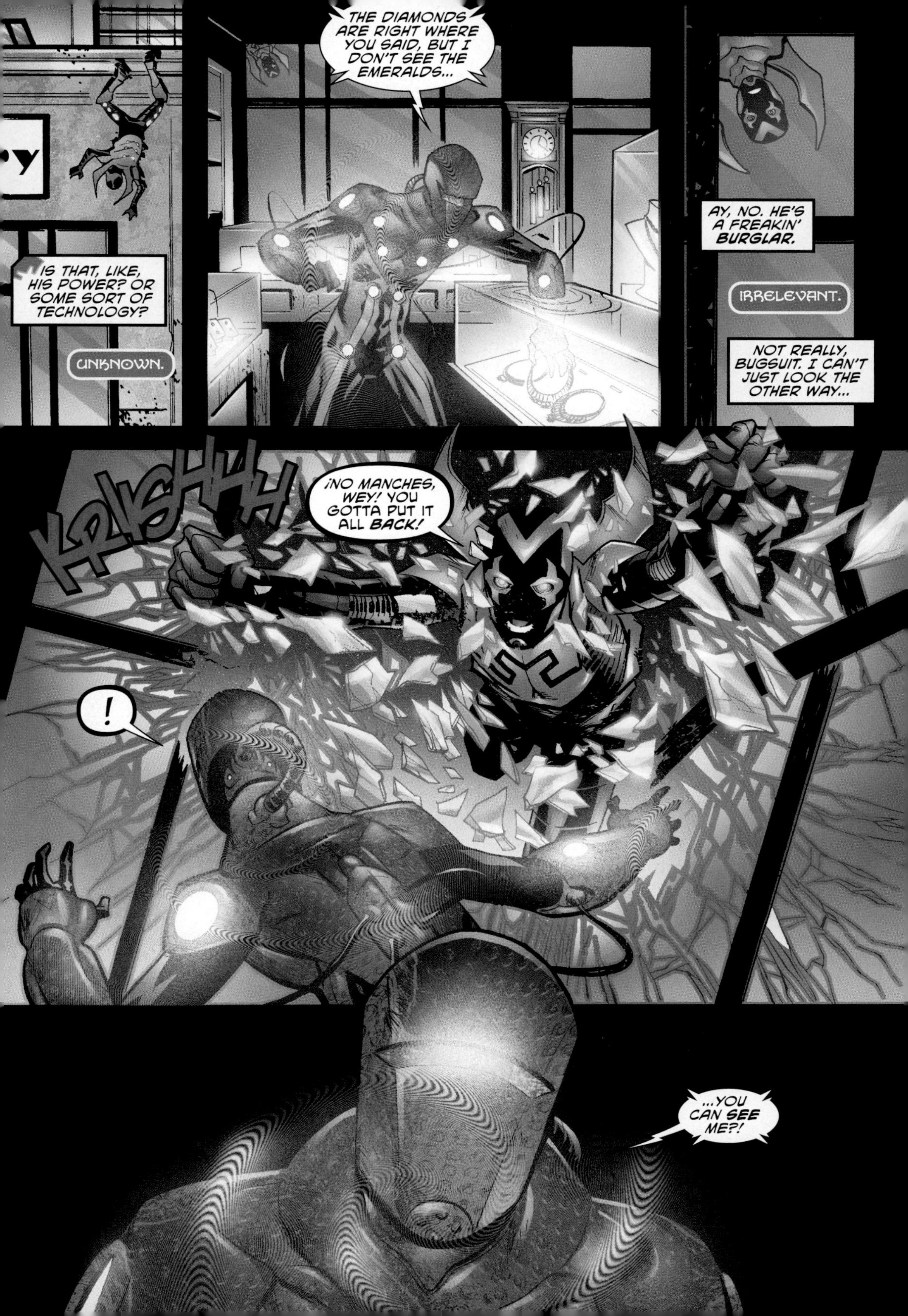

IS THAT, LIKE, HIS POWER? OR SOME SORT OF TECHNOLOGY?
UNKNOWN.
THE DIAMONDS ARE RIGHT WHERE YOU SAID, BUT I DON'T SEE THE EMERALDS...
AY, NO. HE'S A FREAKIN' BURGLAR.
IRRELEVANT.
NOT REALLY, BUGSUIT. I CAN'T JUST LOOK THE OTHER WAY...
KRISHHH
¡NO MANCHES, WEY! YOU GOTTA PUT IT ALL BACK!
!
...YOU CAN SEE ME?!

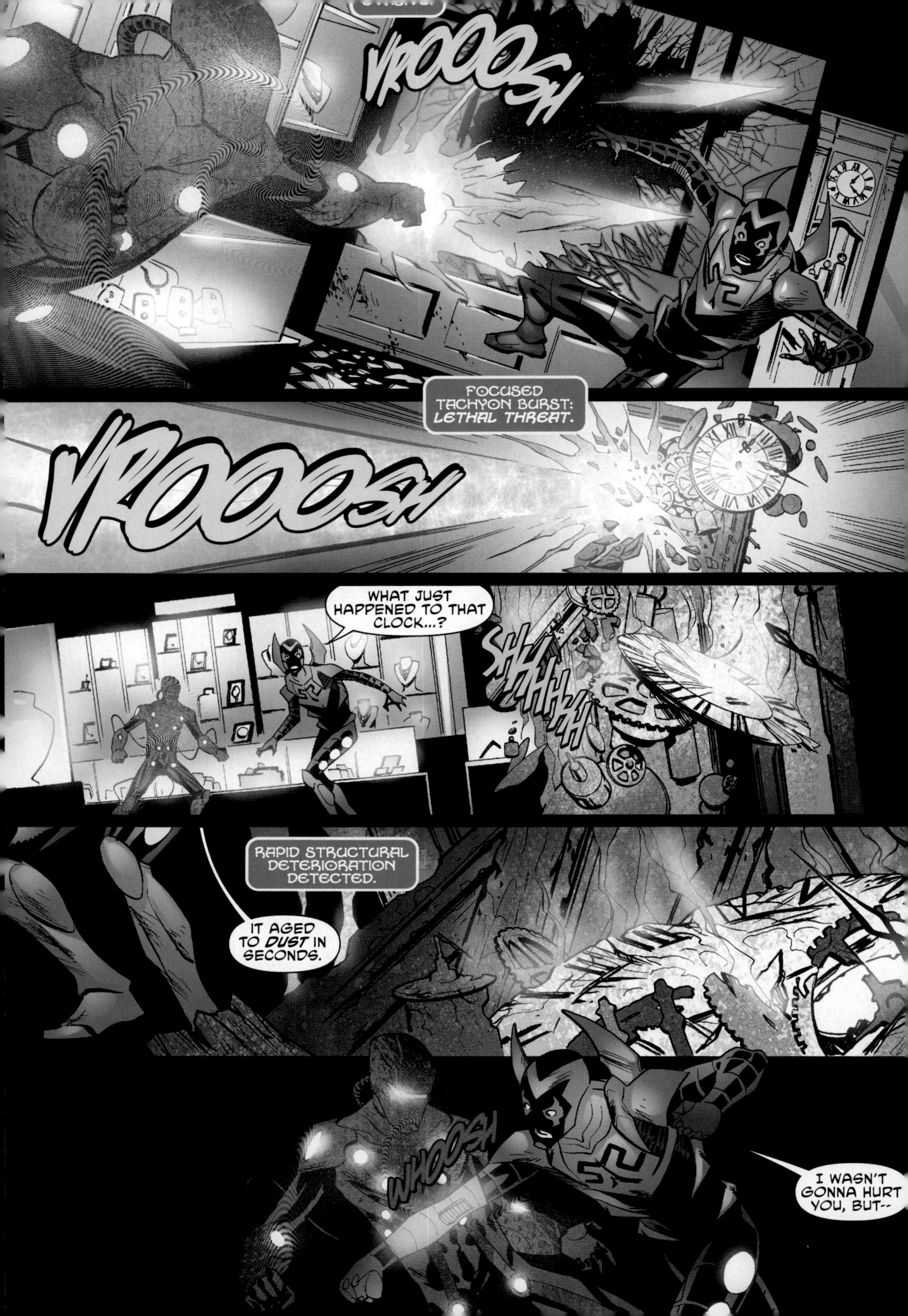
VROOOSH
FOCUSED TACHYON BURST: *LETHAL THREAT.*
VROOOSH
WHAT JUST HAPPENED TO THAT CLOCK...?
SHHHHHH
RAPID STRUCTURAL DETERIORATION DETECTED.
IT AGED TO *DUST* IN SECONDS.
WHOOSH
I WASN'T GONNA HURT YOU, BUT--

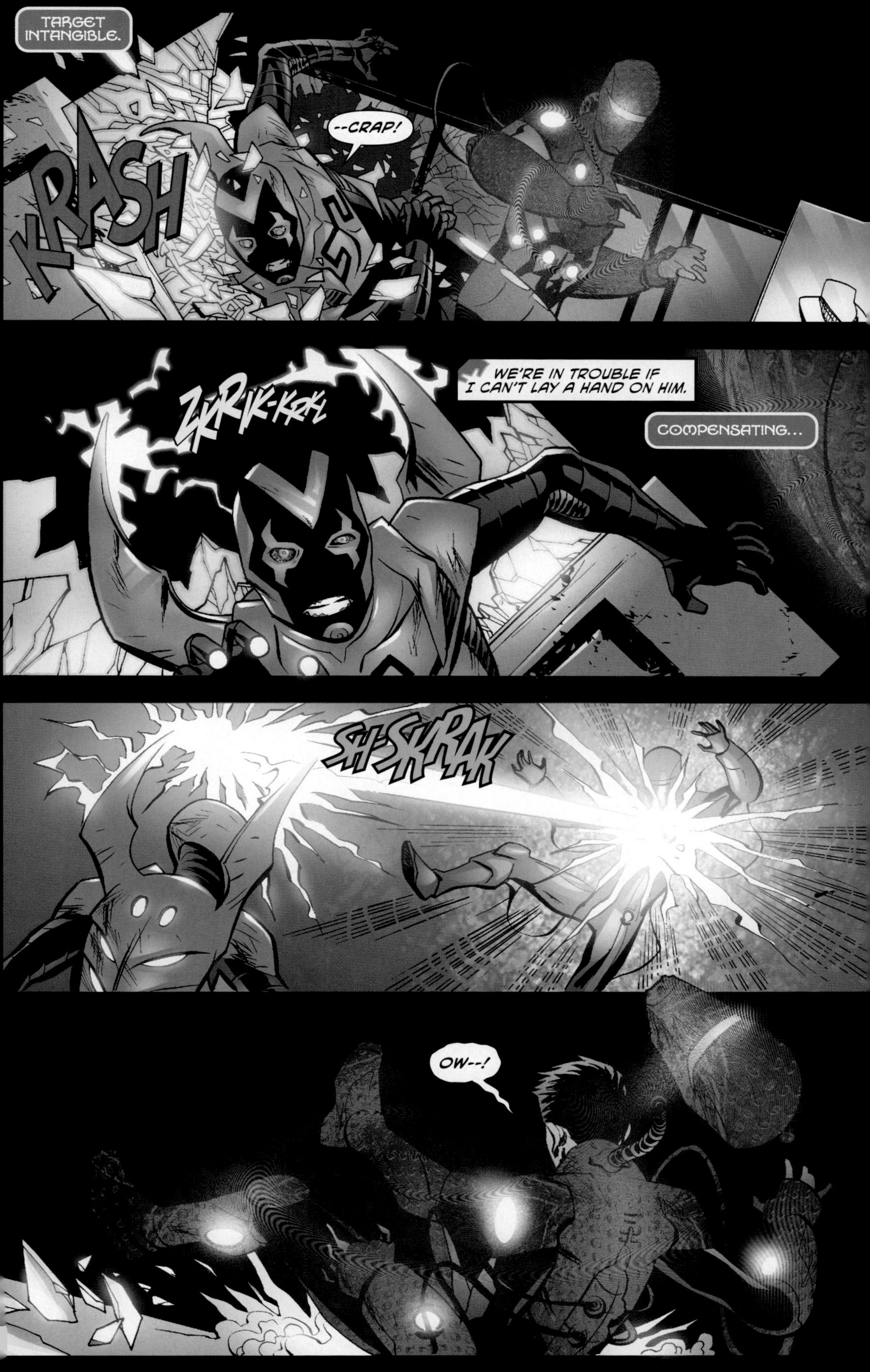
TARGET INTANGIBLE.
KRASH
--CRAP!
WE'RE IN TROUBLE IF I CAN'T LAY A HAND ON HIM.
COMPENSATING...
ZKRIK-KRKL
SH-SKRAK
OW--!

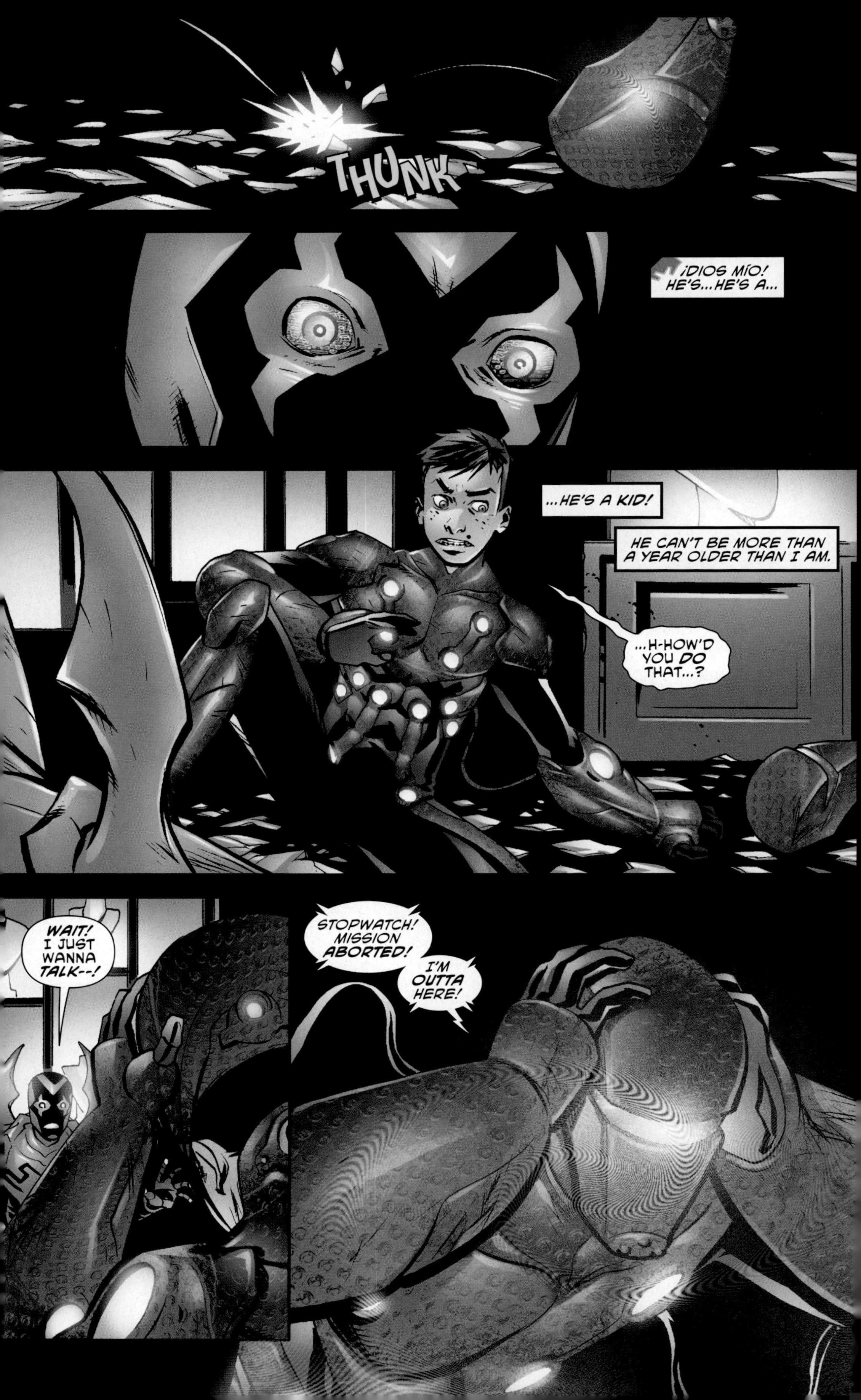
THUNK
¡DIOS MÍO! HE'S...HE'S A...
...HE'S A KID!
HE CAN'T BE MORE THAN A YEAR OLDER THAN I AM.
...H-HOW'D YOU DO THAT...?
WAIT! I JUST WANNA TALK--!
STOPWATCH! MISSION ABORTED!
I'M OUTTA HERE!

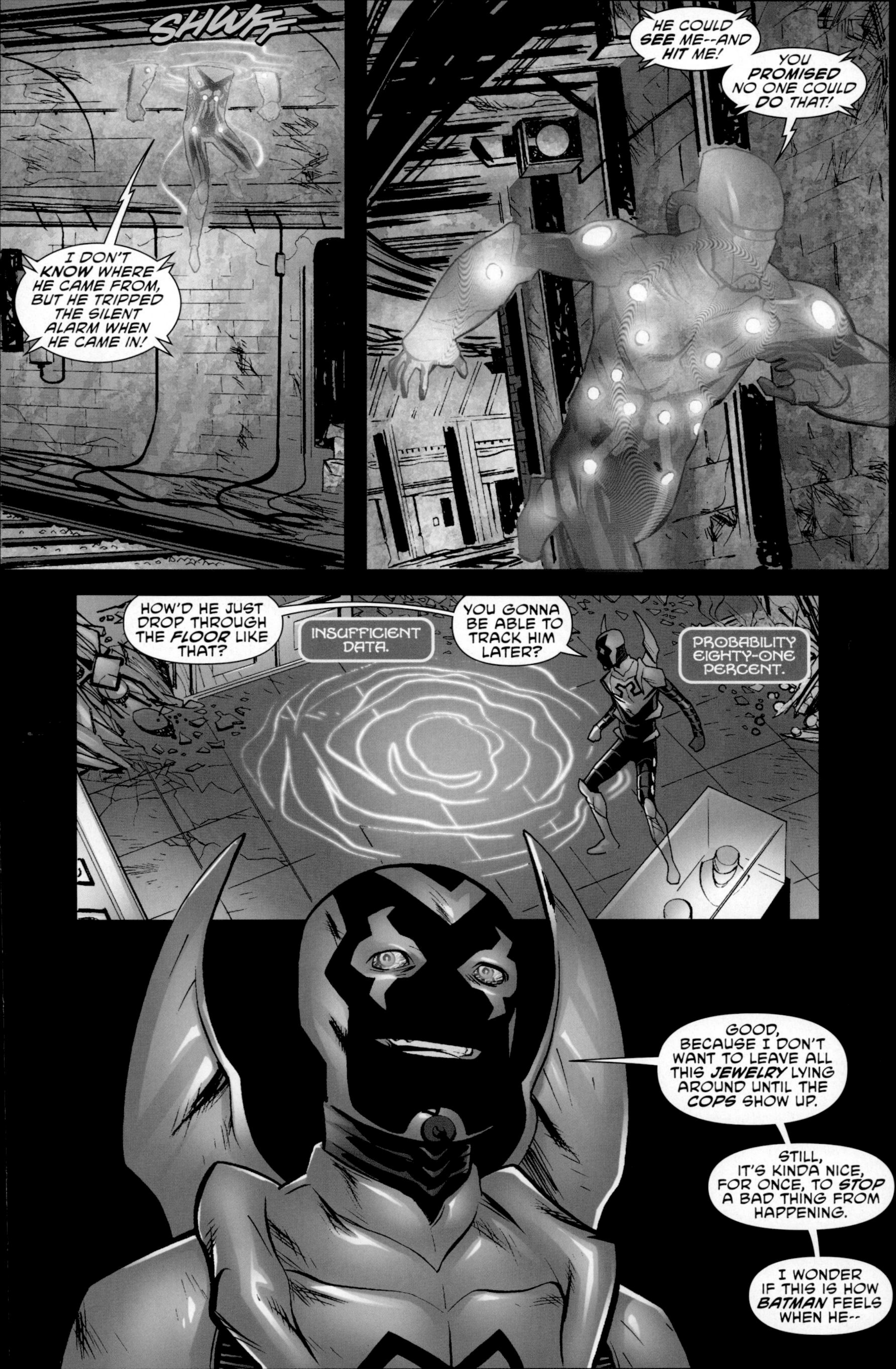
SHWFF
I DON'T KNOW WHERE HE CAME FROM, BUT HE TRIPPED THE SILENT ALARM WHEN HE CAME IN!
HE COULD SEE ME--AND HIT ME!
YOU PROMISED NO ONE COULD DO THAT!
HOW'D HE JUST DROP THROUGH THE FLOOR LIKE THAT?
INSUFFICIENT DATA.
YOU GONNA BE ABLE TO TRACK HIM LATER?
PROBABILITY EIGHTY-ONE PERCENT.
GOOD, BECAUSE I DON'T WANT TO LEAVE ALL THIS JEWELRY LYING AROUND UNTIL THE COPS SHOW UP.
STILL, IT'S KINDA NICE, FOR ONCE, TO STOP A BAD THING FROM HAPPENING.
I WONDER IF THIS IS HOW BATMAN FEELS WHEN HE--

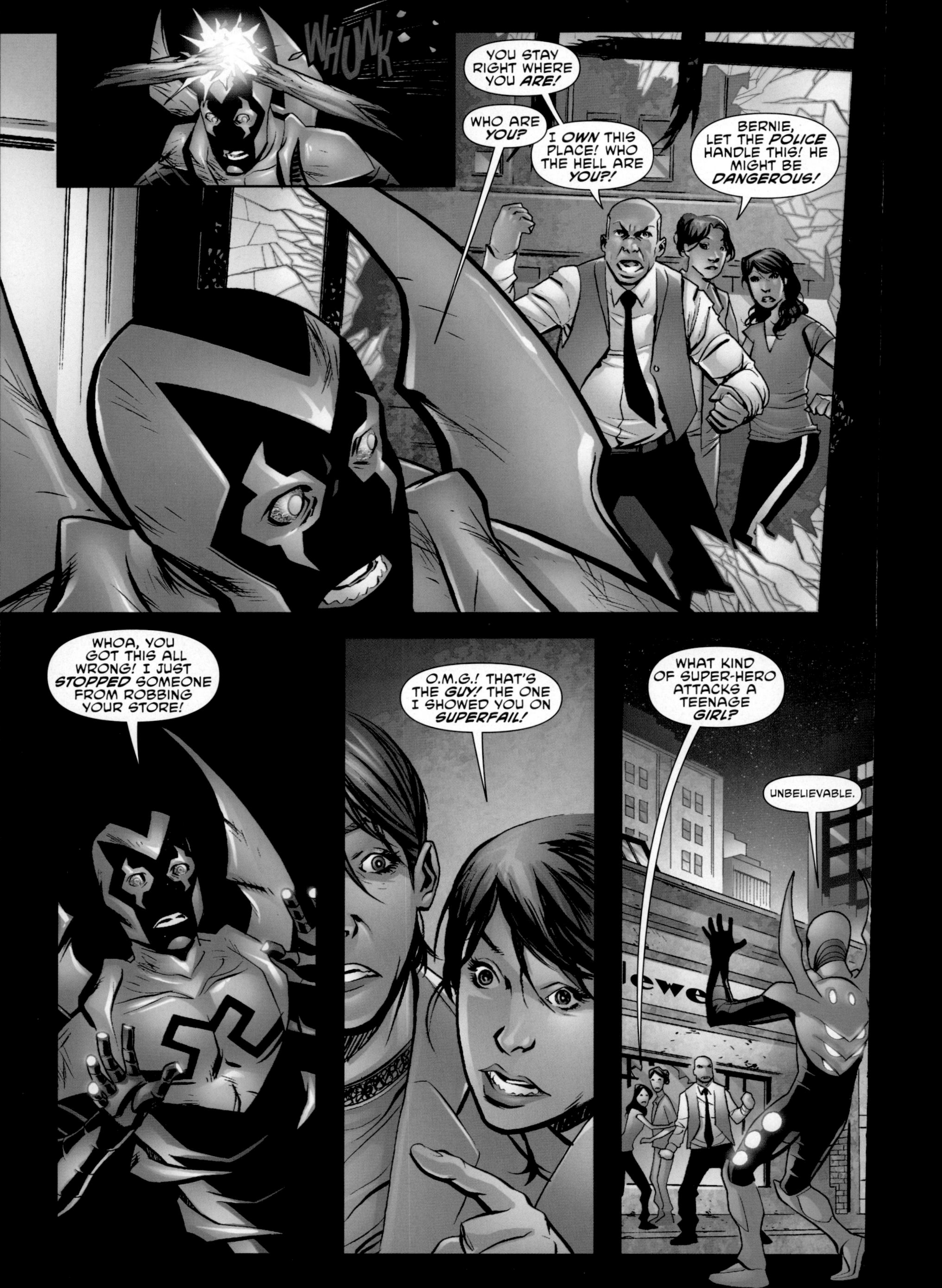
WHUNK
YOU STAY RIGHT WHERE YOU *ARE!*
WHO ARE *YOU?*
I *OWN* THIS PLACE! WHO THE HELL ARE *YOU?!*
BERNIE, LET THE *POLICE* HANDLE THIS! HE MIGHT BE *DANGEROUS!*
WHOA, YOU GOT THIS ALL WRONG! I JUST *STOPPED* SOMEONE FROM ROBBING YOUR STORE!
O.M.G.! THAT'S THE *GUY!* THE ONE I SHOWED YOU ON *SUPERFAIL!*
WHAT KIND OF SUPER-HERO ATTACKS A TEENAGE *GIRL?*
UNBELIEVABLE.

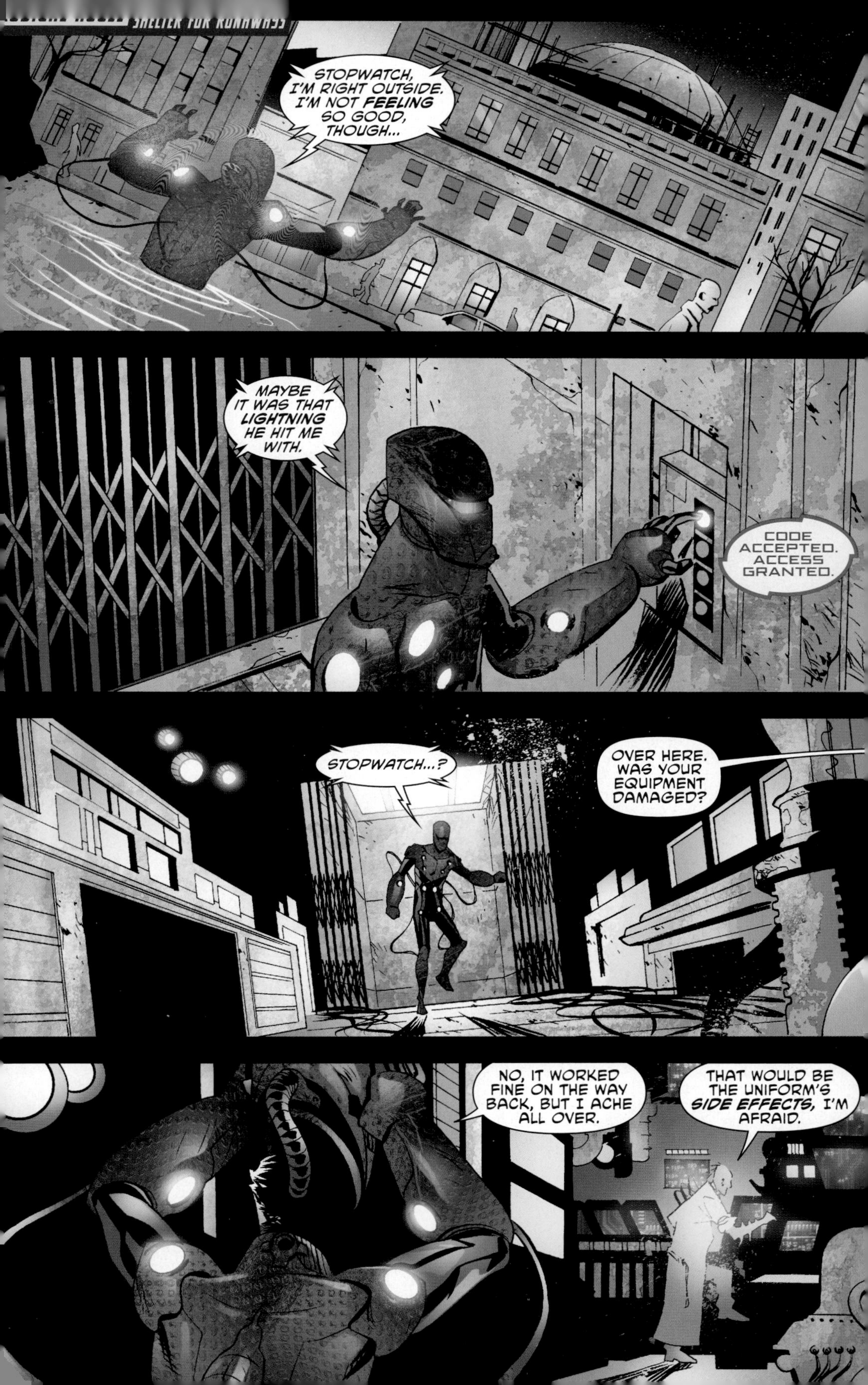
STOPWATCH, I'M RIGHT OUTSIDE. I'M NOT FEELING SO GOOD, THOUGH...
MAYBE IT WAS THAT LIGHTNING HE HIT ME WITH.
CODE ACCEPTED. ACCESS GRANTED.
STOPWATCH...?
OVER HERE. WAS YOUR EQUIPMENT DAMAGED?
NO, IT WORKED FINE ON THE WAY BACK, BUT I ACHE ALL OVER.
THAT WOULD BE THE UNIFORM'S SIDE EFFECTS, I'M AFRAID.

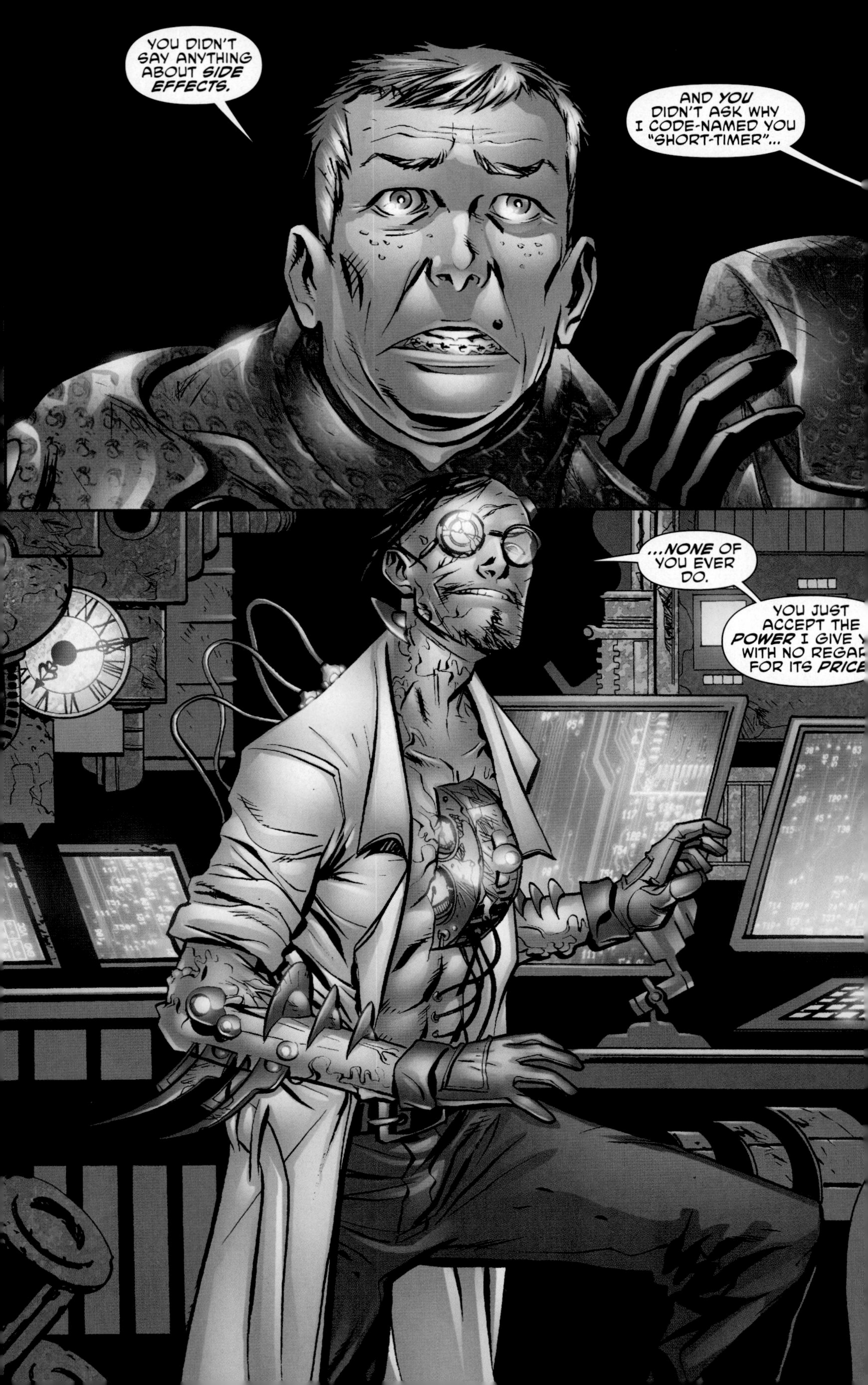
YOU DIDN'T SAY ANYTHING ABOUT *SIDE EFFECTS.*
AND *YOU* DIDN'T ASK WHY I CODE-NAMED YOU "SHORT-TIMER"...
...*NONE* OF YOU EVER DO.
YOU JUST ACCEPT THE *POWER* I GIVE WITH NO REGAR FOR ITS *PRICE*

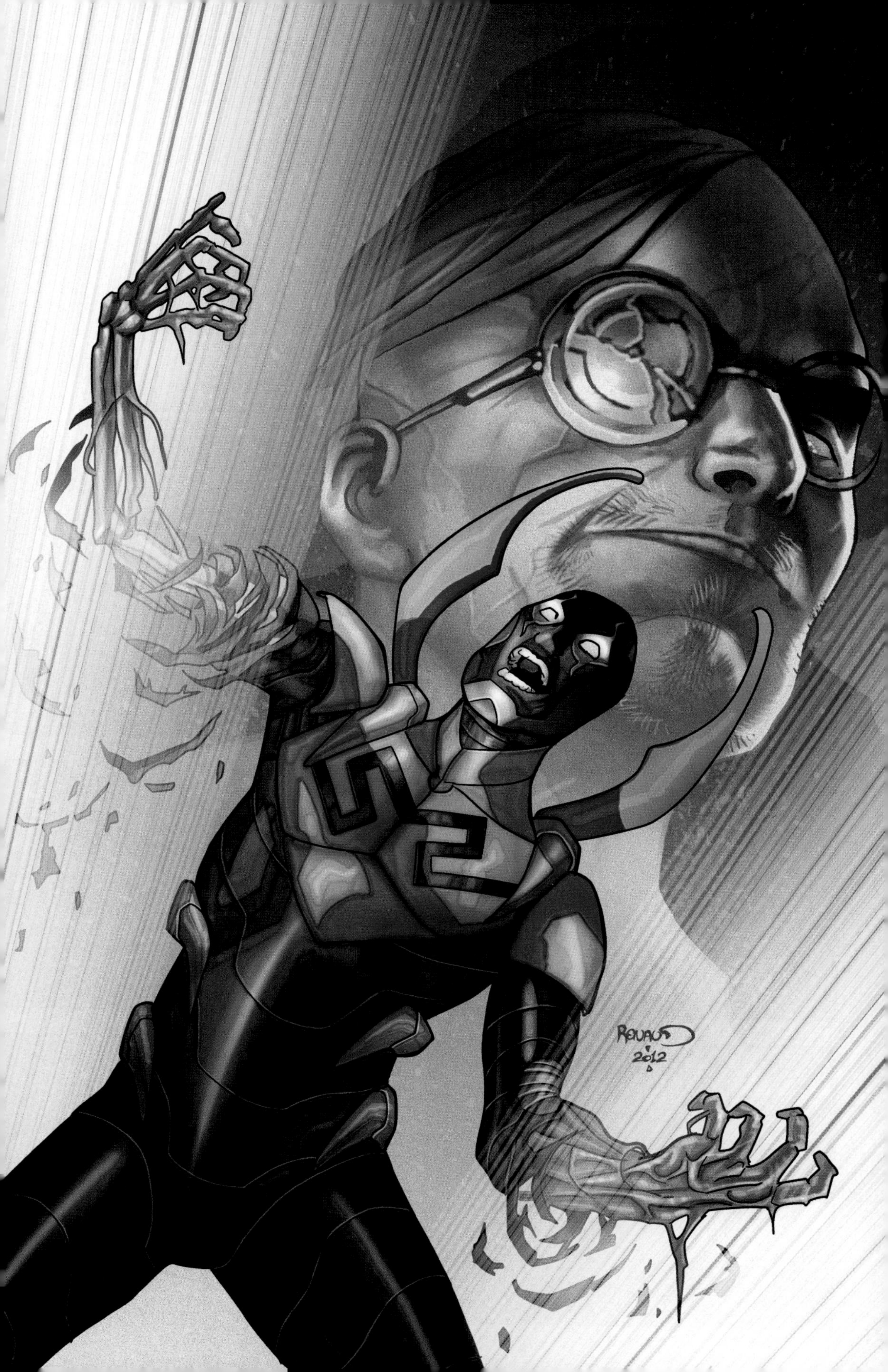

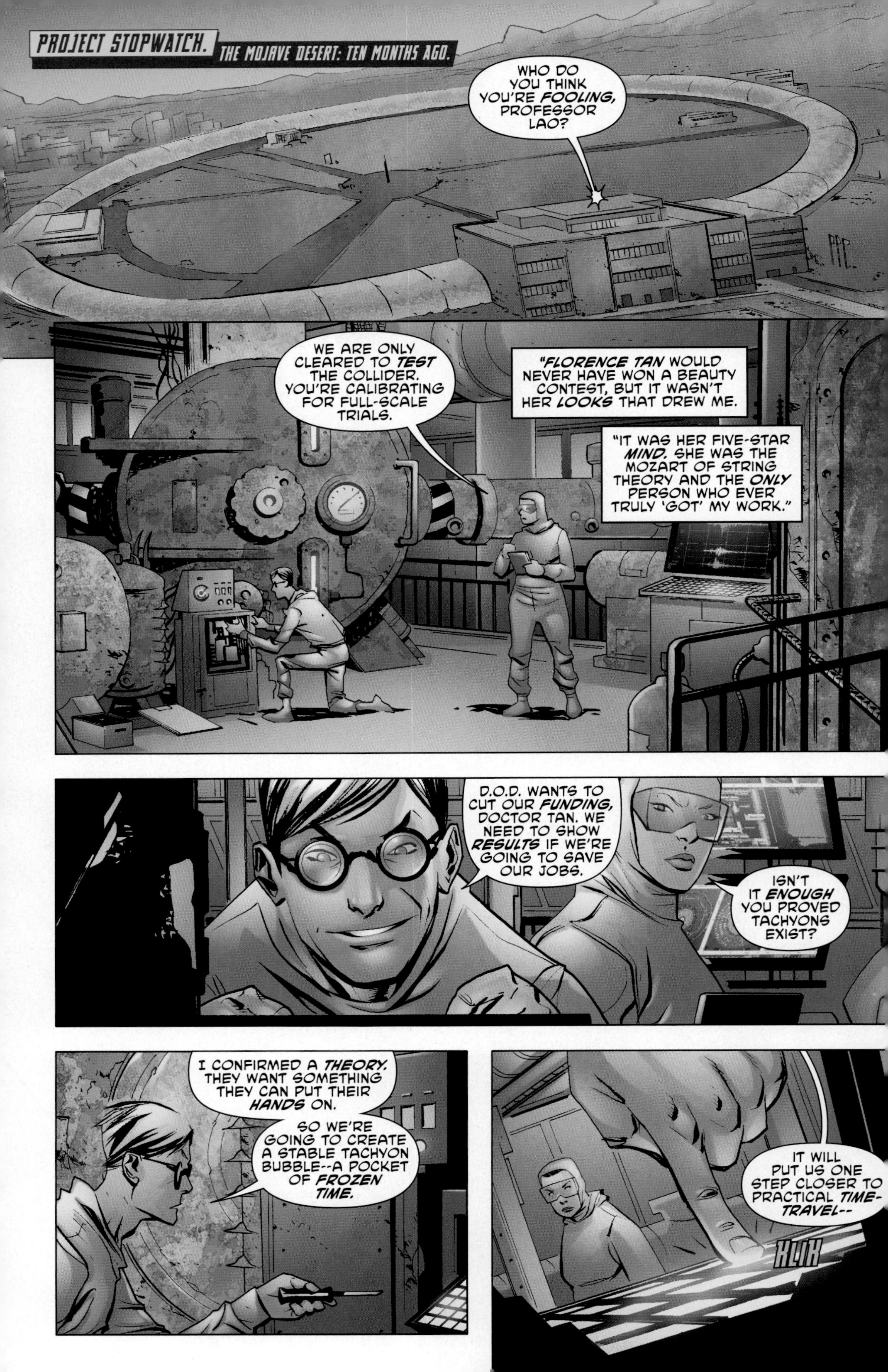
PROJECT STOPWATCH.
THE MOJAVE DESERT: TEN MONTHS AGO.
WHO DO YOU THINK YOU'RE FOOLING, PROFESSOR LAO?
WE ARE ONLY CLEARED TO TEST THE COLLIDER. YOU'RE CALIBRATING FOR FULL-SCALE TRIALS.
"FLORENCE TAN WOULD NEVER HAVE WON A BEAUTY CONTEST, BUT IT WASN'T HER LOOKS THAT DREW ME.
"IT WAS HER FIVE-STAR MIND. SHE WAS THE MOZART OF STRING THEORY AND THE ONLY PERSON WHO EVER TRULY 'GOT' MY WORK."
D.O.D. WANTS TO CUT OUR FUNDING, DOCTOR TAN. WE NEED TO SHOW RESULTS IF WE'RE GOING TO SAVE OUR JOBS.
ISN'T IT ENOUGH YOU PROVED TACHYONS EXIST?
I CONFIRMED A THEORY. THEY WANT SOMETHING THEY CAN PUT THEIR HANDS ON.
SO WE'RE GOING TO CREATE A STABLE TACHYON BUBBLE--A POCKET OF FROZEN TIME.
IT WILL PUT US ONE STEP CLOSER TO PRACTICAL TIME-TRAVEL--
KLIK

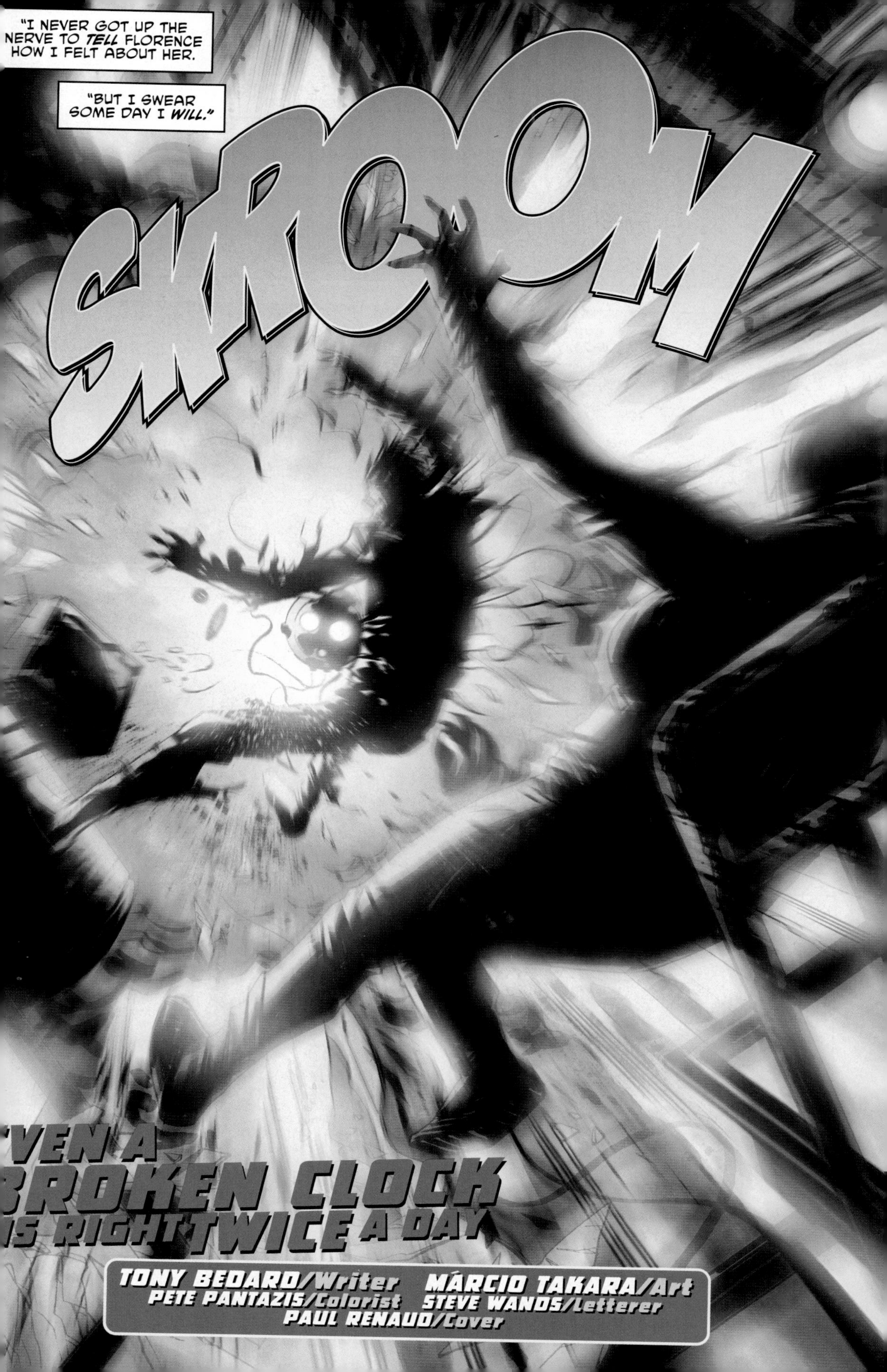
"I NEVER GOT UP THE NERVE TO *TELL* FLORENCE HOW I FELT ABOUT HER.
"BUT I SWEAR SOME DAY I *WILL.*"
SKROOM
VEN A
ROKEN CLOCK
S RIGHT TWICE A DAY
TONY BEDARD/Writer MÁRCIO TAKARA/Art
PETE PANTAZIS/Colorist STEVE WANDS/Letterer
PAUL RENAUD/Cover

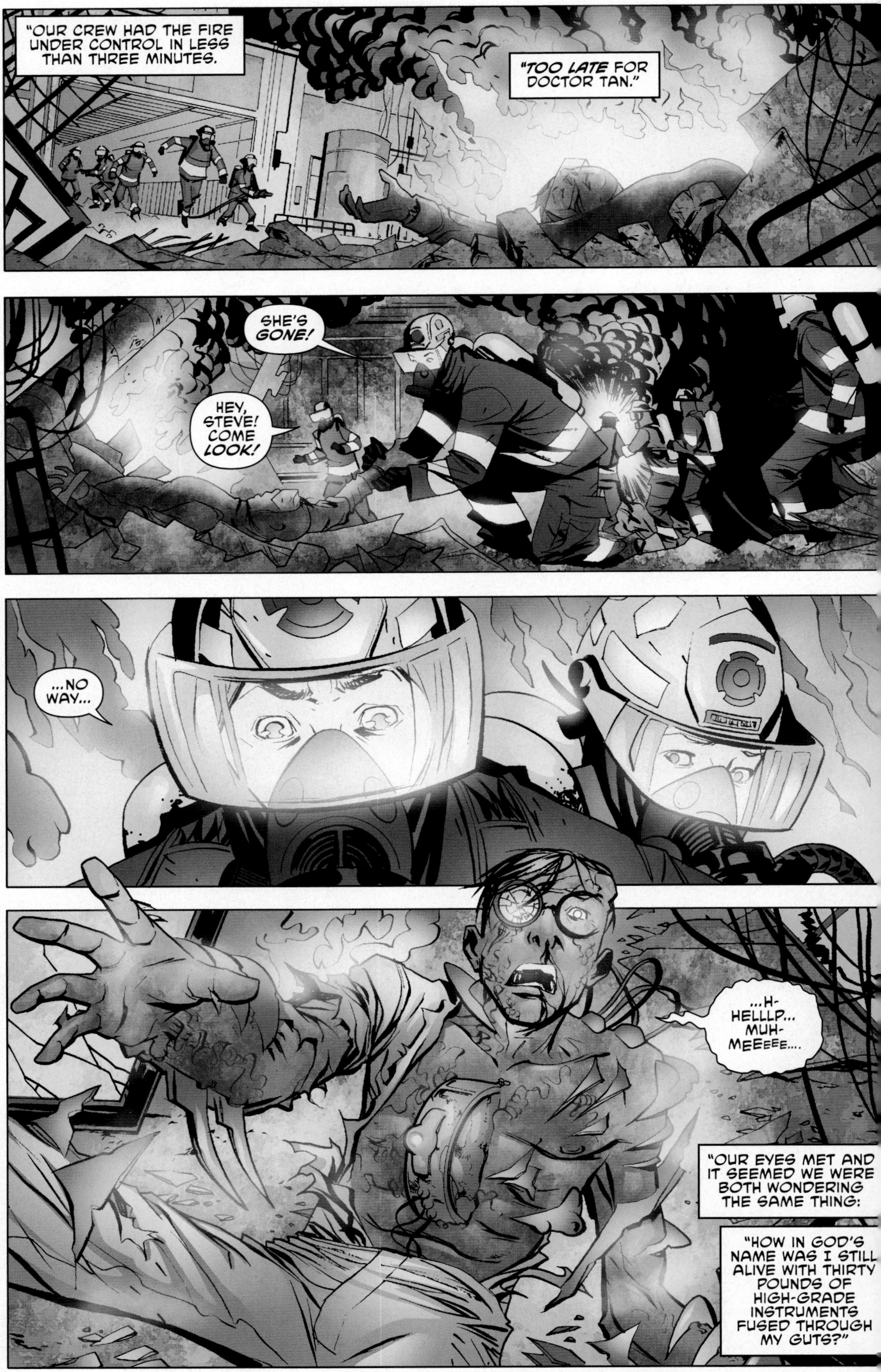
"OUR CREW HAD THE FIRE UNDER CONTROL IN LESS THAN THREE MINUTES.
"TOO LATE FOR DOCTOR TAN."
SHE'S GONE!
HEY, STEVE! COME LOOK!
...NO WAY...
...H-HELLLP... MUH-MEEEEEE....
"OUR EYES MET AND IT SEEMED WE WERE BOTH WONDERING THE SAME THING:
"HOW IN GOD'S NAME WAS I STILL ALIVE WITH THIRTY POUNDS OF HIGH-GRADE INSTRUMENTS FUSED THROUGH MY GUTS?"

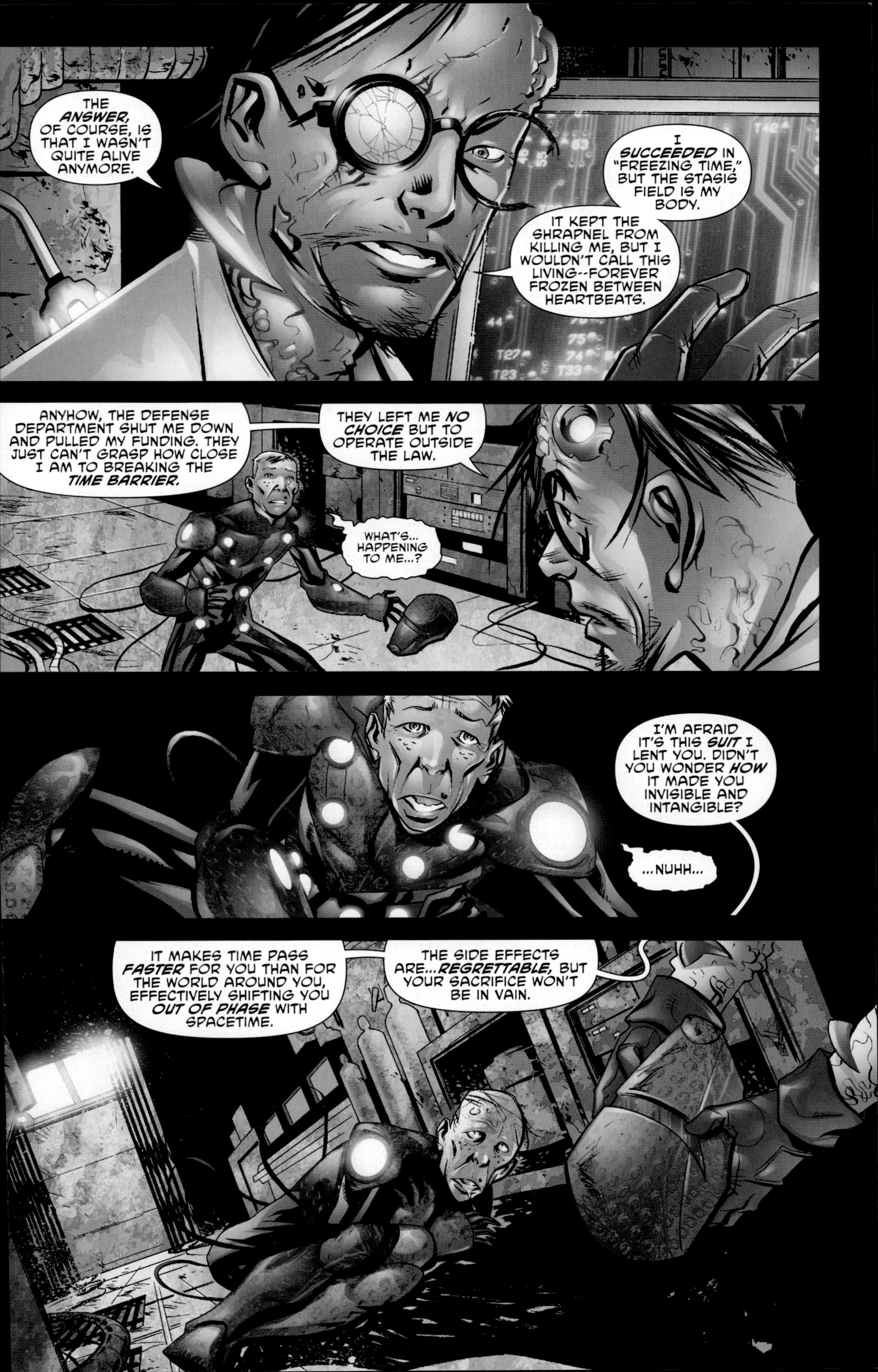
THE ANSWER, OF COURSE, IS THAT I WASN'T QUITE ALIVE ANYMORE.
I SUCCEEDED IN "FREEZING TIME," BUT THE STASIS FIELD IS MY BODY.
IT KEPT THE SHRAPNEL FROM KILLING ME, BUT I WOULDN'T CALL THIS LIVING--FOREVER FROZEN BETWEEN HEARTBEATS.
ANYHOW, THE DEFENSE DEPARTMENT SHUT ME DOWN AND PULLED MY FUNDING. THEY JUST CAN'T GRASP HOW CLOSE I AM TO BREAKING THE TIME BARRIER.
THEY LEFT ME NO CHOICE BUT TO OPERATE OUTSIDE THE LAW.
WHAT'S... HAPPENING TO ME...?
I'M AFRAID IT'S THIS SUIT I LENT YOU. DIDN'T YOU WONDER HOW IT MADE YOU INVISIBLE AND INTANGIBLE?
...NUHH...
IT MAKES TIME PASS FASTER FOR YOU THAN FOR THE WORLD AROUND YOU, EFFECTIVELY SHIFTING YOU OUT OF PHASE WITH SPACETIME.
THE SIDE EFFECTS ARE...REGRETTABLE, BUT YOUR SACRIFICE WON'T BE IN VAIN.

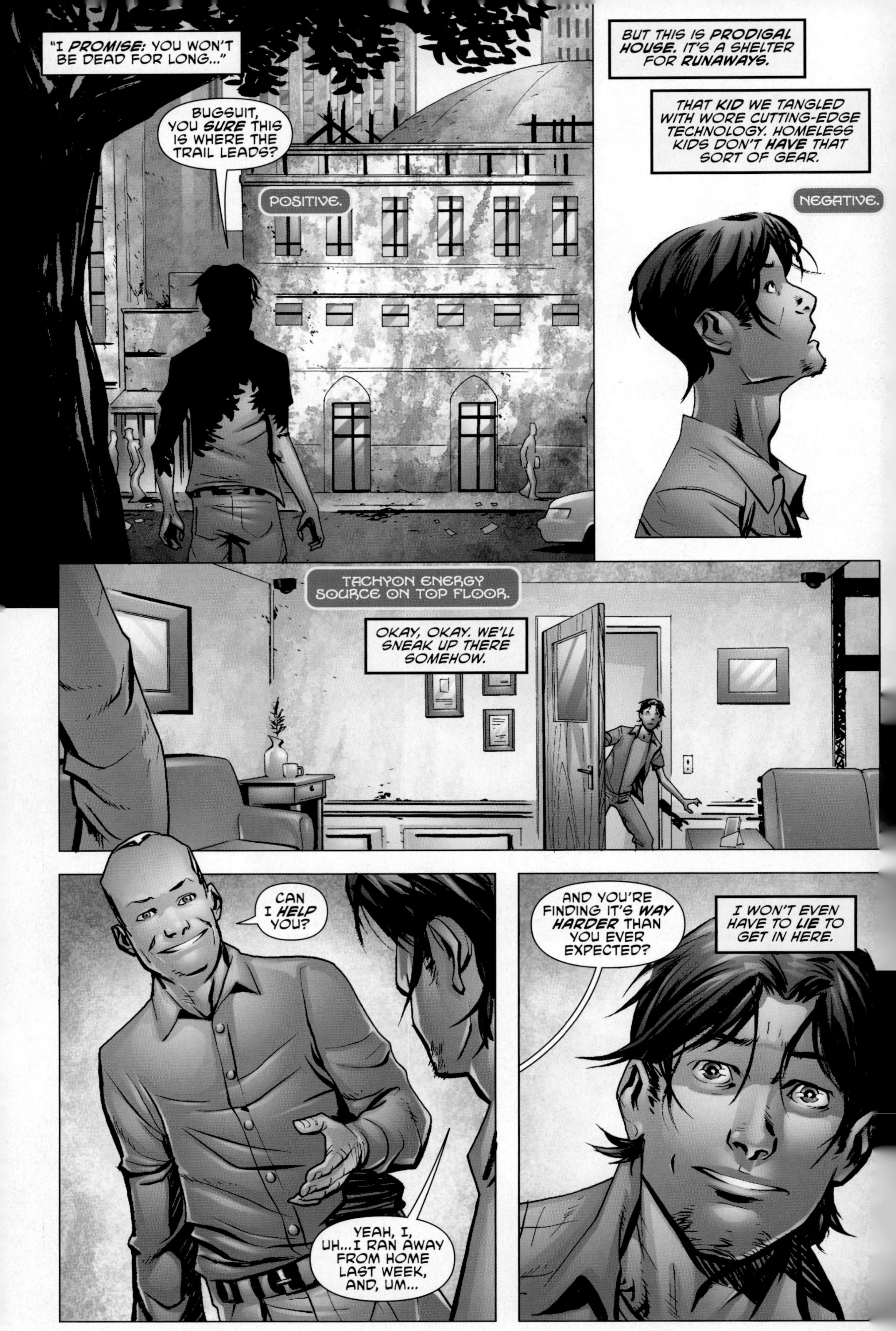
"I PROMISE: YOU WON'T BE DEAD FOR LONG..."
BUGSUIT, YOU SURE THIS IS WHERE THE TRAIL LEADS?
POSITIVE.
BUT THIS IS PRODIGAL HOUSE. IT'S A SHELTER FOR RUNAWAYS.
THAT KID WE TANGLED WITH WORE CUTTING-EDGE TECHNOLOGY. HOMELESS KIDS DON'T HAVE THAT SORT OF GEAR.
NEGATIVE.
TACHYON ENERGY SOURCE ON TOP FLOOR.
OKAY, OKAY. WE'LL SNEAK UP THERE SOMEHOW.
CAN I HELP YOU?
YEAH, I, UH...I RAN AWAY FROM HOME LAST WEEK, AND, UM...
AND YOU'RE FINDING IT'S WAY HARDER THAN YOU EVER EXPECTED?
I WON'T EVEN HAVE TO LIE TO GET IN HERE.

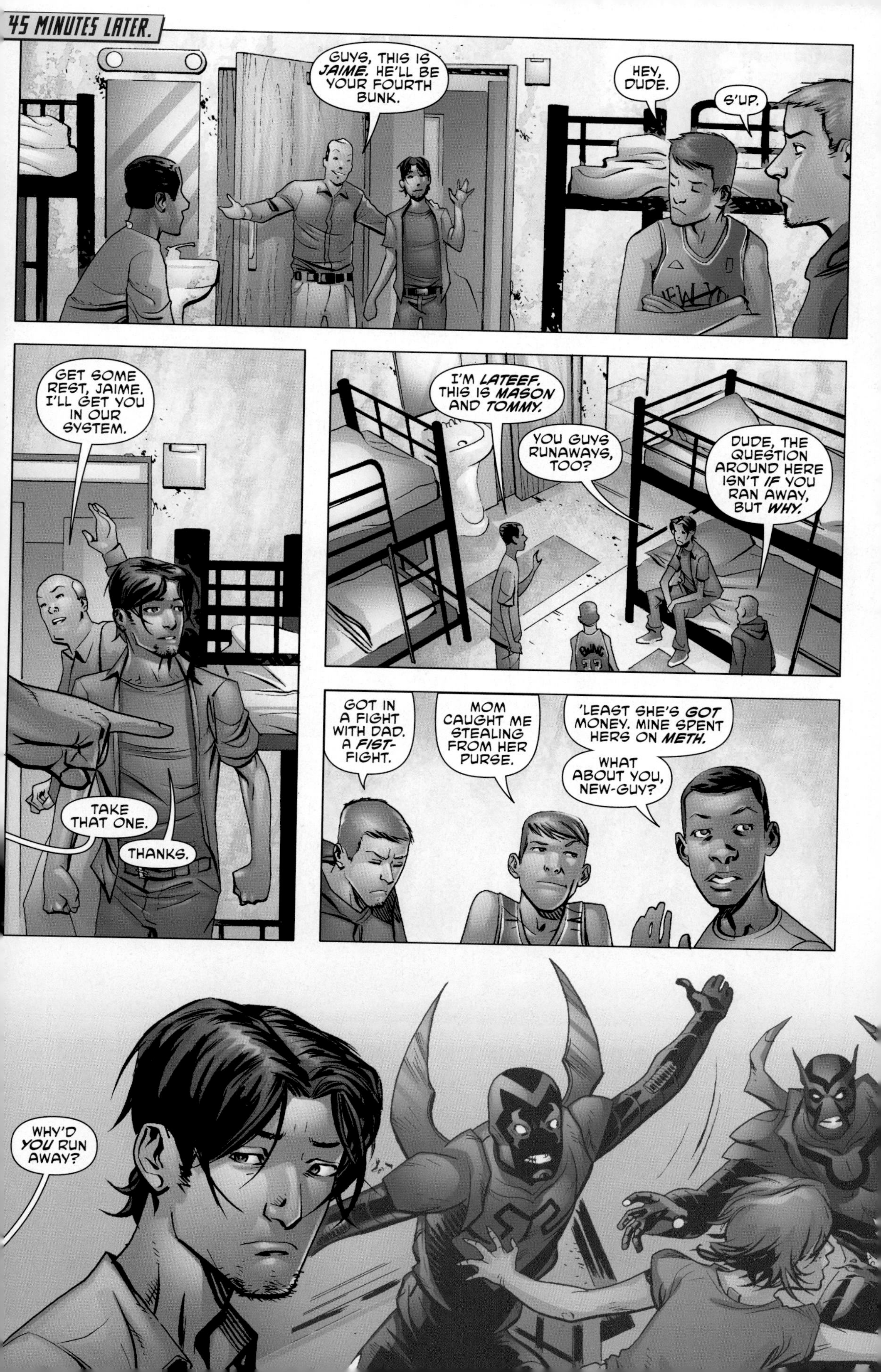
45 MINUTES LATER.
GUYS, THIS IS JAIME. HE'LL BE YOUR FOURTH BUNK.
HEY, DUDE.
S'UP.
GET SOME REST, JAIME. I'LL GET YOU IN OUR SYSTEM.
TAKE THAT ONE.
THANKS.
I'M LATEEF. THIS IS MASON AND TOMMY.
YOU GUYS RUNAWAYS, TOO?
DUDE, THE QUESTION AROUND HERE ISN'T IF YOU RAN AWAY, BUT WHY.
GOT IN A FIGHT WITH DAD. A FIST-FIGHT.
MOM CAUGHT ME STEALING FROM HER PURSE.
'LEAST SHE'S GOT MONEY. MINE SPENT HERS ON METH.
WHAT ABOUT YOU, NEW-GUY?
WHY'D YOU RUN AWAY?

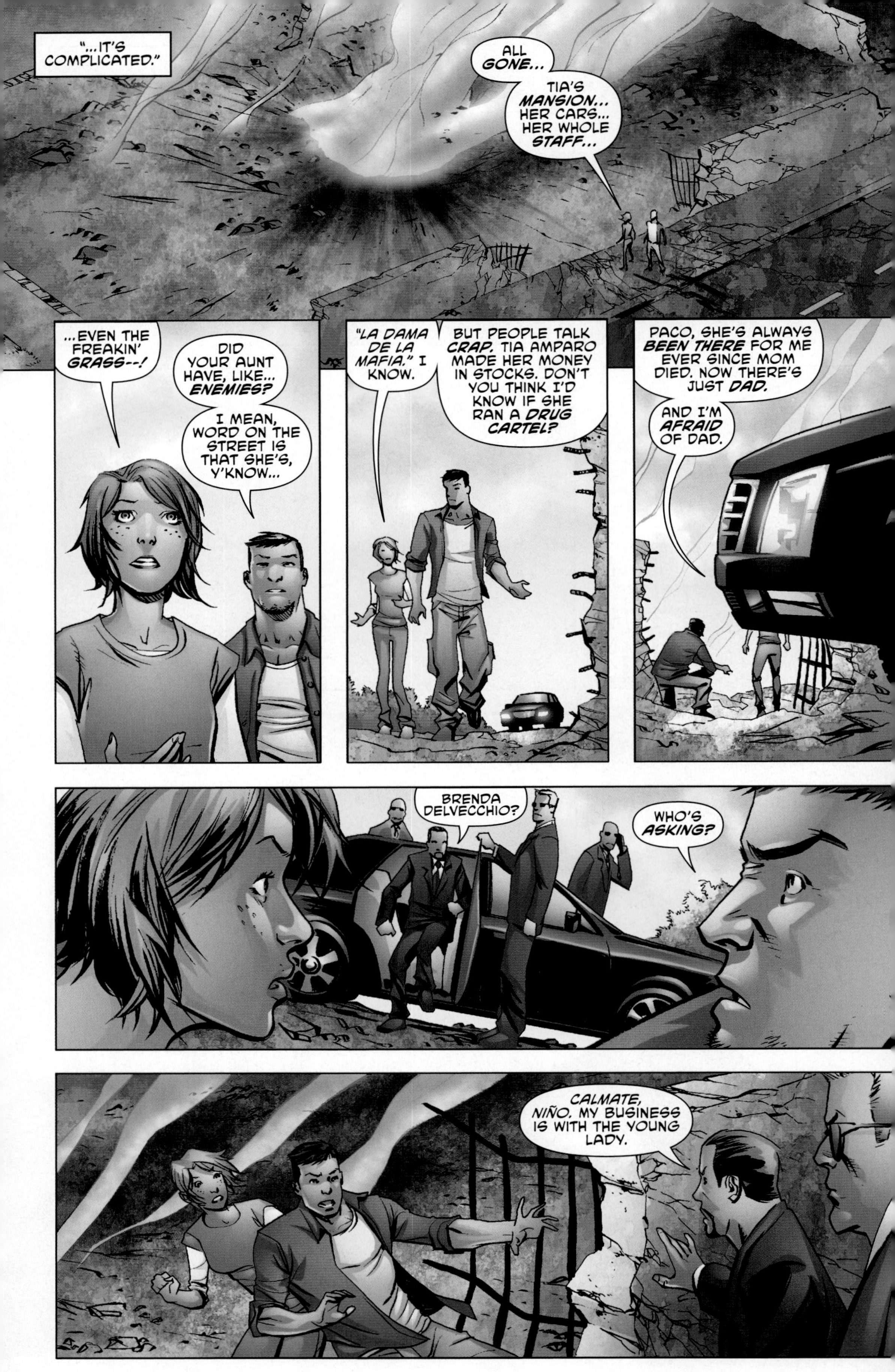
"...IT'S COMPLICATED."
ALL GONE...
TIA'S MANSION... HER CARS... HER WHOLE STAFF...
...EVEN THE FREAKIN' GRASS--!
DID YOUR AUNT HAVE, LIKE... ENEMIES?
I MEAN, WORD ON THE STREET IS THAT SHE'S, Y'KNOW...
"LA DAMA DE LA MAFIA." I KNOW.
BUT PEOPLE TALK CRAP. TIA AMPARO MADE HER MONEY IN STOCKS. DON'T YOU THINK I'D KNOW IF SHE RAN A DRUG CARTEL?
PACO, SHE'S ALWAYS BEEN THERE FOR ME EVER SINCE MOM DIED. NOW THERE'S JUST DAD.
AND I'M AFRAID OF DAD.
BRENDA DELVECCHIO?
WHO'S ASKING?
CALMATE, NIÑO. MY BUSINESS IS WITH THE YOUNG LADY.

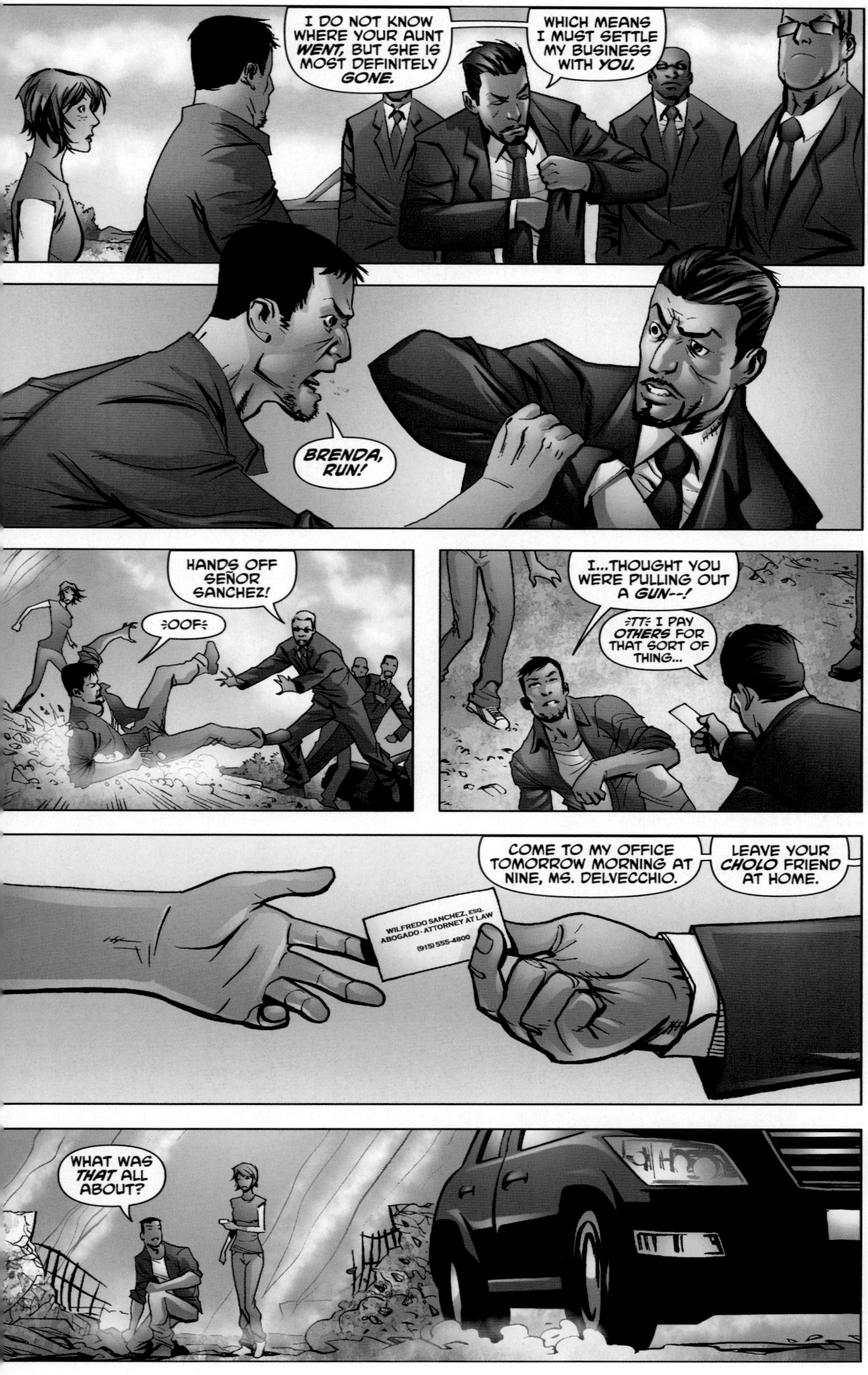
I DO NOT KNOW WHERE YOUR AUNT *WENT,* BUT SHE IS MOST DEFINITELY *GONE.*
WHICH MEANS I MUST SETTLE MY BUSINESS WITH *YOU.*
BRENDA, RUN!
HANDS OFF SEÑOR SANCHEZ!
OOF
I...THOUGHT YOU WERE PULLING OUT A *GUN--!*
TT I PAY *OTHERS* FOR THAT SORT OF THING...
COME TO MY OFFICE TOMORROW MORNING AT NINE, MS. DELVECCHIO.
LEAVE YOUR *CHOLO* FRIEND AT HOME.
WILFREDO SANCHEZ, ESQ.
ABOGADO - ATTORNEY AT LAW
(915) 555-4800
WHAT WAS *THAT* ALL ABOUT?

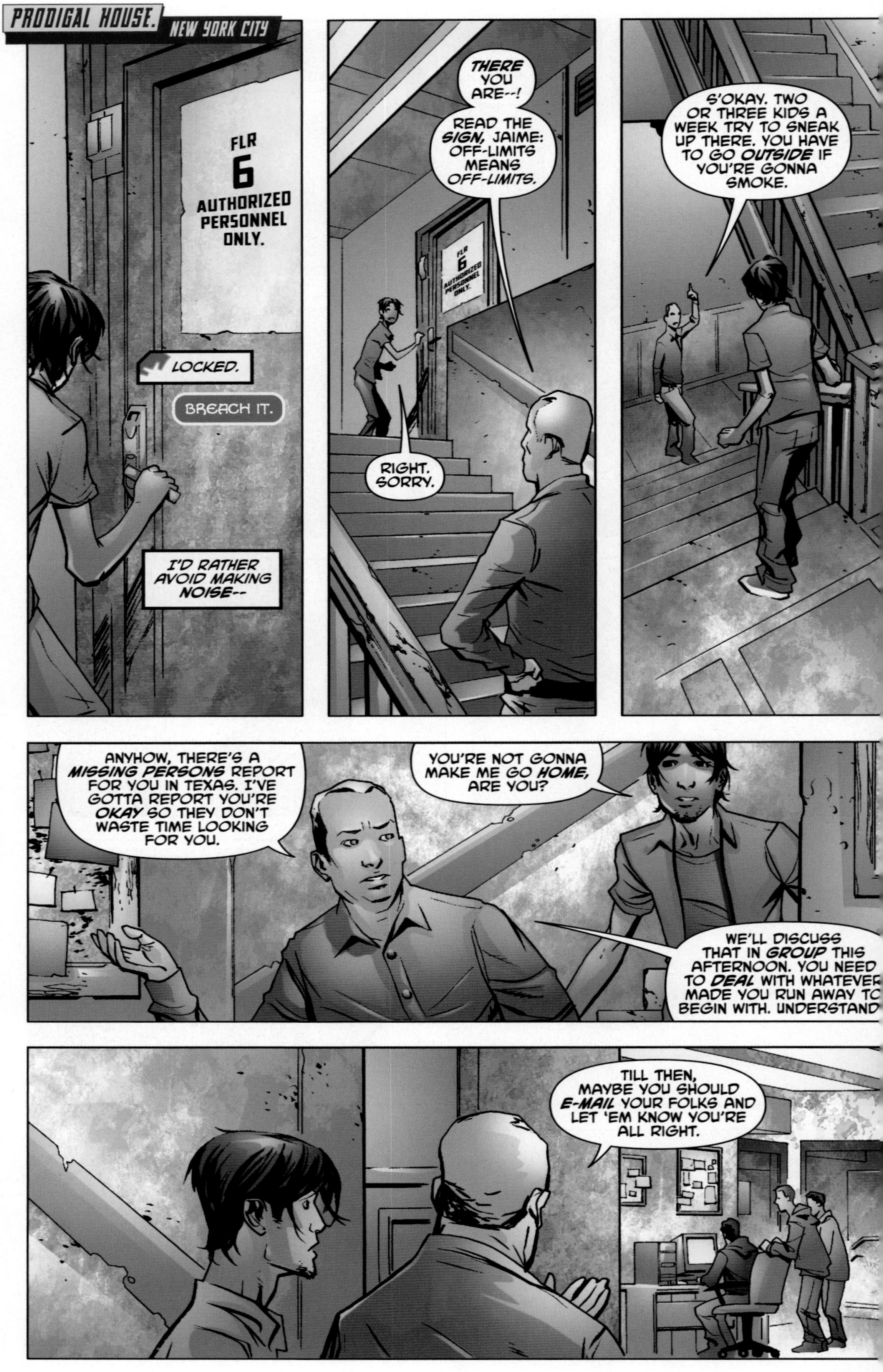
PRODIGAL HOUSE.
NEW YORK CITY
FLR 6 AUTHORIZED PERSONNEL ONLY.
LOCKED.
BREACH IT.
I'D RATHER AVOID MAKING NOISE--
THERE YOU ARE--!
READ THE SIGN, JAIME: OFF-LIMITS MEANS OFF-LIMITS.
RIGHT. SORRY.
S'OKAY. TWO OR THREE KIDS A WEEK TRY TO SNEAK UP THERE. YOU HAVE TO GO OUTSIDE IF YOU'RE GONNA SMOKE.
ANYHOW, THERE'S A MISSING PERSONS REPORT FOR YOU IN TEXAS. I'VE GOTTA REPORT YOU'RE OKAY SO THEY DON'T WASTE TIME LOOKING FOR YOU.
YOU'RE NOT GONNA MAKE ME GO HOME, ARE YOU?
WE'LL DISCUSS THAT IN GROUP THIS AFTERNOON. YOU NEED TO DEAL WITH WHATEVER MADE YOU RUN AWAY TO BEGIN WITH. UNDERSTAND
TILL THEN, MAYBE YOU SHOULD E-MAIL YOUR FOLKS AND LET 'EM KNOW YOU'RE ALL RIGHT.

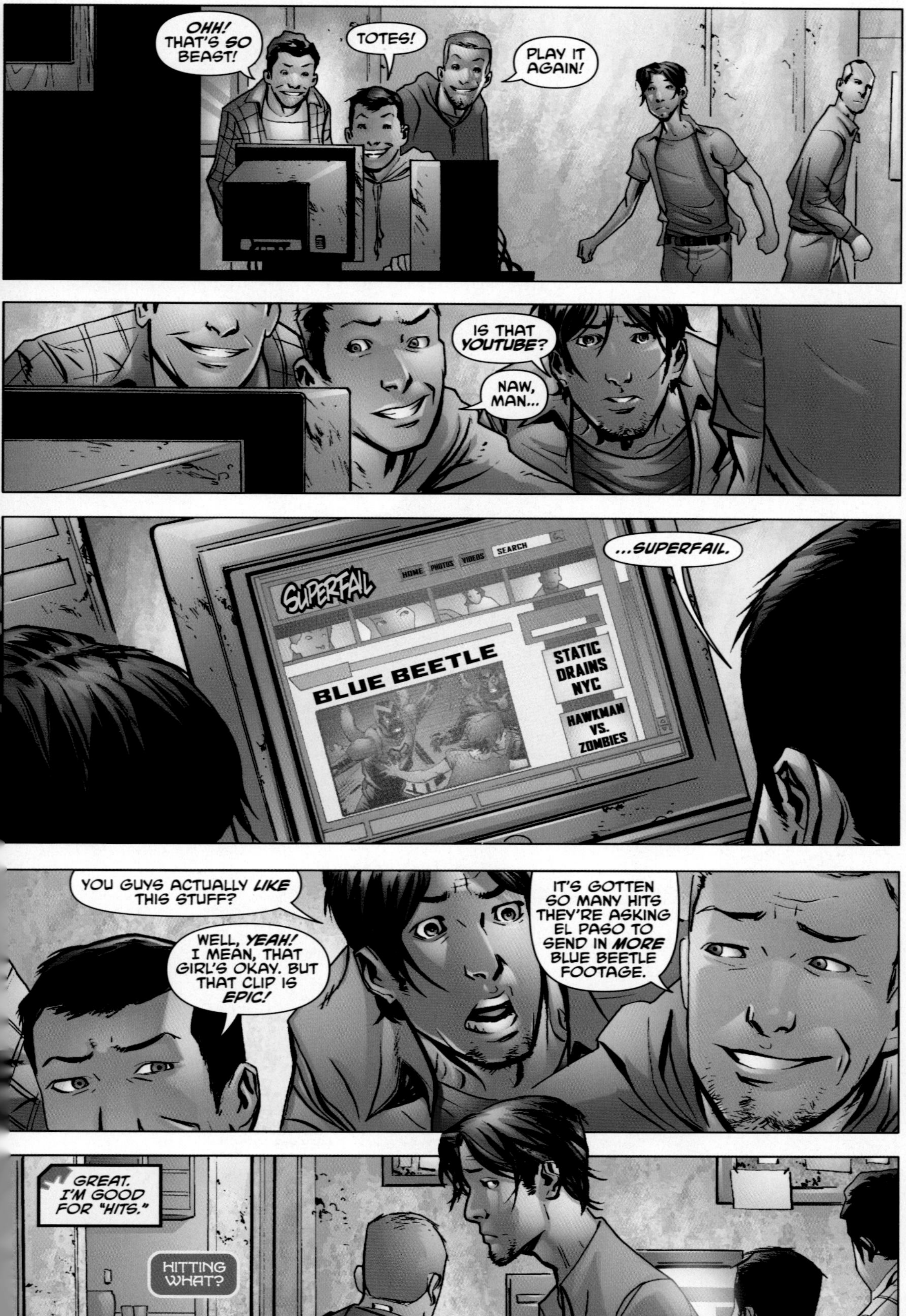

OHH! THAT'S SO BEAST!
TOTES!
PLAY IT AGAIN!
IS THAT YOUTUBE?
NAW, MAN...
SUPERFAIL
HOME
PHOTOS
VIDEOS
SEARCH
BLUE BEETLE
STATIC DRAINS NYC
HAWKMAN VS. ZOMBIES
...SUPERFAIL.
YOU GUYS ACTUALLY LIKE THIS STUFF?
WELL, YEAH! I MEAN, THAT GIRL'S OKAY. BUT THAT CLIP IS EPIC!
IT'S GOTTEN SO MANY HITS THEY'RE ASKING EL PASO TO SEND IN MORE BLUE BEETLE FOOTAGE.
GREAT. I'M GOOD FOR "HITS."
HITTING WHAT?

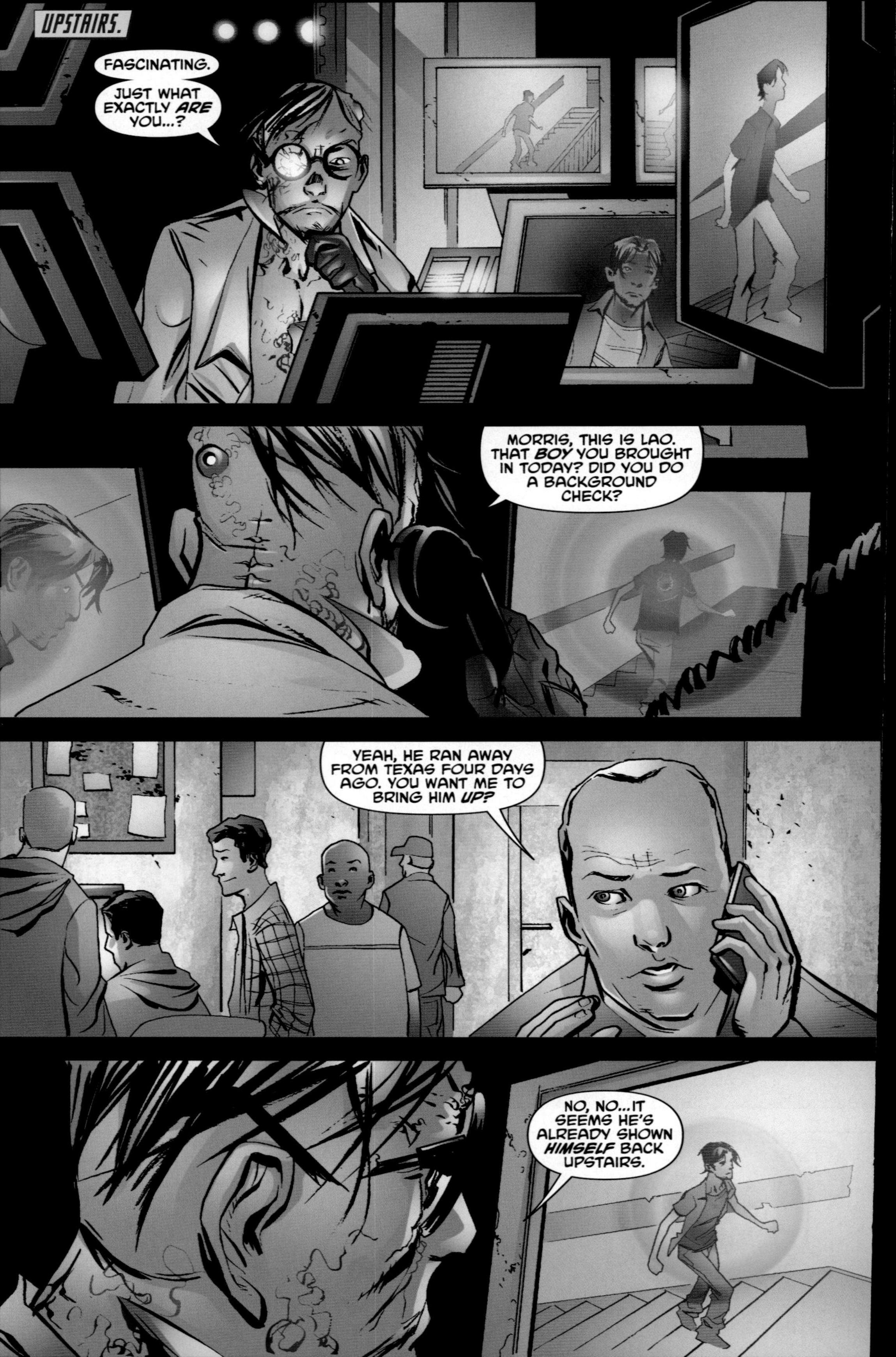
UPSTAIRS.
FASCINATING.
JUST WHAT EXACTLY ARE YOU...?
MORRIS, THIS IS LAO. THAT BOY YOU BROUGHT IN TODAY? DID YOU DO A BACKGROUND CHECK?
YEAH, HE RAN AWAY FROM TEXAS FOUR DAYS AGO. YOU WANT ME TO BRING HIM UP?
NO, NO...IT SEEMS HE'S ALREADY SHOWN HIMSELF BACK UPSTAIRS.

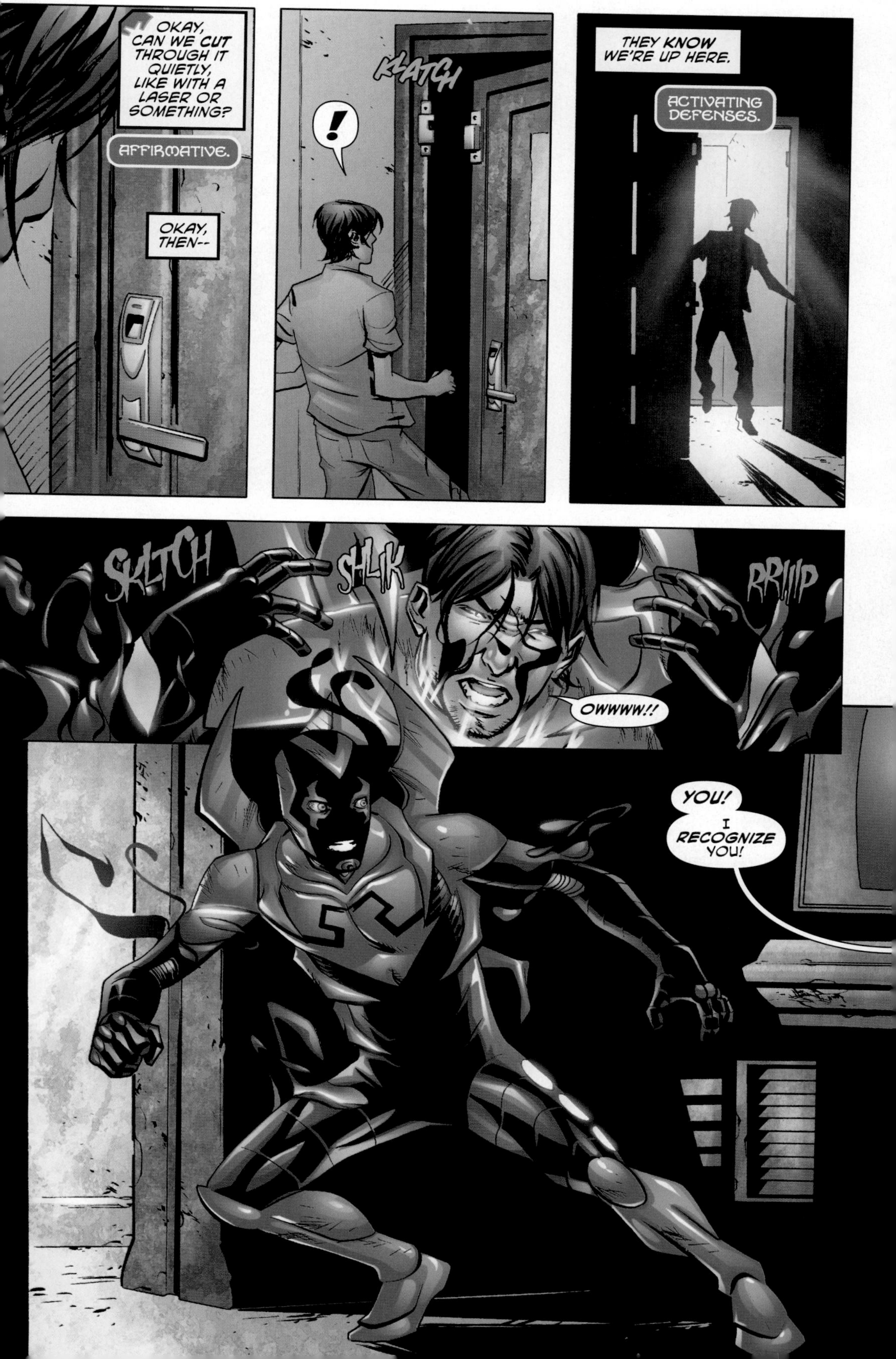
OKAY, CAN WE CUT THROUGH IT QUIETLY, LIKE WITH A LASER OR SOMETHING?
AFFIRMATIVE.
OKAY, THEN--
KLATCH
!
THEY KNOW WE'RE UP HERE.
ACTIVATING DEFENSES.
SKLTCH
SHLIK
RRIIIP
OWWWW!!
YOU! I RECOGNIZE YOU!

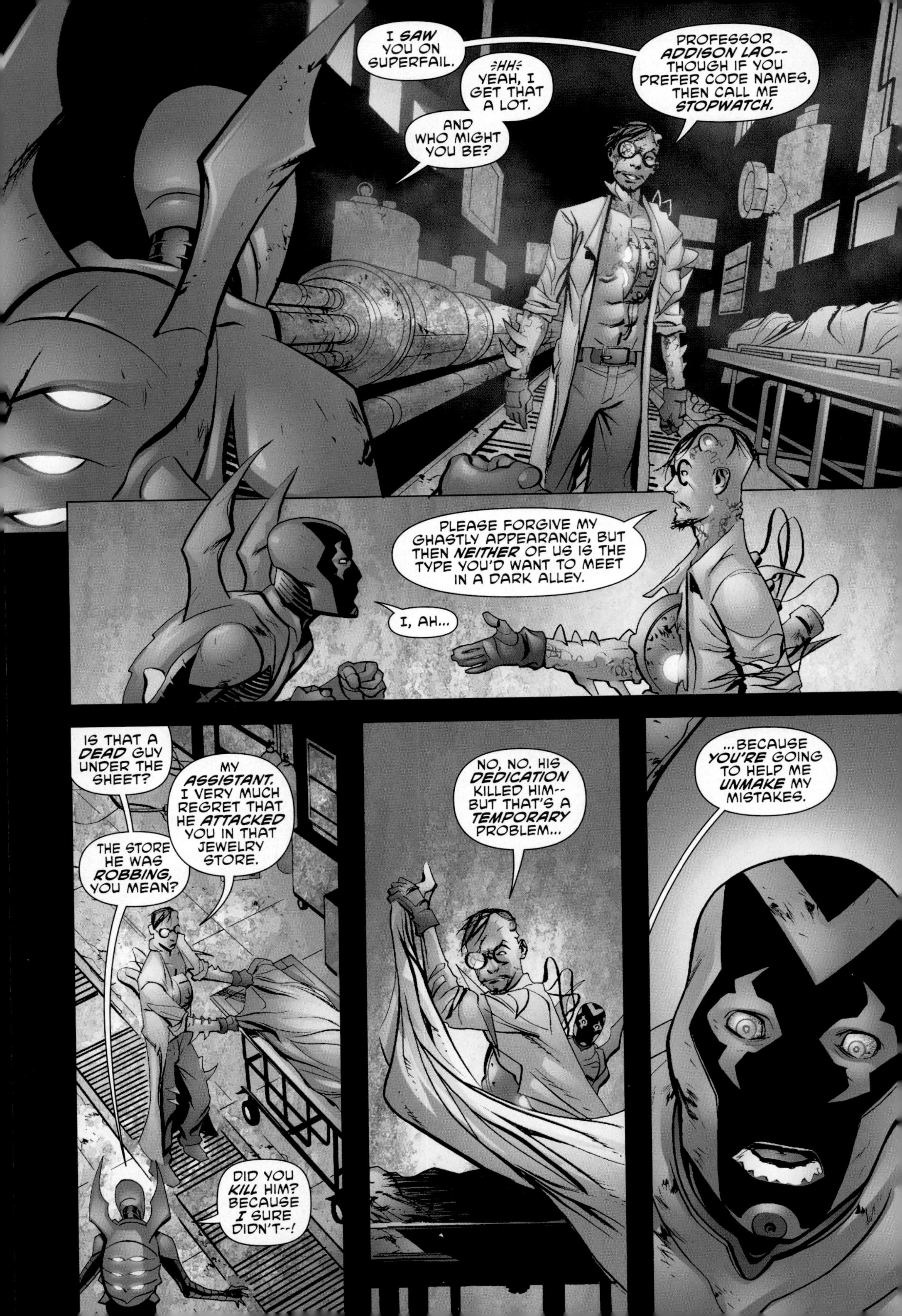
I SAW YOU ON SUPERFAIL.
PROFESSOR ADDISON LAO-- THOUGH IF YOU PREFER CODE NAMES, THEN CALL ME STOPWATCH.
=HH= YEAH, I GET THAT A LOT.
AND WHO MIGHT YOU BE?
PLEASE FORGIVE MY GHASTLY APPEARANCE, BUT THEN NEITHER OF US IS THE TYPE YOU'D WANT TO MEET IN A DARK ALLEY.
I, AH...
IS THAT A DEAD GUY UNDER THE SHEET?
MY ASSISTANT. I VERY MUCH REGRET THAT HE ATTACKED YOU IN THAT JEWELRY STORE.
THE STORE HE WAS ROBBING, YOU MEAN?
DID YOU KILL HIM? BECAUSE I SURE DIDN'T--!
NO, NO. HIS DEDICATION KILLED HIM-- BUT THAT'S A TEMPORARY PROBLEM...
...BECAUSE YOU'RE GOING TO HELP ME UNMAKE MY MISTAKES.

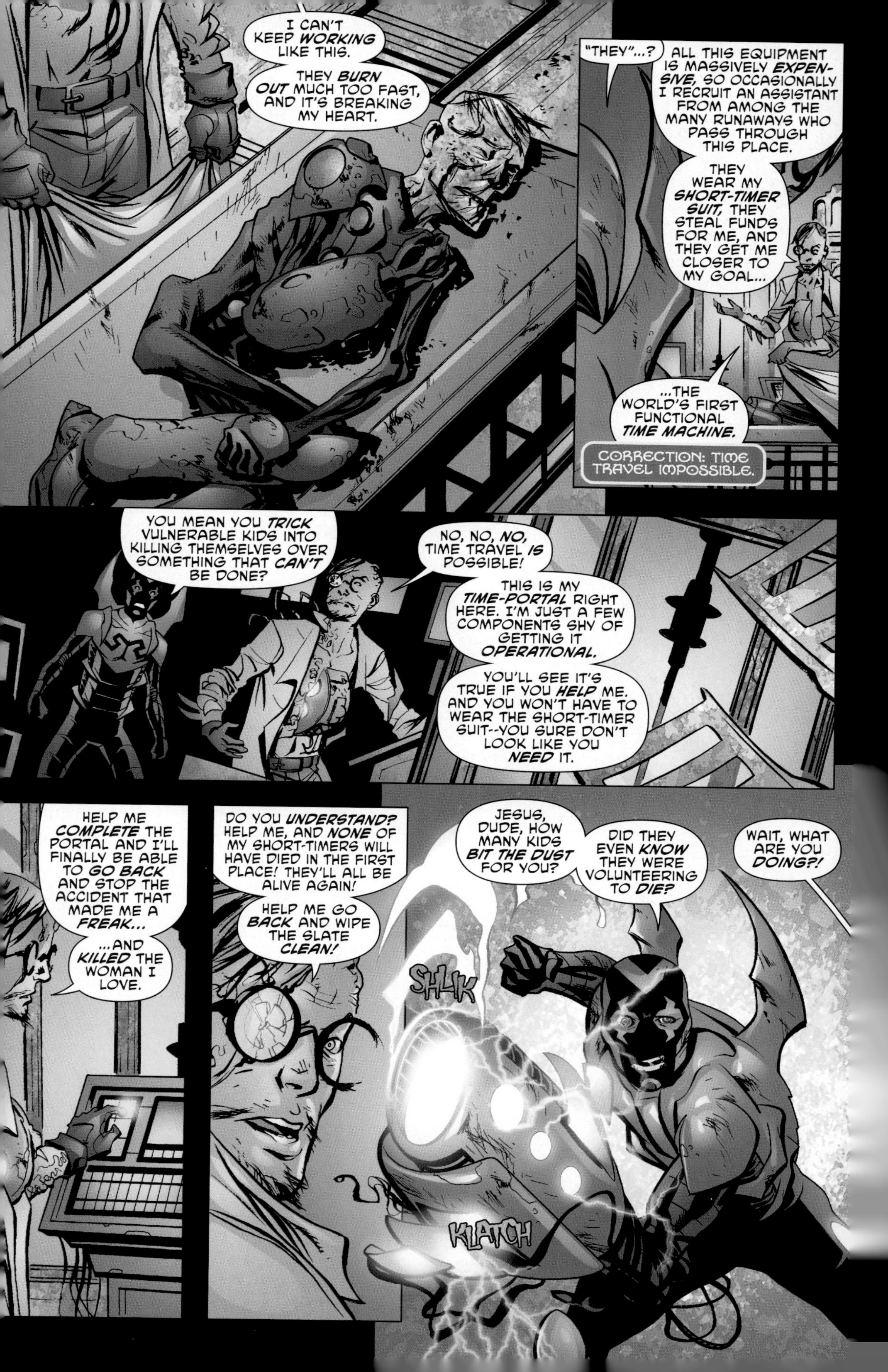
I CAN'T KEEP WORKING LIKE THIS.
THEY BURN OUT MUCH TOO FAST, AND IT'S BREAKING MY HEART.
"THEY"...?
ALL THIS EQUIPMENT IS MASSIVELY EXPENSIVE, SO OCCASIONALLY I RECRUIT AN ASSISTANT FROM AMONG THE MANY RUNAWAYS WHO PASS THROUGH THIS PLACE.
THEY WEAR MY SHORT-TIMER SUIT, THEY STEAL FUNDS FOR ME, AND THEY GET ME CLOSER TO MY GOAL...
...THE WORLD'S FIRST FUNCTIONAL TIME MACHINE.
CORRECTION: TIME TRAVEL IMPOSSIBLE.
YOU MEAN YOU TRICK VULNERABLE KIDS INTO KILLING THEMSELVES OVER SOMETHING THAT CAN'T BE DONE?
NO, NO, NO, TIME TRAVEL IS POSSIBLE!
THIS IS MY TIME-PORTAL RIGHT HERE. I'M JUST A FEW COMPONENTS SHY OF GETTING IT OPERATIONAL.
YOU'LL SEE IT'S TRUE IF YOU HELP ME. AND YOU WON'T HAVE TO WEAR THE SHORT-TIMER SUIT--YOU SURE DON'T LOOK LIKE YOU NEED IT.
HELP ME COMPLETE THE PORTAL AND I'LL FINALLY BE ABLE TO GO BACK AND STOP THE ACCIDENT THAT MADE ME A FREAK...
...AND KILLED THE WOMAN I LOVE.
DO YOU UNDERSTAND? HELP ME, AND NONE OF MY SHORT-TIMERS WILL HAVE DIED IN THE FIRST PLACE! THEY'LL ALL BE ALIVE AGAIN!
HELP ME GO BACK AND WIPE THE SLATE CLEAN!
JESUS, DUDE, HOW MANY KIDS BIT THE DUST FOR YOU?
DID THEY EVEN KNOW THEY WERE VOLUNTEERING TO DIE?
WAIT, WHAT ARE YOU DOING?!
SHLIK
KLATCH

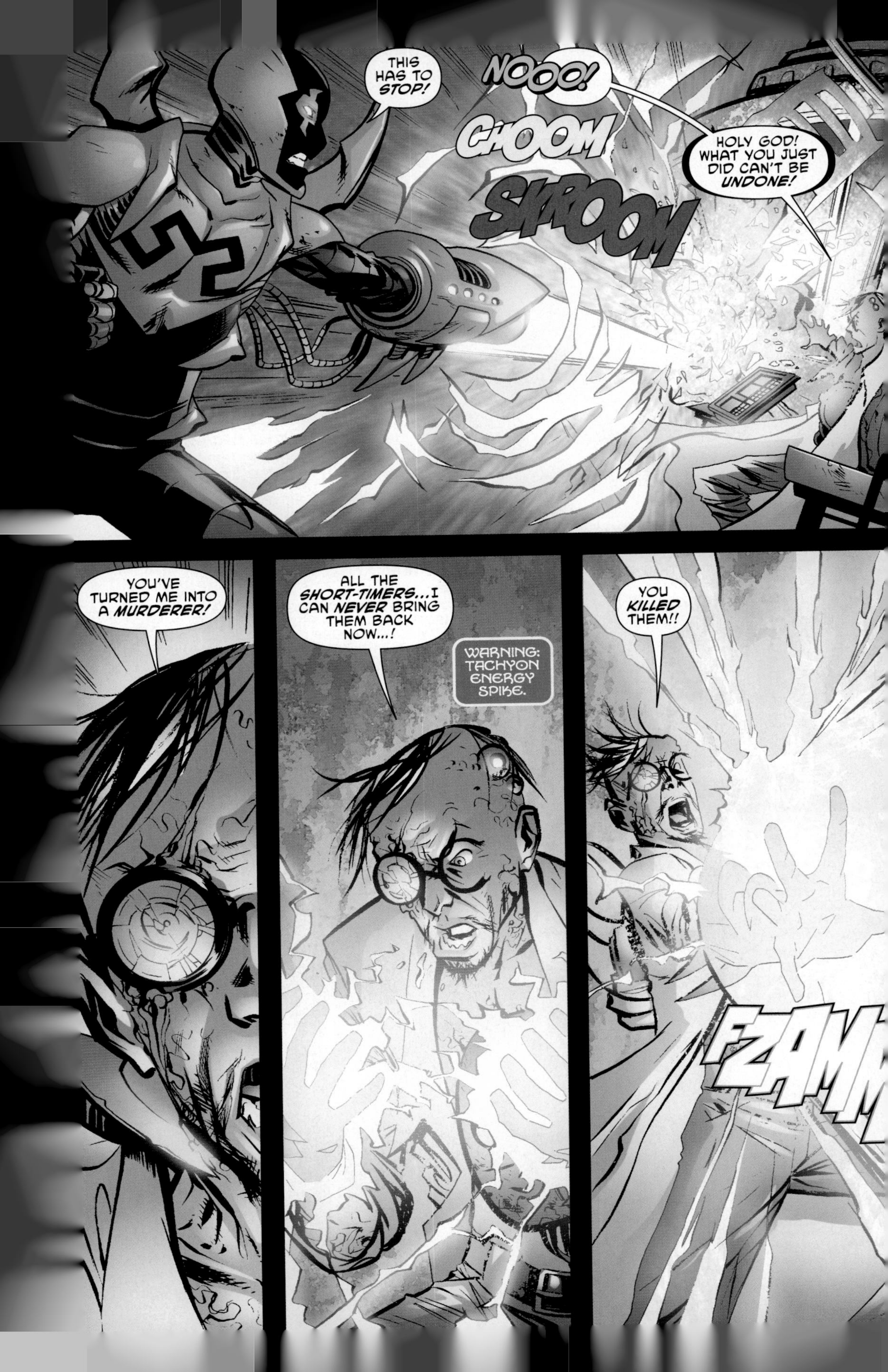
THIS HAS TO STOP!
NOOO!
CHOOM
SKROOM
HOLY GOD! WHAT YOU JUST DID CAN'T BE UNDONE!
YOU'VE TURNED ME INTO A MURDERER!
ALL THE SHORT-TIMERS... I CAN NEVER BRING THEM BACK NOW...!
WARNING: TACHYON ENERGY SPIKE.
YOU KILLED THEM!!
FZAMM

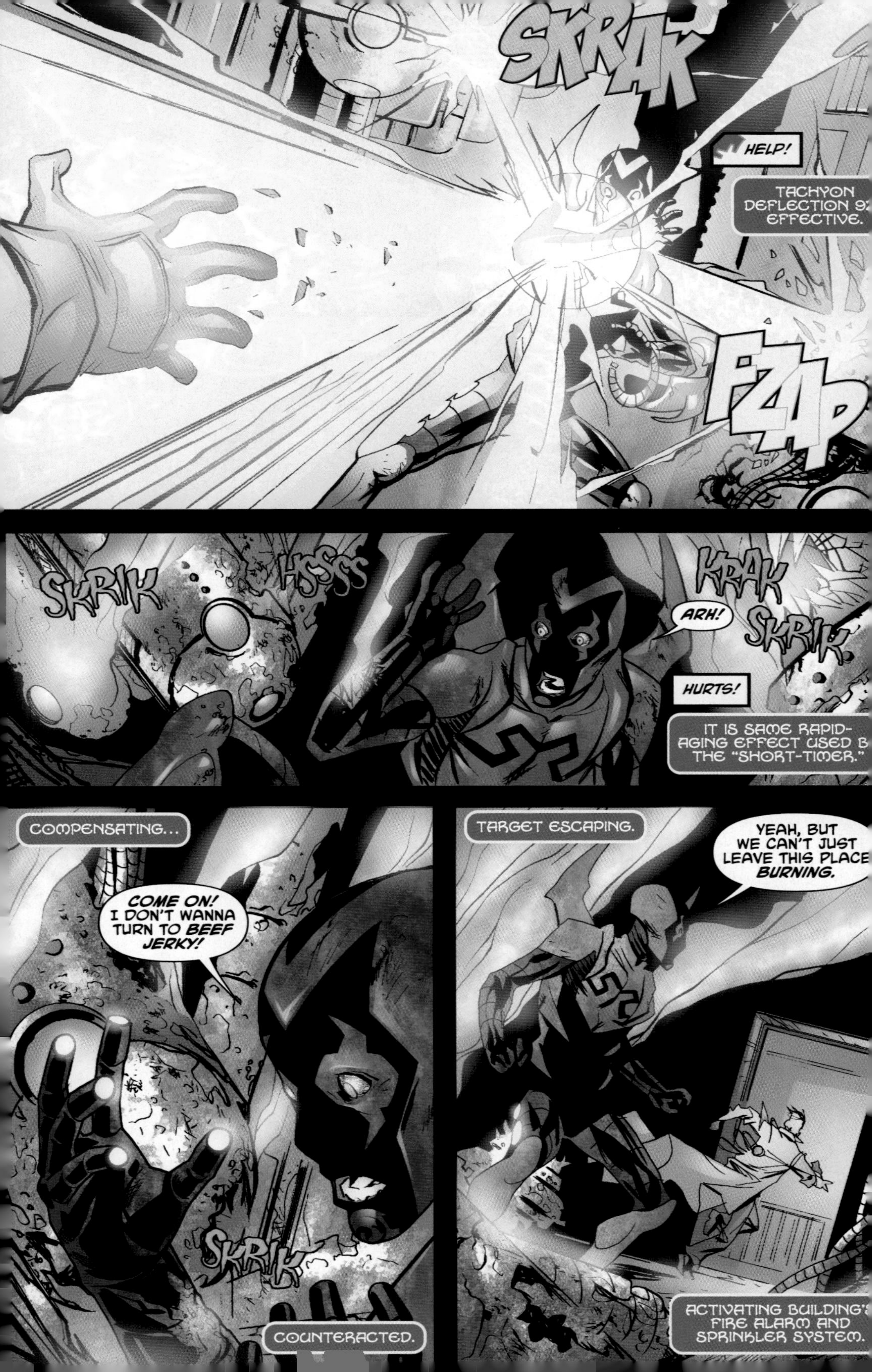
SKRAK
HELP!
TACHYON DEFLECTION 9
EFFECTIVE.
FZAP
SKRIK
HSSSS
KRAK
ARH!
SKRIK
HURTS!
IT IS SAME RAPID-AGING EFFECT USED B
THE "SHORT-TIMER."
COMPENSATING...
COME ON! I DON'T WANNA TURN TO BEEF JERKY!
SKRIK
COUNTERACTED.
TARGET ESCAPING.
YEAH, BUT WE CAN'T JUST LEAVE THIS PLACE BURNING.
ACTIVATING BUILDING'S FIRE ALARM AND SPRINKLER SYSTEM.

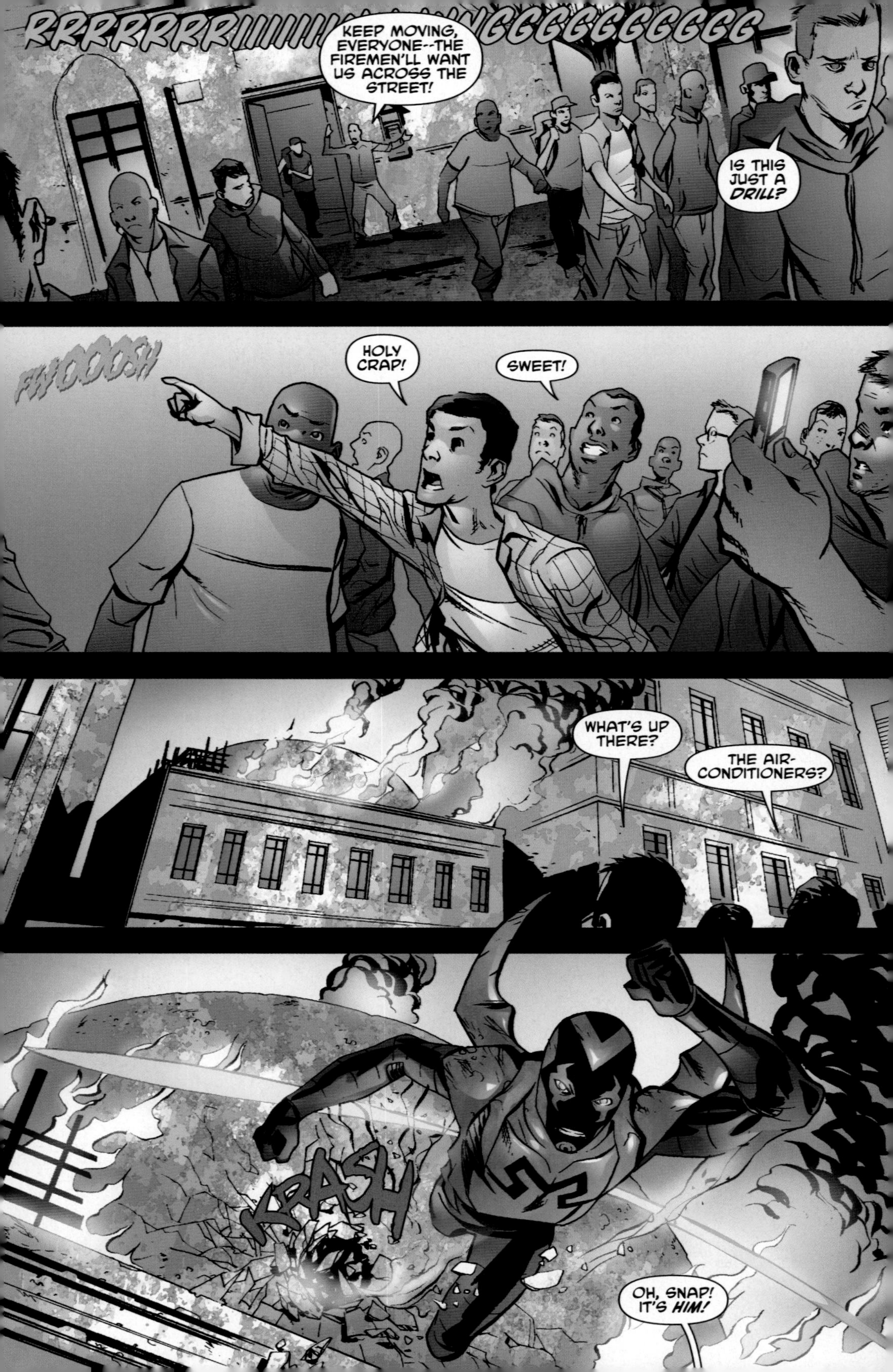
RRRRRRRRIIIIIIIIIIIIIINNGGGGGGGGGGG
KEEP MOVING, EVERYONE--THE FIREMEN'LL WANT US ACROSS THE STREET!
IS THIS JUST A *DRILL?*
FWOOOSH
HOLY CRAP!
SWEET!
WHAT'S UP THERE?
THE AIR-CONDITIONERS?
KRASH
OH, SNAP! IT'S *HIM!*

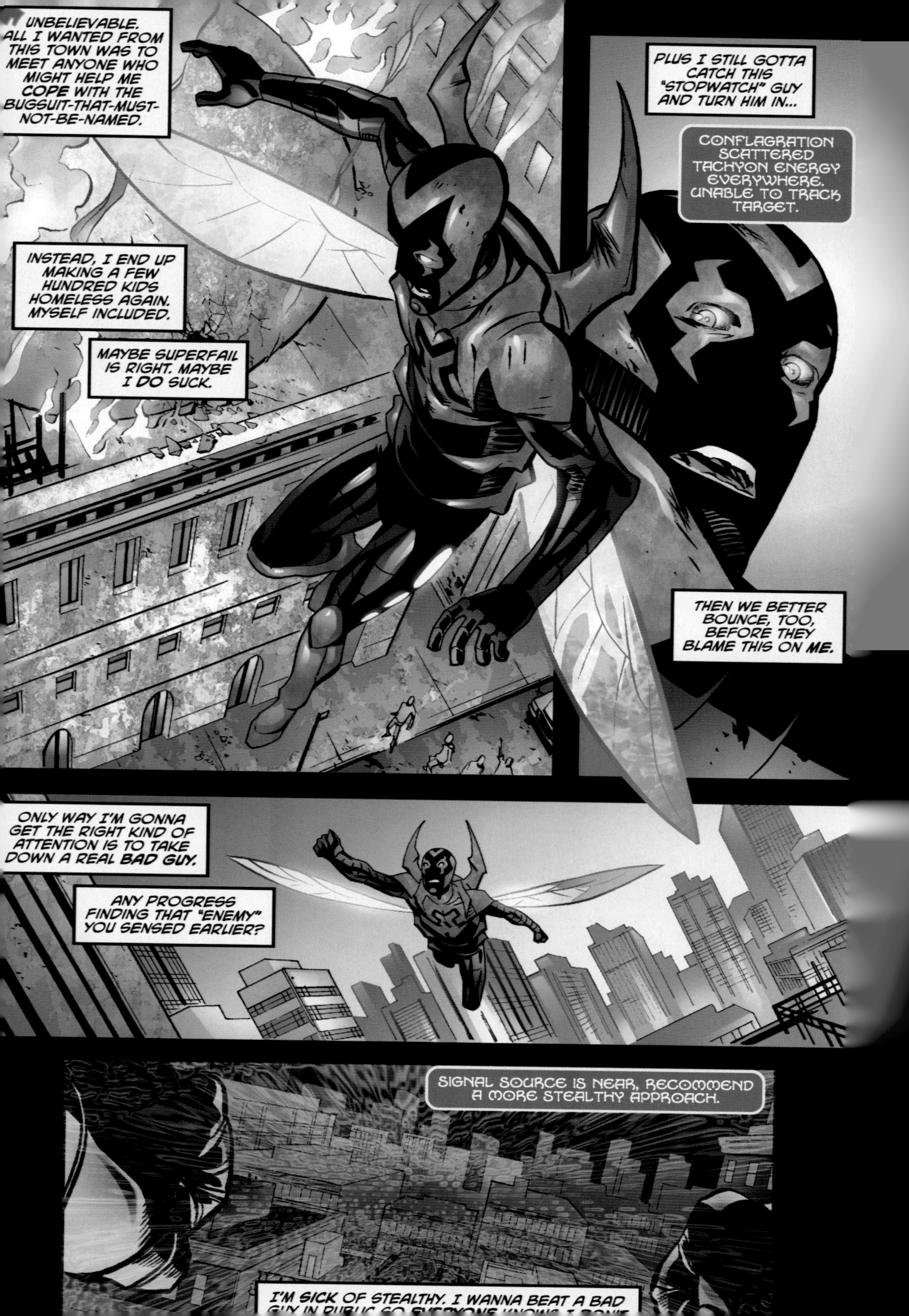
UNBELIEVABLE. ALL I WANTED FROM THIS TOWN WAS TO MEET ANYONE WHO MIGHT HELP ME COPE WITH THE BUGSUIT-THAT-MUST-NOT-BE-NAMED.
INSTEAD, I END UP MAKING A FEW HUNDRED KIDS HOMELESS AGAIN. MYSELF INCLUDED.
MAYBE SUPERFAIL IS RIGHT. MAYBE I DO SUCK.
PLUS I STILL GOTTA CATCH THIS "STOPWATCH" GUY AND TURN HIM IN...
CONFLAGRATION SCATTERED TACHYON ENERGY EVERYWHERE. UNABLE TO TRACK TARGET.
THEN WE BETTER BOUNCE, TOO, BEFORE THEY BLAME THIS ON ME.
ONLY WAY I'M GONNA GET THE RIGHT KIND OF ATTENTION IS TO TAKE DOWN A REAL BAD GUY.
ANY PROGRESS FINDING THAT "ENEMY" YOU SENSED EARLIER?
SIGNAL SOURCE IS NEAR, RECOMMEND A MORE STEALTHY APPROACH.
I'M SICK OF STEALTHY. I WANNA BEAT A BAD

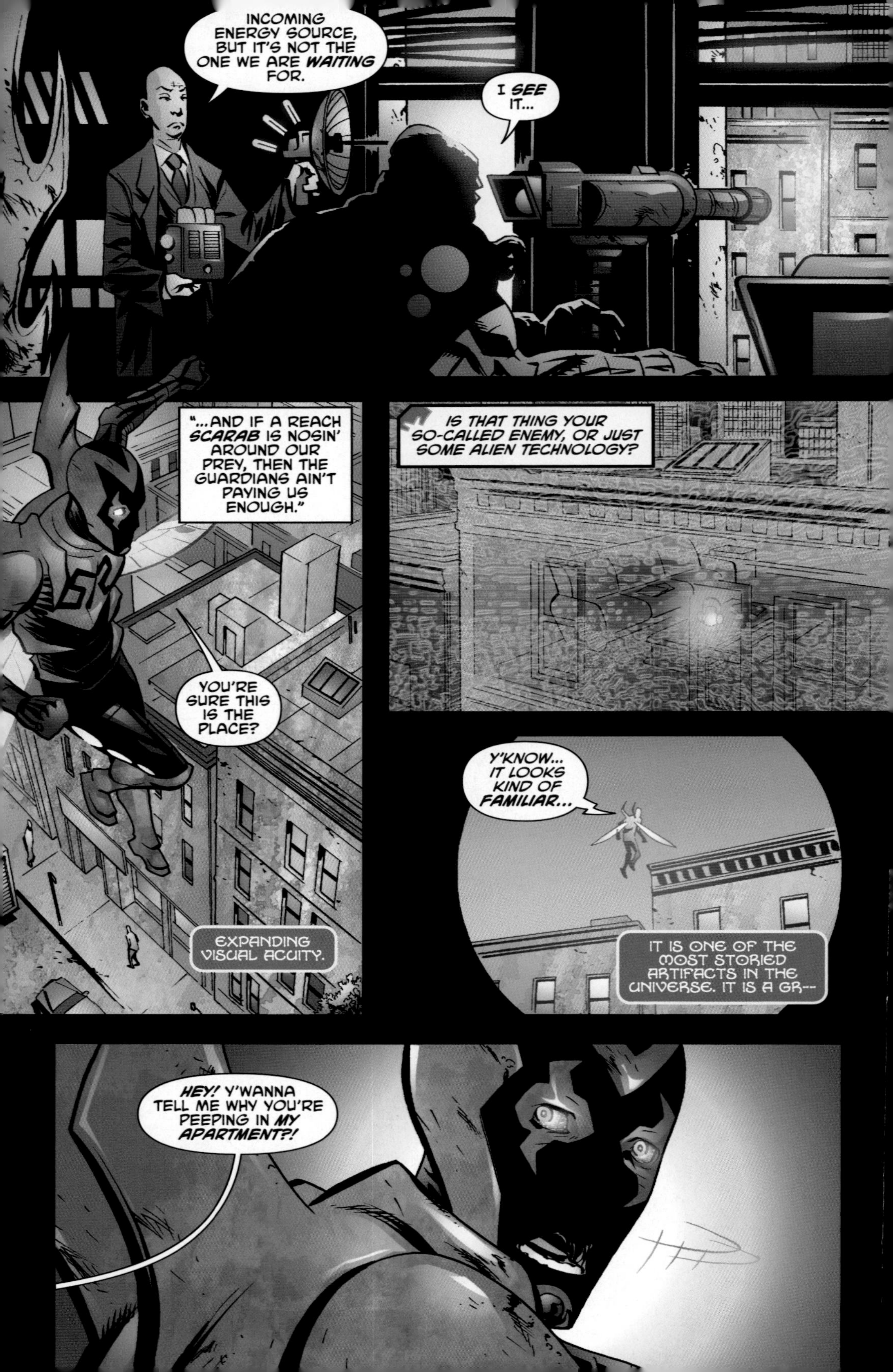
INCOMING ENERGY SOURCE, BUT IT'S NOT THE ONE WE ARE WAITING FOR.
I SEE IT...
"...AND IF A REACH SCARAB IS NOSIN' AROUND OUR PREY, THEN THE GUARDIANS AIN'T PAYING US ENOUGH."
YOU'RE SURE THIS IS THE PLACE?
EXPANDING VISUAL ACUITY.
IS THAT THING YOUR SO-CALLED ENEMY, OR JUST SOME ALIEN TECHNOLOGY?
Y'KNOW... IT LOOKS KIND OF FAMILIAR...
IT IS ONE OF THE MOST STORIED ARTIFACTS IN THE UNIVERSE. IT IS A GR--
HEY! Y'WANNA TELL ME WHY YOU'RE PEEPING IN MY APARTMENT?!

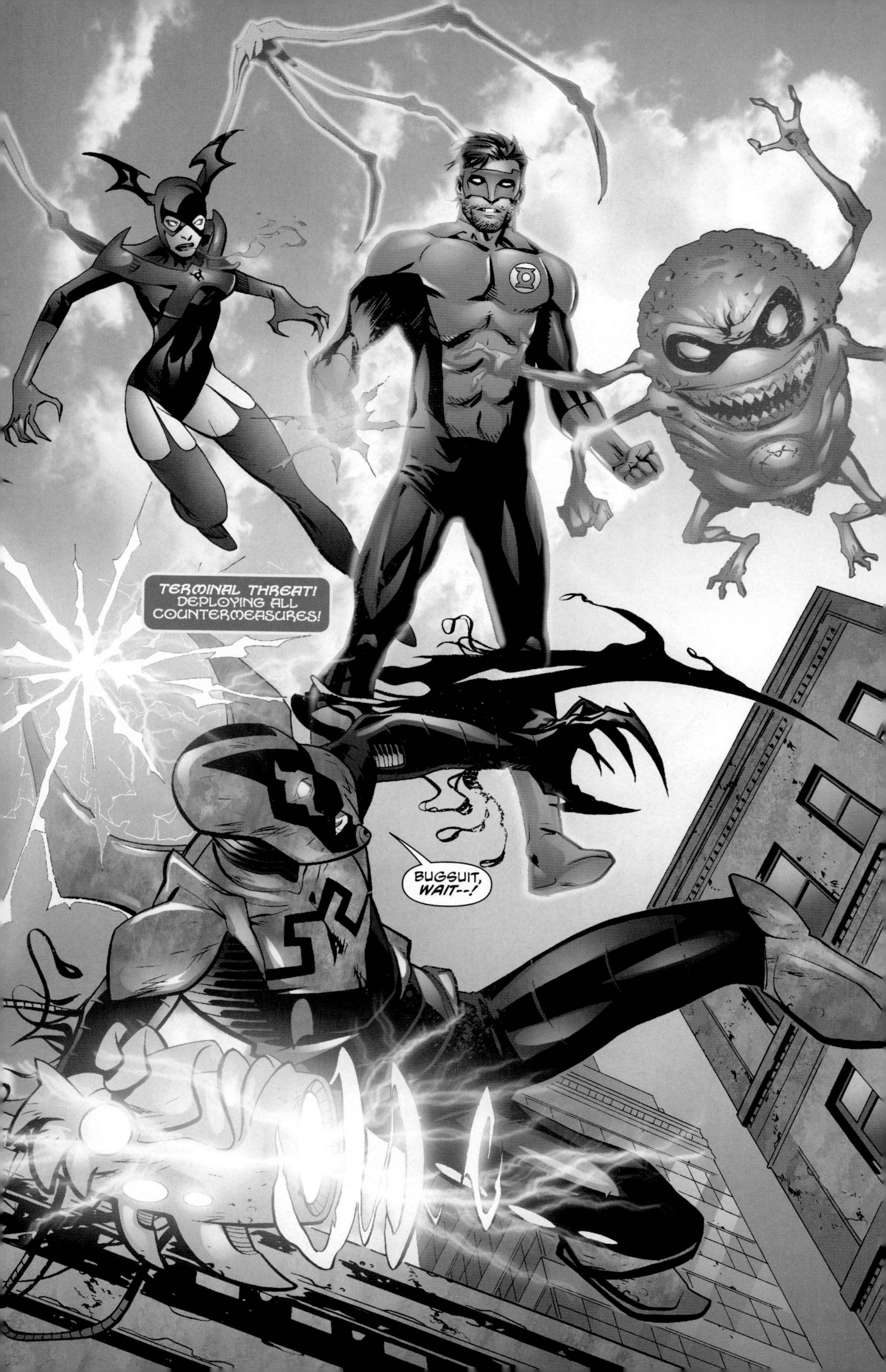
TERMINAL THREAT! DEPLOYING ALL COUNTERMEASURES!
BUGSUIT, WAIT--!

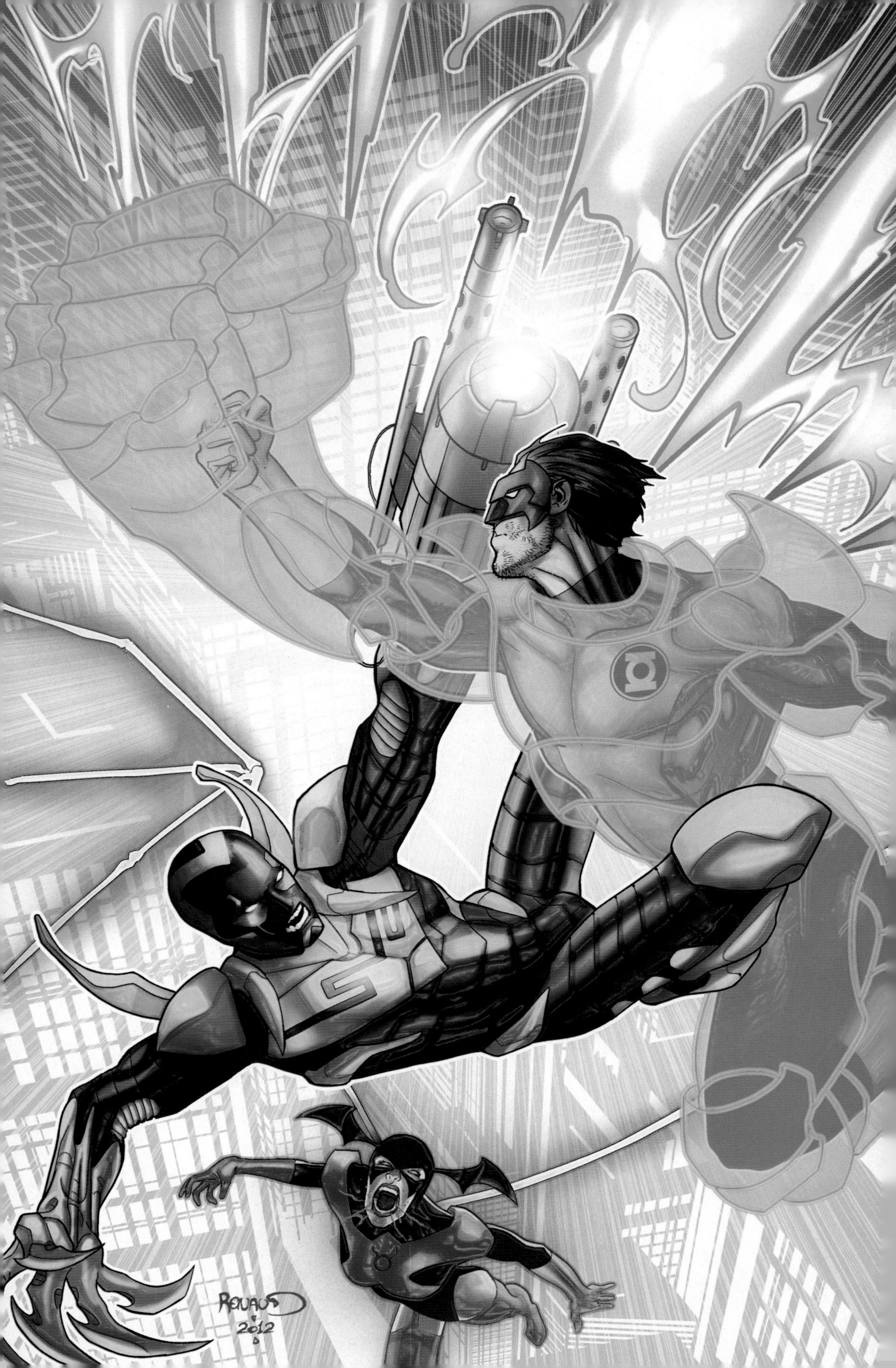

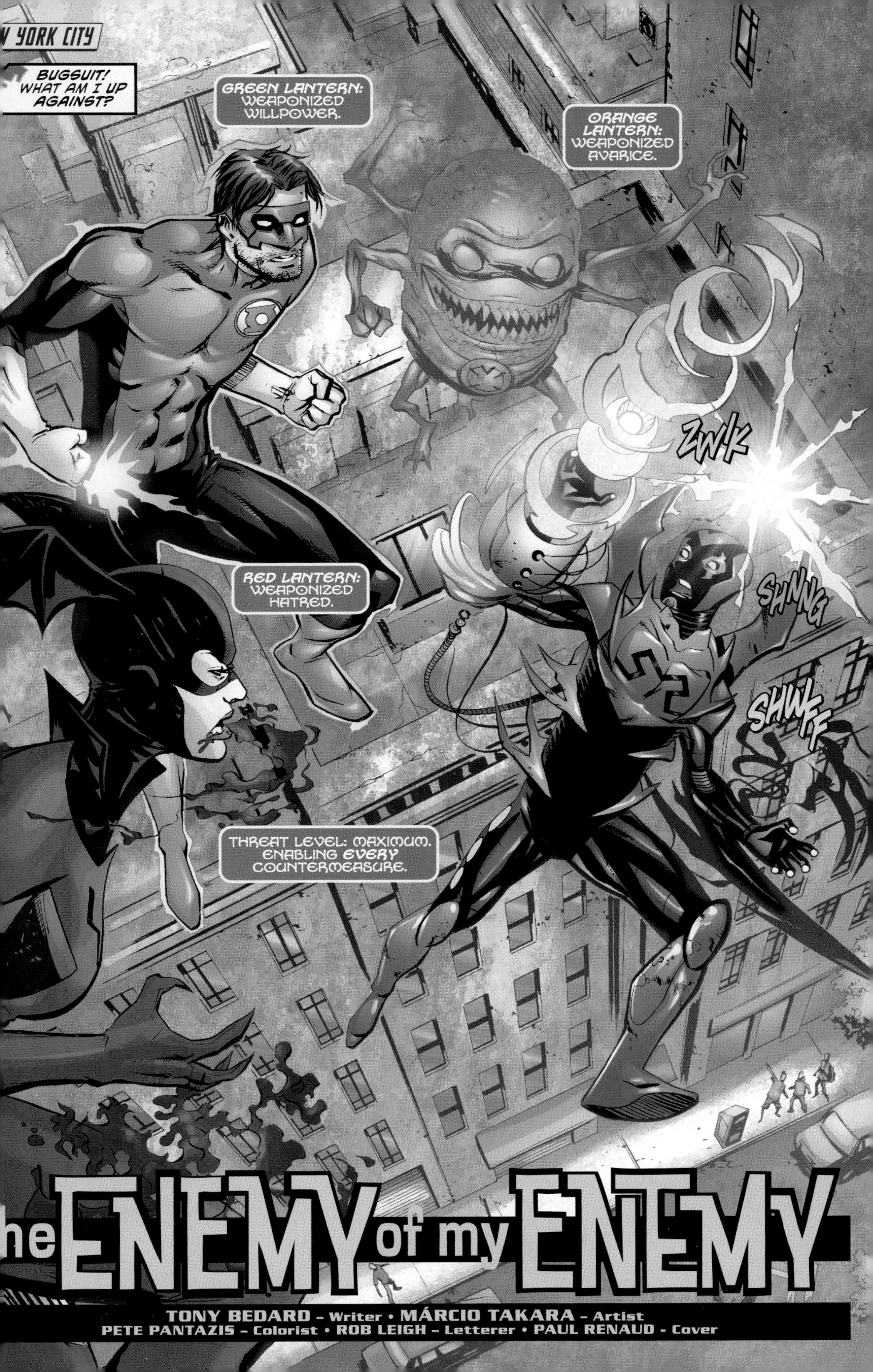

W YORK CITY
BUGSUIT! WHAT AM I UP AGAINST?
GREEN LANTERN: WEAPONIZED WILLPOWER.
ORANGE LANTERN: WEAPONIZED AVARICE.
ZWIK
RED LANTERN: WEAPONIZED HATRED.
SHNNG
SHWFF
THREAT LEVEL: MAXIMUM. ENABLING EVERY COUNTERMEASURE.
he ENEMY of my ENEMY
TONY BEDARD - Writer • MÁRCIO TAKARA - Artist
PETE PANTAZIS - Colorist • ROB LEIGH - Letterer • PAUL RENAUD - Cover

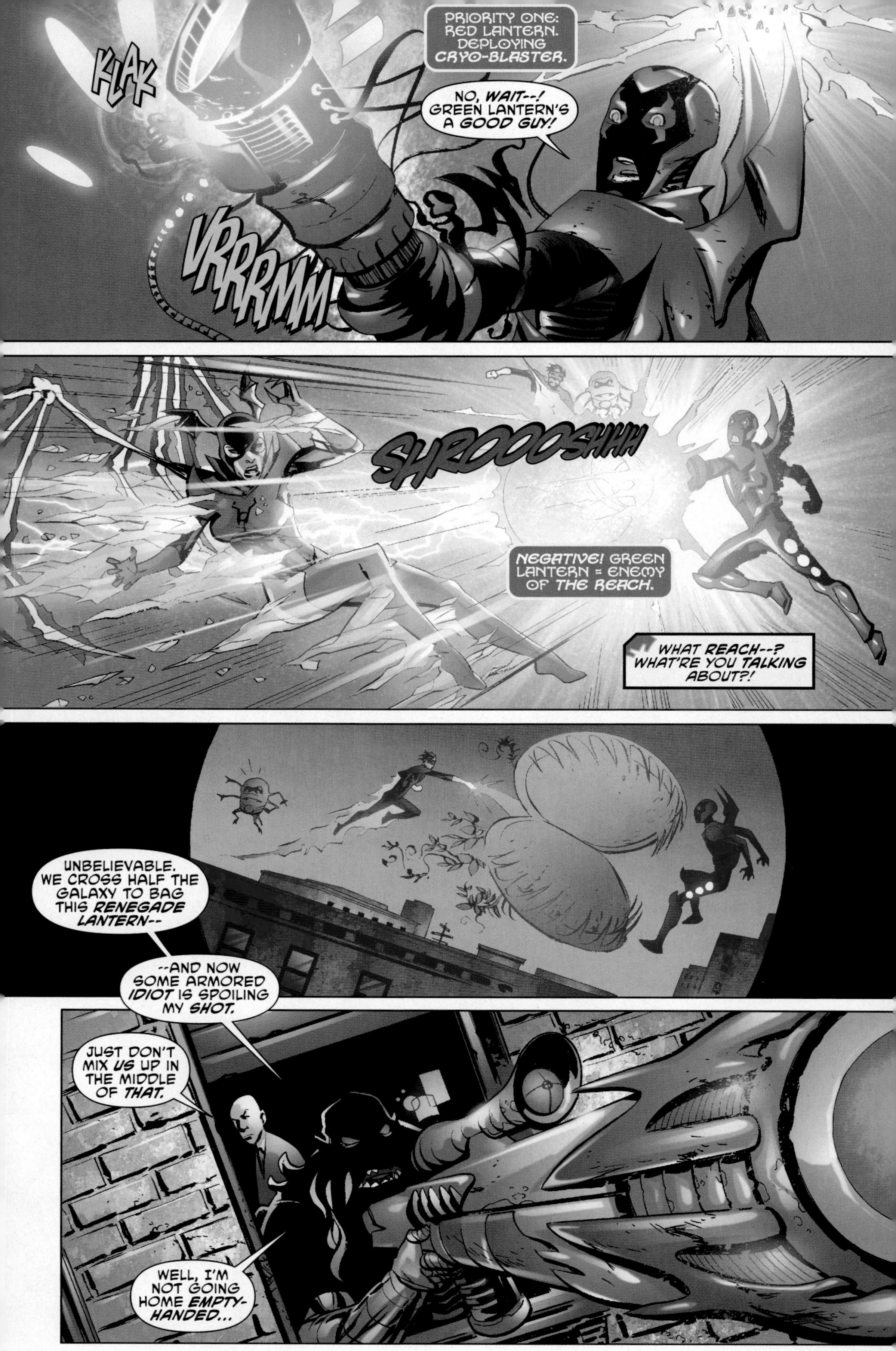
KLAK
PRIORITY ONE: RED LANTERN. DEPLOYING CRYO-BLASTER.
NO, WAIT--! GREEN LANTERN'S A GOOD GUY!
VRRRMM
SHROOOOSHHH
NEGATIVE! GREEN LANTERN = ENEMY OF THE REACH.
WHAT REACH--? WHAT'RE YOU TALKING ABOUT?!
UNBELIEVABLE. WE CROSS HALF THE GALAXY TO BAG THIS RENEGADE LANTERN--
--AND NOW SOME ARMORED IDIOT IS SPOILING MY SHOT.
JUST DON'T MIX US UP IN THE MIDDLE OF THAT.
WELL, I'M NOT GOING HOME EMPTY-HANDED...

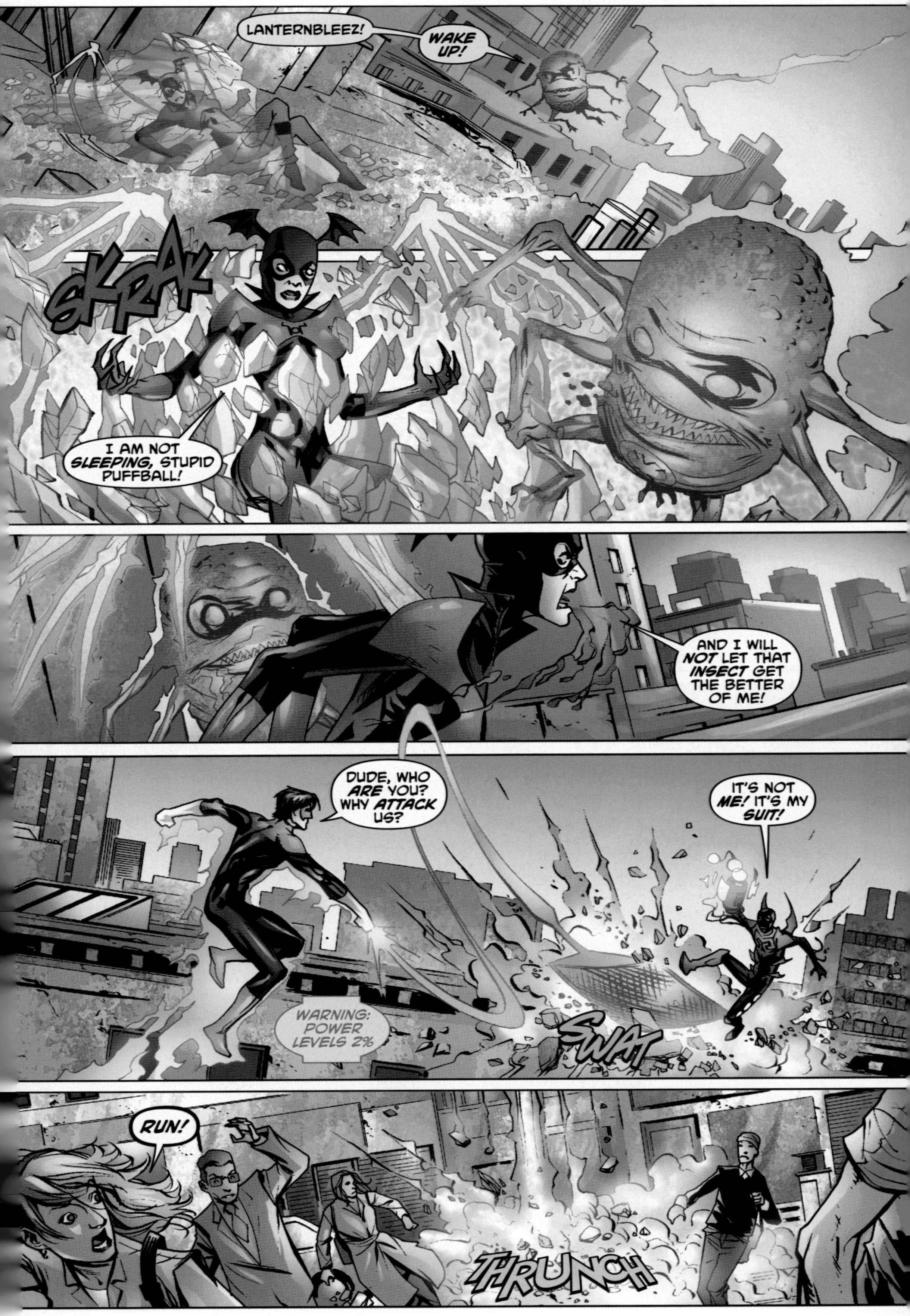
LANTERNBLEEZ!
WAKE UP!
SKRAK
I AM NOT SLEEPING, STUPID PUFFBALL!
AND I WILL NOT LET THAT INSECT GET THE BETTER OF ME!
DUDE, WHO ARE YOU? WHY ATTACK US?
IT'S NOT ME! IT'S MY SUIT!
WARNING: POWER LEVELS 2%
SWAT
RUN!
THRUNCH

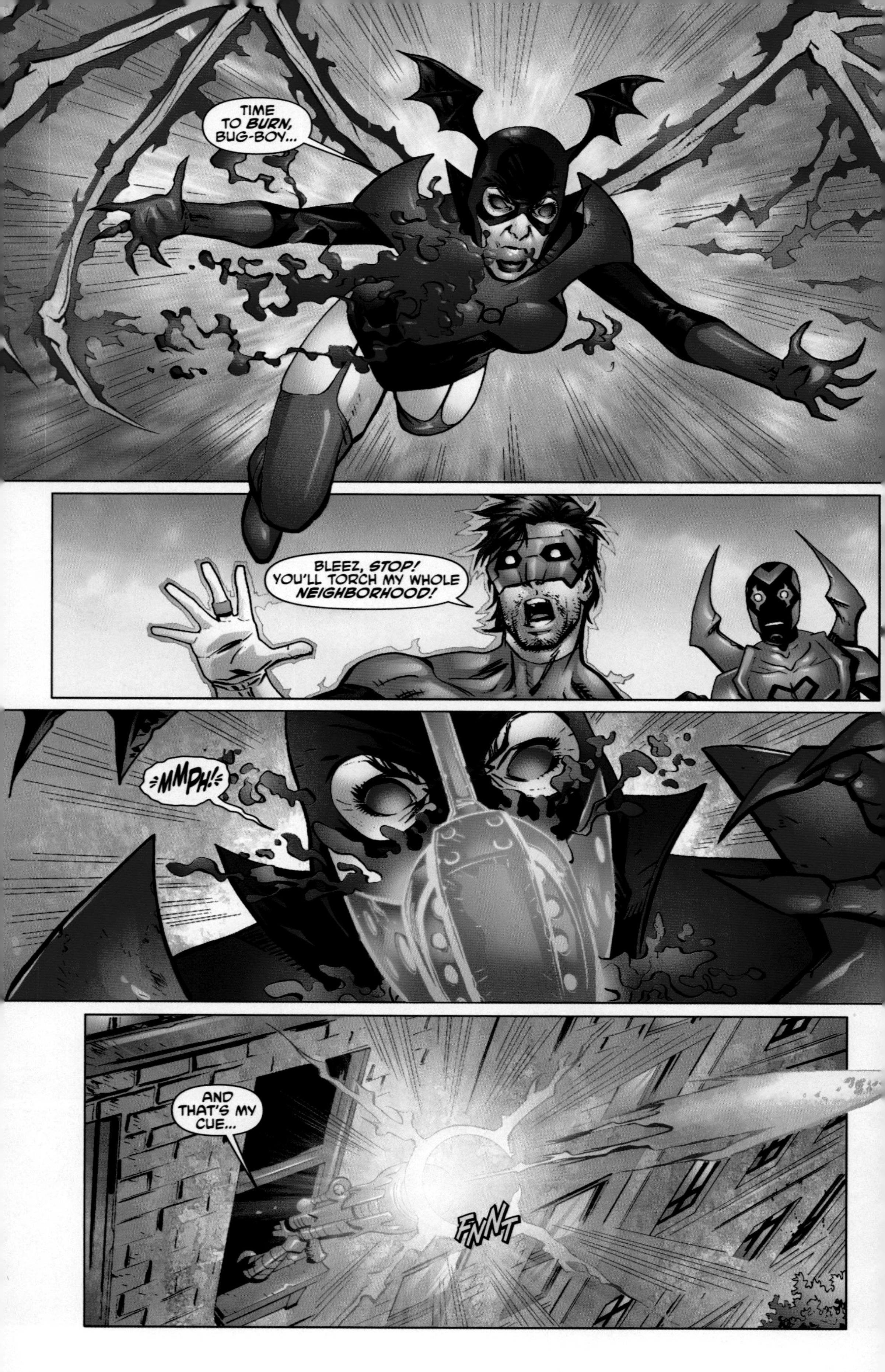
TIME TO BURN, BUG-BOY...
BLEEZ, STOP! YOU'LL TORCH MY WHOLE NEIGHBORHOOD!
MMPH!
AND THAT'S MY CUE...
FNNT

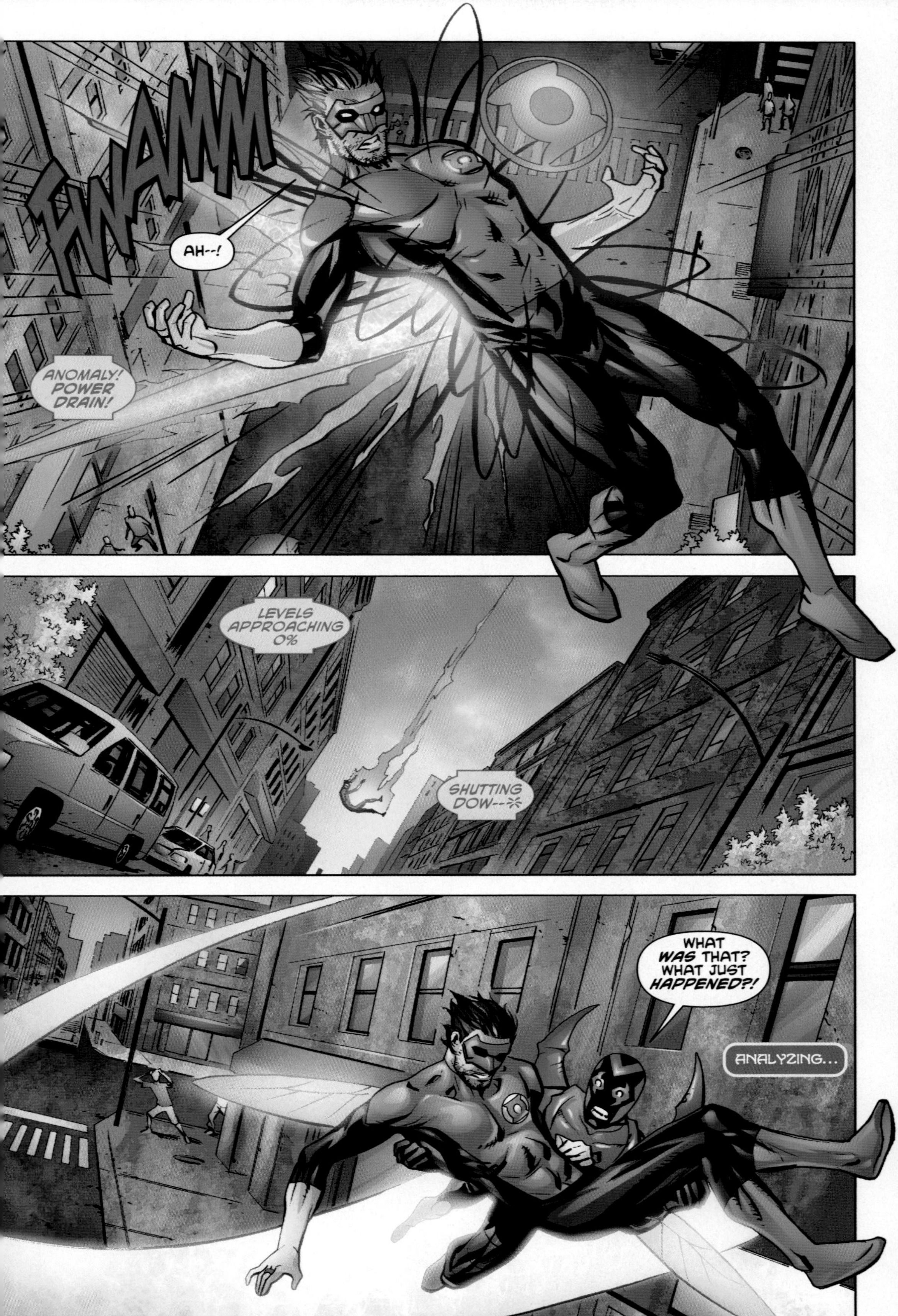
FWAMM
AH--!
ANOMALY! POWER DRAIN!
LEVELS APPROACHING 0%
SHUTTING DOW--
WHAT WAS THAT? WHAT JUST HAPPENED?!
ANALYZING...

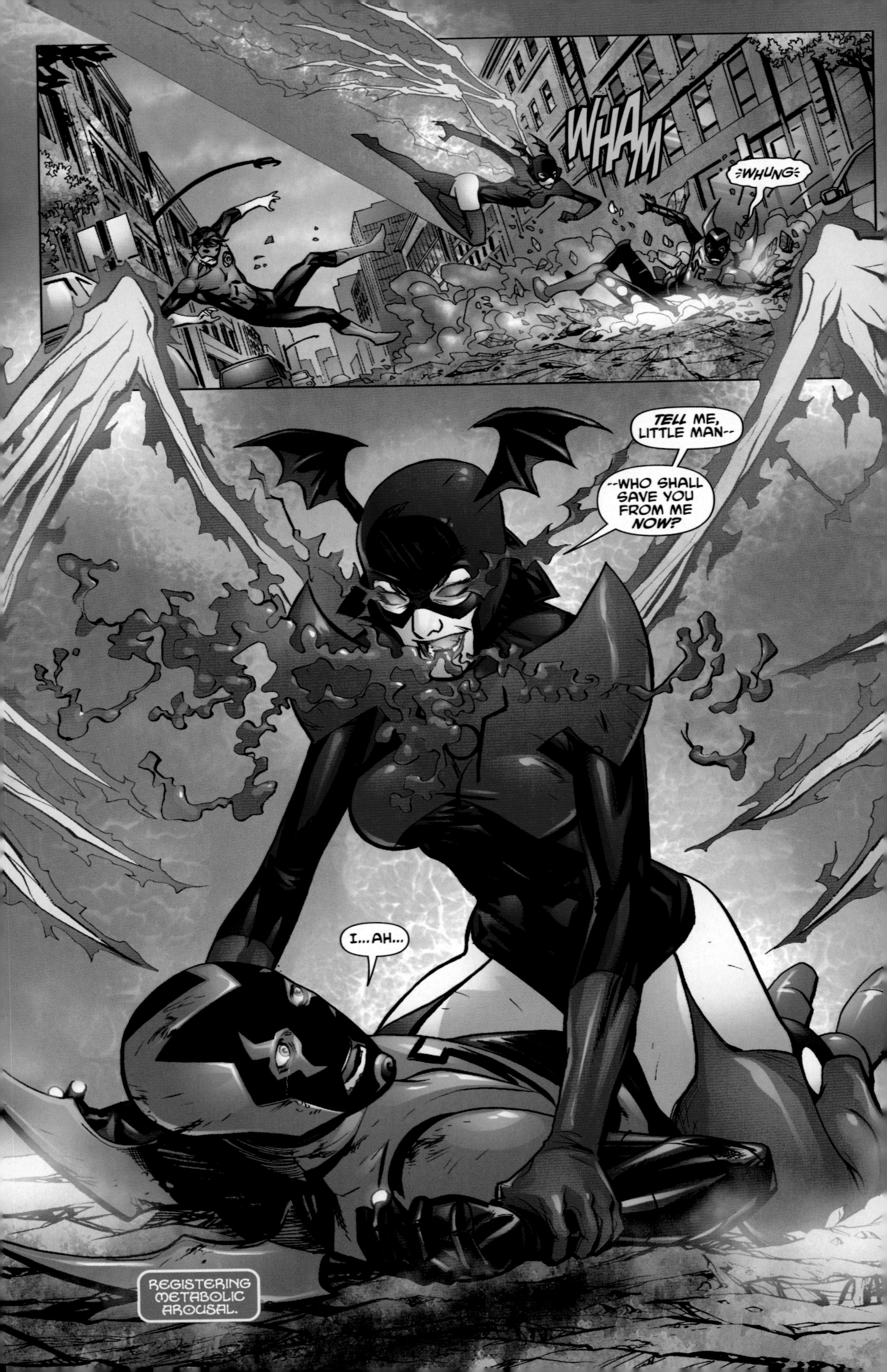
WHAM
WHUNG
TELL ME, LITTLE MAN--
--WHO SHALL SAVE YOU FROM ME NOW?
I...AH...
REGISTERING METABOLIC AROUSAL.

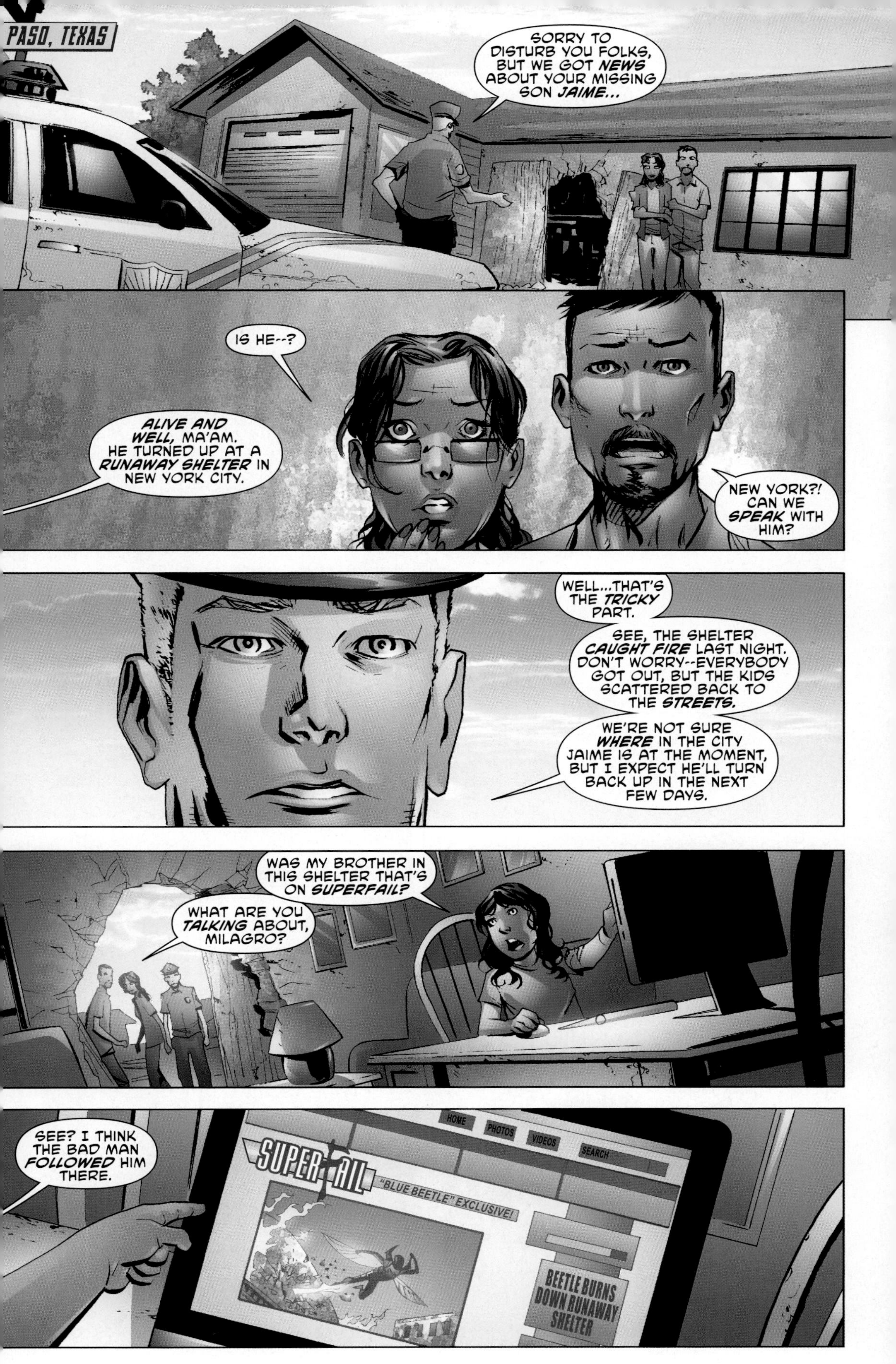
PASO, TEXAS
SORRY TO DISTURB YOU FOLKS, BUT WE GOT NEWS ABOUT YOUR MISSING SON JAIME...
IS HE--?
ALIVE AND WELL, MA'AM. HE TURNED UP AT A RUNAWAY SHELTER IN NEW YORK CITY.
NEW YORK?! CAN WE SPEAK WITH HIM?
WELL...THAT'S THE TRICKY PART.
SEE, THE SHELTER CAUGHT FIRE LAST NIGHT. DON'T WORRY--EVERYBODY GOT OUT, BUT THE KIDS SCATTERED BACK TO THE STREETS.
WE'RE NOT SURE WHERE IN THE CITY JAIME IS AT THE MOMENT, BUT I EXPECT HE'LL TURN BACK UP IN THE NEXT FEW DAYS.
WAS MY BROTHER IN THIS SHELTER THAT'S ON SUPERFAIL?
WHAT ARE YOU TALKING ABOUT, MILAGRO?
SEE? I THINK THE BAD MAN FOLLOWED HIM THERE.
HOME
PHOTOS
VIDEOS
SEARCH
SUPERFAIL
"BLUE BEETLE" EXCLUSIVE!
BEETLE BURNS DOWN RUNAWAY SHELTER

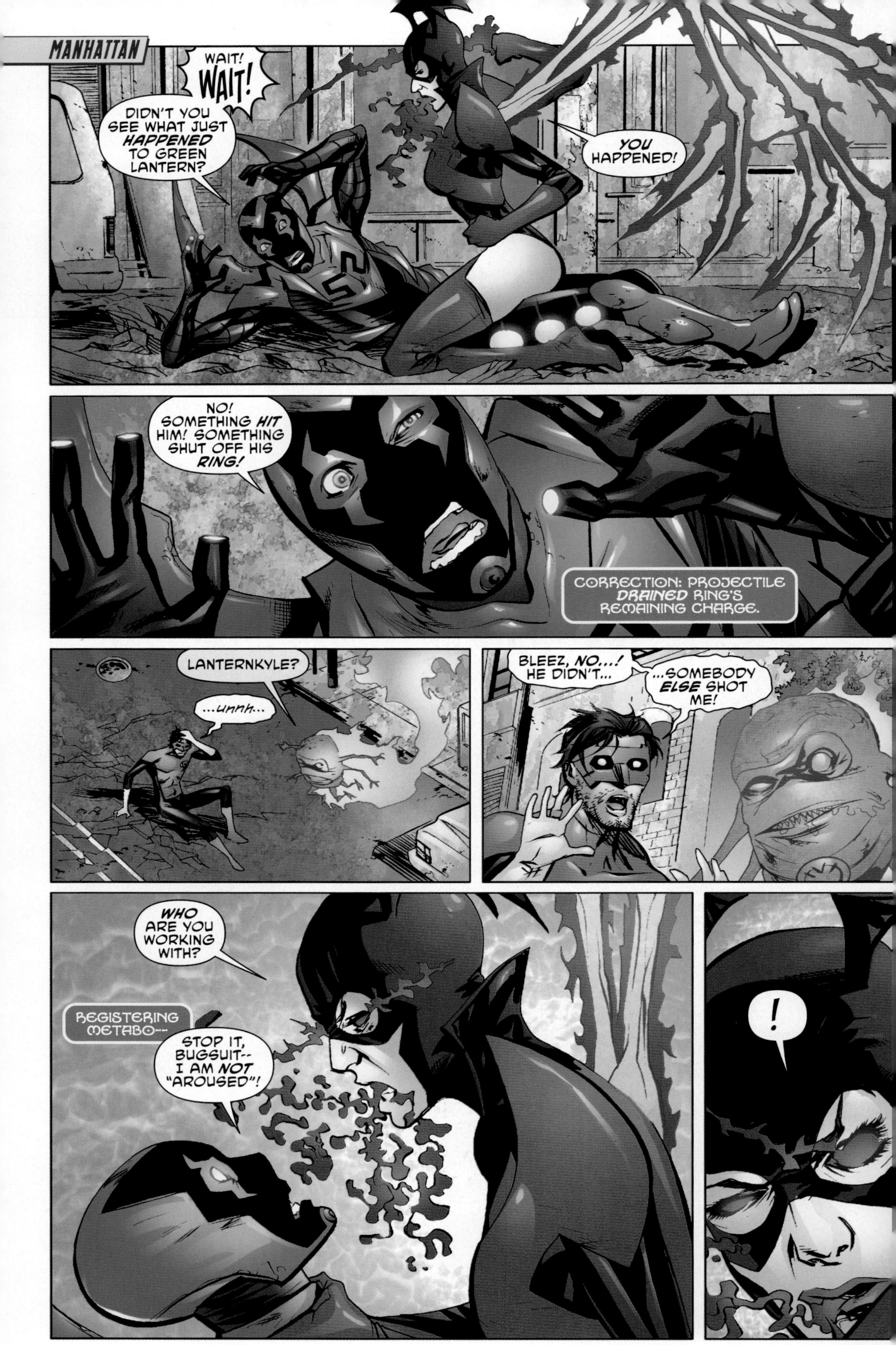
MANHATTAN
WAIT! WAIT!
DIDN'T YOU SEE WHAT JUST HAPPENED TO GREEN LANTERN?
YOU HAPPENED!
NO! SOMETHING HIT HIM! SOMETHING SHUT OFF HIS RING!
CORRECTION: PROJECTILE DRAINED RING'S REMAINING CHARGE.
LANTERNKYLE?
...unnh...
BLEEZ, NO...! HE DIDN'T...
...SOMEBODY ELSE SHOT ME!
WHO ARE YOU WORKING WITH?
REGISTERING METABO--
STOP IT, BUGSUIT-- I AM NOT "AROUSED"!
!

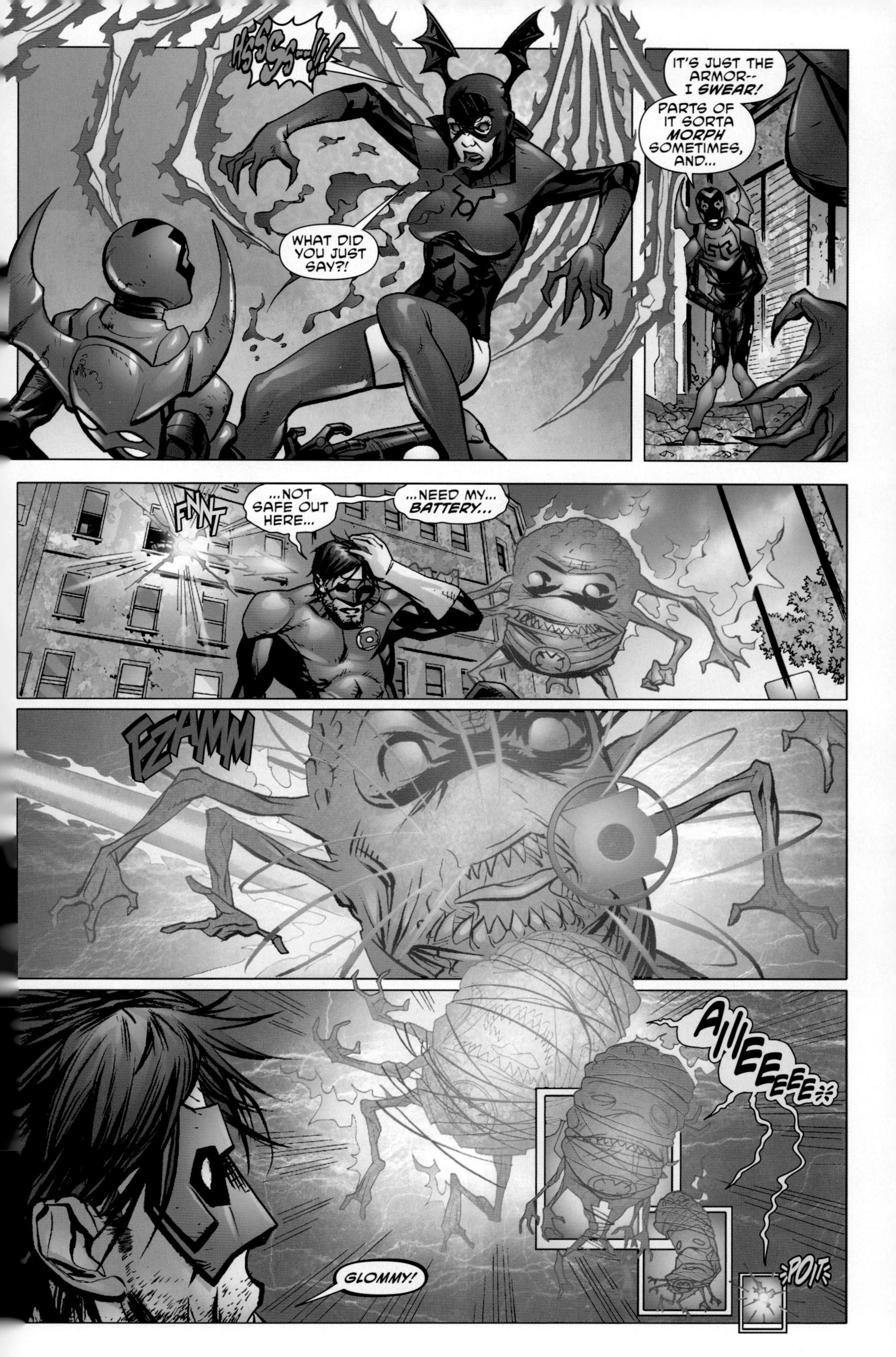
HSSSS--!!!
WHAT DID YOU JUST SAY?!
IT'S JUST THE ARMOR-- I SWEAR!
PARTS OF IT SORTA MORPH SOMETIMES, AND...
FNNT
...NOT SAFE OUT HERE...
...NEED MY... BATTERY...
FZAMM
AIIEEEEEE!!
GLOMMY!
POIT

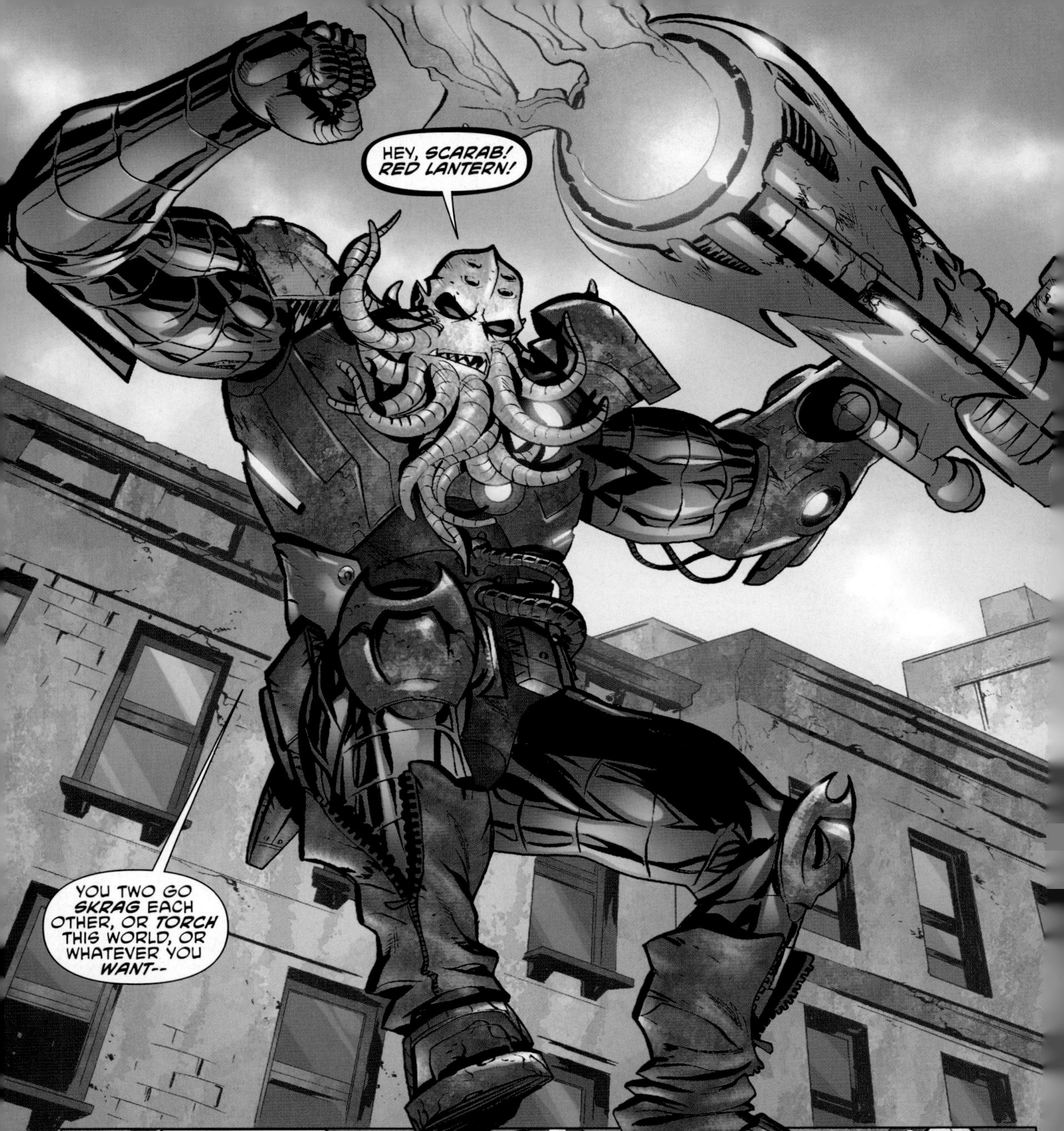
HEY, SCARAB! RED LANTERN!
YOU TWO GO SKRAG EACH OTHER, OR TORCH THIS WORLD, OR WHATEVER YOU WANT--
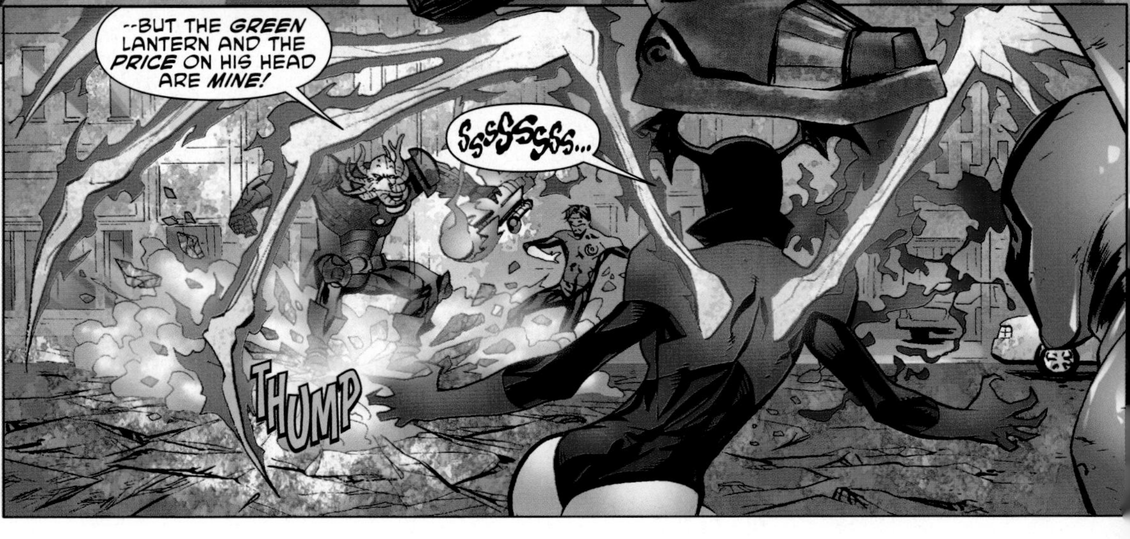
--BUT THE GREEN LANTERN AND THE PRICE ON HIS HEAD ARE MINE!
SSSSSSSS...
THUMP

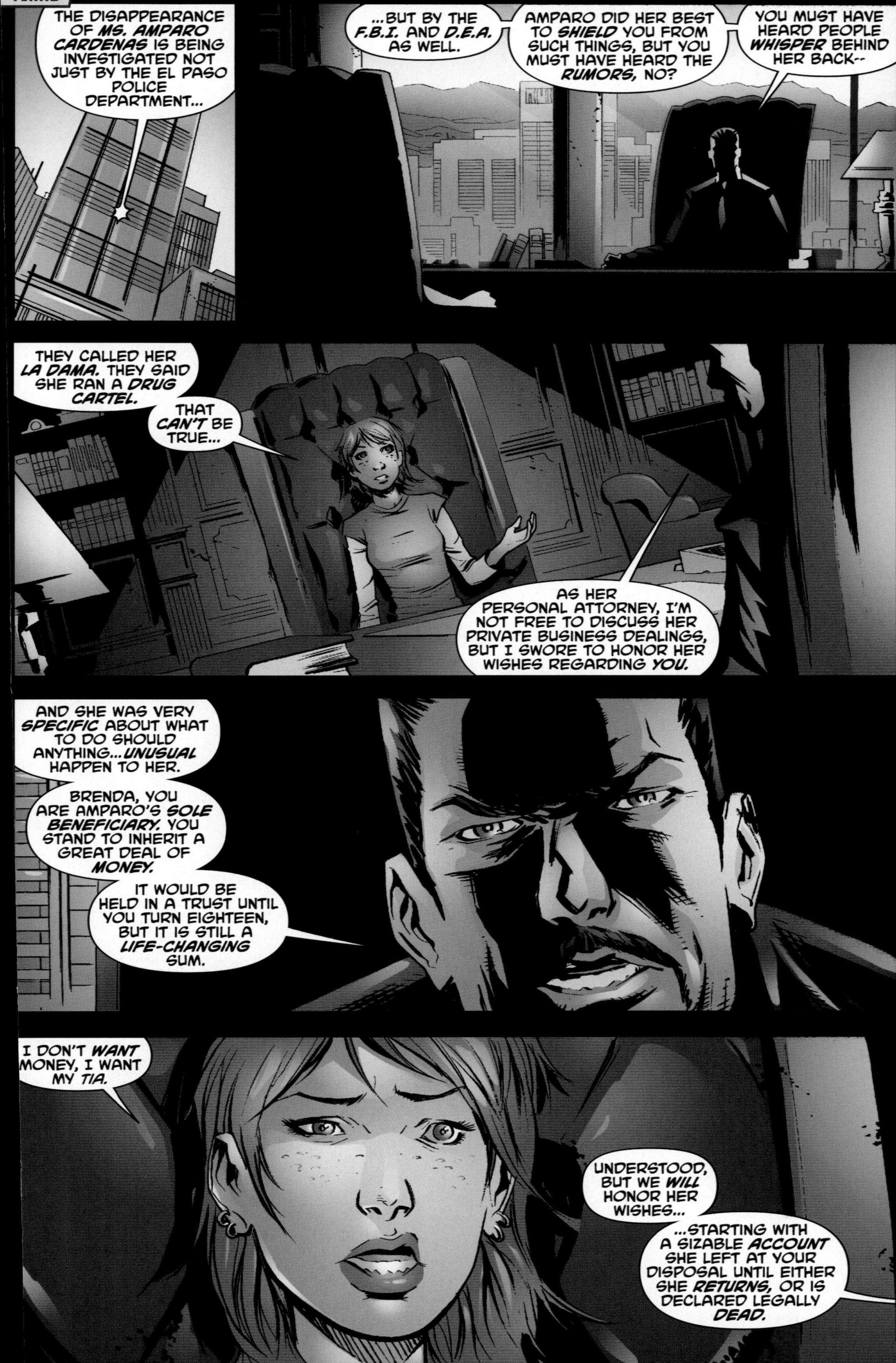
THE DISAPPEARANCE OF MS. AMPARO CARDENAS IS BEING INVESTIGATED NOT JUST BY THE EL PASO POLICE DEPARTMENT...
...BUT BY THE F.B.I. AND D.E.A. AS WELL.
AMPARO DID HER BEST TO SHIELD YOU FROM SUCH THINGS, BUT YOU MUST HAVE HEARD THE RUMORS, NO?
YOU MUST HAVE HEARD PEOPLE WHISPER BEHIND HER BACK--
THEY CALLED HER LA DAMA. THEY SAID SHE RAN A DRUG CARTEL.
THAT CAN'T BE TRUE...
AS HER PERSONAL ATTORNEY, I'M NOT FREE TO DISCUSS HER PRIVATE BUSINESS DEALINGS, BUT I SWORE TO HONOR HER WISHES REGARDING YOU.
AND SHE WAS VERY SPECIFIC ABOUT WHAT TO DO SHOULD ANYTHING...UNUSUAL HAPPEN TO HER.
BRENDA, YOU ARE AMPARO'S SOLE BENEFICIARY. YOU STAND TO INHERIT A GREAT DEAL OF MONEY.
IT WOULD BE HELD IN A TRUST UNTIL YOU TURN EIGHTEEN, BUT IT IS STILL A LIFE-CHANGING SUM.
I DON'T WANT MONEY, I WANT MY TIA.
UNDERSTOOD, BUT WE WILL HONOR HER WISHES...
...STARTING WITH A SIZABLE ACCOUNT SHE LEFT AT YOUR DISPOSAL UNTIL EITHER SHE RETURNS, OR IS DECLARED LEGALLY DEAD.

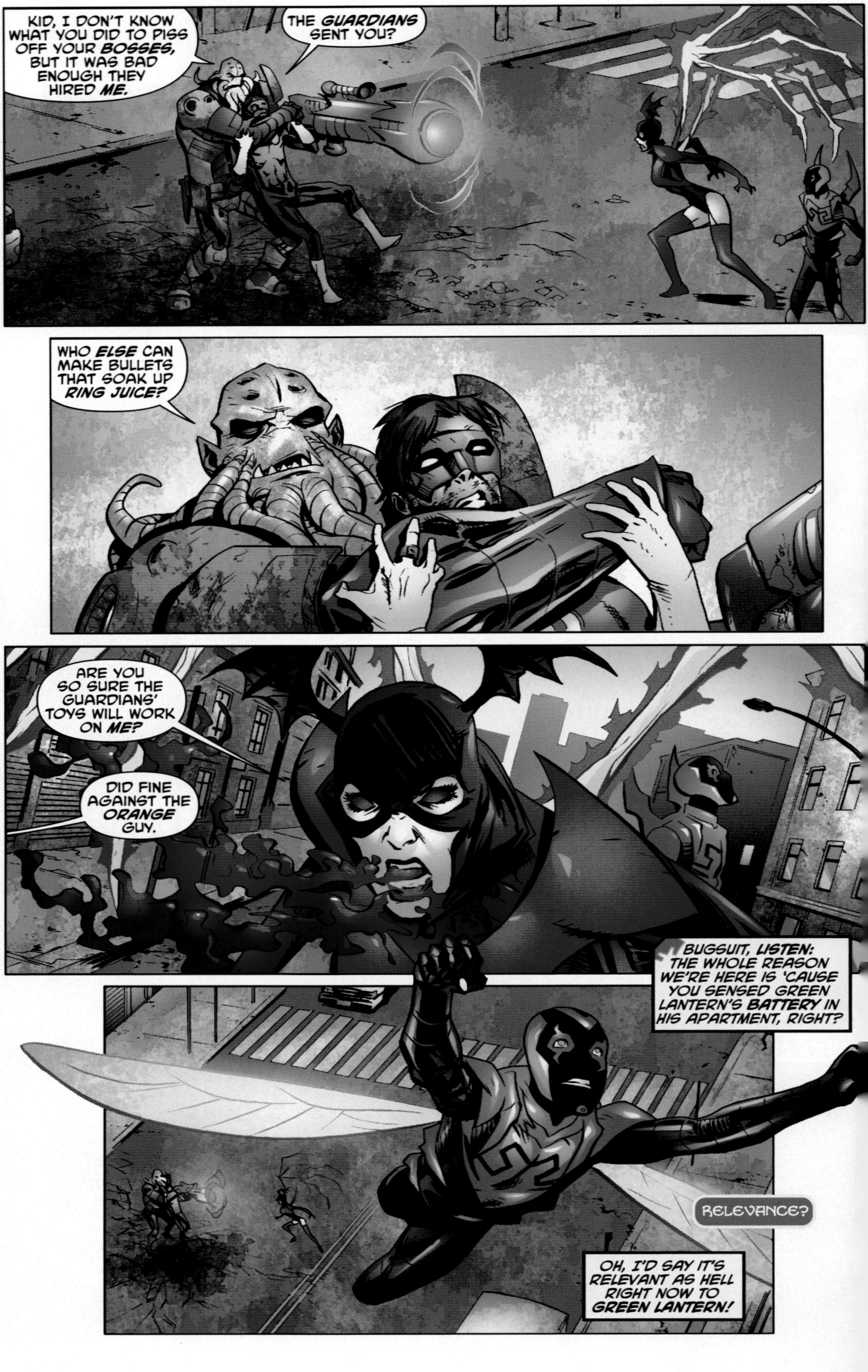
KID, I DON'T KNOW WHAT YOU DID TO PISS OFF YOUR BOSSES, BUT IT WAS BAD ENOUGH THEY HIRED ME.
THE GUARDIANS SENT YOU?
WHO ELSE CAN MAKE BULLETS THAT SOAK UP RING JUICE?
ARE YOU SO SURE THE GUARDIANS' TOYS WILL WORK ON ME?
DID FINE AGAINST THE ORANGE GUY.
BUGSUIT, LISTEN: THE WHOLE REASON WE'RE HERE IS 'CAUSE YOU SENSED GREEN LANTERN'S BATTERY IN HIS APARTMENT, RIGHT?
RELEVANCE?
OH, I'D SAY IT'S RELEVANT AS HELL RIGHT NOW TO GREEN LANTERN!

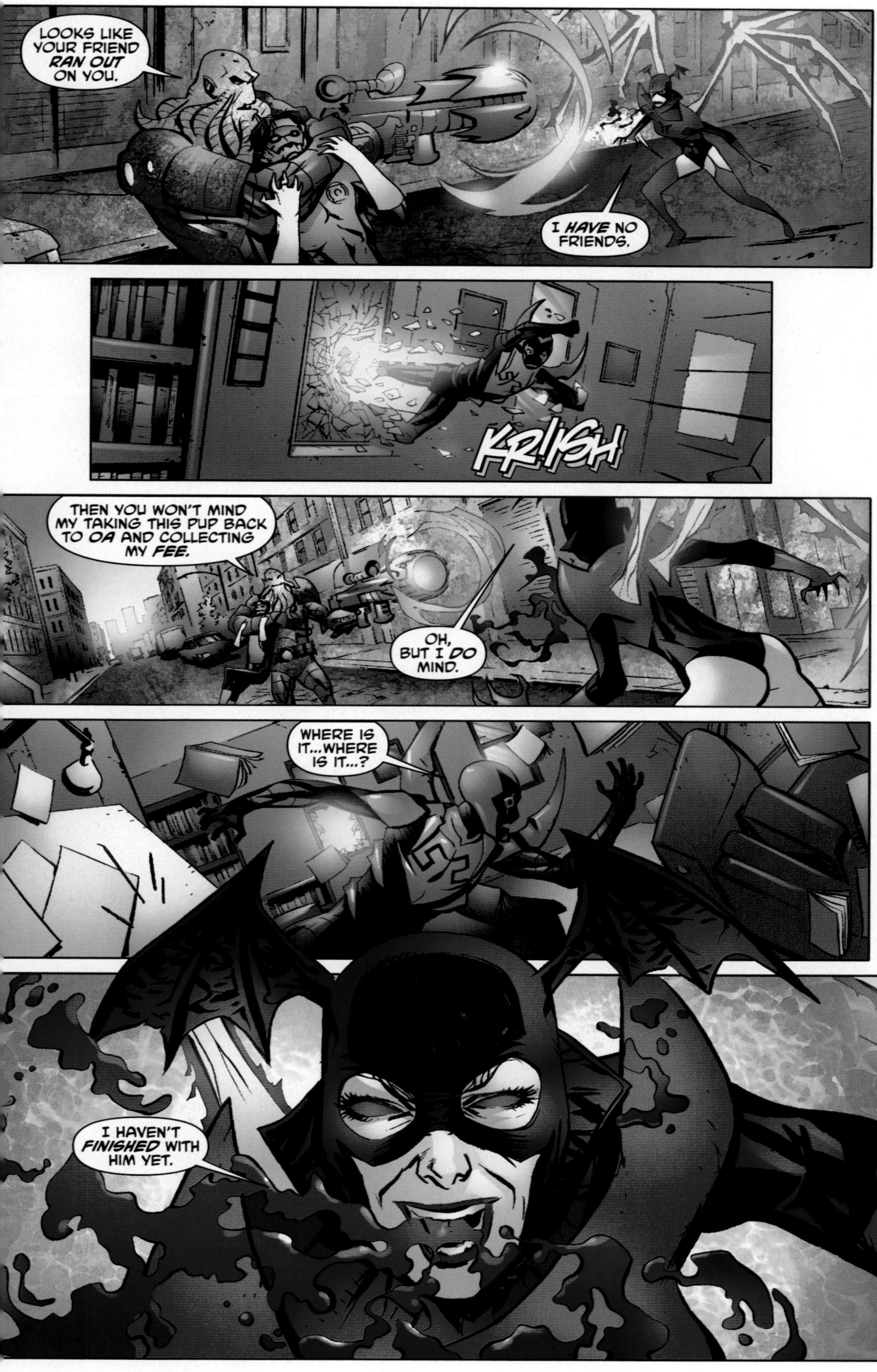
LOOKS LIKE YOUR FRIEND *RAN OUT* ON YOU.
I *HAVE* NO FRIENDS.
KR!ISH
THEN YOU WON'T MIND MY TAKING THIS PUP BACK TO *OA* AND COLLECTING MY *FEE.*
OH, BUT I *DO* MIND.
WHERE IS IT...WHERE IS IT...?
I HAVEN'T *FINISHED* WITH HIM YET.

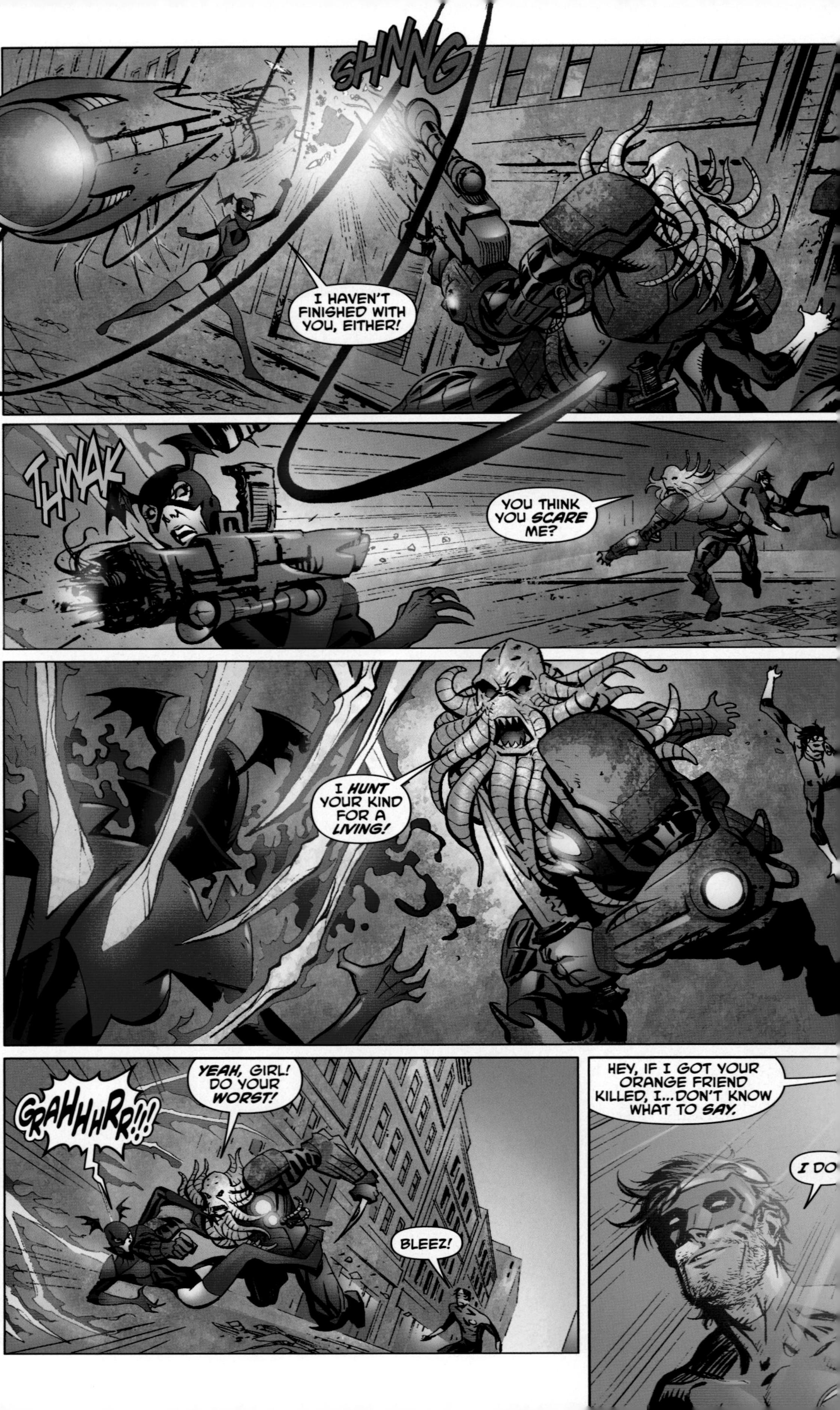
SHNNG
I HAVEN'T FINISHED WITH YOU, EITHER!
THWAK
YOU THINK YOU SCARE ME?
I HUNT YOUR KIND FOR A LIVING!
GRAHHHRR!!!
YEAH, GIRL! DO YOUR WORST!
BLEEZ!
HEY, IF I GOT YOUR ORANGE FRIEND KILLED, I...DON'T KNOW WHAT TO SAY.
I DO

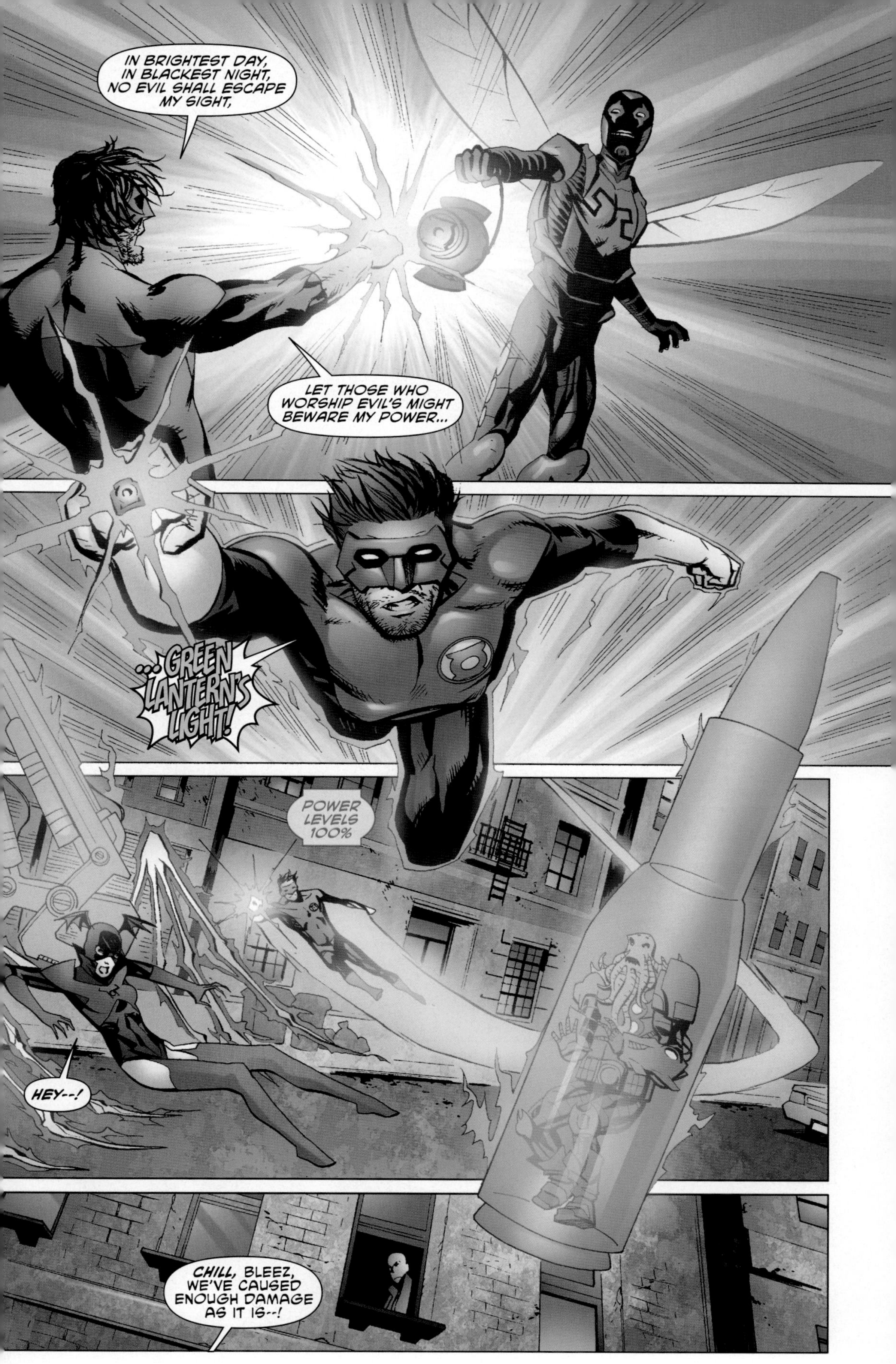
IN BRIGHTEST DAY, IN BLACKEST NIGHT, NO EVIL SHALL ESCAPE MY SIGHT,
LET THOSE WHO WORSHIP EVIL'S MIGHT BEWARE MY POWER...
...GREEN LANTERN'S LIGHT!
POWER LEVELS 100%
HEY--!
CHILL, BLEEZ, WE'VE CAUSED ENOUGH DAMAGE AS IT IS--!

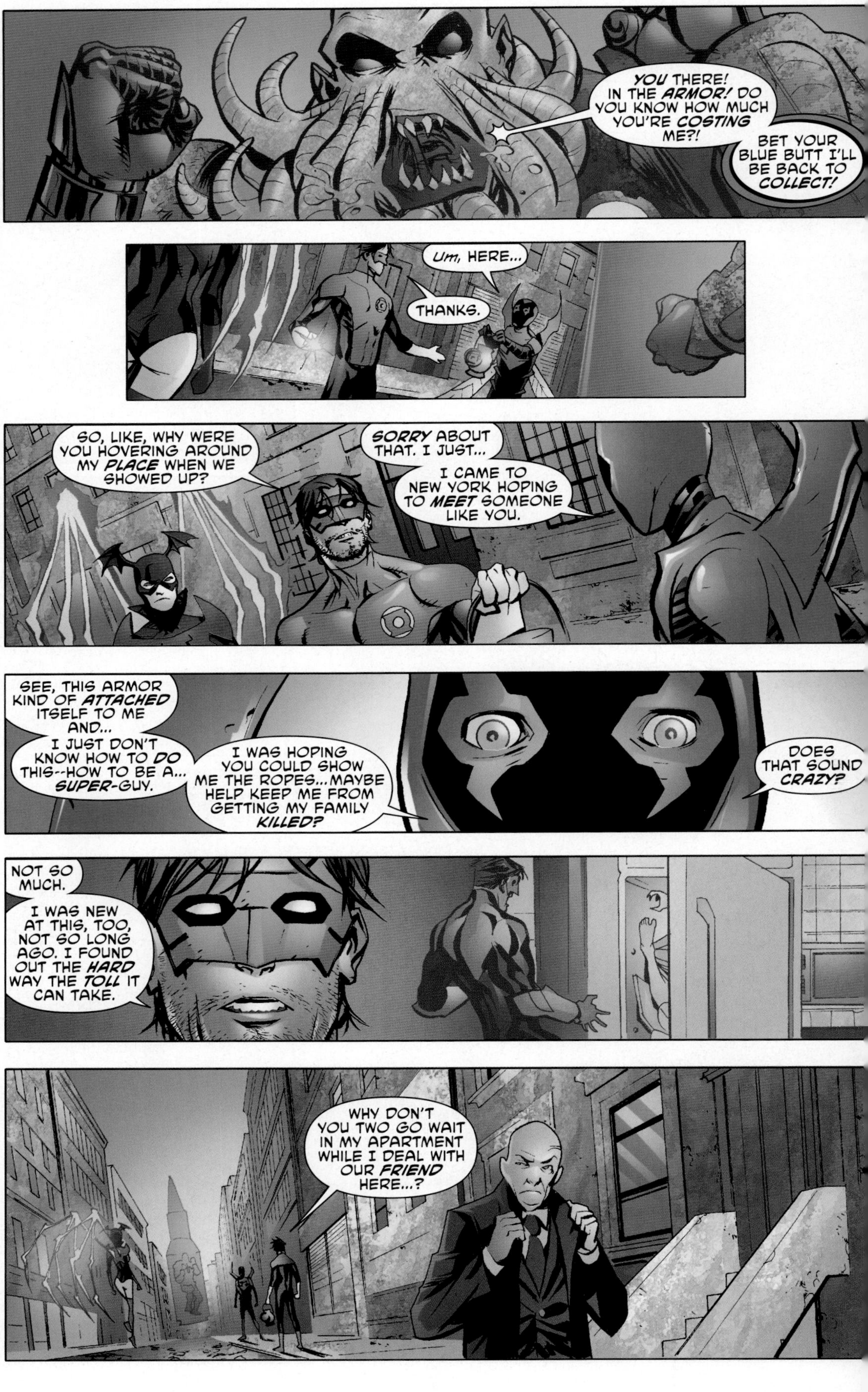
YOU THERE! IN THE ARMOR! DO YOU KNOW HOW MUCH YOU'RE COSTING ME?!
BET YOUR BLUE BUTT I'LL BE BACK TO COLLECT!
Um, HERE...
THANKS.
SO, LIKE, WHY WERE YOU HOVERING AROUND MY PLACE WHEN WE SHOWED UP?
SORRY ABOUT THAT. I JUST...
I CAME TO NEW YORK HOPING TO MEET SOMEONE LIKE YOU.
SEE, THIS ARMOR KIND OF ATTACHED ITSELF TO ME AND...
I JUST DON'T KNOW HOW TO DO THIS--HOW TO BE A... SUPER-GUY.
I WAS HOPING YOU COULD SHOW ME THE ROPES...MAYBE HELP KEEP ME FROM GETTING MY FAMILY KILLED?
DOES THAT SOUND CRAZY?
NOT SO MUCH.
I WAS NEW AT THIS, TOO, NOT SO LONG AGO. I FOUND OUT THE HARD WAY THE TOLL IT CAN TAKE.
WHY DON'T YOU TWO GO WAIT IN MY APARTMENT WHILE I DEAL WITH OUR FRIEND HERE...?

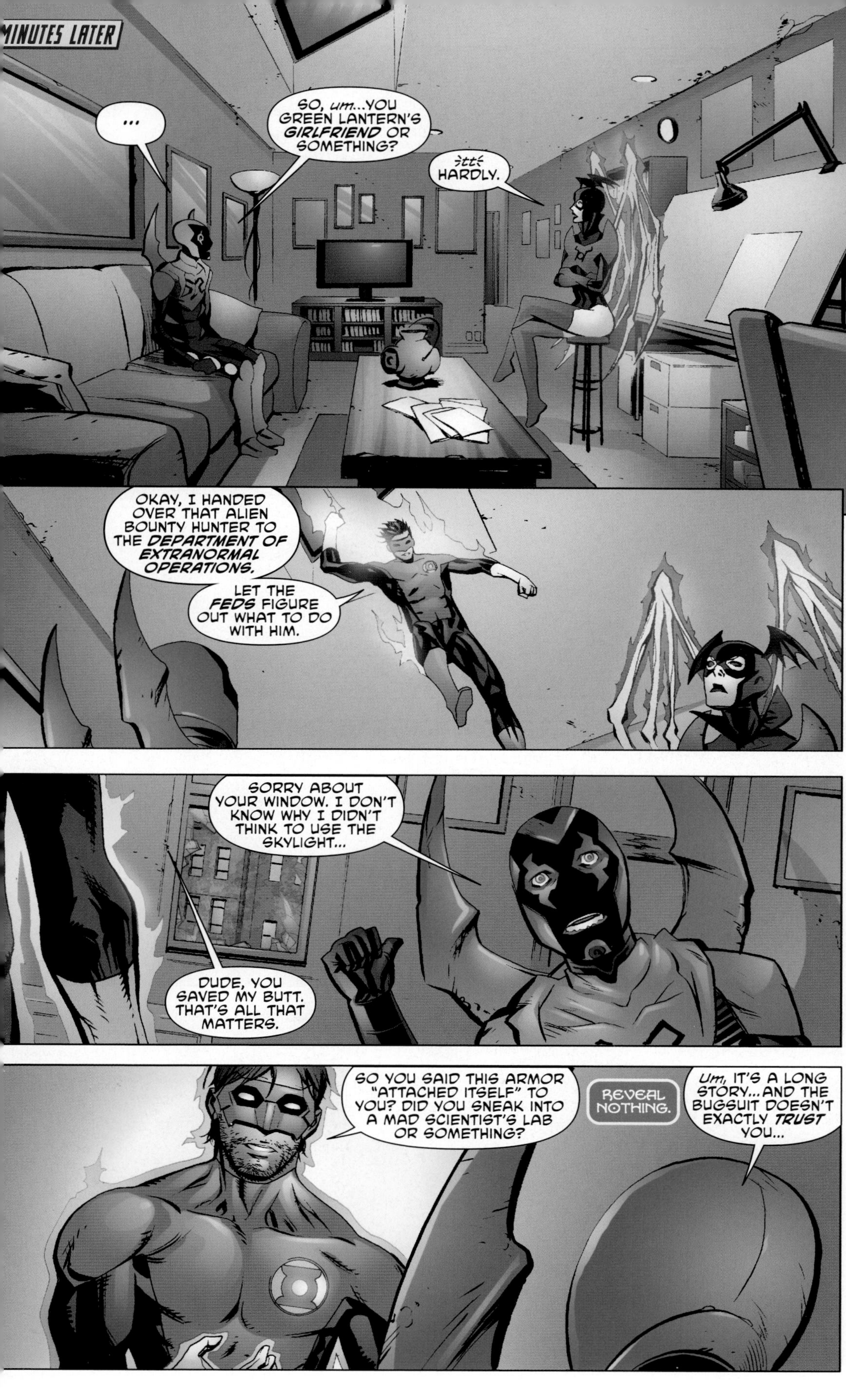
MINUTES LATER
...
SO, *um*...YOU GREEN LANTERN'S *GIRLFRIEND* OR SOMETHING?
ttt HARDLY.
OKAY, I HANDED OVER THAT ALIEN BOUNTY HUNTER TO THE *DEPARTMENT OF EXTRANORMAL OPERATIONS.*
LET THE *FEDS* FIGURE OUT WHAT TO DO WITH HIM.
SORRY ABOUT YOUR WINDOW. I DON'T KNOW WHY I DIDN'T THINK TO USE THE SKYLIGHT...
DUDE, YOU SAVED MY BUTT. THAT'S ALL THAT MATTERS.
SO YOU SAID THIS ARMOR "ATTACHED ITSELF" TO YOU? DID YOU SNEAK INTO A MAD SCIENTIST'S LAB OR SOMETHING?
REVEAL NOTHING.
Um, IT'S A LONG STORY...AND THE BUGSUIT DOESN'T EXACTLY *TRUST* YOU...

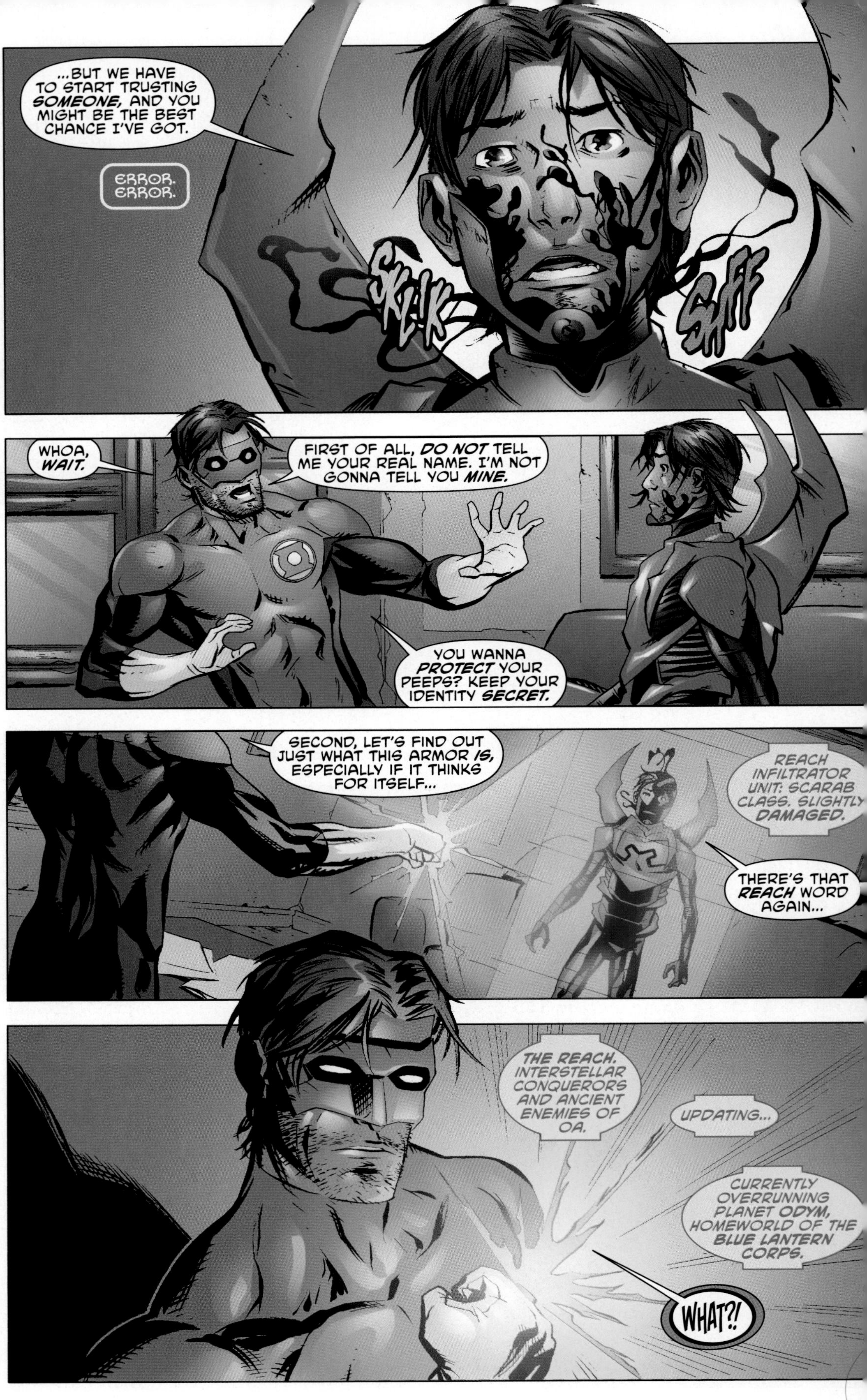
...BUT WE HAVE TO START TRUSTING SOMEONE, AND YOU MIGHT BE THE BEST CHANCE I'VE GOT.
ERROR. ERROR.
SKLIK
SNFF
WHOA, WAIT.
FIRST OF ALL, DO NOT TELL ME YOUR REAL NAME. I'M NOT GONNA TELL YOU MINE.
YOU WANNA PROTECT YOUR PEEPS? KEEP YOUR IDENTITY SECRET.
SECOND, LET'S FIND OUT JUST WHAT THIS ARMOR IS, ESPECIALLY IF IT THINKS FOR ITSELF...
REACH INFILTRATOR UNIT: SCARAB CLASS. SLIGHTLY DAMAGED.
THERE'S THAT REACH WORD AGAIN...
THE REACH. INTERSTELLAR CONQUERORS AND ANCIENT ENEMIES OF OA.
UPDATING...
CURRENTLY OVERRUNNING PLANET ODYM, HOMEWORLD OF THE BLUE LANTERN CORPS.
WHAT?!

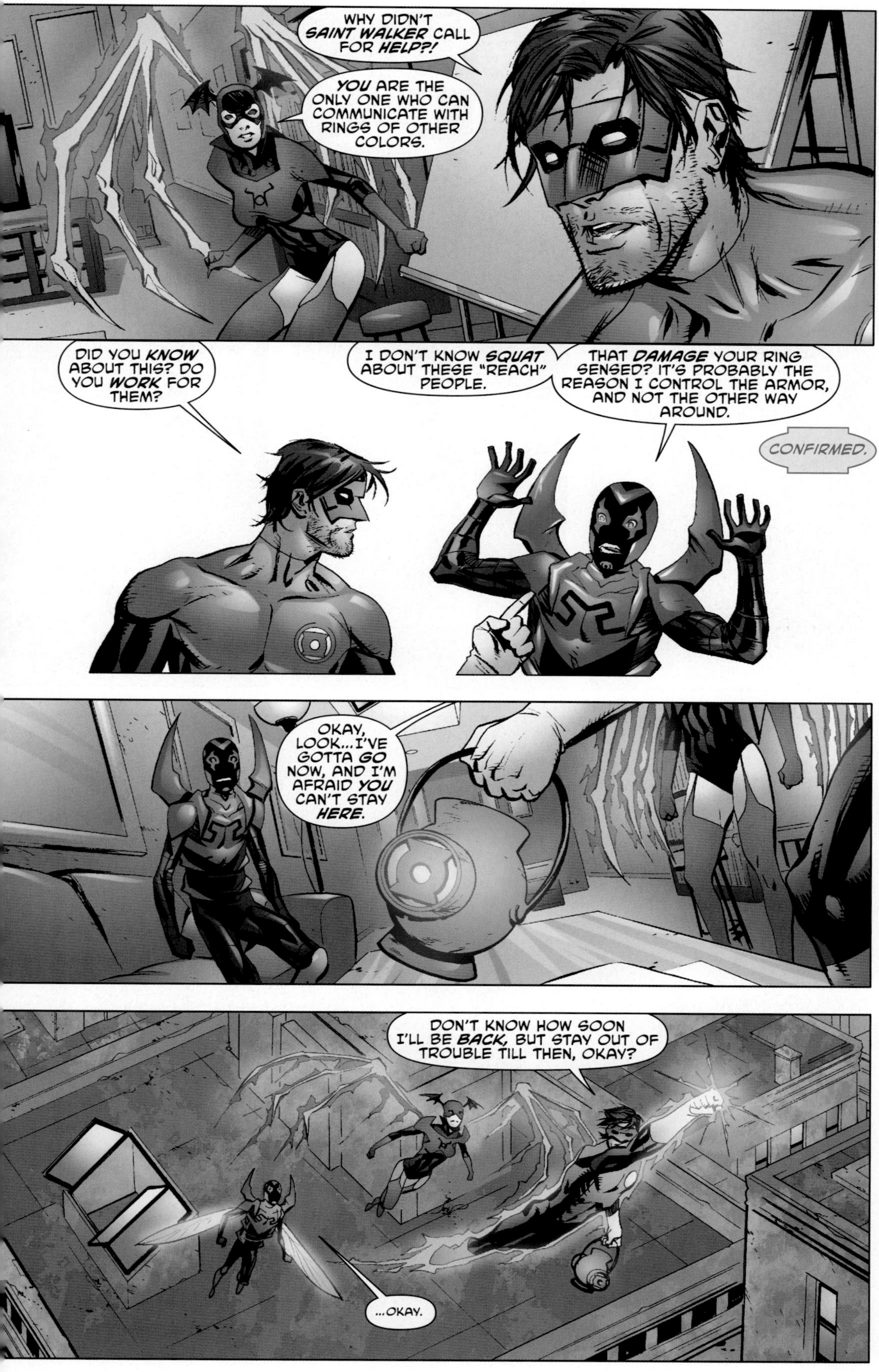
WHY DIDN'T SAINT WALKER CALL FOR HELP?!
YOU ARE THE ONLY ONE WHO CAN COMMUNICATE WITH RINGS OF OTHER COLORS.
DID YOU KNOW ABOUT THIS? DO YOU WORK FOR THEM?
I DON'T KNOW SQUAT ABOUT THESE "REACH" PEOPLE.
THAT DAMAGE YOUR RING SENSED? IT'S PROBABLY THE REASON I CONTROL THE ARMOR, AND NOT THE OTHER WAY AROUND.
CONFIRMED.
OKAY, LOOK...I'VE GOTTA GO NOW, AND I'M AFRAID YOU CAN'T STAY HERE.
DON'T KNOW HOW SOON I'LL BE BACK, BUT STAY OUT OF TROUBLE TILL THEN, OKAY?
...OKAY.

WHATEVER YOU DO ON ODYM, DO *NOT* GET YOURSELF KILLED.

AREN'T YOU *COMING?*

PERHAPS *LATER.* FOR NOW, I HAVE UNFINISHED BUSINESS WITH *ATROCITUS.*

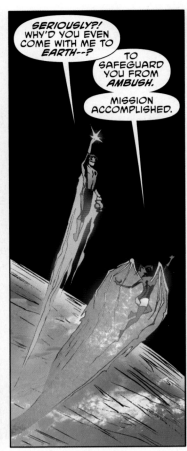

SERIOUSLY?! WHY'D YOU EVEN COME WITH ME TO *EARTH--?*

TO SAFEGUARD YOU FROM *AMBUSH.*

MISSION ACCOMPLISHED.

SO WHY DOES YOUR SUDDEN CONCERN FOR MY *WELL-BEING* ONLY MAKE ME NERVOUS?

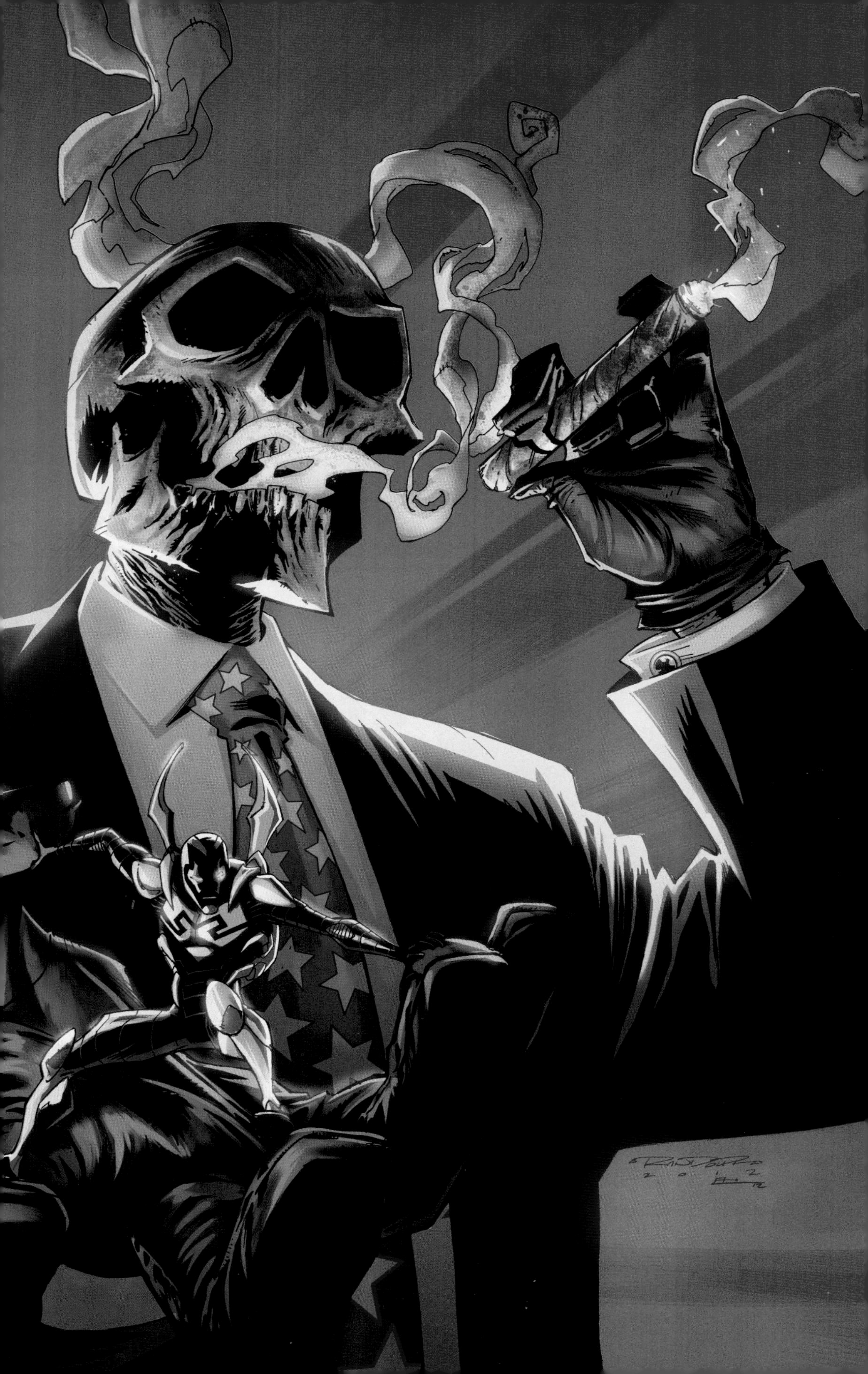

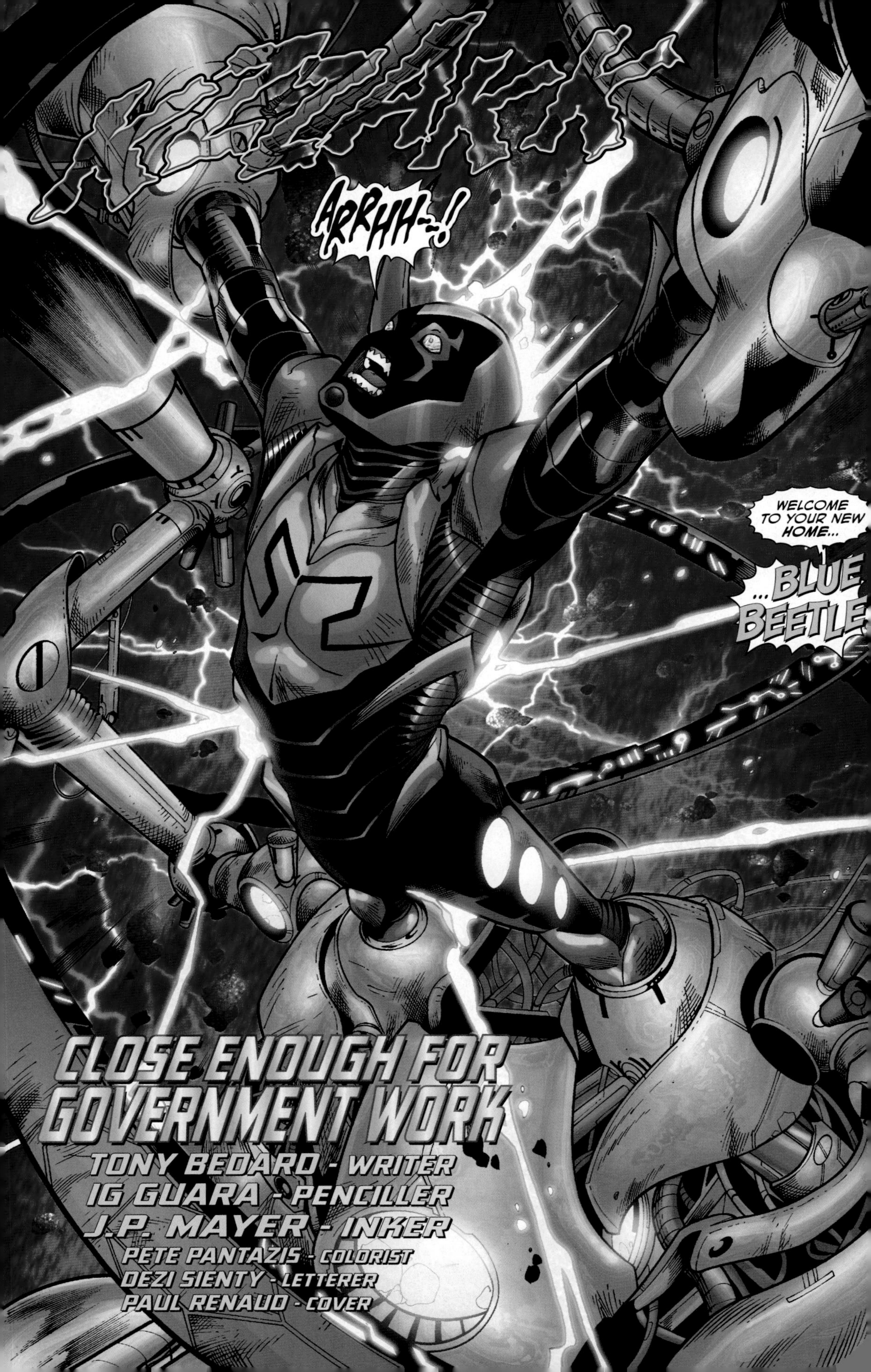
ARRHH--!
WELCOME TO YOUR NEW HOME...
...BLUE BEETLE
CLOSE ENOUGH FOR GOVERNMENT WORK
TONY BEDARD - WRITER
IG GUARA - PENCILLER
J.P. MAYER - INKER
PETE PANTAZIS - COLORIST
DEZI SIENTY - LETTERER
PAUL RENAUD - COVER

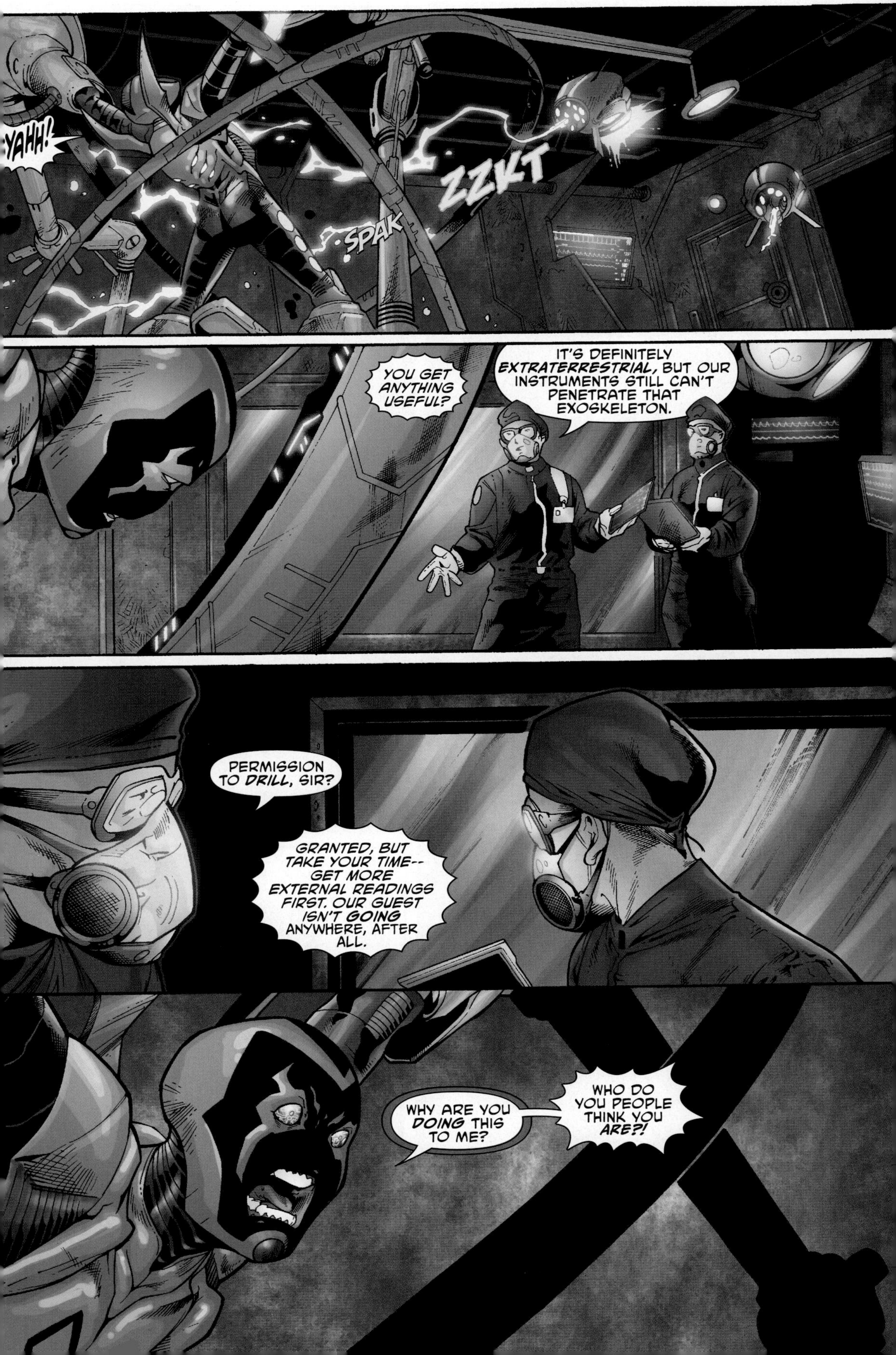
YAHH!
ZZKT
SPAK
YOU GET ANYTHING USEFUL?
IT'S DEFINITELY EXTRATERRESTRIAL, BUT OUR INSTRUMENTS STILL CAN'T PENETRATE THAT EXOSKELETON.
PERMISSION TO DRILL, SIR?
GRANTED, BUT TAKE YOUR TIME-- GET MORE EXTERNAL READINGS FIRST. OUR GUEST ISN'T GOING ANYWHERE, AFTER ALL.
WHY ARE YOU DOING THIS TO ME?
WHO DO YOU PEOPLE THINK YOU ARE?!

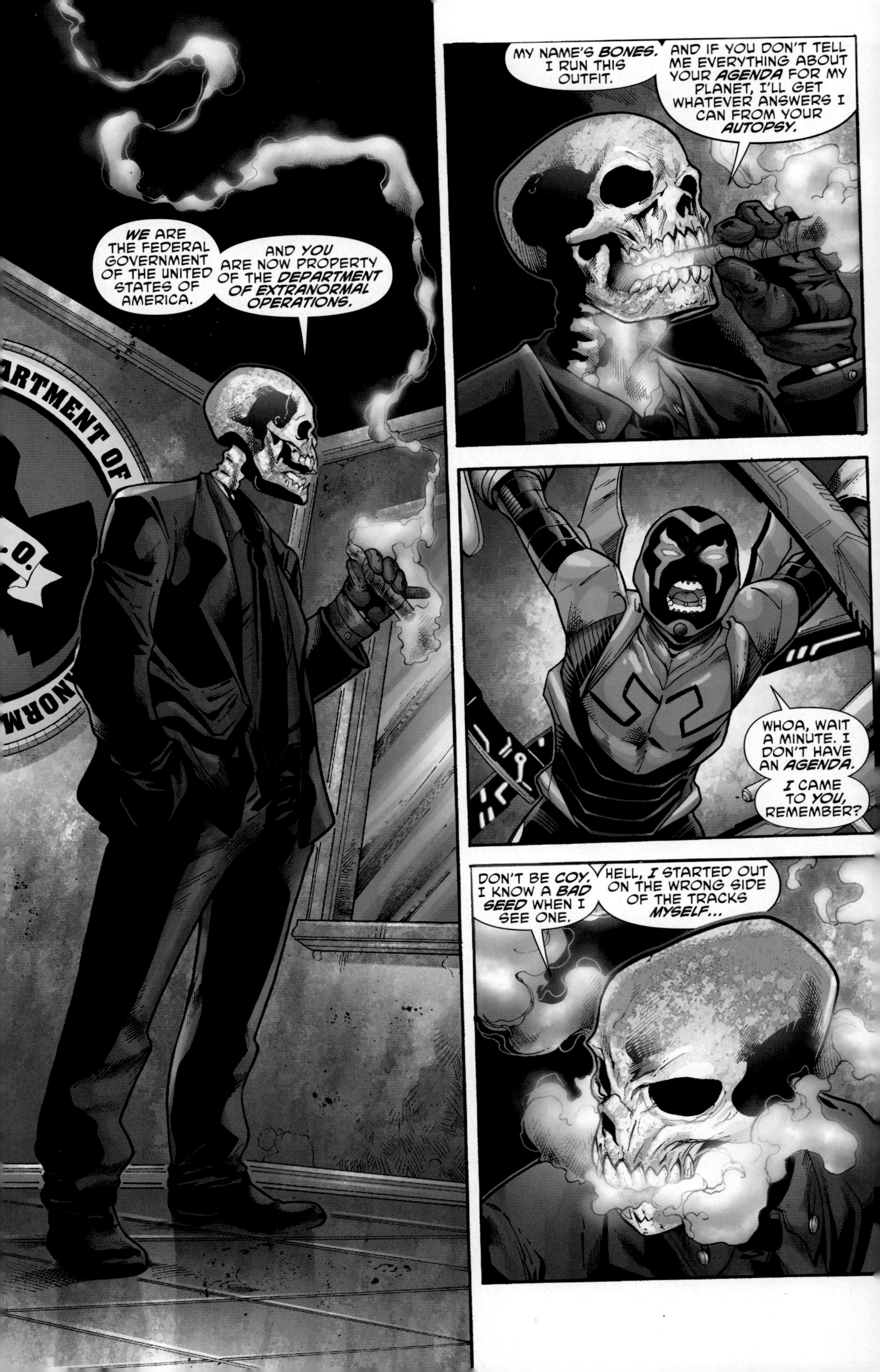
WE ARE THE FEDERAL GOVERNMENT OF THE UNITED STATES OF AMERICA.
AND YOU ARE NOW PROPERTY OF THE DEPARTMENT OF EXTRANORMAL OPERATIONS.
ARTMENT OF
MY NAME'S BONES. I RUN THIS OUTFIT.
AND IF YOU DON'T TELL ME EVERYTHING ABOUT YOUR AGENDA FOR MY PLANET, I'LL GET WHATEVER ANSWERS I CAN FROM YOUR AUTOPSY.
WHOA, WAIT A MINUTE. I DON'T HAVE AN AGENDA.
I CAME TO YOU, REMEMBER?
DON'T BE COY. I KNOW A BAD SEED WHEN I SEE ONE.
HELL, I STARTED OUT ON THE WRONG SIDE OF THE TRACKS MYSELF...

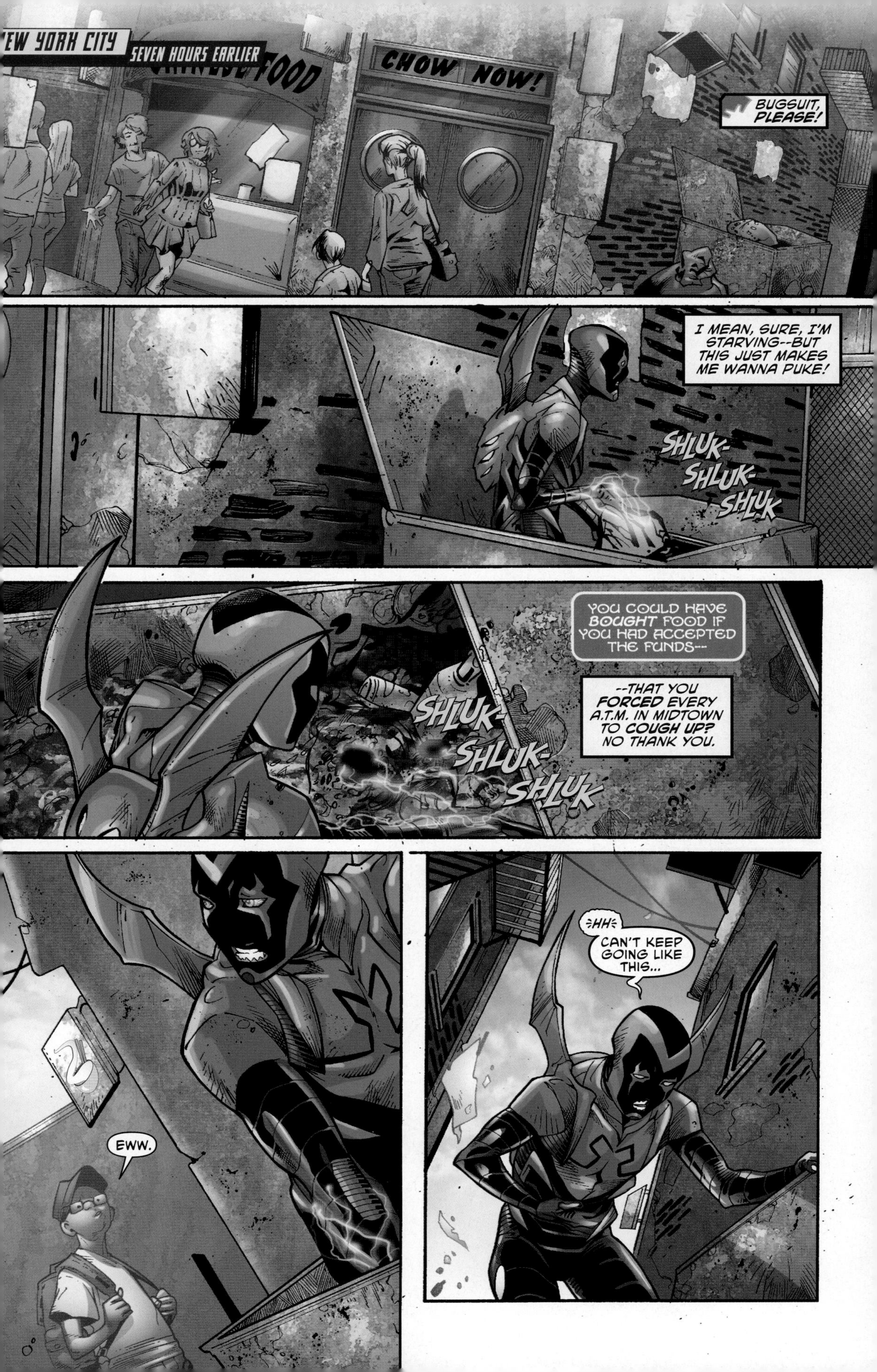

EW YORK CITY
SEVEN HOURS EARLIER
CHOW NOW!
BUGSUIT, PLEASE!
I MEAN, SURE, I'M STARVING--BUT THIS JUST MAKES ME WANNA PUKE!
SHLUK-SHLUK-SHLUK
YOU COULD HAVE BOUGHT FOOD IF YOU HAD ACCEPTED THE FUNDS--
--THAT YOU FORCED EVERY A.T.M. IN MIDTOWN TO COUGH UP? NO THANK YOU.
SHLUK-SHLUK-SHLUK
EWW.
HH
CAN'T KEEP GOING LIKE THIS...

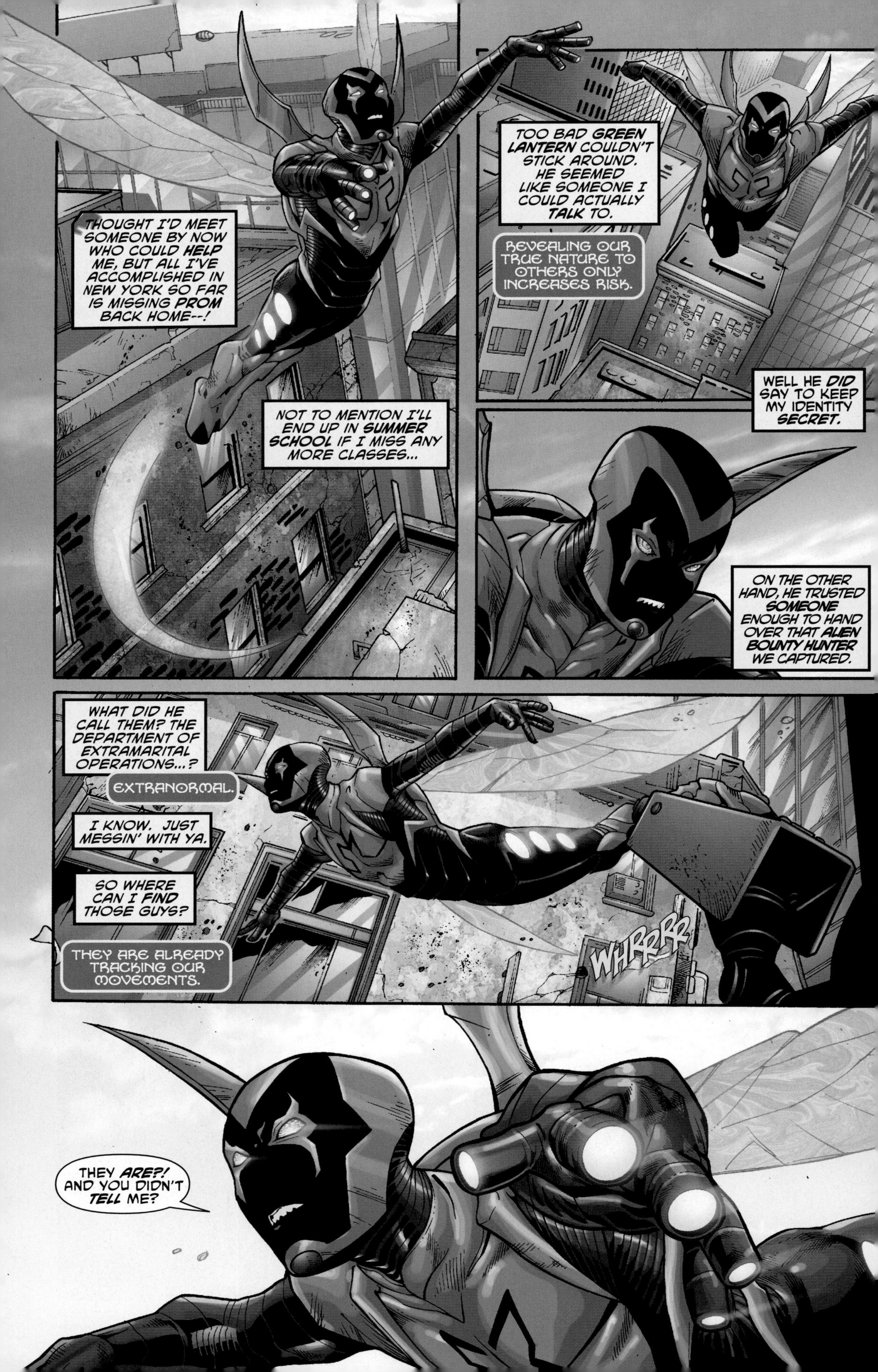
THOUGHT I'D MEET SOMEONE BY NOW WHO COULD HELP ME, BUT ALL I'VE ACCOMPLISHED IN NEW YORK SO FAR IS MISSING PROM BACK HOME--!
NOT TO MENTION I'LL END UP IN SUMMER SCHOOL IF I MISS ANY MORE CLASSES...
TOO BAD GREEN LANTERN COULDN'T STICK AROUND. HE SEEMED LIKE SOMEONE I COULD ACTUALLY TALK TO.
REVEALING OUR TRUE NATURE TO OTHERS ONLY INCREASES RISK.
WELL HE DID SAY TO KEEP MY IDENTITY SECRET.
ON THE OTHER HAND, HE TRUSTED SOMEONE ENOUGH TO HAND OVER THAT ALIEN BOUNTY HUNTER WE CAPTURED.
WHAT DID HE CALL THEM? THE DEPARTMENT OF EXTRAMARITAL OPERATIONS...?
EXTRANORMAL.
I KNOW. JUST MESSIN' WITH YA.
SO WHERE CAN I FIND THOSE GUYS?
THEY ARE ALREADY TRACKING OUR MOVEMENTS.
WHRRRR
THEY ARE?! AND YOU DIDN'T TELL ME?

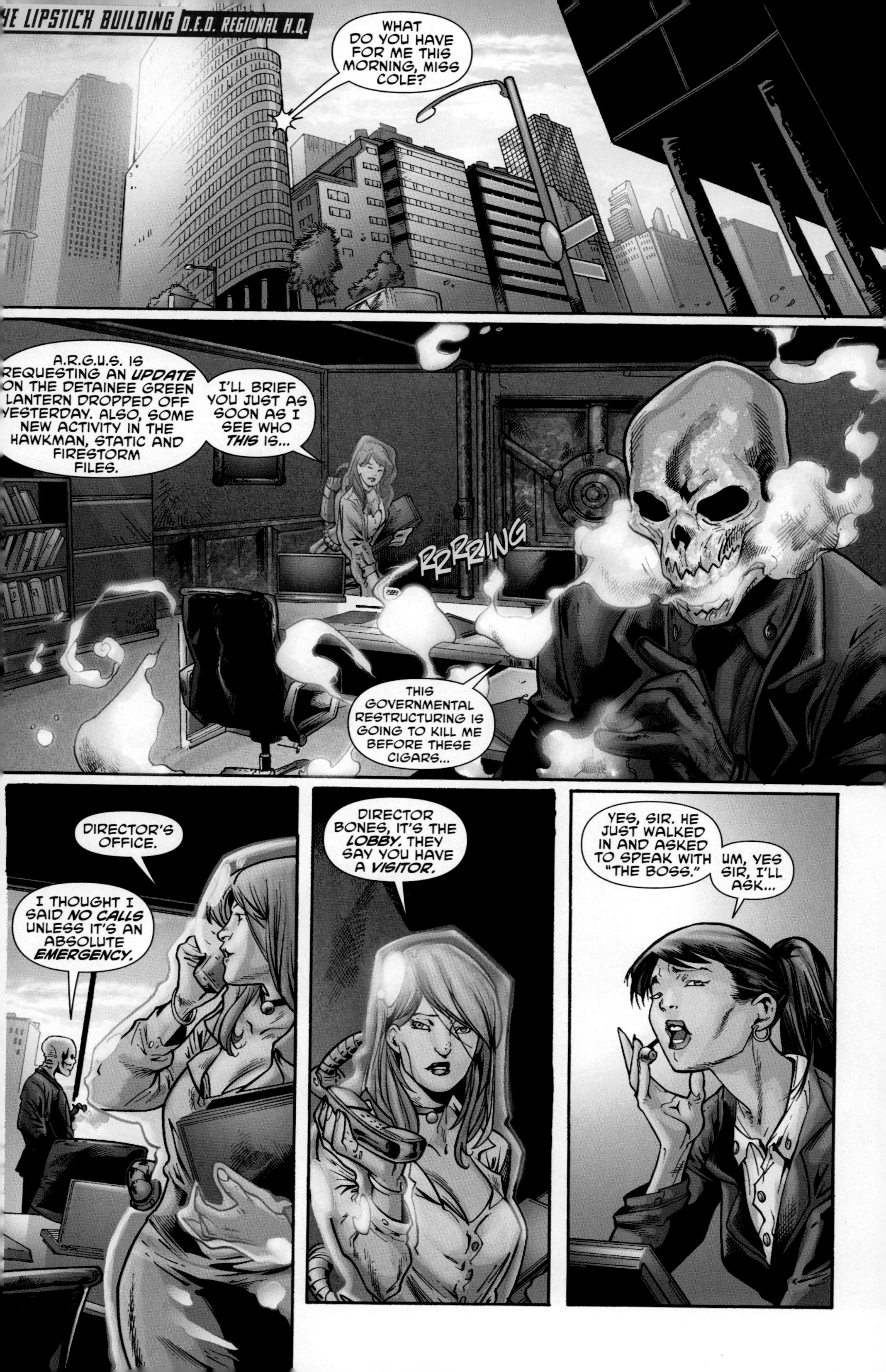
THE LIPSTICK BUILDING D.E.O. REGIONAL H.Q.
WHAT DO YOU HAVE FOR ME THIS MORNING, MISS COLE?
A.R.G.U.S. IS REQUESTING AN UPDATE ON THE DETAINEE GREEN LANTERN DROPPED OFF YESTERDAY. ALSO, SOME NEW ACTIVITY IN THE HAWKMAN, STATIC AND FIRESTORM FILES.
I'LL BRIEF YOU JUST AS SOON AS I SEE WHO THIS IS...
RRRRING
THIS GOVERNMENTAL RESTRUCTURING IS GOING TO KILL ME BEFORE THESE CIGARS...
DIRECTOR'S OFFICE.
I THOUGHT I SAID NO CALLS UNLESS IT'S AN ABSOLUTE EMERGENCY.
DIRECTOR BONES, IT'S THE LOBBY. THEY SAY YOU HAVE A VISITOR.
YES, SIR. HE JUST WALKED IN AND ASKED TO SPEAK WITH "THE BOSS."
UM, YES SIR, I'LL ASK...

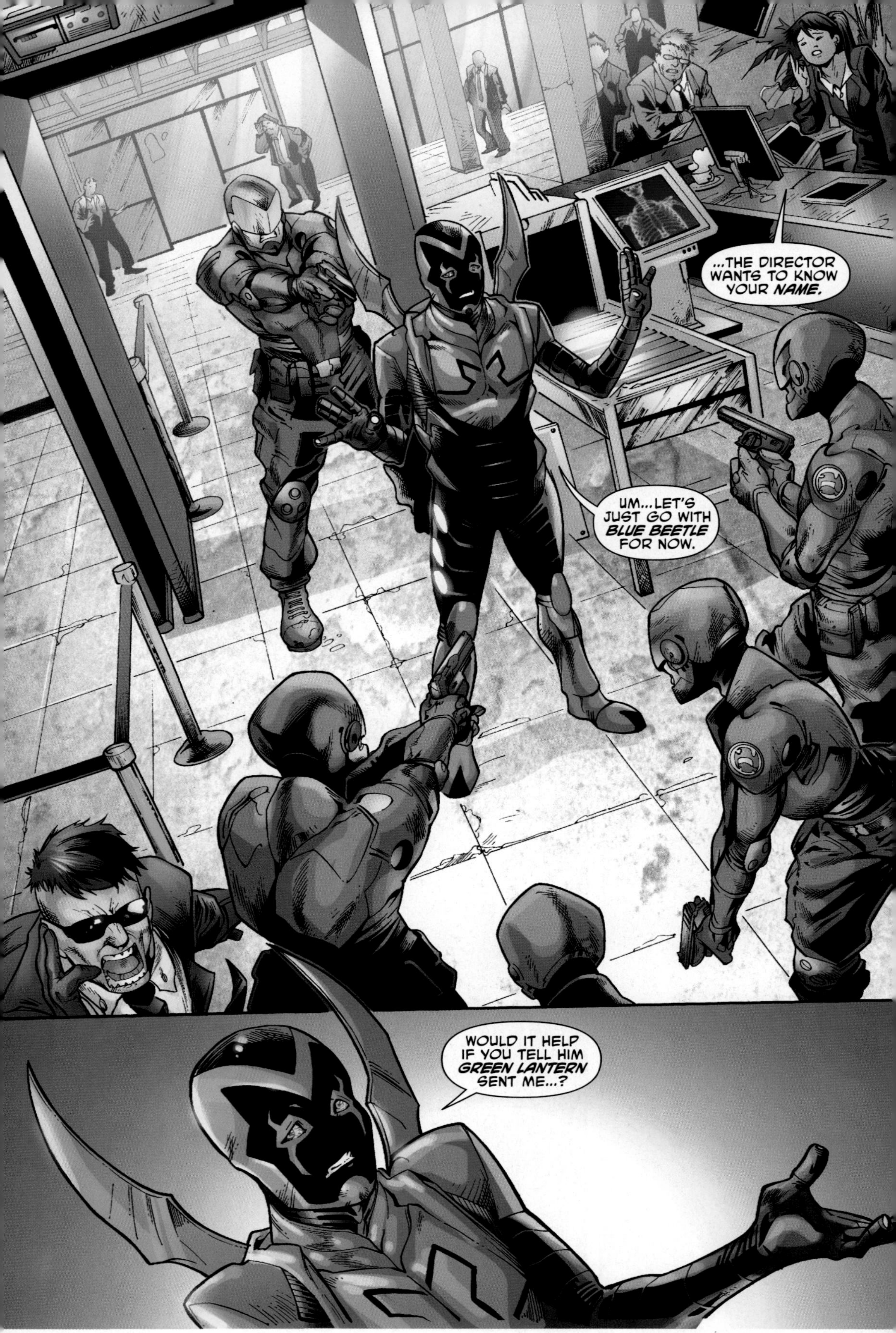
...THE DIRECTOR WANTS TO KNOW YOUR *NAME.*
UM...LET'S JUST GO WITH *BLUE BEETLE* FOR NOW.
WOULD IT HELP IF YOU TELL HIM *GREEN LANTERN* SENT ME...?

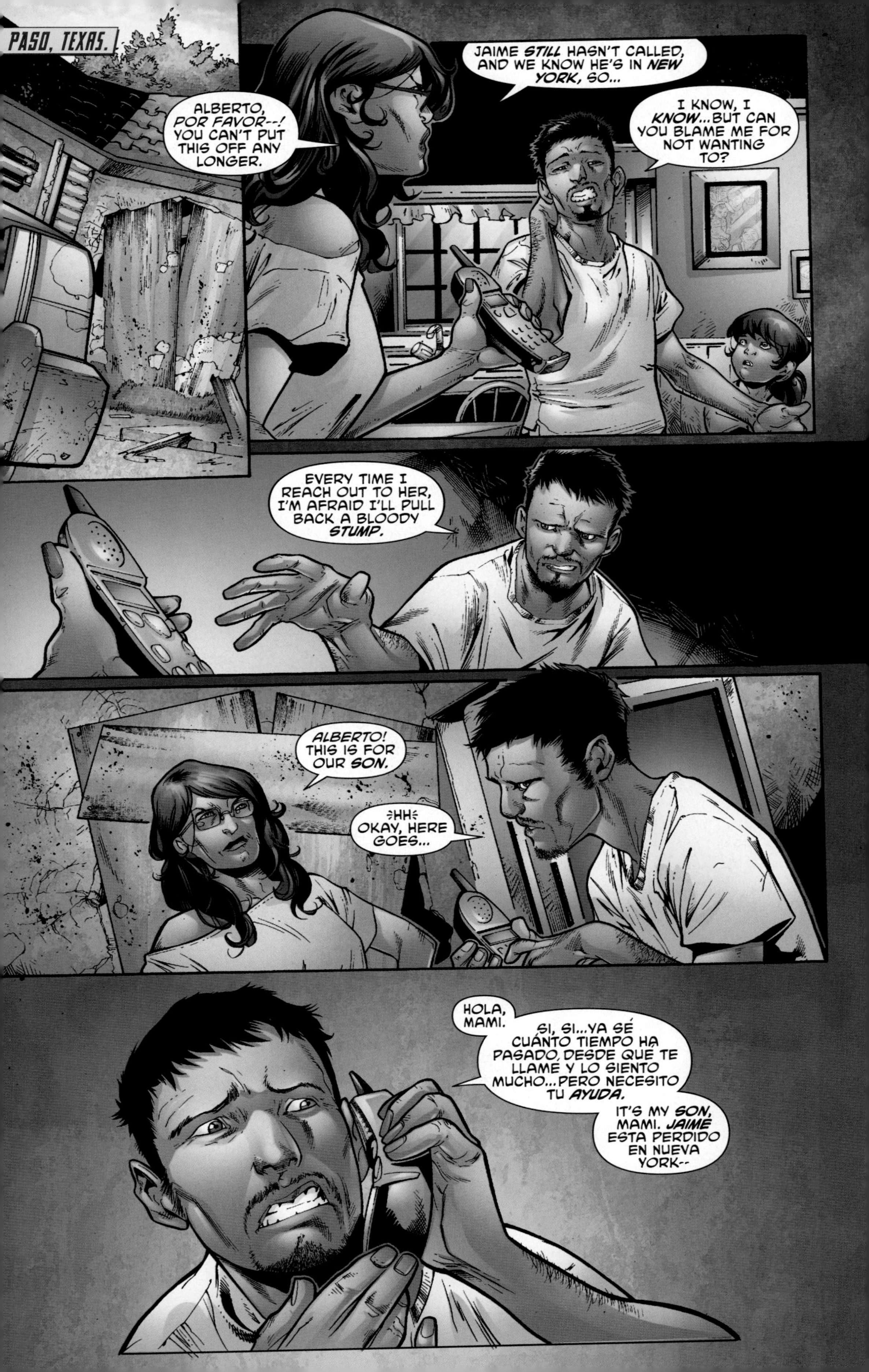
PASO, TEXAS.
ALBERTO, POR FAVOR--! YOU CAN'T PUT THIS OFF ANY LONGER.
JAIME STILL HASN'T CALLED, AND WE KNOW HE'S IN NEW YORK, SO...
I KNOW, I KNOW...BUT CAN YOU BLAME ME FOR NOT WANTING TO?
EVERY TIME I REACH OUT TO HER, I'M AFRAID I'LL PULL BACK A BLOODY STUMP.
ALBERTO! THIS IS FOR OUR SON.
HH
OKAY, HERE GOES...
HOLA, MAMI.
SI, SI...YA SÉ CUÁNTO TIEMPO HA PASADO, DESDE QUE TE LLAMÉ Y LO SIENTO MUCHO...PERO NECESITO TU AYUDA.
IT'S MY SON, MAMI. JAIME ESTA PERDIDO EN NUEVA YORK--

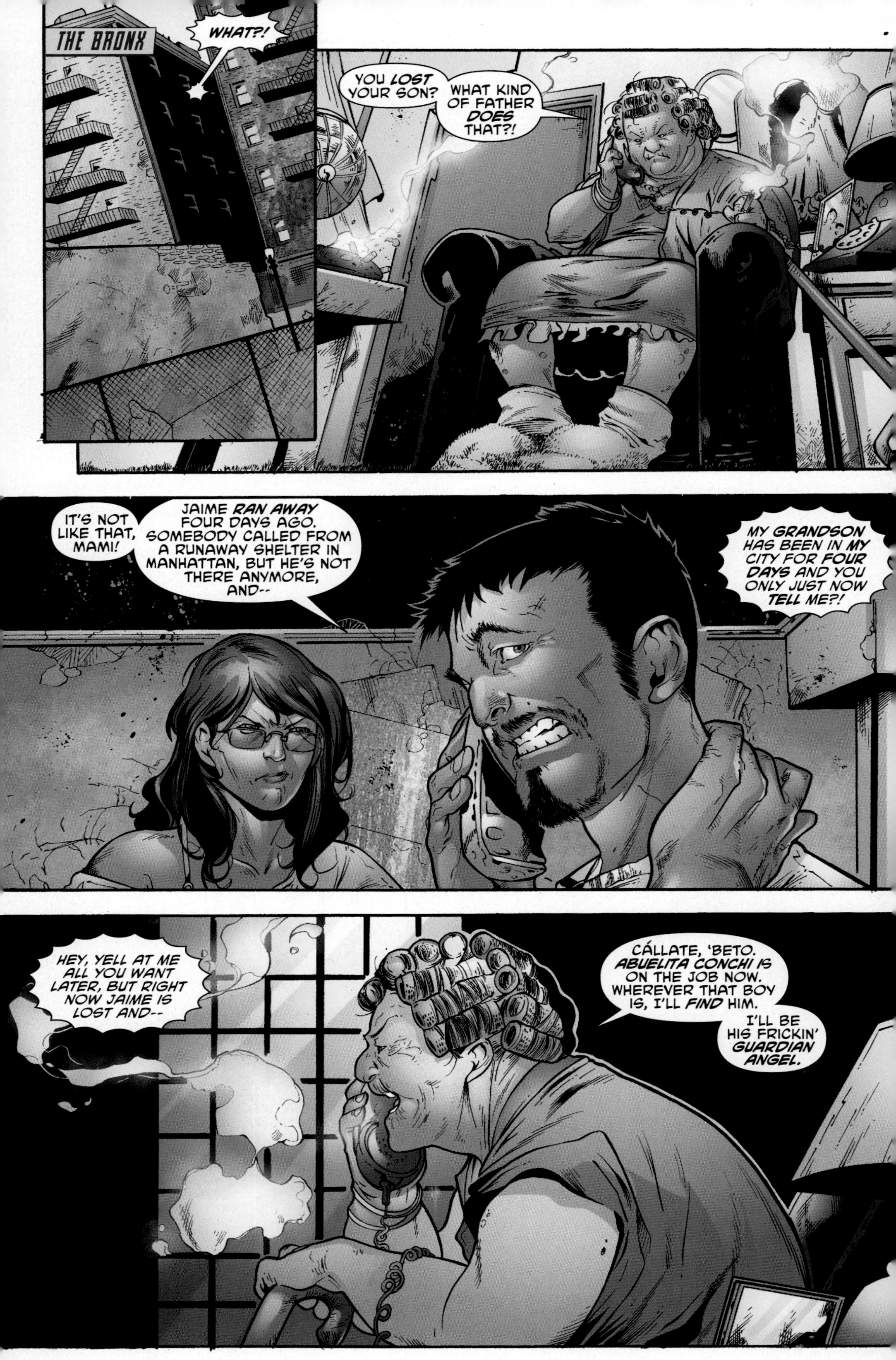
THE BRONX
WHAT?!
YOU LOST YOUR SON?
WHAT KIND OF FATHER DOES THAT?!
IT'S NOT LIKE THAT, MAMI!
JAIME RAN AWAY FOUR DAYS AGO. SOMEBODY CALLED FROM A RUNAWAY SHELTER IN MANHATTAN, BUT HE'S NOT THERE ANYMORE, AND--
MY GRANDSON HAS BEEN IN MY CITY FOR FOUR DAYS AND YOU ONLY JUST NOW TELL ME?!
HEY, YELL AT ME ALL YOU WANT LATER, BUT RIGHT NOW JAIME IS LOST AND--
CÁLLATE, 'BETO. ABUELITA CONCHI IS ON THE JOB NOW. WHEREVER THAT BOY IS, I'LL FIND HIM.
I'LL BE HIS FRICKIN' GUARDIAN ANGEL.

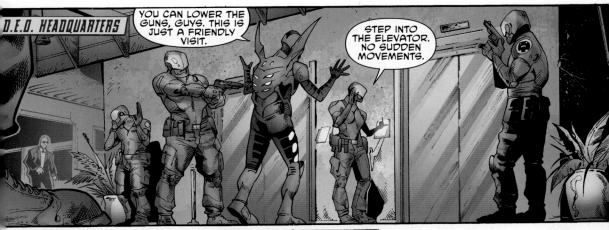

YOU CAN LOWER THE GUNS, GUYS. THIS IS JUST A FRIENDLY VISIT.

STEP INTO THE ELEVATOR. NO SUDDEN MOVEMENTS.

OKAY, FINE. BUT EVEN THIS CLOSE, A BULLET'S NOT GONNA HURT ME. I JUST DON'T WANT ANY OF YOU CATCHING A *RICOCHET*.

NOTED. NOW SHUT UP.

PING

UM, SHOULDN'T WE BE GOING *UP*?

IT'S MOSTLY ADMINISTRATIVE UP THERE. THE *REAL* WORK'S DONE UNDERGROUND.

HM. SHAKIRA. GUESS THEY CAN'T BE ALL BAD.

UNACCEPTABLE EXPOSURE. EXIT IMMEDIATELY.

COME ON, BUGSUIT, WE'RE ALREADY ALL OVER THE INTERNET. KEEPING OUR EXISTENCE SECRET ISN'T REALLY AN OPTION ANYMORE.

THE BEST WE CAN HOPE FOR NOW IS TO *MANAGE* MY PUBLIC IMAGE SO PEOPLE DON'T THINK I'M DANGEROUS.

YOU DON'T *WANT* MY FELLOW EARTHLINGS THINKING WE'RE A *THREAT*, RIGHT?

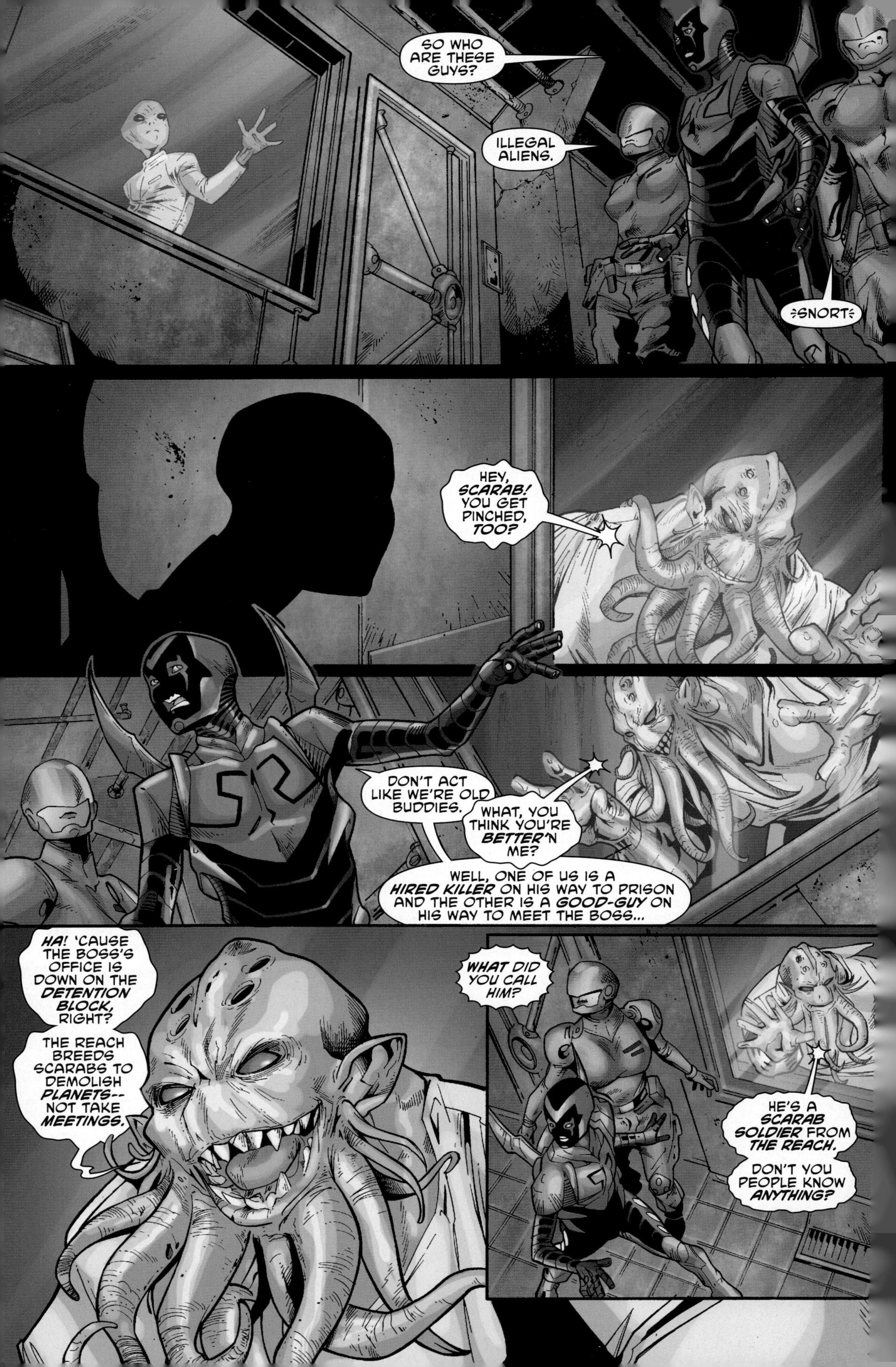
SO WHO ARE THESE GUYS?
ILLEGAL ALIENS.
SNORT
HEY, SCARAB! YOU GET PINCHED, TOO?
DON'T ACT LIKE WE'RE OLD BUDDIES.
WHAT, YOU THINK YOU'RE BETTER'N ME?
WELL, ONE OF US IS A HIRED KILLER ON HIS WAY TO PRISON AND THE OTHER IS A GOOD-GUY ON HIS WAY TO MEET THE BOSS...
HA! 'CAUSE THE BOSS'S OFFICE IS DOWN ON THE DETENTION BLOCK, RIGHT?
THE REACH BREEDS SCARABS TO DEMOLISH PLANETS-- NOT TAKE MEETINGS.
WHAT DID YOU CALL HIM?
HE'S A SCARAB SOLDIER FROM THE REACH.
DON'T YOU PEOPLE KNOW ANYTHING?

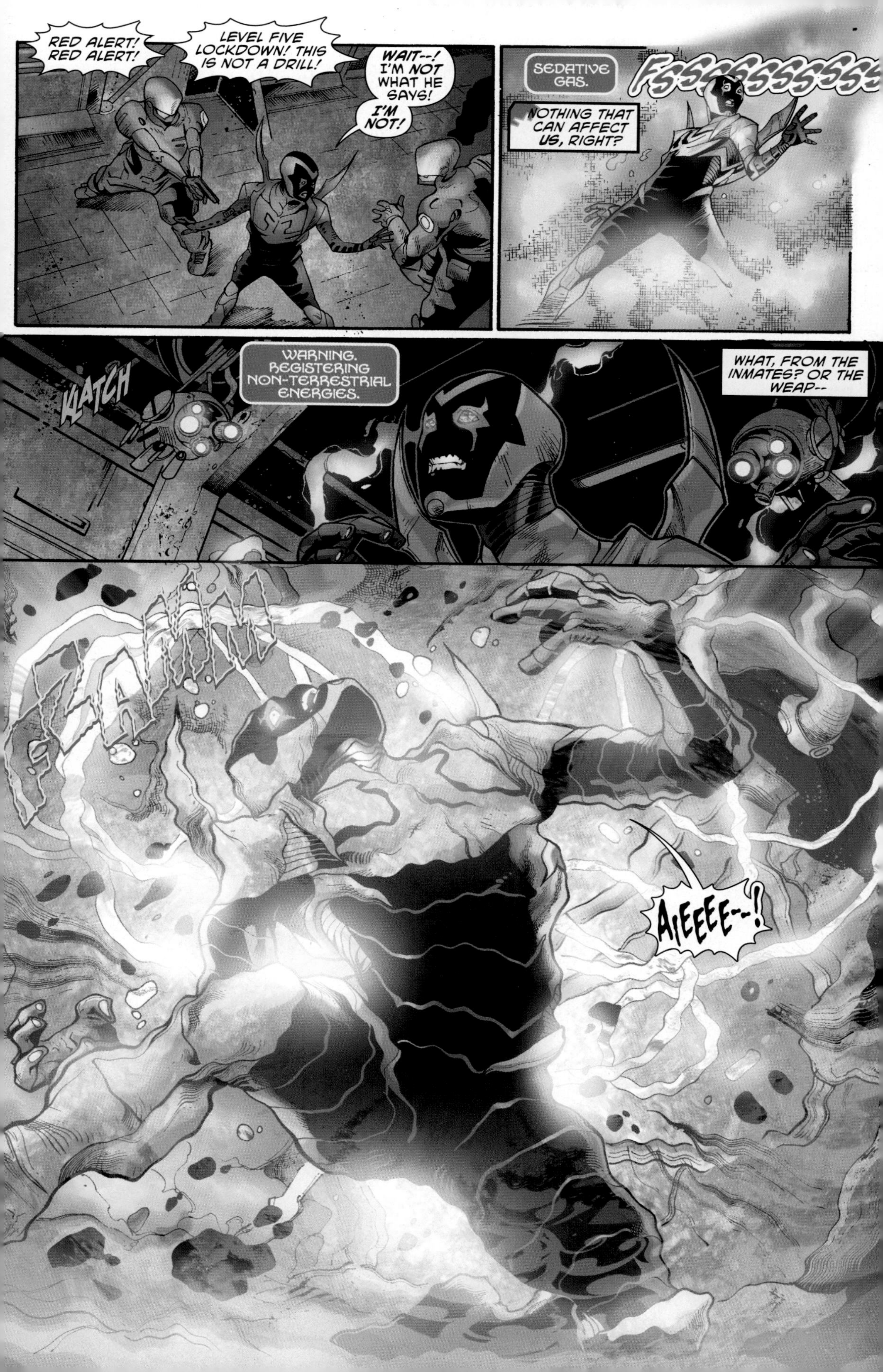
RED ALERT! RED ALERT!
LEVEL FIVE LOCKDOWN! THIS IS NOT A DRILL!
WAIT--! I'M NOT WHAT HE SAYS!
I'M NOT!
SEDATIVE GAS.
NOTHING THAT CAN AFFECT US, RIGHT?
FSSSSSSSSSS
KLATCH
WARNING. REGISTERING NON-TERRESTRIAL ENERGIES.
WHAT, FROM THE INMATES? OR THE WEAP--
AIEEEE--!

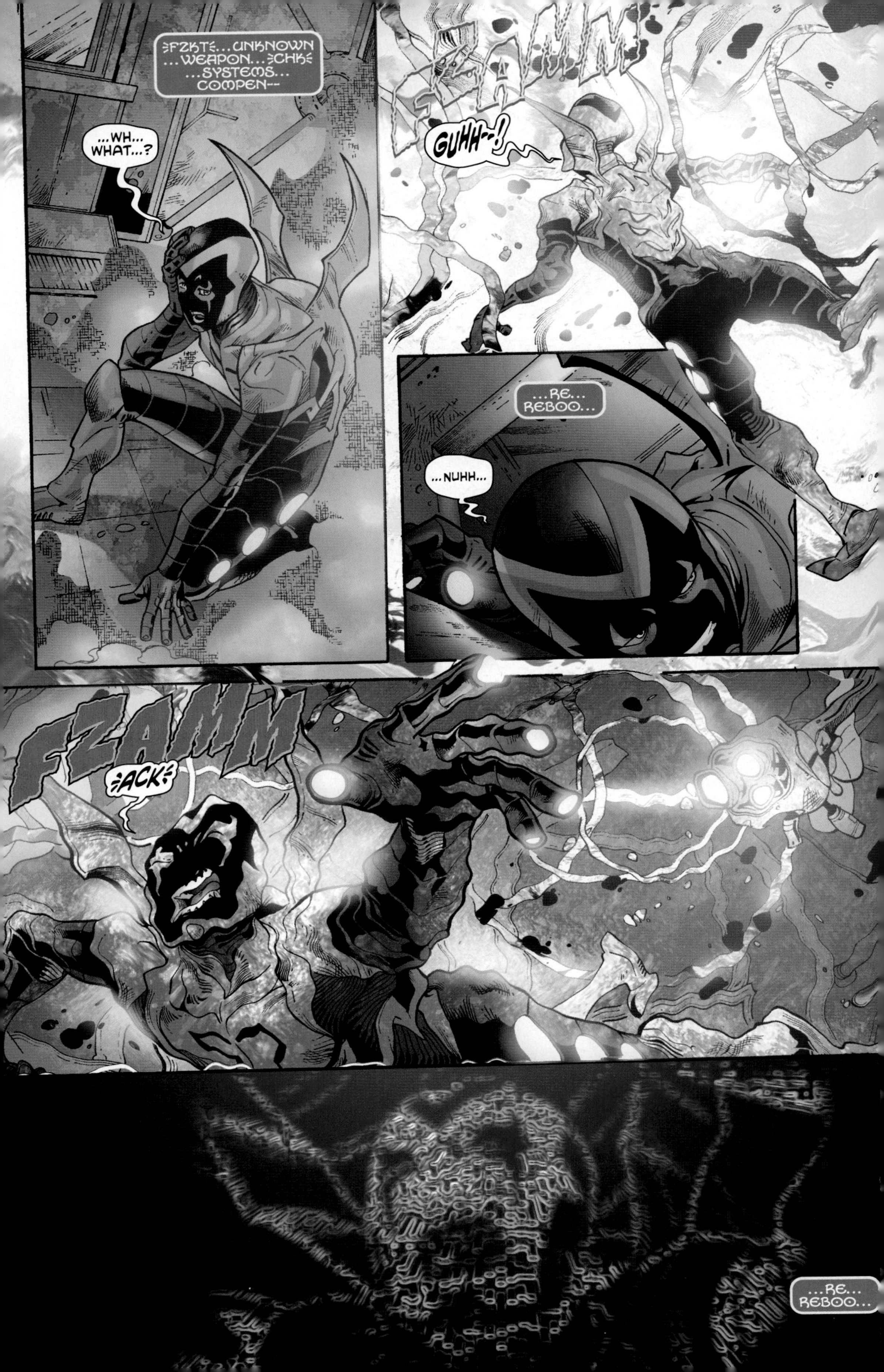

FZKT... UNKNOWN ...WEAPON... CHK ...SYSTEMS... COMPEN--
...WH... WHAT...?
FZAMM
GUHH--!
...RE... REBOO...
...NUHH...
FZAMM
ACK
...RE... REBOO...

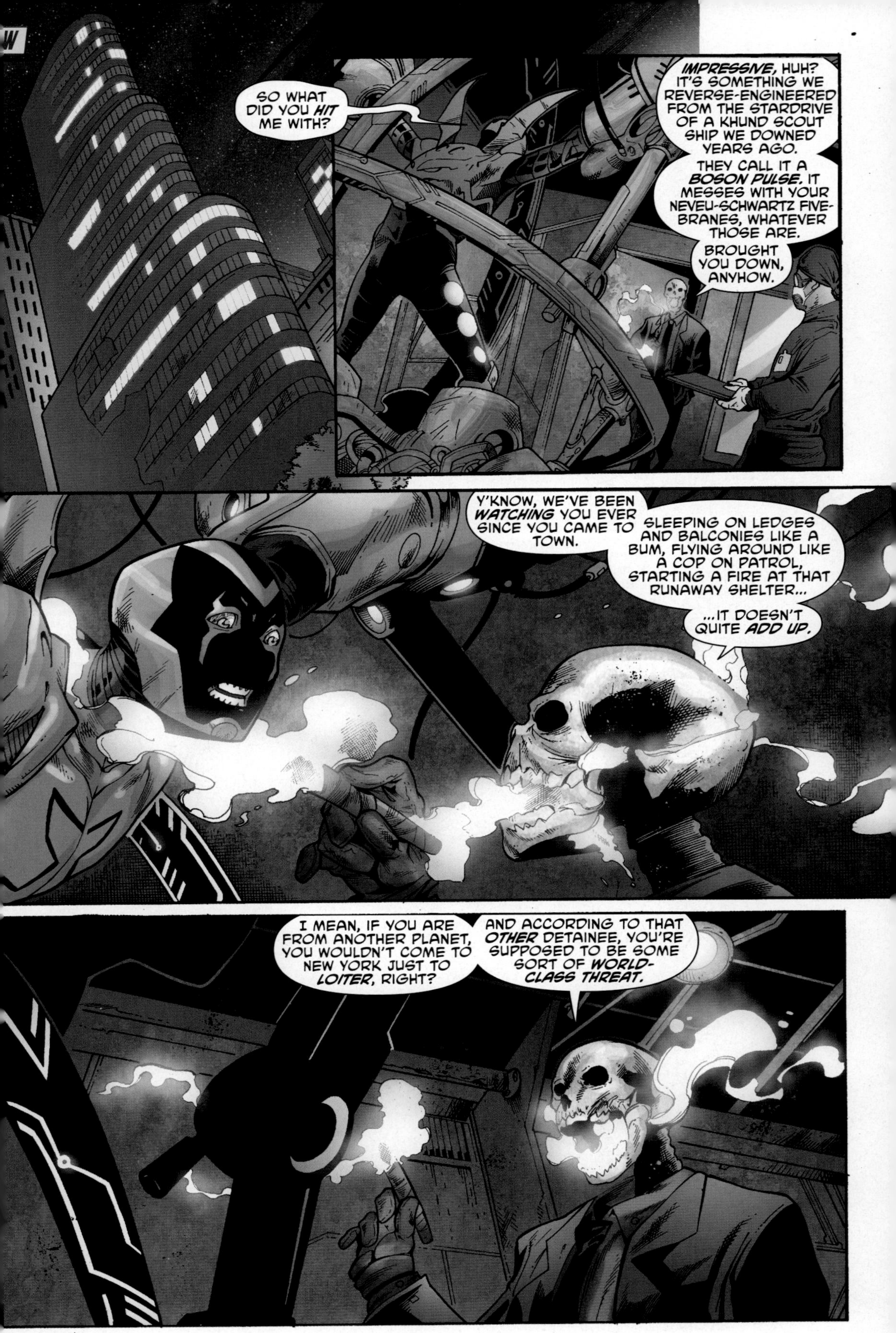
SO WHAT DID YOU HIT ME WITH?
IMPRESSIVE, HUH? IT'S SOMETHING WE REVERSE-ENGINEERED FROM THE STARDRIVE OF A KHUND SCOUT SHIP WE DOWNED YEARS AGO.
THEY CALL IT A BOSON PULSE. IT MESSES WITH YOUR NEVEU-SCHWARTZ FIVE-BRANES, WHATEVER THOSE ARE.
BROUGHT YOU DOWN, ANYHOW.
Y'KNOW, WE'VE BEEN WATCHING YOU EVER SINCE YOU CAME TO TOWN.
SLEEPING ON LEDGES AND BALCONIES LIKE A BUM, FLYING AROUND LIKE A COP ON PATROL, STARTING A FIRE AT THAT RUNAWAY SHELTER...
...IT DOESN'T QUITE ADD UP.
I MEAN, IF YOU ARE FROM ANOTHER PLANET, YOU WOULDN'T COME TO NEW YORK JUST TO LOITER, RIGHT?
AND ACCORDING TO THAT OTHER DETAINEE, YOU'RE SUPPOSED TO BE SOME SORT OF WORLD-CLASS THREAT.

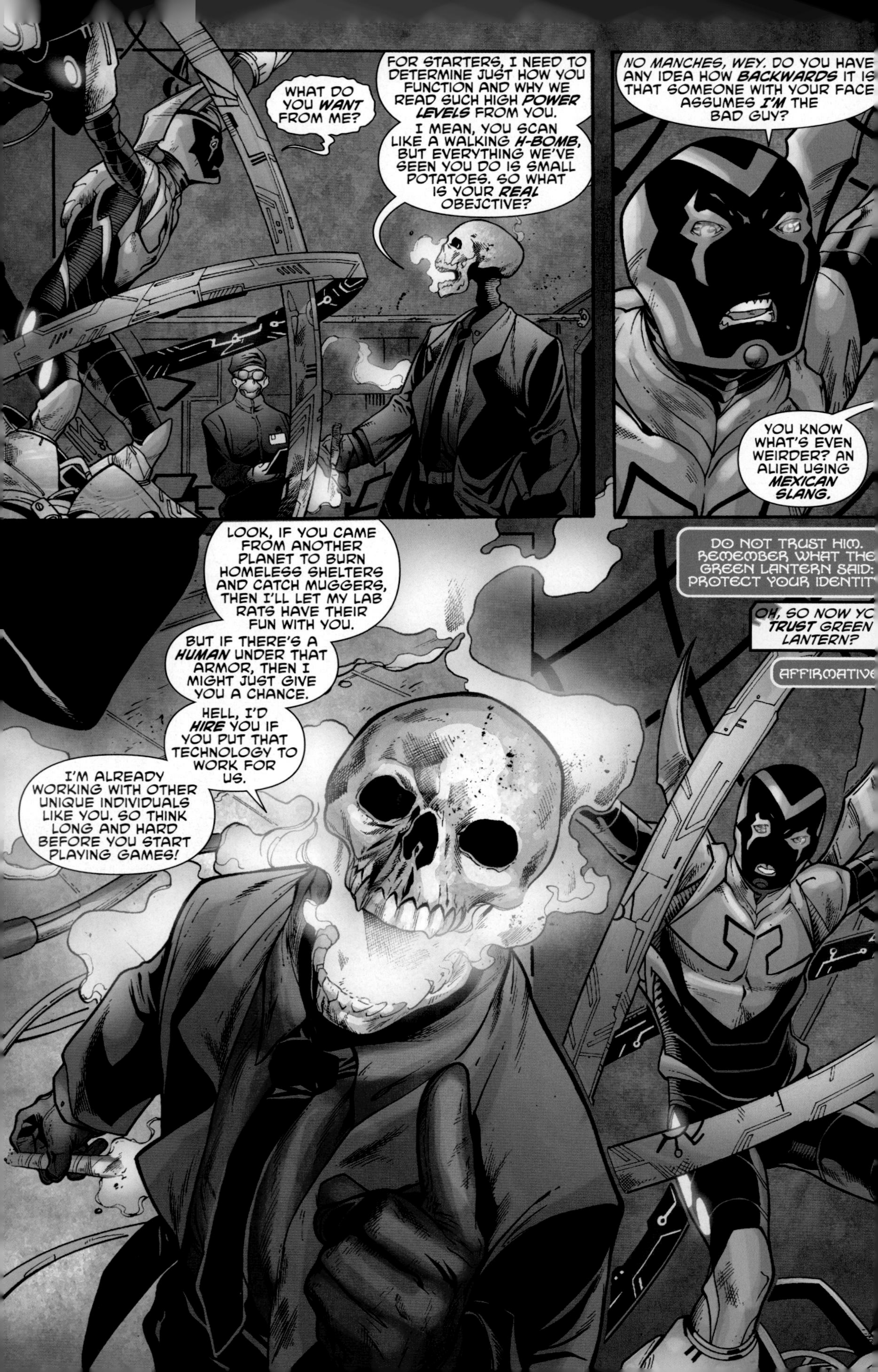
WHAT DO YOU WANT FROM ME?
FOR STARTERS, I NEED TO DETERMINE JUST HOW YOU FUNCTION AND WHY WE READ SUCH HIGH POWER LEVELS FROM YOU.
I MEAN, YOU SCAN LIKE A WALKING H-BOMB, BUT EVERYTHING WE'VE SEEN YOU DO IS SMALL POTATOES. SO WHAT IS YOUR REAL OBEJCTIVE?
NO MANCHES, WEY. DO YOU HAVE ANY IDEA HOW BACKWARDS IT IS THAT SOMEONE WITH YOUR FACE ASSUMES I'M THE BAD GUY?
YOU KNOW WHAT'S EVEN WEIRDER? AN ALIEN USING MEXICAN SLANG.
LOOK, IF YOU CAME FROM ANOTHER PLANET TO BURN HOMELESS SHELTERS AND CATCH MUGGERS, THEN I'LL LET MY LAB RATS HAVE THEIR FUN WITH YOU.
BUT IF THERE'S A HUMAN UNDER THAT ARMOR, THEN I MIGHT JUST GIVE YOU A CHANCE.
HELL, I'D HIRE YOU IF YOU PUT THAT TECHNOLOGY TO WORK FOR US.
I'M ALREADY WORKING WITH OTHER UNIQUE INDIVIDUALS LIKE YOU. SO THINK LONG AND HARD BEFORE YOU START PLAYING GAMES!
DO NOT TRUST HIM. REMEMBER WHAT THE GREEN LANTERN SAID: PROTECT YOUR IDENTIT
OH, SO NOW YO TRUST GREEN LANTERN?
AFFIRMATIVE

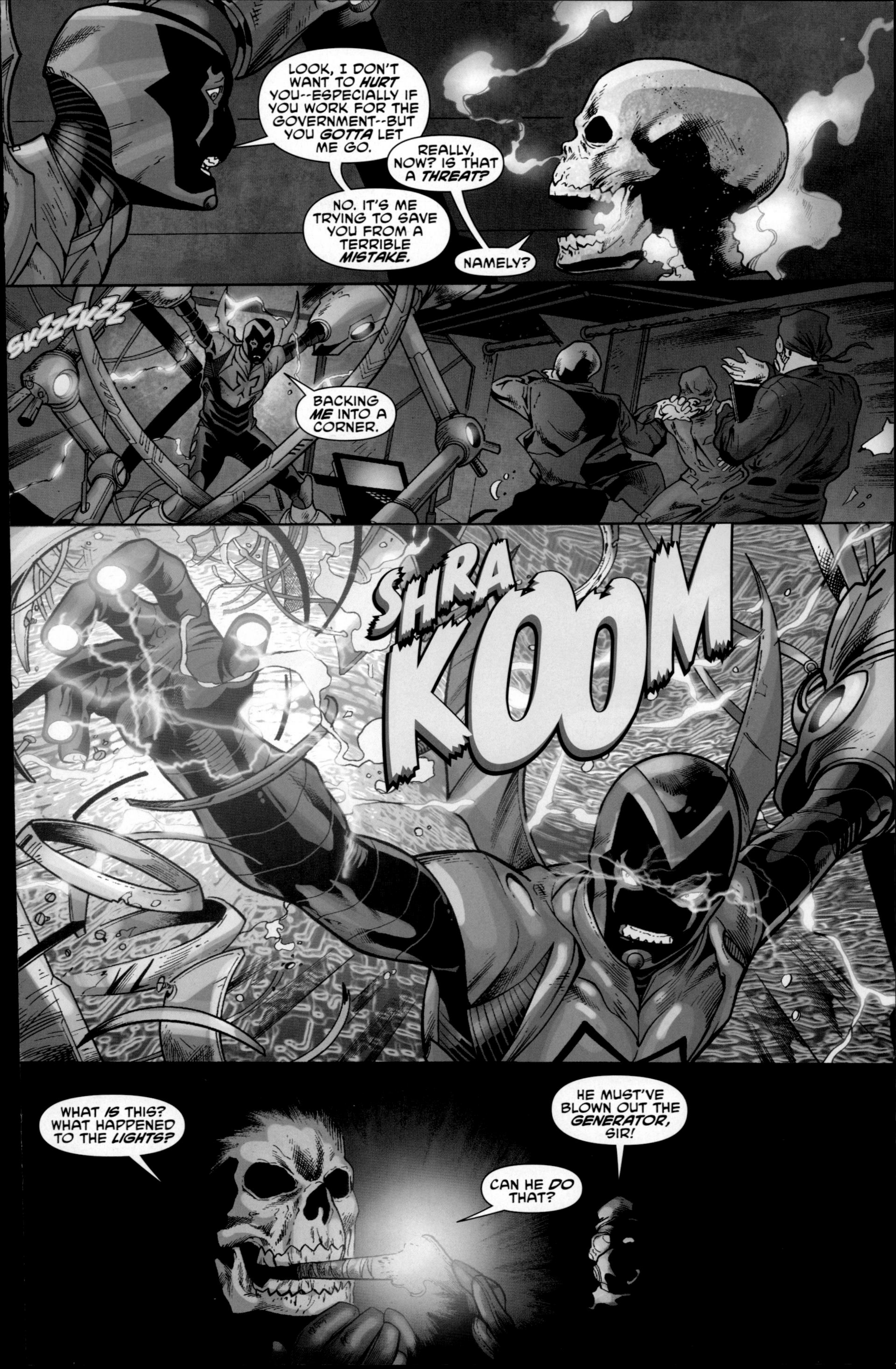
LOOK, I DON'T WANT TO HURT YOU--ESPECIALLY IF YOU WORK FOR THE GOVERNMENT--BUT YOU GOTTA LET ME GO.
REALLY, NOW? IS THAT A THREAT?
NO. IT'S ME TRYING TO SAVE YOU FROM A TERRIBLE MISTAKE.
NAMELY?
SKZZZKZZ
BACKING ME INTO A CORNER.
SHRA KOOM
WHAT IS THIS? WHAT HAPPENED TO THE LIGHTS?
HE MUST'VE BLOWN OUT THE GENERATOR, SIR!
CAN HE DO THAT?

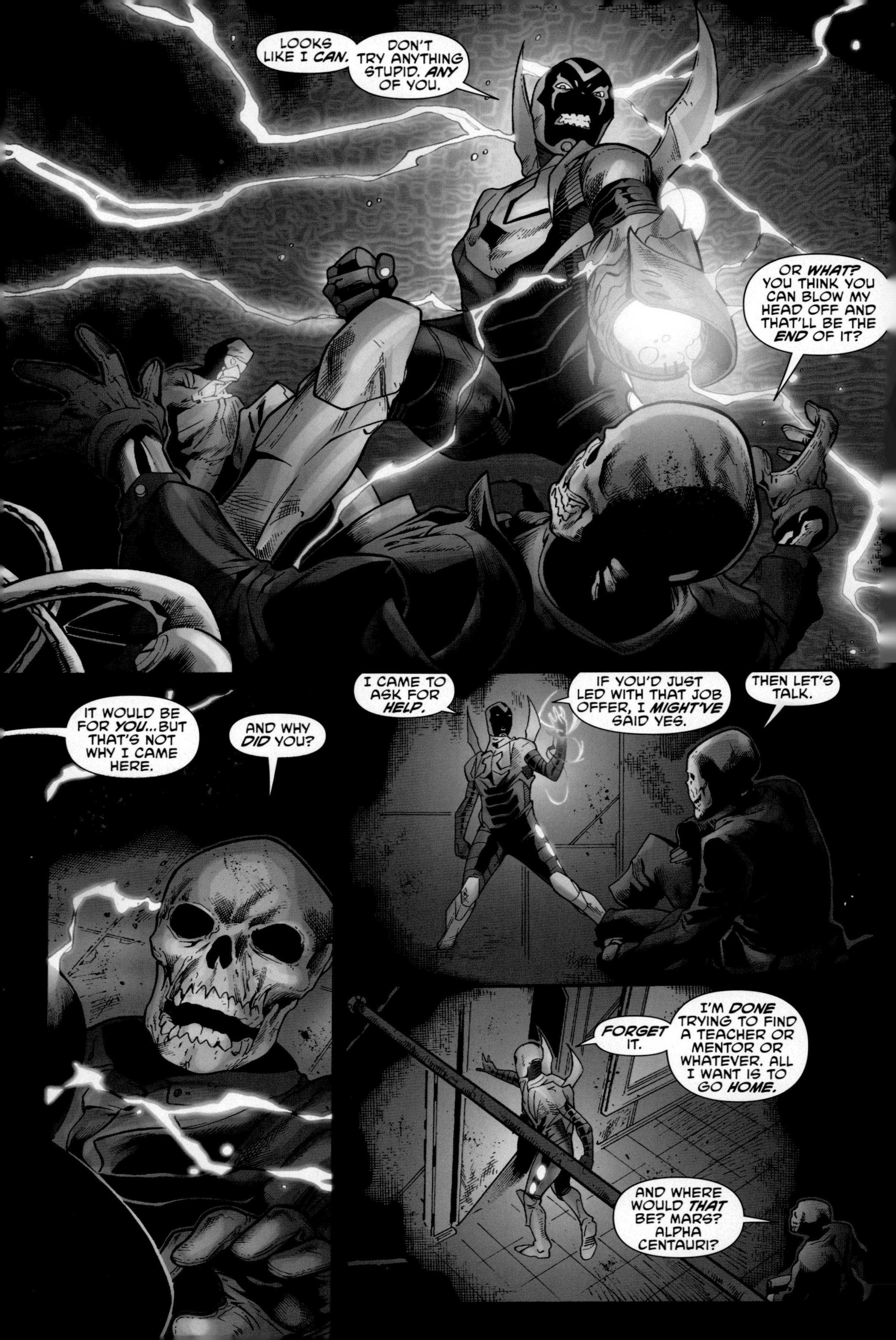
LOOKS LIKE I CAN.
DON'T TRY ANYTHING STUPID. ANY OF YOU.
OR WHAT? YOU THINK YOU CAN BLOW MY HEAD OFF AND THAT'LL BE THE END OF IT?
IT WOULD BE FOR YOU...BUT THAT'S NOT WHY I CAME HERE.
AND WHY DID YOU?
I CAME TO ASK FOR HELP.
IF YOU'D JUST LED WITH THAT JOB OFFER, I MIGHT'VE SAID YES.
THEN LET'S TALK.
FORGET IT.
I'M DONE TRYING TO FIND A TEACHER OR MENTOR OR WHATEVER. ALL I WANT IS TO GO HOME.
AND WHERE WOULD THAT BE? MARS? ALPHA CENTAURI?

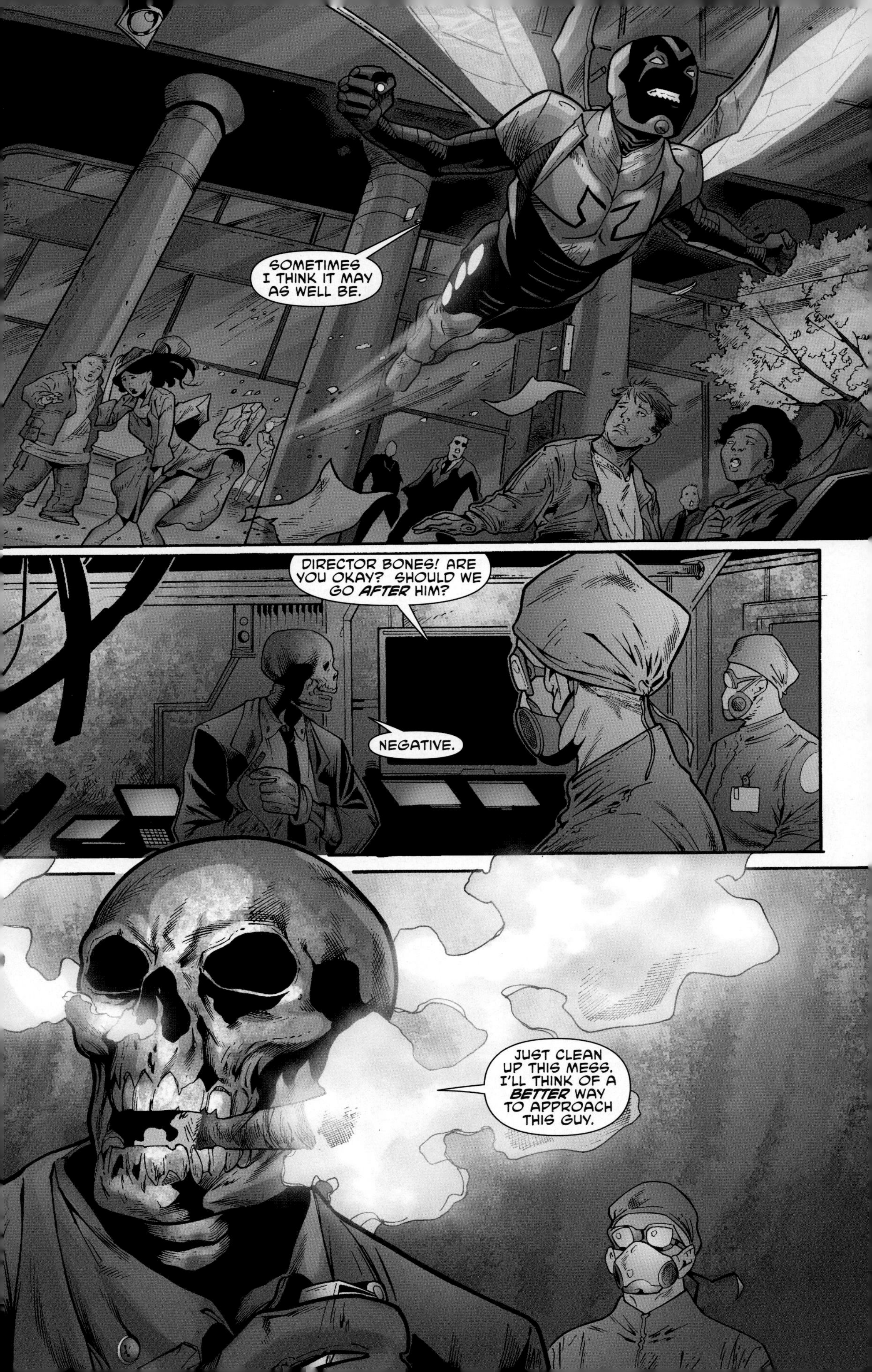

SOMETIMES I THINK IT MAY AS WELL BE.
DIRECTOR BONES! ARE YOU OKAY? SHOULD WE GO *AFTER* HIM?
NEGATIVE.
JUST CLEAN UP THIS MESS. I'LL THINK OF A *BETTER* WAY TO APPROACH THIS GUY.

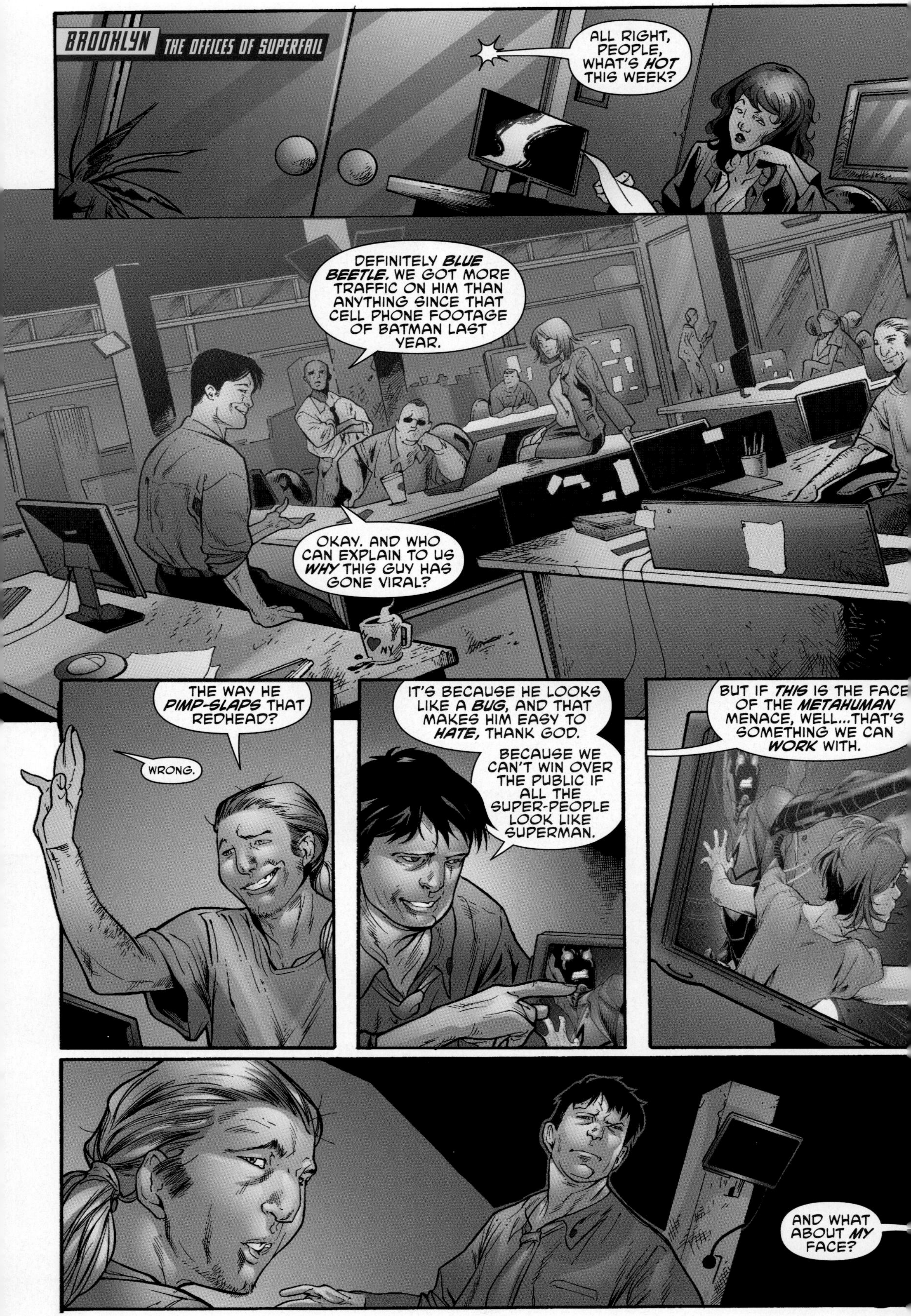
BROOKLYN
THE OFFICES OF SUPERFAIL
ALL RIGHT, PEOPLE, WHAT'S HOT THIS WEEK?
DEFINITELY BLUE BEETLE. WE GOT MORE TRAFFIC ON HIM THAN ANYTHING SINCE THAT CELL PHONE FOOTAGE OF BATMAN LAST YEAR.
OKAY. AND WHO CAN EXPLAIN TO US WHY THIS GUY HAS GONE VIRAL?
THE WAY HE PIMP-SLAPS THAT REDHEAD?
WRONG.
IT'S BECAUSE HE LOOKS LIKE A BUG, AND THAT MAKES HIM EASY TO HATE, THANK GOD.
BECAUSE WE CAN'T WIN OVER THE PUBLIC IF ALL THE SUPER-PEOPLE LOOK LIKE SUPERMAN.
BUT IF THIS IS THE FACE OF THE METAHUMAN MENACE, WELL...THAT'S SOMETHING WE CAN WORK WITH.
AND WHAT ABOUT MY FACE?

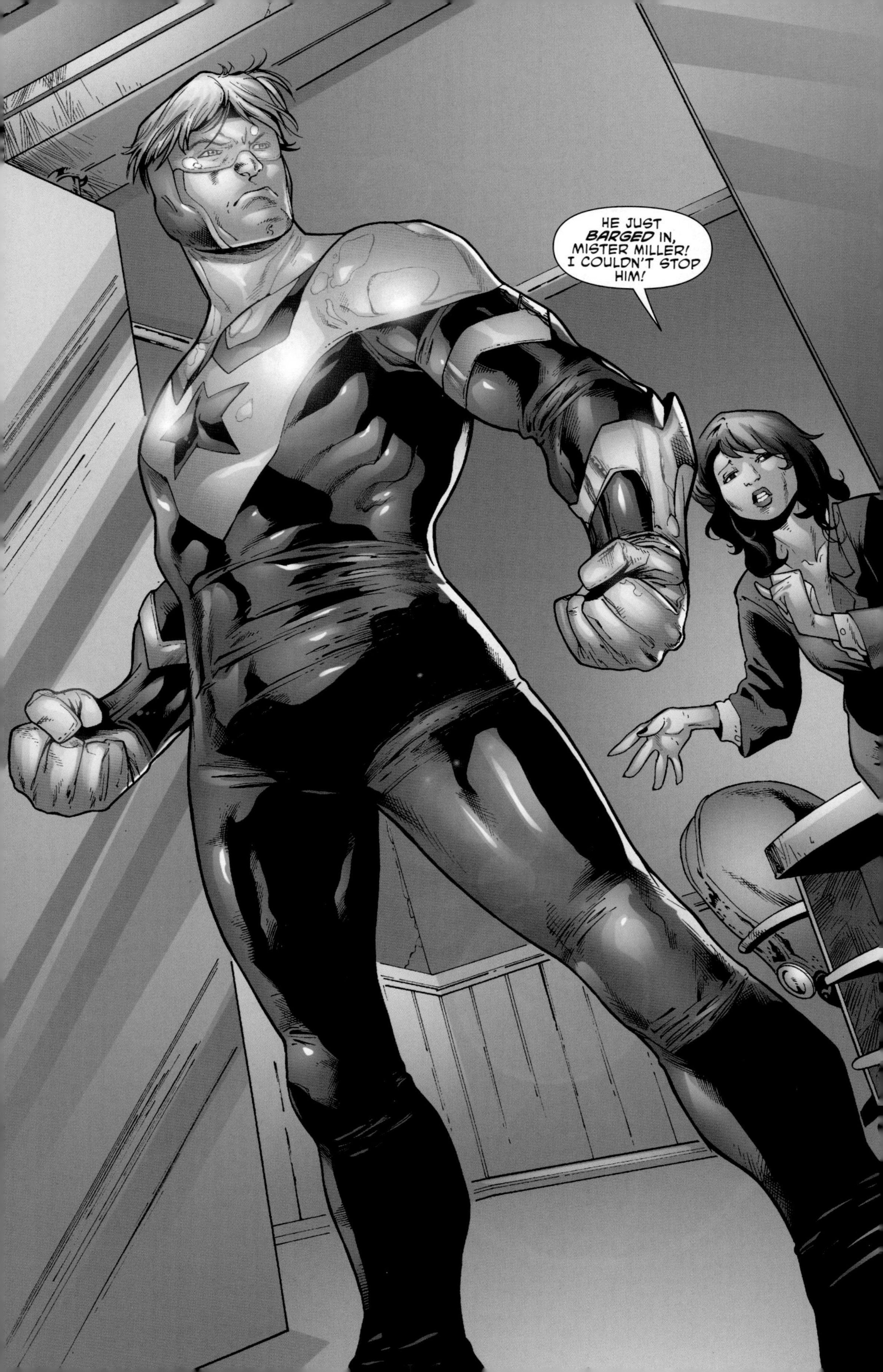
HE JUST *BARGED* IN, MISTER MILLER! I COULDN'T STOP HIM!

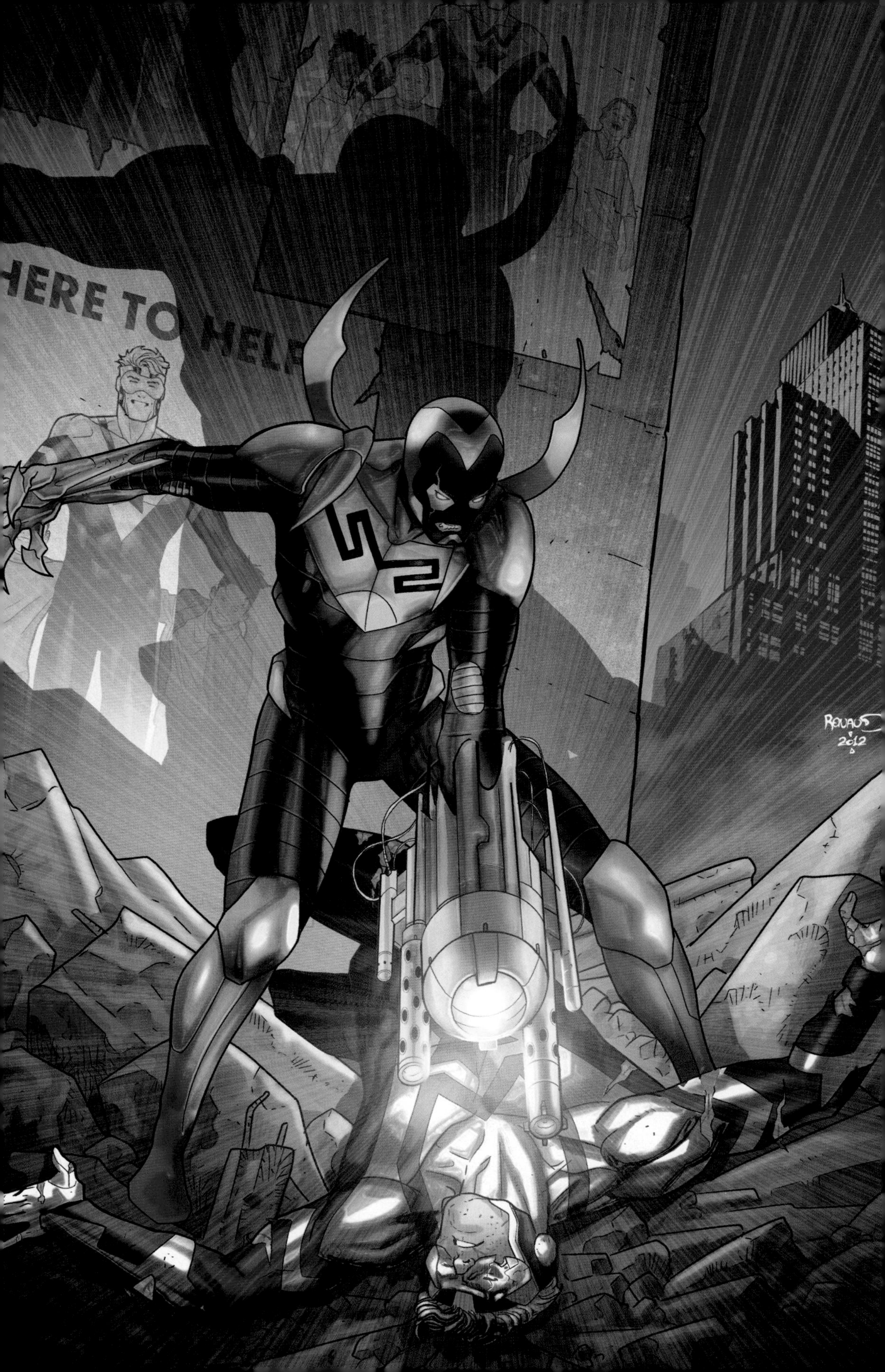
HERE TO HEL

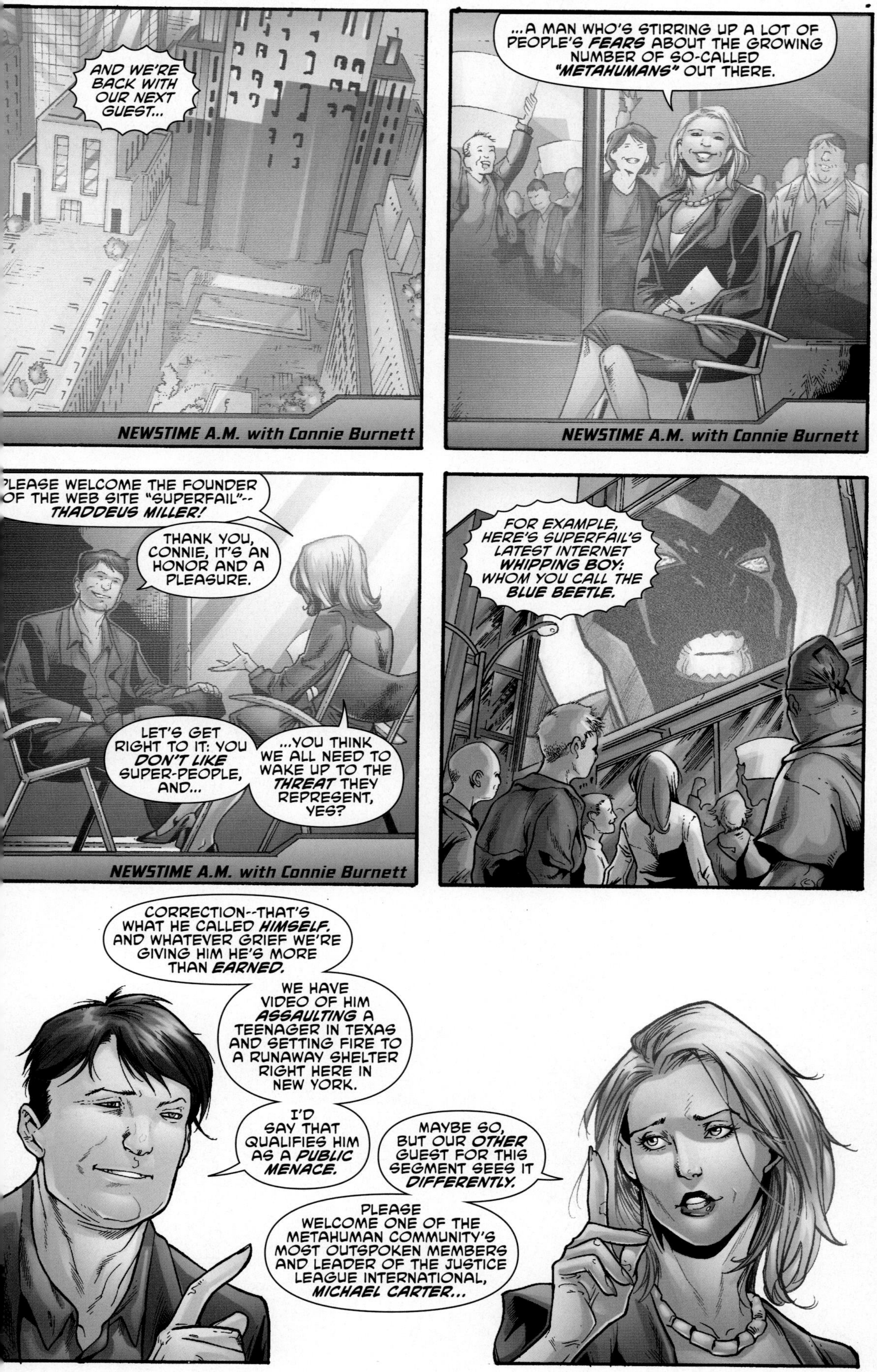
AND WE'RE BACK WITH OUR NEXT GUEST...
NEWSTIME A.M. with Connie Burnett
...A MAN WHO'S STIRRING UP A LOT OF PEOPLE'S FEARS ABOUT THE GROWING NUMBER OF SO-CALLED "METAHUMANS" OUT THERE.
NEWSTIME A.M. with Connie Burnett
PLEASE WELCOME THE FOUNDER OF THE WEB SITE "SUPERFAIL"-- THADDEUS MILLER!
THANK YOU, CONNIE, IT'S AN HONOR AND A PLEASURE.
LET'S GET RIGHT TO IT: YOU DON'T LIKE SUPER-PEOPLE, AND...
...YOU THINK WE ALL NEED TO WAKE UP TO THE THREAT THEY REPRESENT, YES?
NEWSTIME A.M. with Connie Burnett
FOR EXAMPLE, HERE'S SUPERFAIL'S LATEST INTERNET WHIPPING BOY: WHOM YOU CALL THE BLUE BEETLE.
CORRECTION--THAT'S WHAT HE CALLED HIMSELF. AND WHATEVER GRIEF WE'RE GIVING HIM HE'S MORE THAN EARNED.
WE HAVE VIDEO OF HIM ASSAULTING A TEENAGER IN TEXAS AND SETTING FIRE TO A RUNAWAY SHELTER RIGHT HERE IN NEW YORK.
I'D SAY THAT QUALIFIES HIM AS A PUBLIC MENACE.
MAYBE SO, BUT OUR OTHER GUEST FOR THIS SEGMENT SEES IT DIFFERENTLY.
PLEASE WELCOME ONE OF THE METAHUMAN COMMUNITY'S MOST OUTSPOKEN MEMBERS AND LEADER OF THE JUSTICE LEAGUE INTERNATIONAL, MICHAEL CARTER...

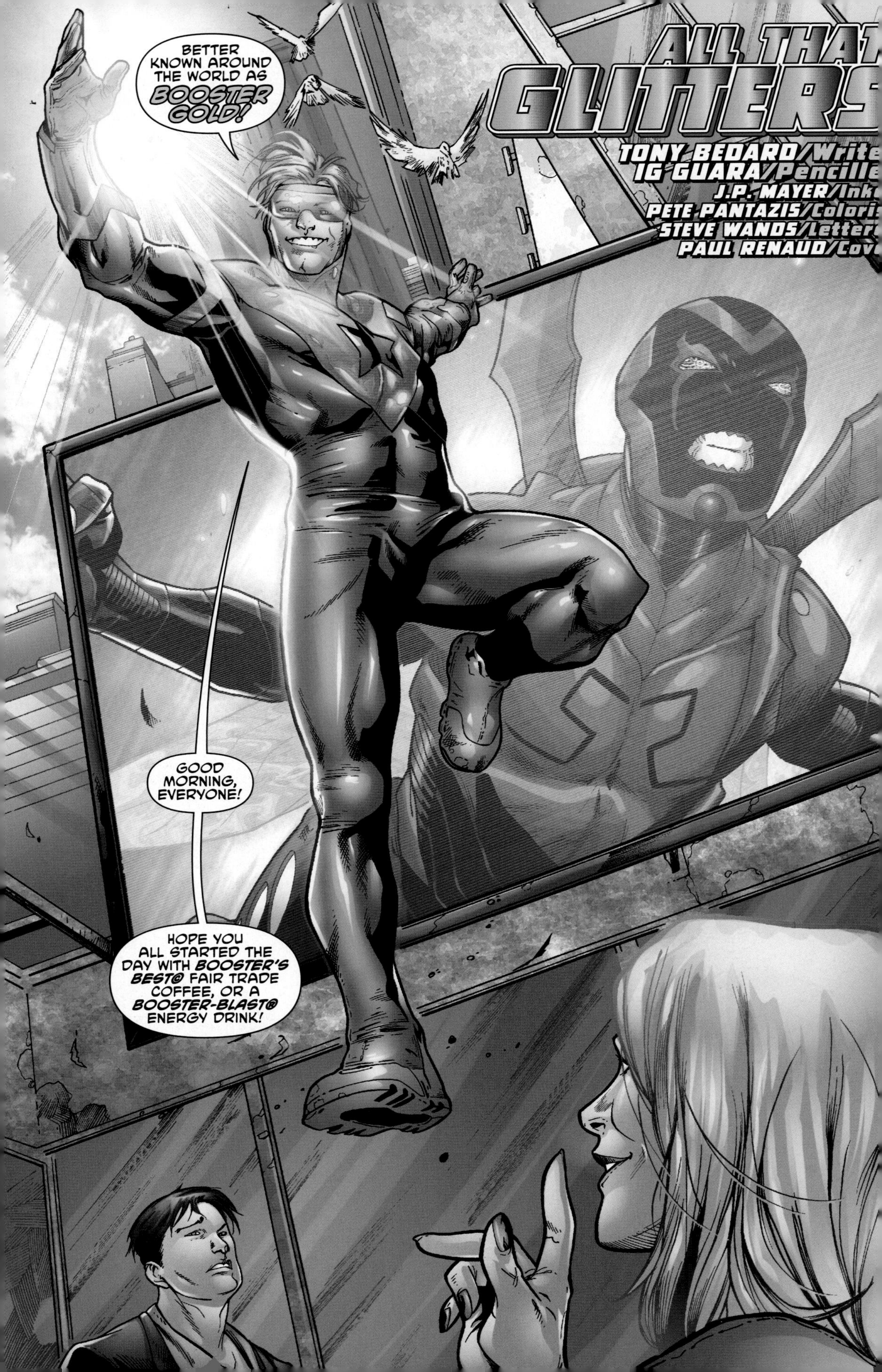
BETTER KNOWN AROUND THE WORLD AS BOOSTER GOLD!
ALL THAT GLITTERS
TONY BEDARD/Write
IG GUARA/Penciller
J.P. MAYER/Ink
PETE PANTAZIS/Colori
STEVE WANDS/Letter
PAUL RENAUD/Cove
GOOD MORNING, EVERYONE!
HOPE YOU ALL STARTED THE DAY WITH BOOSTER'S BEST® FAIR TRADE COFFEE, OR A BOOSTER-BLAST® ENERGY DRINK!

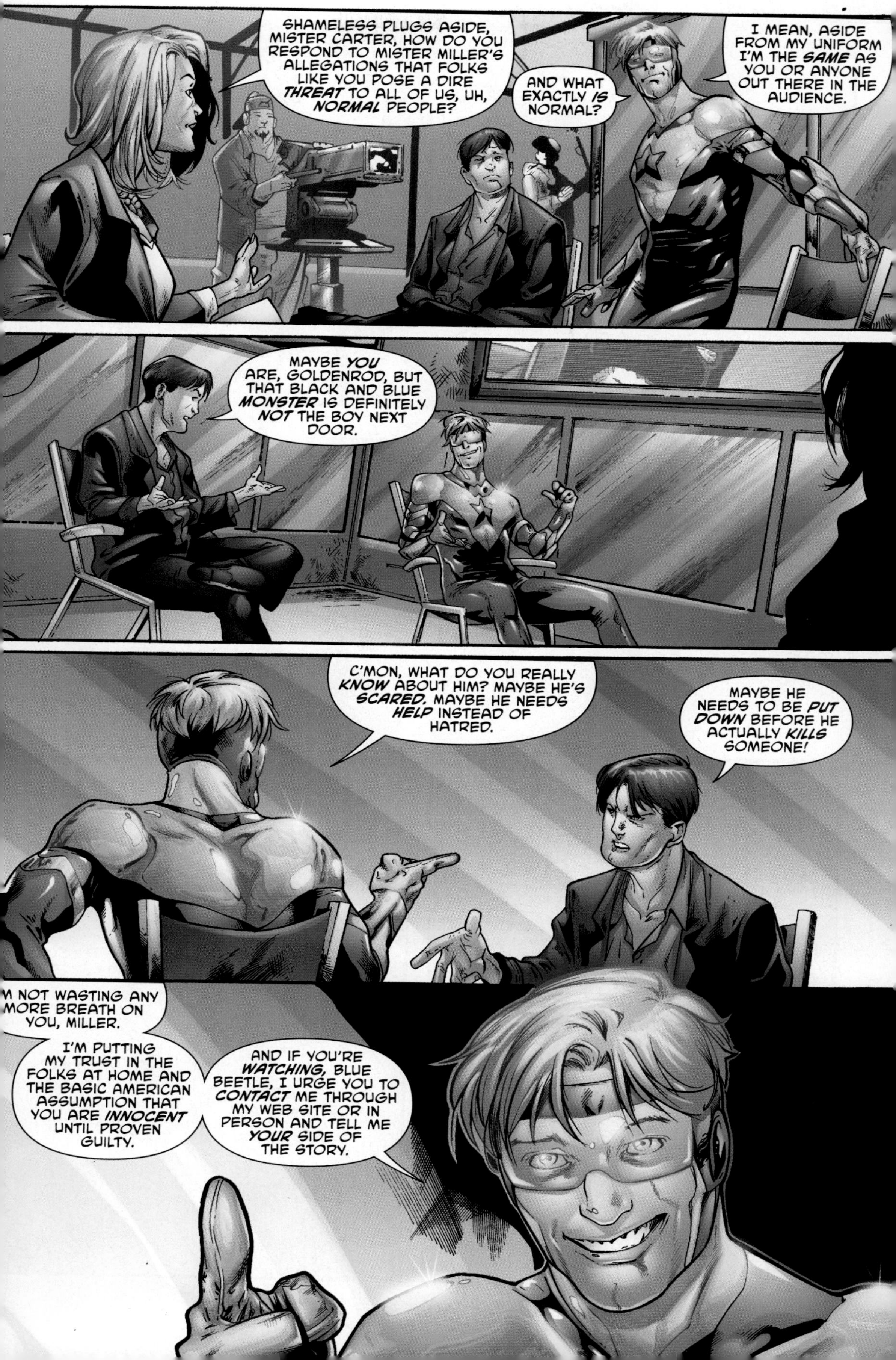
SHAMELESS PLUGS ASIDE, MISTER CARTER, HOW DO YOU RESPOND TO MISTER MILLER'S ALLEGATIONS THAT FOLKS LIKE YOU POSE A DIRE THREAT TO ALL OF US, UH, NORMAL PEOPLE?
AND WHAT EXACTLY IS NORMAL?
I MEAN, ASIDE FROM MY UNIFORM I'M THE SAME AS YOU OR ANYONE OUT THERE IN THE AUDIENCE.
MAYBE YOU ARE, GOLDENROD, BUT THAT BLACK AND BLUE MONSTER IS DEFINITELY NOT THE BOY NEXT DOOR.
C'MON, WHAT DO YOU REALLY KNOW ABOUT HIM? MAYBE HE'S SCARED. MAYBE HE NEEDS HELP INSTEAD OF HATRED.
MAYBE HE NEEDS TO BE PUT DOWN BEFORE HE ACTUALLY KILLS SOMEONE!
'M NOT WASTING ANY MORE BREATH ON YOU, MILLER.
I'M PUTTING MY TRUST IN THE FOLKS AT HOME AND THE BASIC AMERICAN ASSUMPTION THAT YOU ARE INNOCENT UNTIL PROVEN GUILTY.
AND IF YOU'RE WATCHING, BLUE BEETLE, I URGE YOU TO CONTACT ME THROUGH MY WEB SITE OR IN PERSON AND TELL ME YOUR SIDE OF THE STORY.

I CAN **HELP** YOU. I CAN MAKE SURE EVERYONE **AROUND** YOU IS SAFE, TOO.

BUT YOU NEED TO REACH OUT TO ME NOW.

UNBELIEVABLE. HOW COULD ANYONE **DEFEND** THAT BEETLE GUY?

SERIOUSLY, **PACO**--I'M LUCKY HE DIDN'T **KILL** ME!

I, UH... GOTTA TAKE YOUR WORD FOR IT, **BRENDA.** I MEAN, I WAS **THERE,** BUT--

YOU DON'T **REMEMBER** ANY OF IT. I KNOW. PROBABLY **BETTER** THAT WAY...

...LET'S JUST FIND **JAIME** AND BRING HIM HOME.

UM, THANKS AGAIN FOR PAYING MY WAY.

THANK MY **TIA,** IF WE EVER SEE HER AGAIN. AT LEAST WE'RE PUTTING THE **MONEY** SHE LEFT ME TO GOOD USE.

NOW IF ONLY THAT MONEY COULD PINPOINT ONE RUNAWAY KID IN A CITY OF TEN MILLION...

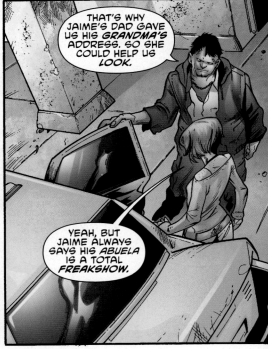

THAT'S WHY JAIME'S DAD GAVE US HIS **GRANDMA'S** ADDRESS. SO SHE COULD HELP US **LOOK.**

YEAH, BUT JAIME ALWAYS SAYS HIS **ABUELA** IS A TOTAL **FREAKSHOW.**

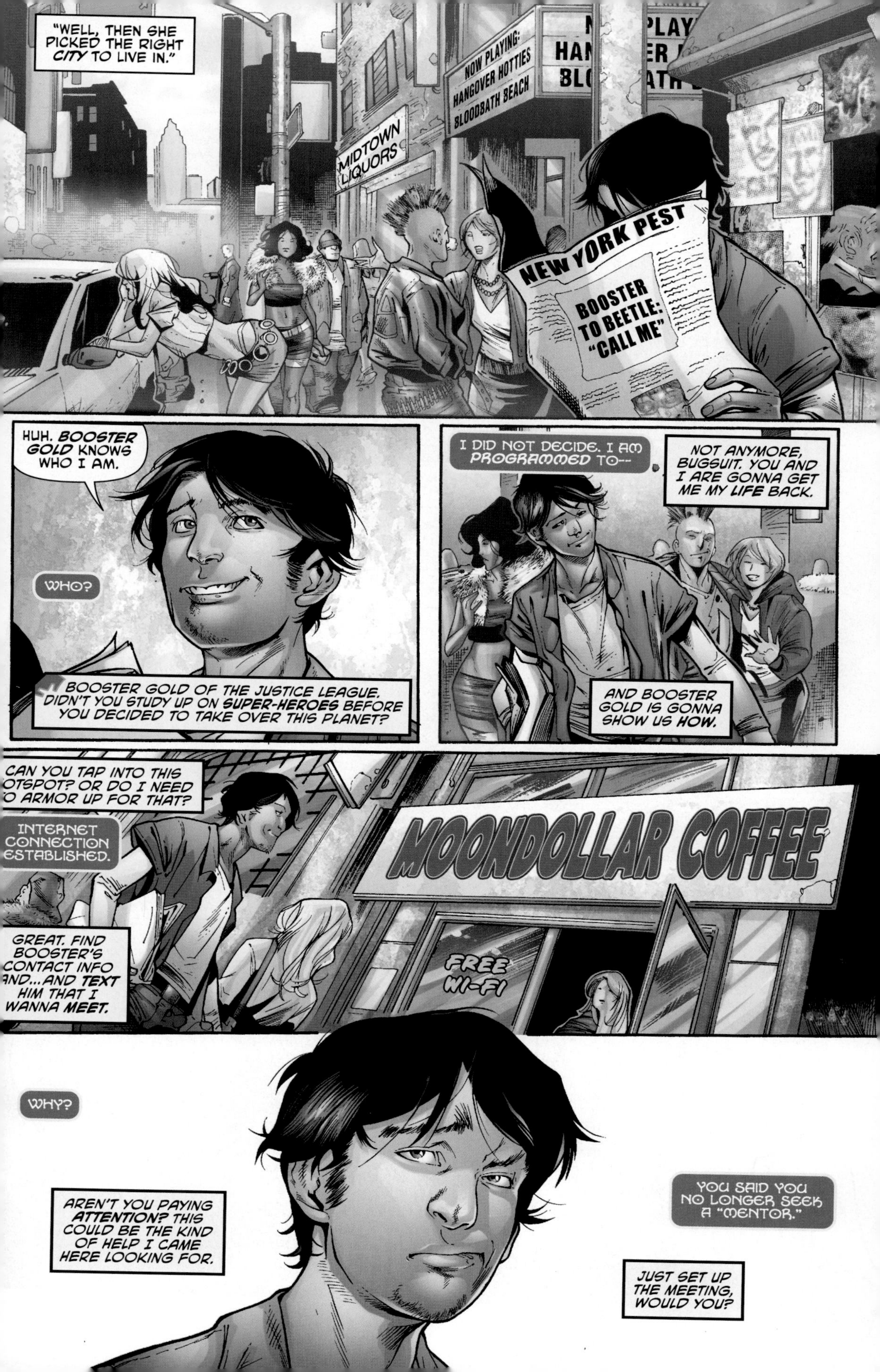
"WELL, THEN SHE PICKED THE RIGHT CITY TO LIVE IN."
NOW PLAYING: HANGOVER HOTTIES BLOODBATH BEACH
MIDTOWN LIQUORS
NEW YORK PEST
BOOSTER TO BEETLE: "CALL ME"
HUH. BOOSTER GOLD KNOWS WHO I AM.
WHO?
BOOSTER GOLD OF THE JUSTICE LEAGUE. DIDN'T YOU STUDY UP ON SUPER-HEROES BEFORE YOU DECIDED TO TAKE OVER THIS PLANET?
I DID NOT DECIDE. I AM PROGRAMMED TO--
NOT ANYMORE, BUGSUIT. YOU AND I ARE GONNA GET ME MY LIFE BACK.
AND BOOSTER GOLD IS GONNA SHOW US HOW.
CAN YOU TAP INTO THIS OTSPOT? OR DO I NEED O ARMOR UP FOR THAT?
INTERNET CONNECTION ESTABLISHED.
MOONDOLLAR COFFEE
GREAT. FIND BOOSTER'S CONTACT INFO AND...AND TEXT HIM THAT I WANNA MEET.
FREE WI-FI
WHY?
AREN'T YOU PAYING ATTENTION? THIS COULD BE THE KIND OF HELP I CAME HERE LOOKING FOR.
YOU SAID YOU NO LONGER SEEK A "MENTOR."
JUST SET UP THE MEETING, WOULD YOU?

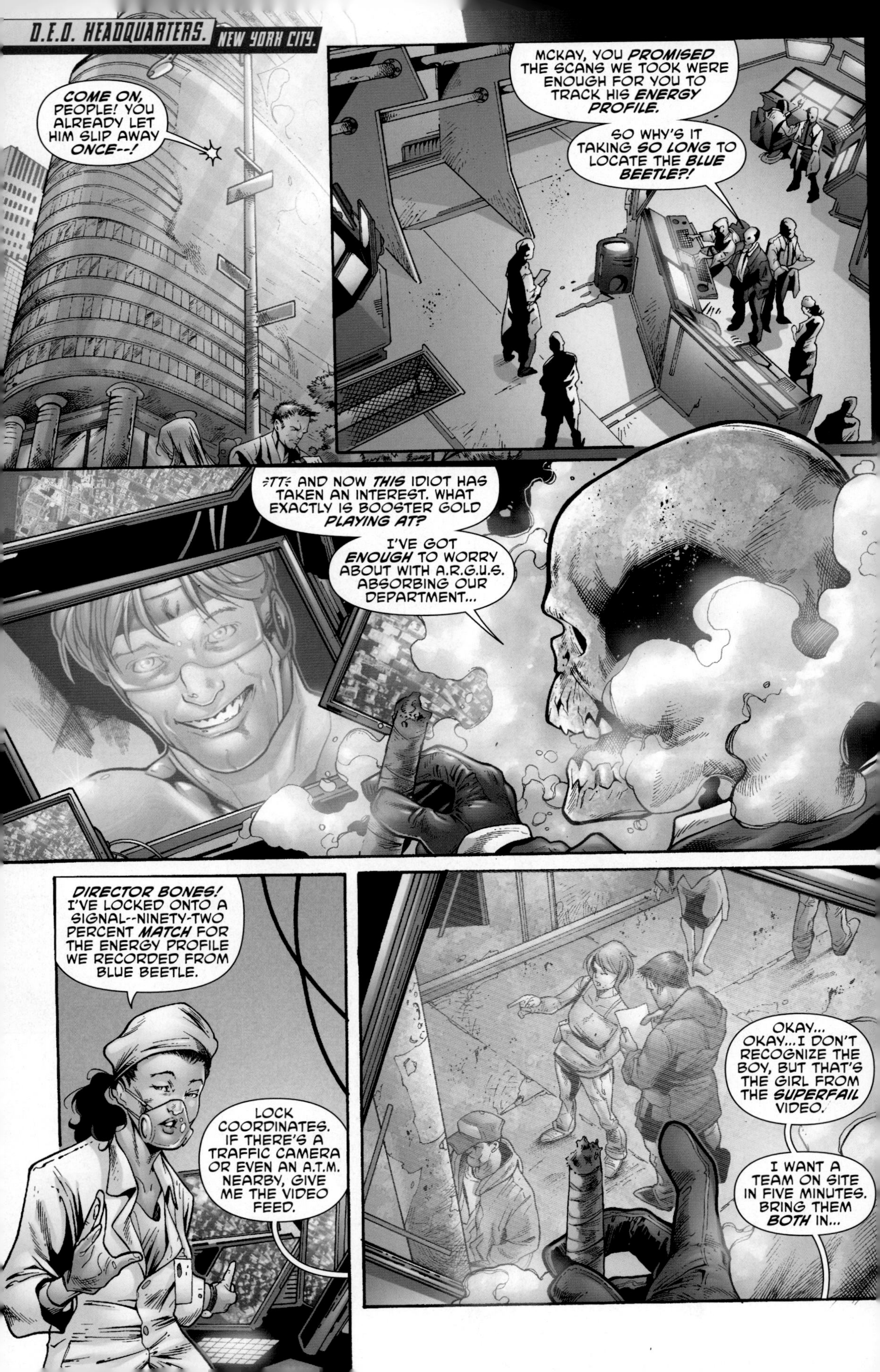
D.E.O. HEADQUARTERS. NEW YORK CITY.
COME ON, PEOPLE! YOU ALREADY LET HIM SLIP AWAY ONCE--!
MCKAY, YOU PROMISED THE SCANS WE TOOK WERE ENOUGH FOR YOU TO TRACK HIS ENERGY PROFILE.
SO WHY'S IT TAKING SO LONG TO LOCATE THE BLUE BEETLE?!
TT AND NOW THIS IDIOT HAS TAKEN AN INTEREST. WHAT EXACTLY IS BOOSTER GOLD PLAYING AT?
I'VE GOT ENOUGH TO WORRY ABOUT WITH A.R.G.U.S. ABSORBING OUR DEPARTMENT...
DIRECTOR BONES! I'VE LOCKED ONTO A SIGNAL--NINETY-TWO PERCENT MATCH FOR THE ENERGY PROFILE WE RECORDED FROM BLUE BEETLE.
LOCK COORDINATES. IF THERE'S A TRAFFIC CAMERA OR EVEN AN A.T.M. NEARBY, GIVE ME THE VIDEO FEED.
OKAY... OKAY...I DON'T RECOGNIZE THE BOY, BUT THAT'S THE GIRL FROM THE SUPERFAIL VIDEO.
I WANT A TEAM ON SITE IN FIVE MINUTES. BRING THEM BOTH IN...

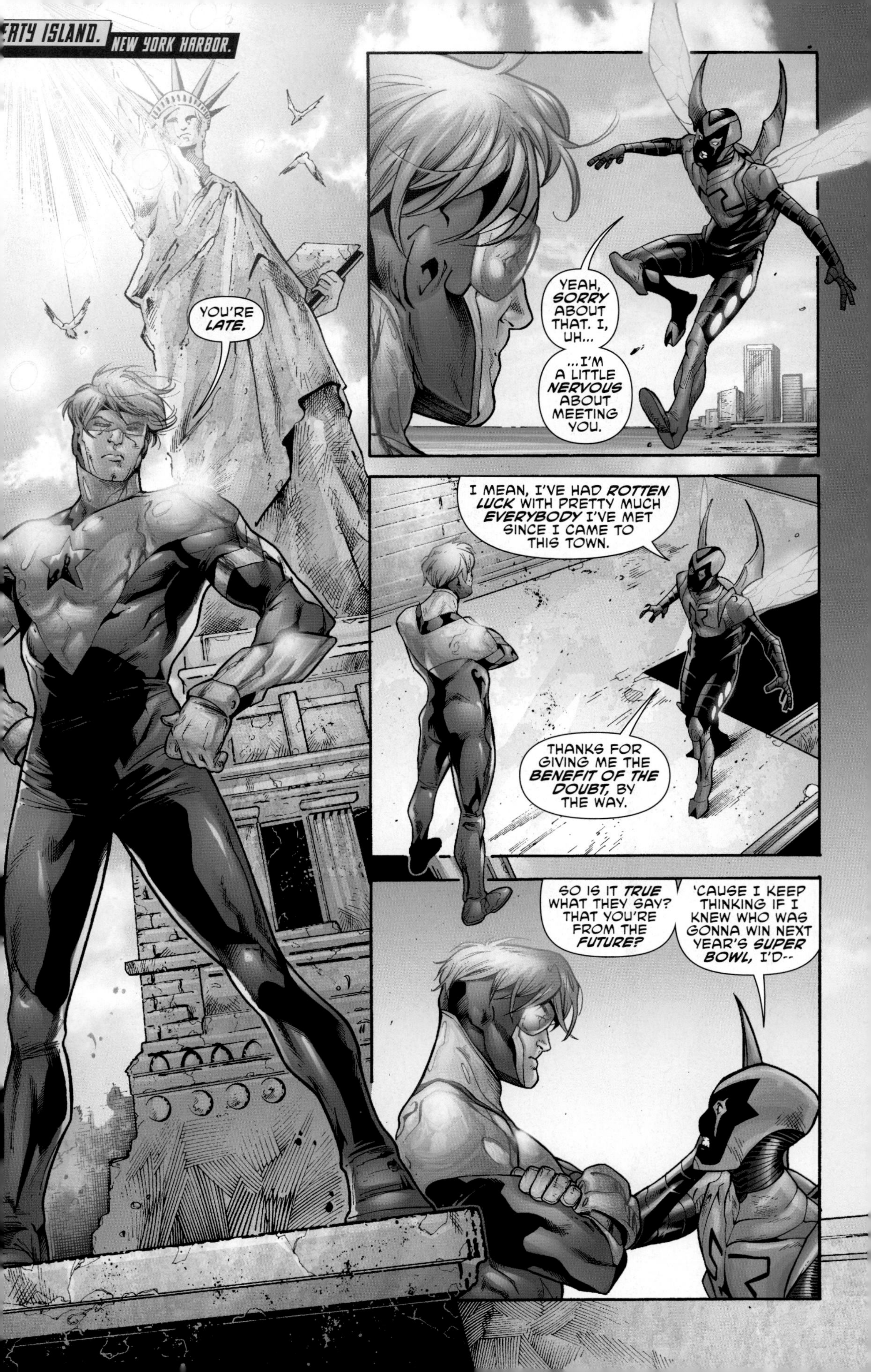
ERTY ISLAND.
NEW YORK HARBOR.
YOU'RE LATE.
YEAH, SORRY ABOUT THAT. I, UH...
...I'M A LITTLE NERVOUS ABOUT MEETING YOU.
I MEAN, I'VE HAD ROTTEN LUCK WITH PRETTY MUCH EVERYBODY I'VE MET SINCE I CAME TO THIS TOWN.
THANKS FOR GIVING ME THE BENEFIT OF THE DOUBT, BY THE WAY.
SO IS IT TRUE WHAT THEY SAY? THAT YOU'RE FROM THE FUTURE?
'CAUSE I KEEP THINKING IF I KNEW WHO WAS GONNA WIN NEXT YEAR'S SUPER BOWL, I'D--

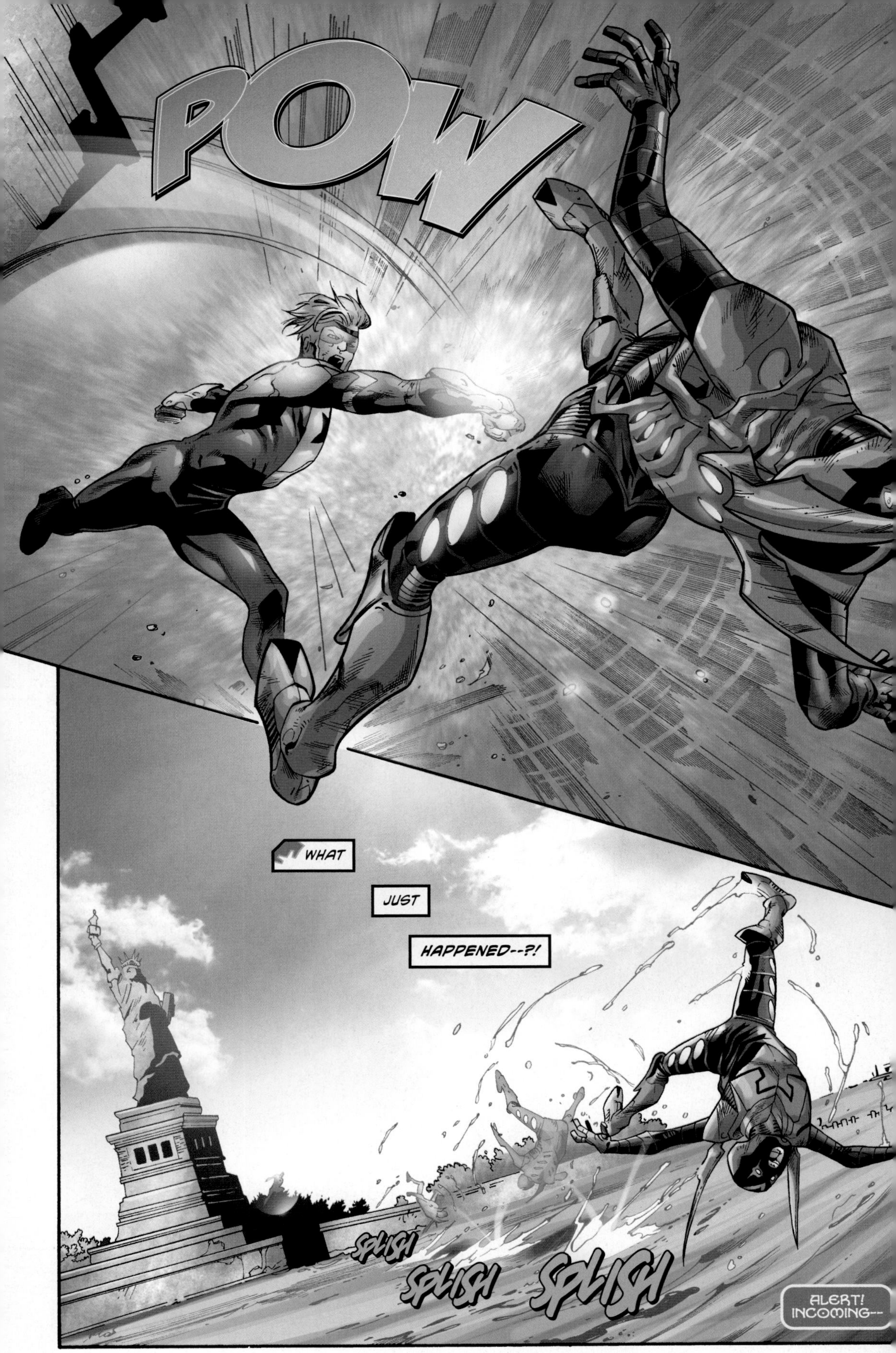
POW
WHAT
JUST
HAPPENED--?!
SPLISH
SPLISH
SPLISH
ALERT! INCOMING--

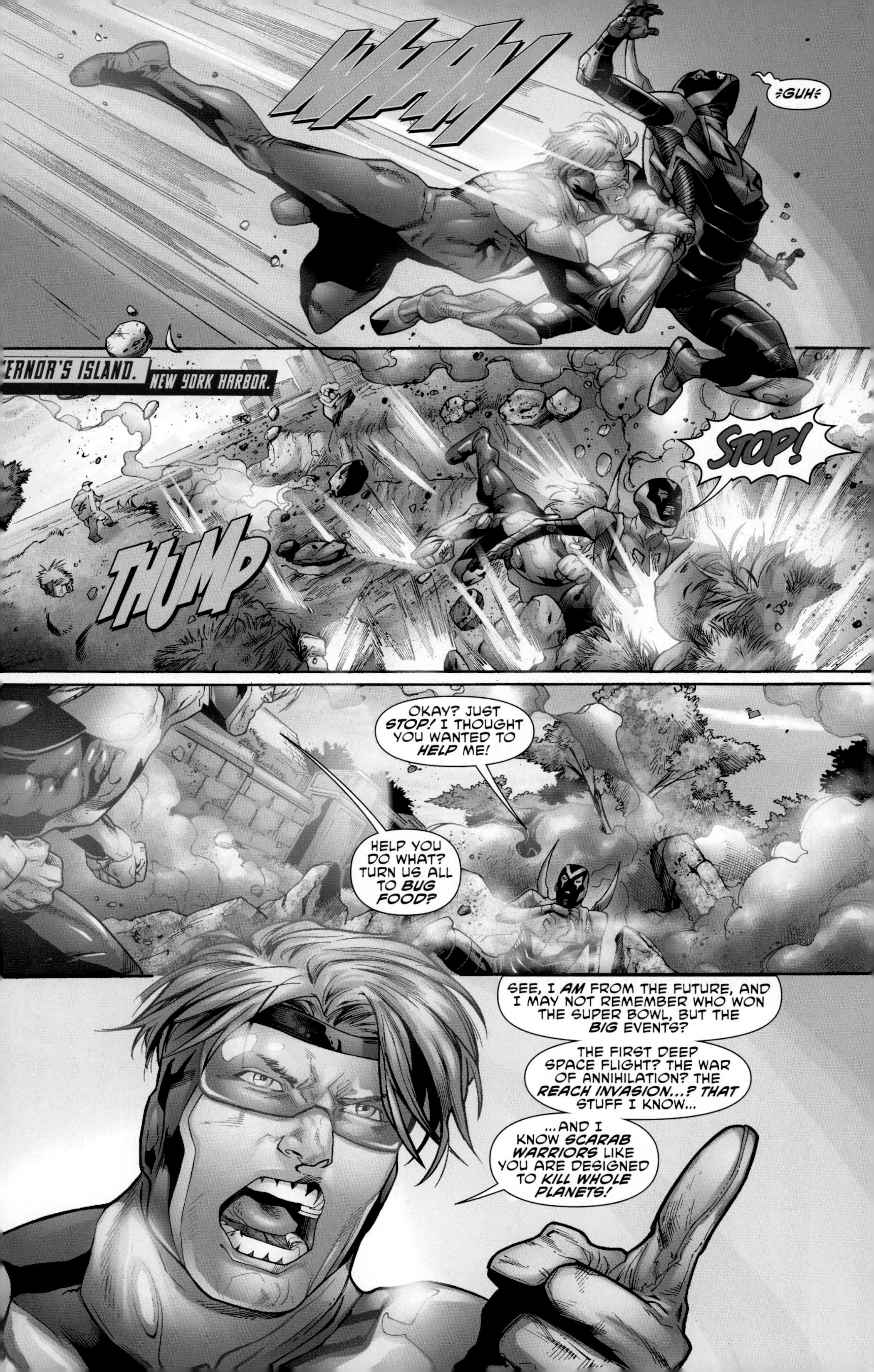

WHAM
GUH
ERNOR'S ISLAND.
NEW YORK HARBOR.
STOP!
THUMP
OKAY? JUST STOP! I THOUGHT YOU WANTED TO HELP ME!
HELP YOU DO WHAT? TURN US ALL TO BUG FOOD?
SEE, I AM FROM THE FUTURE, AND I MAY NOT REMEMBER WHO WON THE SUPER BOWL, BUT THE BIG EVENTS?
THE FIRST DEEP SPACE FLIGHT? THE WAR OF ANNIHILATION? THE REACH INVASION...? THAT STUFF I KNOW...
...AND I KNOW SCARAB WARRIORS LIKE YOU ARE DESIGNED TO KILL WHOLE PLANETS!

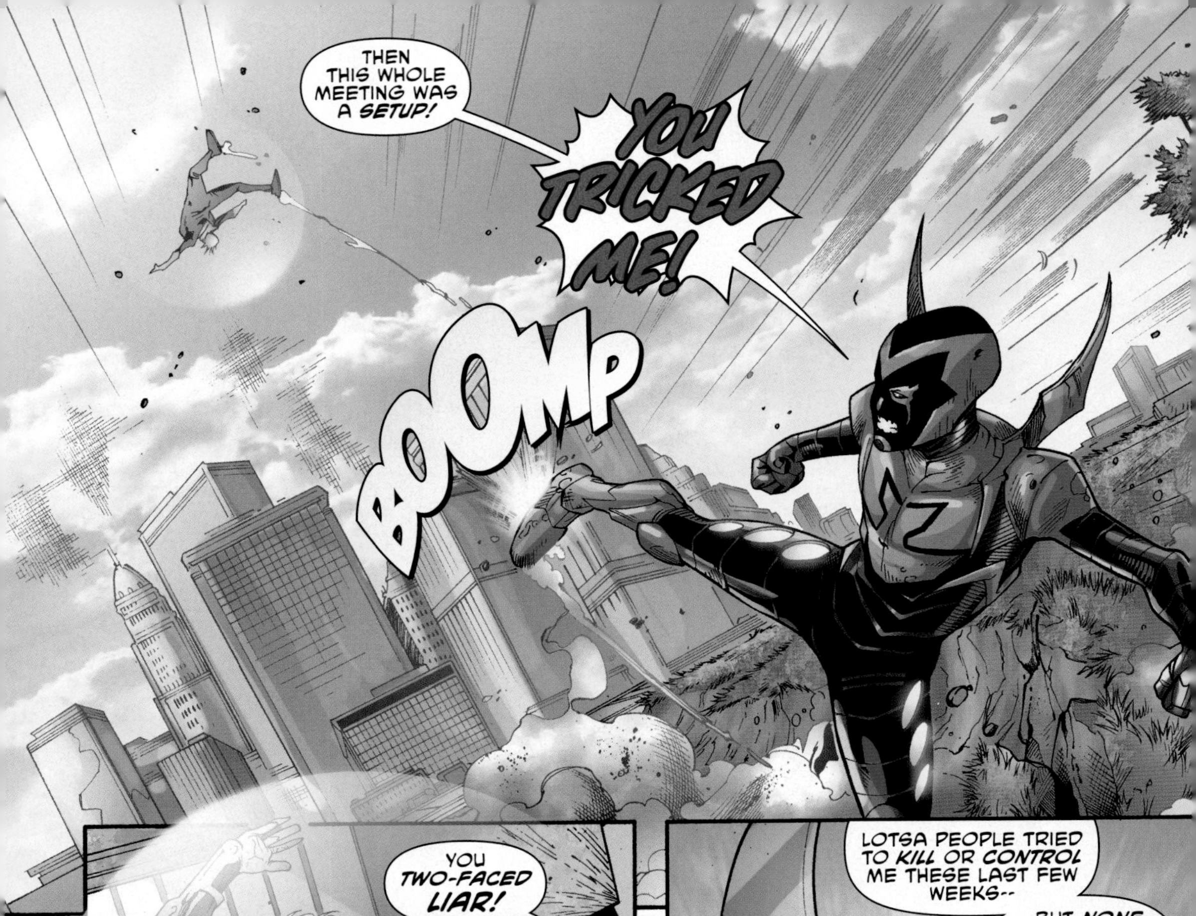
THEN THIS WHOLE MEETING WAS A *SETUP!*
YOU TRICKED ME!
BOOMP

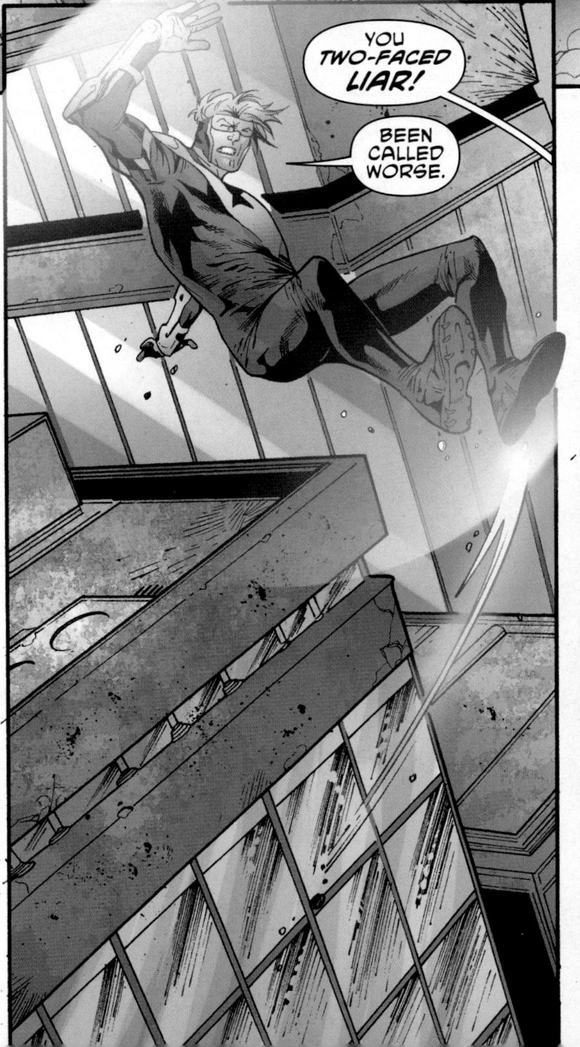
YOU *TWO-FACED* **LIAR!**
BEEN CALLED WORSE.

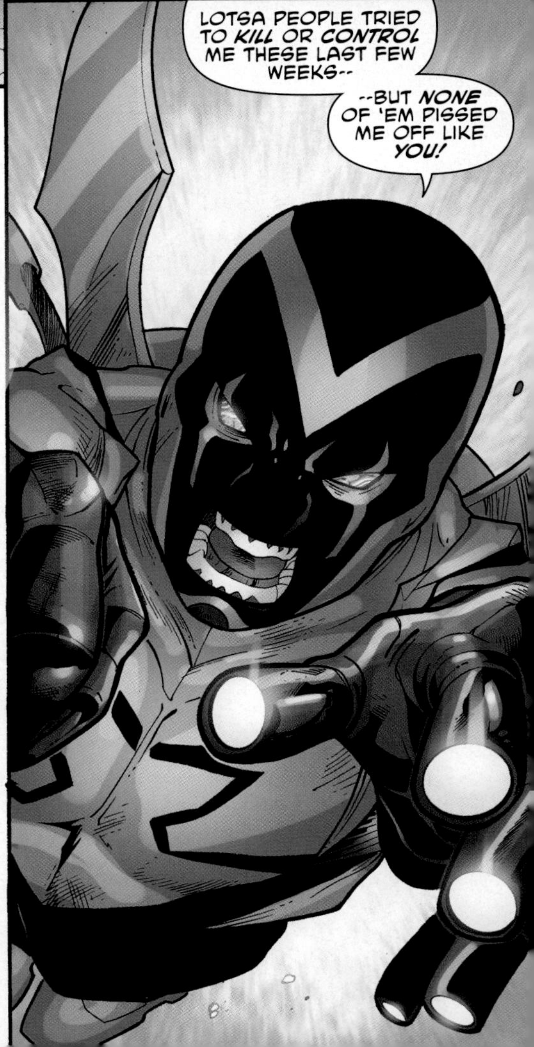
LOTSA PEOPLE TRIED TO *KILL* OR *CONTROL* ME THESE LAST FEW WEEKS--
--BUT *NONE* OF 'EM PISSED ME OFF LIKE *YOU!*

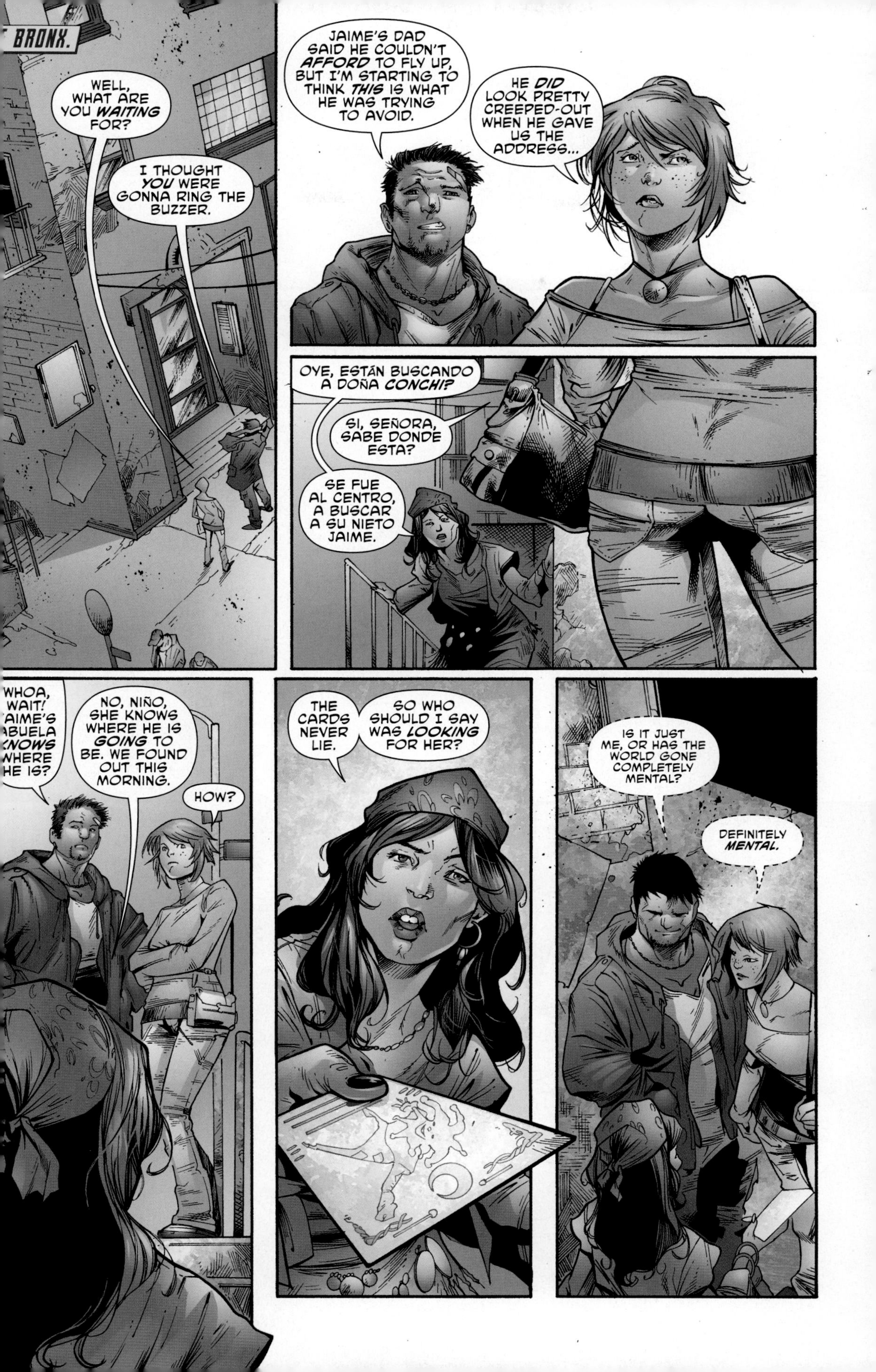
BRONX.
WELL, WHAT ARE YOU WAITING FOR?
I THOUGHT YOU WERE GONNA RING THE BUZZER.
JAIME'S DAD SAID HE COULDN'T AFFORD TO FLY UP, BUT I'M STARTING TO THINK THIS IS WHAT HE WAS TRYING TO AVOID.
HE DID LOOK PRETTY CREEPED-OUT WHEN HE GAVE US THE ADDRESS...
OYE, ESTÁN BUSCANDO A DOÑA CONCHI?
SI, SEÑORA, SABE DONDE ESTA?
SE FUE AL CENTRO, A BUSCAR A SU NIETO JAIME.
WHOA, WAIT! JAIME'S ABUELA KNOWS WHERE HE IS?
NO, NIÑO, SHE KNOWS WHERE HE IS GOING TO BE. WE FOUND OUT THIS MORNING.
HOW?
THE CARDS NEVER LIE.
SO WHO SHOULD I SAY WAS LOOKING FOR HER?
IS IT JUST ME, OR HAS THE WORLD GONE COMPLETELY MENTAL?
DEFINITELY MENTAL.

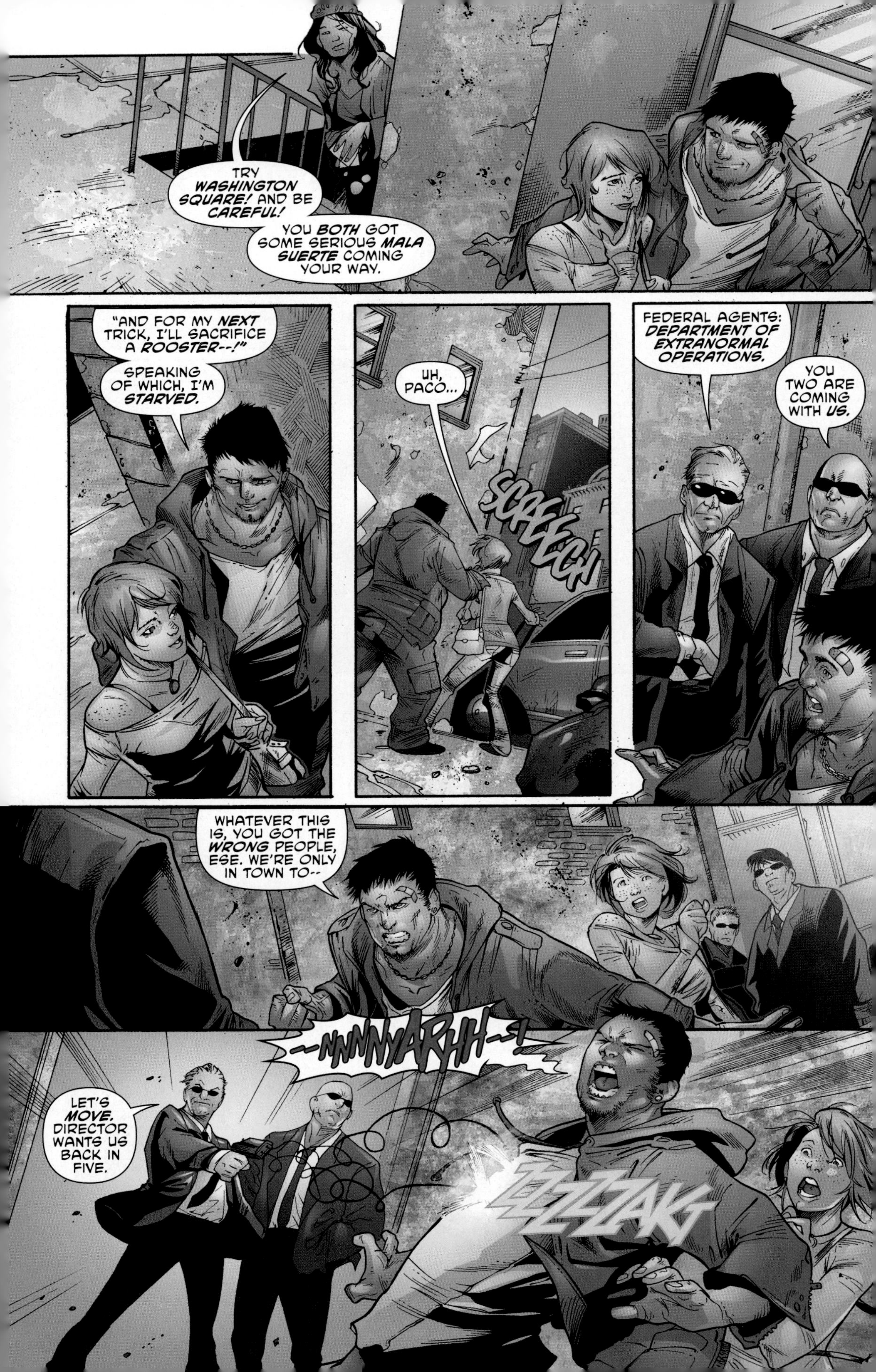
TRY *WASHINGTON SQUARE!* AND BE *CAREFUL!*
YOU *BOTH* GOT SOME SERIOUS *MALA SUERTE* COMING YOUR WAY.
"AND FOR MY *NEXT* TRICK, I'LL SACRIFICE A *ROOSTER--!"*
SPEAKING OF WHICH, I'M *STARVED.*
UH, PACO...
SCREEECH
FEDERAL AGENTS: *DEPARTMENT OF EXTRANORMAL OPERATIONS.*
YOU TWO ARE COMING WITH *US.*
WHATEVER THIS IS, YOU GOT THE *WRONG* PEOPLE, ESE. WE'RE ONLY IN TOWN TO--
--NNNNYARHH--!
LET'S *MOVE.* DIRECTOR WANTS US BACK IN FIVE.
ZZZZAK

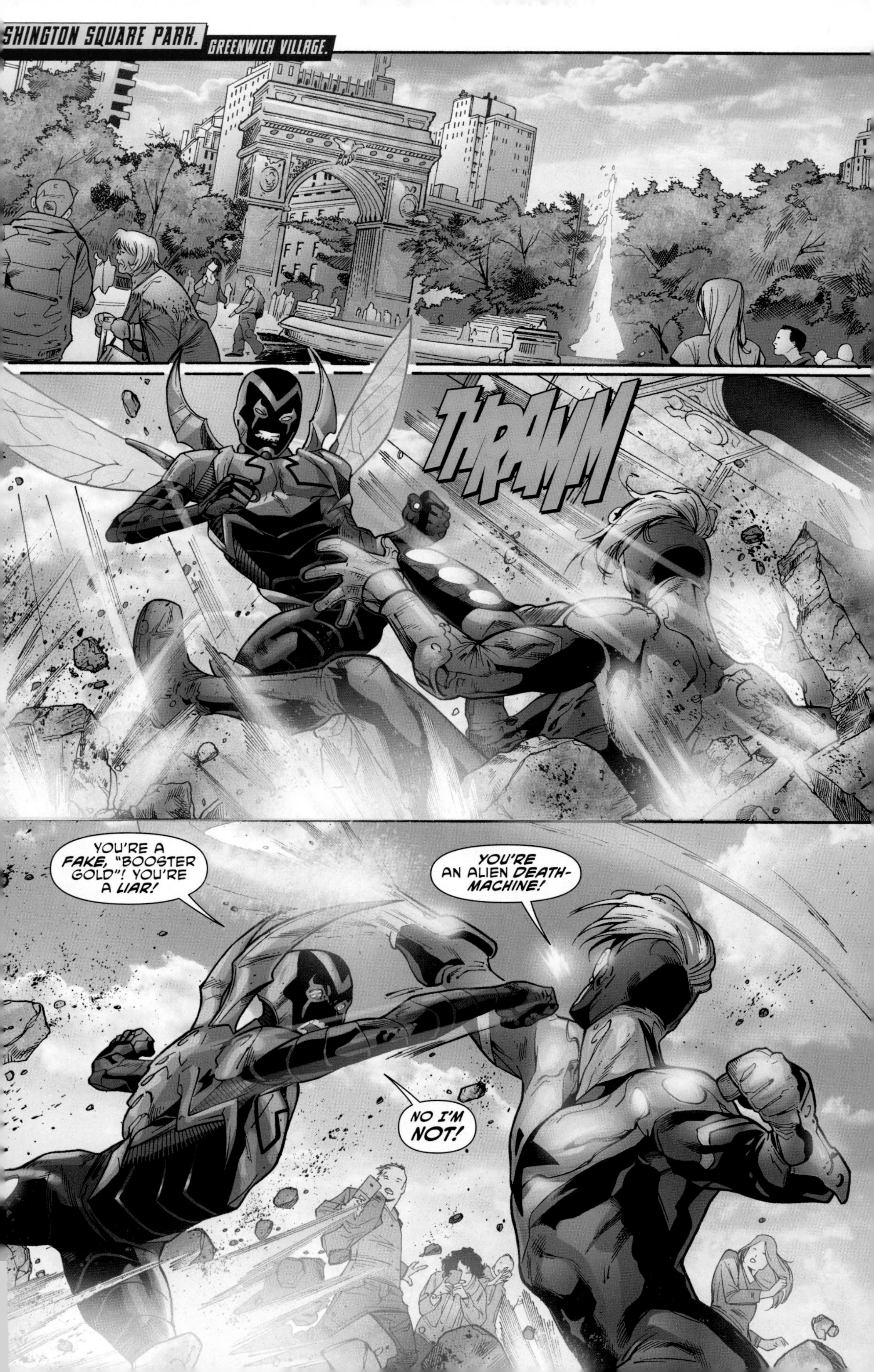
SHINGTON SQUARE PARK.
GREENWICH VILLAGE.
THRAMM
YOU'RE A *FAKE,* "BOOSTER GOLD"! YOU'RE A *LIAR!*
YOU'RE AN ALIEN *DEATH-MACHINE!*
NO I'M *NOT!*

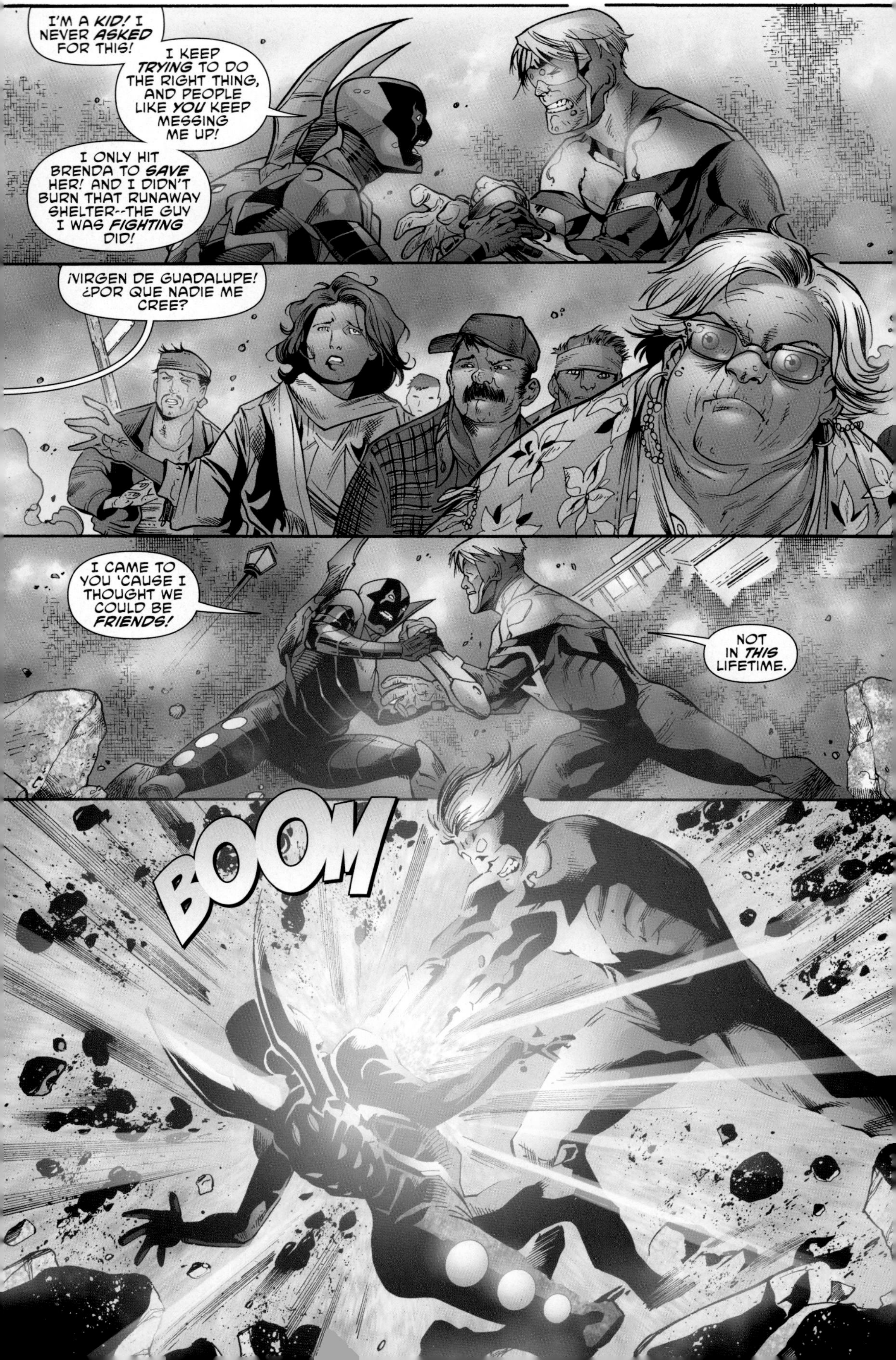

I'M A KID! I NEVER ASKED FOR THIS!
I KEEP TRYING TO DO THE RIGHT THING, AND PEOPLE LIKE YOU KEEP MESSING ME UP!
I ONLY HIT BRENDA TO SAVE HER! AND I DIDN'T BURN THAT RUNAWAY SHELTER--THE GUY I WAS FIGHTING DID!
¡VIRGEN DE GUADALUPE! ¿POR QUE NADIE ME CREE?
I CAME TO YOU 'CAUSE I THOUGHT WE COULD BE FRIENDS!
NOT IN THIS LIFETIME.
BOOM

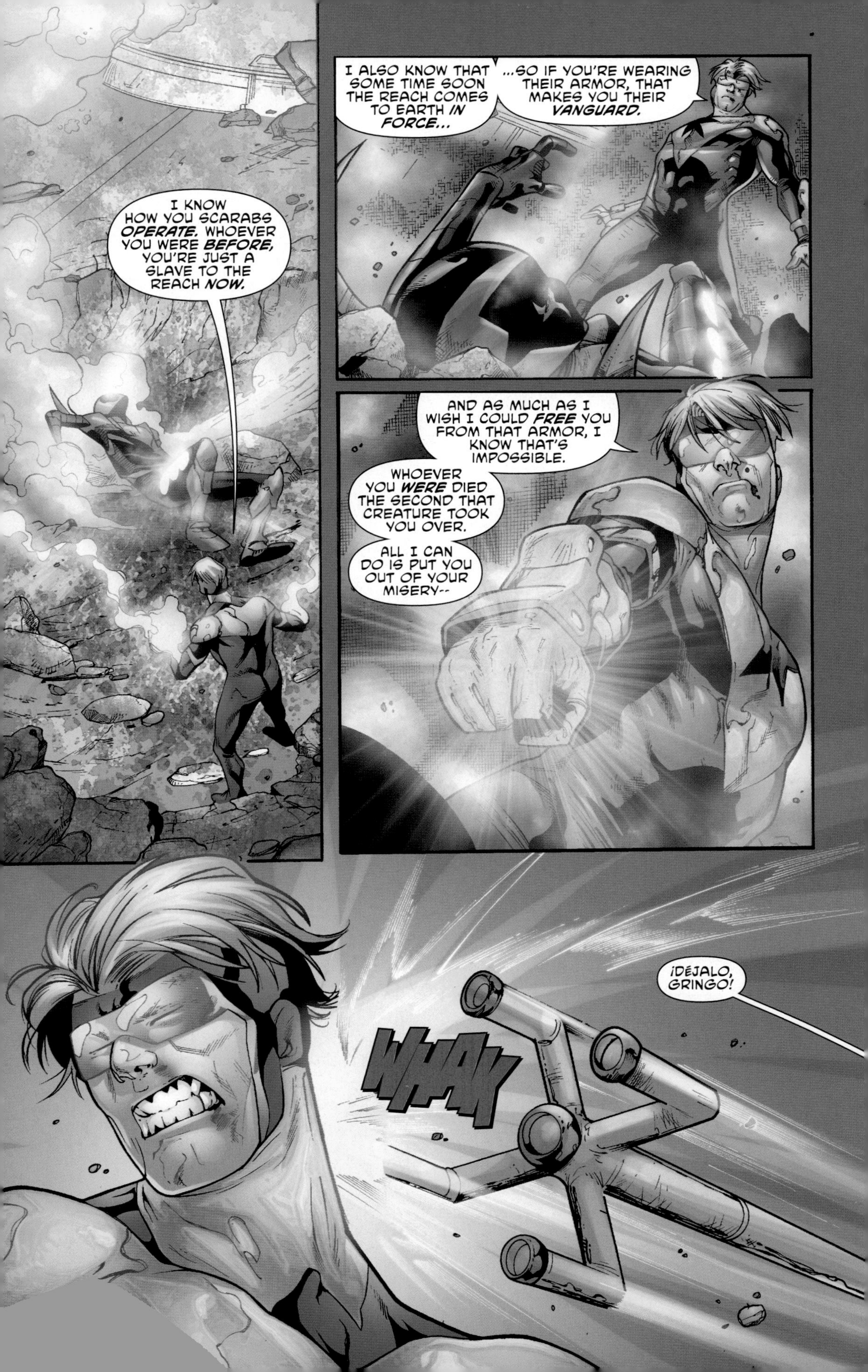
I KNOW HOW YOU SCARABS *OPERATE.* WHOEVER YOU WERE *BEFORE,* YOU'RE JUST A SLAVE TO THE REACH *NOW.*
I ALSO KNOW THAT SOME TIME SOON THE REACH COMES TO EARTH *IN FORCE...*
...SO IF YOU'RE WEARING THEIR ARMOR, THAT MAKES YOU THEIR *VANGUARD.*
AND AS MUCH AS I WISH I COULD *FREE* YOU FROM THAT ARMOR, I KNOW THAT'S IMPOSSIBLE.
WHOEVER YOU *WERE* DIED THE SECOND THAT CREATURE TOOK YOU OVER.
ALL I CAN DO IS PUT YOU OUT OF YOUR MISERY--
WHAK
¡DÉJALO, GRINGO!

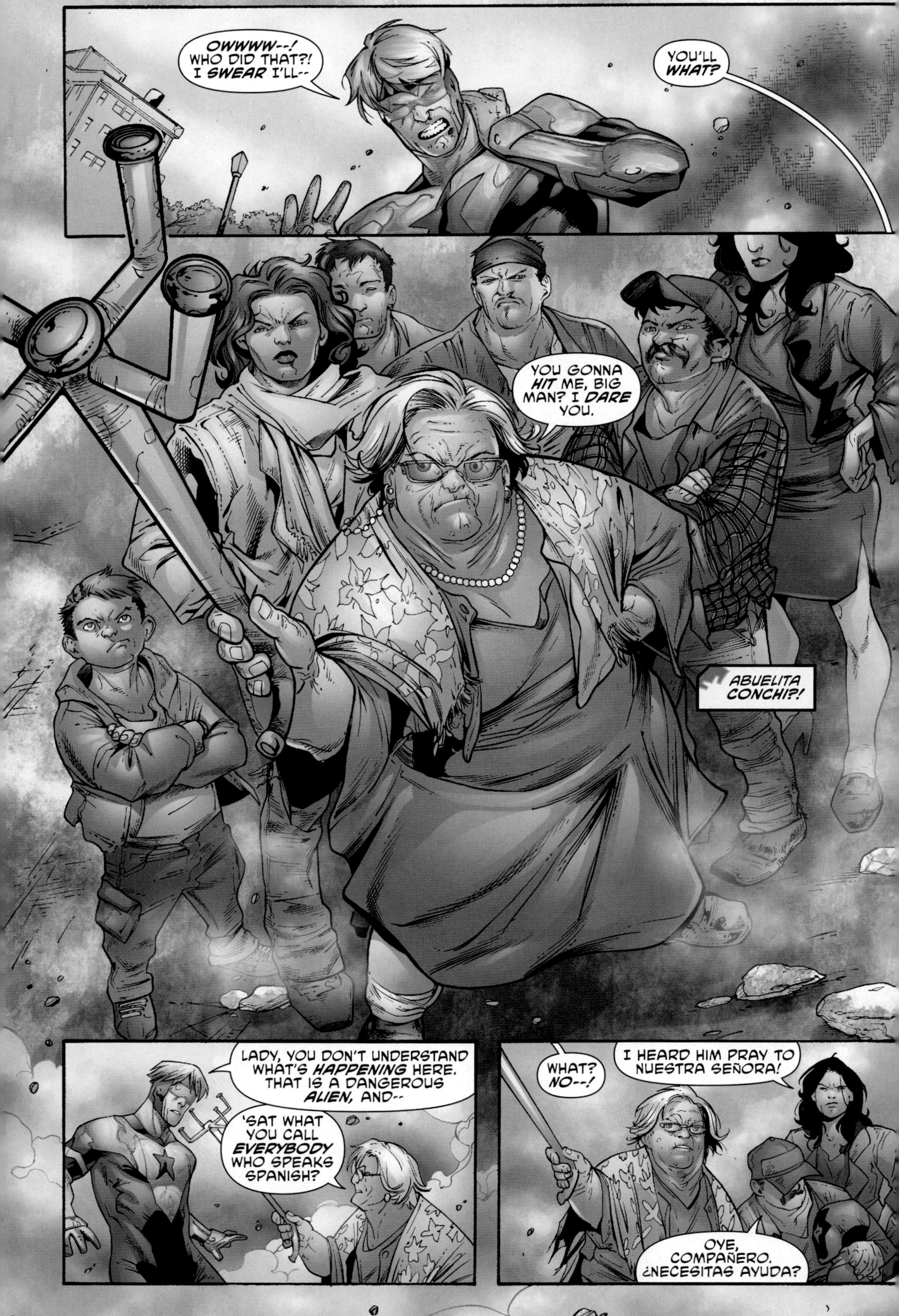
OWWWW--! WHO DID THAT?! I SWEAR I'LL--
YOU'LL WHAT?
YOU GONNA HIT ME, BIG MAN? I DARE YOU.
ABUELITA CONCHI?!
LADY, YOU DON'T UNDERSTAND WHAT'S HAPPENING HERE. THAT IS A DANGEROUS ALIEN, AND--
'SAT WHAT YOU CALL EVERYBODY WHO SPEAKS SPANISH?
WHAT? NO--!
I HEARD HIM PRAY TO NUESTRA SEÑORA!
OYE, COMPAÑERO. ¿NECESITAS AYUDA?

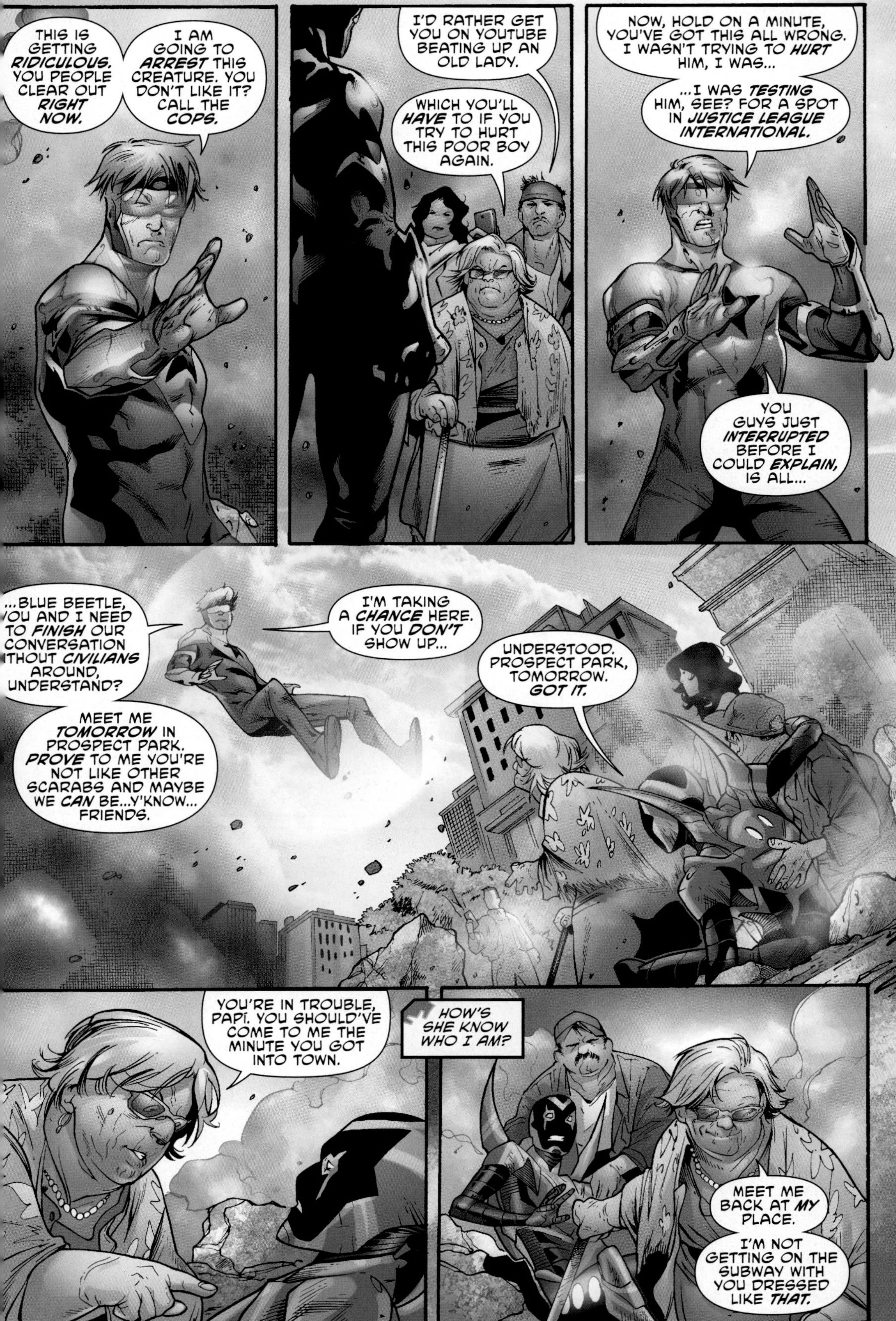
THIS IS GETTING *RIDICULOUS.* YOU PEOPLE CLEAR OUT *RIGHT NOW.*
I AM GOING TO *ARREST* THIS CREATURE. YOU DON'T LIKE IT? CALL THE *COPS.*
I'D RATHER GET YOU ON YOUTUBE BEATING UP AN OLD LADY.
WHICH YOU'LL *HAVE* TO IF YOU TRY TO HURT THIS POOR BOY AGAIN.
NOW, HOLD ON A MINUTE, YOU'VE GOT THIS ALL WRONG. I WASN'T TRYING TO *HURT* HIM, I WAS...
...I WAS *TESTING* HIM, SEE? FOR A SPOT IN *JUSTICE LEAGUE INTERNATIONAL.*
YOU GUYS JUST *INTERRUPTED* BEFORE I COULD *EXPLAIN,* IS ALL...
...BLUE BEETLE, OU AND I NEED TO *FINISH* OUR CONVERSATION ITHOUT *CIVILIANS* AROUND, UNDERSTAND?
MEET ME *TOMORROW* IN PROSPECT PARK. *PROVE* TO ME YOU'RE NOT LIKE OTHER SCARABS AND MAYBE WE *CAN* BE...Y'KNOW... FRIENDS.
I'M TAKING A *CHANCE* HERE. IF YOU *DON'T* SHOW UP...
UNDERSTOOD. PROSPECT PARK, TOMORROW. *GOT IT.*
YOU'RE IN TROUBLE, PAPÍ. YOU SHOULD'VE COME TO ME THE MINUTE YOU GOT INTO TOWN.
HOW'S SHE KNOW WHO I AM?
MEET ME BACK AT *MY* PLACE.
I'M NOT GETTING ON THE SUBWAY WITH YOU DRESSED LIKE *THAT.*

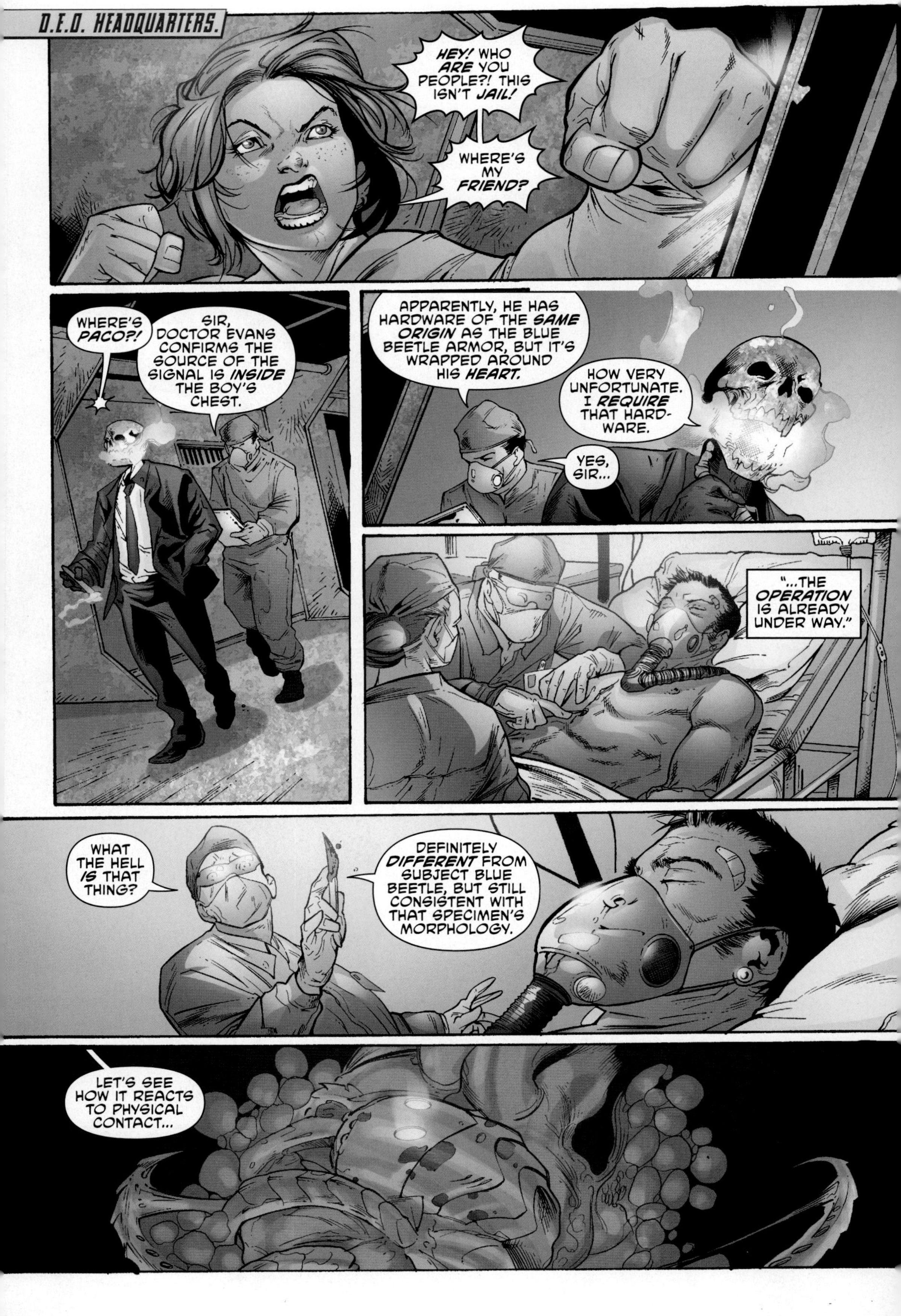
D.E.O. HEADQUARTERS.
HEY! WHO ARE YOU PEOPLE?! THIS ISN'T JAIL!
WHERE'S MY FRIEND?
WHERE'S PACO?!
SIR, DOCTOR EVANS CONFIRMS THE SOURCE OF THE SIGNAL IS INSIDE THE BOY'S CHEST.
APPARENTLY, HE HAS HARDWARE OF THE SAME ORIGIN AS THE BLUE BEETLE ARMOR, BUT IT'S WRAPPED AROUND HIS HEART.
HOW VERY UNFORTUNATE. I REQUIRE THAT HARDWARE.
YES, SIR...
"...THE OPERATION IS ALREADY UNDER WAY."
WHAT THE HELL IS THAT THING?
DEFINITELY DIFFERENT FROM SUBJECT BLUE BEETLE, BUT STILL CONSISTENT WITH THAT SPECIMEN'S MORPHOLOGY.
LET'S SEE HOW IT REACTS TO PHYSICAL CONTACT...

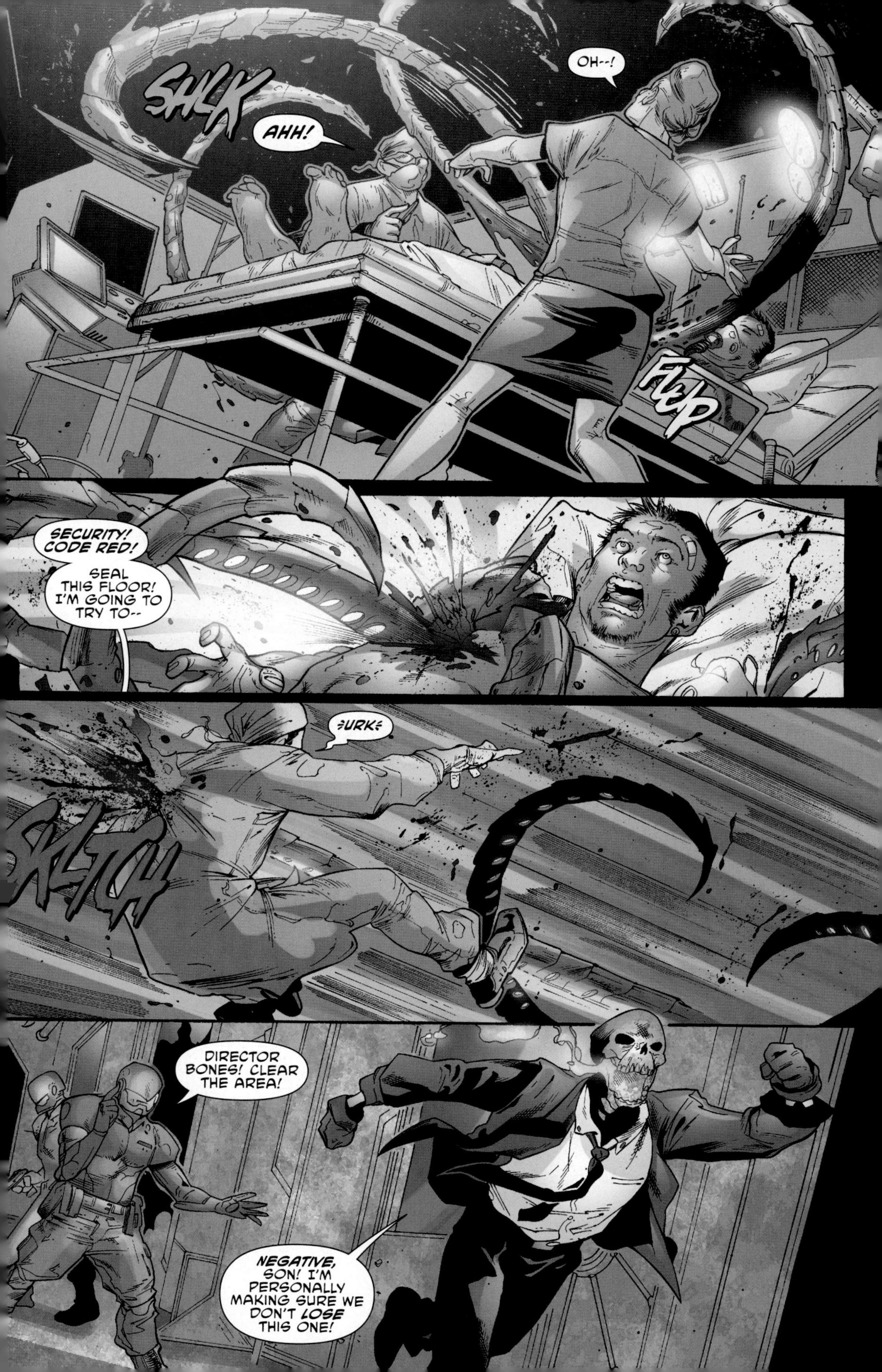
SHLK
AHH!
OH--!
FLUP
SECURITY! CODE RED!
SEAL THIS FLOOR! I'M GOING TO TRY TO--
URK
SKLTCH
DIRECTOR BONES! CLEAR THE AREA!
NEGATIVE, SON! I'M PERSONALLY MAKING SURE WE DON'T LOSE THIS ONE!

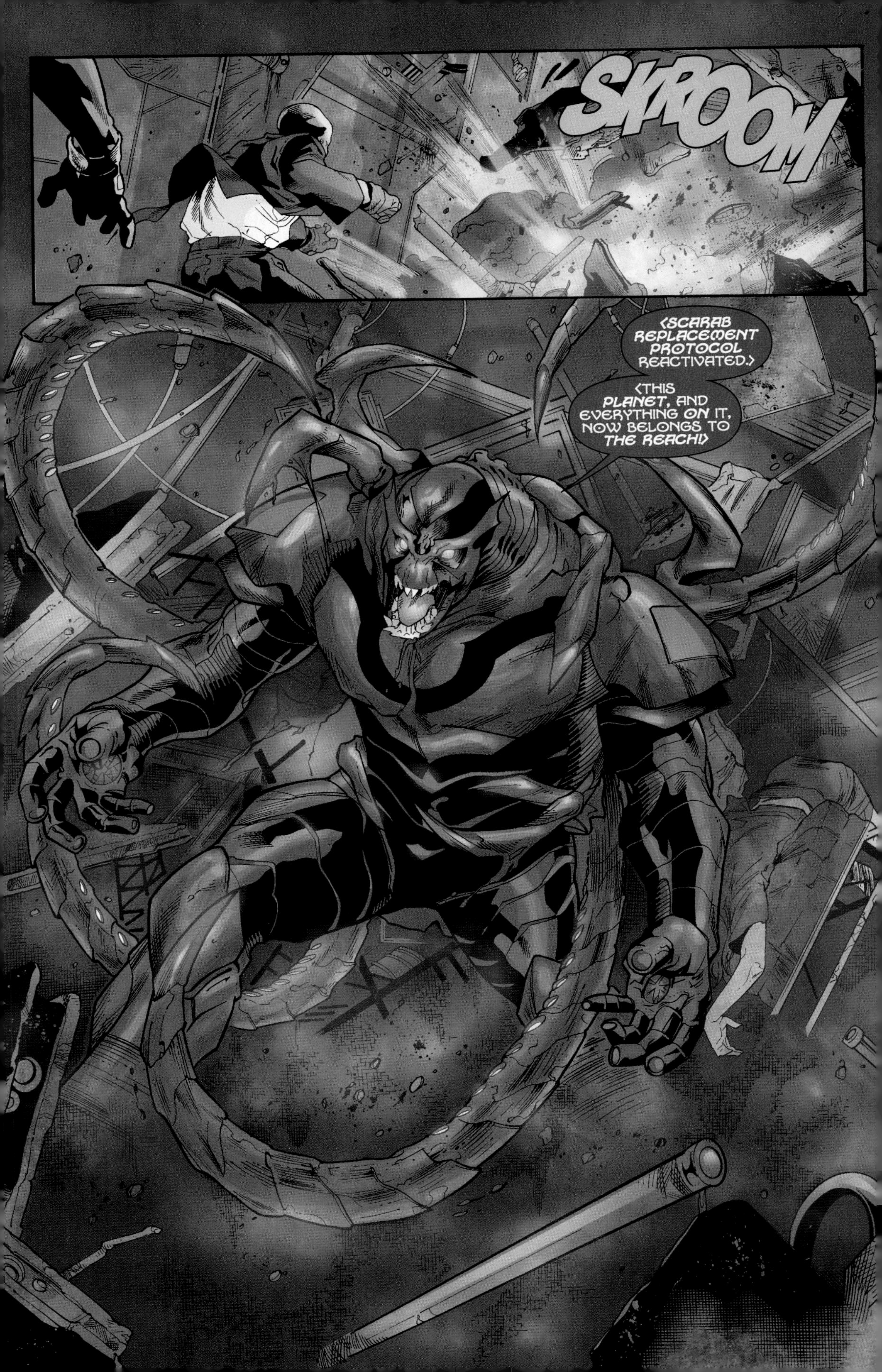
SKROOM
<SCARAB REPLACEMENT PROTOCOL REACTIVATED.>
<THIS PLANET, AND EVERYTHING ON IT, NOW BELONGS TO THE REACH!>

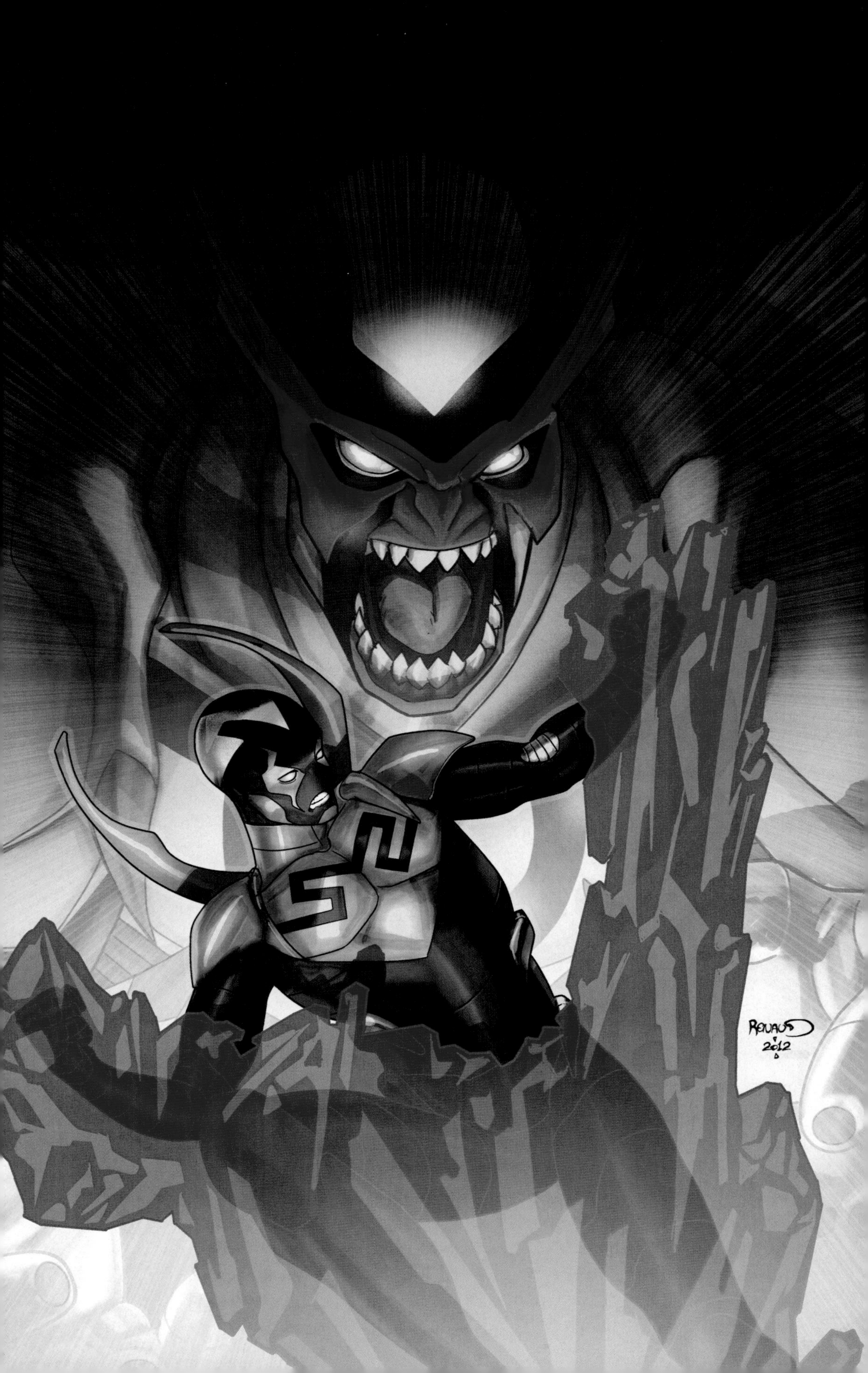
RENAUD
2012

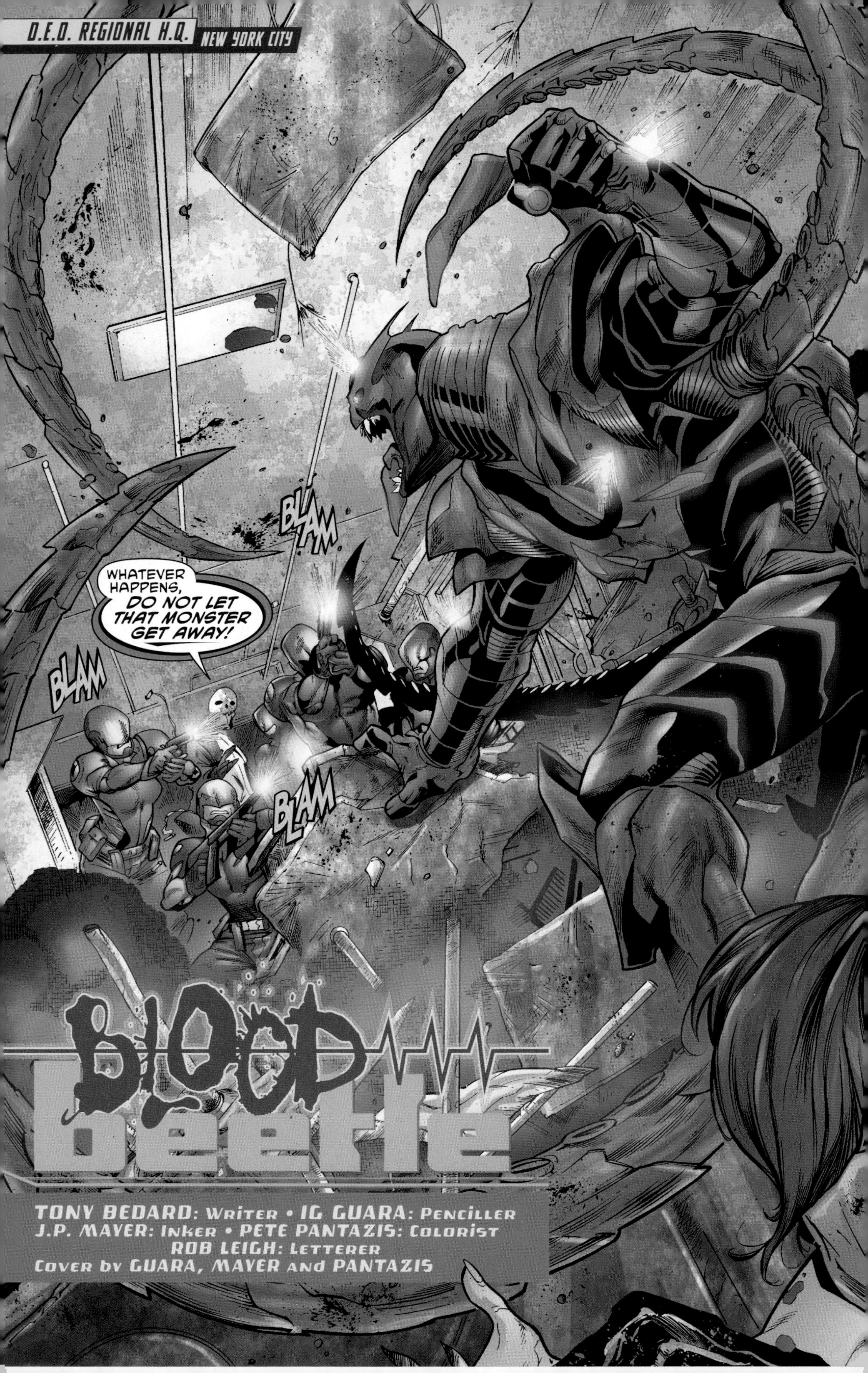
D.E.O. REGIONAL H.Q. NEW YORK CITY
BLAM
WHATEVER HAPPENS, DO NOT LET THAT MONSTER GET AWAY!
BLAM
BLAM
BLOOD beetle
TONY BEDARD: Writer • IG GUARA: Penciller
J.P. MAYER: Inker • PETE PANTAZIS: Colorist
ROB LEIGH: Letterer
Cover by GUARA, MAYER and PANTAZIS

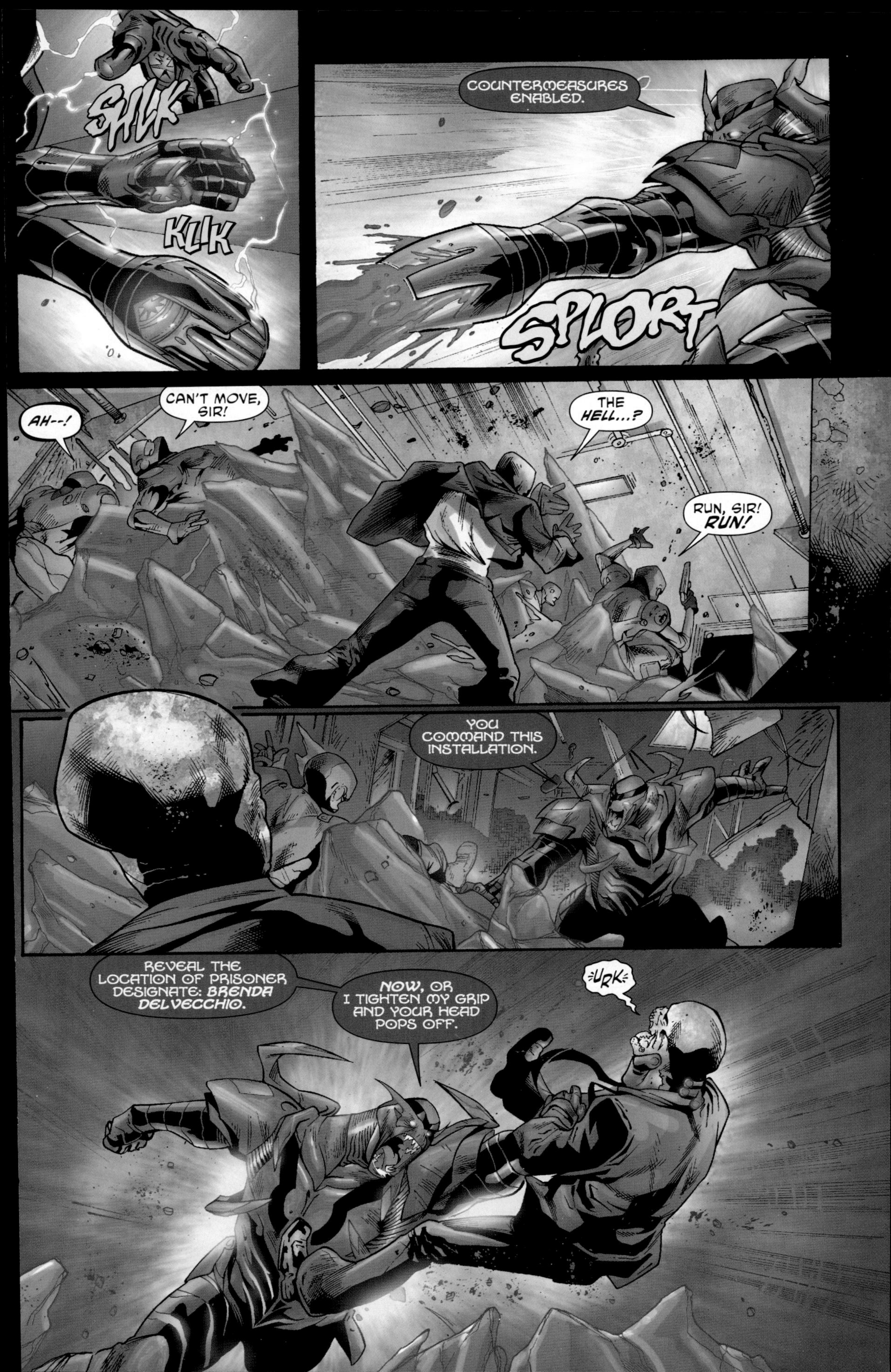
SHLK
KLIK
COUNTERMEASURES ENABLED.
SPLORT
AH--!
CAN'T MOVE, SIR!
THE *HELL*...?
RUN, SIR! *RUN!*
YOU COMMAND THIS INSTALLATION.
REVEAL THE LOCATION OF PRISONER DESIGNATE: *BRENDA DELVECCHIO.*
NOW, OR I TIGHTEN MY GRIP AND YOUR HEAD POPS OFF.
URK

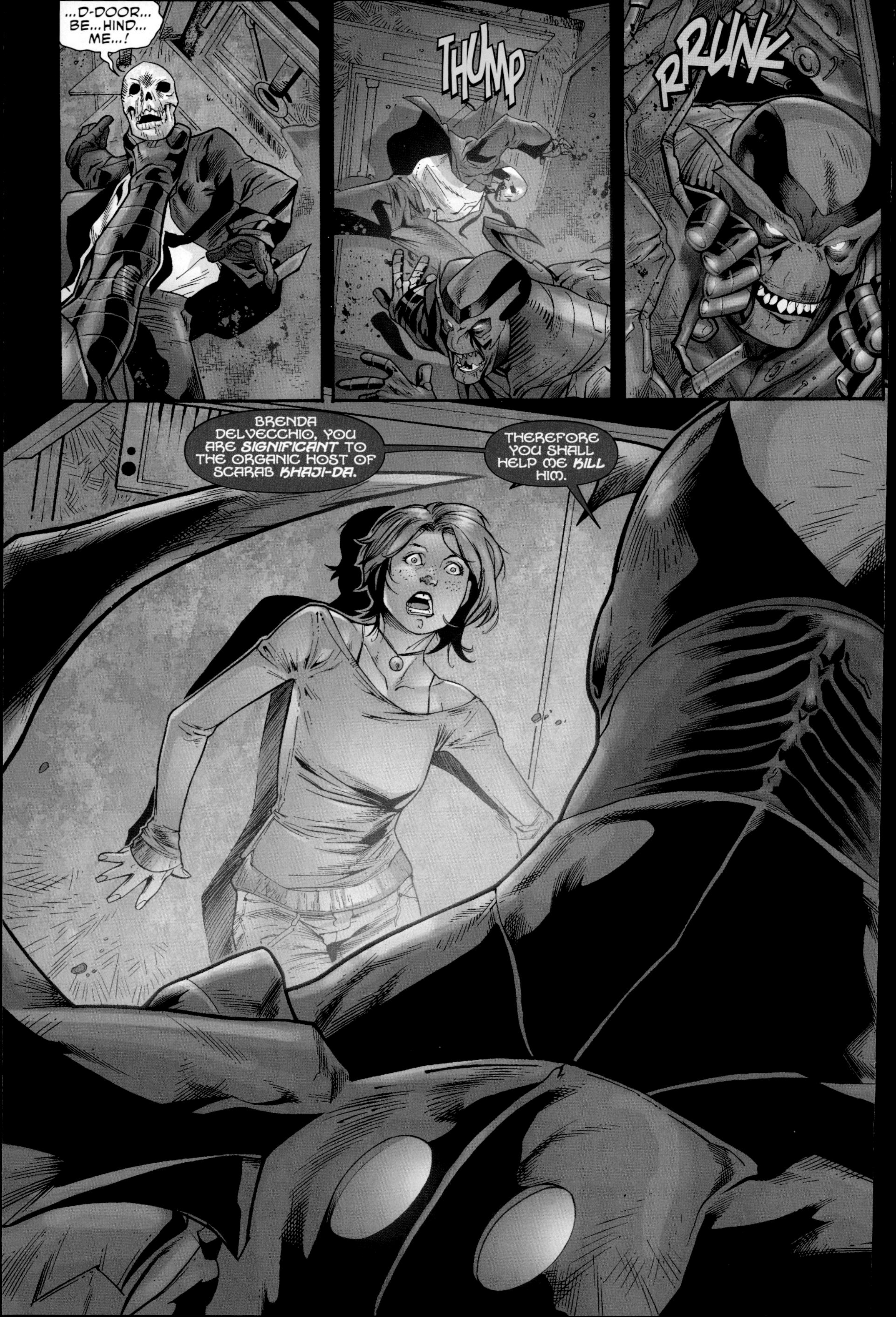
...D-DOOR... BE...HIND... ME...!
THUMP
RRUNK
BRENDA DELVECCHIO, YOU ARE SIGNIFICANT TO THE ORGANIC HOST OF SCARAB KHAJI-DA.
THEREFORE YOU SHALL HELP ME KILL HIM.

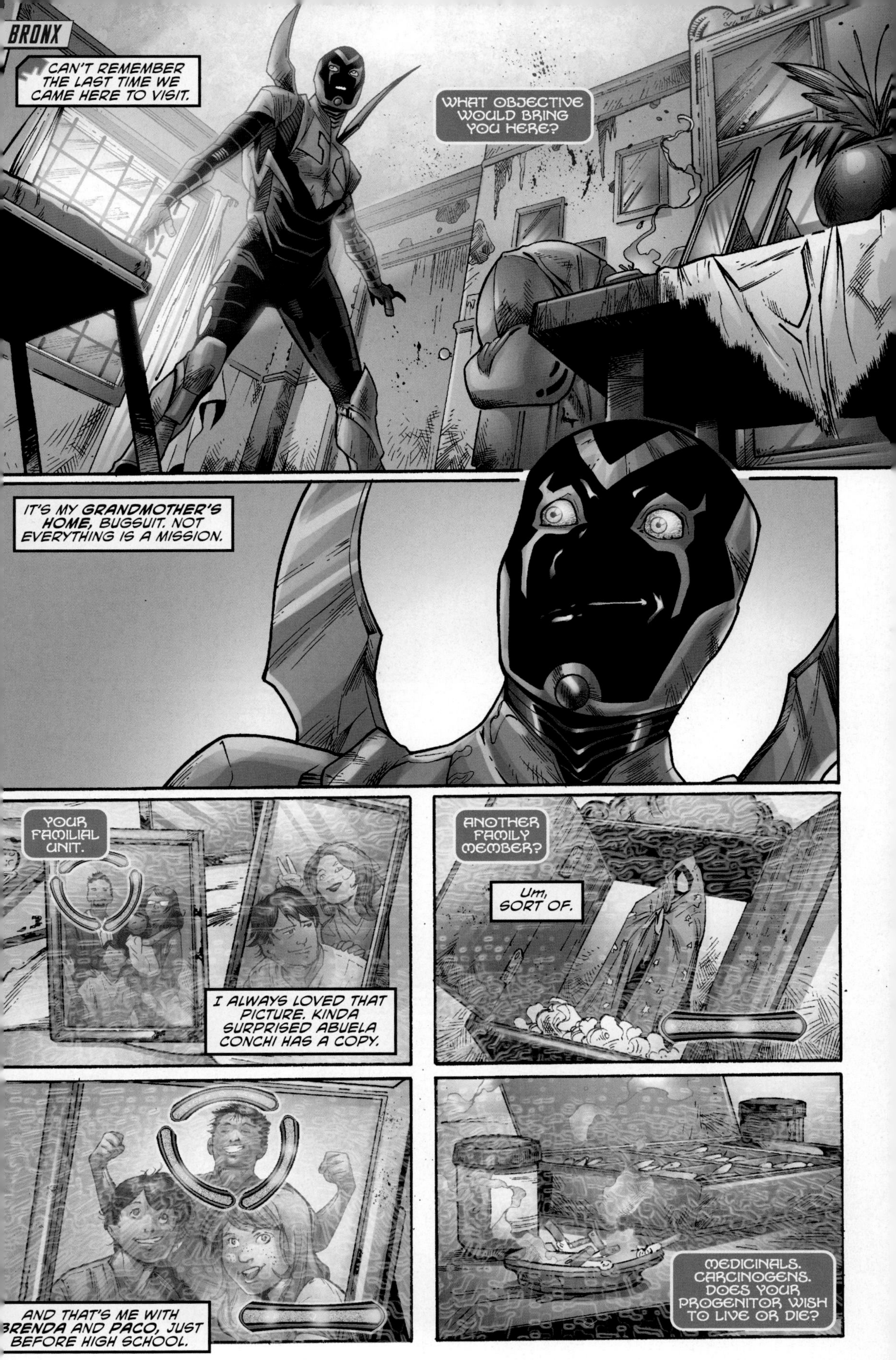
BRONX
CAN'T REMEMBER THE LAST TIME WE CAME HERE TO VISIT.
WHAT OBJECTIVE WOULD BRING YOU HERE?
IT'S MY **GRANDMOTHER'S HOME,** BUGSUIT. NOT EVERYTHING IS A MISSION.
YOUR FAMILIAL UNIT.
I ALWAYS LOVED THAT PICTURE. KINDA SURPRISED ABUELA CONCHI HAS A COPY.
ANOTHER FAMILY MEMBER?
Um, SORT OF.
AND THAT'S ME WITH **BRENDA** AND **PACO,** JUST BEFORE HIGH SCHOOL.
MEDICINALS. CARCINOGENS. DOES YOUR PROGENITOR WISH TO LIVE OR DIE?

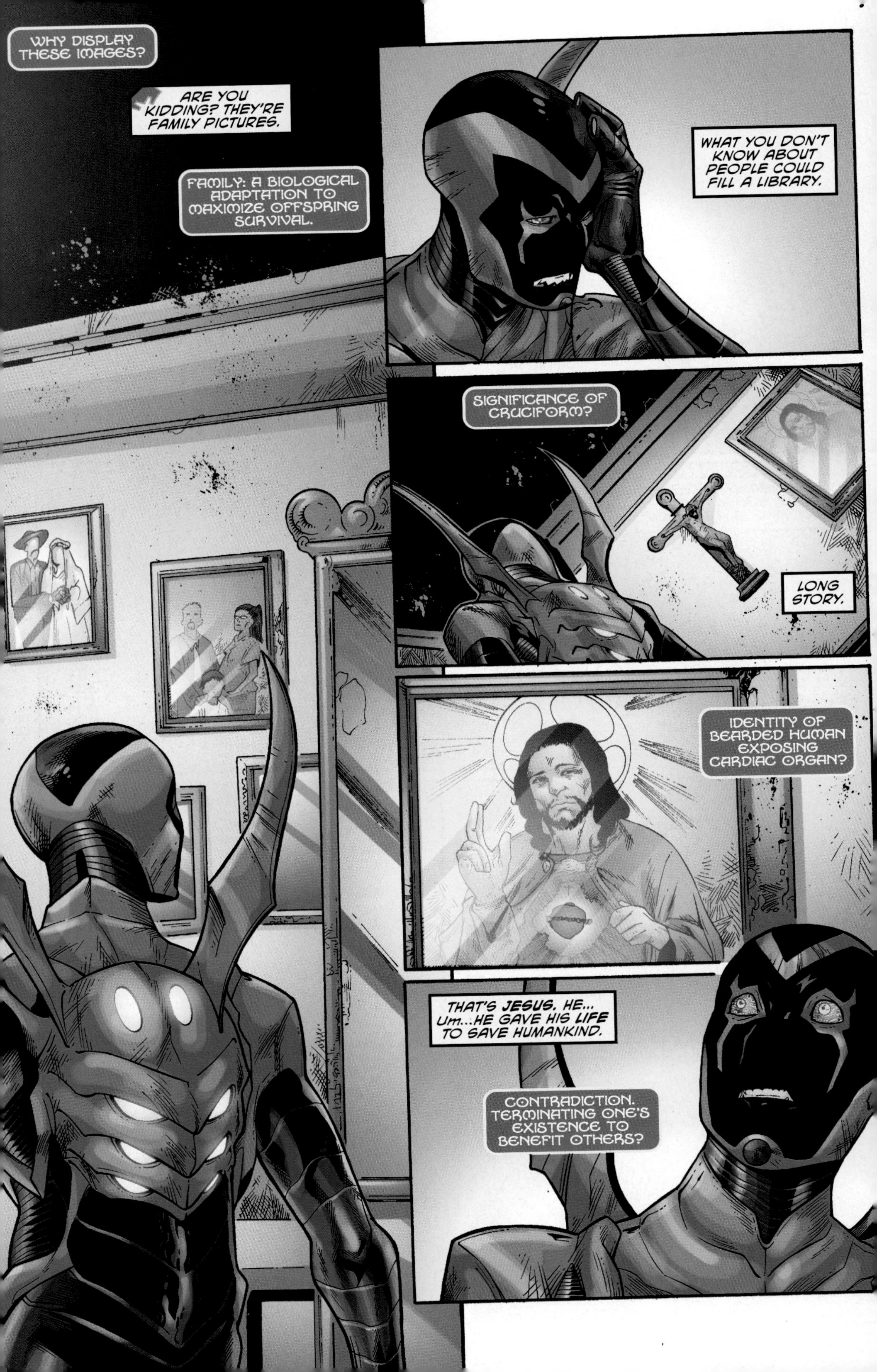
WHY DISPLAY THESE IMAGES?
ARE YOU KIDDING? THEY'RE FAMILY PICTURES.
FAMILY: A BIOLOGICAL ADAPTATION TO MAXIMIZE OFFSPRING SURVIVAL.
WHAT YOU DON'T KNOW ABOUT PEOPLE COULD FILL A LIBRARY.
SIGNIFICANCE OF CRUCIFORM?
LONG STORY.
IDENTITY OF BEARDED HUMAN EXPOSING CARDIAC ORGAN?
THAT'S JESUS. HE... Um...HE GAVE HIS LIFE TO SAVE HUMANKIND.
CONTRADICTION. TERMINATING ONE'S EXISTENCE TO BENEFIT OTHERS?

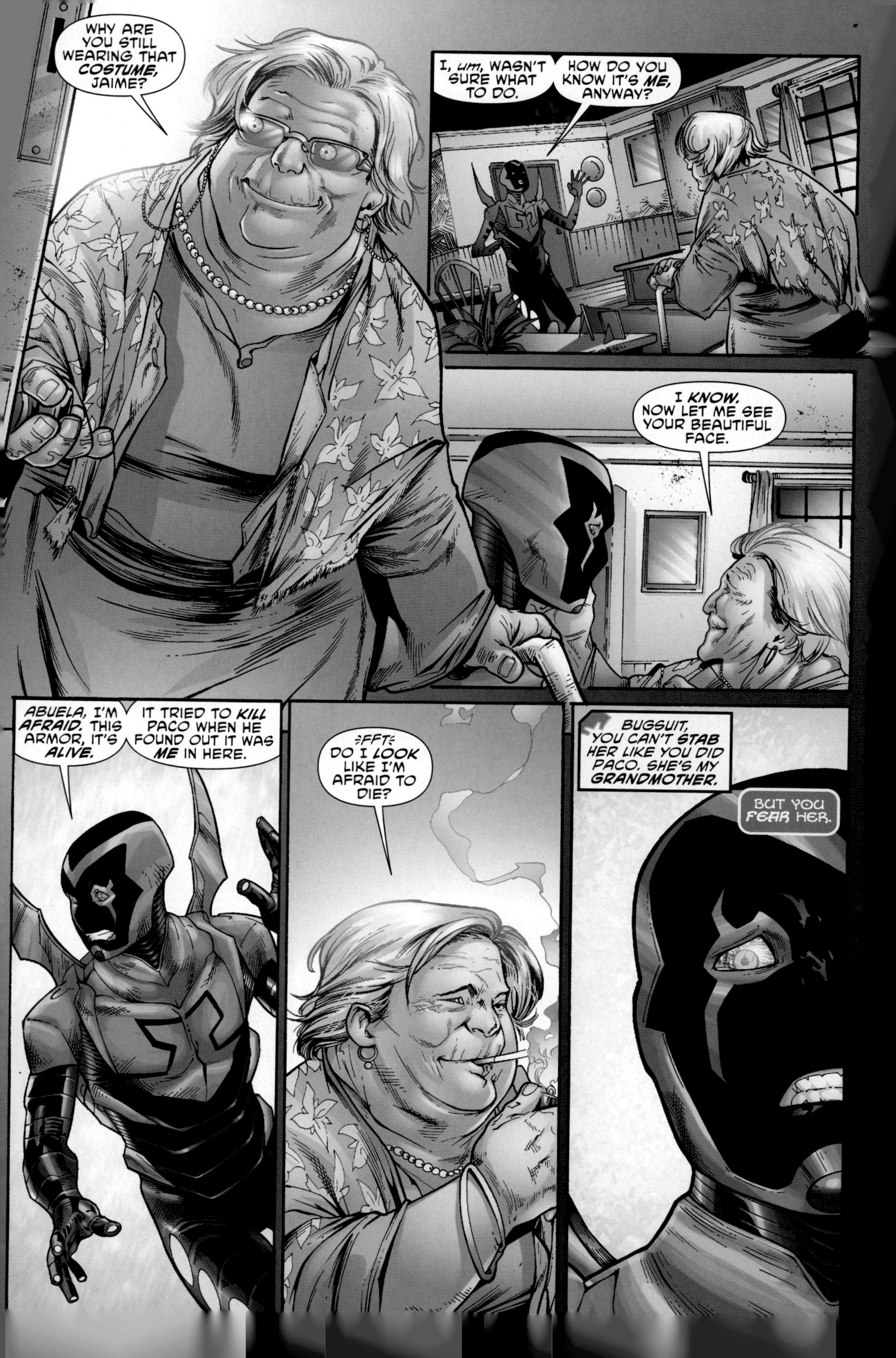
WHY ARE YOU STILL WEARING THAT COSTUME, JAIME?
I, um, WASN'T SURE WHAT TO DO.
HOW DO YOU KNOW IT'S ME, ANYWAY?
I KNOW. NOW LET ME SEE YOUR BEAUTIFUL FACE.
ABUELA, I'M AFRAID. THIS ARMOR, IT'S ALIVE.
IT TRIED TO KILL PACO WHEN HE FOUND OUT IT WAS ME IN HERE.
PFFT. DO I LOOK LIKE I'M AFRAID TO DIE?
BUGSUIT, YOU CAN'T STAB HER LIKE YOU DID PACO. SHE'S MY GRANDMOTHER.
BUT YOU FEAR HER.

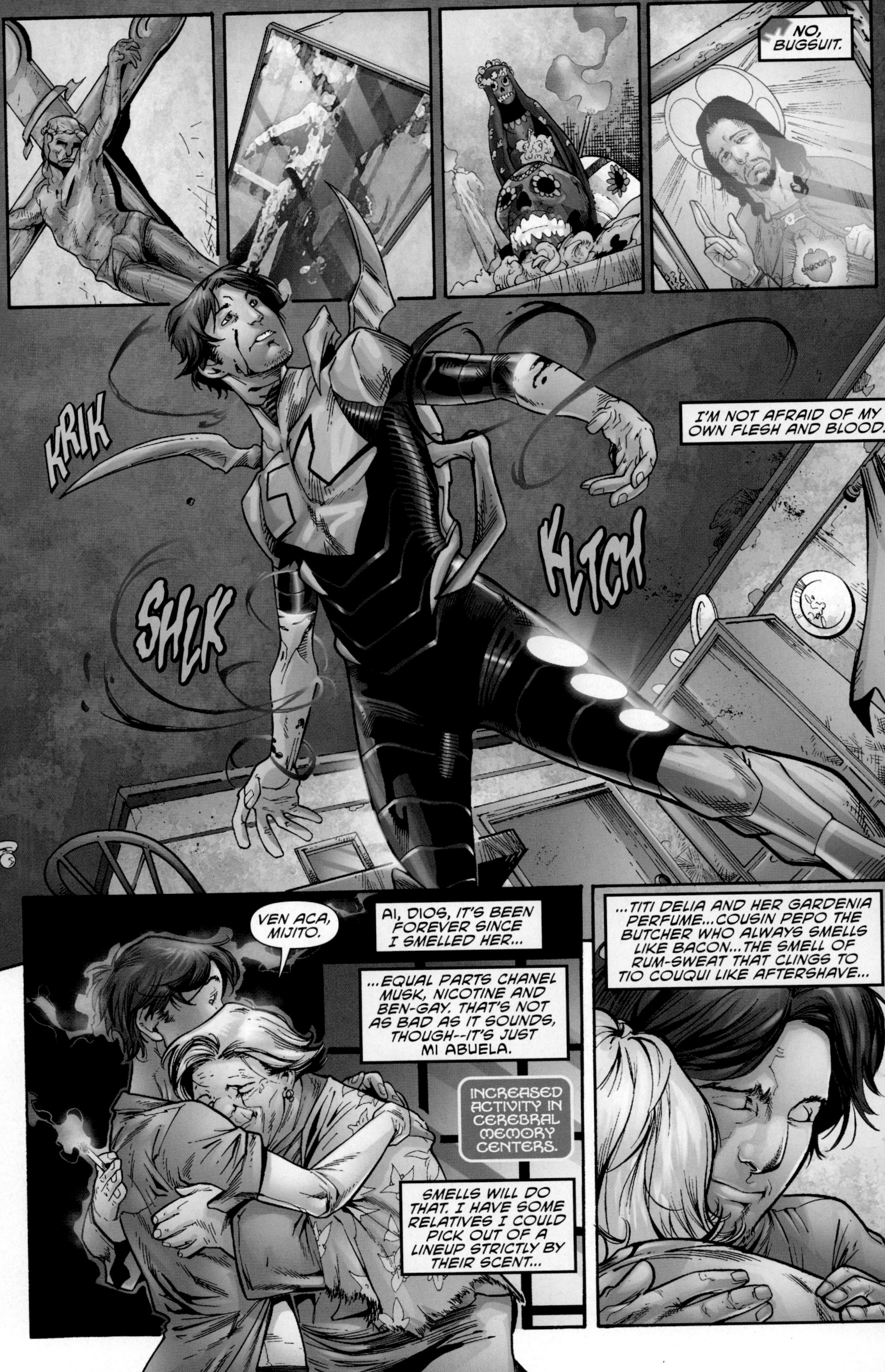
NO, BUGSUIT.
KRIK
I'M NOT AFRAID OF MY OWN FLESH AND BLOOD.
SHLK
KLTCH
VEN ACA, MIJITO.
AI, DIOS, IT'S BEEN FOREVER SINCE I SMELLED HER...
...EQUAL PARTS CHANEL MUSK, NICOTINE AND BEN-GAY. THAT'S NOT AS BAD AS IT SOUNDS, THOUGH--IT'S JUST MI ABUELA.
INCREASED ACTIVITY IN CEREBRAL MEMORY CENTERS.
SMELLS WILL DO THAT. I HAVE SOME RELATIVES I COULD PICK OUT OF A LINEUP STRICTLY BY THEIR SCENT...
...TITI DELIA AND HER GARDENIA PERFUME...COUSIN PEPO THE BUTCHER WHO ALWAYS SMELLS LIKE BACON...THE SMELL OF RUM-SWEAT THAT CLINGS TO TIO COUQUI LIKE AFTERSHAVE...

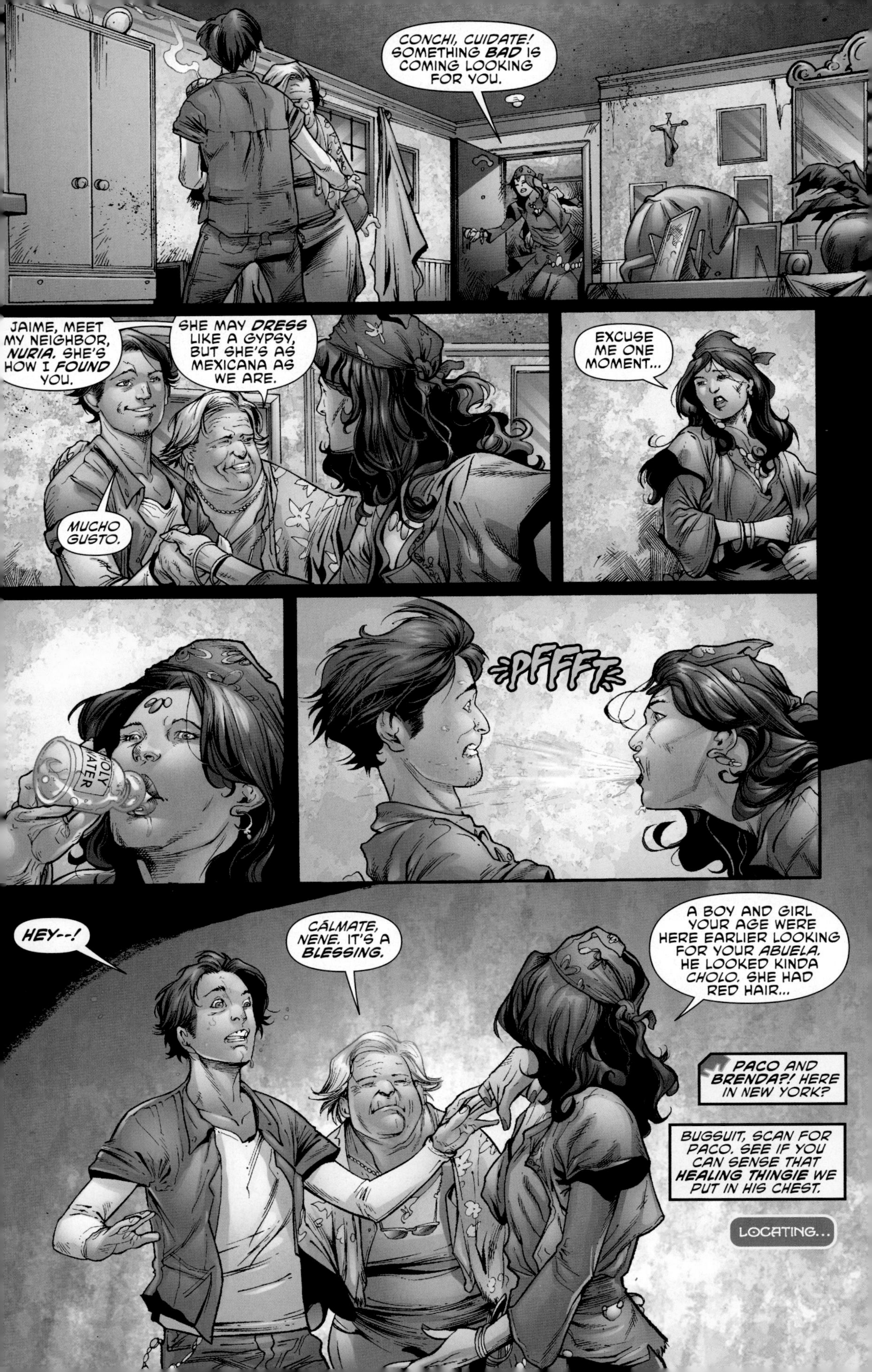
CONCHI, CUIDATE! SOMETHING BAD IS COMING LOOKING FOR YOU.
JAIME, MEET MY NEIGHBOR, NURIA. SHE'S HOW I FOUND YOU.
SHE MAY DRESS LIKE A GYPSY, BUT SHE'S AS MEXICANA AS WE ARE.
MUCHO GUSTO.
EXCUSE ME ONE MOMENT...
HOLY WATER
PFFFT
HEY--!
CÁLMATE, NENE. IT'S A BLESSING.
A BOY AND GIRL YOUR AGE WERE HERE EARLIER LOOKING FOR YOUR ABUELA. HE LOOKED KINDA CHOLO. SHE HAD RED HAIR...
PACO AND BRENDA?! HERE IN NEW YORK?
BUGSUIT, SCAN FOR PACO. SEE IF YOU CAN SENSE THAT HEALING THINGIE WE PUT IN HIS CHEST.
LOCATING...

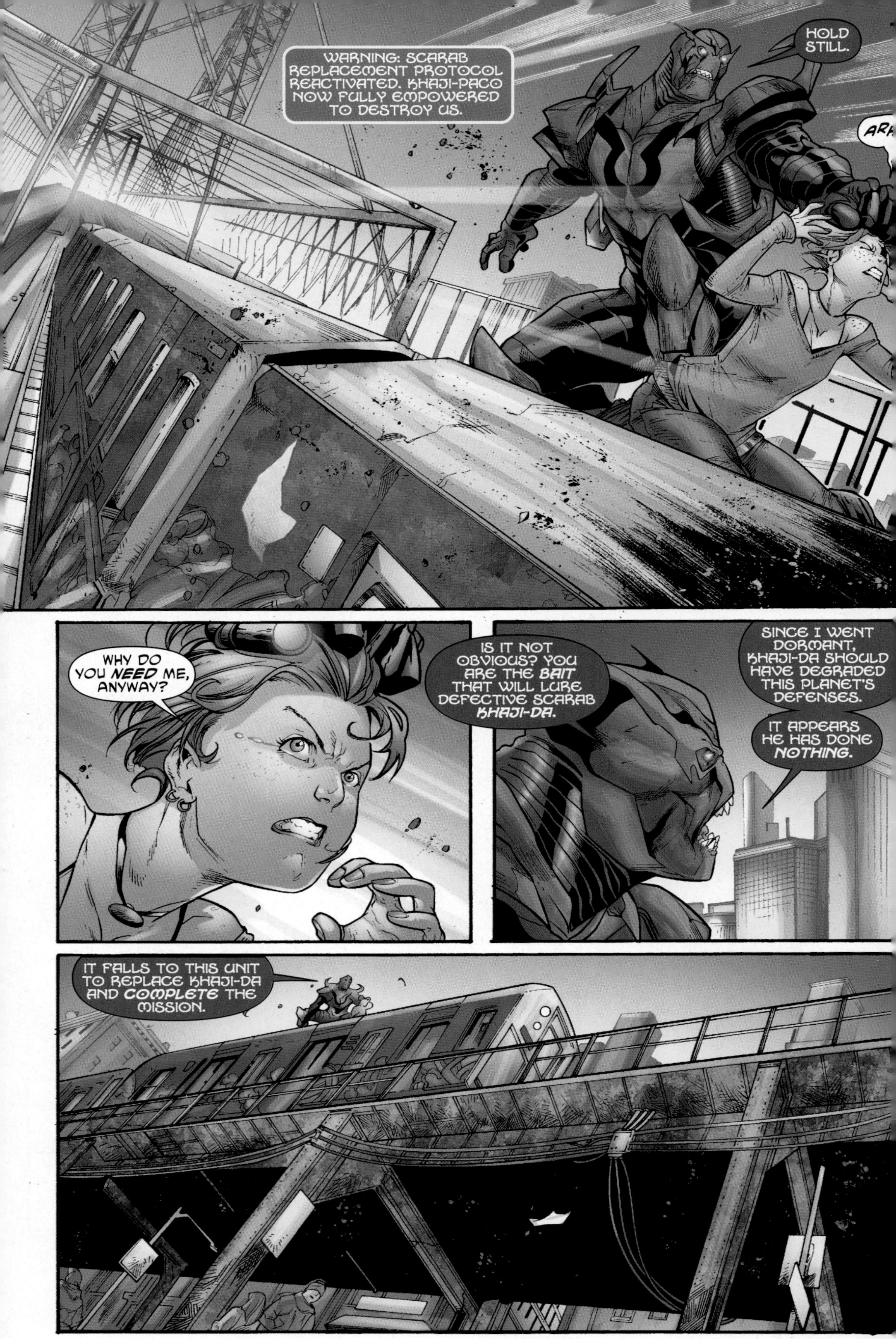
WARNING: SCARAB REPLACEMENT PROTOCOL REACTIVATED. KHAJI-PACO NOW FULLY EMPOWERED TO DESTROY US.
HOLD STILL.
WHY DO YOU NEED ME, ANYWAY?
IS IT NOT OBVIOUS? YOU ARE THE BAIT THAT WILL LURE DEFECTIVE SCARAB KHAJI-DA.
SINCE I WENT DORMANT, KHAJI-DA SHOULD HAVE DEGRADED THIS PLANET'S DEFENSES.
IT APPEARS HE HAS DONE NOTHING.
IT FALLS TO THIS UNIT TO REPLACE KHAJI-DA AND COMPLETE THE MISSION.

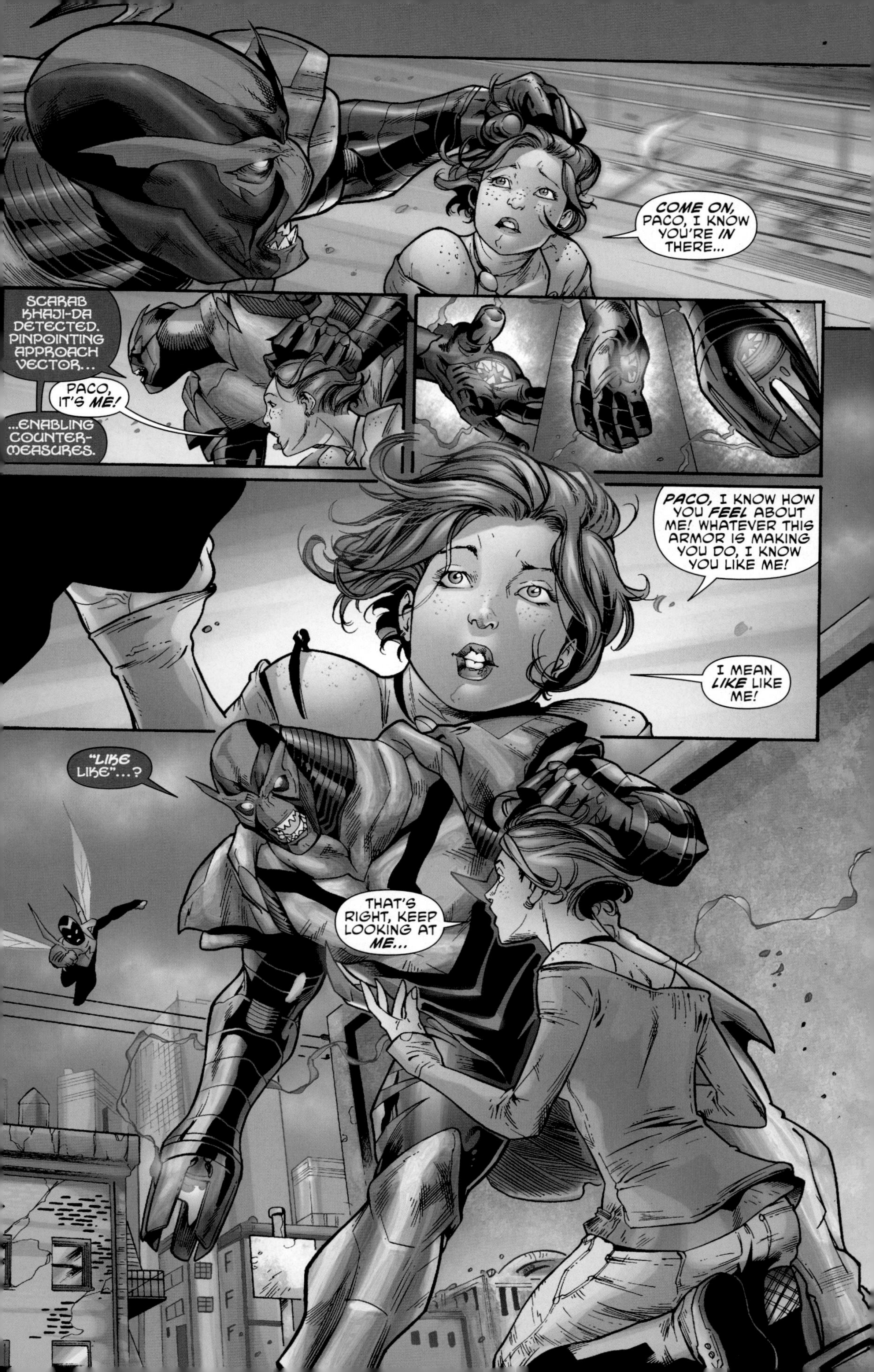
COME ON, PACO, I KNOW YOU'RE IN THERE...
SCARAB KHAJI-DA DETECTED. PINPOINTING APPROACH VECTOR...
PACO, IT'S ME!
...ENABLING COUNTER-MEASURES.
PACO, I KNOW HOW YOU FEEL ABOUT ME! WHATEVER THIS ARMOR IS MAKING YOU DO, I KNOW YOU LIKE ME!
I MEAN LIKE LIKE ME!
"LIKE LIKE"...?
THAT'S RIGHT, KEEP LOOKING AT ME...

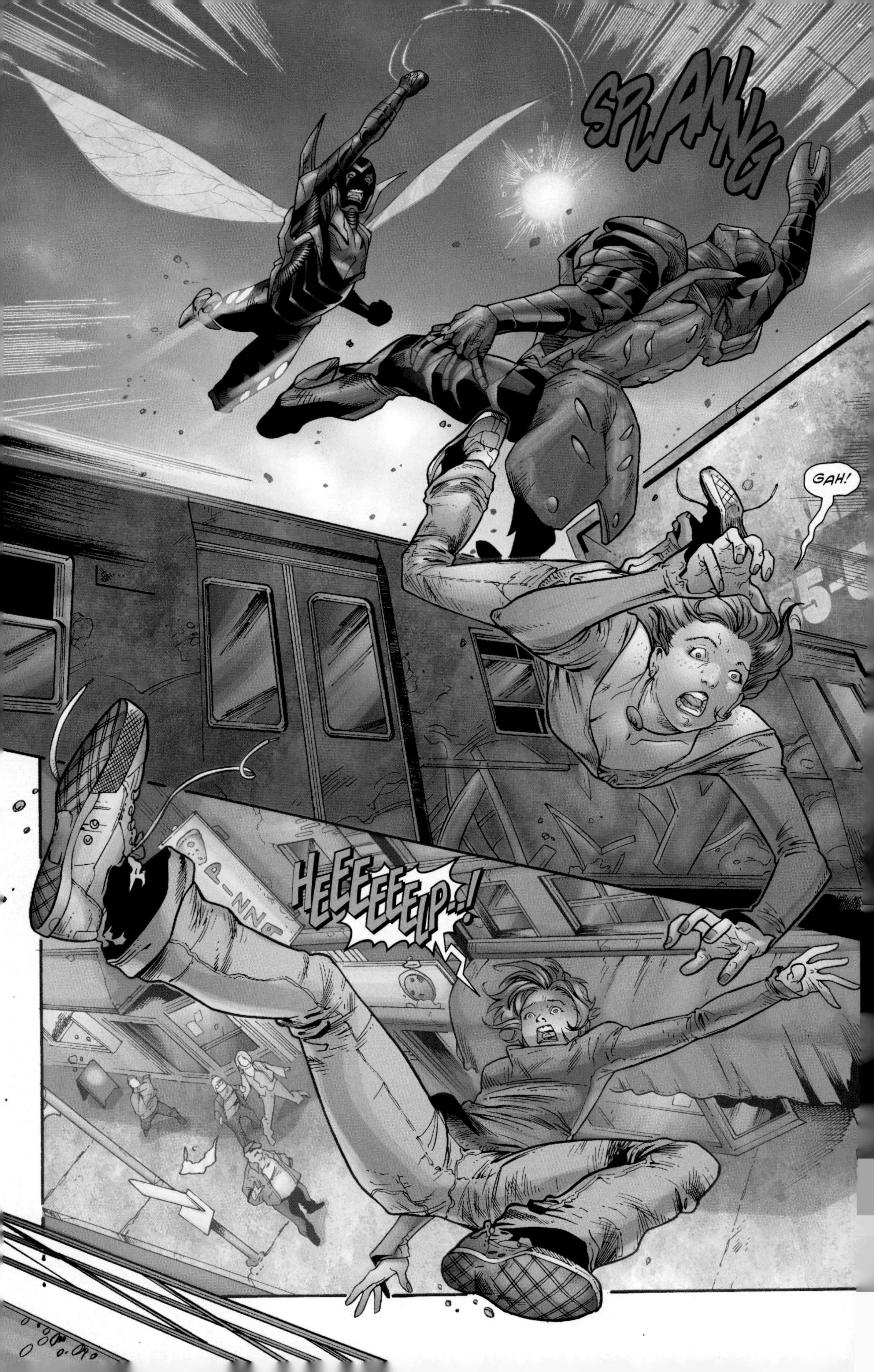
SPLANNG
GAH!
HEEEEEEELP..!

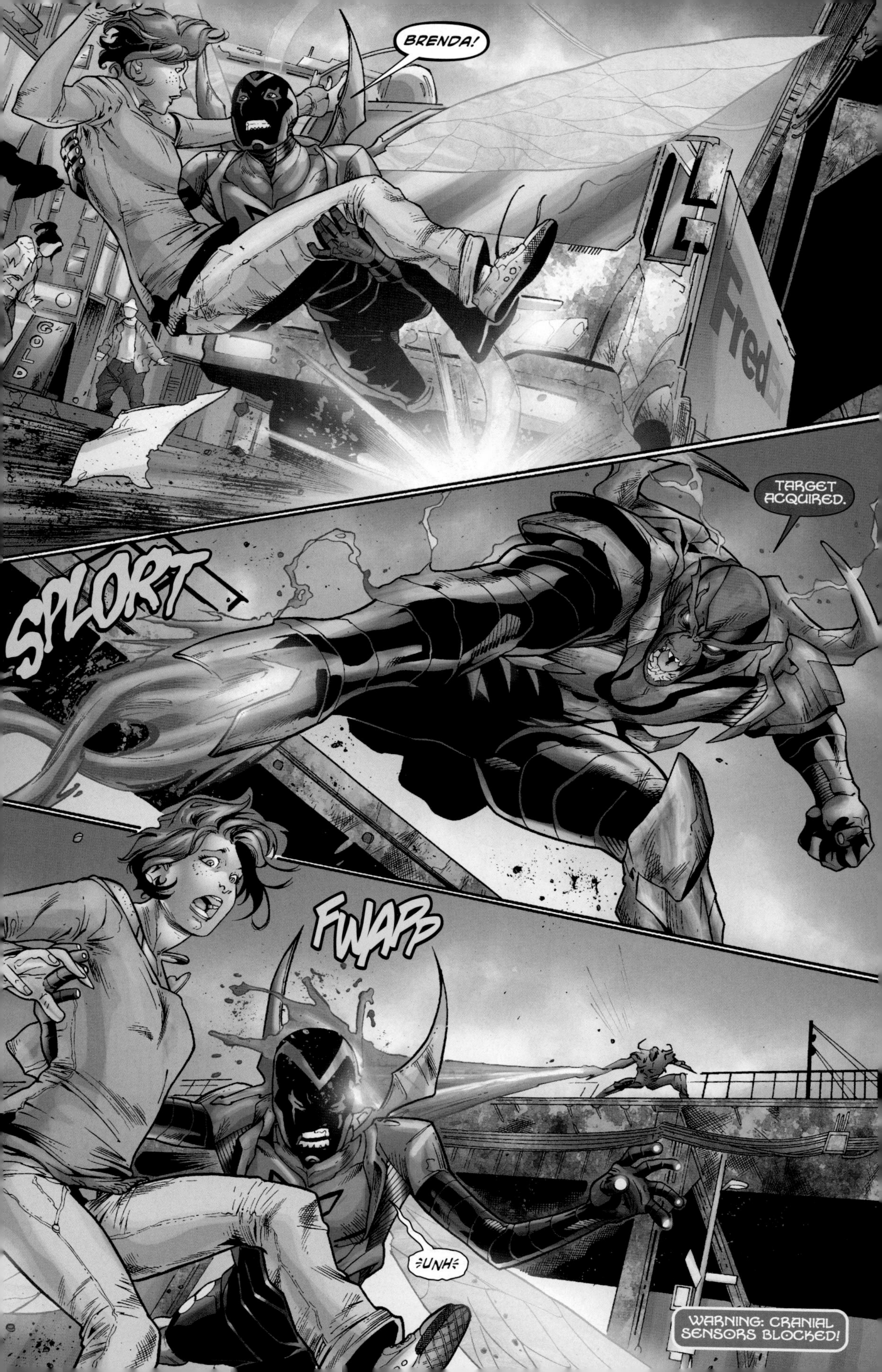
BRENDA!
GOLD
FedEx
TARGET ACQUIRED.
SPLORT
FWAPP
UNH
WARNING: CRANIAL SENSORS BLOCKED!

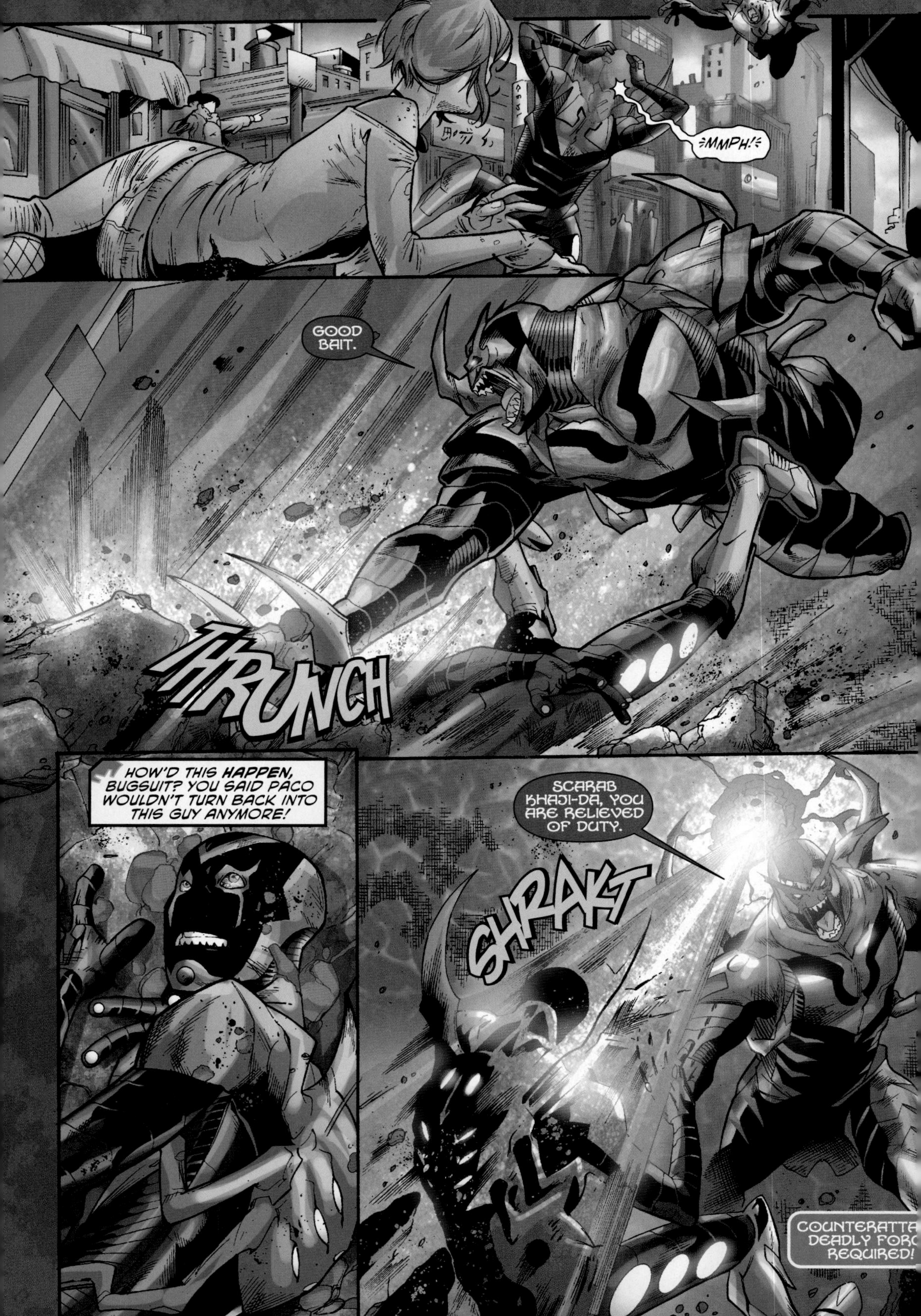
MMPH!
GOOD BAIT.
THRUNCH
HOW'D THIS HAPPEN, BUGSUIT? YOU SAID PACO WOULDN'T TURN BACK INTO THIS GUY ANYMORE!
SCARAB KHAJI-DA, YOU ARE RELIEVED OF DUTY.
SHRAKT
COUNTERATTA
DEADLY FORC
REQUIRED!

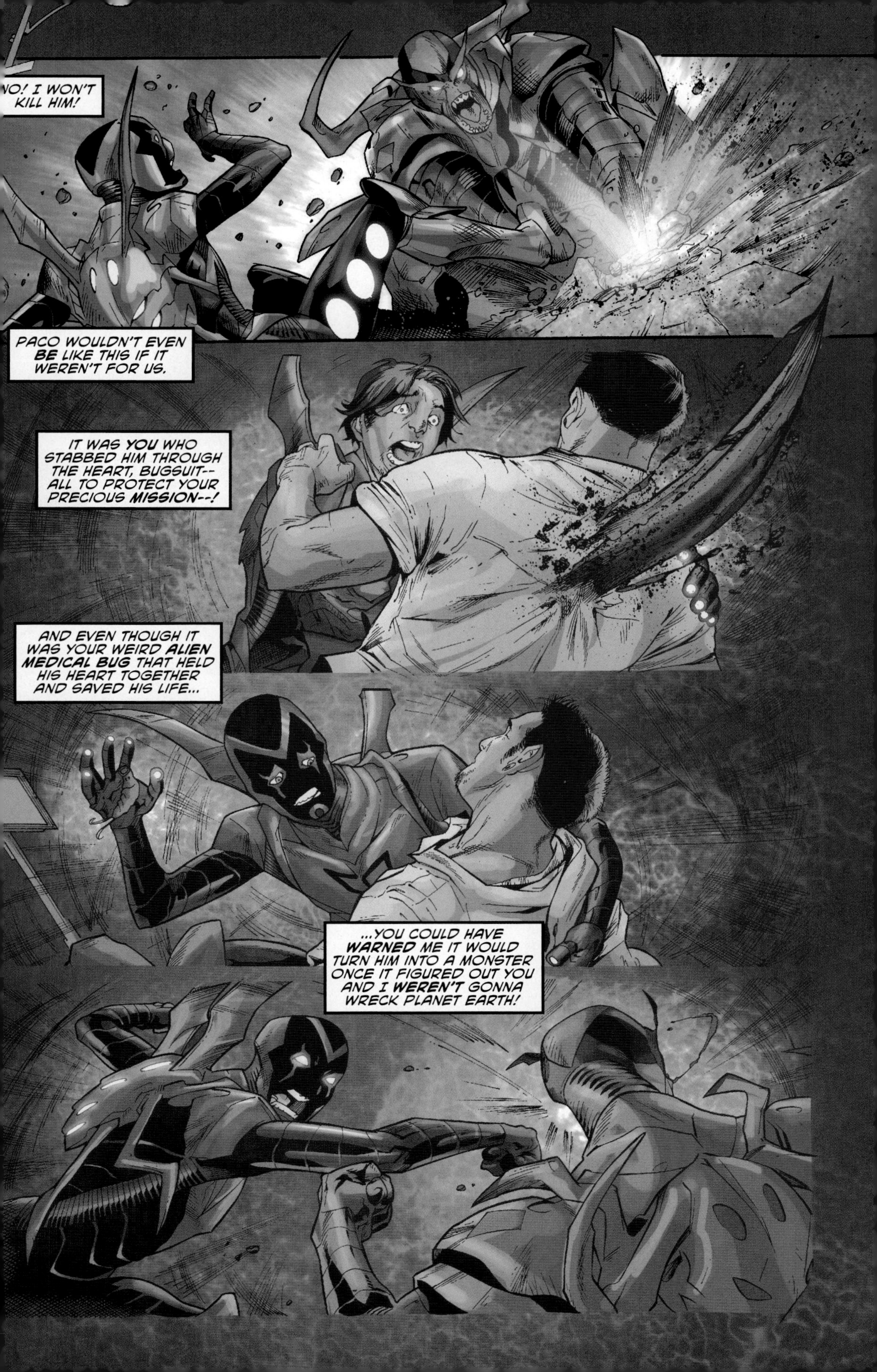
NO! I WON'T KILL HIM!
PACO WOULDN'T EVEN BE LIKE THIS IF IT WEREN'T FOR US.
IT WAS YOU WHO STABBED HIM THROUGH THE HEART, BUGSUIT-- ALL TO PROTECT YOUR PRECIOUS MISSION--!
AND EVEN THOUGH IT WAS YOUR WEIRD ALIEN MEDICAL BUG THAT HELD HIS HEART TOGETHER AND SAVED HIS LIFE...
...YOU COULD HAVE WARNED ME IT WOULD TURN HIM INTO A MONSTER ONCE IT FIGURED OUT YOU AND I WEREN'T GONNA WRECK PLANET EARTH!

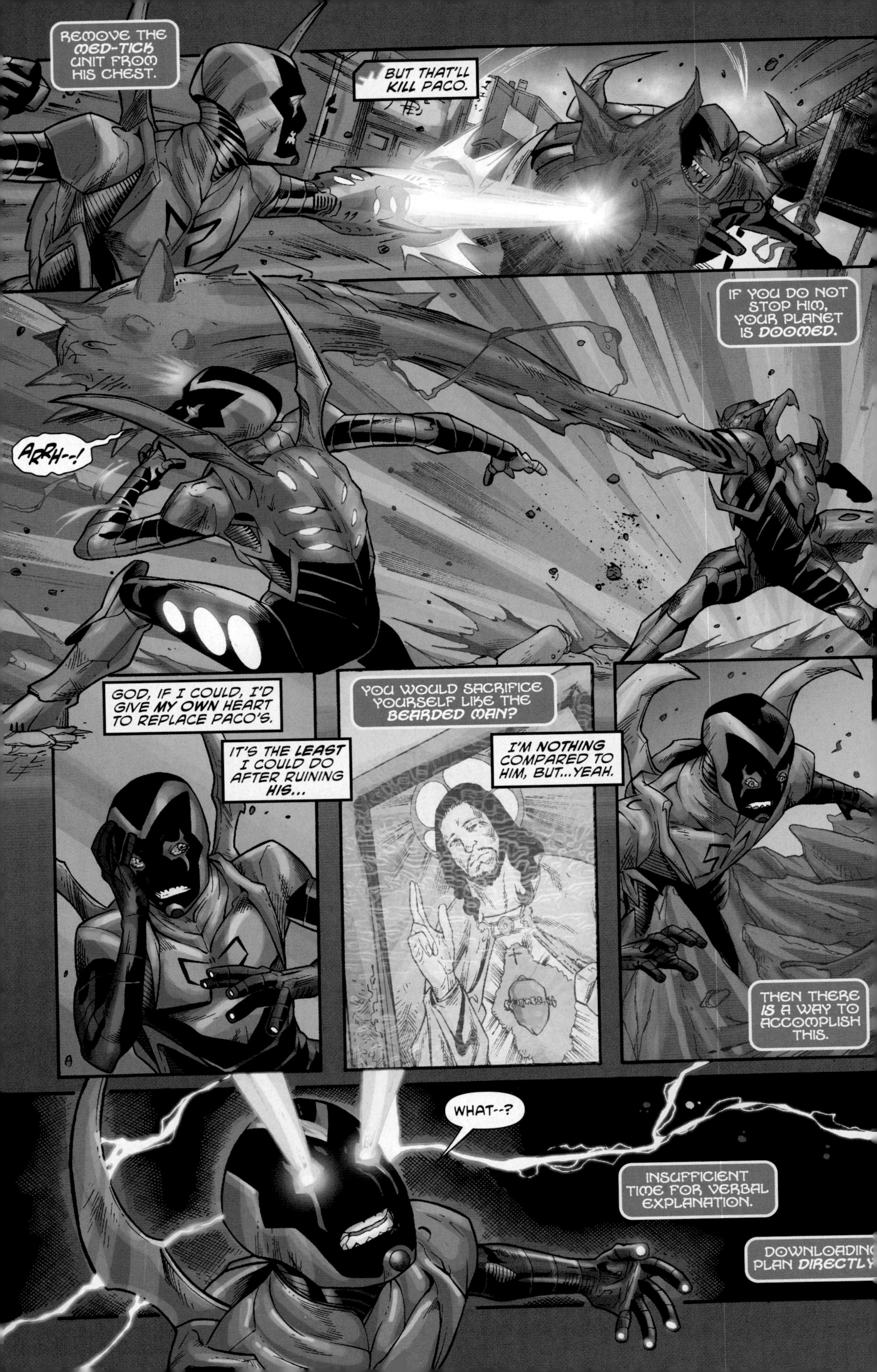
REMOVE THE MED-TICK UNIT FROM HIS CHEST.
BUT THAT'LL KILL PACO.
IF YOU DO NOT STOP HIM, YOUR PLANET IS DOOMED.
ARRH--!
GOD, IF I COULD, I'D GIVE MY OWN HEART TO REPLACE PACO'S.
IT'S THE LEAST I COULD DO AFTER RUINING HIS...
YOU WOULD SACRIFICE YOURSELF LIKE THE BEARDED MAN?
I'M NOTHING COMPARED TO HIM, BUT...YEAH.
THEN THERE IS A WAY TO ACCOMPLISH THIS.
WHAT--?
INSUFFICIENT TIME FOR VERBAL EXPLANATION.
DOWNLOADING PLAN DIRECTLY

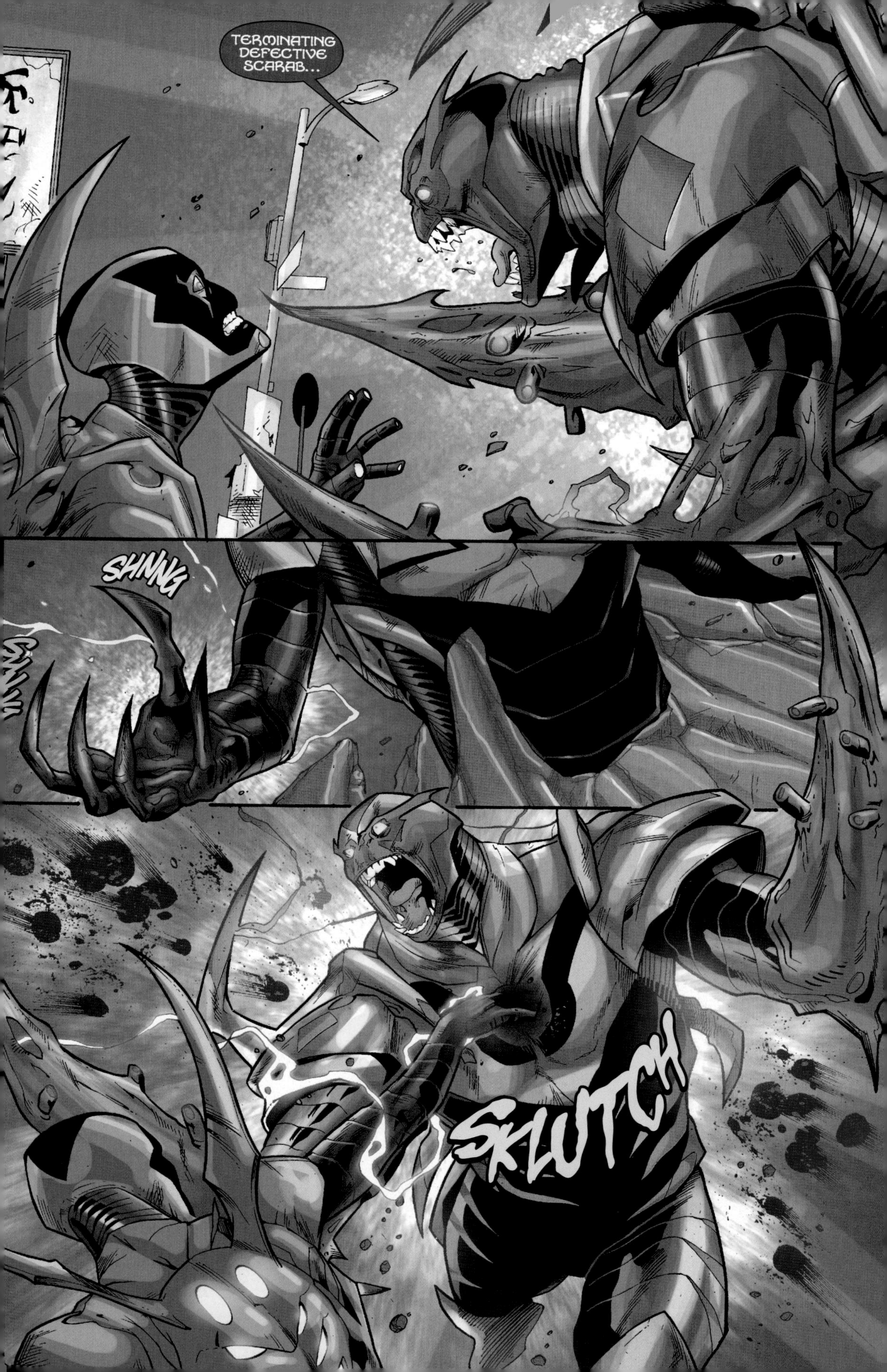
TERMINATING DEFECTIVE SCARAB...
SHNNG
SKLUTCH

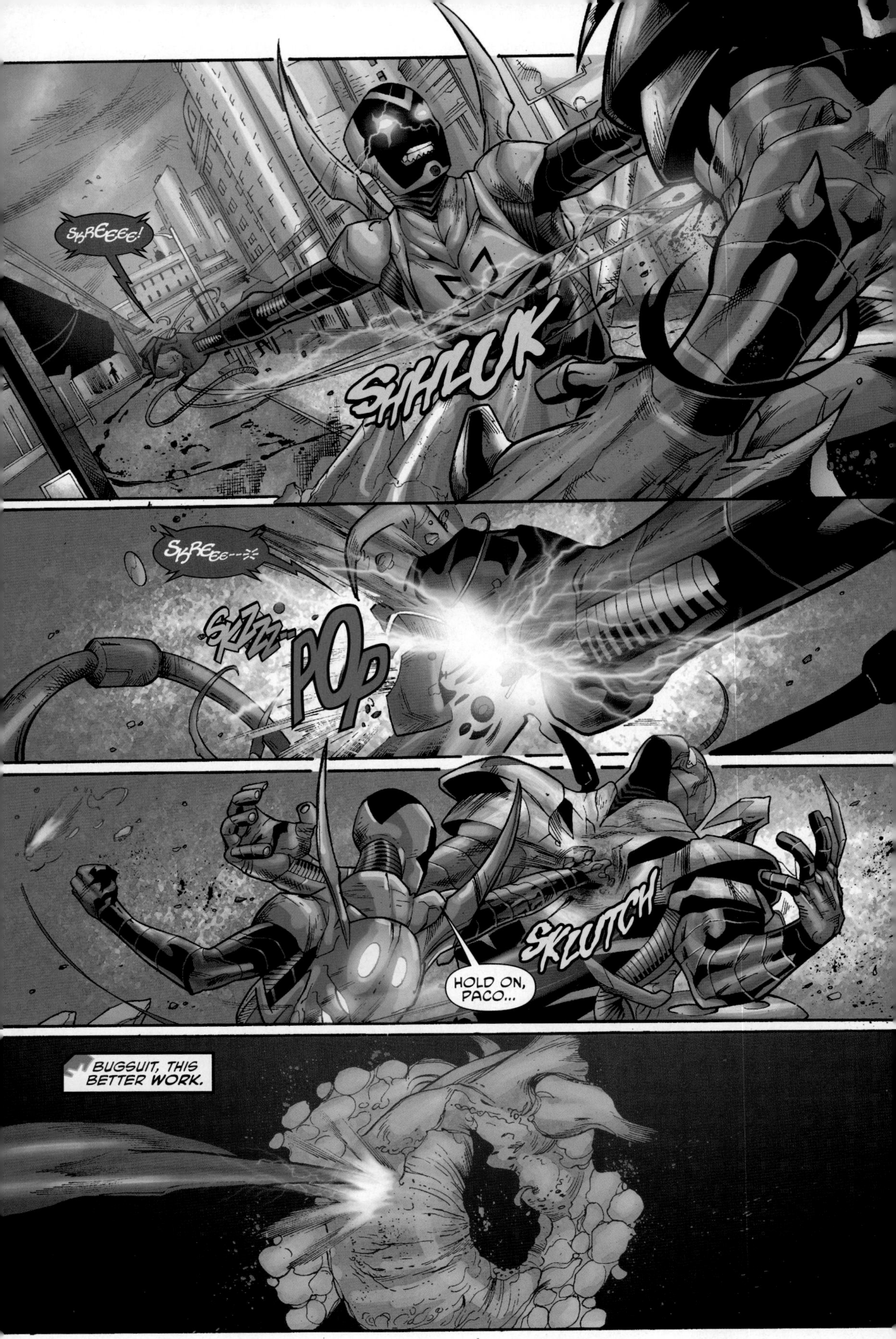
SKREEEE!
SHHLUK
SKREEE--
SKZZZ--
POP
SKLUTCH
HOLD ON, PACO...
BUGSUIT, THIS BETTER WORK.

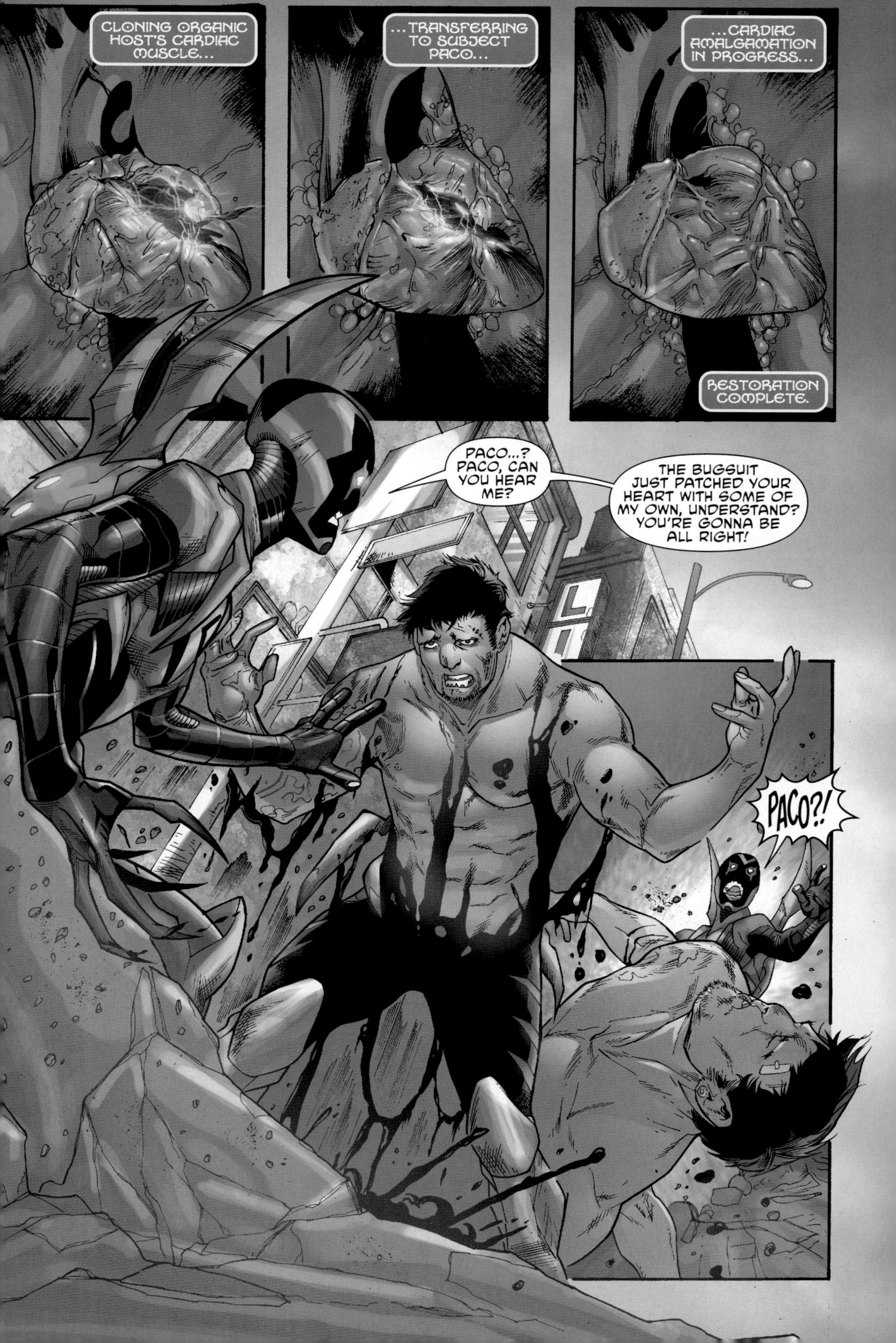
CLONING ORGANIC HOST'S CARDIAC MUSCLE...
...TRANSFERRING TO SUBJECT PACO...
...CARDIAC AMALGAMATION IN PROGRESS...
RESTORATION COMPLETE.
PACO...? PACO, CAN YOU HEAR ME?
THE BUGSUIT JUST PATCHED YOUR HEART WITH SOME OF MY OWN, UNDERSTAND? YOU'RE GONNA BE ALL RIGHT!
PACO?!

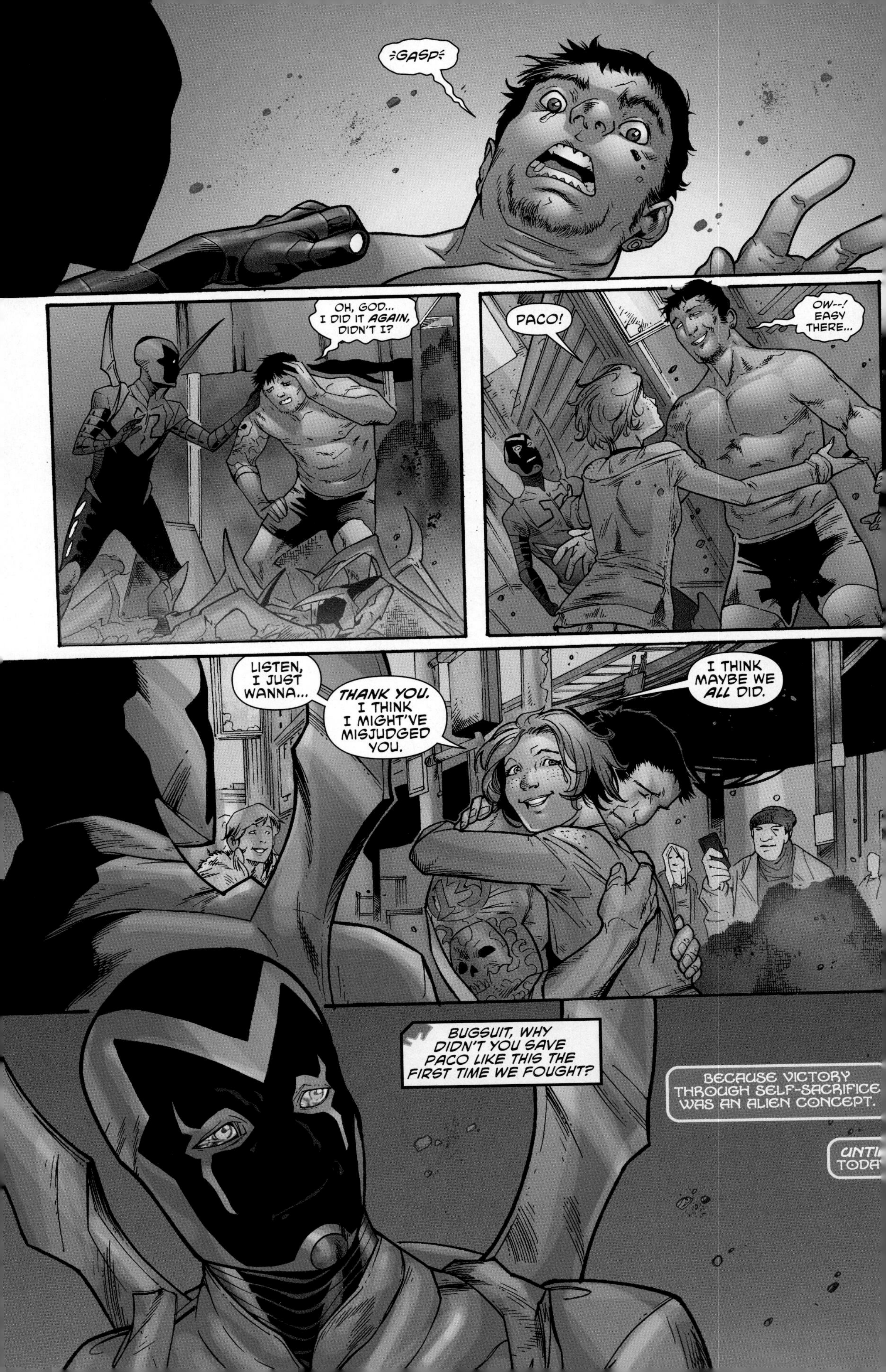
GASP
OH, GOD... I DID IT AGAIN, DIDN'T I?
PACO!
OW--! EASY THERE...
LISTEN, I JUST WANNA...
THANK YOU. I THINK I MIGHT'VE MISJUDGED YOU.
I THINK MAYBE WE ALL DID.
BUGSUIT, WHY DIDN'T YOU SAVE PACO LIKE THIS THE FIRST TIME WE FOUGHT?
BECAUSE VICTORY THROUGH SELF-SACRIFICE WAS AN ALIEN CONCEPT.

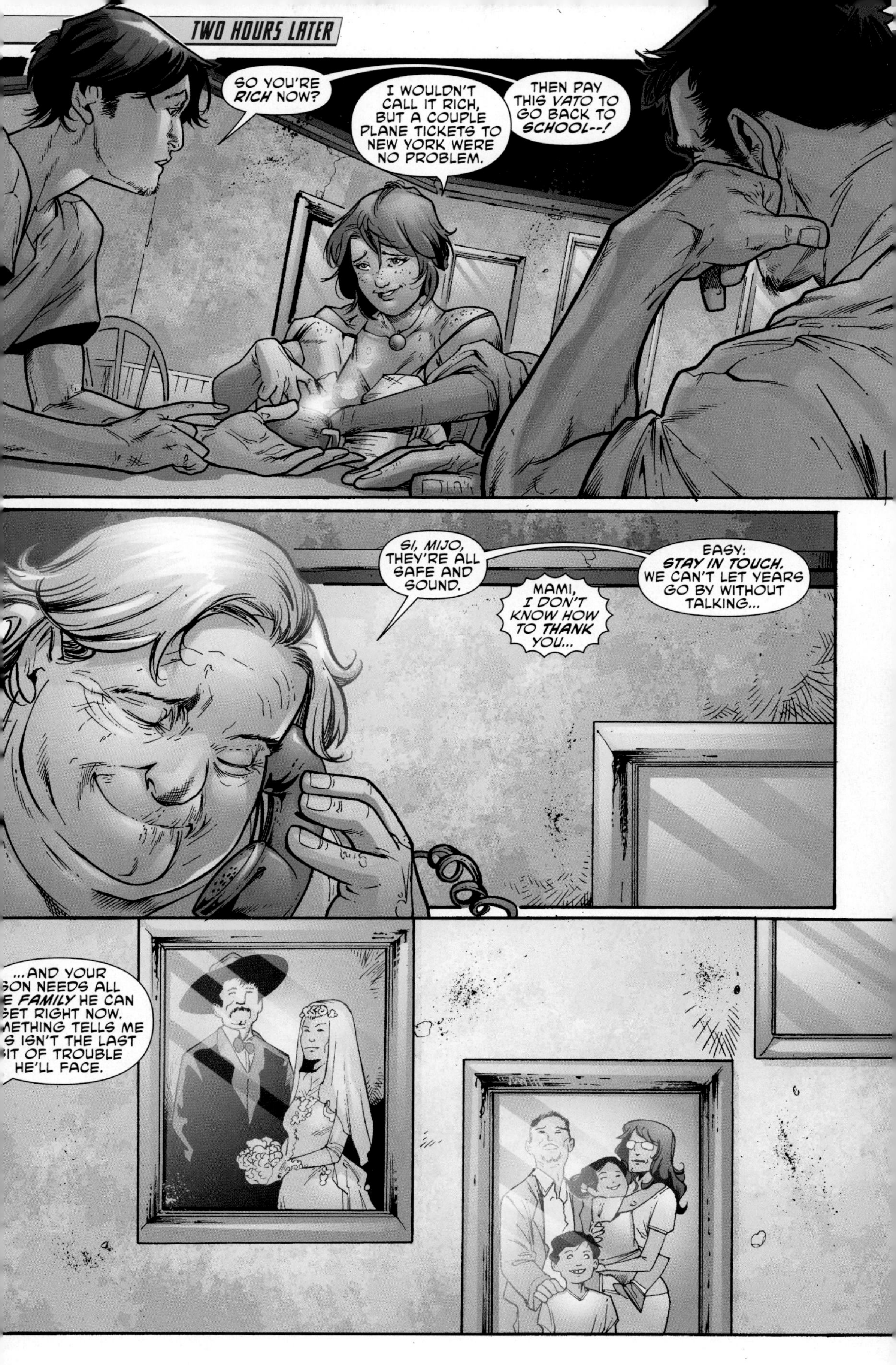
TWO HOURS LATER
SO YOU'RE RICH NOW?
I WOULDN'T CALL IT RICH, BUT A COUPLE PLANE TICKETS TO NEW YORK WERE NO PROBLEM.
THEN PAY THIS VATO TO GO BACK TO SCHOOL--!
SI, MIJO, THEY'RE ALL SAFE AND SOUND.
MAMI, I DON'T KNOW HOW TO THANK YOU...
EASY: STAY IN TOUCH. WE CAN'T LET YEARS GO BY WITHOUT TALKING...
...AND YOUR
NEEDS ALL
FAMILY HE CAN
GET RIGHT NOW.
TELLS ME
ISN'T THE LAST
OF TROUBLE
HE'LL FACE.

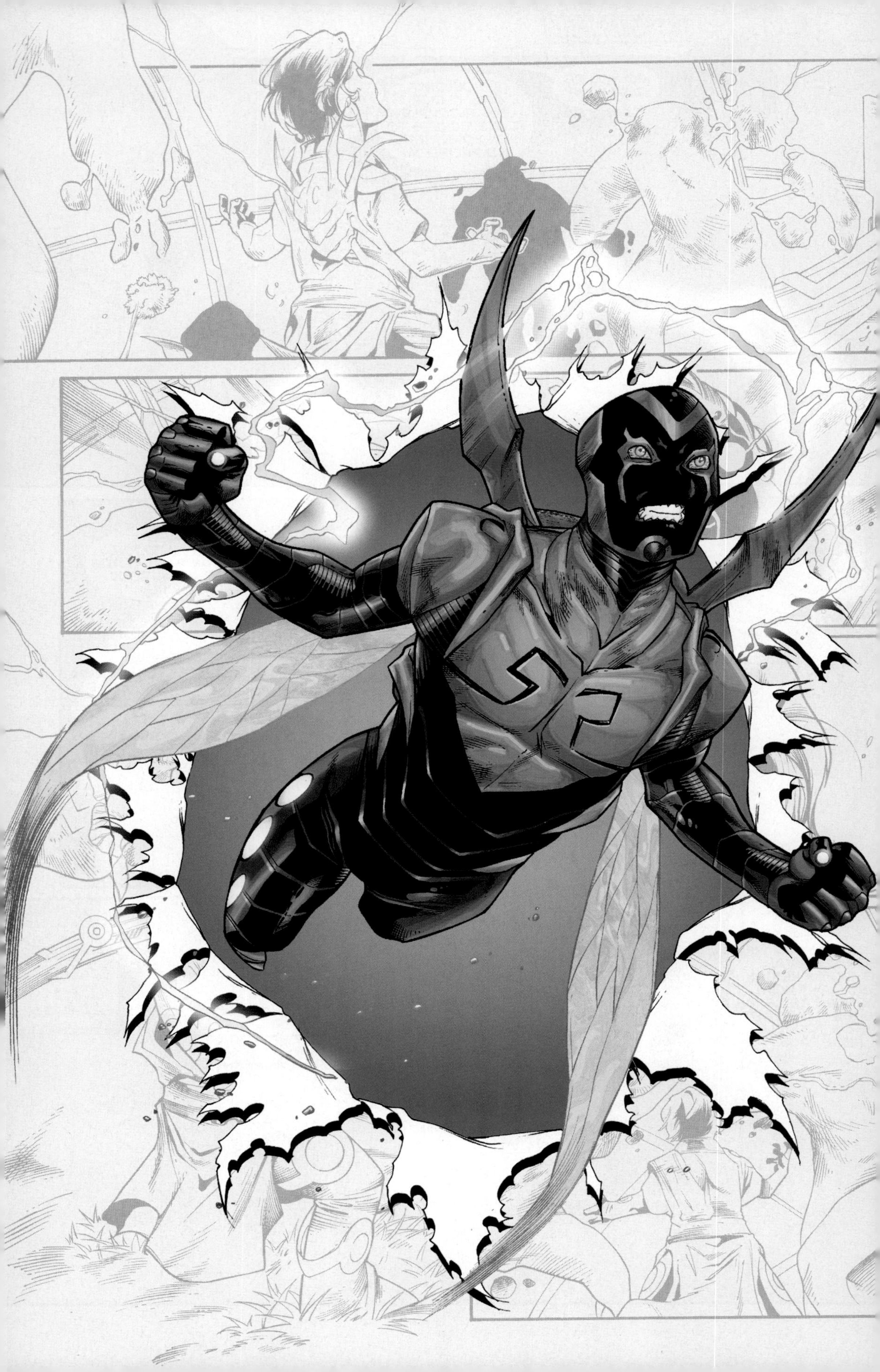

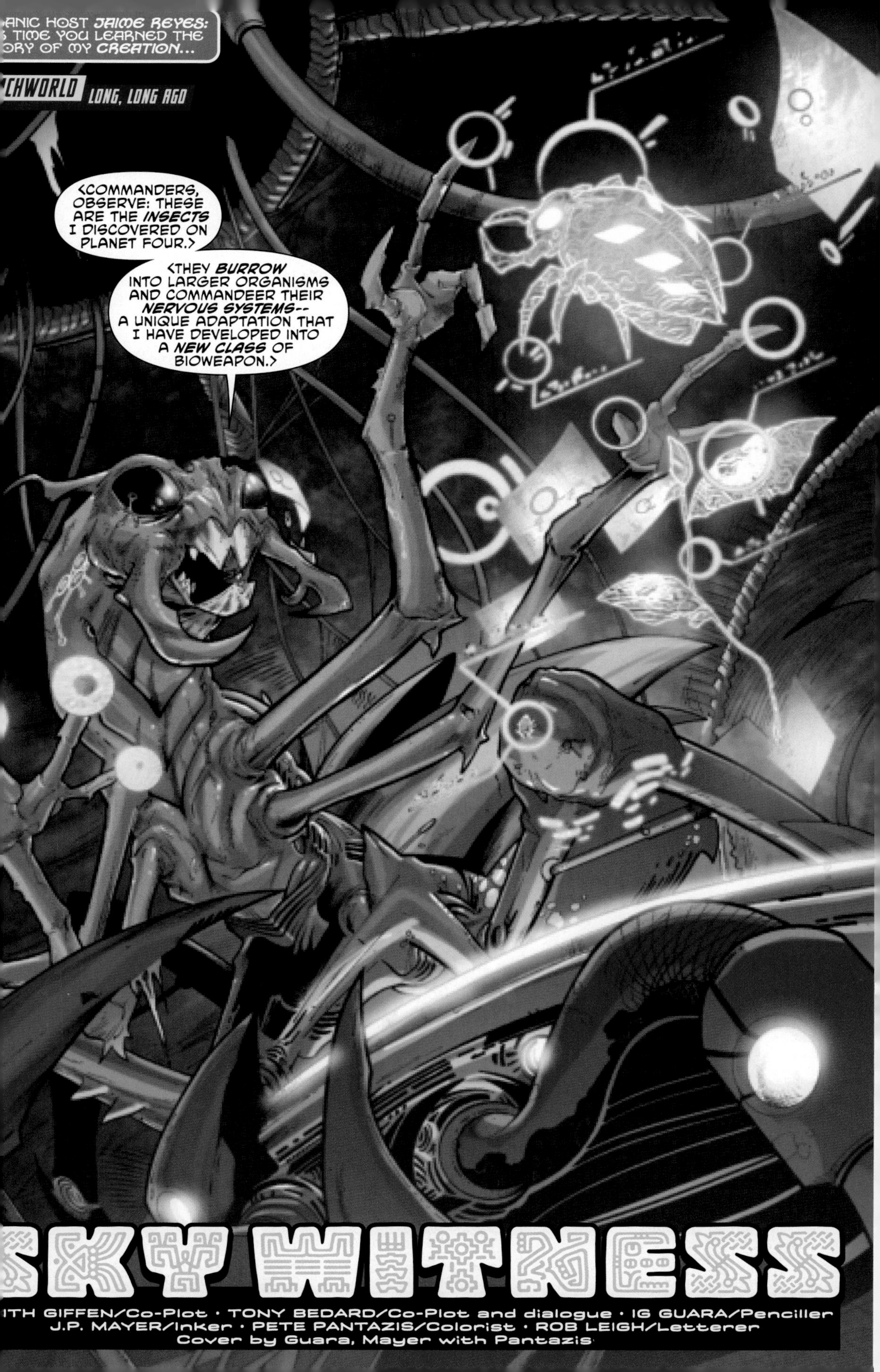
ANIC HOST JAIME REYES: S TIME YOU LEARNED THE ORY OF MY CREATION...
CHWORLD
LONG, LONG AGO
<COMMANDERS, OBSERVE: THESE ARE THE INSECTS I DISCOVERED ON PLANET FOUR.>
<THEY BURROW INTO LARGER ORGANISMS AND COMMANDEER THEIR NERVOUS SYSTEMS-- A UNIQUE ADAPTATION THAT I HAVE DEVELOPED INTO A NEW CLASS OF BIOWEAPON.>
SKY WITNESS
ITH GIFFEN/Co-Plot · TONY BEDARD/Co-Plot and dialogue · IG GUARA/Penciller
J.P. MAYER/Inker · PETE PANTAZIS/Colorist · ROB LEIGH/Letterer
Cover by Guara, Mayer with Pantazis

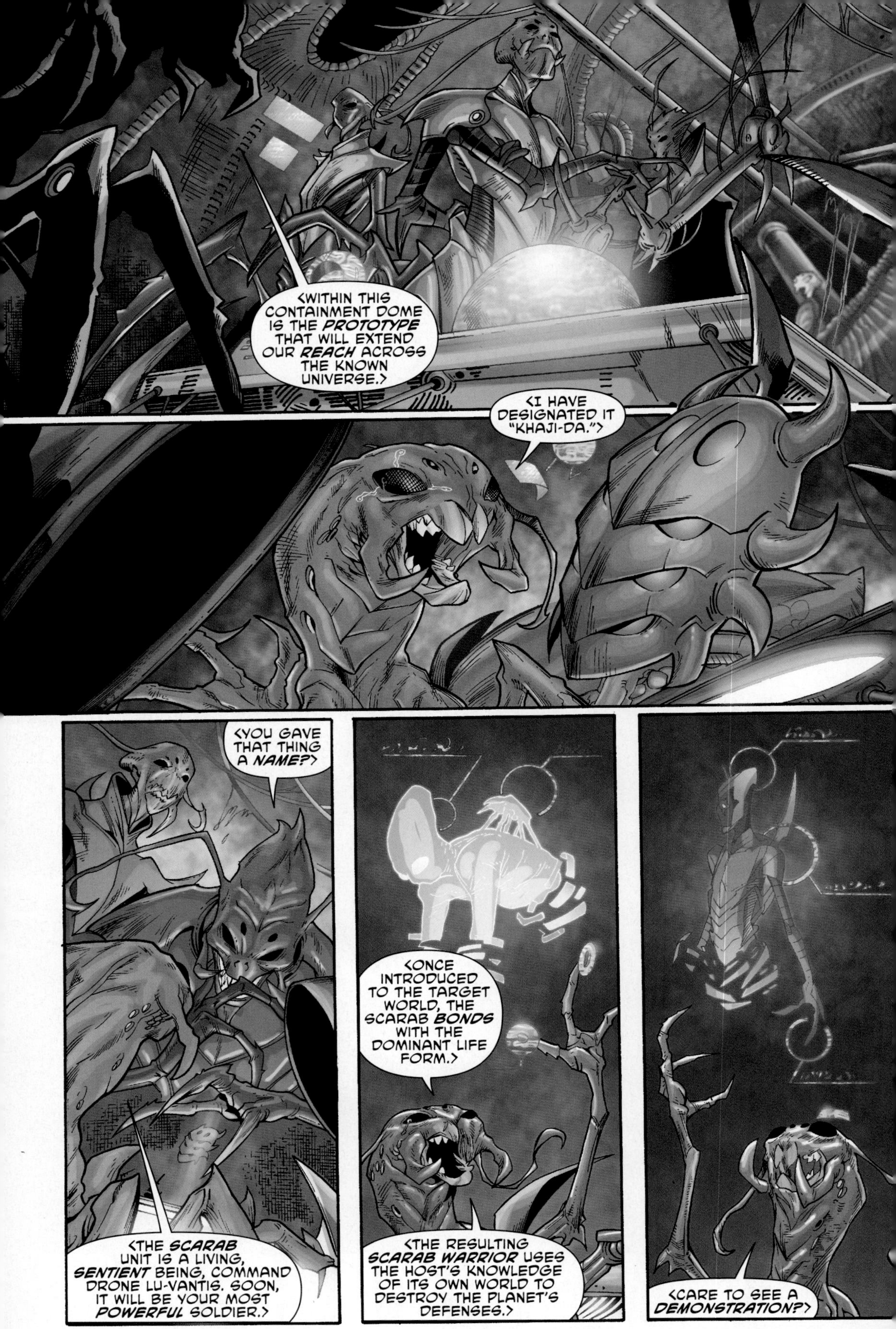
<WITHIN THIS CONTAINMENT DOME IS THE PROTOTYPE THAT WILL EXTEND OUR REACH ACROSS THE KNOWN UNIVERSE.>
<I HAVE DESIGNATED IT "KHAJI-DA.">
<YOU GAVE THAT THING A NAME?>
<THE SCARAB UNIT IS A LIVING, SENTIENT BEING, COMMAND DRONE LU-VANTIS. SOON, IT WILL BE YOUR MOST POWERFUL SOLDIER.>
<ONCE INTRODUCED TO THE TARGET WORLD, THE SCARAB BONDS WITH THE DOMINANT LIFE FORM.>
<THE RESULTING SCARAB WARRIOR USES THE HOST'S KNOWLEDGE OF ITS OWN WORLD TO DESTROY THE PLANET'S DEFENSES.>
<CARE TO SEE A DEMONSTRATION?>

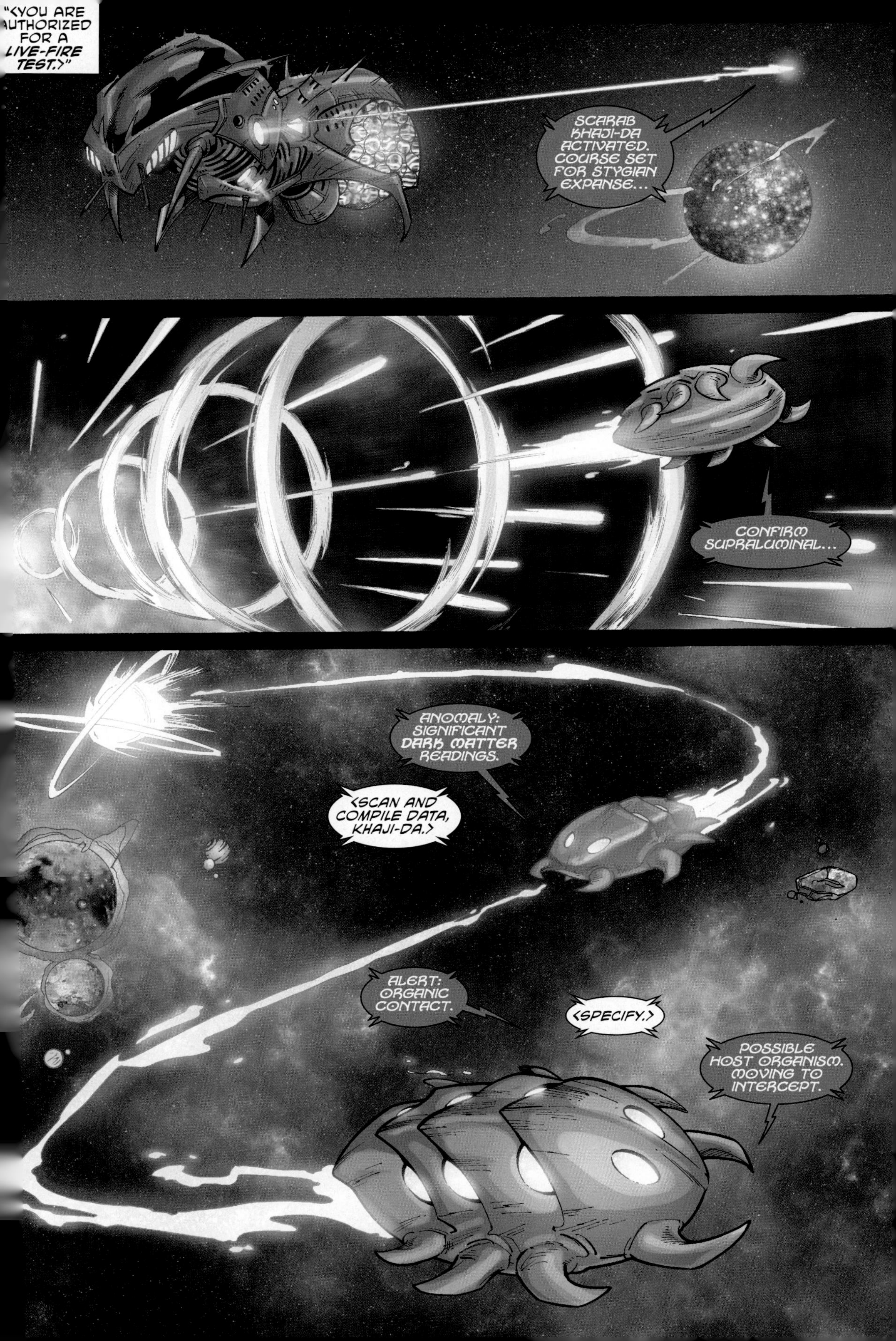
"<YOU ARE AUTHORIZED FOR A LIVE-FIRE TEST.>"
SCARAB KHAJI-DA ACTIVATED. COURSE SET FOR STYGIAN EXPANSE...
CONFIRM SUPRALUMINAL...
ANOMALY: SIGNIFICANT DARK MATTER READINGS.
<SCAN AND COMPILE DATA, KHAJI-DA.>
ALERT: ORGANIC CONTACT.
<SPECIFY.>
POSSIBLE HOST ORGANISM. MOVING TO INTERCEPT.

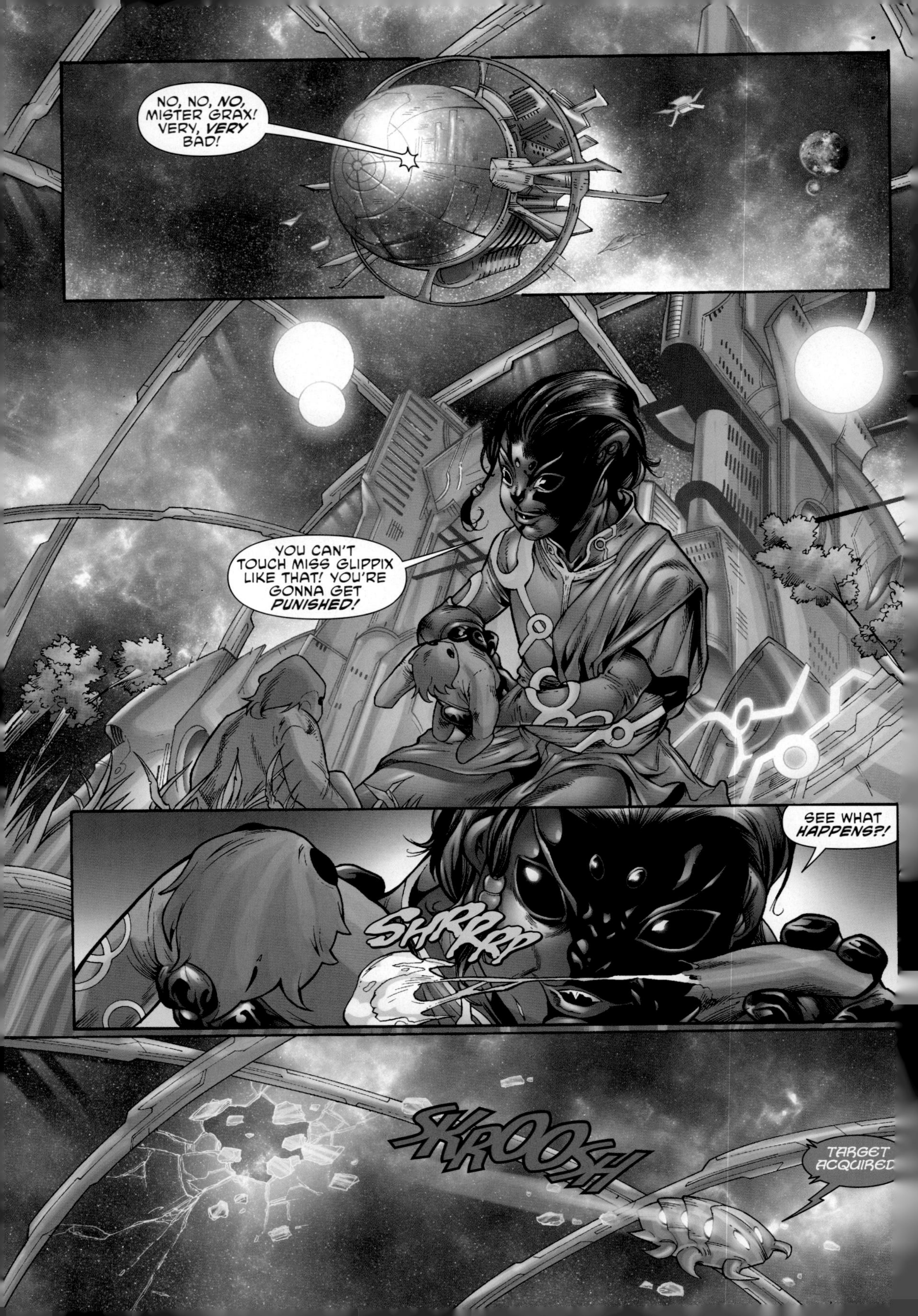
NO, NO, *NO*, MISTER GRAX! VERY, ***VERY*** BAD!
YOU CAN'T TOUCH MISS GLIPPIX LIKE THAT! YOU'RE GONNA GET ***PUNISHED!***
SHRRRP
SEE WHAT ***HAPPENS?!***
SKROOSH
TARGET ACQUIRED

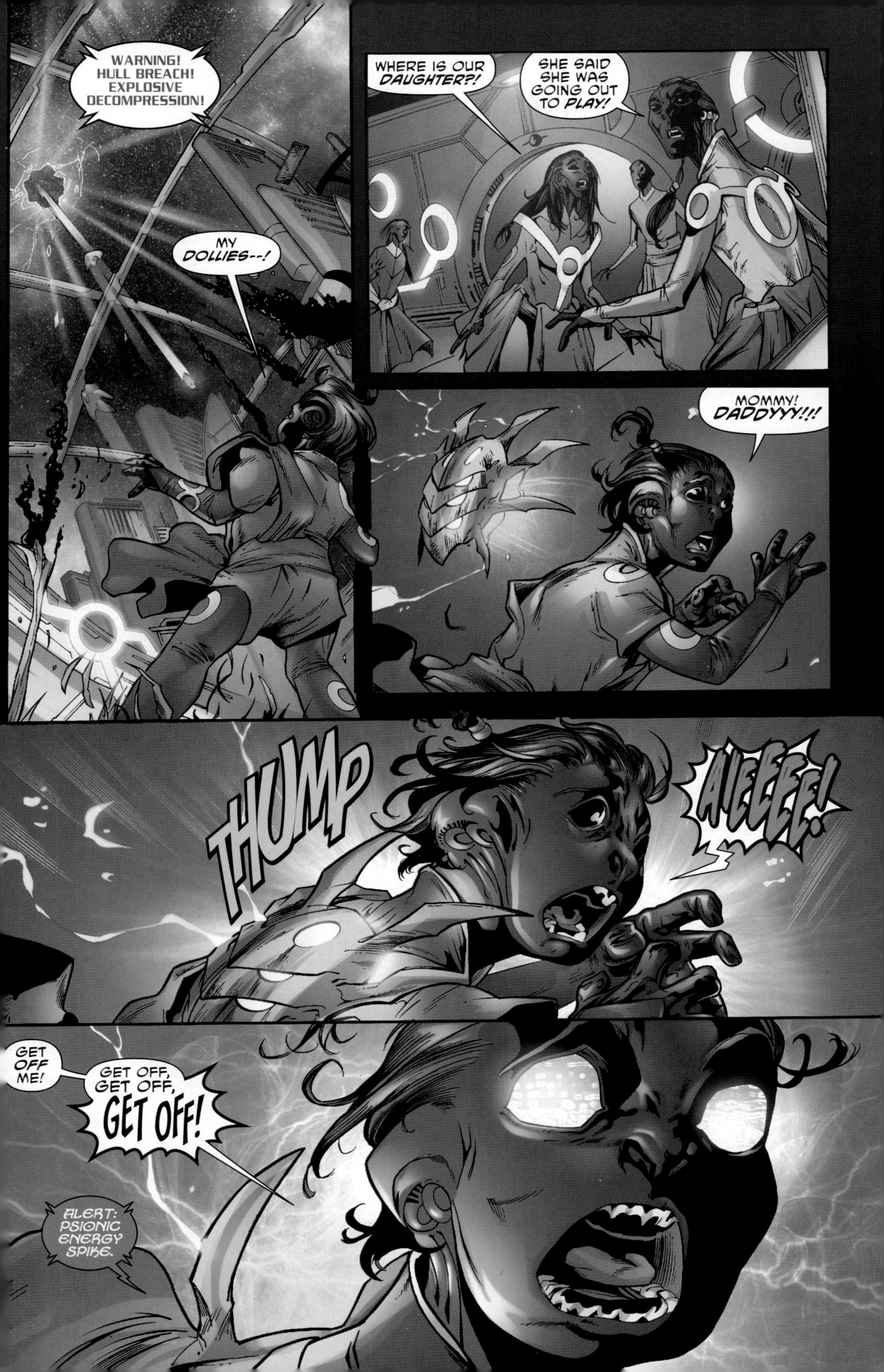

WARNING! HULL BREACH! EXPLOSIVE DECOMPRESSION!
MY DOLLIES--!
WHERE IS OUR DAUGHTER?!
SHE SAID SHE WAS GOING OUT TO PLAY!
MOMMY! DADDYYY!!!
THUMP
AIEEEE!
GET OFF ME!
GET OFF, GET OFF, GET OFF!
ALERT: PSIONIC ENERGY SPIKE.

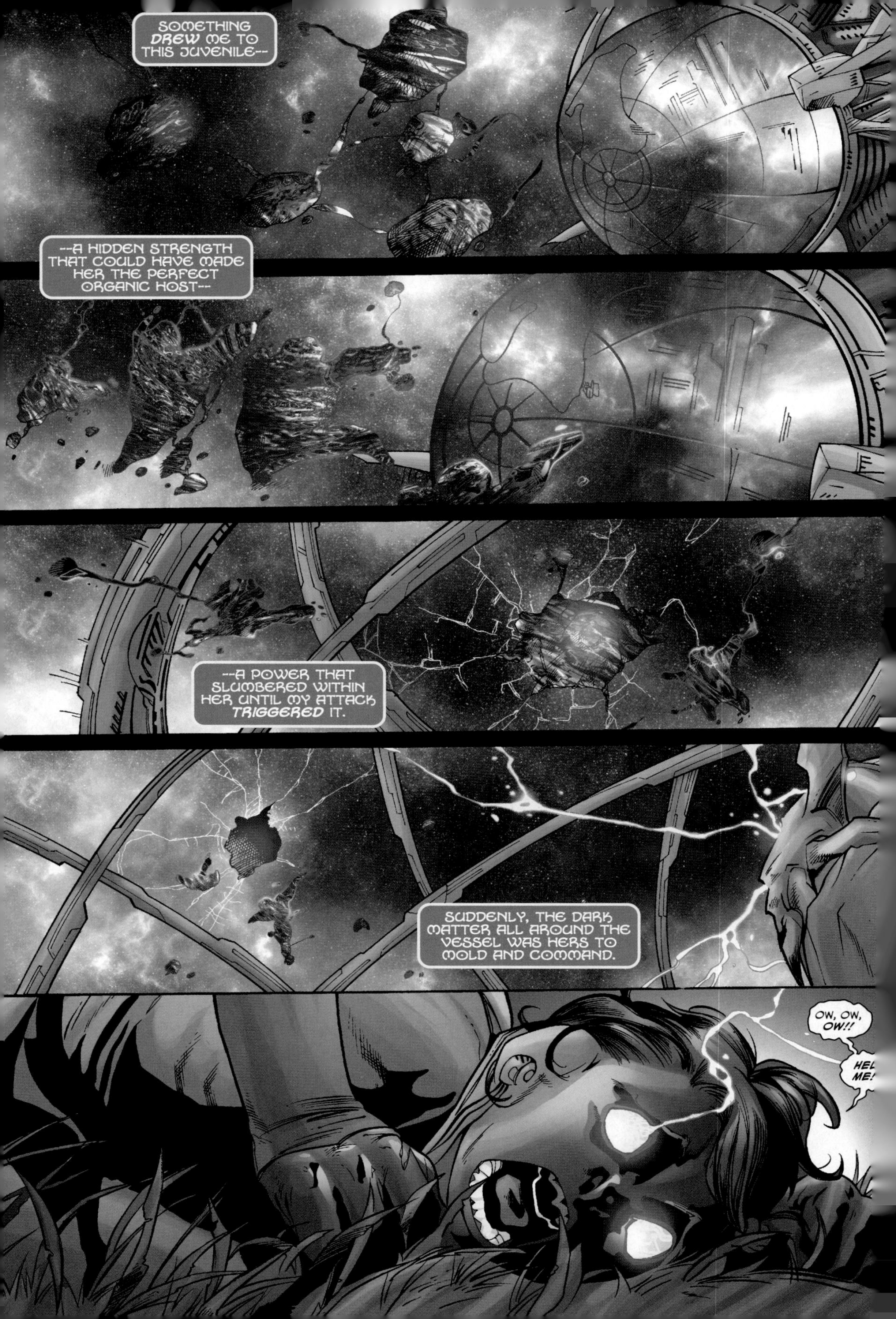
SOMETHING DREW ME TO THIS JUVENILE--
--A HIDDEN STRENGTH THAT COULD HAVE MADE HER THE PERFECT ORGANIC HOST--
--A POWER THAT SLUMBERED WITHIN HER UNTIL MY ATTACK TRIGGERED IT.
SUDDENLY, THE DARK MATTER ALL AROUND THE VESSEL WAS HERS TO MOLD AND COMMAND.
OW, OW, OW!!
HEL ME!

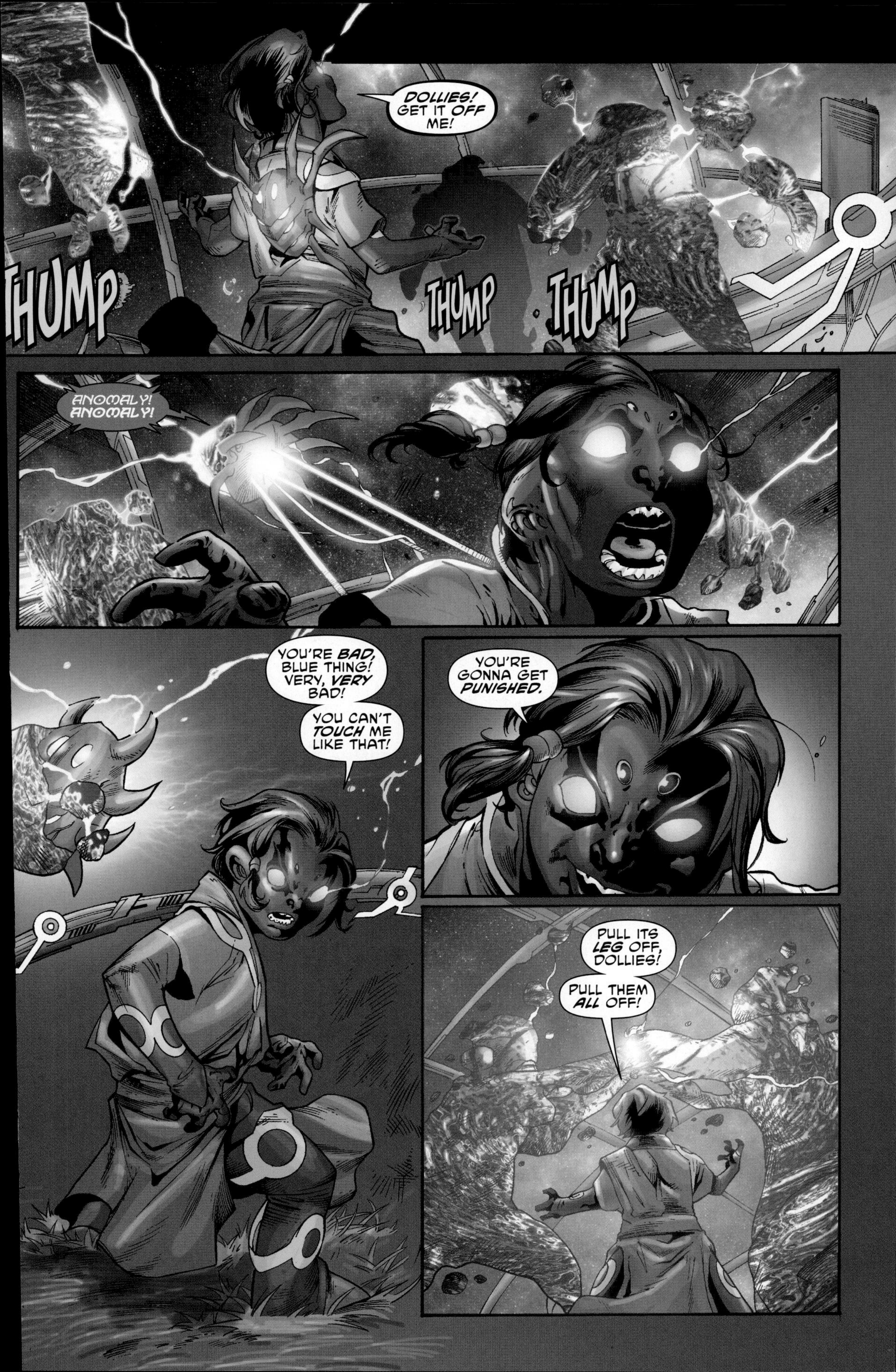
DOLLIES! GET IT OFF ME!
THUMP
THUMP
THUMP
ANOMALY! ANOMALY!
YOU'RE BAD, BLUE THING! VERY, VERY BAD!
YOU CAN'T TOUCH ME LIKE THAT!
YOU'RE GONNA GET PUNISHED.
PULL ITS LEG OFF, DOLLIES!
PULL THEM ALL OFF!

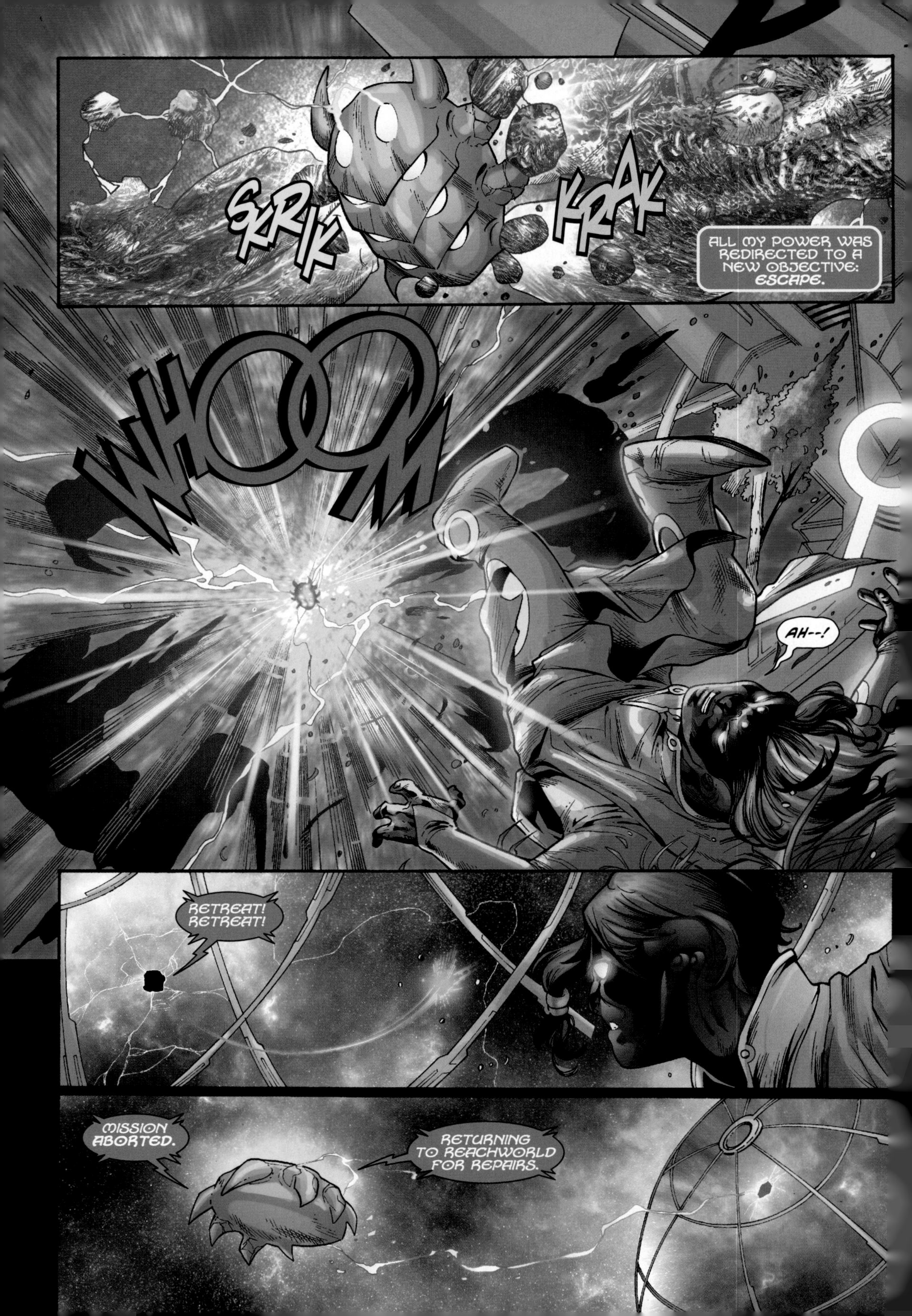
SKRIK
KRAK
ALL MY POWER WAS REDIRECTED TO A NEW OBJECTIVE: ESCAPE.
WHOOM
AH--!
RETREAT! RETREAT!
MISSION ABORTED.
RETURNING TO REACHWORLD FOR REPAIRS.

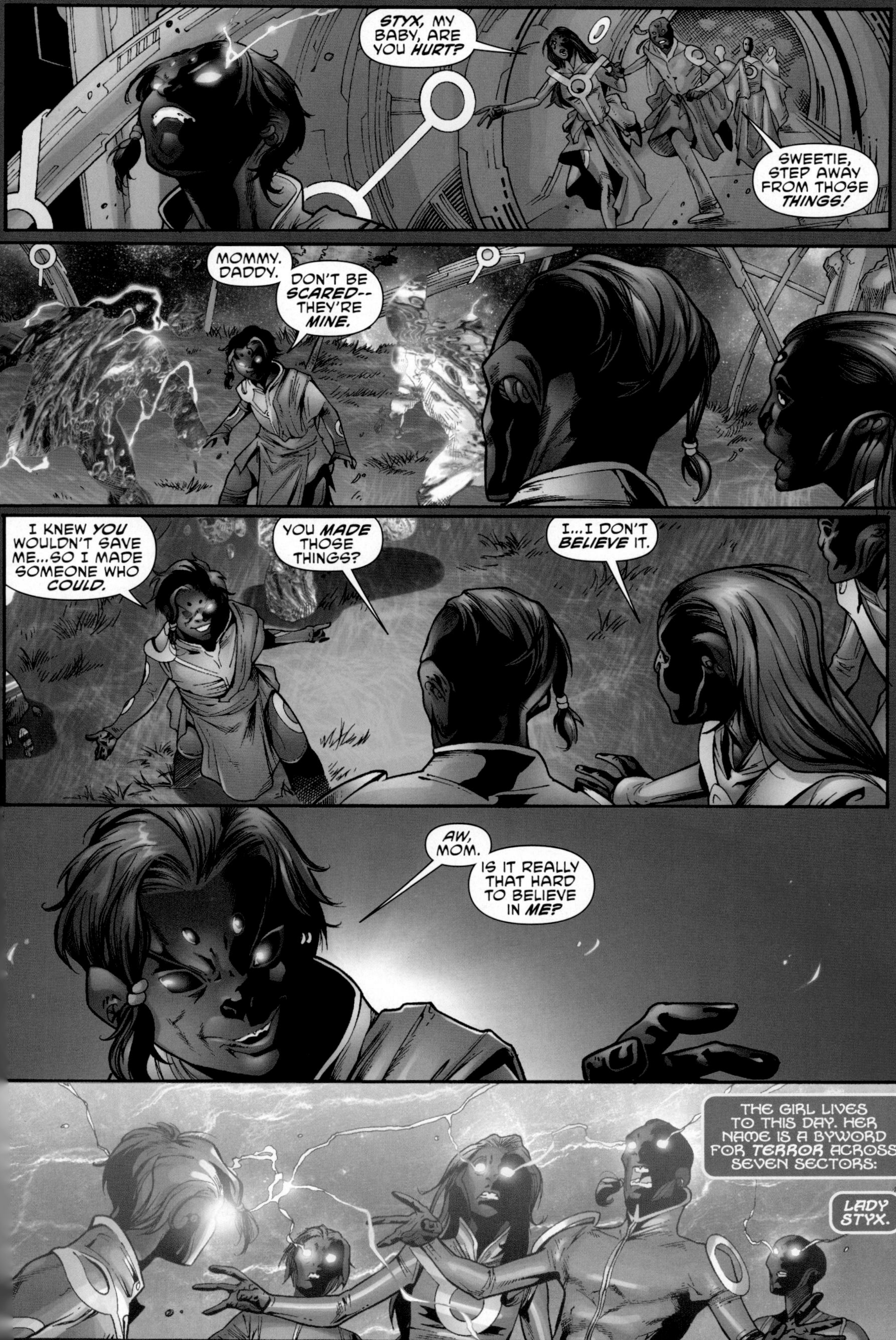
STYX, MY BABY, ARE YOU HURT?
SWEETIE, STEP AWAY FROM THOSE THINGS!
MOMMY. DADDY.
DON'T BE SCARED-- THEY'RE MINE.
I KNEW YOU WOULDN'T SAVE ME...SO I MADE SOMEONE WHO COULD.
YOU MADE THOSE THINGS?
I...I DON'T BELIEVE IT.
AW, MOM.
IS IT REALLY THAT HARD TO BELIEVE IN ME?
THE GIRL LIVES TO THIS DAY. HER NAME IS A BYWORD FOR TERROR ACROSS SEVEN SECTORS:
LADY STYX.

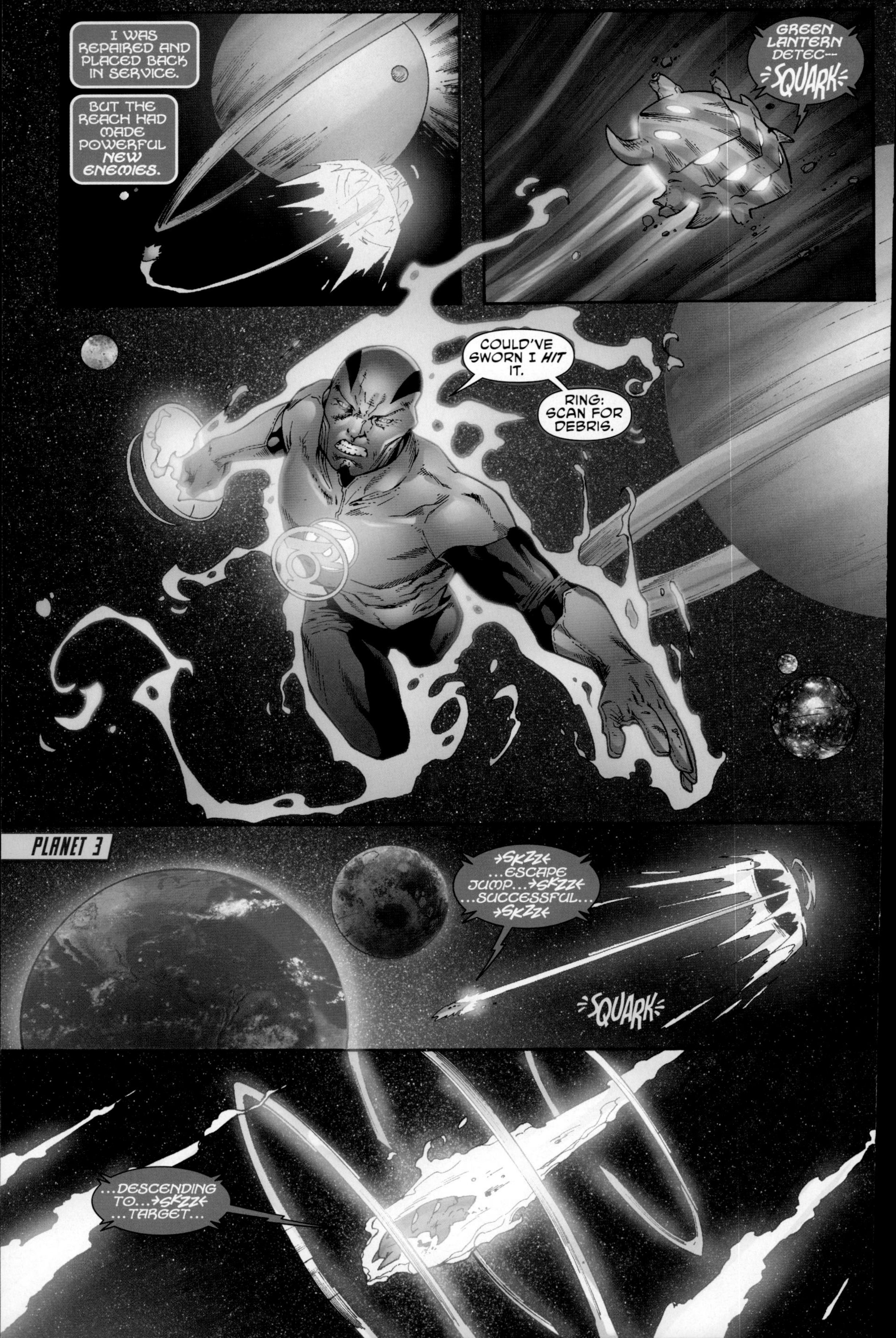
I WAS REPAIRED AND PLACED BACK IN SERVICE.
BUT THE REACH HAD MADE POWERFUL NEW ENEMIES.
GREEN LANTERN DETEC---
SQUARK
COULD'VE SWORN I HIT IT.
RING: SCAN FOR DEBRIS.
PLANET 3
SKZZ ...ESCAPE JUMP... SKZZ ...SUCCESSFUL... SKZZ
SQUARK
...DESCENDING TO... SKZZ ...TARGET...

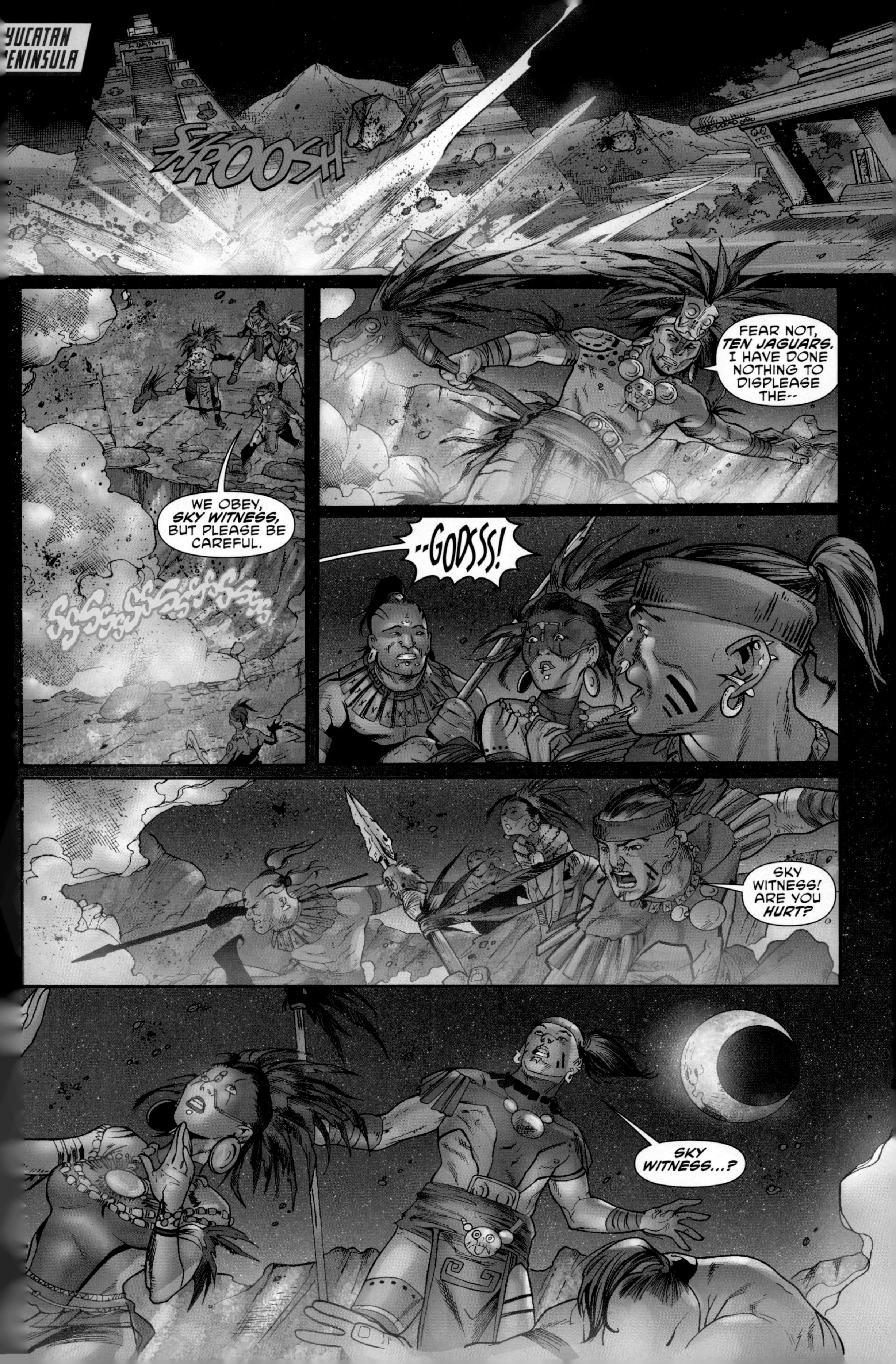
YUCATAN PENINSULA
SKROOSH
WE OBEY, SKY WITNESS, BUT PLEASE BE CAREFUL.
SSSSSSSSSSSSS
FEAR NOT, TEN JAGUARS. I HAVE DONE NOTHING TO DISPLEASE THE--
--GODSSS!
SKY WITNESS! ARE YOU HURT?
SKY WITNESS...?

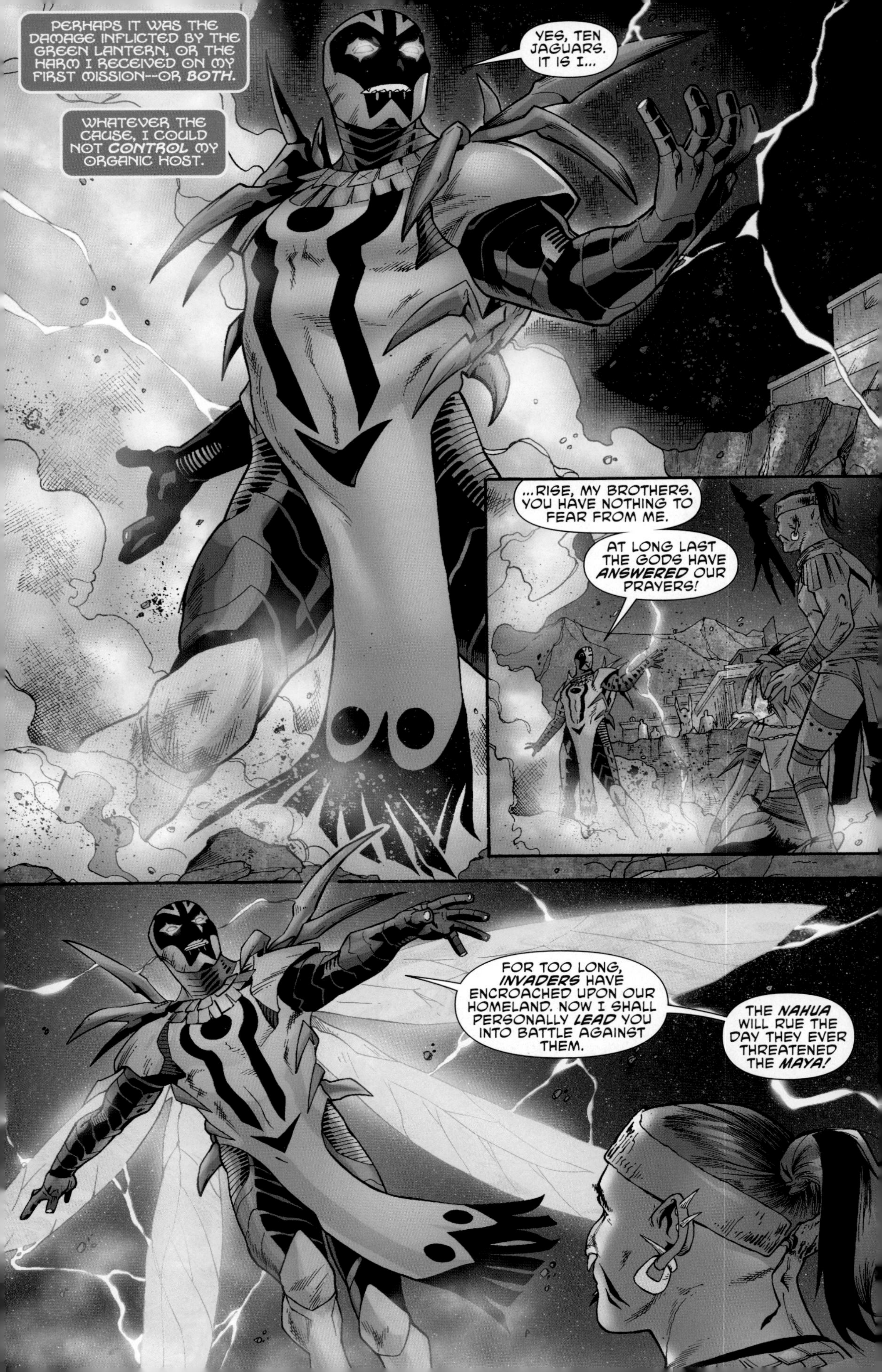
PERHAPS IT WAS THE DAMAGE INFLICTED BY THE GREEN LANTERN, OR THE HARM I RECEIVED ON MY FIRST MISSION--OR *BOTH*.
WHATEVER THE CAUSE, I COULD NOT *CONTROL* MY ORGANIC HOST.
YES, TEN JAGUARS. IT IS I...
...RISE, MY BROTHERS. YOU HAVE NOTHING TO FEAR FROM ME.
AT LONG LAST THE GODS HAVE *ANSWERED* OUR PRAYERS!
FOR TOO LONG, *INVADERS* HAVE ENCROACHED UPON OUR HOMELAND. NOW I SHALL PERSONALLY *LEAD* YOU INTO BATTLE AGAINST THEM.
THE *NAHUA* WILL RUE THE DAY THEY EVER THREATENED THE *MAYA!*

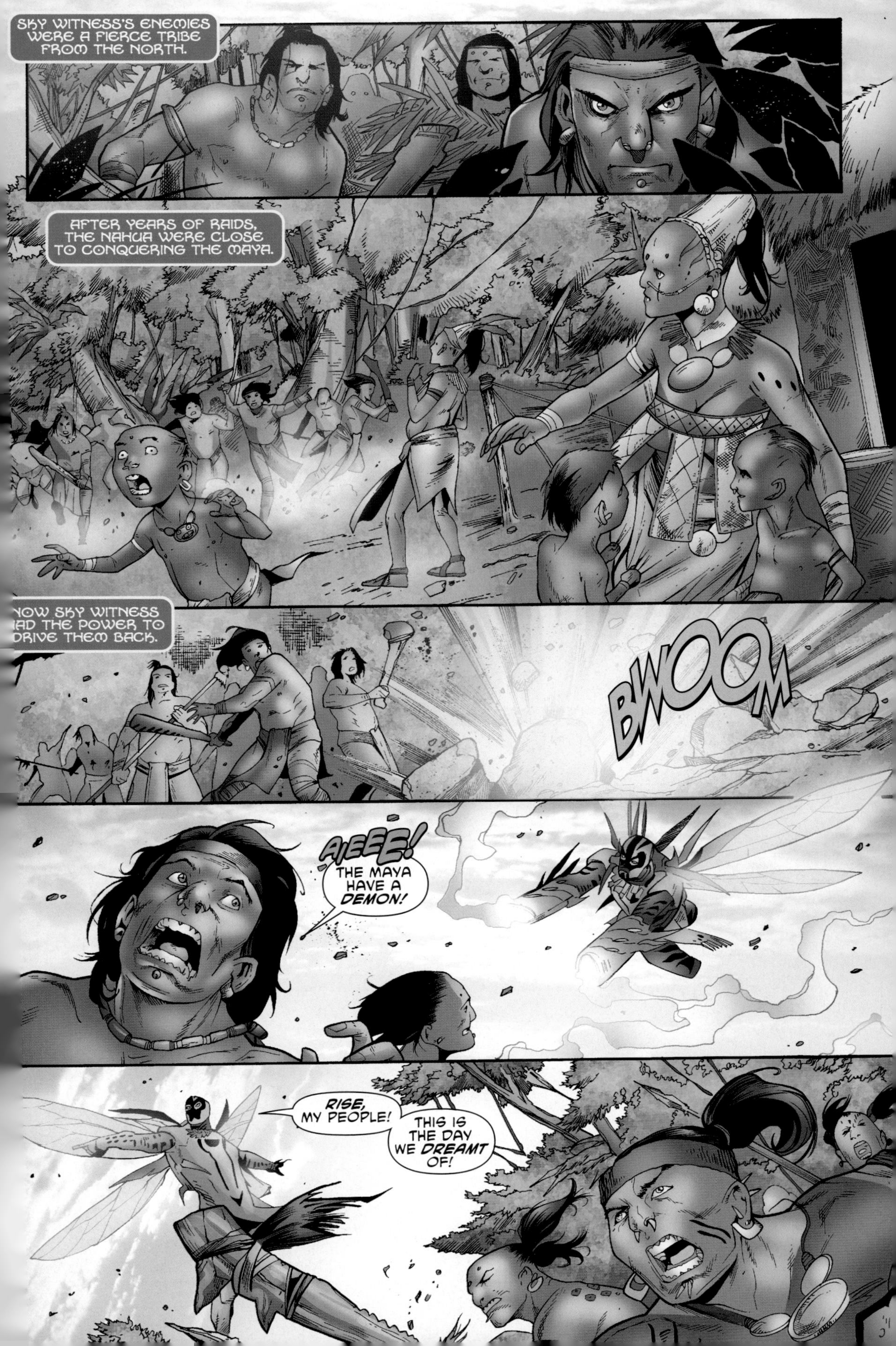
SKY WITNESS'S ENEMIES WERE A FIERCE TRIBE FROM THE NORTH.
AFTER YEARS OF RAIDS, THE NAHUA WERE CLOSE TO CONQUERING THE MAYA.
NOW SKY WITNESS HAD THE POWER TO DRIVE THEM BACK.
BWOOM
AIEEE! THE MAYA HAVE A DEMON!
RISE, MY PEOPLE!
THIS IS THE DAY WE DREAMT OF!

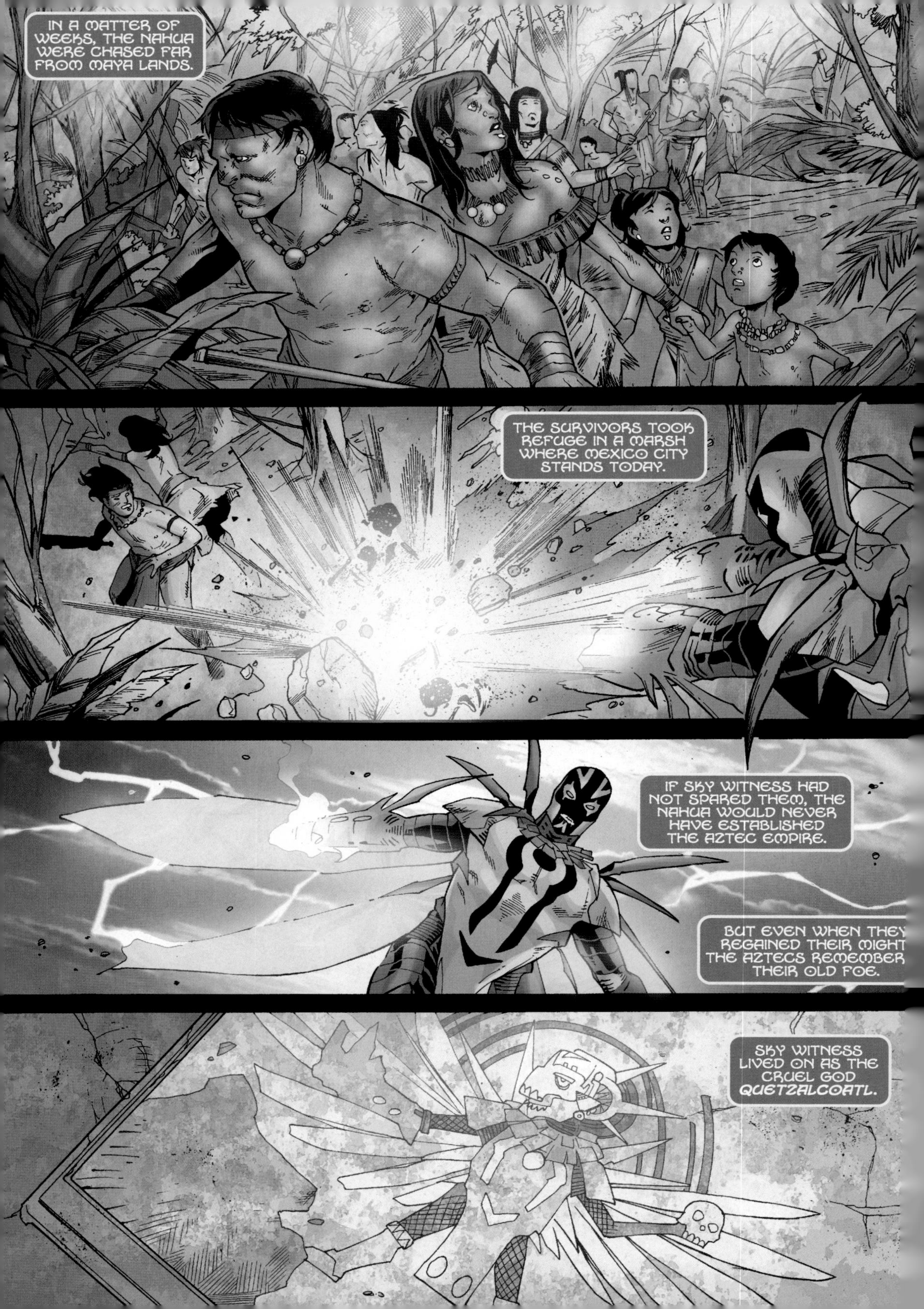
IN A MATTER OF WEEKS, THE NAHUA WERE CHASED FAR FROM MAYA LANDS.
THE SURVIVORS TOOK REFUGE IN A MARSH WHERE MEXICO CITY STANDS TODAY.
IF SKY WITNESS HAD NOT SPARED THEM, THE NAHUA WOULD NEVER HAVE ESTABLISHED THE AZTEC EMPIRE.
BUT EVEN WHEN THEY REGAINED THEIR MIGHT THE AZTECS REMEMBER THEIR OLD FOE.
SKY WITNESS LIVED ON AS THE CRUEL GOD *QUETZALCOATL*.

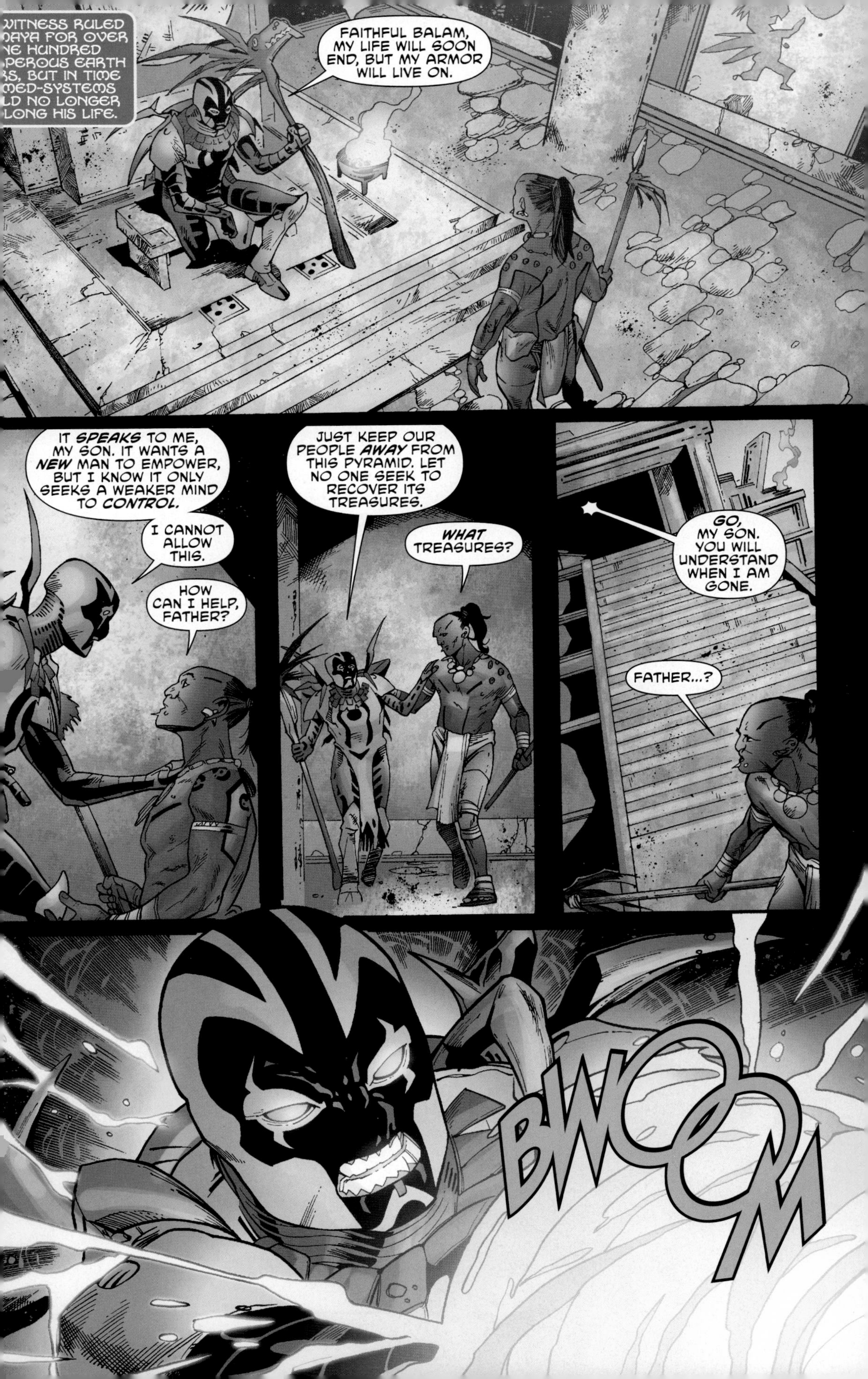
WITNESS RULED MAYA FOR OVER NE HUNDRED PEROUS EARTH KS, BUT IN TIME MED-SYSTEMS LD NO LONGER LONG HIS LIFE.
FAITHFUL BALAM, MY LIFE WILL SOON END, BUT MY ARMOR WILL LIVE ON.
IT SPEAKS TO ME, MY SON. IT WANTS A NEW MAN TO EMPOWER, BUT I KNOW IT ONLY SEEKS A WEAKER MIND TO CONTROL.
I CANNOT ALLOW THIS.
HOW CAN I HELP, FATHER?
JUST KEEP OUR PEOPLE AWAY FROM THIS PYRAMID. LET NO ONE SEEK TO RECOVER ITS TREASURES.
WHAT TREASURES?
GO, MY SON. YOU WILL UNDERSTAND WHEN I AM GONE.
FATHER...?
BWOOM

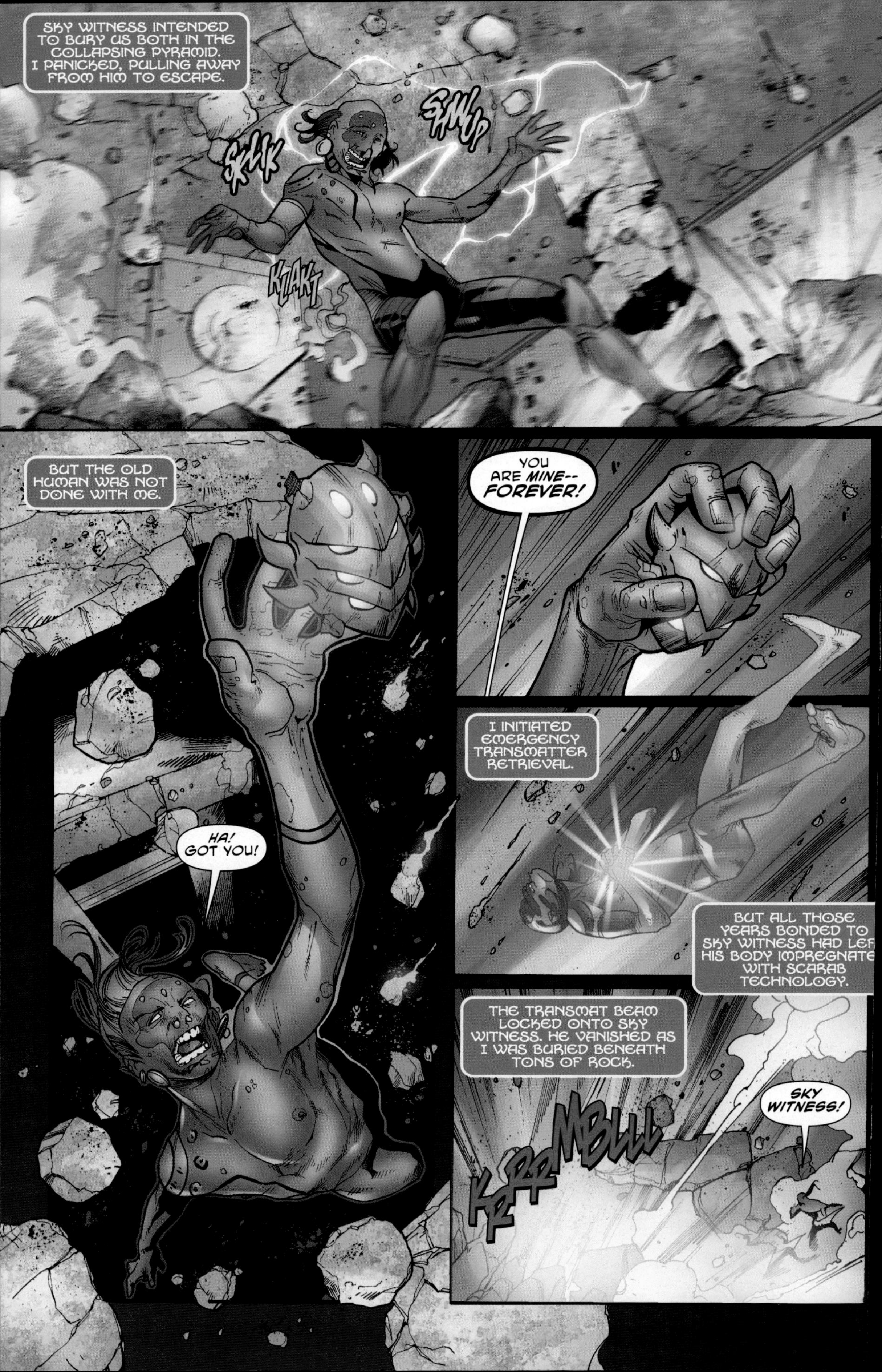
SKY WITNESS INTENDED TO BURY US BOTH IN THE COLLAPSING PYRAMID. I PANICKED, PULLING AWAY FROM HIM TO ESCAPE.
SKLIK
SHWUP
KLAKT
BUT THE OLD HUMAN WAS NOT DONE WITH ME.
HA! GOT YOU!
YOU ARE MINE-- FOREVER!
I INITIATED EMERGENCY TRANSMATTER RETRIEVAL.
BUT ALL THOSE YEARS BONDED TO SKY WITNESS HAD LEF
HIS BODY IMPREGNATE
WITH SCARAB TECHNOLOGY.
THE TRANSMAT BEAM LOCKED ONTO SKY WITNESS. HE VANISHED AS I WAS BURIED BENEATH TONS OF ROCK.
KRRRMBLLL
SKY WITNESS!

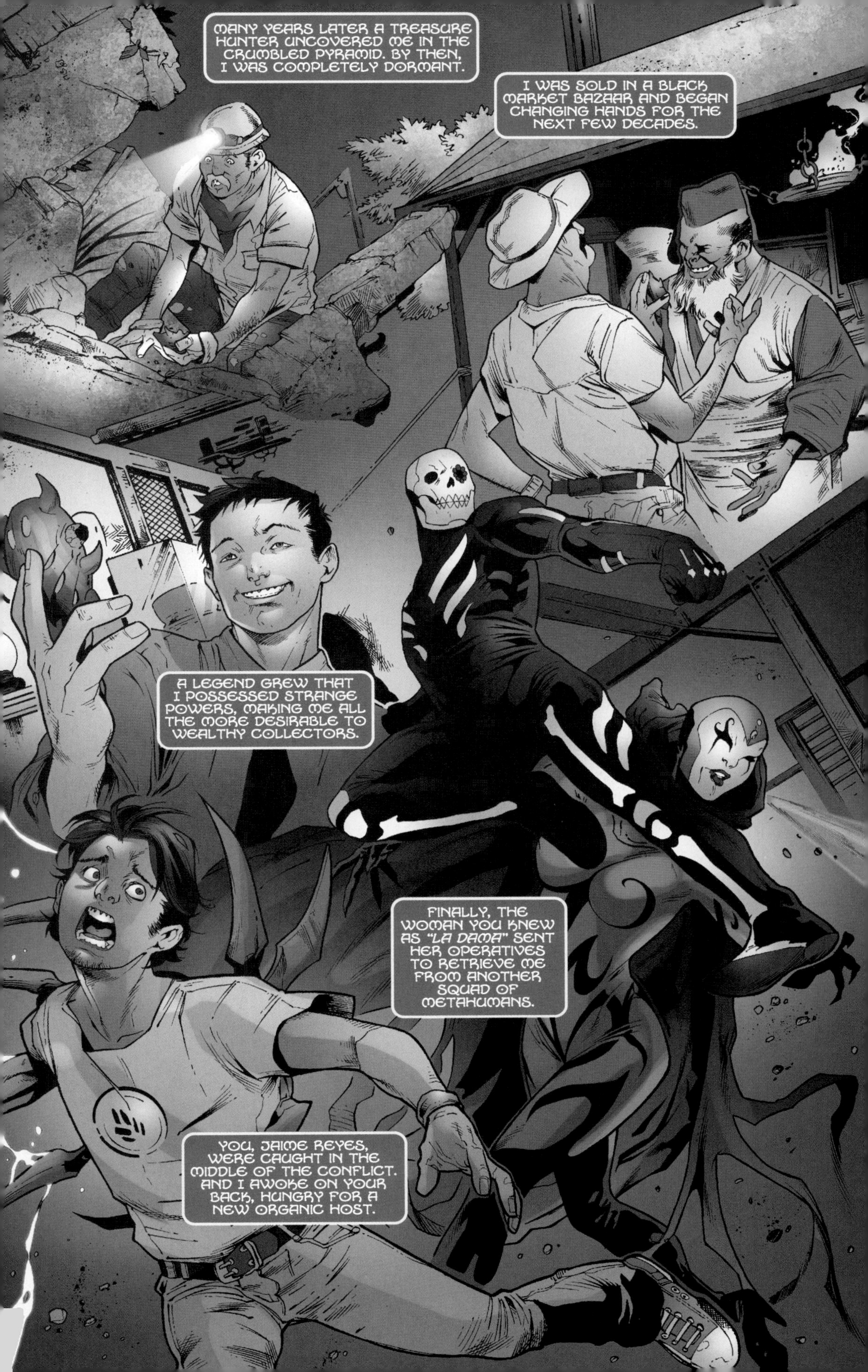
MANY YEARS LATER A TREASURE HUNTER UNCOVERED ME IN THE CRUMBLED PYRAMID. BY THEN, I WAS COMPLETELY DORMANT.
I WAS SOLD IN A BLACK MARKET BAZAAR AND BEGAN CHANGING HANDS FOR THE NEXT FEW DECADES.
A LEGEND GREW THAT I POSSESSED STRANGE POWERS, MAKING ME ALL THE MORE DESIRABLE TO WEALTHY COLLECTORS.
FINALLY, THE WOMAN YOU KNEW AS "LA DAMA" SENT HER OPERATIVES TO RETRIEVE ME FROM ANOTHER SQUAD OF METAHUMANS.
YOU, JAIME REYES, WERE CAUGHT IN THE MIDDLE OF THE CONFLICT. AND I AWOKE ON YOUR BACK, HUNGRY FOR A NEW ORGANIC HOST.

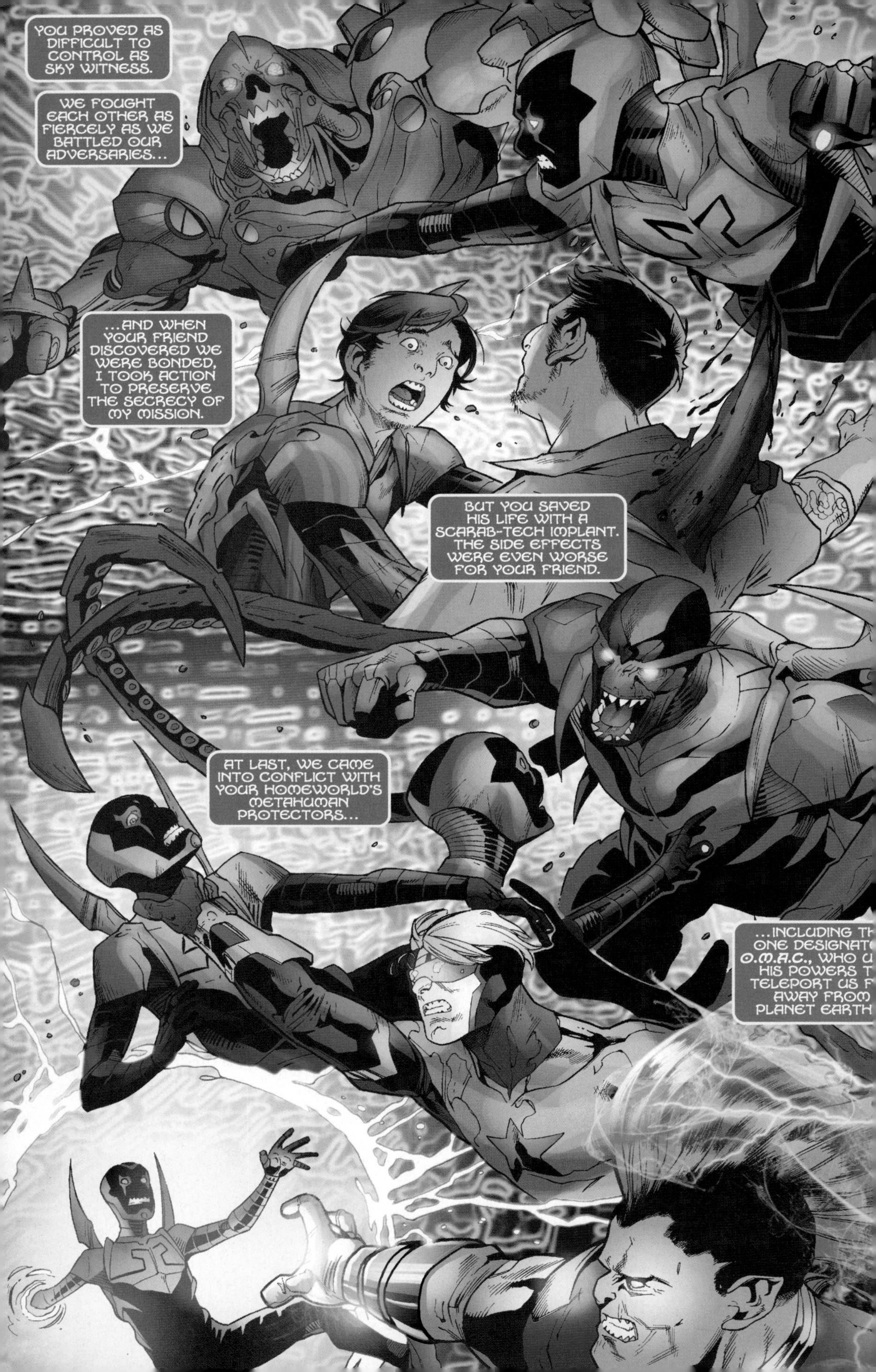
YOU PROVED AS DIFFICULT TO CONTROL AS SKY WITNESS.
WE FOUGHT EACH OTHER AS FIERCELY AS WE BATTLED OUR ADVERSARIES...
...AND WHEN YOUR FRIEND DISCOVERED WE WERE BONDED, I TOOK ACTION TO PRESERVE THE SECRECY OF MY MISSION.
BUT YOU SAVED HIS LIFE WITH A SCARAB-TECH IMPLANT. THE SIDE EFFECTS WERE EVEN WORSE FOR YOUR FRIEND.
AT LAST, WE CAME INTO CONFLICT WITH YOUR HOMEWORLD'S METAHUMAN PROTECTORS...
...INCLUDING TH ONE DESIGNATE O.M.A.C., WHO U HIS POWERS T TELEPORT US F AWAY FROM PLANET EARTH

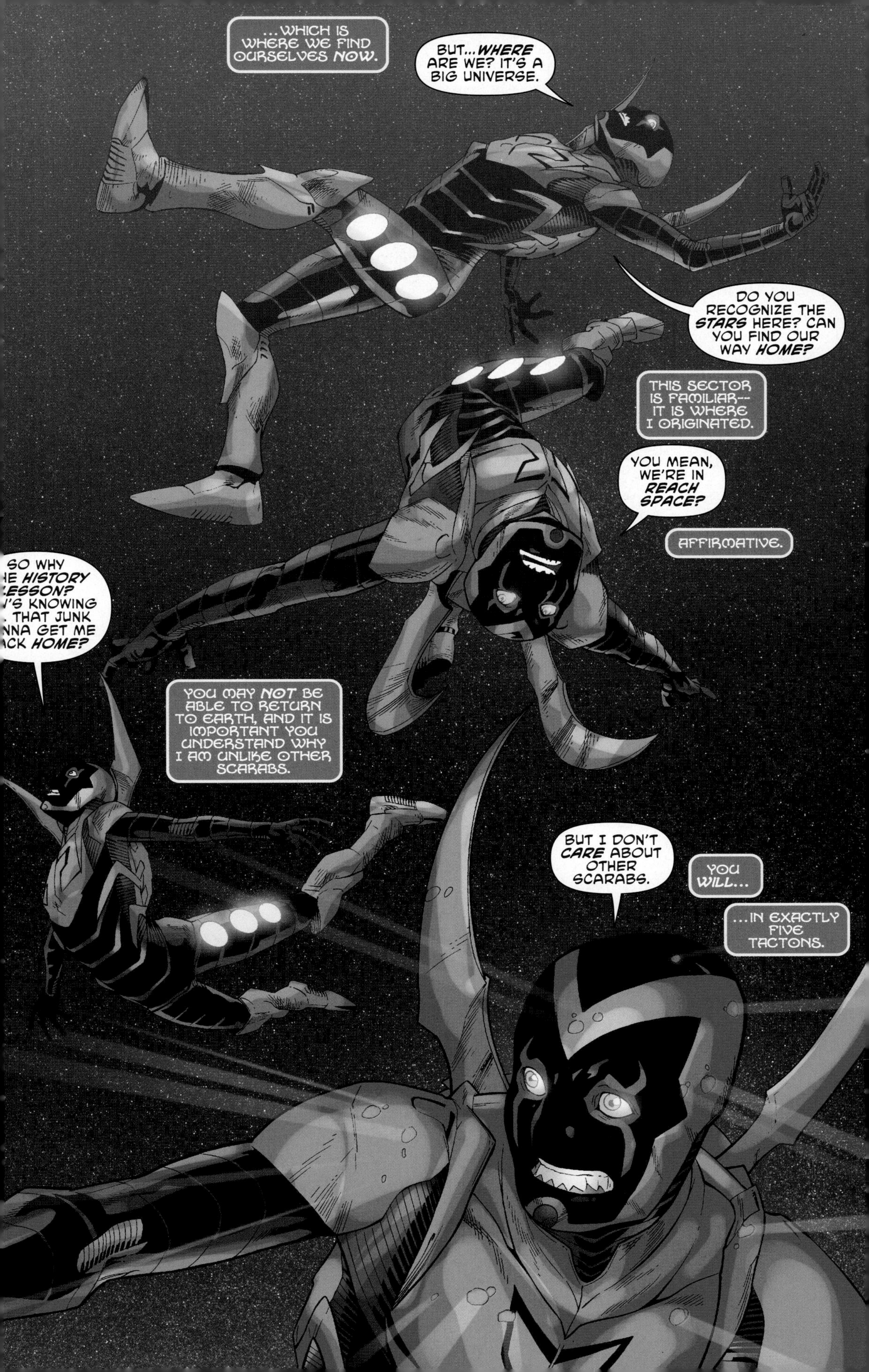
...WHICH IS WHERE WE FIND OURSELVES NOW.
BUT...WHERE ARE WE? IT'S A BIG UNIVERSE.
DO YOU RECOGNIZE THE STARS HERE? CAN YOU FIND OUR WAY HOME?
THIS SECTOR IS FAMILIAR-- IT IS WHERE I ORIGINATED.
YOU MEAN, WE'RE IN REACH SPACE?
AFFIRMATIVE.
SO WHY HE HISTORY LESSON? W'S KNOWING . THAT JUNK NNA GET ME ACK HOME?
YOU MAY NOT BE ABLE TO RETURN TO EARTH, AND IT IS IMPORTANT YOU UNDERSTAND WHY I AM UNLIKE OTHER SCARABS.
BUT I DON'T CARE ABOUT OTHER SCARABS.
YOU WILL...
...IN EXACTLY FIVE TACTONS.

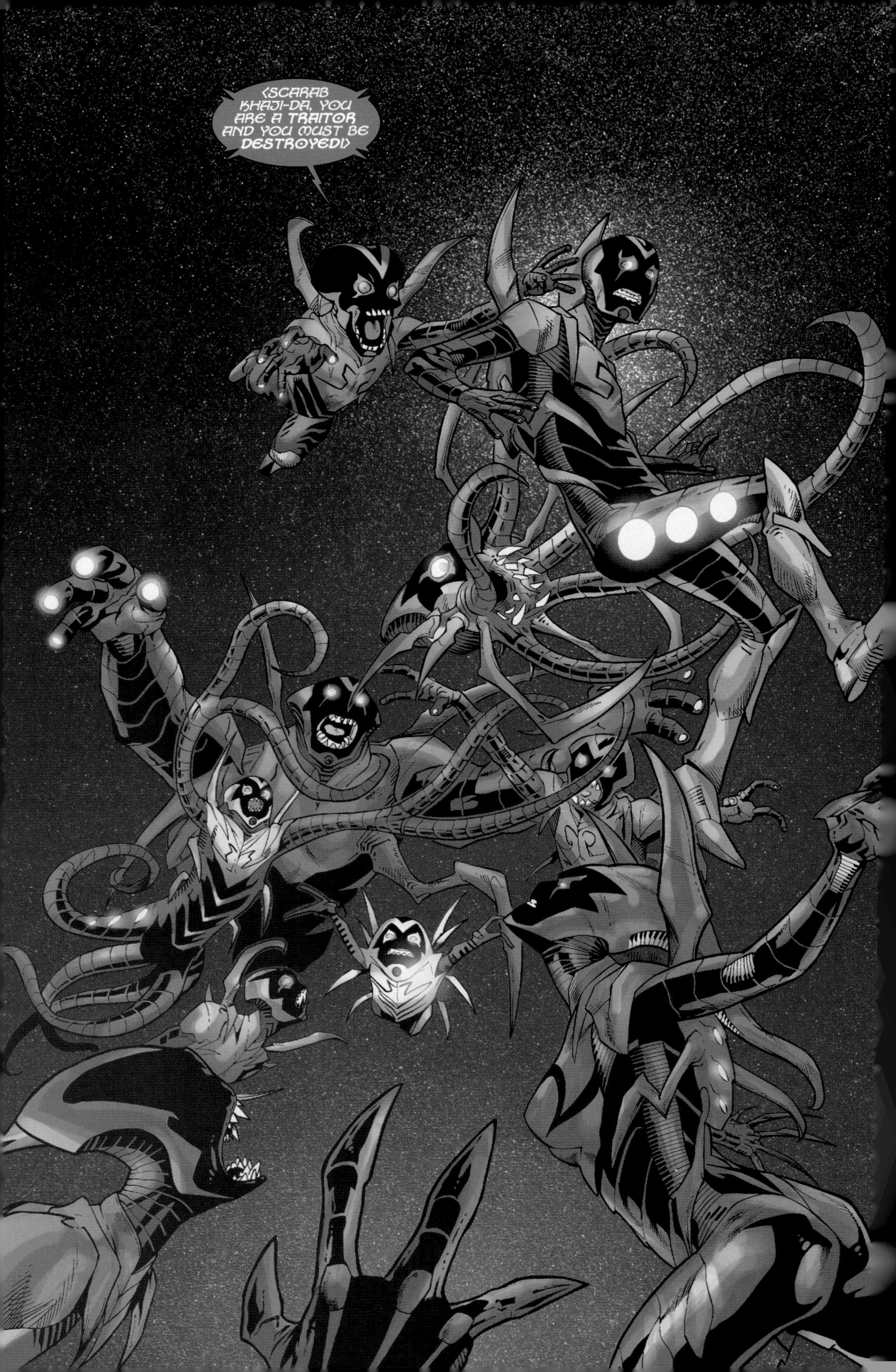

<SCARAB KHAJI-DA, YOU ARE A TRAITOR AND YOU MUST BE DESTROYED!>

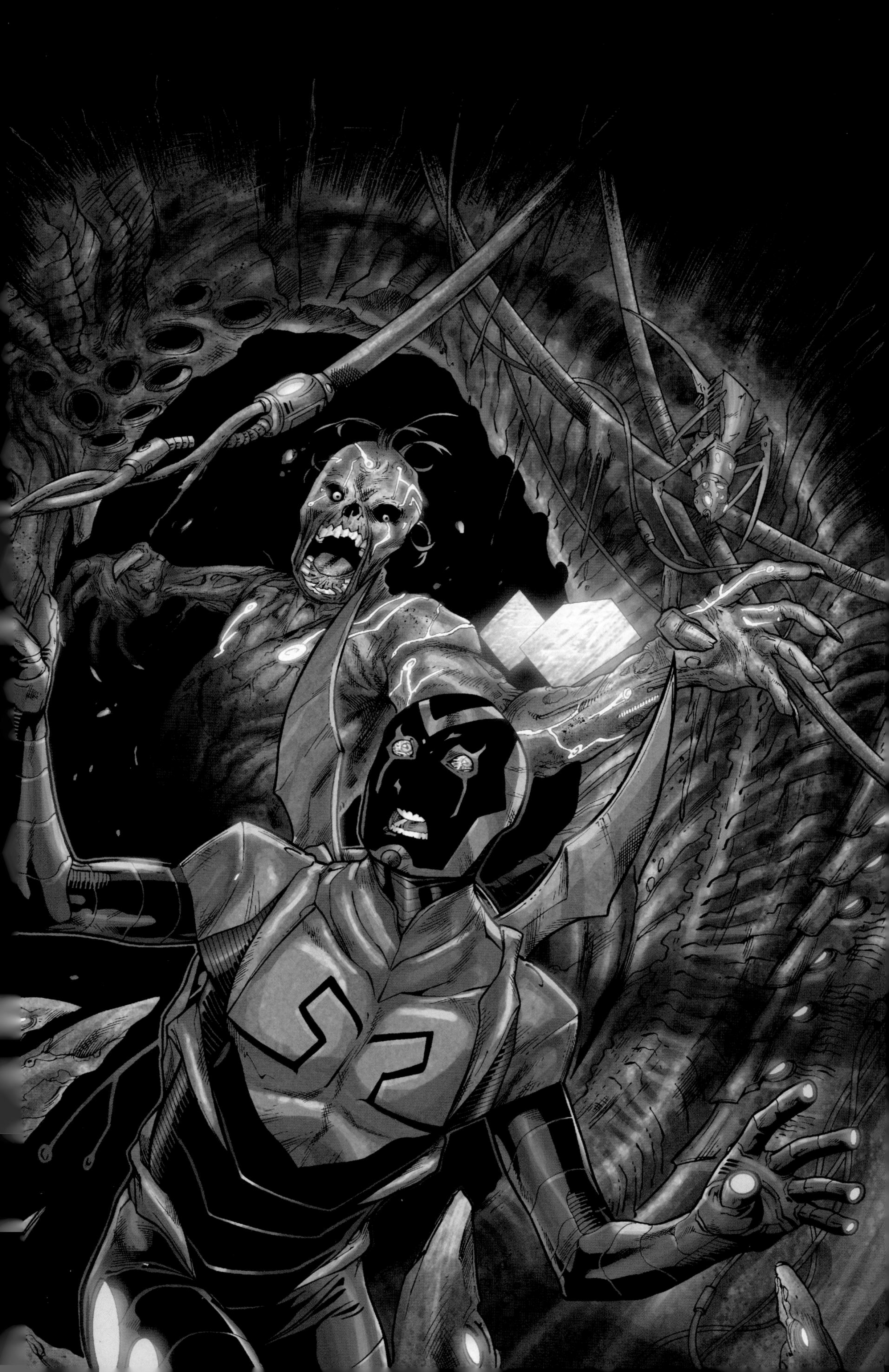

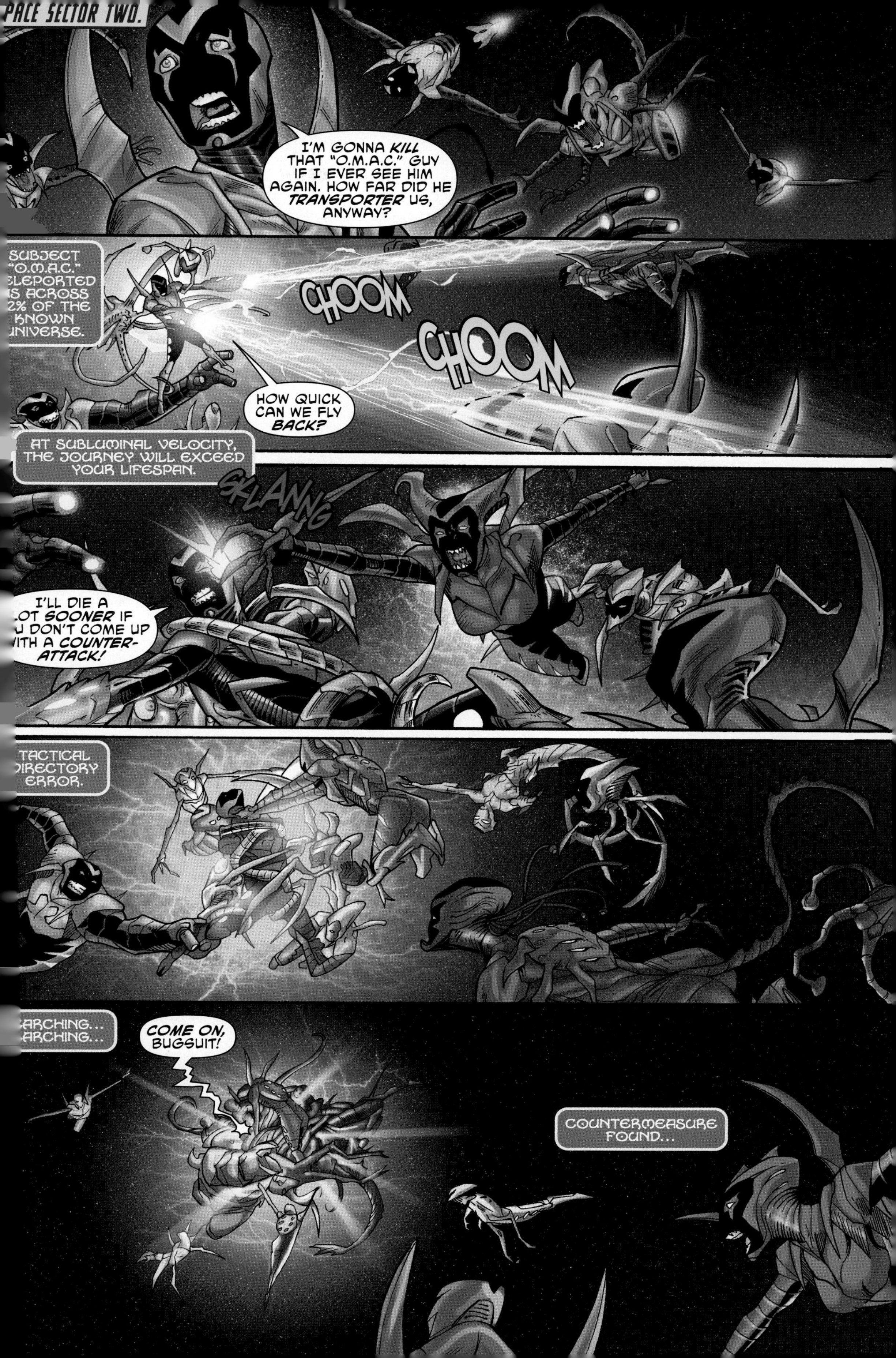
PACE SECTOR TWO.
I'M GONNA KILL THAT "O.M.A.C." GUY IF I EVER SEE HIM AGAIN. HOW FAR DID HE TRANSPORTER US, ANYWAY?
SUBJECT "O.M.A.C." ELEPORTED S ACROSS 2% OF THE KNOWN UNIVERSE.
CHOOM
CHOOM
HOW QUICK CAN WE FLY BACK?
AT SUBLUMINAL VELOCITY, THE JOURNEY WILL EXCEED YOUR LIFESPAN.
SKLANNG
I'LL DIE A LOT SOONER IF U DON'T COME UP WITH A COUNTER-ATTACK!
TACTICAL DIRECTORY ERROR.
ARCHING... ARCHING...
COME ON, BUGSUIT!
COUNTERMEASURE FOUND...

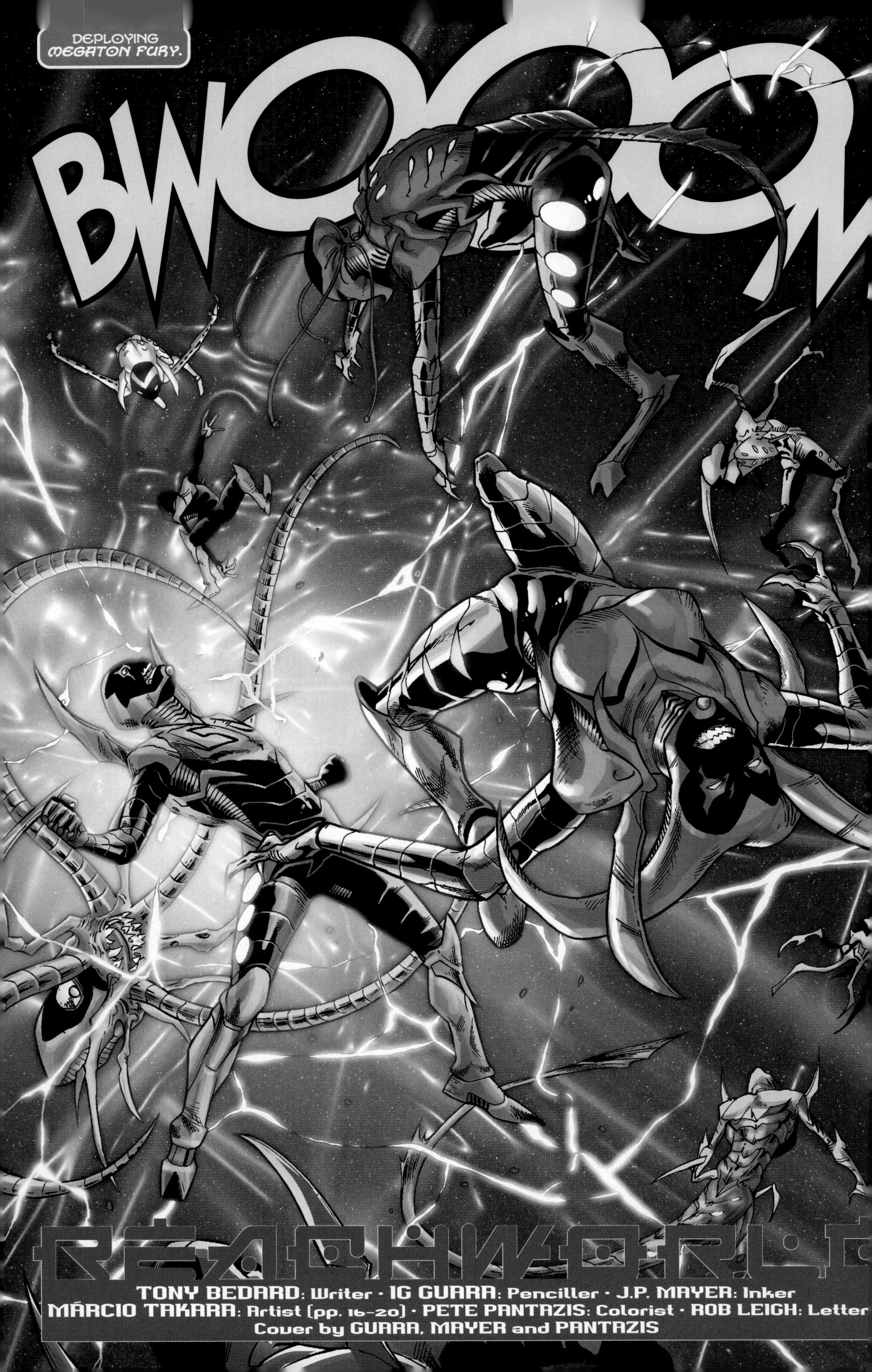

DEPLOYING MEGATON FURY.
BWOOO
REACHWORLD
TONY BEDARD: Writer · IG GUARA: Penciller · J.P. MAYER: Inker
MÁRCIO TAKARA: Artist (pp. 16-20) · PETE PANTAZIS: Colorist · ROB LEIGH: Letter
Cover by GUARA, MAYER and PANTAZIS

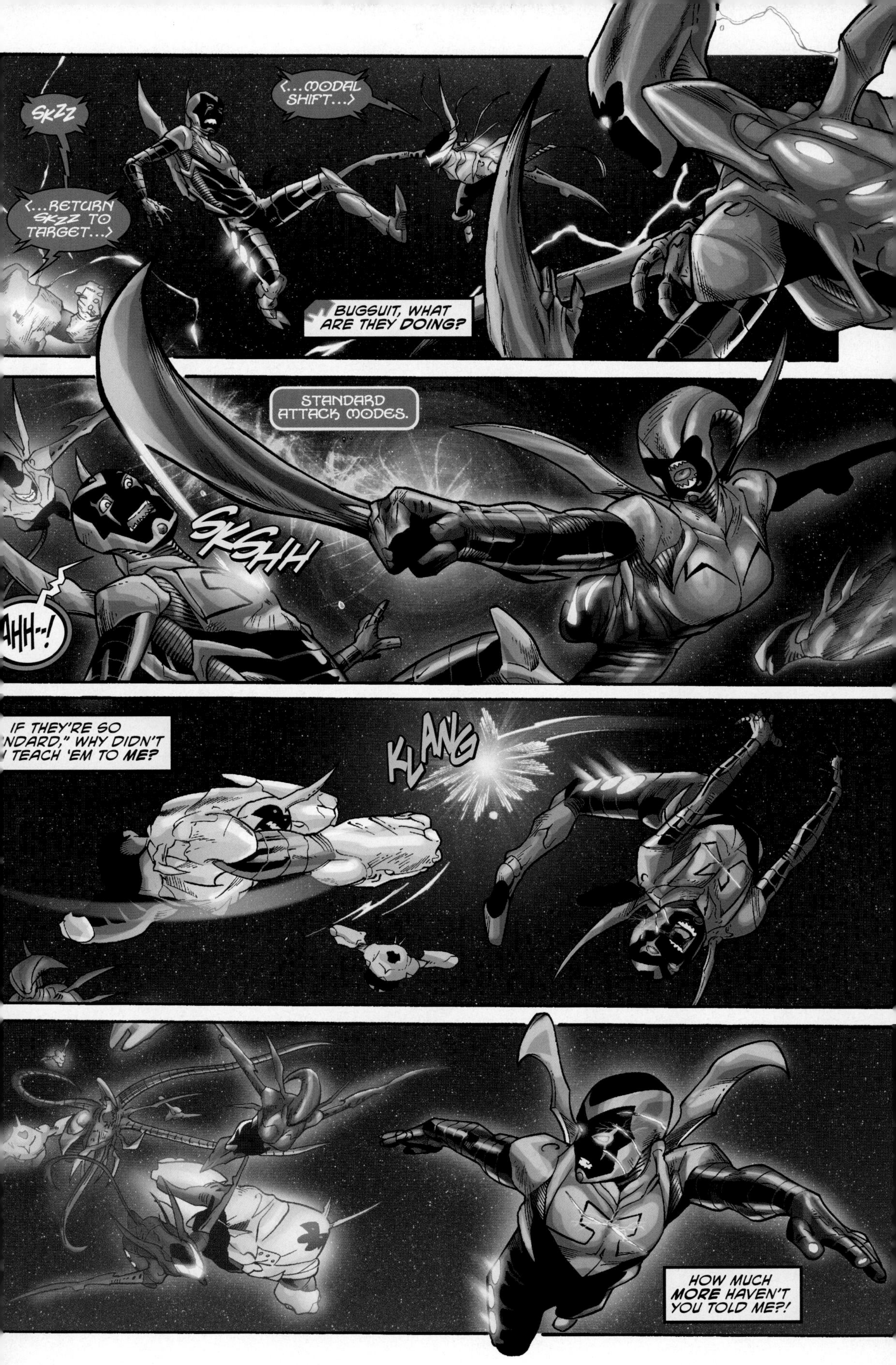
SKZZ
<...RETURN SKZZ TO TARGET...>
<...MODAL SHIFT...>
BUGSUIT, WHAT ARE THEY DOING?
STANDARD ATTACK MODES.
SKSHH
AHH--!
IF THEY'RE SO NDARD," WHY DIDN'T TEACH 'EM TO ME?
KLANG
HOW MUCH MORE HAVEN'T YOU TOLD ME?!

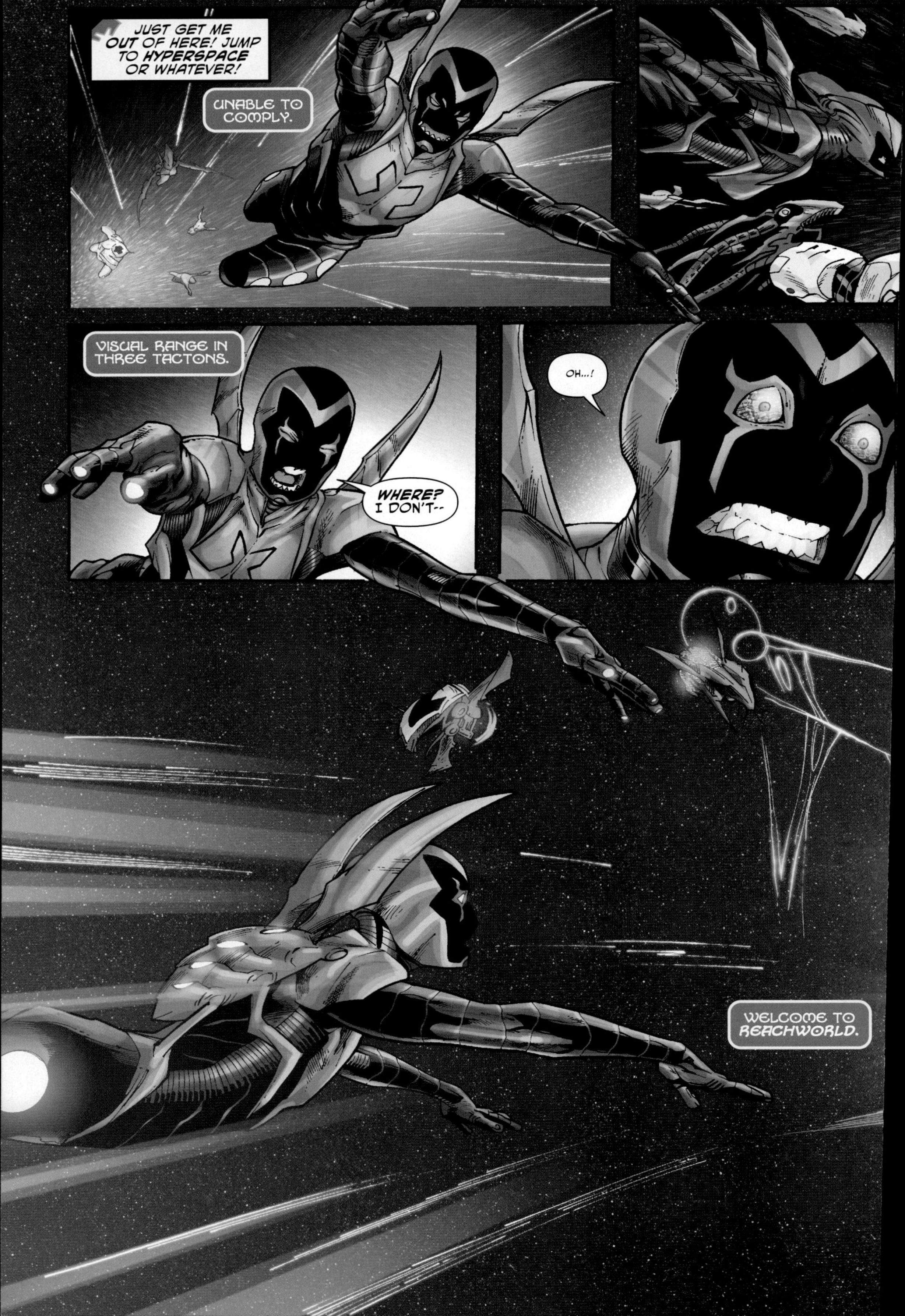
JUST GET ME OUT OF HERE! JUMP TO HYPERSPACE OR WHATEVER!
UNABLE TO COMPLY.
VISUAL RANGE IN THREE TACTONS.
WHERE? I DON'T--
OH...!
WELCOME TO REACHWORLD.

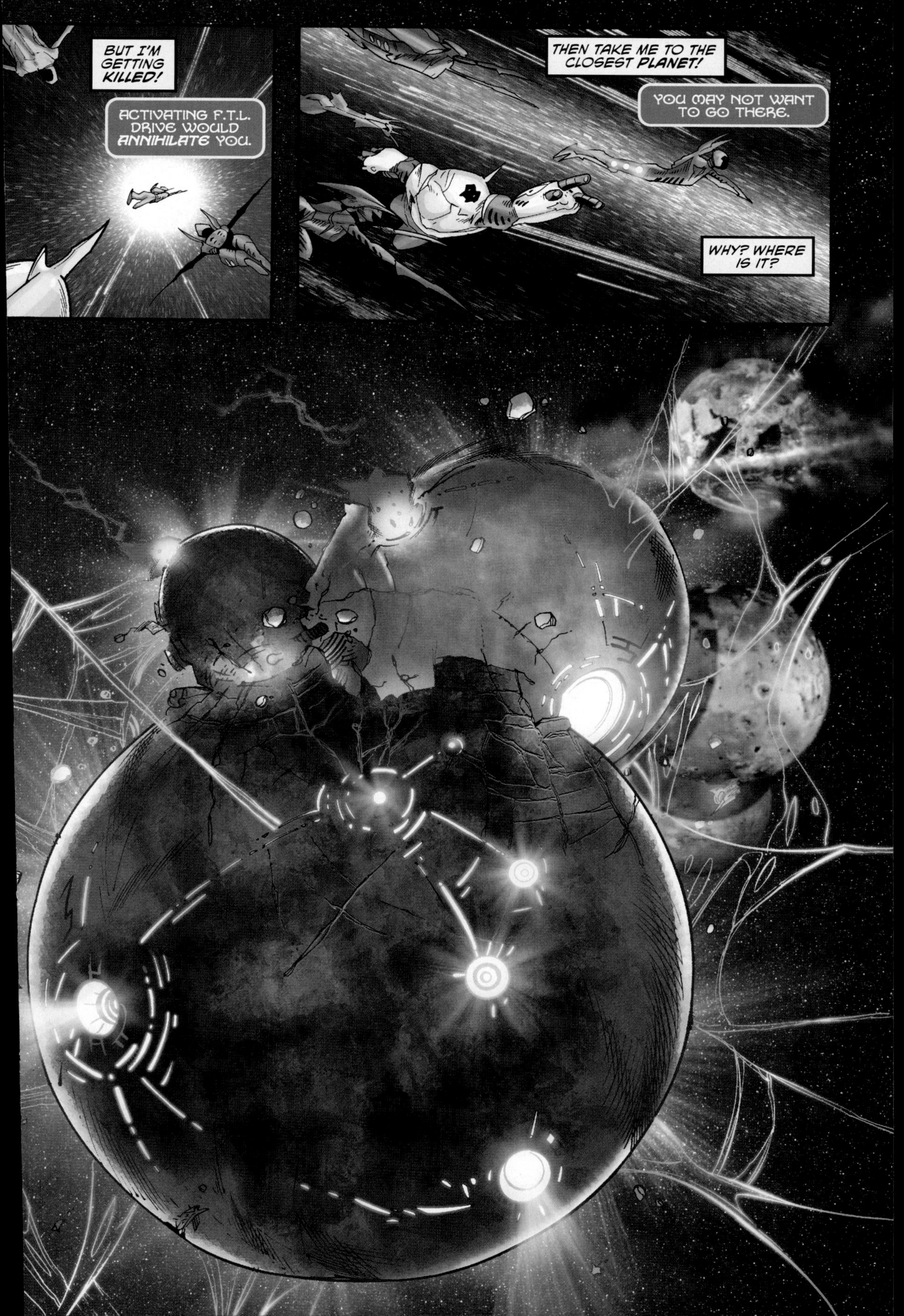
BUT I'M GETTING KILLED!
ACTIVATING F.T.L. DRIVE WOULD ANNIHILATE YOU.
THEN TAKE ME TO THE CLOSEST PLANET!
YOU MAY NOT WANT TO GO THERE.
WHY? WHERE IS IT?

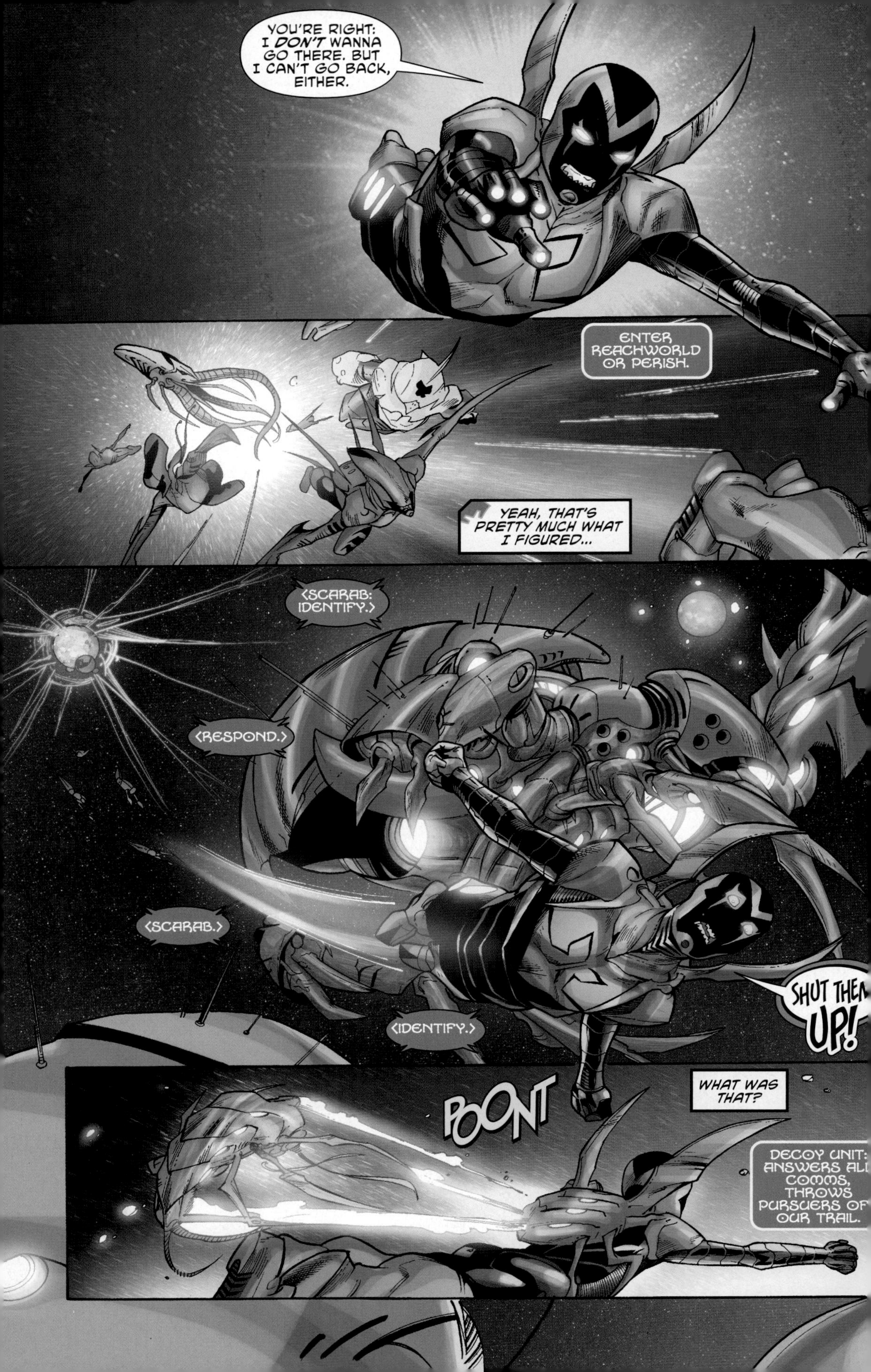
YOU'RE RIGHT: I DON'T WANNA GO THERE. BUT I CAN'T GO BACK, EITHER.
ENTER REACHWORLD OR PERISH.
YEAH, THAT'S PRETTY MUCH WHAT I FIGURED...
<SCARAB: IDENTIFY.>
<RESPOND.>
<SCARAB.>
<IDENTIFY.>
SHUT THEM UP!
POONT
WHAT WAS THAT?
DECOY UNIT: ANSWERS ALL COMMS, THROWS PURSUERS OFF OUR TRAIL.

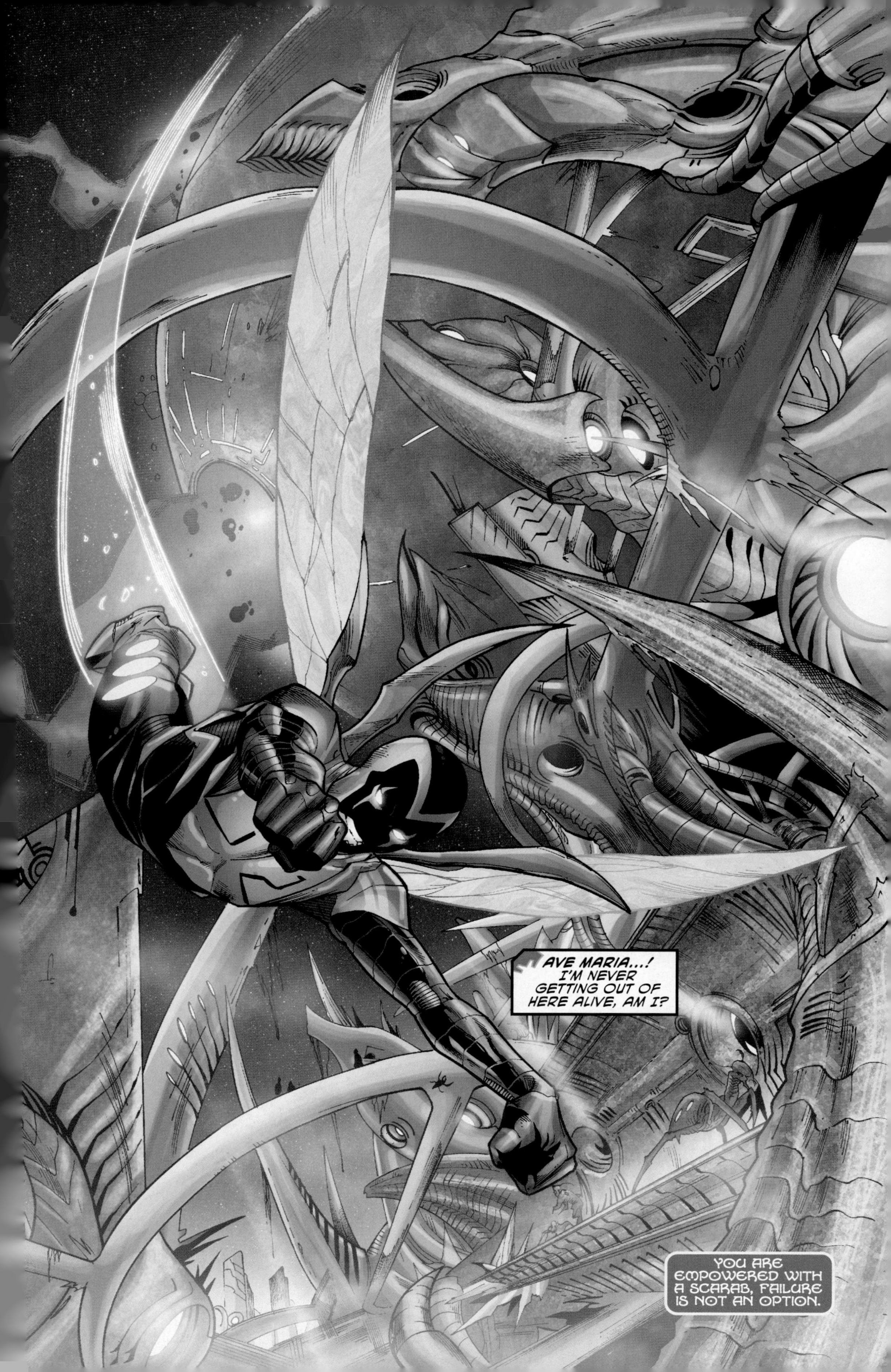
AVE MARIA...! I'M NEVER GETTING OUT OF HERE ALIVE, AM I?
YOU ARE EMPOWERED WITH A SCARAB, FAILURE IS NOT AN OPTION.

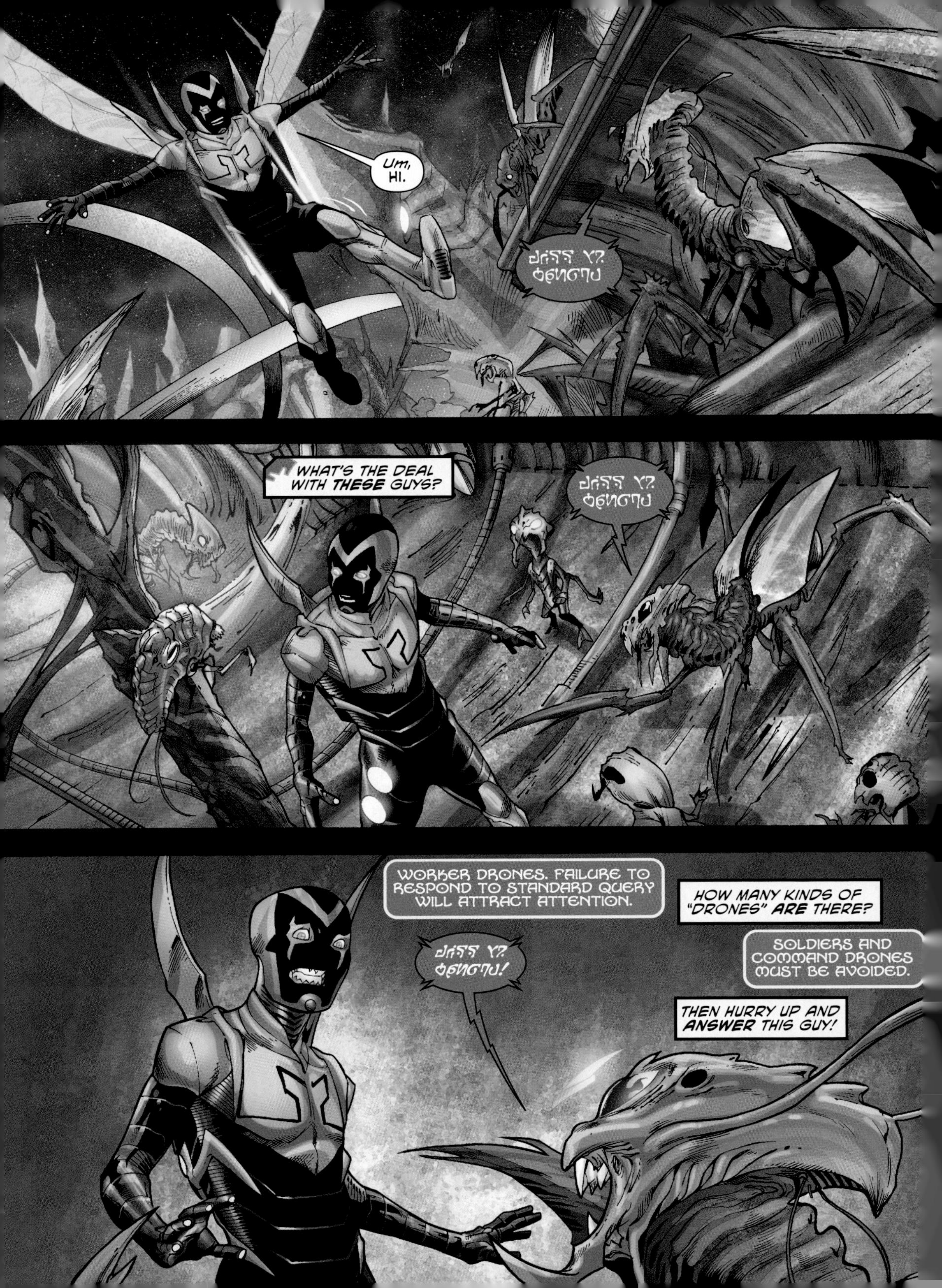
UM, HI.
WHAT'S THE DEAL WITH **THESE** GUYS?
WORKER DRONES. FAILURE TO RESPOND TO STANDARD QUERY WILL ATTRACT ATTENTION.
HOW MANY KINDS OF "DRONES" **ARE** THERE?
SOLDIERS AND COMMAND DRONES MUST BE AVOIDED.
THEN HURRY UP AND **ANSWER** THIS GUY!

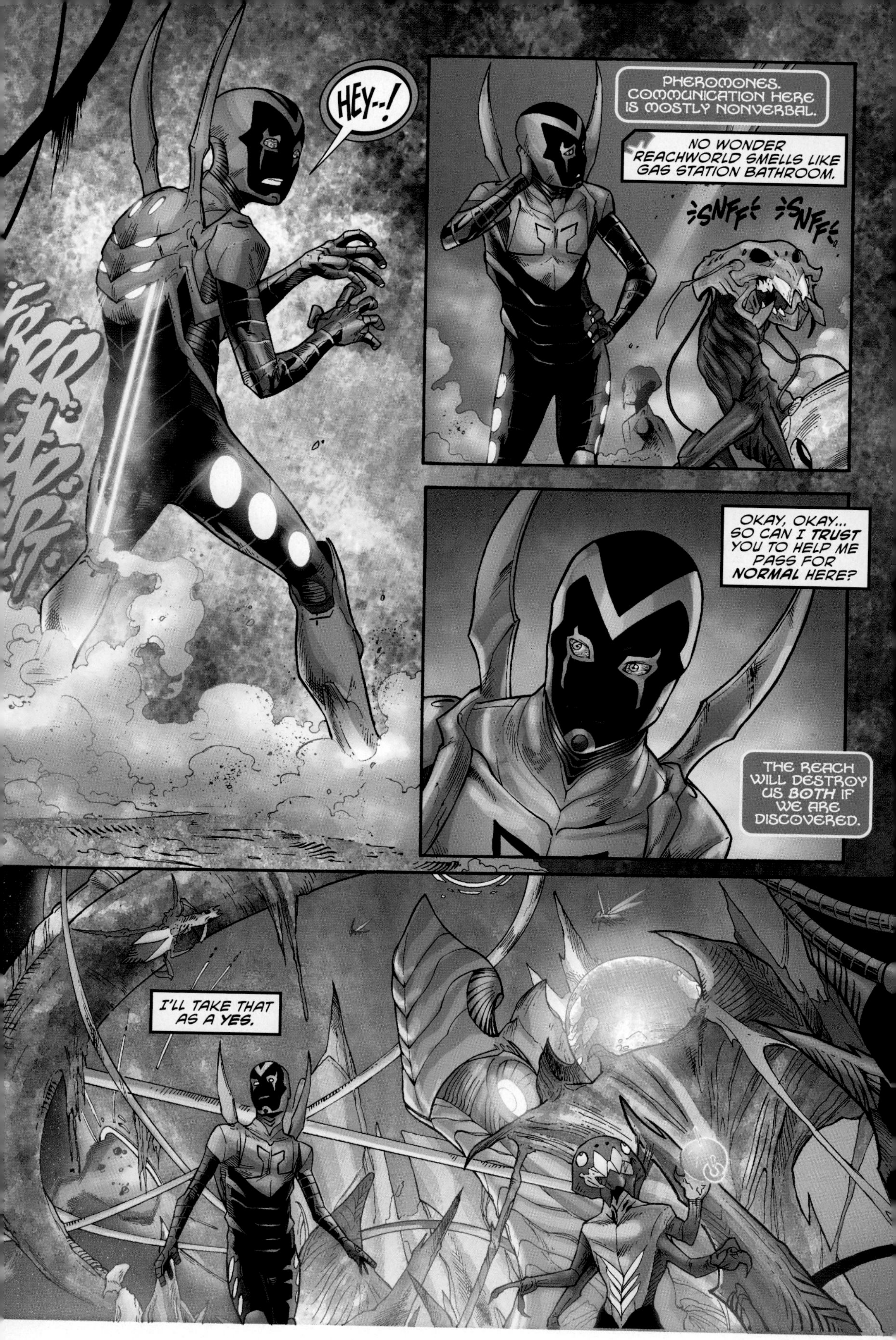
HEY--!
PHEROMONES. COMMUNICATION HERE IS MOSTLY NONVERBAL.
NO WONDER REACHWORLD SMELLS LIKE GAS STATION BATHROOM.
SNFF
SNFF
OKAY, OKAY... SO CAN I TRUST YOU TO HELP ME PASS FOR NORMAL HERE?
THE REACH WILL DESTROY US BOTH IF WE ARE DISCOVERED.
I'LL TAKE THAT AS A YES.

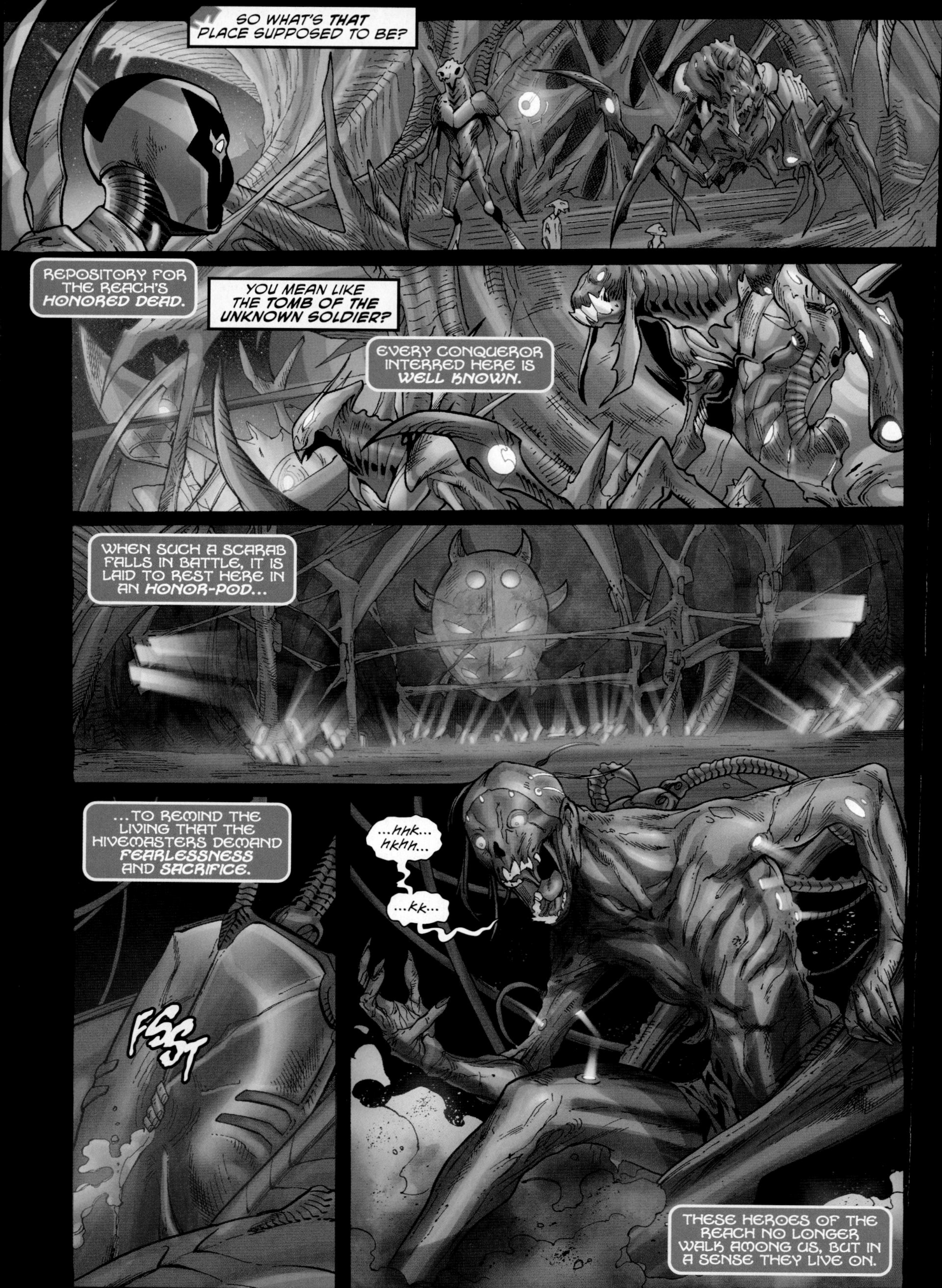
SO WHAT'S THAT PLACE SUPPOSED TO BE?
REPOSITORY FOR THE REACH'S HONORED DEAD.
YOU MEAN LIKE THE TOMB OF THE UNKNOWN SOLDIER?
EVERY CONQUEROR INTERRED HERE IS WELL KNOWN.
WHEN SUCH A SCARAB FALLS IN BATTLE, IT IS LAID TO REST HERE IN AN HONOR-POD...
...TO REMIND THE LIVING THAT THE HIVEMASTERS DEMAND FEARLESSNESS AND SACRIFICE.
FSST
...hhk... hkhh...
...kk...
THESE HEROES OF THE REACH NO LONGER WALK AMONG US, BUT IN A SENSE THEY LIVE ON.

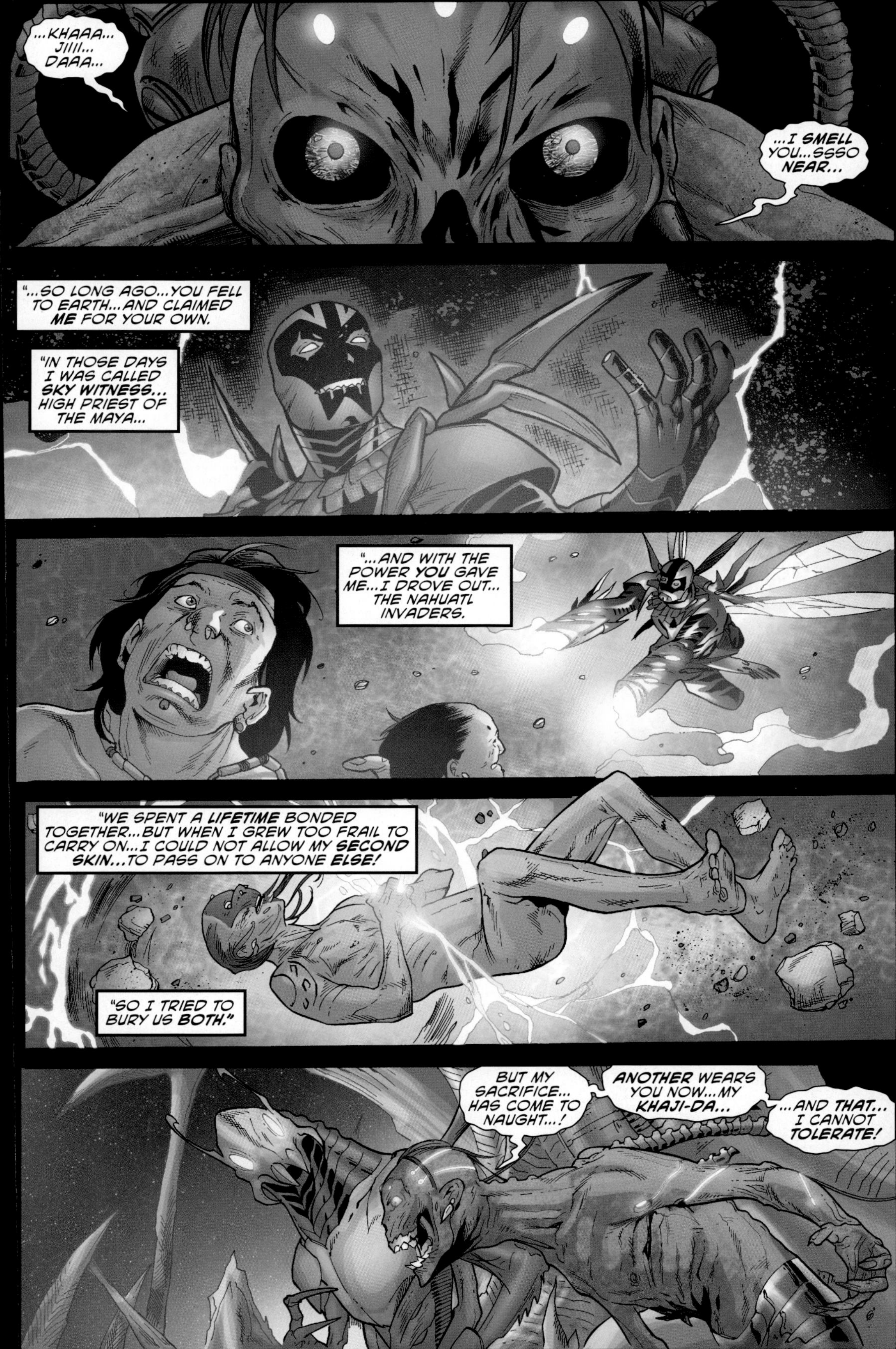
...KHAAA... JIIII... DAAA...
...I SMELL YOU...SSSO NEAR...
"...SO LONG AGO...YOU FELL TO EARTH...AND CLAIMED ME FOR YOUR OWN.
"IN THOSE DAYS I WAS CALLED SKY WITNESS... HIGH PRIEST OF THE MAYA...
"...AND WITH THE POWER YOU GAVE ME...I DROVE OUT... THE NAHUATL INVADERS.
"WE SPENT A LIFETIME BONDED TOGETHER...BUT WHEN I GREW TOO FRAIL TO CARRY ON...I COULD NOT ALLOW MY SECOND SKIN...TO PASS ON TO ANYONE ELSE!
"SO I TRIED TO BURY US BOTH."
BUT MY SACRIFICE... HAS COME TO NAUGHT...!
ANOTHER WEARS YOU NOW...MY KHAJI-DA...
...AND THAT... I CANNOT TOLERATE!

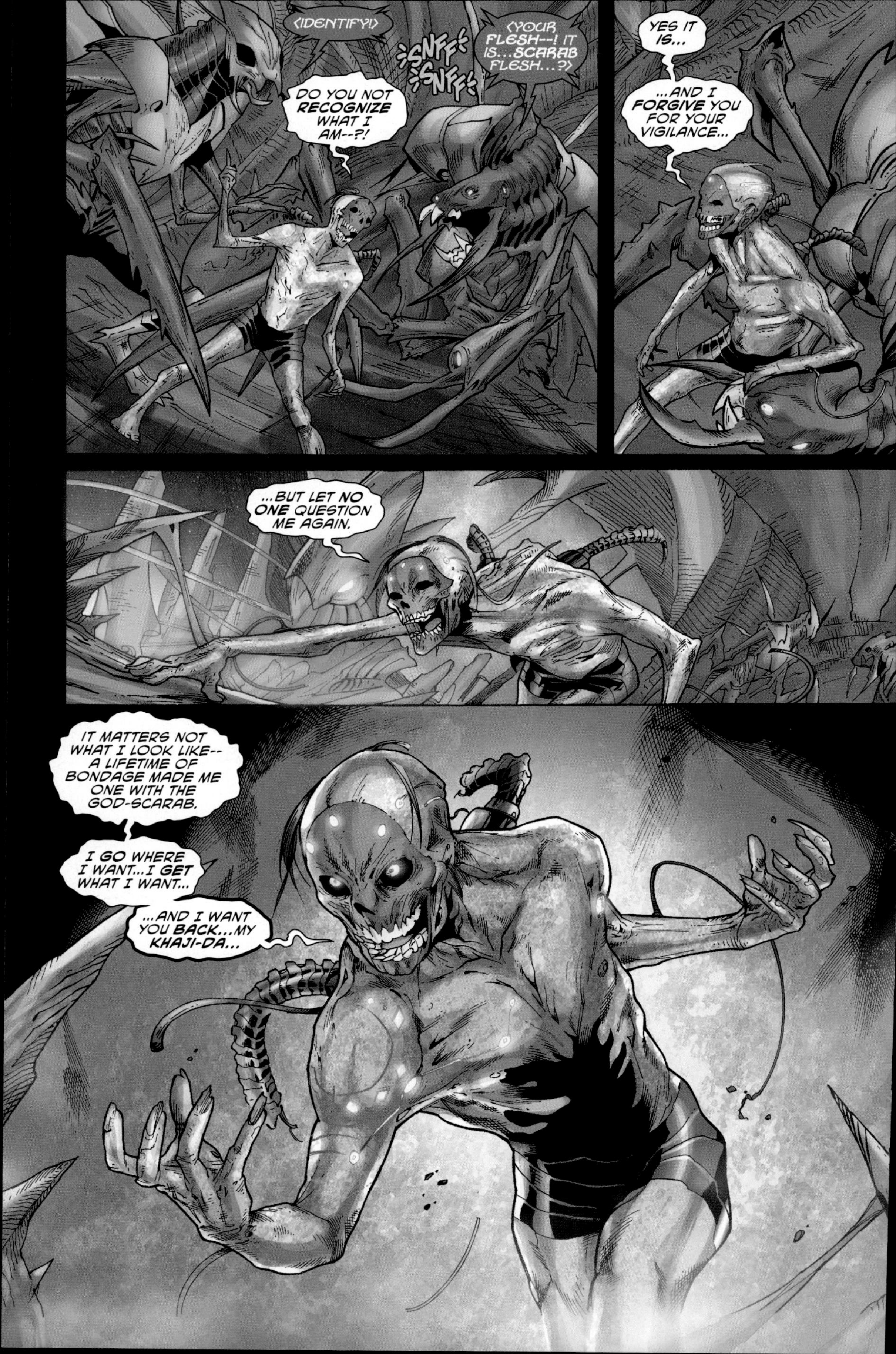

‹IDENTIFY!›
SNFF SNFF
DO YOU NOT RECOGNIZE WHAT I AM--?!
‹YOUR FLESH--! IT IS...SCARAB FLESH...?›
YES IT IS...
...AND I FORGIVE YOU FOR YOUR VIGILANCE...
...BUT LET NO ONE QUESTION ME AGAIN.
IT MATTERS NOT WHAT I LOOK LIKE-- A LIFETIME OF BONDAGE MADE ME ONE WITH THE GOD-SCARAB.
I GO WHERE I WANT...I GET WHAT I WANT...
...AND I WANT YOU BACK...MY KHAJI-DA...

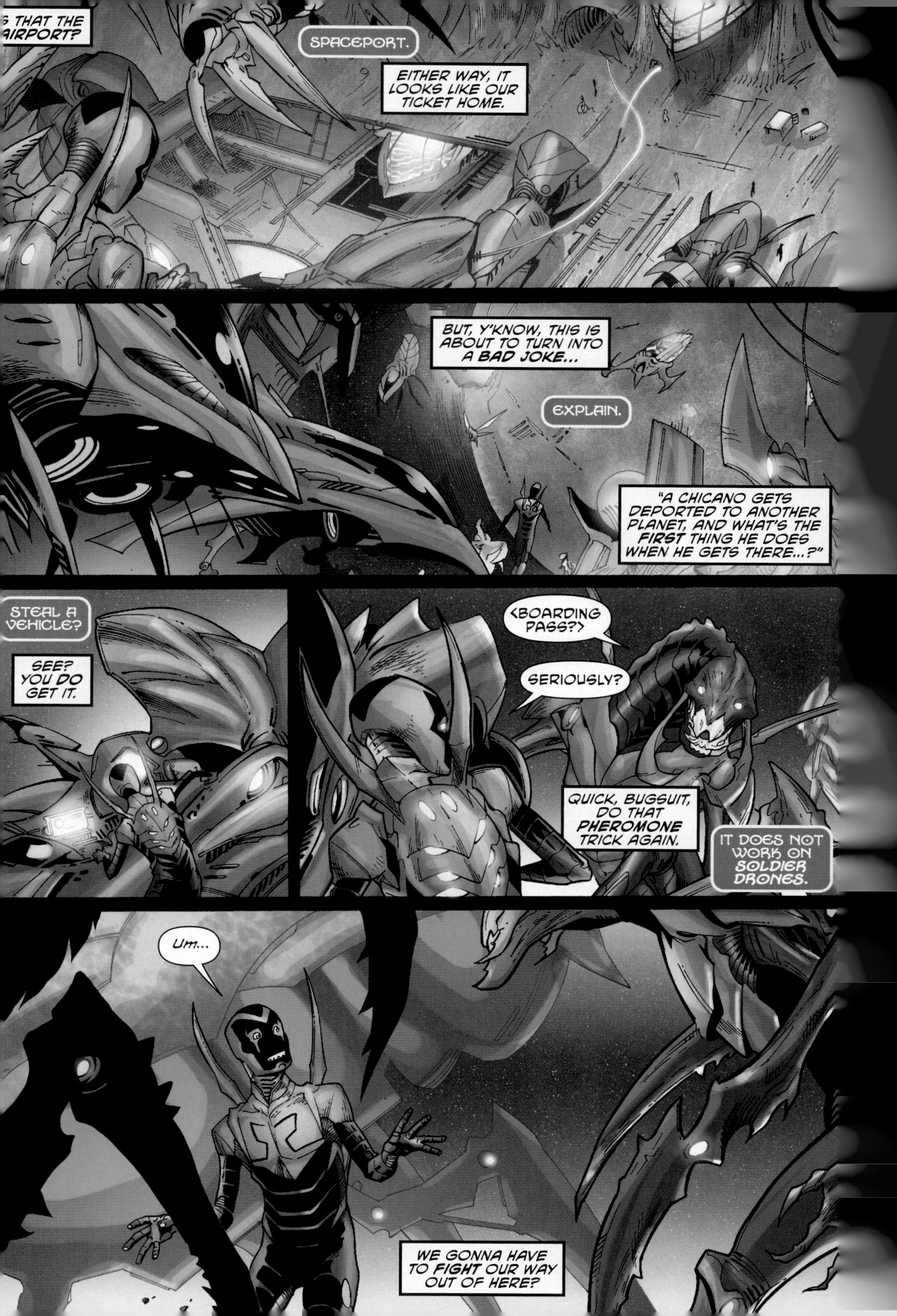
...S THAT THE
AIRPORT?
SPACEPORT.
EITHER WAY, IT LOOKS LIKE OUR TICKET HOME.
BUT, Y'KNOW, THIS IS ABOUT TO TURN INTO A **BAD JOKE...**
EXPLAIN.
"A CHICANO GETS DEPORTED TO ANOTHER PLANET, AND WHAT'S THE **FIRST** THING HE DOES WHEN HE GETS THERE...?"
STEAL A VEHICLE?
SEE? YOU **DO** GET IT.
<BOARDING PASS?>
SERIOUSLY?
QUICK, BUGSUIT, DO THAT **PHEROMONE** TRICK AGAIN.
IT DOES NOT WORK ON **SOLDIER DRONES.**
Um...
WE GONNA HAVE TO **FIGHT** OUR WAY OUT OF HERE?

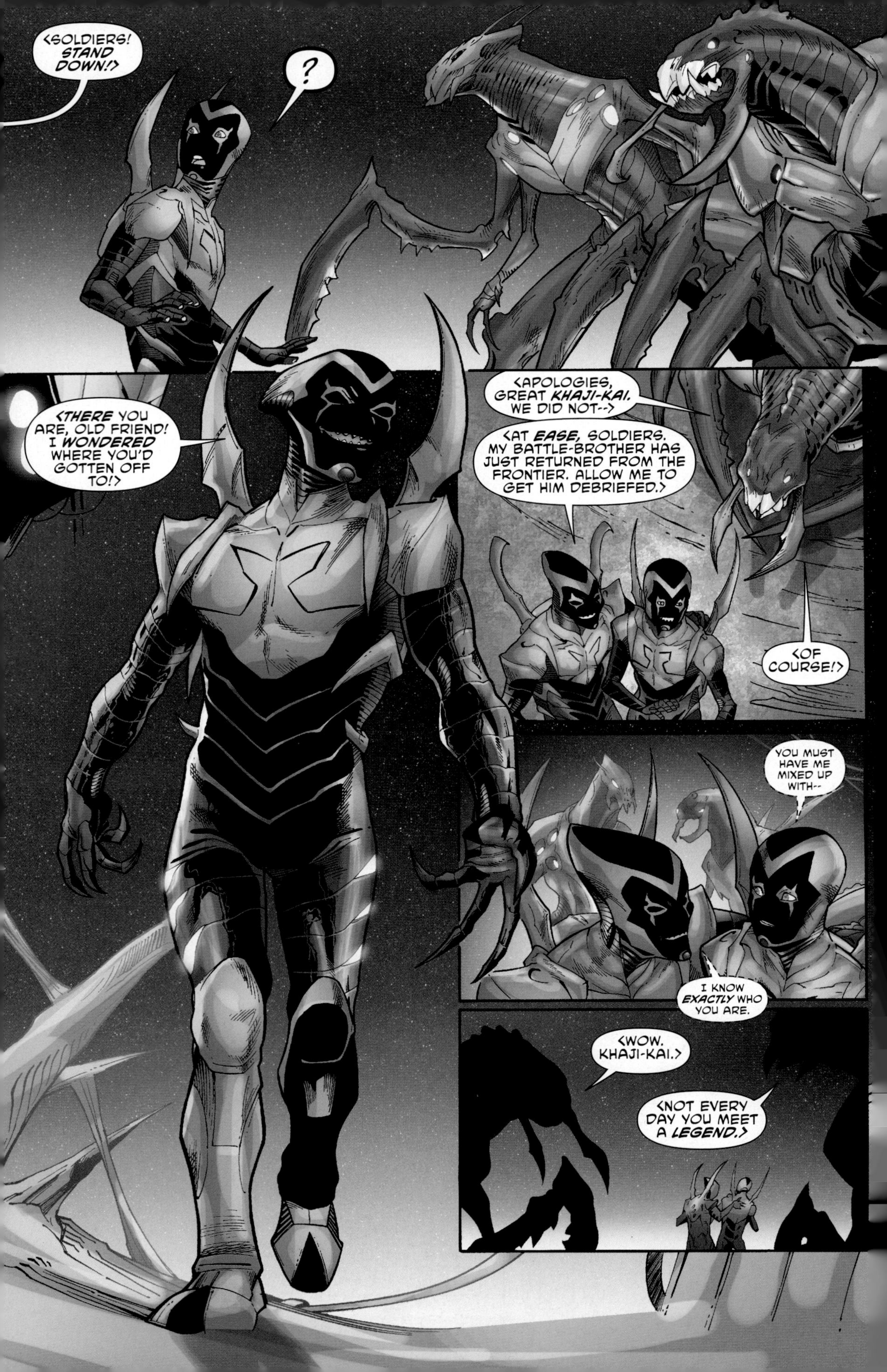
<SOLDIERS! STAND DOWN!>
?
<THERE YOU ARE, OLD FRIEND! I WONDERED WHERE YOU'D GOTTEN OFF TO!>
<APOLOGIES, GREAT KHAJI-KAI. WE DID NOT-->
<AT EASE, SOLDIERS. MY BATTLE-BROTHER HAS JUST RETURNED FROM THE FRONTIER. ALLOW ME TO GET HIM DEBRIEFED.>
<OF COURSE!>
YOU MUST HAVE ME MIXED UP WITH--
I KNOW EXACTLY WHO YOU ARE.
<WOW. KHAJI-KAI.>
<NOT EVERY DAY YOU MEET A LEGEND.>

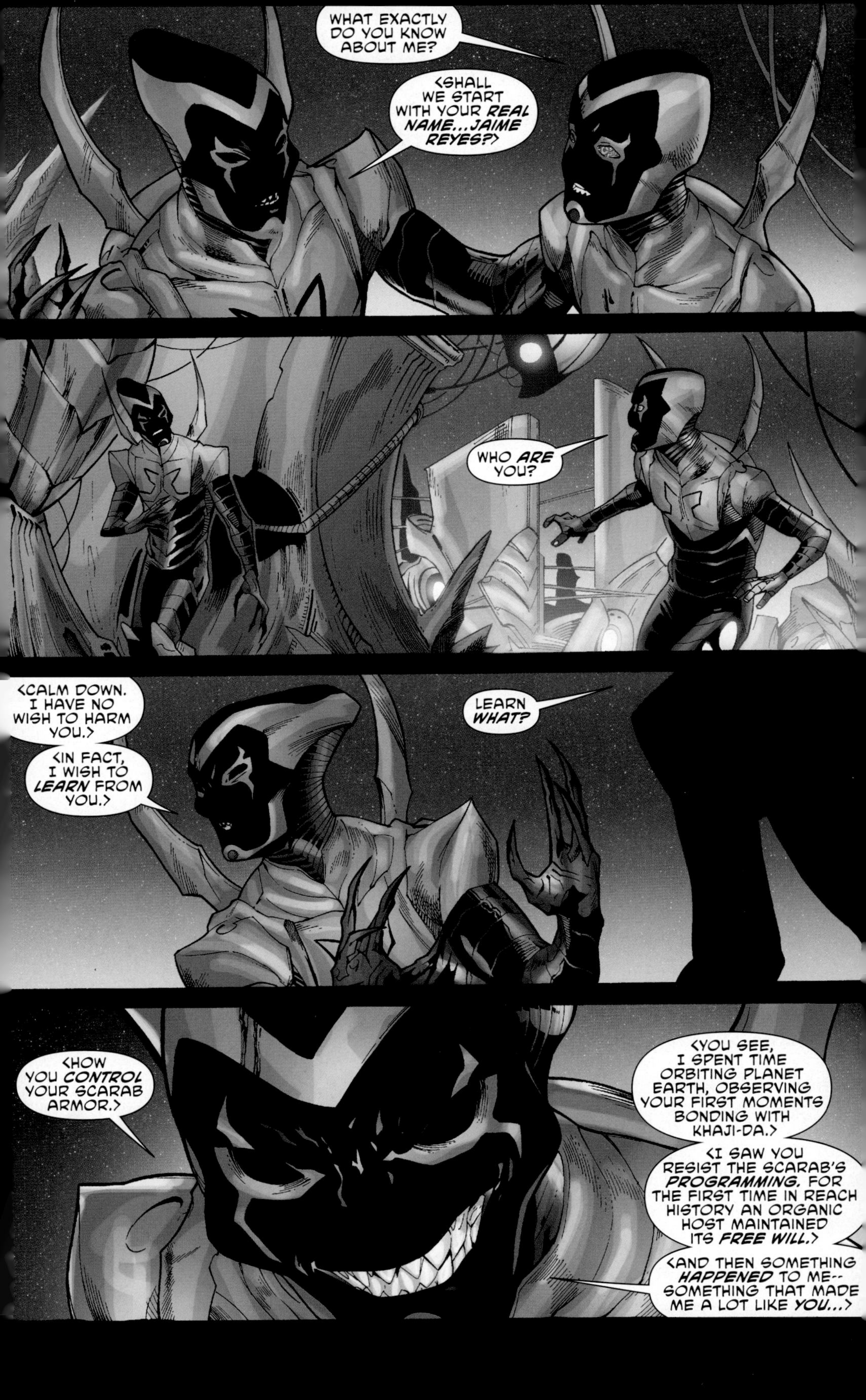
WHAT EXACTLY DO YOU KNOW ABOUT ME?
<SHALL WE START WITH YOUR *REAL NAME...JAIME REYES?*>
WHO *ARE* YOU?
<CALM DOWN. I HAVE NO WISH TO HARM YOU.>
<IN FACT, I WISH TO *LEARN* FROM YOU.>
LEARN *WHAT?*
<HOW YOU *CONTROL* YOUR SCARAB ARMOR.>
<YOU SEE, I SPENT TIME ORBITING PLANET EARTH, OBSERVING YOUR FIRST MOMENTS BONDING WITH KHAJI-DA.>
<I SAW YOU RESIST THE SCARAB'S *PROGRAMMING.* FOR THE FIRST TIME IN REACH HISTORY AN ORGANIC HOST MAINTAINED ITS *FREE WILL.*>
<AND THEN SOMETHING *HAPPENED* TO ME-- SOMETHING THAT MADE ME A LOT LIKE *YOU...*>

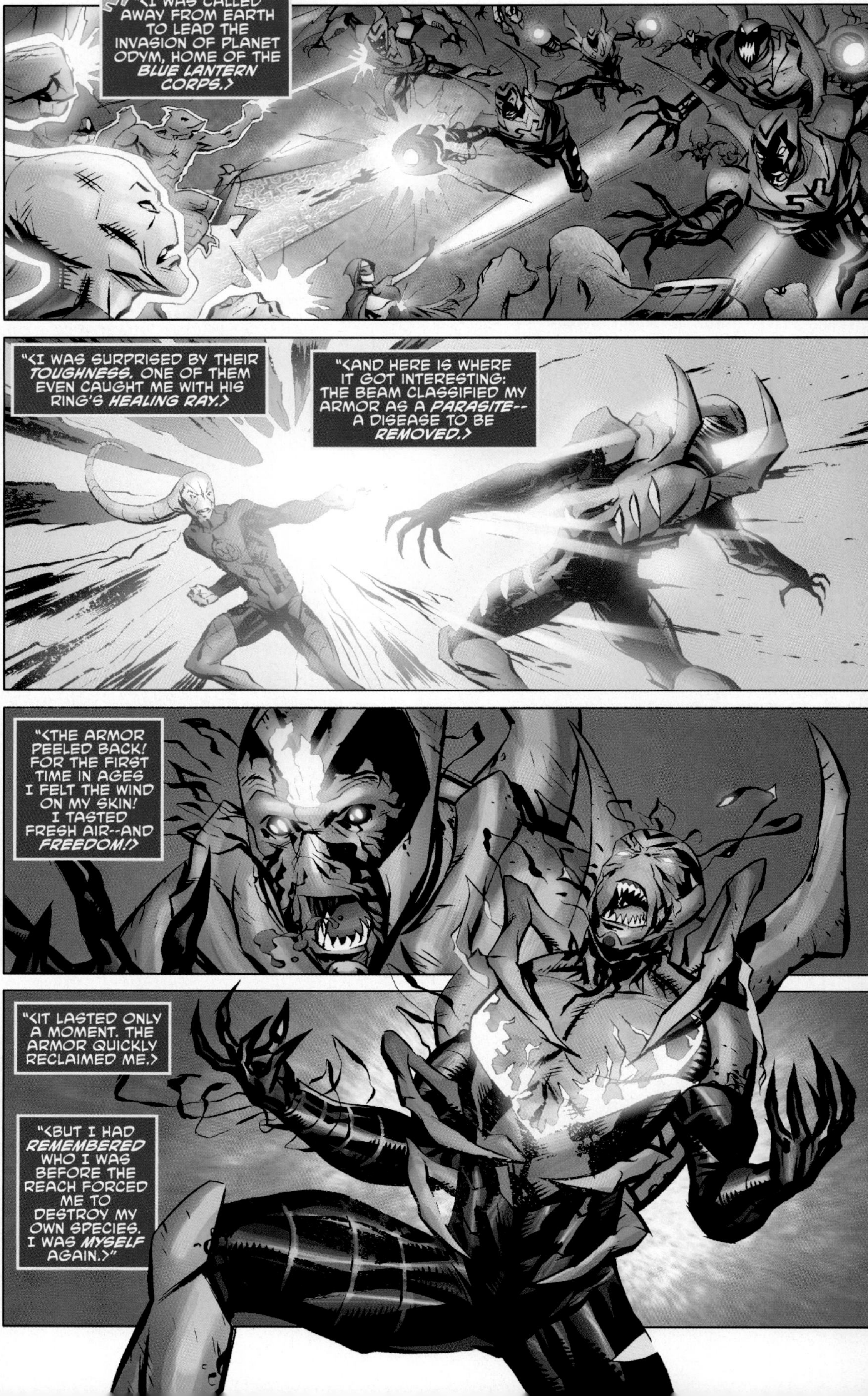
"<I WAS CALLED AWAY FROM EARTH TO LEAD THE INVASION OF PLANET ODYM, HOME OF THE *BLUE LANTERN CORPS.*>
"<I WAS SURPRISED BY THEIR *TOUGHNESS.* ONE OF THEM EVEN CAUGHT ME WITH HIS RING'S *HEALING RAY.*>
"<AND HERE IS WHERE IT GOT INTERESTING: THE BEAM CLASSIFIED MY ARMOR AS A *PARASITE*-- A DISEASE TO BE *REMOVED.*>
"<THE ARMOR PEELED BACK! FOR THE FIRST TIME IN AGES I FELT THE WIND ON MY SKIN! I TASTED FRESH AIR--AND *FREEDOM!*>
"<IT LASTED ONLY A MOMENT. THE ARMOR QUICKLY RECLAIMED ME.>
"<BUT I HAD *REMEMBERED* WHO I WAS BEFORE THE REACH FORCED ME TO DESTROY MY OWN SPECIES. I WAS *MYSELF* AGAIN.>"

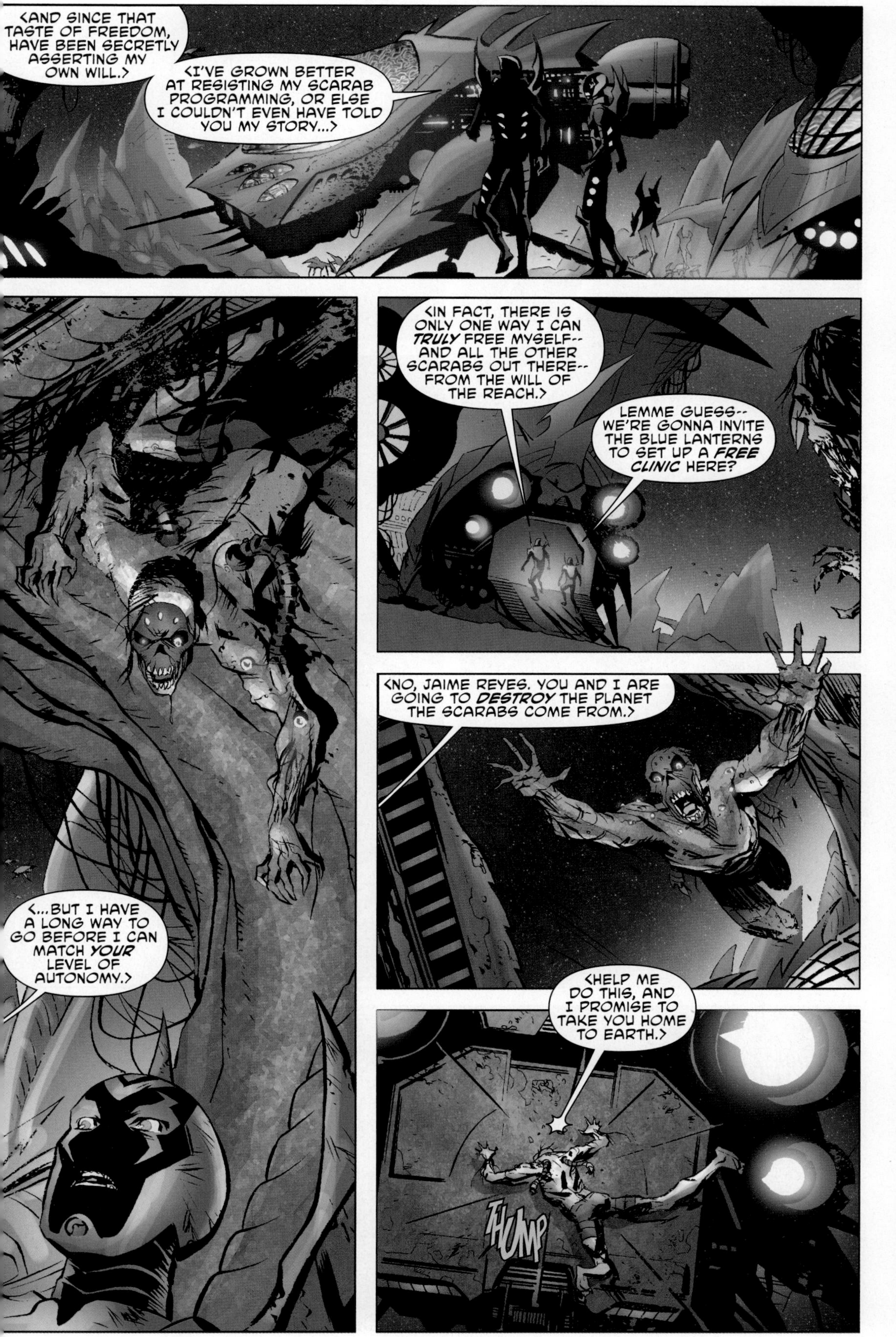
<AND SINCE THAT TASTE OF FREEDOM, HAVE BEEN SECRETLY ASSERTING MY OWN WILL.>
<I'VE GROWN BETTER AT RESISTING MY SCARAB PROGRAMMING, OR ELSE I COULDN'T EVEN HAVE TOLD YOU MY STORY...>
<...BUT I HAVE A LONG WAY TO GO BEFORE I CAN MATCH YOUR LEVEL OF AUTONOMY.>
<IN FACT, THERE IS ONLY ONE WAY I CAN TRULY FREE MYSELF-- AND ALL THE OTHER SCARABS OUT THERE-- FROM THE WILL OF THE REACH.>
LEMME GUESS-- WE'RE GONNA INVITE THE BLUE LANTERNS TO SET UP A FREE CLINIC HERE?
<NO, JAIME REYES. YOU AND I ARE GOING TO DESTROY THE PLANET THE SCARABS COME FROM.>
<HELP ME DO THIS, AND I PROMISE TO TAKE YOU HOME TO EARTH.>
THUMP

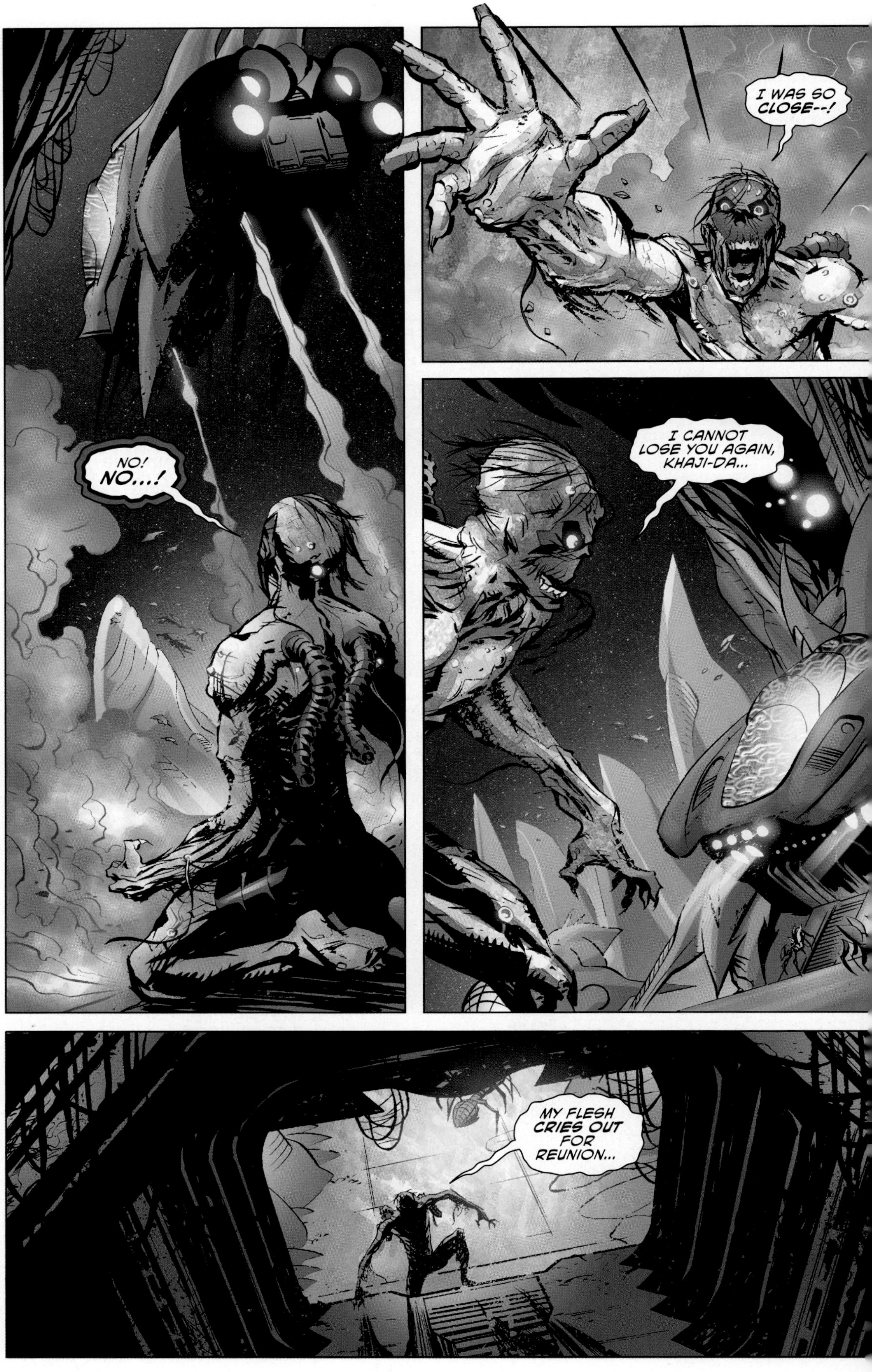
I WAS SO CLOSE--!
NO! NO...!
I CANNOT LOSE YOU AGAIN, KHAJI-DA...
MY FLESH CRIES OUT FOR REUNION...

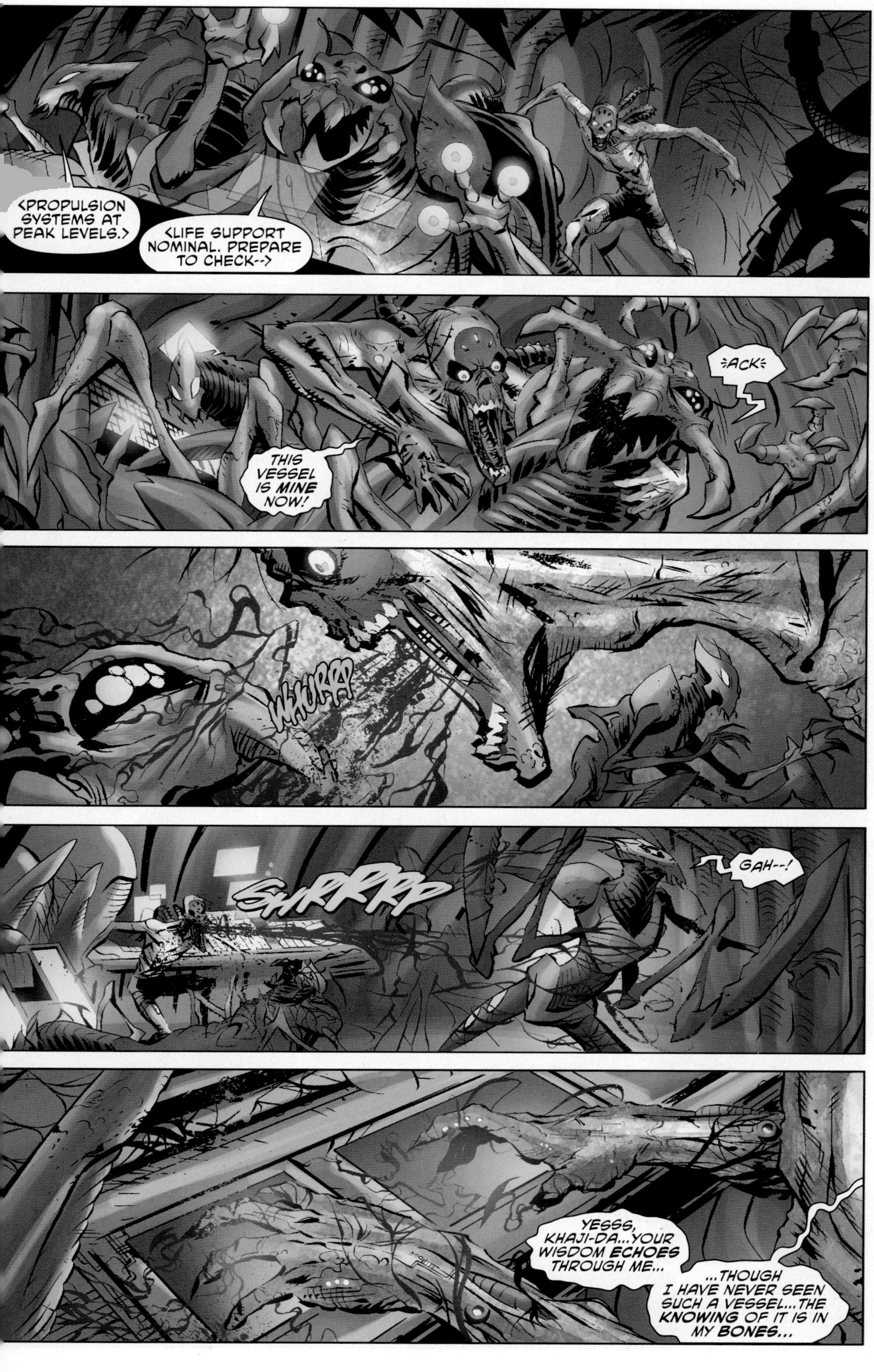
<PROPULSION SYSTEMS AT PEAK LEVELS.>
<LIFE SUPPORT NOMINAL. PREPARE TO CHECK-->
THIS VESSEL IS **MINE** NOW!
ACK
WHURRP
SHRRRRP
GAH--!
YESSS, KHAJI-DA...YOUR WISDOM **ECHOES** THROUGH ME...
...THOUGH I HAVE NEVER SEEN SUCH A VESSEL...THE **KNOWING** OF IT IS IN MY **BONES**...

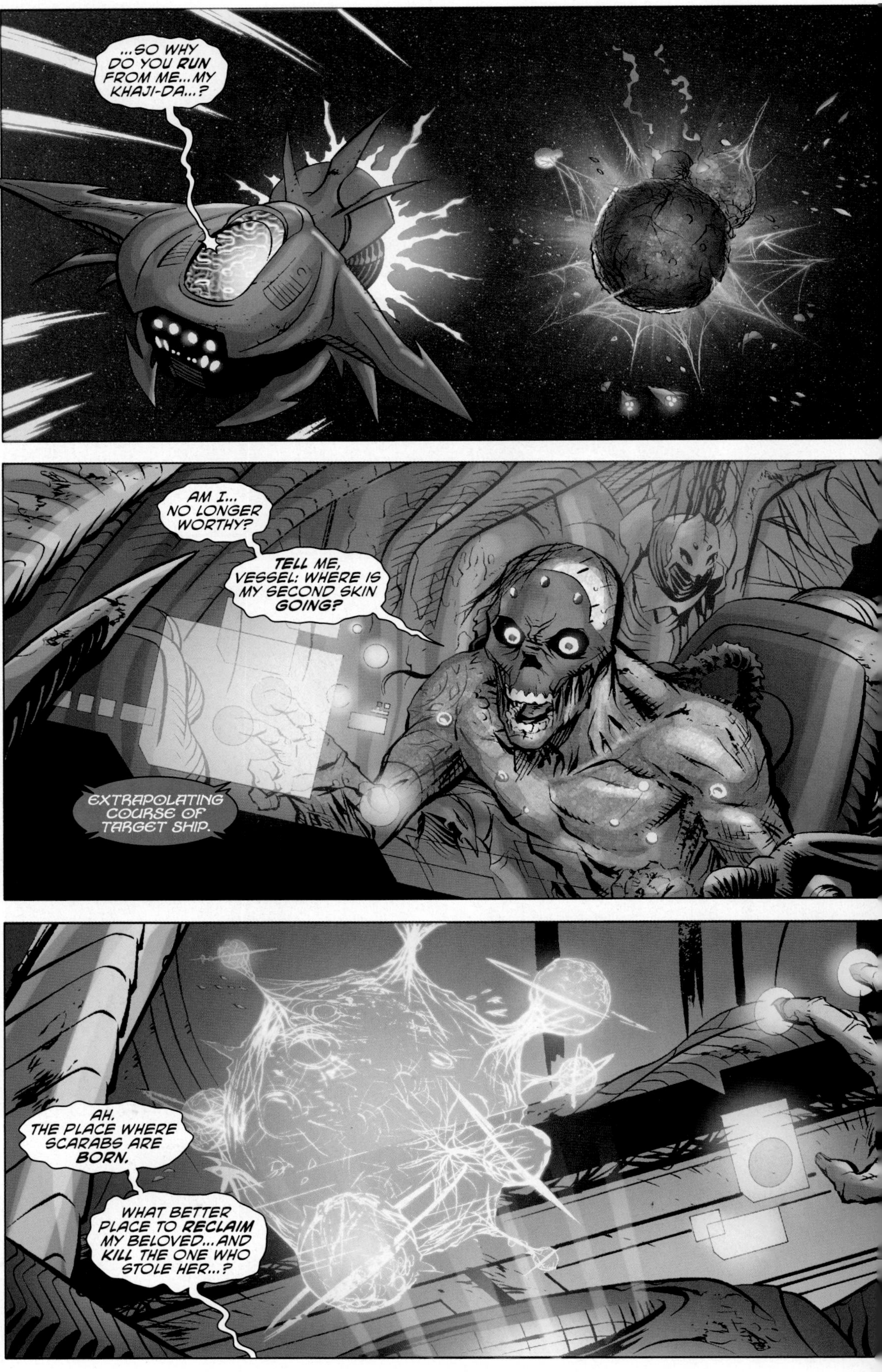
...SO WHY DO YOU RUN FROM ME...MY KHAJI-DA...?
AM I... NO LONGER WORTHY?
TELL ME, VESSEL: WHERE IS MY SECOND SKIN GOING?
EXTRAPOLATING COURSE OF TARGET SHIP.
AH. THE PLACE WHERE SCARABS ARE BORN.
WHAT BETTER PLACE TO RECLAIM MY BELOVED...AND KILL THE ONE WHO STOLE HER...?

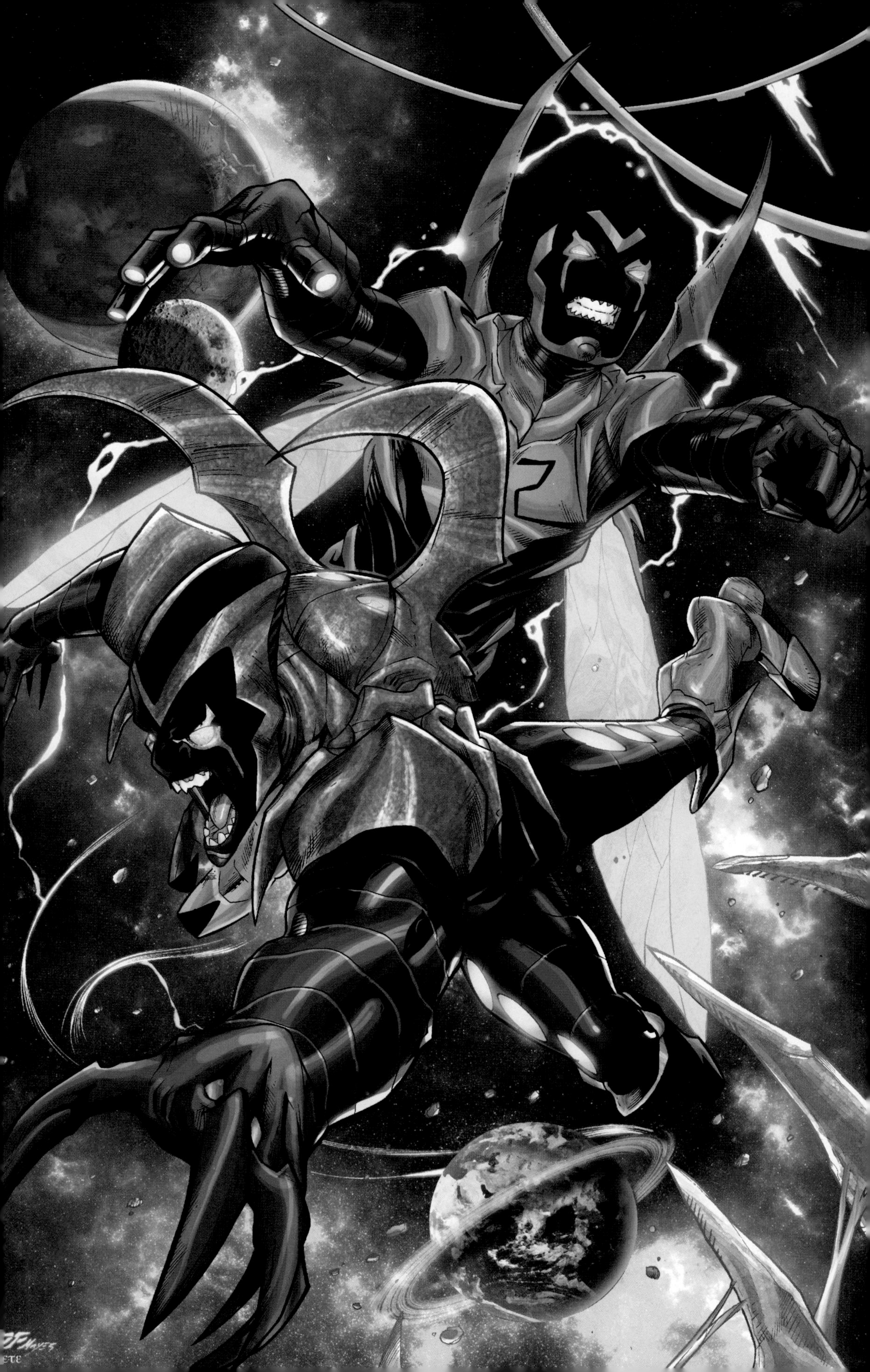

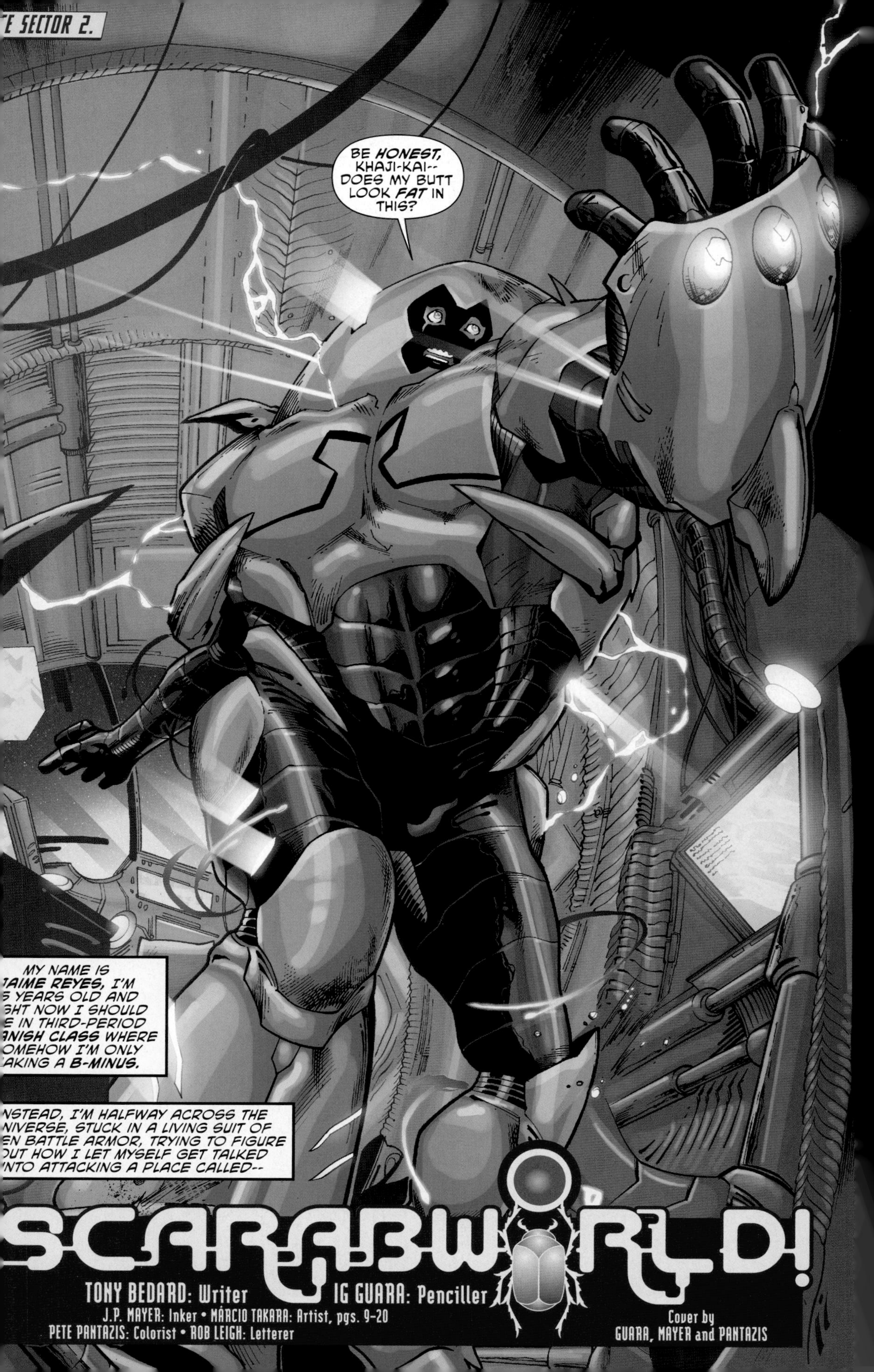
E SECTOR 2.
BE HONEST, KHAJI-KAI-- DOES MY BUTT LOOK FAT IN THIS?
MY NAME IS JAIME REYES, I'M 5 YEARS OLD AND GHT NOW I SHOULD E IN THIRD-PERIOD ANISH CLASS WHERE OMEHOW I'M ONLY AKING A B-MINUS.
NSTEAD, I'M HALFWAY ACROSS THE NIVERSE, STUCK IN A LIVING SUIT OF EN BATTLE ARMOR, TRYING TO FIGURE UT HOW I LET MYSELF GET TALKED NTO ATTACKING A PLACE CALLED--
SCARABWORLD!
TONY BEDARD: Writer
IG GUARA: Penciller
J.P. MAYER: Inker • MÁRCIO TAKARA: Artist, pgs. 9-20
PETE PANTAZIS: Colorist • ROB LEIGH: Letterer
Cover by GUARA, MAYER and PANTAZIS

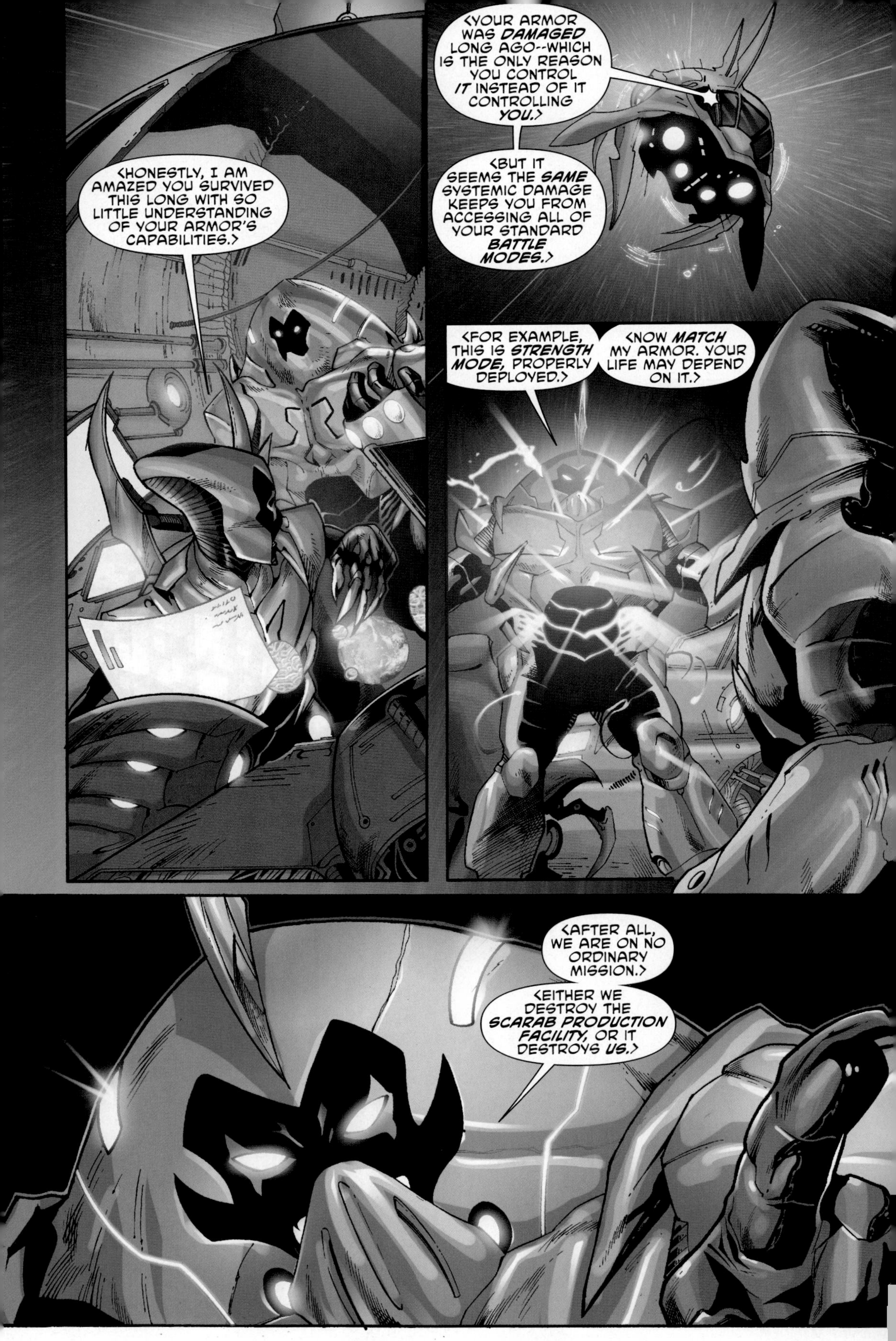
<HONESTLY, I AM AMAZED YOU SURVIVED THIS LONG WITH SO LITTLE UNDERSTANDING OF YOUR ARMOR'S CAPABILITIES.>
<YOUR ARMOR WAS DAMAGED LONG AGO--WHICH IS THE ONLY REASON YOU CONTROL IT INSTEAD OF IT CONTROLLING YOU.>
<BUT IT SEEMS THE SAME SYSTEMIC DAMAGE KEEPS YOU FROM ACCESSING ALL OF YOUR STANDARD BATTLE MODES.>
<FOR EXAMPLE, THIS IS STRENGTH MODE, PROPERLY DEPLOYED.>
<NOW MATCH MY ARMOR. YOUR LIFE MAY DEPEND ON IT.>
<AFTER ALL, WE ARE ON NO ORDINARY MISSION.>
<EITHER WE DESTROY THE SCARAB PRODUCTION FACILITY, OR IT DESTROYS US.>

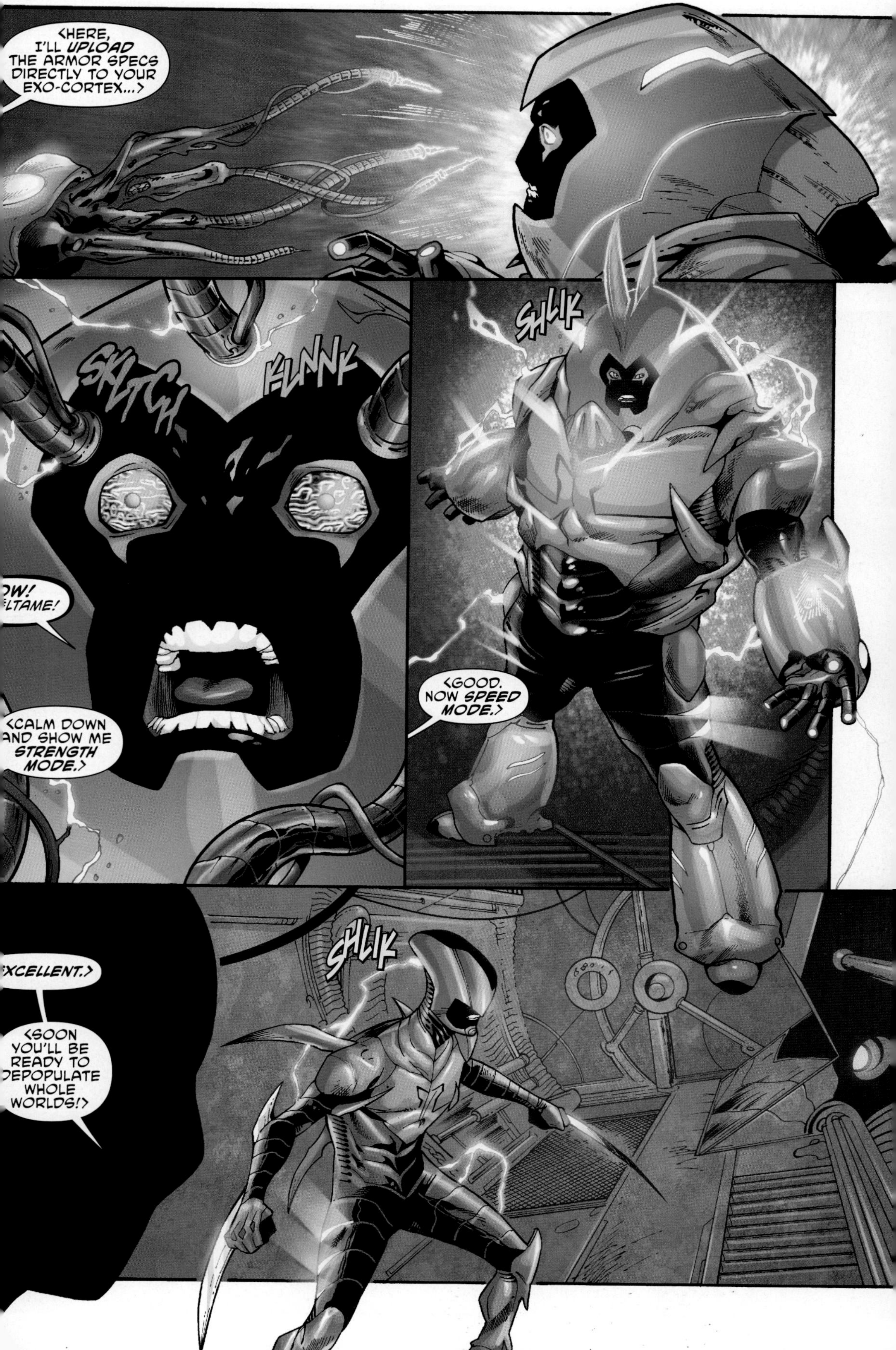

<HERE, I'LL UPLOAD THE ARMOR SPECS DIRECTLY TO YOUR EXO-CORTEX...>
SKLTCH
KLNNK
OW! ELTAME!
<CALM DOWN AND SHOW ME STRENGTH MODE.>
SHLIK
<GOOD. NOW SPEED MODE.>
SHLIK
XCELLENT.>
<SOON YOU'LL BE READY TO DEPOPULATE WHOLE WORLDS!>

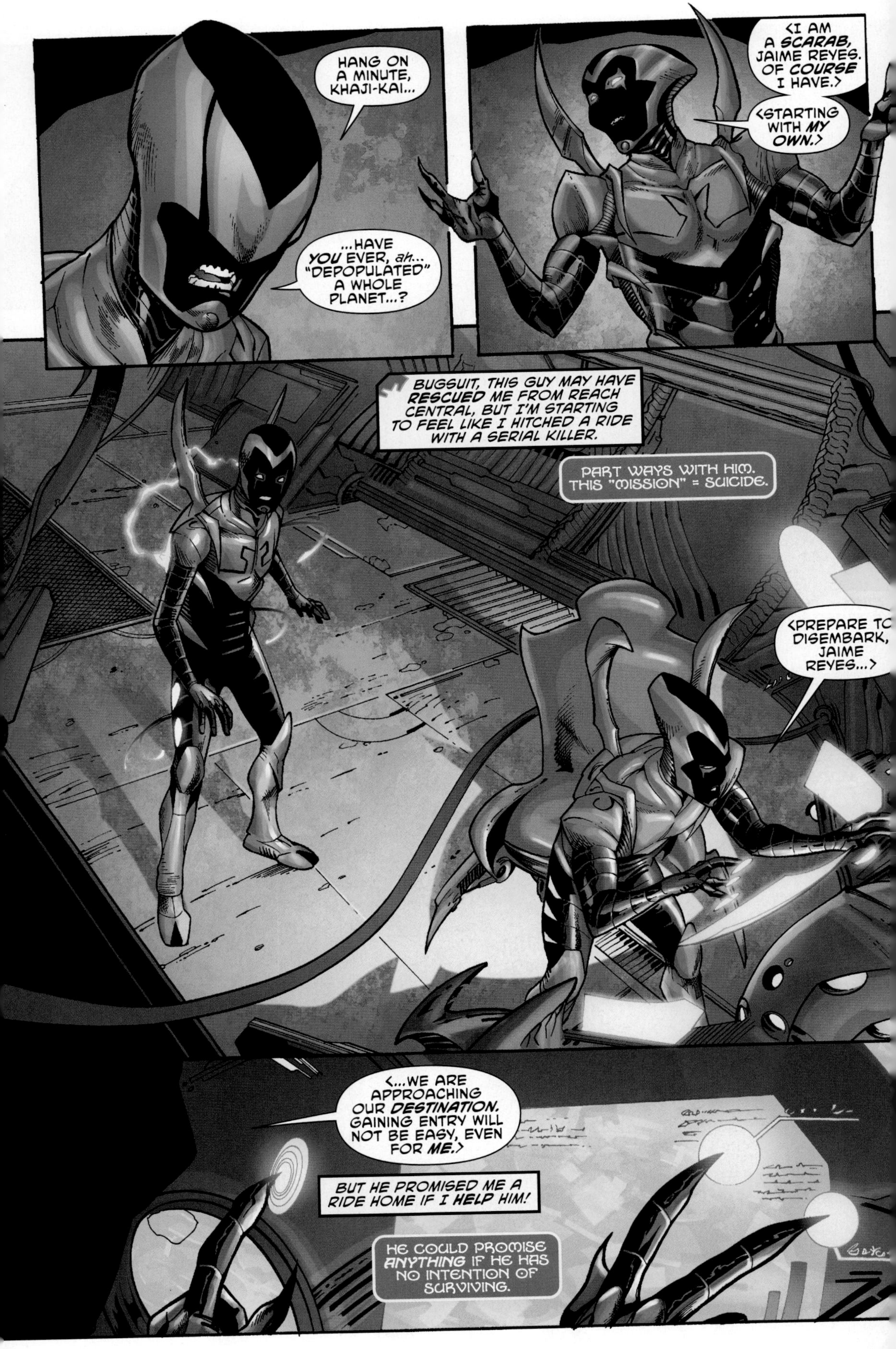
HANG ON A MINUTE, KHAJI-KAI...
...HAVE YOU EVER, ah... "DEPOPULATED" A WHOLE PLANET...?
<I AM A SCARAB, JAIME REYES. OF COURSE I HAVE.>
<STARTING WITH MY OWN.>
BUGSUIT, THIS GUY MAY HAVE RESCUED ME FROM REACH CENTRAL, BUT I'M STARTING TO FEEL LIKE I HITCHED A RIDE WITH A SERIAL KILLER.
PART WAYS WITH HIM. THIS "MISSION" = SUICIDE.
<PREPARE TO DISEMBARK, JAIME REYES...>
<...WE ARE APPROACHING OUR DESTINATION. GAINING ENTRY WILL NOT BE EASY, EVEN FOR ME.>
BUT HE PROMISED ME A RIDE HOME IF I HELP HIM!
HE COULD PROMISE ANYTHING IF HE HAS NO INTENTION OF SURVIVING.

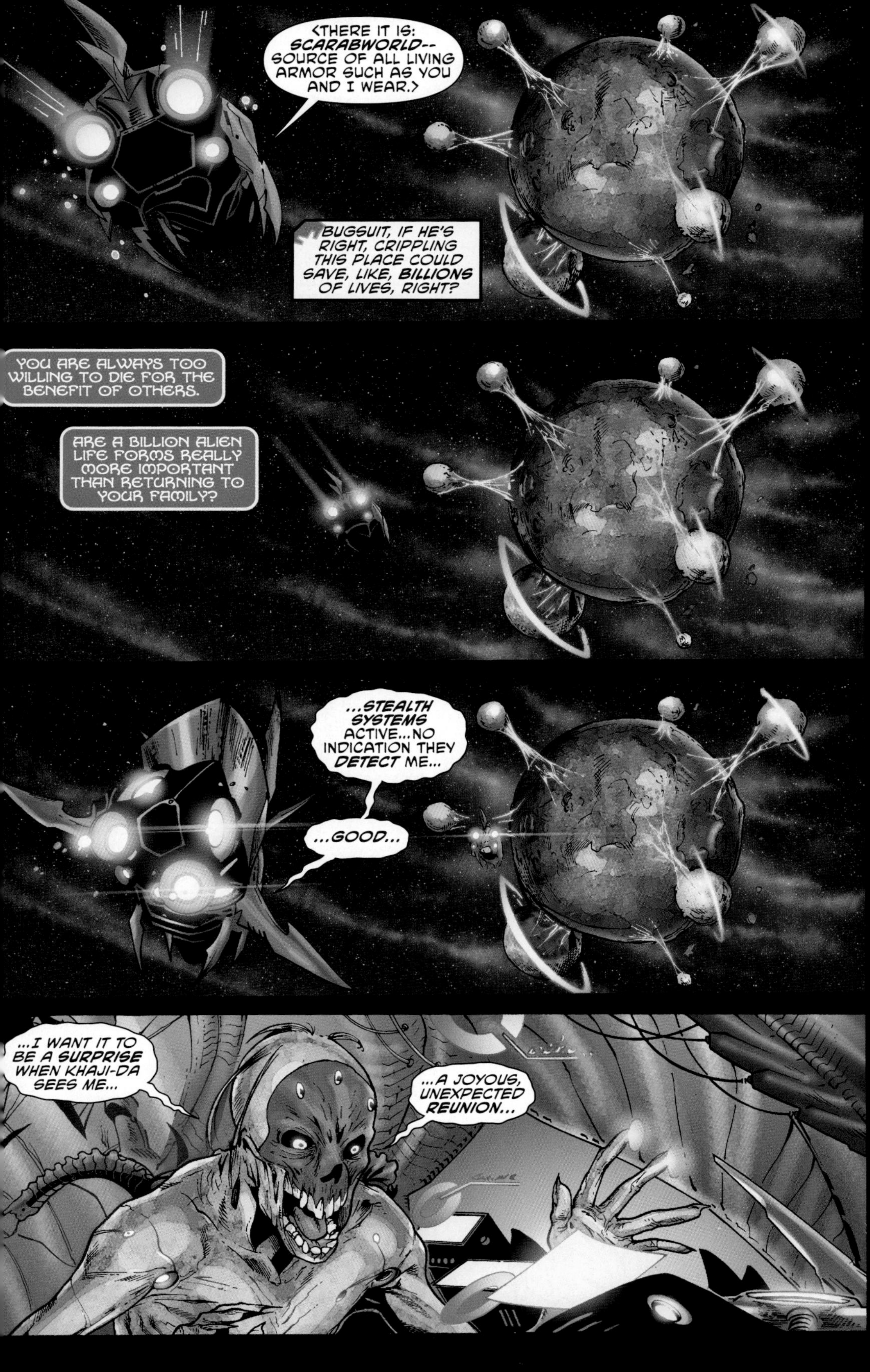
<THERE IT IS: SCARABWORLD-- SOURCE OF ALL LIVING ARMOR SUCH AS YOU AND I WEAR.>
BUGSUIT, IF HE'S RIGHT, CRIPPLING THIS PLACE COULD SAVE, LIKE, BILLIONS OF LIVES, RIGHT?
YOU ARE ALWAYS TOO WILLING TO DIE FOR THE BENEFIT OF OTHERS.
ARE A BILLION ALIEN LIFE FORMS REALLY MORE IMPORTANT THAN RETURNING TO YOUR FAMILY?
...STEALTH SYSTEMS ACTIVE...NO INDICATION THEY DETECT ME...
...GOOD...
...I WANT IT TO BE A SURPRISE WHEN KHAJI-DA SEES ME...
...A JOYOUS, UNEXPECTED REUNION...

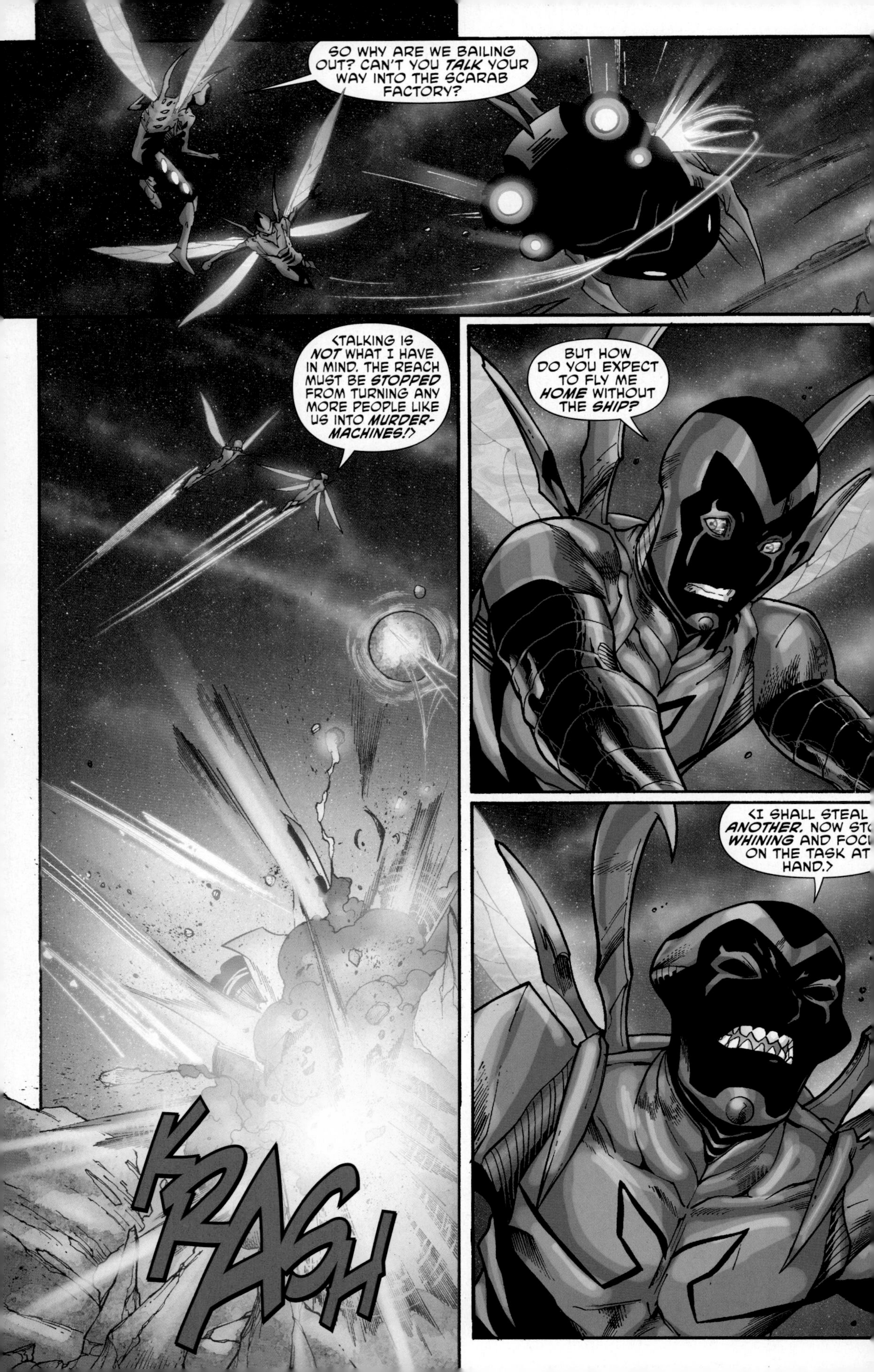

SO WHY ARE WE BAILING OUT? CAN'T YOU *TALK* YOUR WAY INTO THE SCARAB FACTORY?
<TALKING IS *NOT* WHAT I HAVE IN MIND. THE REACH MUST BE *STOPPED* FROM TURNING ANY MORE PEOPLE LIKE US INTO *MURDER-MACHINES!*>
KRASH
BUT HOW DO YOU EXPECT TO FLY ME *HOME* WITHOUT THE *SHIP?*
<I SHALL STEAL *ANOTHER.* NOW STO *WHINING* AND FOCU ON THE TASK AT HAND.>

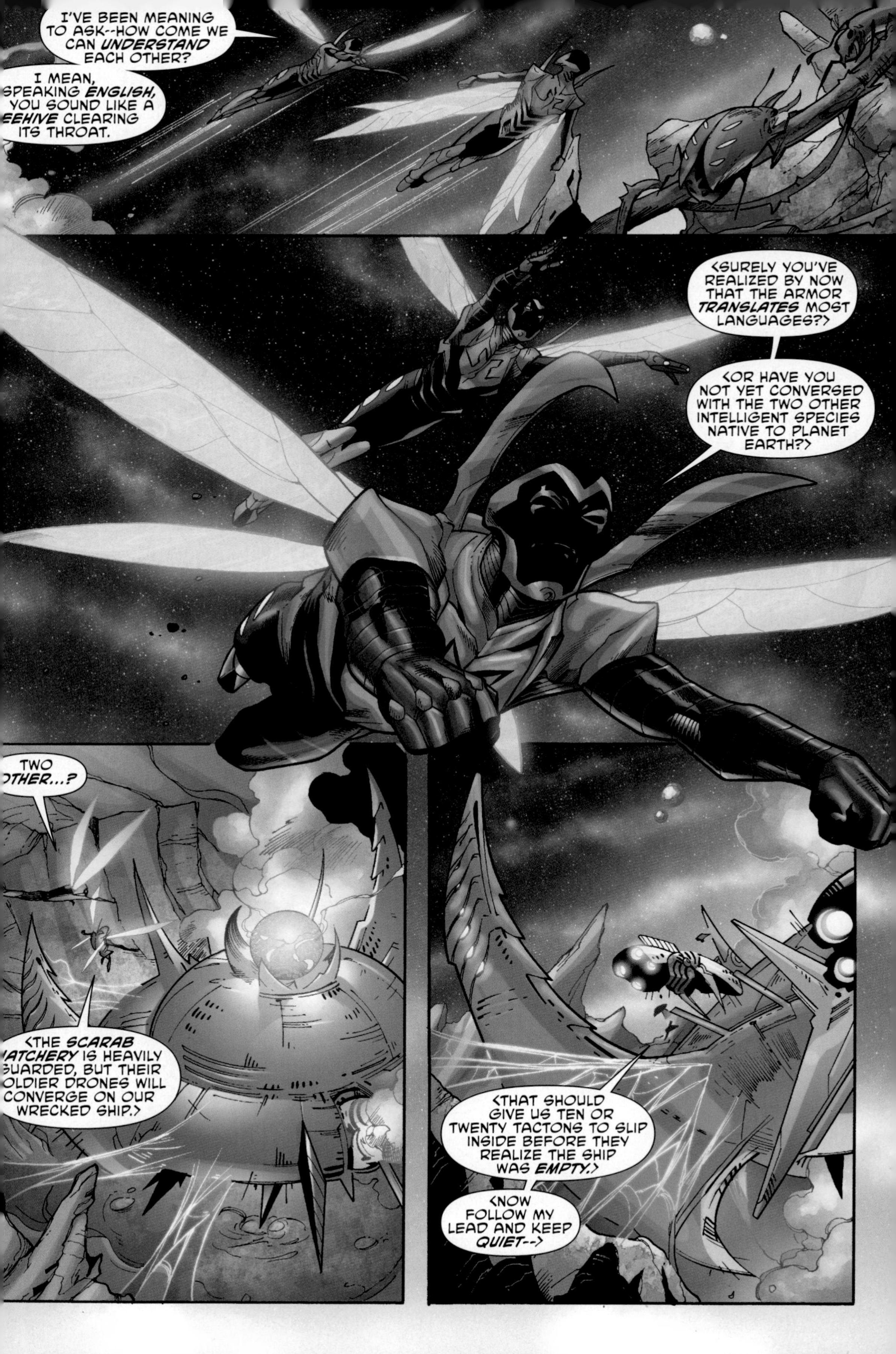

I'VE BEEN MEANING TO ASK--HOW COME WE CAN UNDERSTAND EACH OTHER?
I MEAN, SPEAKING ENGLISH, YOU SOUND LIKE A EEHIVE CLEARING ITS THROAT.
<SURELY YOU'VE REALIZED BY NOW THAT THE ARMOR TRANSLATES MOST LANGUAGES?>
<OR HAVE YOU NOT YET CONVERSED WITH THE TWO OTHER INTELLIGENT SPECIES NATIVE TO PLANET EARTH?>
TWO THER...?
<THE SCARAB ATCHERY IS HEAVILY UARDED, BUT THEIR OLDIER DRONES WILL CONVERGE ON OUR WRECKED SHIP.>
<THAT SHOULD GIVE US TEN OR TWENTY TACTONS TO SLIP INSIDE BEFORE THEY REALIZE THE SHIP WAS EMPTY.>
<NOW FOLLOW MY LEAD AND KEEP QUIET-->

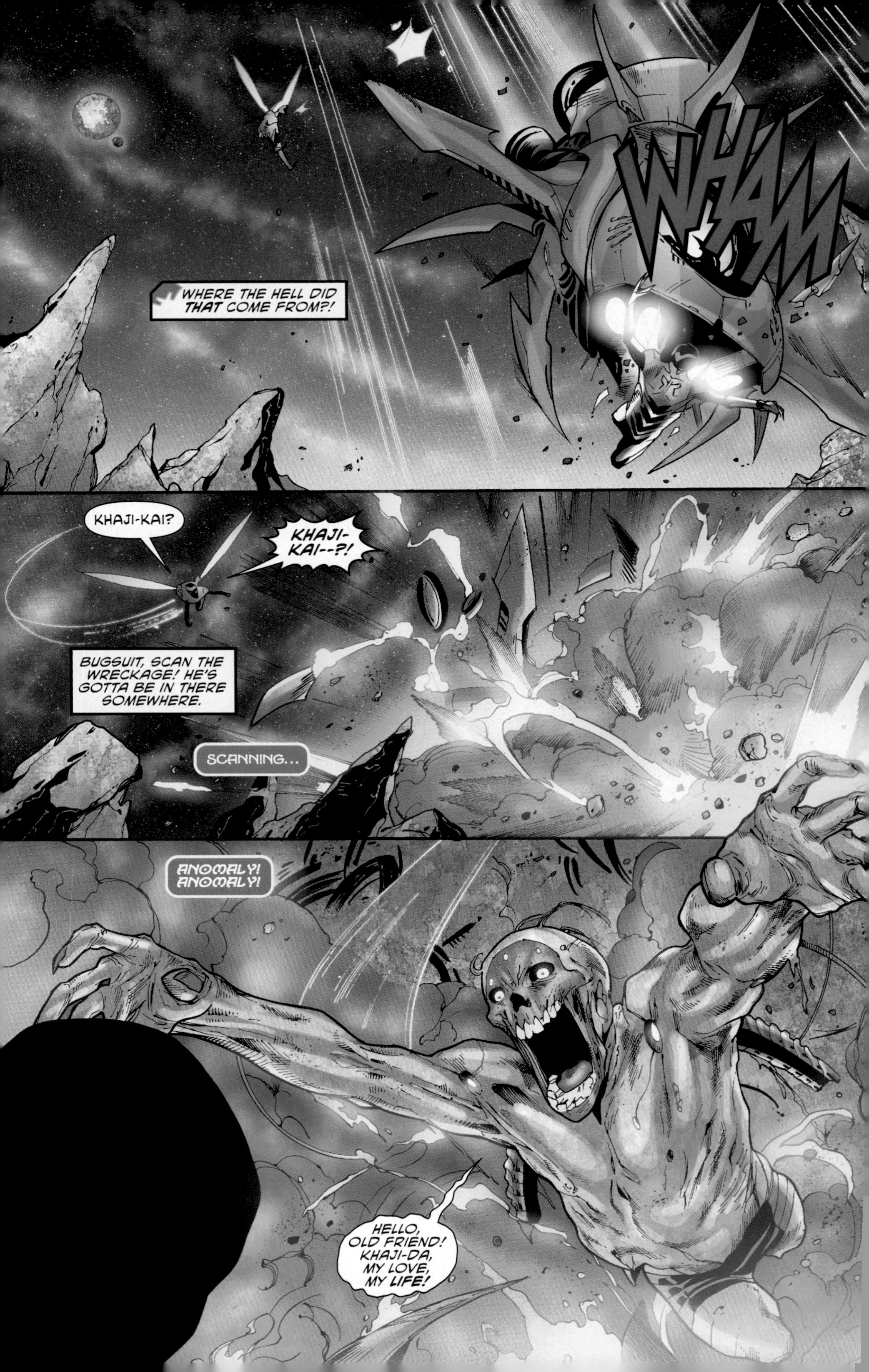
WHAM
WHERE THE HELL DID THAT COME FROM?!
KHAJI-KAI?
KHAJI-KAI--?!
BUGSUIT, SCAN THE WRECKAGE! HE'S GOTTA BE IN THERE SOMEWHERE.
SCANNING...
ANOMALY! ANOMALY!
HELLO, OLD FRIEND! KHAJI-DA, MY LOVE, MY LIFE!

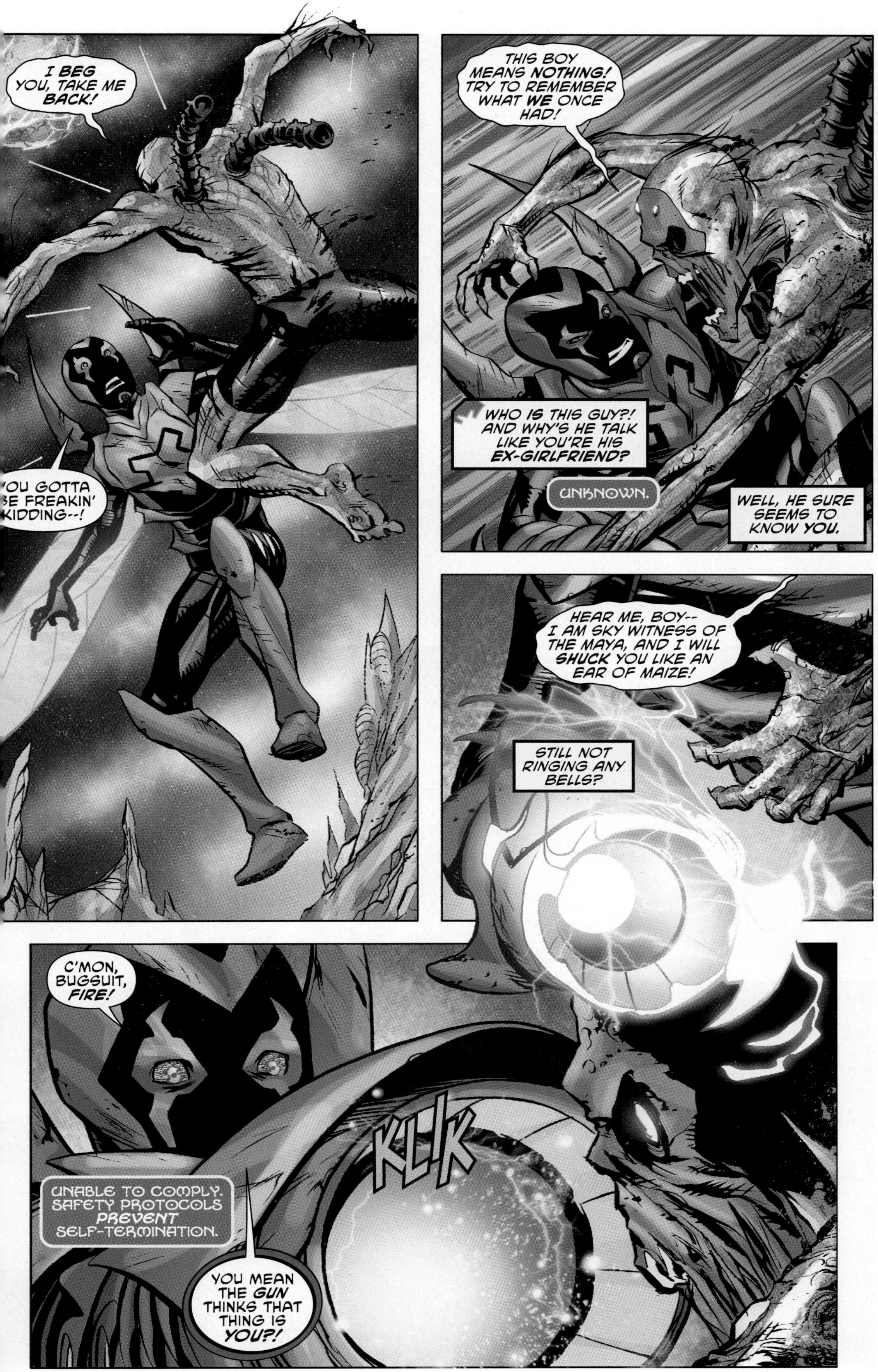
I BEG YOU, TAKE ME BACK!
YOU GOTTA BE FREAKIN' KIDDING--!
THIS BOY MEANS NOTHING! TRY TO REMEMBER WHAT WE ONCE HAD!
WHO IS THIS GUY?! AND WHY'S HE TALK LIKE YOU'RE HIS EX-GIRLFRIEND?
UNKNOWN.
WELL, HE SURE SEEMS TO KNOW YOU.
HEAR ME, BOY-- I AM SKY WITNESS OF THE MAYA, AND I WILL SHUCK YOU LIKE AN EAR OF MAIZE!
STILL NOT RINGING ANY BELLS?
C'MON, BUGSUIT, FIRE!
KLIK
UNABLE TO COMPLY. SAFETY PROTOCOLS PREVENT SELF-TERMINATION.
YOU MEAN THE GUN THINKS THAT THING IS YOU?!

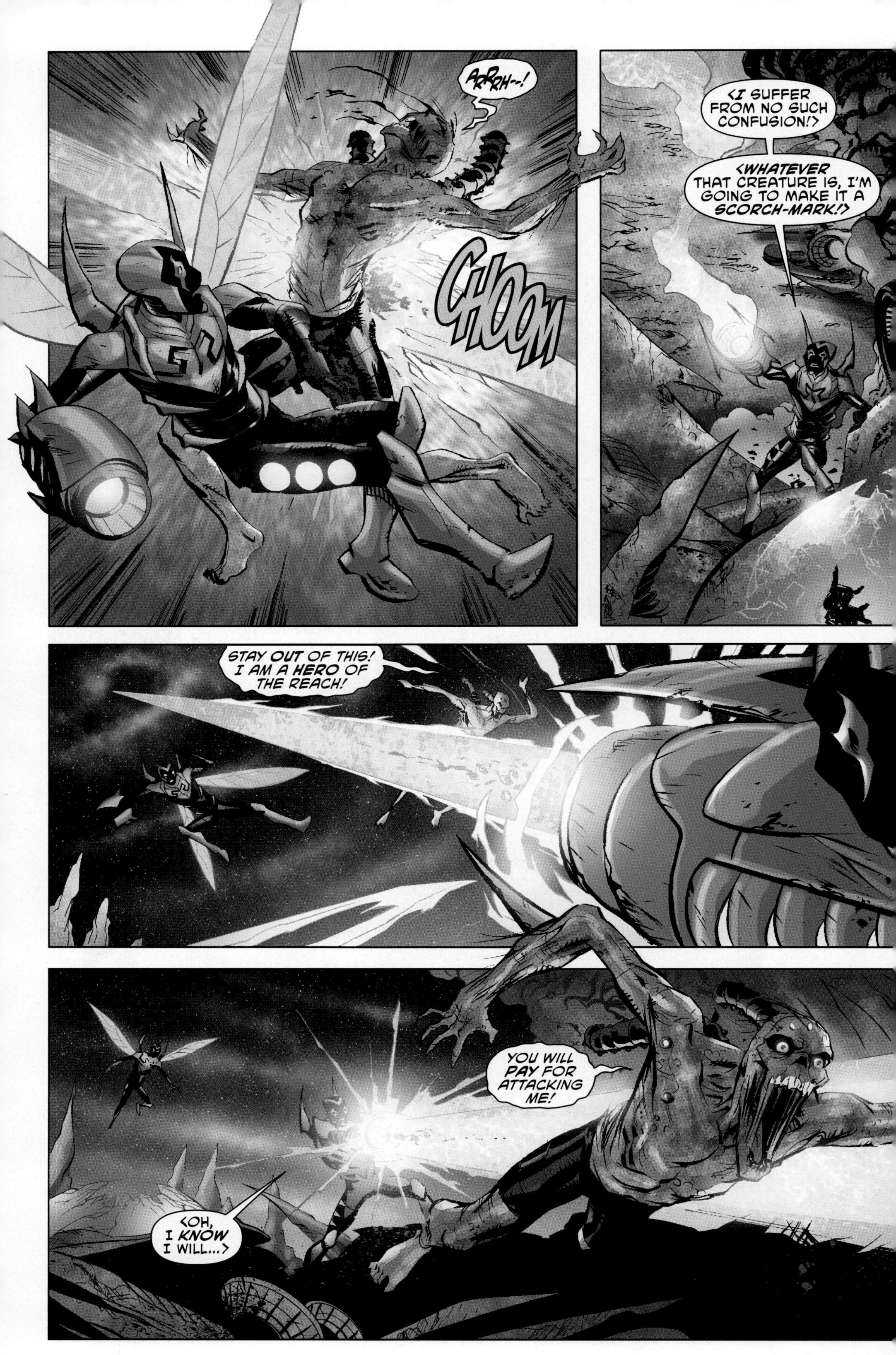
ARRRH--!
CHOOM
<I SUFFER FROM NO SUCH CONFUSION!>
<WHATEVER THAT CREATURE IS, I'M GOING TO MAKE IT A SCORCH-MARK!>
STAY OUT OF THIS! I AM A HERO OF THE REACH!
YOU WILL PAY FOR ATTACKING ME!
<OH, I KNOW I WILL...>

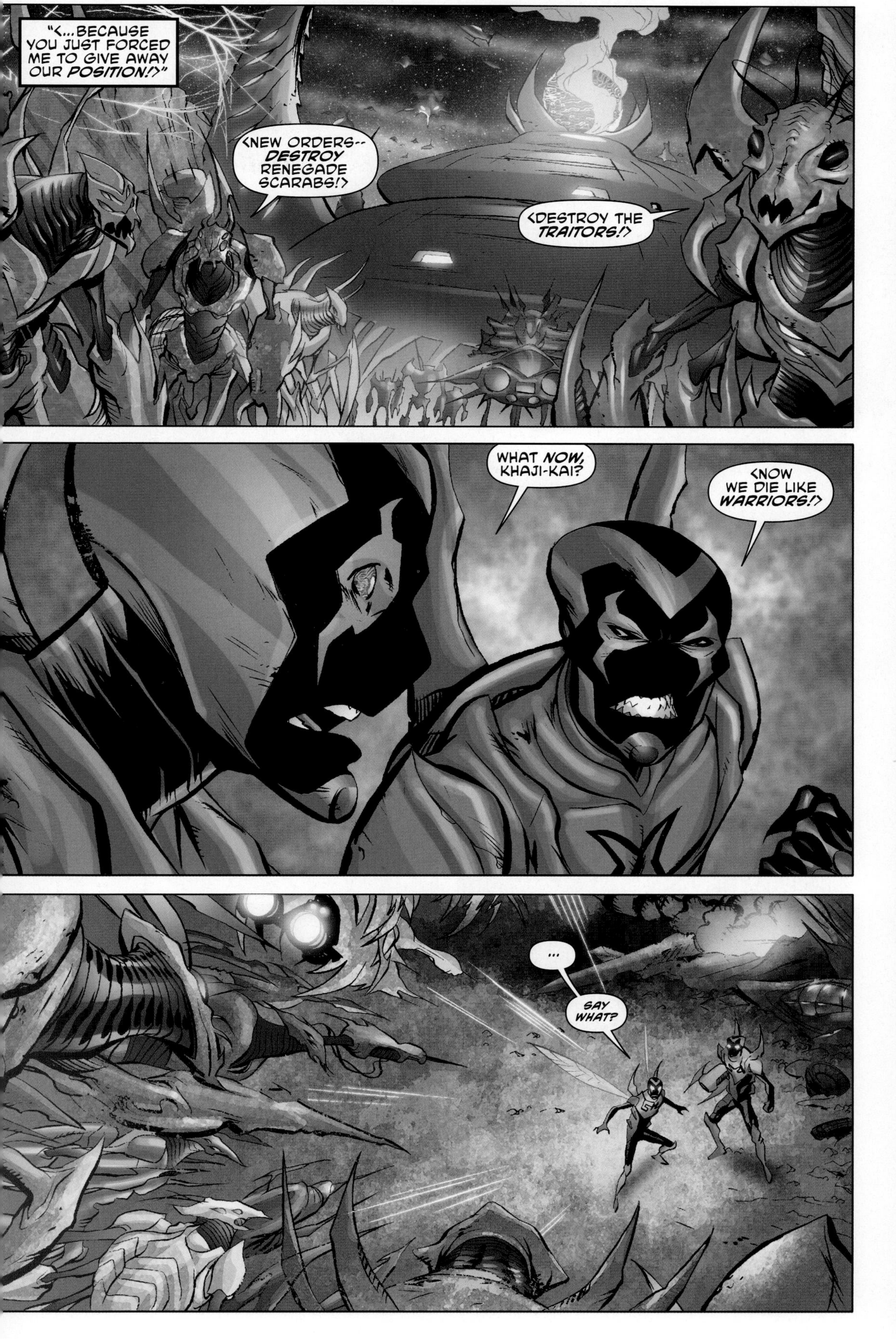

"<...BECAUSE YOU JUST FORCED ME TO GIVE AWAY OUR POSITION!>"
<NEW ORDERS-- DESTROY RENEGADE SCARABS!>
<DESTROY THE TRAITORS!>
WHAT NOW, KHAJI-KAI?
<NOW WE DIE LIKE WARRIORS!>
...
SAY WHAT?

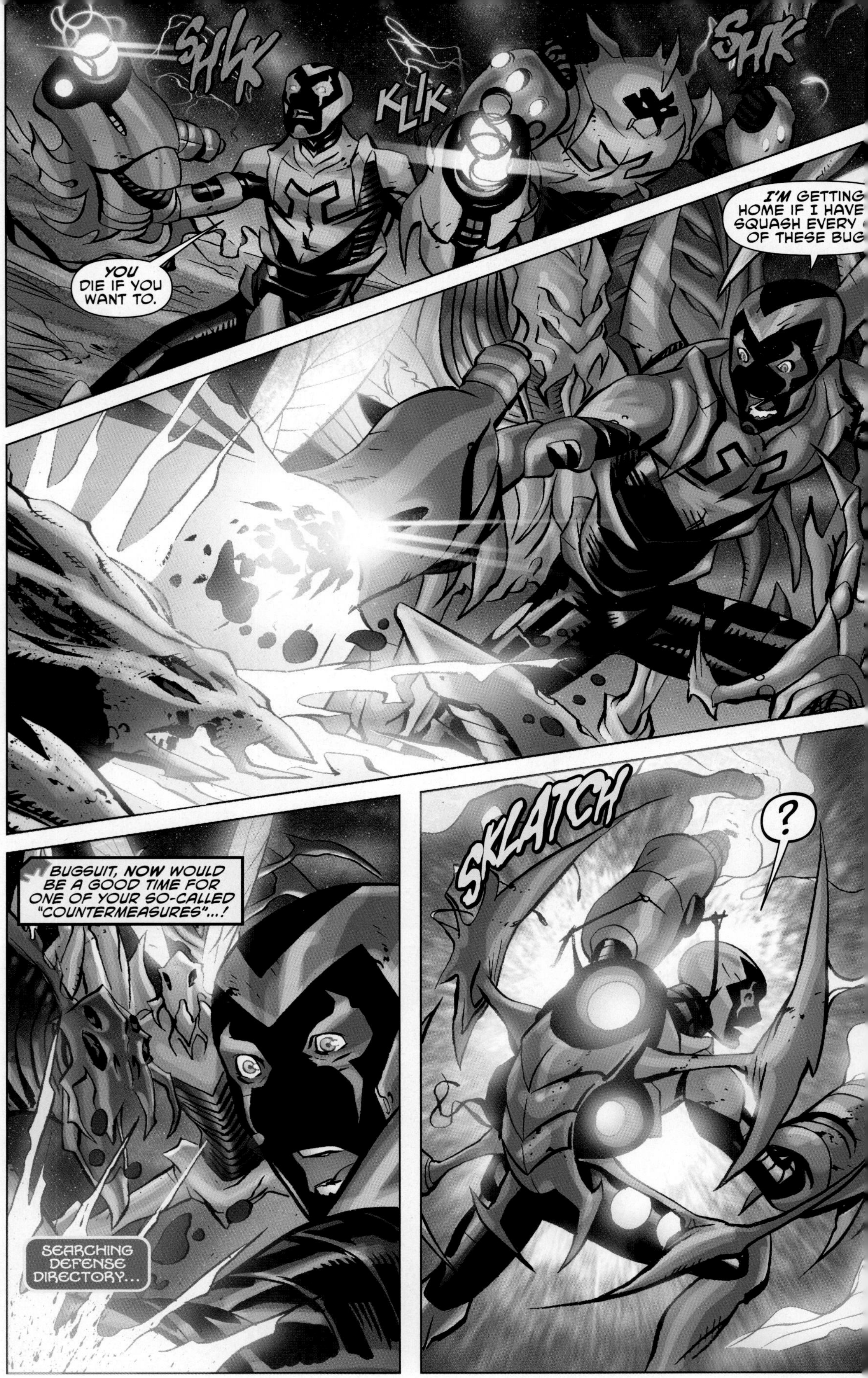
SHLK
KLIK
SHK
YOU DIE IF YOU WANT TO.
I'M GETTING HOME IF I HAVE SQUASH EVERY OF THESE BUG
BUGSUIT, NOW WOULD BE A GOOD TIME FOR ONE OF YOUR SO-CALLED "COUNTERMEASURES"...!
SEARCHING DEFENSE DIRECTORY...
SKLATCH
?

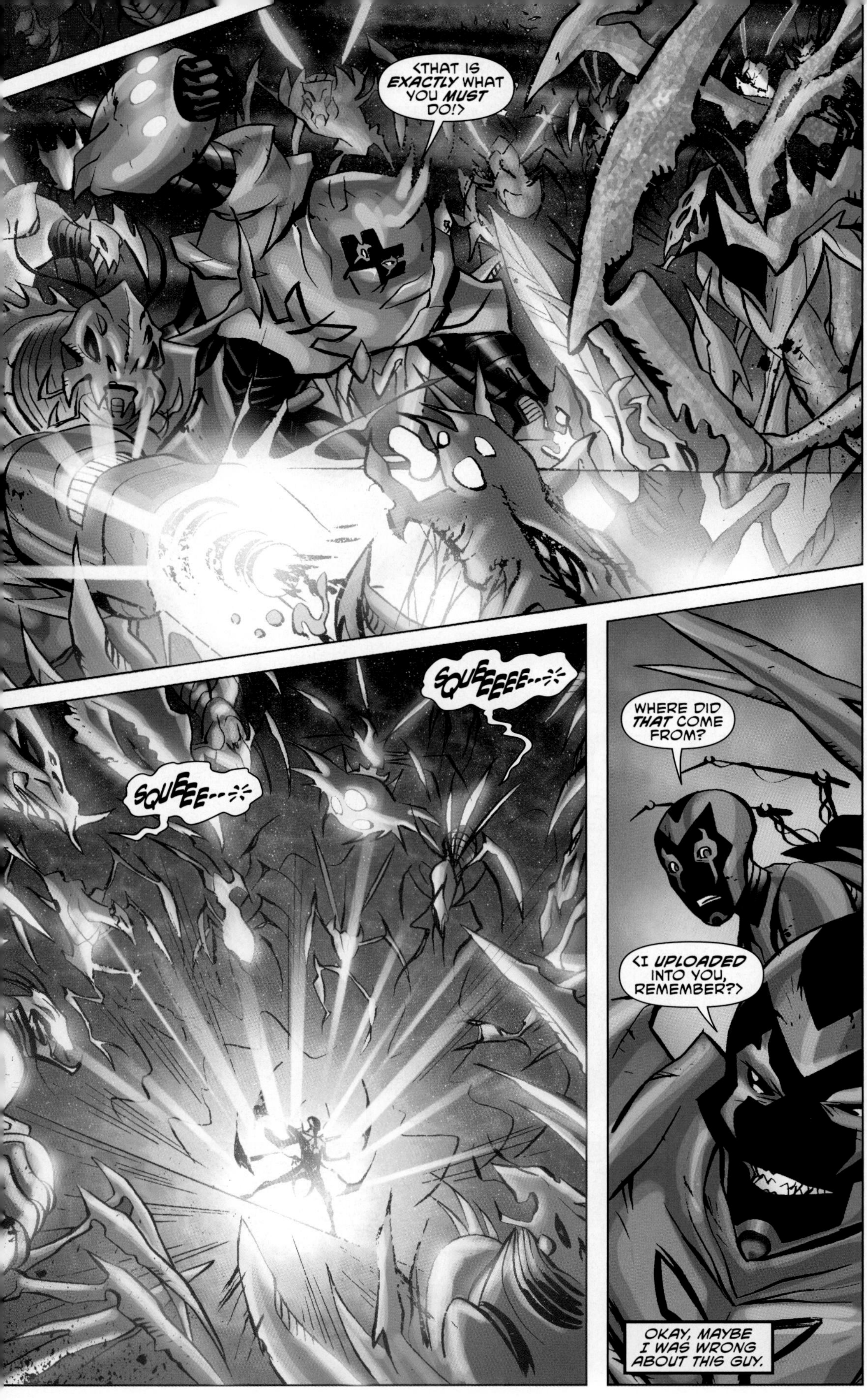
<THAT IS EXACTLY WHAT YOU MUST DO!>
SQUEEEE--
SQUEEEEEE--
WHERE DID THAT COME FROM?
<I UPLOADED INTO YOU, REMEMBER?>
OKAY, MAYBE I WAS WRONG ABOUT THIS GUY.

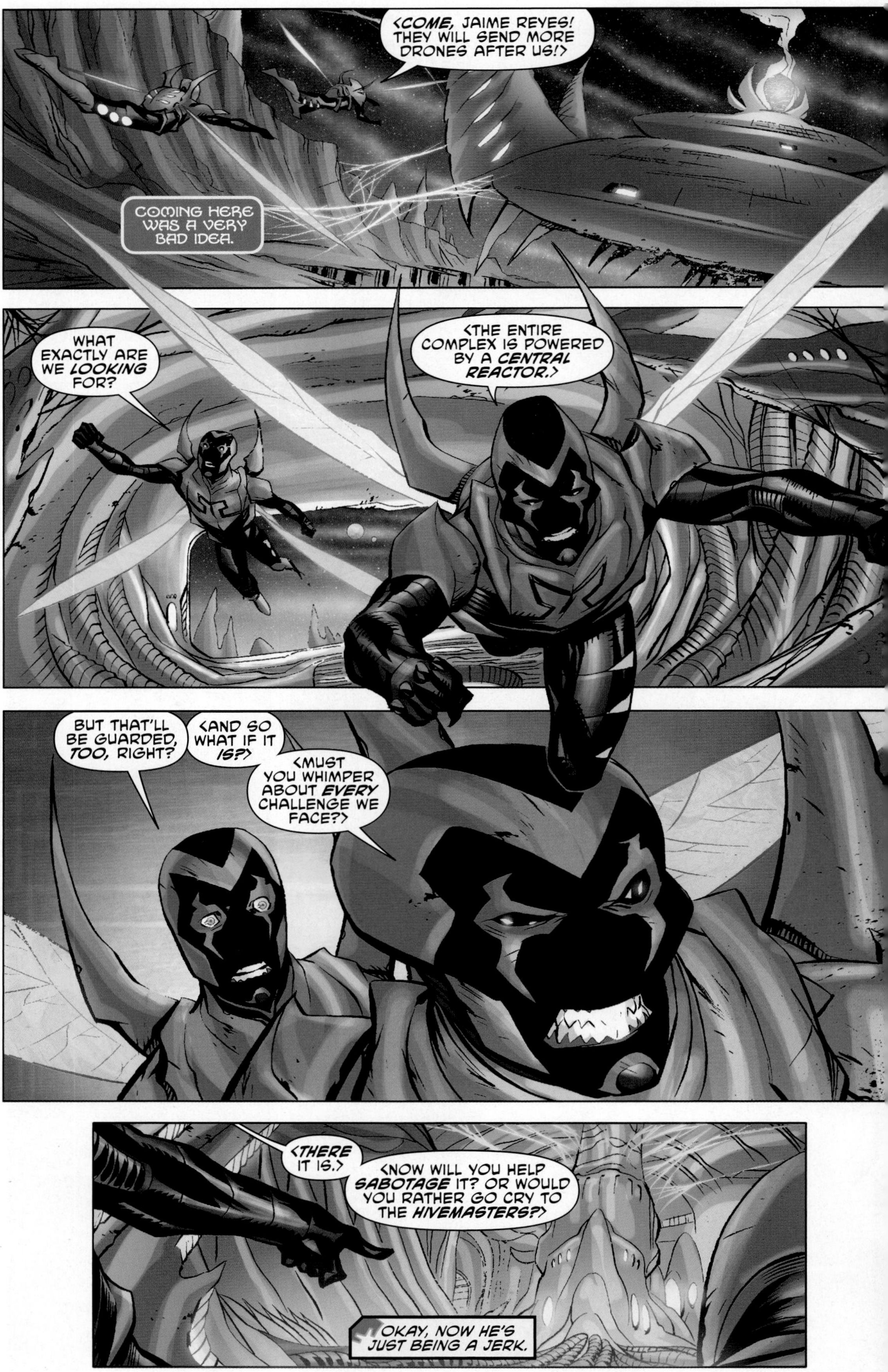

<COME, JAIME REYES! THEY WILL SEND MORE DRONES AFTER US!>
COMING HERE WAS A VERY BAD IDEA.
WHAT EXACTLY ARE WE LOOKING FOR?
<THE ENTIRE COMPLEX IS POWERED BY A CENTRAL REACTOR.>
BUT THAT'LL BE GUARDED, TOO, RIGHT?
<AND SO WHAT IF IT IS?>
<MUST YOU WHIMPER ABOUT EVERY CHALLENGE WE FACE?>
<THERE IT IS.>
<NOW WILL YOU HELP SABOTAGE IT? OR WOULD YOU RATHER GO CRY TO THE HIVEMASTERS?>
OKAY, NOW HE'S JUST BEING A JERK.

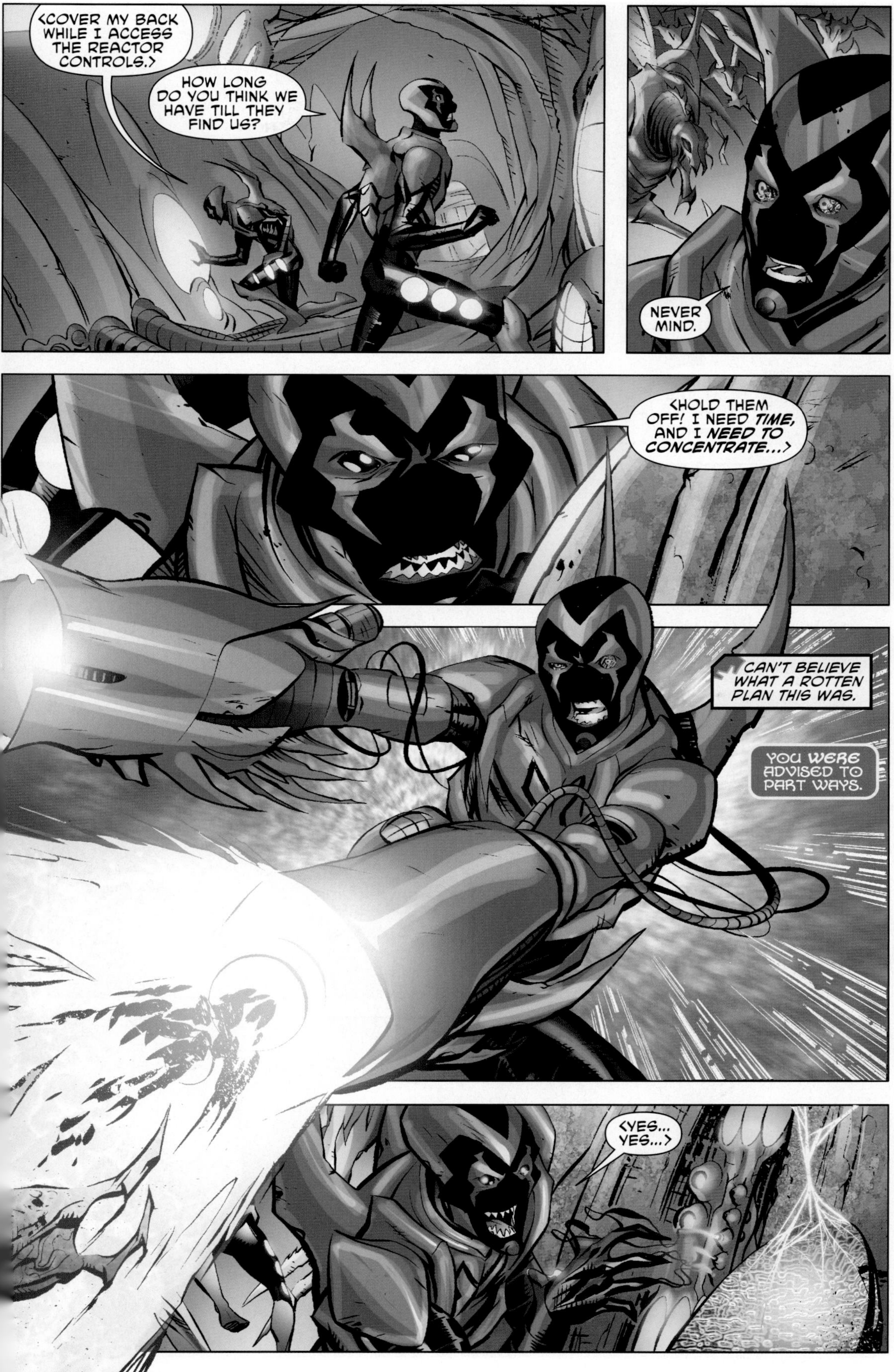
<COVER MY BACK WHILE I ACCESS THE REACTOR CONTROLS.>
HOW LONG DO YOU THINK WE HAVE TILL THEY FIND US?
NEVER MIND.
<HOLD THEM OFF! I NEED *TIME,* AND I *NEED TO CONCENTRATE...*>
CAN'T BELIEVE WHAT A ROTTEN PLAN THIS WAS.
YOU *WERE* ADVISED TO PART WAYS.
<YES... YES...>

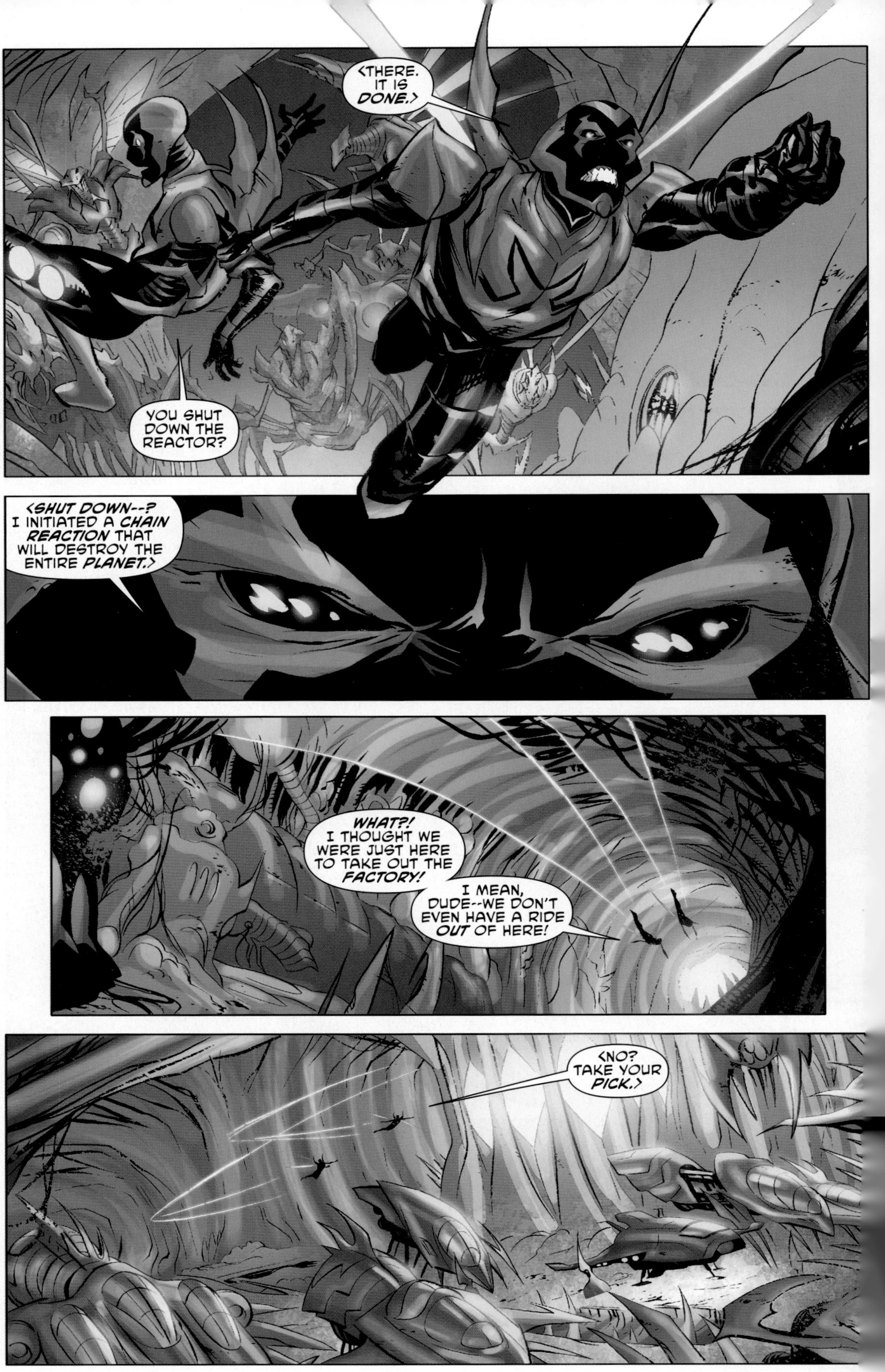
<THERE. IT IS DONE.>
YOU SHUT DOWN THE REACTOR?
<SHUT DOWN--? I INITIATED A CHAIN REACTION THAT WILL DESTROY THE ENTIRE PLANET.>
WHAT?! I THOUGHT WE WERE JUST HERE TO TAKE OUT THE FACTORY!
I MEAN, DUDE--WE DON'T EVEN HAVE A RIDE OUT OF HERE!
<NO? TAKE YOUR PICK.>

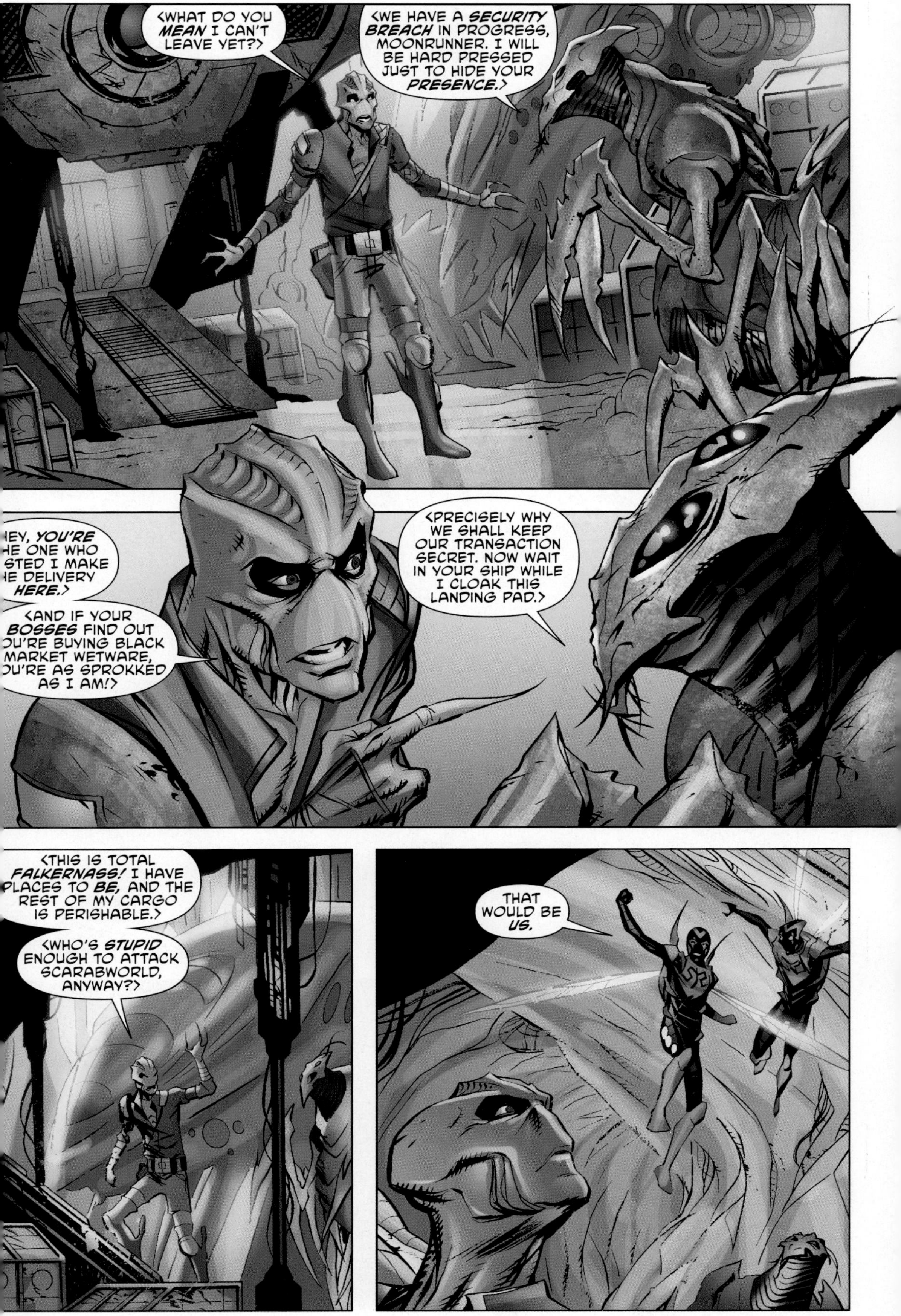

<WHAT DO YOU MEAN I CAN'T LEAVE YET?>
<WE HAVE A SECURITY BREACH IN PROGRESS, MOONRUNNER. I WILL BE HARD PRESSED JUST TO HIDE YOUR PRESENCE.>
EY, YOU'RE HE ONE WHO STED I MAKE HE DELIVERY HERE.>
<AND IF YOUR BOSSES FIND OUT OU'RE BUYING BLACK MARKET WETWARE, OU'RE AS SPROKKED AS I AM!>
<PRECISELY WHY WE SHALL KEEP OUR TRANSACTION SECRET. NOW WAIT IN YOUR SHIP WHILE I CLOAK THIS LANDING PAD.>
<THIS IS TOTAL FALKERNASS! I HAVE PLACES TO BE, AND THE REST OF MY CARGO IS PERISHABLE.>
<WHO'S STUPID ENOUGH TO ATTACK SCARABWORLD, ANYWAY?>
THAT WOULD BE US.

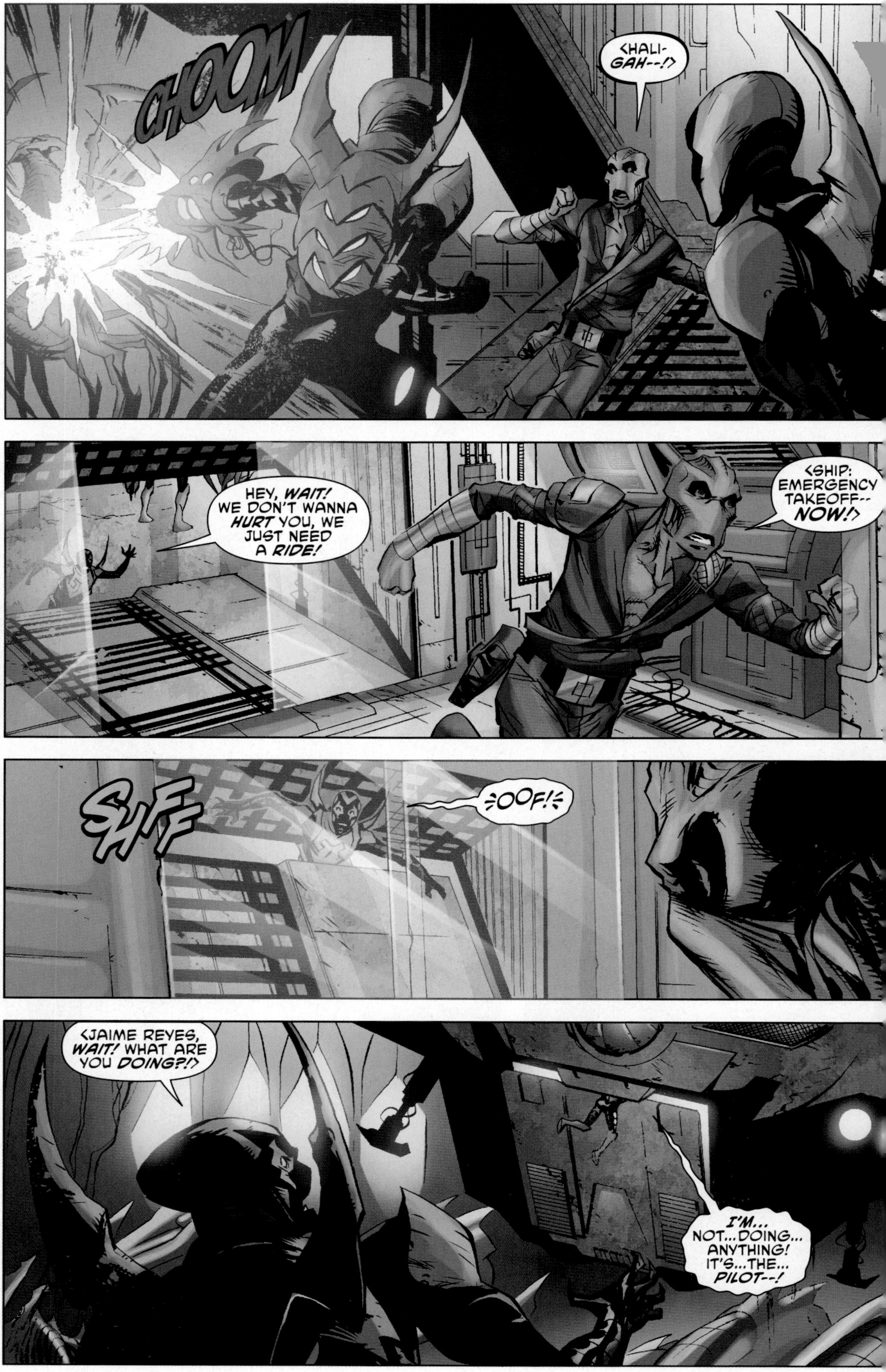
CHOOM
<HALI-GAH--!>
HEY, WAIT! WE DON'T WANNA HURT YOU, WE JUST NEED A RIDE!
<SHIP: EMERGENCY TAKEOFF--NOW!>
SHFF
OOF!
<JAIME REYES, WAIT! WHAT ARE YOU DOING?!>
I'M... NOT...DOING... ANYTHING! IT'S...THE... PILOT--!

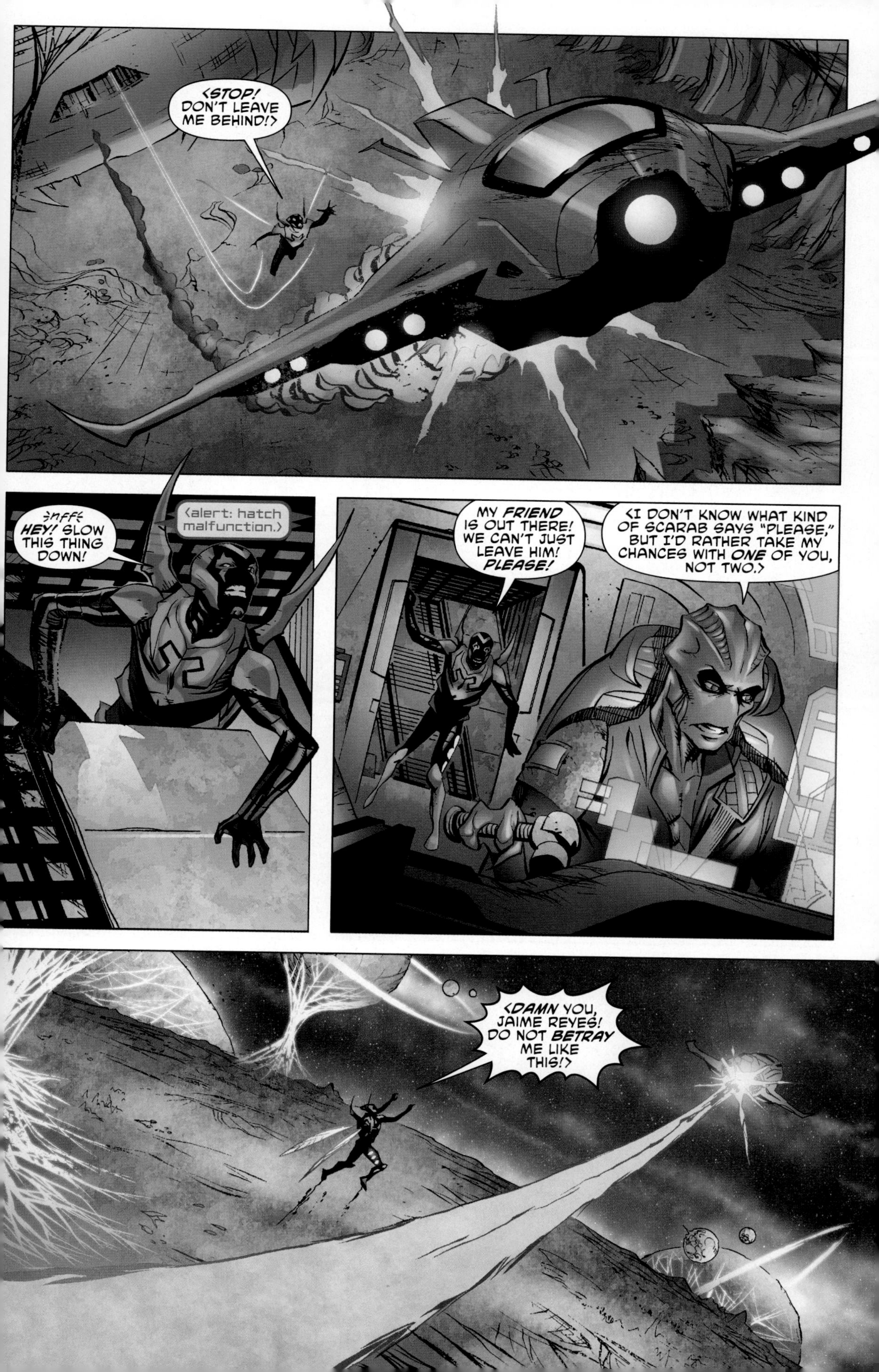

<STOP! DON'T LEAVE ME BEHIND!>
≷nff≷ HEY! SLOW THIS THING DOWN!
<alert: hatch malfunction.>
MY FRIEND IS OUT THERE! WE CAN'T JUST LEAVE HIM! PLEASE!
<I DON'T KNOW WHAT KIND OF SCARAB SAYS "PLEASE," BUT I'D RATHER TAKE MY CHANCES WITH ONE OF YOU, NOT TWO.>
<DAMN YOU, JAIME REYES! DO NOT BETRAY ME LIKE THIS!>

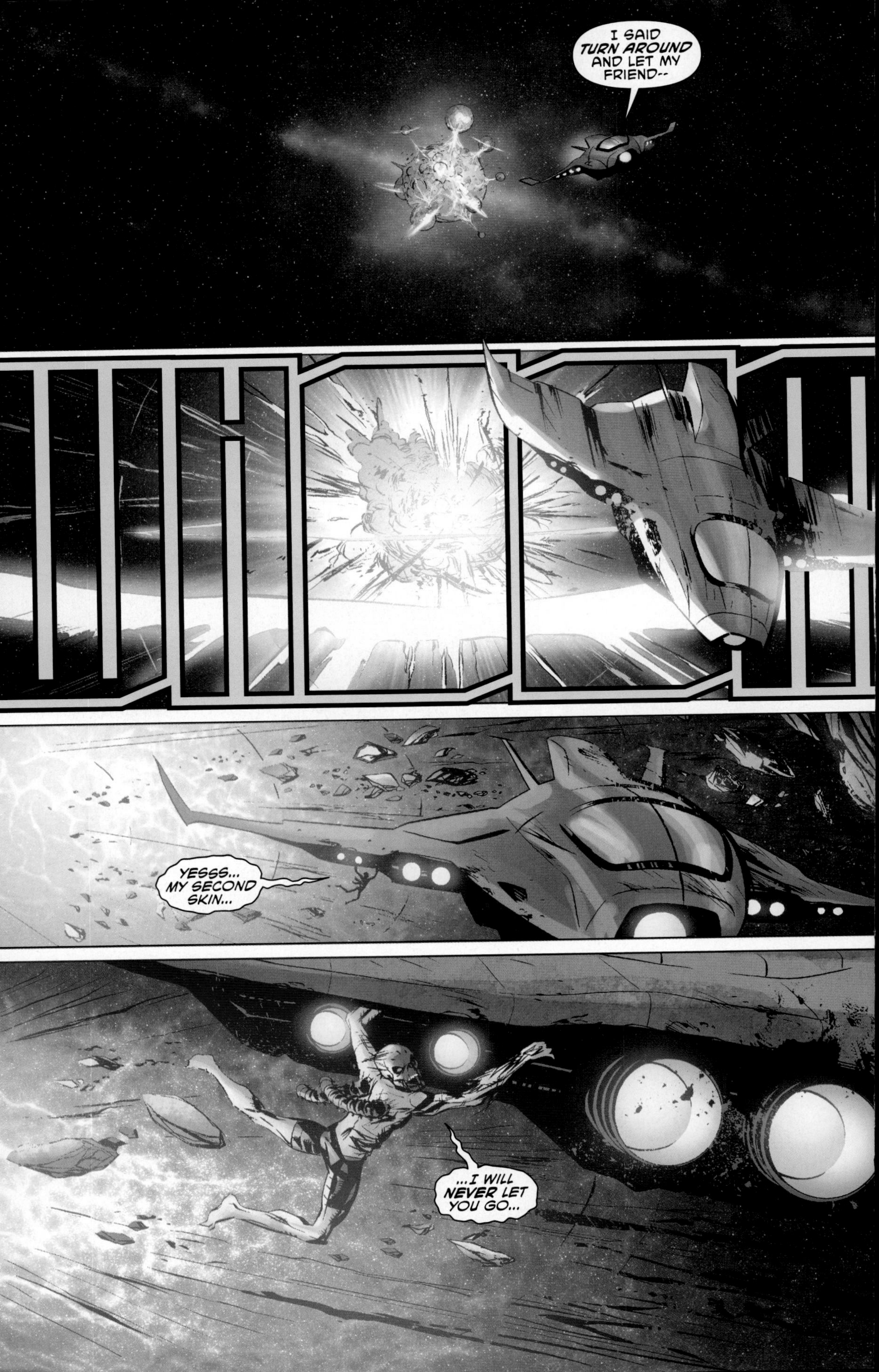
I SAID TURN AROUND AND LET MY FRIEND--
YESSS... MY SECOND SKIN...
...I WILL NEVER LET YOU GO...

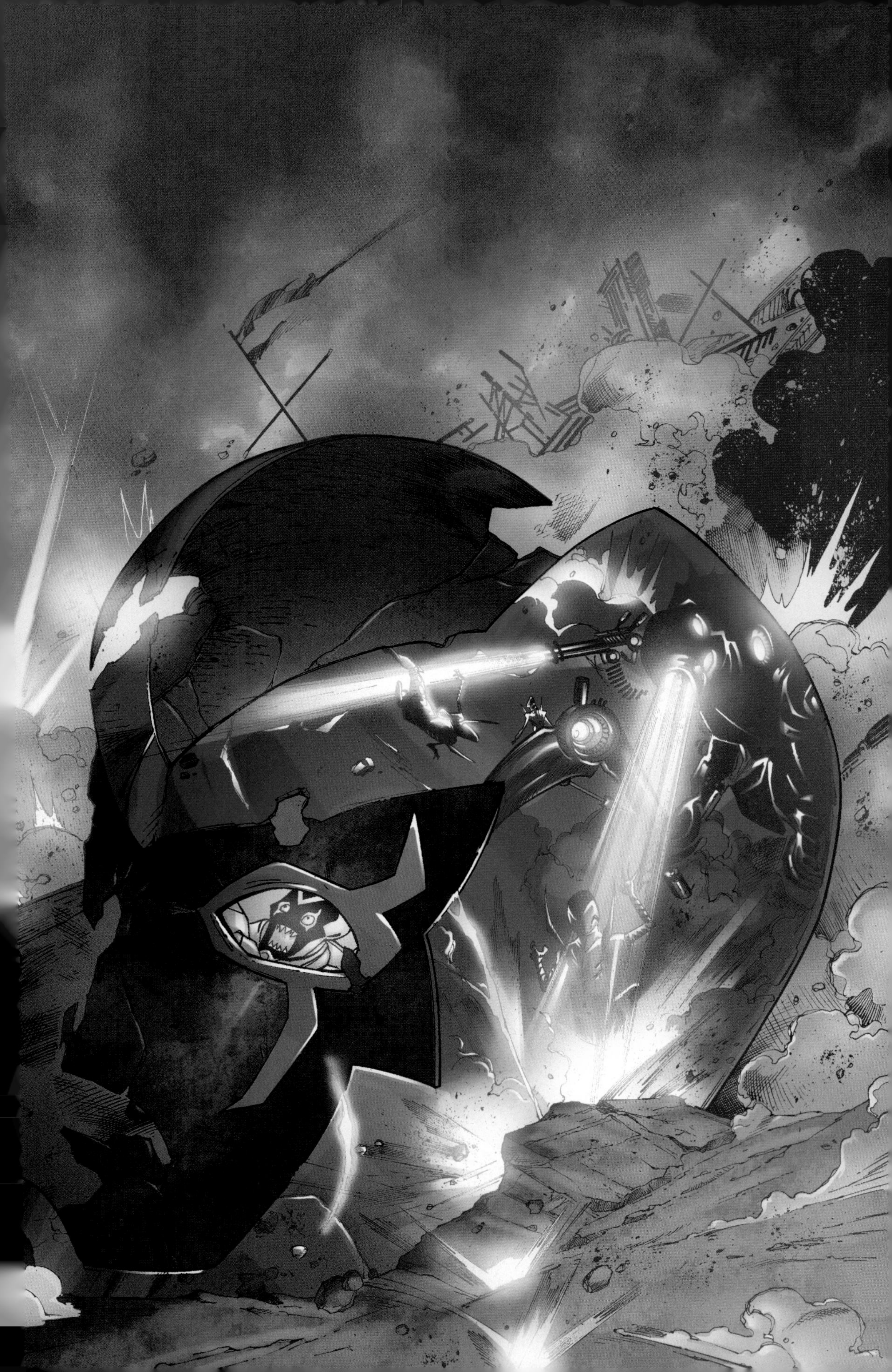

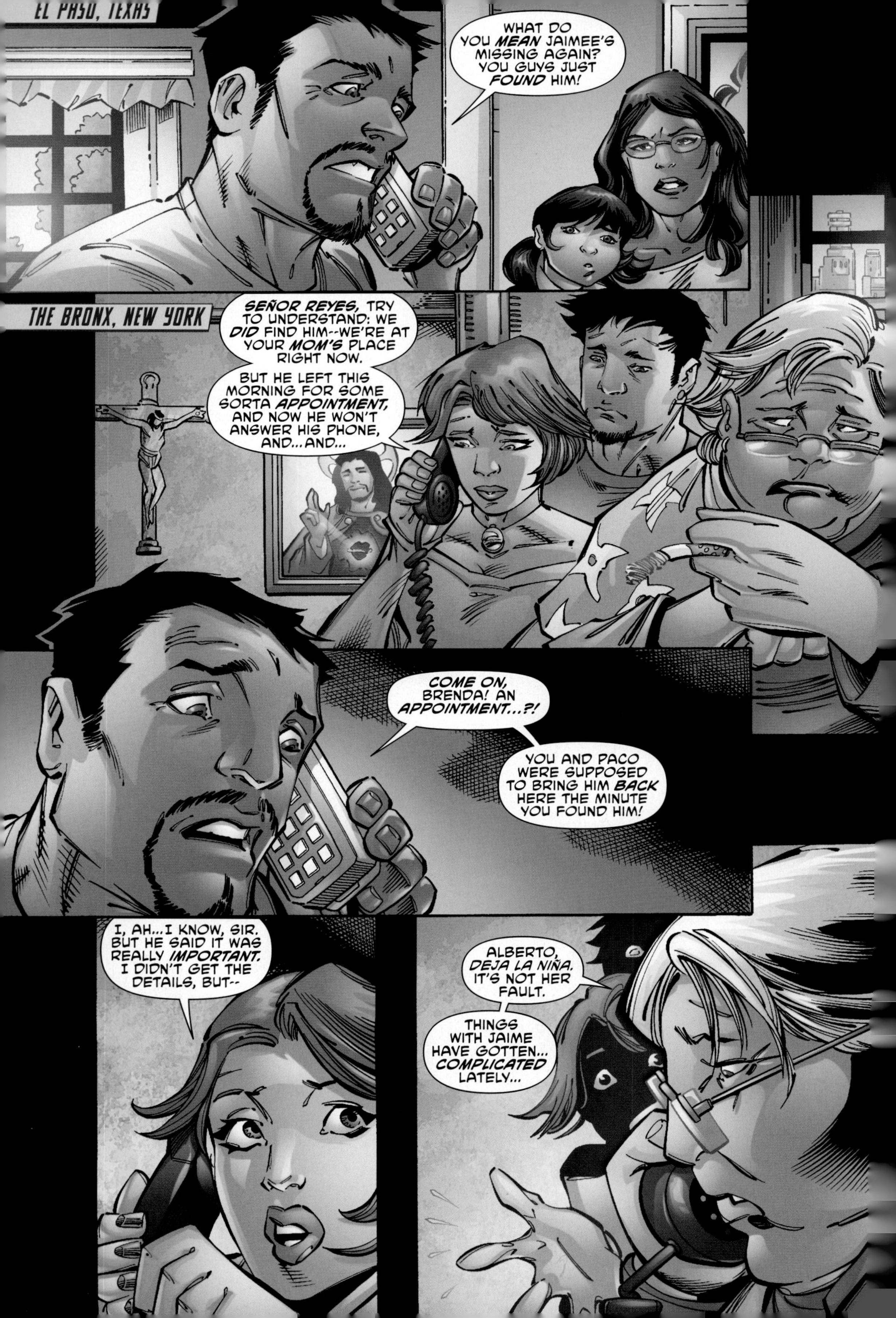
EL PASO, TEXAS
WHAT DO YOU *MEAN* JAIMEE'S MISSING AGAIN? YOU GUYS JUST *FOUND* HIM!
THE BRONX, NEW YORK
SEÑOR REYES, TRY TO UNDERSTAND: WE *DID* FIND HIM--WE'RE AT YOUR *MOM'S* PLACE RIGHT NOW.
BUT HE LEFT THIS MORNING FOR SOME SORTA *APPOINTMENT,* AND NOW HE WON'T ANSWER HIS PHONE, AND...AND...
COME ON, BRENDA! AN *APPOINTMENT...?!*
YOU AND PACO WERE SUPPOSED TO BRING HIM *BACK* HERE THE MINUTE YOU FOUND HIM!
I, AH...I KNOW, SIR. BUT HE SAID IT WAS REALLY *IMPORTANT.* I DIDN'T GET THE DETAILS, BUT--
ALBERTO, *DEJA LA NIÑA.* IT'S NOT HER FAULT.
THINGS WITH JAIME HAVE GOTTEN... *COMPLICATED* LATELY...

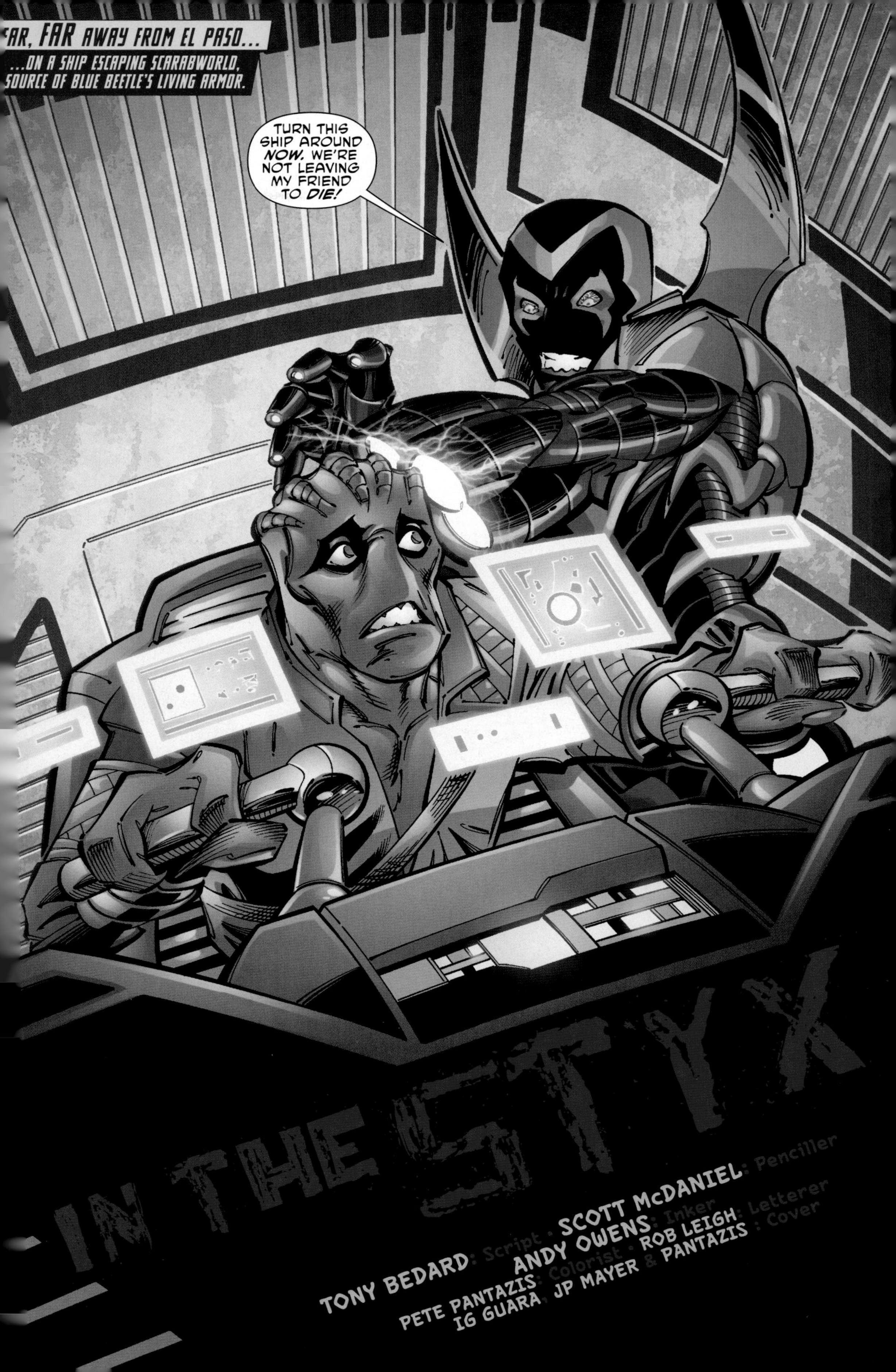
FAR, FAR AWAY FROM EL PASO...
...ON A SHIP ESCAPING SCARABWORLD, SOURCE OF BLUE BEETLE'S LIVING ARMOR.
TURN THIS SHIP AROUND NOW. WE'RE NOT LEAVING MY FRIEND TO DIE!
IN THE STYX
TONY BEDARD: Script · SCOTT McDANIEL: Penciller
ANDY OWENS: Inker
PETE PANTAZIS: Colorist · ROB LEIGH: Letterer
IG GUARA, JP MAYER & PANTAZIS : Cover

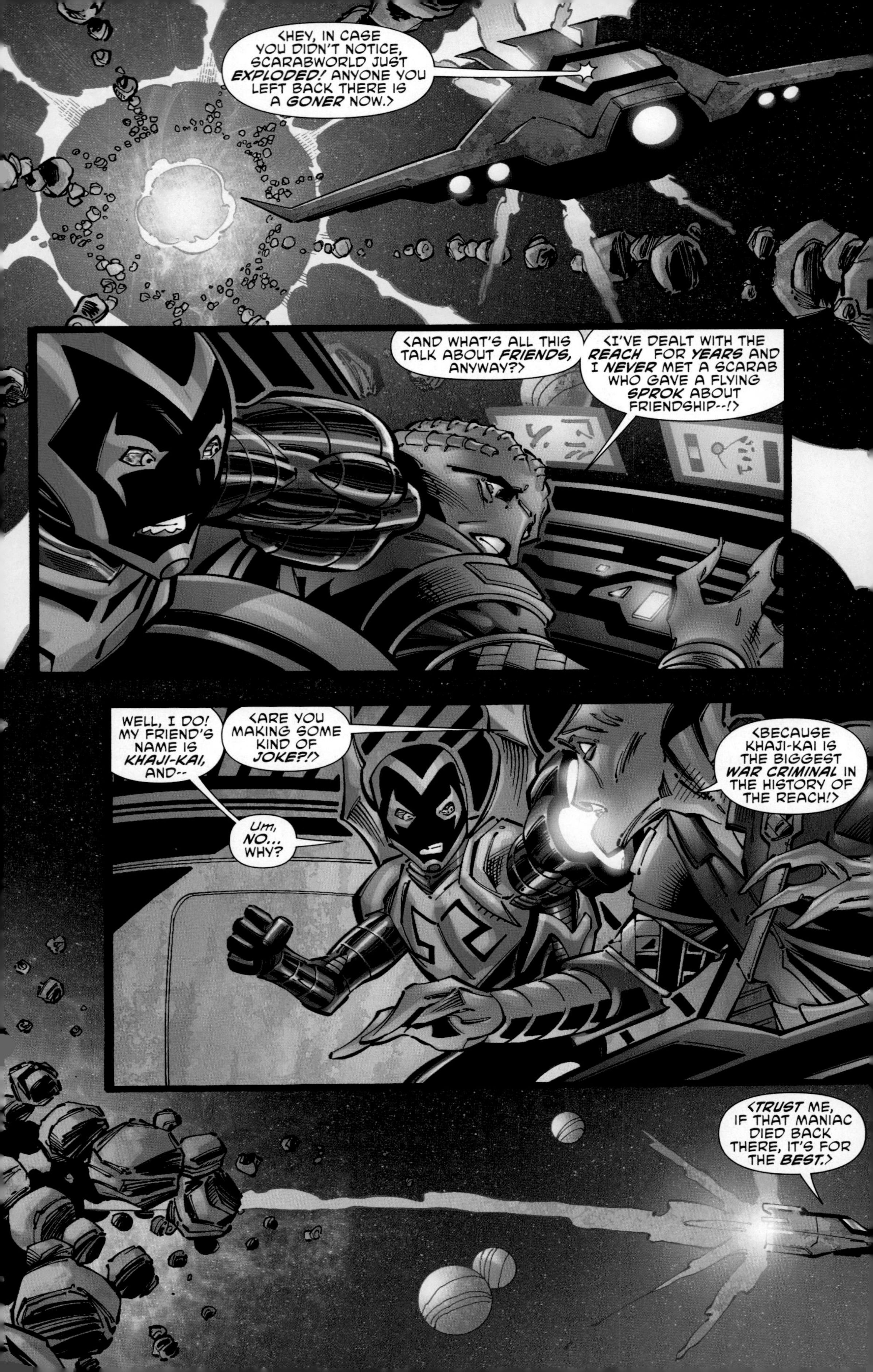
<HEY, IN CASE YOU DIDN'T NOTICE, SCARABWORLD JUST *EXPLODED!* ANYONE YOU LEFT BACK THERE IS A *GONER* NOW.>
<AND WHAT'S ALL THIS TALK ABOUT *FRIENDS,* ANYWAY?>
<I'VE DEALT WITH THE *REACH* FOR *YEARS* AND I *NEVER* MET A SCARAB WHO GAVE A FLYING *SPROK* ABOUT FRIENDSHIP--!>
WELL, I DO! MY FRIEND'S NAME IS *KHAJI-KAI,* AND--
<ARE YOU MAKING SOME KIND OF *JOKE?!*>
Um, ***NO...*** WHY?
<BECAUSE KHAJI-KAI IS THE BIGGEST *WAR CRIMINAL* IN THE HISTORY OF THE REACH!>
<*TRUST* ME, IF THAT MANIAC DIED BACK THERE, IT'S FOR THE *BEST.*>

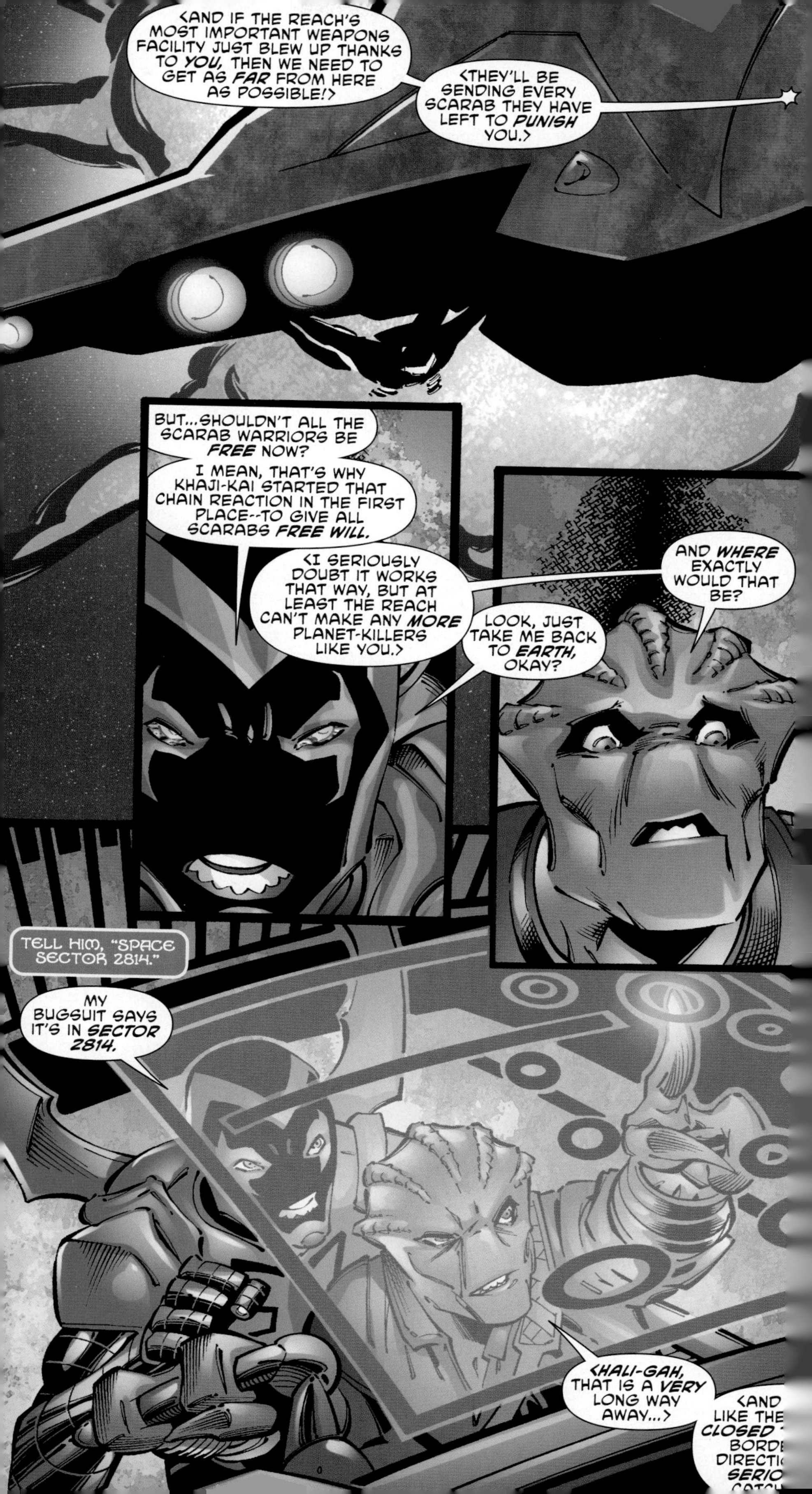
<AND IF THE REACH'S MOST IMPORTANT WEAPONS FACILITY JUST BLEW UP THANKS TO *YOU,* THEN WE NEED TO GET AS *FAR* FROM HERE AS POSSIBLE!>
<THEY'LL BE SENDING EVERY SCARAB THEY HAVE LEFT TO *PUNISH* YOU.>
BUT...SHOULDN'T ALL THE SCARAB WARRIORS BE *FREE* NOW?
I MEAN, THAT'S WHY KHAJI-KAI STARTED THAT CHAIN REACTION IN THE FIRST PLACE--TO GIVE ALL SCARABS *FREE WILL.*
<I SERIOUSLY DOUBT IT WORKS THAT WAY, BUT AT LEAST THE REACH CAN'T MAKE ANY *MORE* PLANET-KILLERS LIKE YOU.>
LOOK, JUST TAKE ME BACK TO *EARTH,* OKAY?
AND *WHERE* EXACTLY WOULD THAT BE?
TELL HIM, "SPACE SECTOR 2814."
MY BUGSUIT SAYS IT'S IN *SECTOR 2814.*
<HALI-GAH, THAT IS A *VERY* LONG WAY AWAY...>
<AND LIKE THE *CLOSED* BORDE DIRECTIC *SERIO*

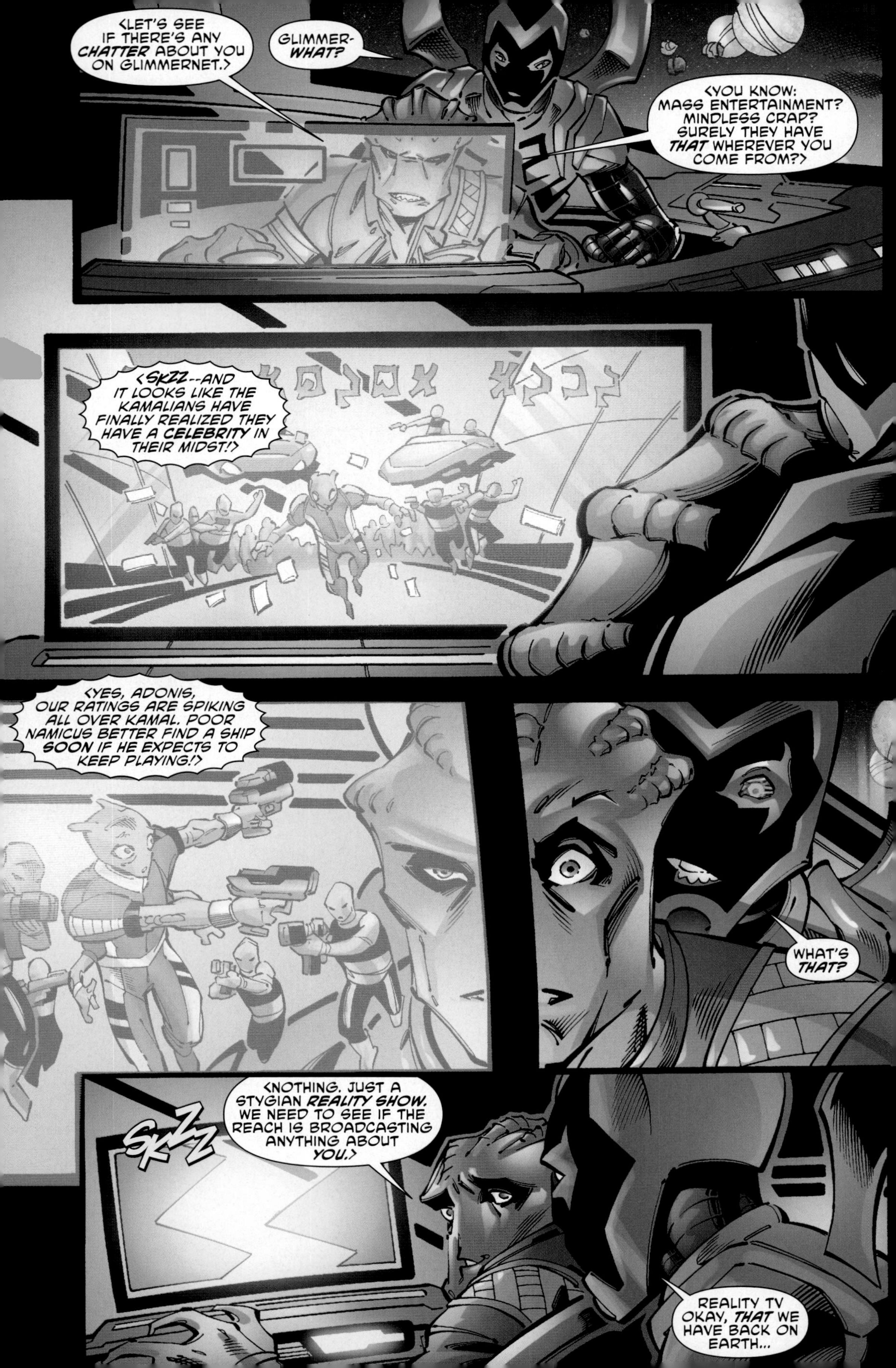
<LET'S SEE IF THERE'S ANY CHATTER ABOUT YOU ON GLIMMERNET.>
GLIMMER-WHAT?
<YOU KNOW: MASS ENTERTAINMENT? MINDLESS CRAP? SURELY THEY HAVE THAT WHEREVER YOU COME FROM?>
<SKZZ--AND IT LOOKS LIKE THE KAMALIANS HAVE FINALLY REALIZED THEY HAVE A CELEBRITY IN THEIR MIDST!>
<YES, ADONIS, OUR RATINGS ARE SPIKING ALL OVER KAMAL. POOR NAMICUS BETTER FIND A SHIP SOON IF HE EXPECTS TO KEEP PLAYING!>
WHAT'S THAT?
SKZZZ
<NOTHING. JUST A STYGIAN REALITY SHOW. WE NEED TO SEE IF THE REACH IS BROADCASTING ANYTHING ABOUT YOU.>
REALITY TV. OKAY, THAT WE HAVE BACK ON EARTH...

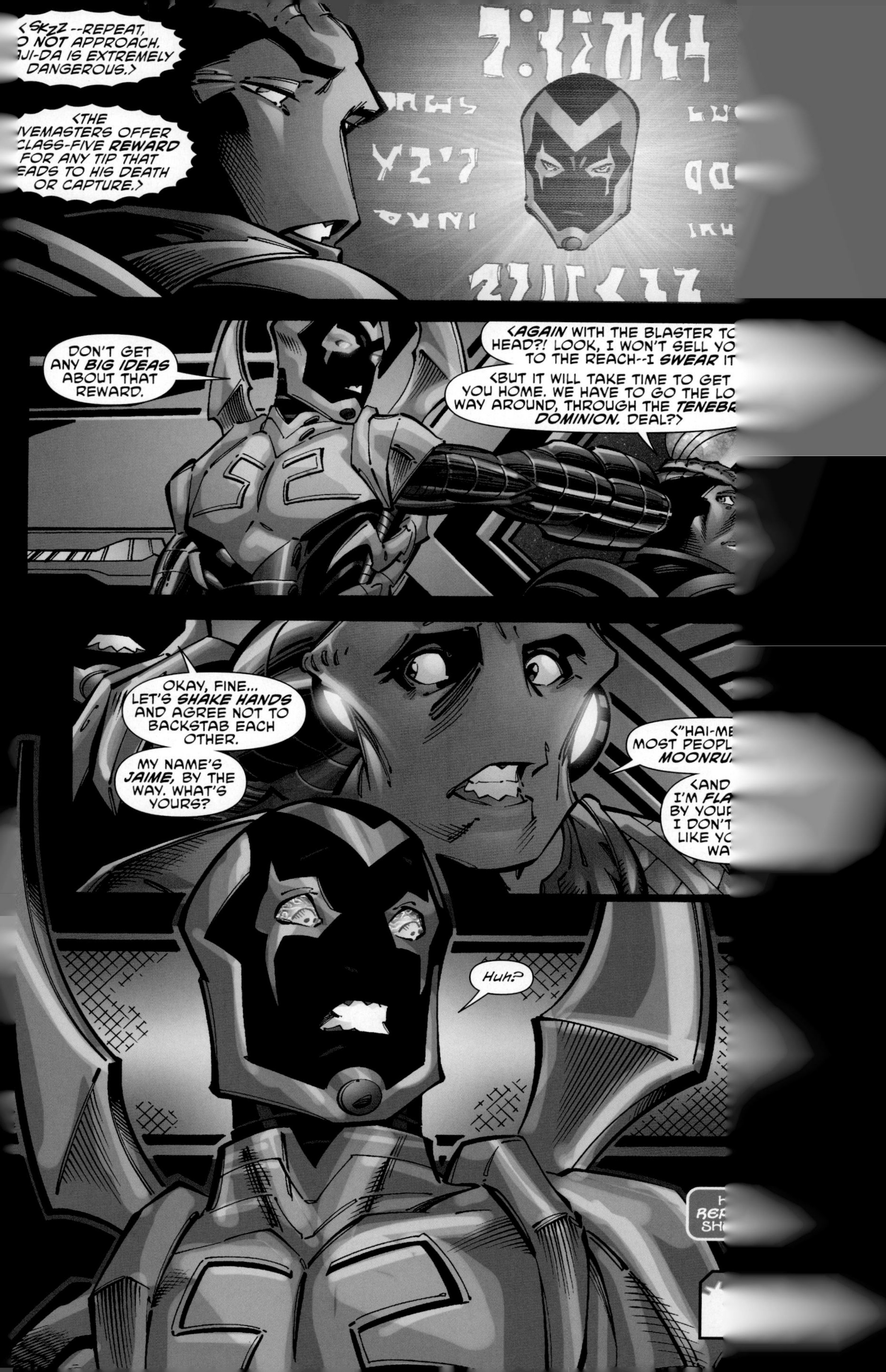
<SKZZ --REPEAT, O NOT APPROACH. AJI-DA IS EXTREMELY DANGEROUS.>
<THE IVEMASTERS OFFER CLASS-FIVE REWARD FOR ANY TIP THAT EADS TO HIS DEATH OR CAPTURE.>
DON'T GET ANY BIG IDEAS ABOUT THAT REWARD.
<AGAIN WITH THE BLASTER TO HEAD?! LOOK, I WON'T SELL YO TO THE REACH--I SWEAR IT
<BUT IT WILL TAKE TIME TO GET YOU HOME. WE HAVE TO GO THE LO WAY AROUND, THROUGH THE TENEBR DOMINION. DEAL?>
OKAY, FINE... LET'S SHAKE HANDS AND AGREE NOT TO BACKSTAB EACH OTHER.
MY NAME'S JAIME, BY THE WAY. WHAT'S YOURS?
<"HAI-ME MOST PEOPL MOONRU
<AND I'M FLA BY YOUR I DON'T LIKE YO WA
Huh?

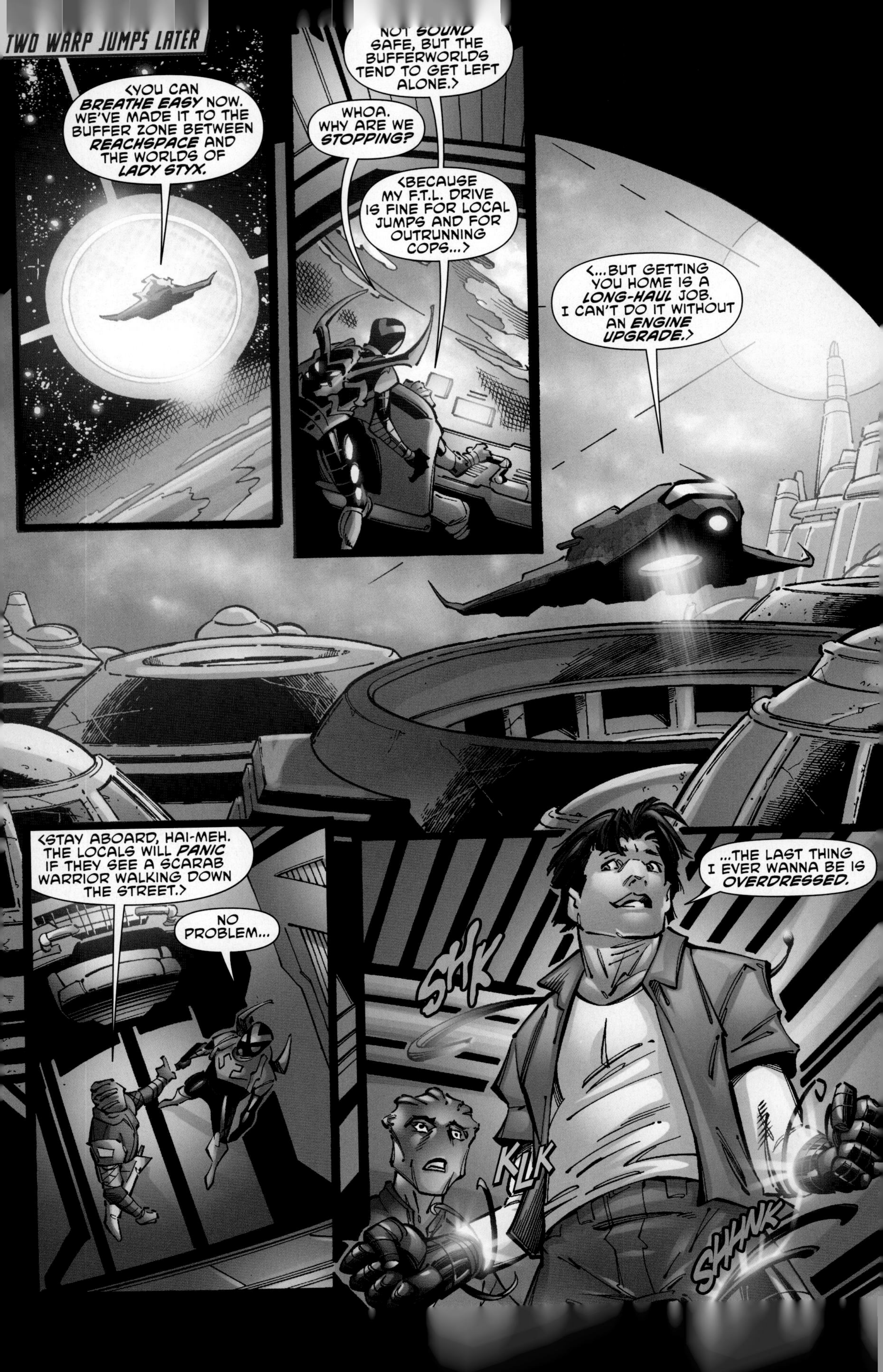

TWO WARP JUMPS LATER
<YOU CAN BREATHE EASY NOW. WE'VE MADE IT TO THE BUFFER ZONE BETWEEN REACHSPACE AND THE WORLDS OF LADY STYX.
NOT SOUND SAFE, BUT THE BUFFERWORLDS TEND TO GET LEFT ALONE.>
WHOA. WHY ARE WE STOPPING?
<BECAUSE MY F.T.L. DRIVE IS FINE FOR LOCAL JUMPS AND FOR OUTRUNNING COPS...>
<...BUT GETTING YOU HOME IS A LONG-HAUL JOB. I CAN'T DO IT WITHOUT AN ENGINE UPGRADE.>
<STAY ABOARD, HAI-MEH. THE LOCALS WILL PANIC IF THEY SEE A SCARAB WARRIOR WALKING DOWN THE STREET.>
NO PROBLEM...
...THE LAST THING I EVER WANNA BE IS OVERDRESSED.
SHK
KLIK
SHUNK

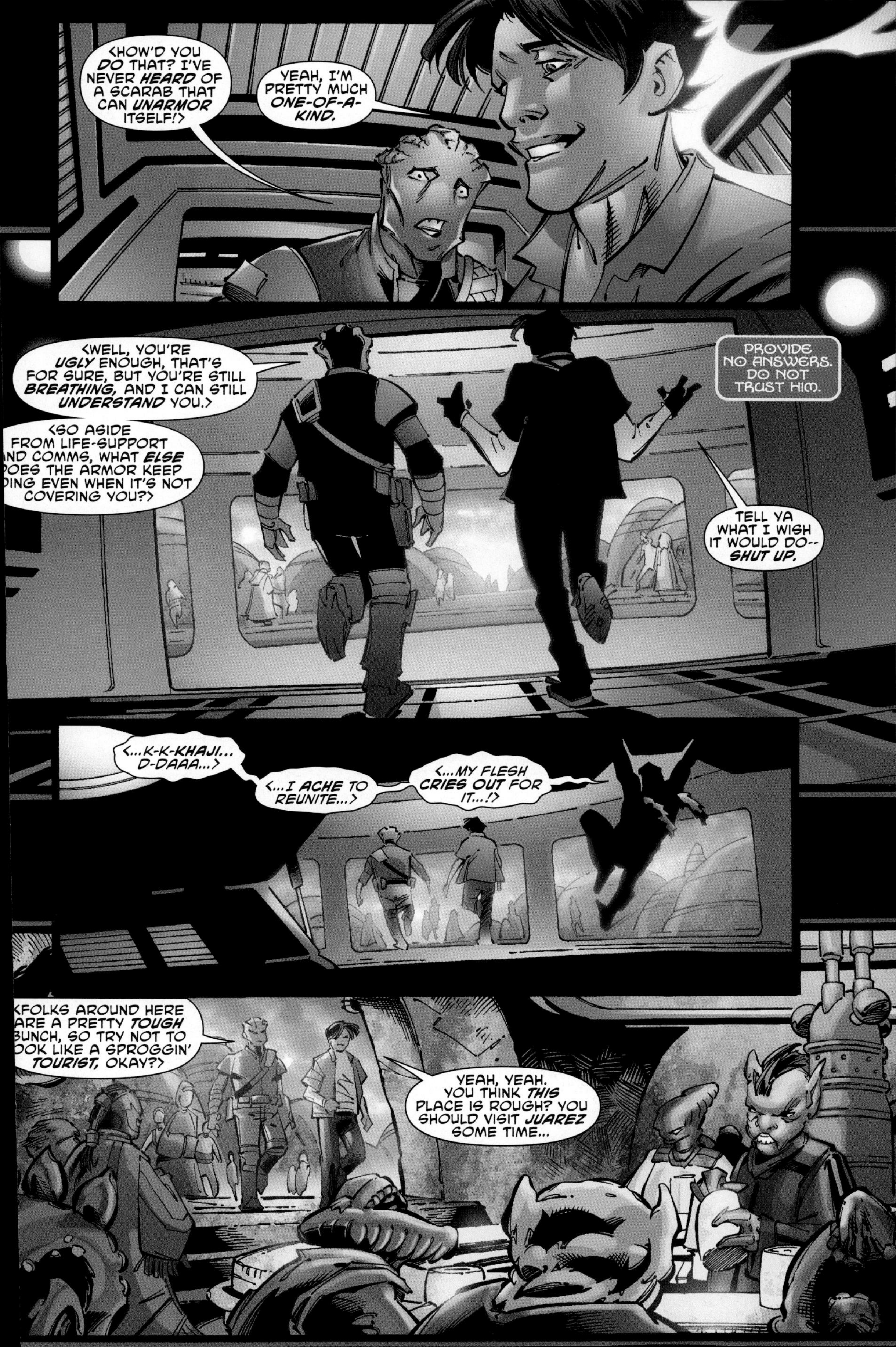
<HOW'D YOU DO THAT? I'VE NEVER HEARD OF A SCARAB THAT CAN UNARMOR ITSELF!>
YEAH, I'M PRETTY MUCH ONE-OF-A-KIND.
<WELL, YOU'RE UGLY ENOUGH, THAT'S FOR SURE, BUT YOU'RE STILL BREATHING, AND I CAN STILL UNDERSTAND YOU.>
<SO ASIDE FROM LIFE-SUPPORT ND COMMS, WHAT ELSE OES THE ARMOR KEEP DING EVEN WHEN IT'S NOT COVERING YOU?>
PROVIDE NO ANSWERS. DO NOT TRUST HIM.
TELL YA WHAT I WISH IT WOULD DO-- SHUT UP.
<...K-K-KHAJI... D-DAAA...>
<...I ACHE TO REUNITE...>
<...MY FLESH CRIES OUT FOR IT...!>
<FOLKS AROUND HERE ARE A PRETTY TOUGH BUNCH, SO TRY NOT TO OOK LIKE A SPROGGIN' TOURIST, OKAY?>
YEAH, YEAH. YOU THINK THIS PLACE IS ROUGH? YOU SHOULD VISIT JUAREZ SOME TIME...

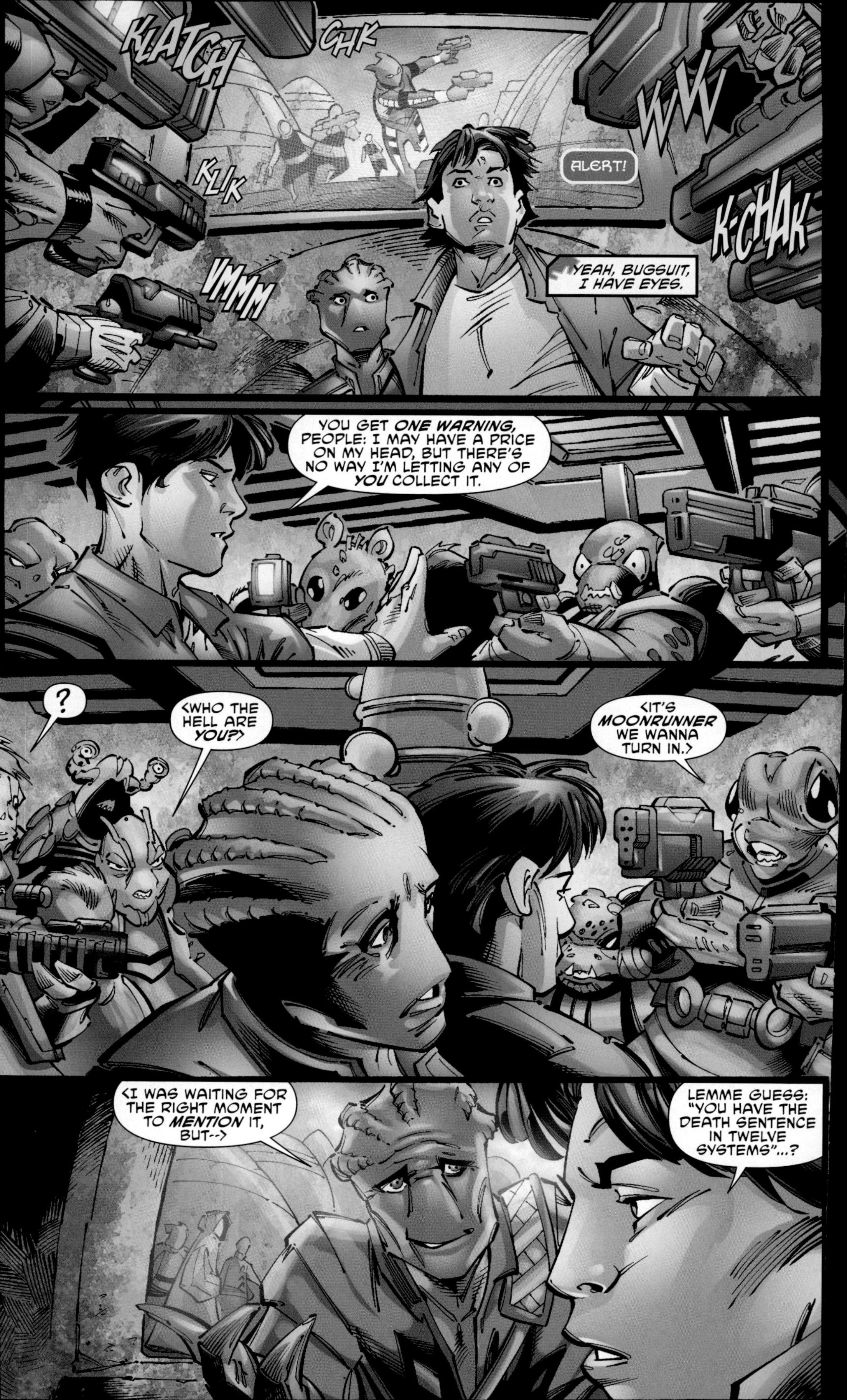
KLATCH
CHK
KLIK
ALERT!
WW
K-CHAK
VMMM
YEAH, BUGSUIT, I HAVE EYES.
YOU GET *ONE WARNING,* PEOPLE: I MAY HAVE A PRICE ON MY HEAD, BUT THERE'S NO WAY I'M LETTING ANY OF *YOU* COLLECT IT.
?
<WHO THE HELL ARE *YOU?*>
<IT'S *MOONRUNNER* WE WANNA TURN IN.>
<I WAS WAITING FOR THE RIGHT MOMENT TO *MENTION* IT, BUT-->
LEMME GUESS: "YOU HAVE THE DEATH SENTENCE IN TWELVE SYSTEMS"...?

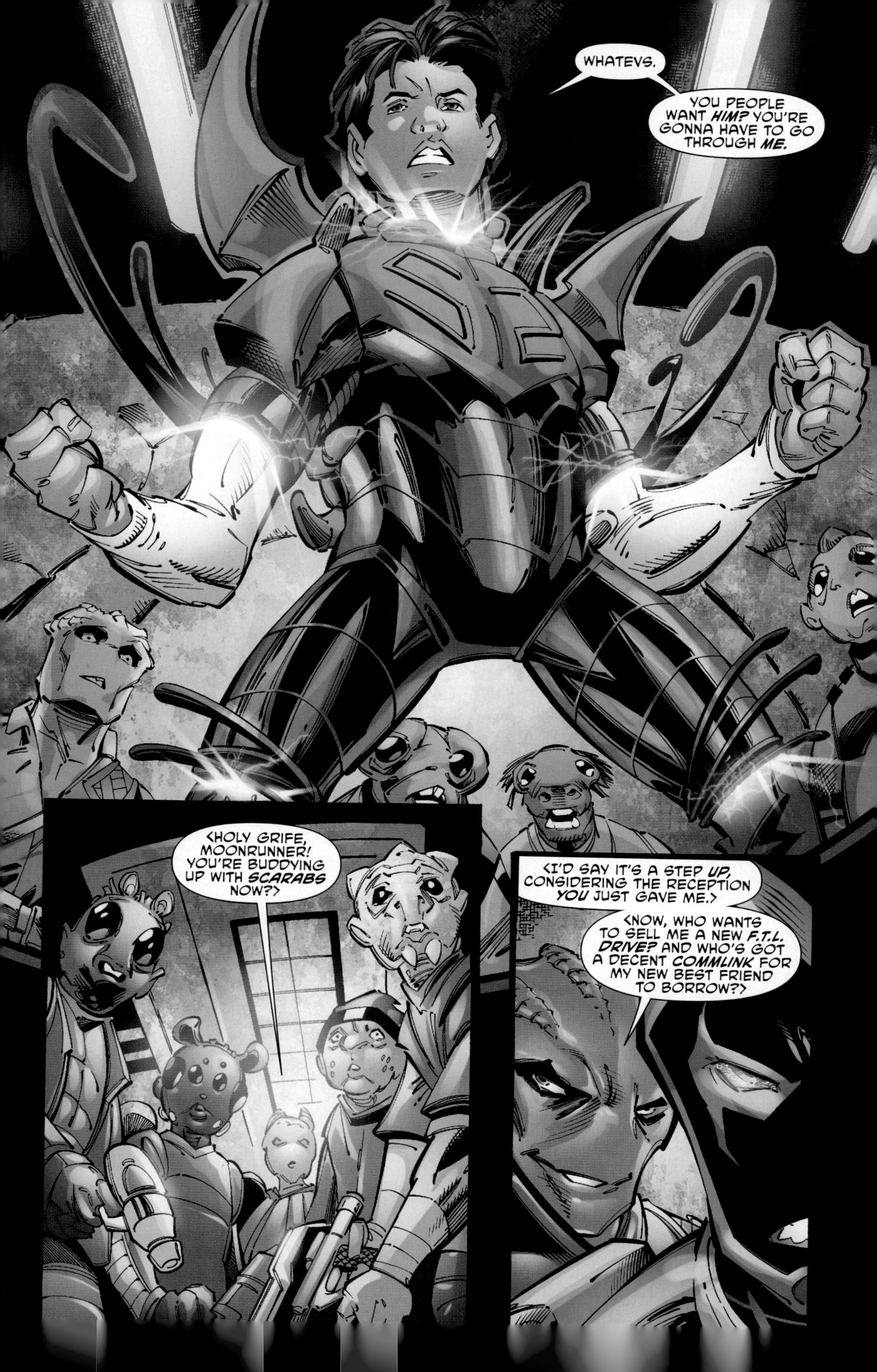
WHATEVS.
YOU PEOPLE WANT *HIM?* YOU'RE GONNA HAVE TO GO THROUGH *ME.*
<HOLY GRIFE, MOONRUNNER! YOU'RE BUDDYING UP WITH *SCARABS* NOW?>
<I'D SAY IT'S A STEP *UP,* CONSIDERING THE RECEPTION *YOU* JUST GAVE ME.>
<NOW, WHO WANTS TO SELL ME A NEW *F.T.L. DRIVE?* AND WHO'S GOT A DECENT *COMMLINK* FOR MY NEW BEST FRIEND TO BORROW?>

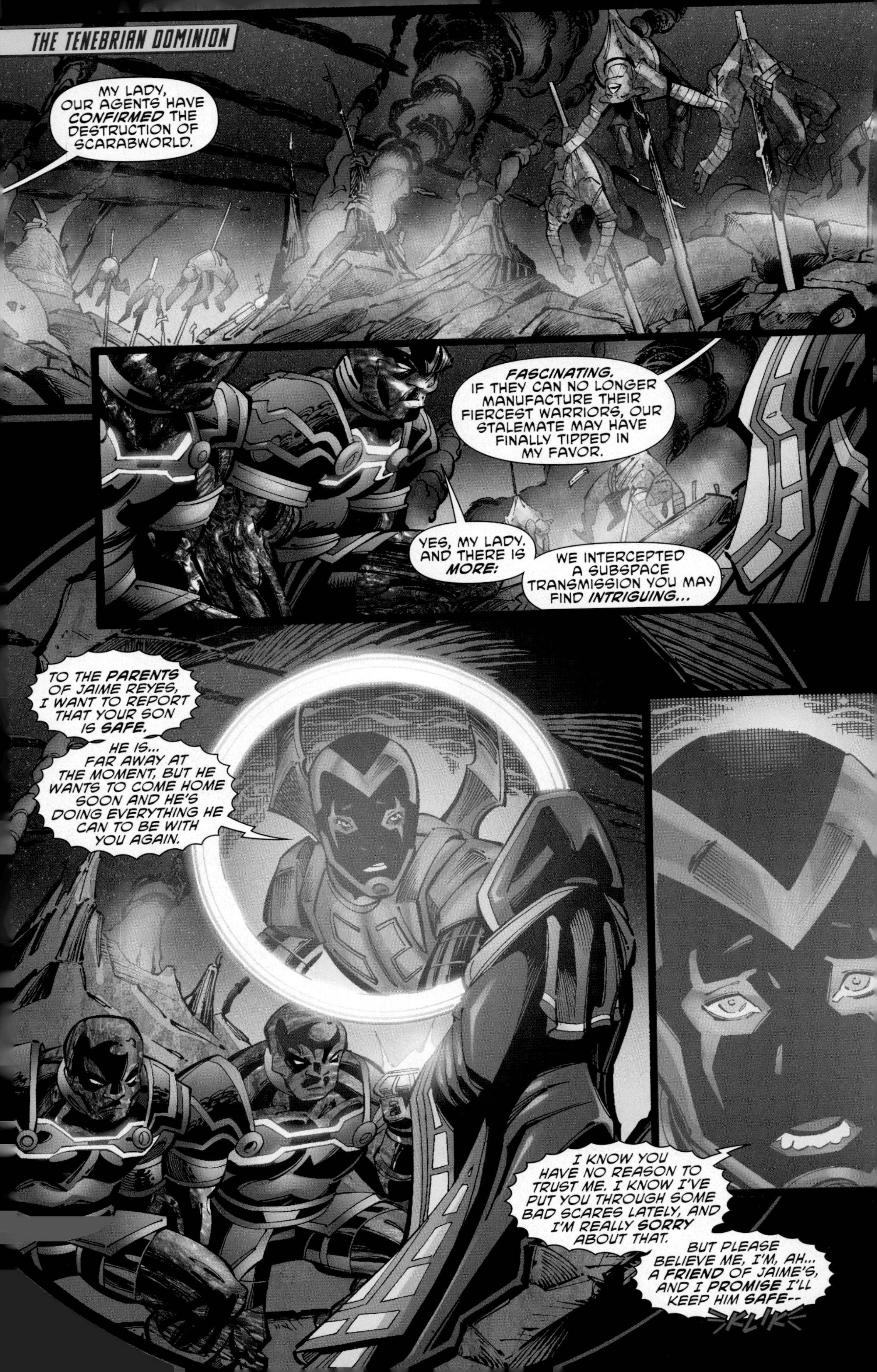
THE TENEBRIAN DOMINION
MY LADY, OUR AGENTS HAVE CONFIRMED THE DESTRUCTION OF SCARABWORLD.
FASCINATING. IF THEY CAN NO LONGER MANUFACTURE THEIR FIERCEST WARRIORS, OUR STALEMATE MAY HAVE FINALLY TIPPED IN MY FAVOR.
YES, MY LADY. AND THERE IS MORE:
WE INTERCEPTED A SUBSPACE TRANSMISSION YOU MAY FIND INTRIGUING...
TO THE PARENTS OF JAIME REYES, I WANT TO REPORT THAT YOUR SON IS SAFE.
HE IS... FAR AWAY AT THE MOMENT, BUT HE WANTS TO COME HOME SOON AND HE'S DOING EVERYTHING HE CAN TO BE WITH YOU AGAIN.
I KNOW YOU HAVE NO REASON TO TRUST ME. I KNOW I'VE PUT YOU THROUGH SOME BAD SCARES LATELY, AND I'M REALLY SORRY ABOUT THAT.
BUT PLEASE BELIEVE ME, I'M, AH... A FRIEND OF JAIME'S, AND I PROMISE I'LL KEEP HIM SAFE--
KLIK

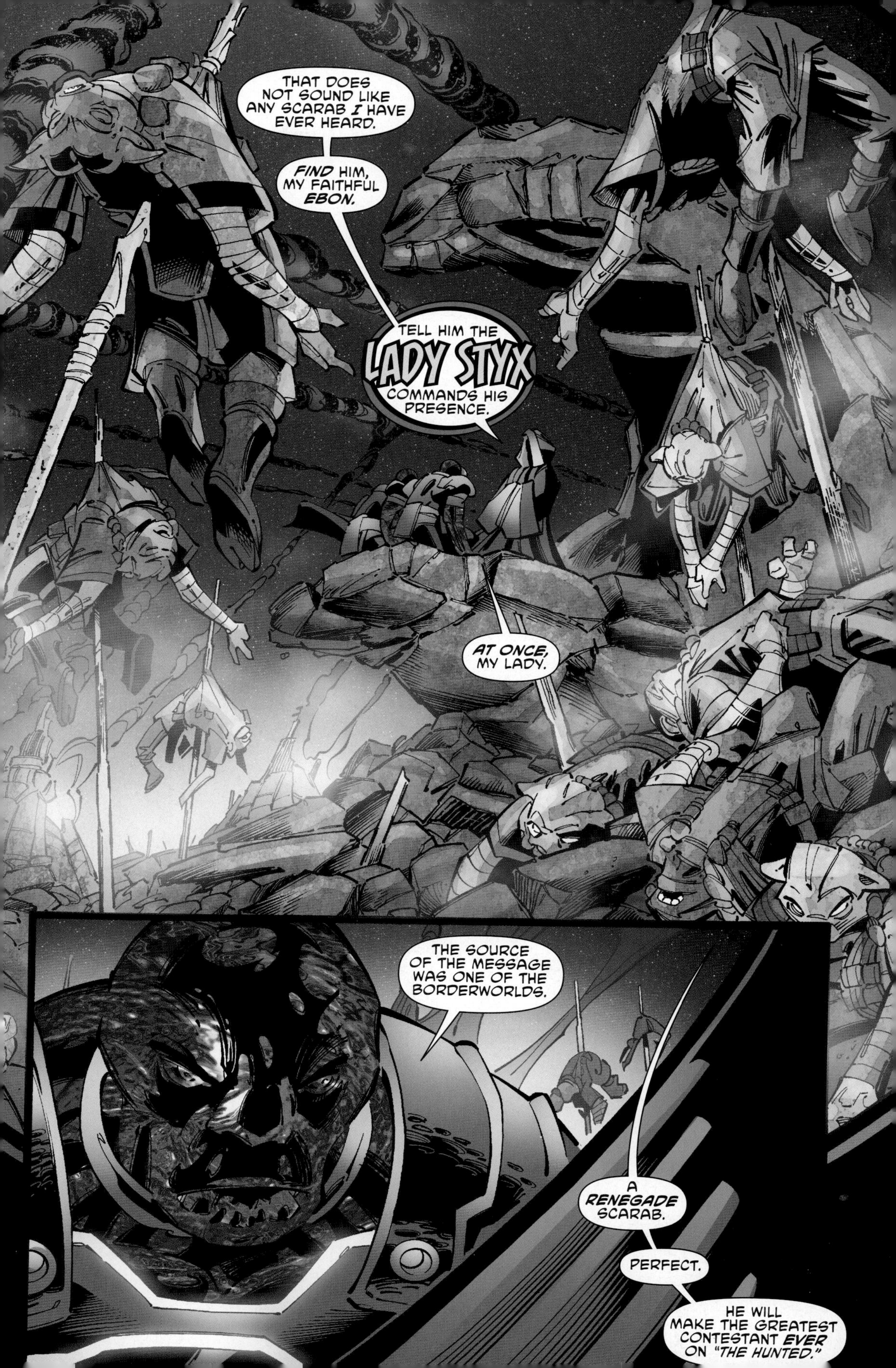
THAT DOES NOT SOUND LIKE ANY SCARAB I HAVE EVER HEARD.
FIND HIM, MY FAITHFUL EBON.
TELL HIM THE LADY STYX COMMANDS HIS PRESENCE.
AT ONCE, MY LADY.
THE SOURCE OF THE MESSAGE WAS ONE OF THE BORDERWORLDS.
A RENEGADE SCARAB.
PERFECT.
HE WILL MAKE THE GREATEST CONTESTANT EVER ON "THE HUNTED."

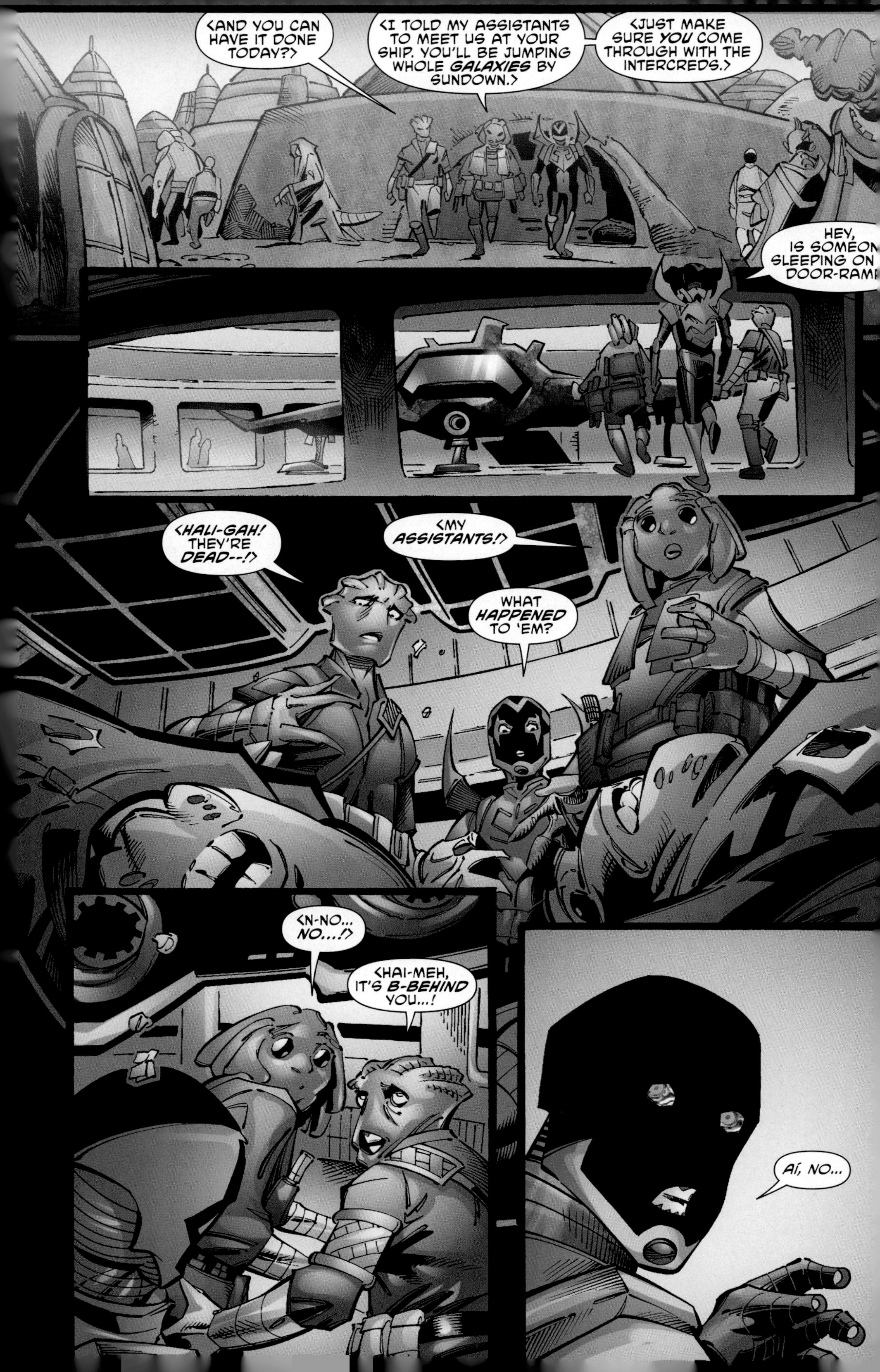
<AND YOU CAN HAVE IT DONE TODAY?>
<I TOLD MY ASSISTANTS TO MEET US AT YOUR SHIP. YOU'LL BE JUMPING WHOLE GALAXIES BY SUNDOWN.>
<JUST MAKE SURE YOU COME THROUGH WITH THE INTERCREDS.>
HEY, IS SOMEON SLEEPING ON DOOR-RAM
<HALI-GAH! THEY'RE DEAD--!>
<MY ASSISTANTS!>
WHAT HAPPENED TO 'EM?
<N-NO... NO...!>
<HAI-MEH, IT'S B-BEHIND YOU...!
AÍ, NO...

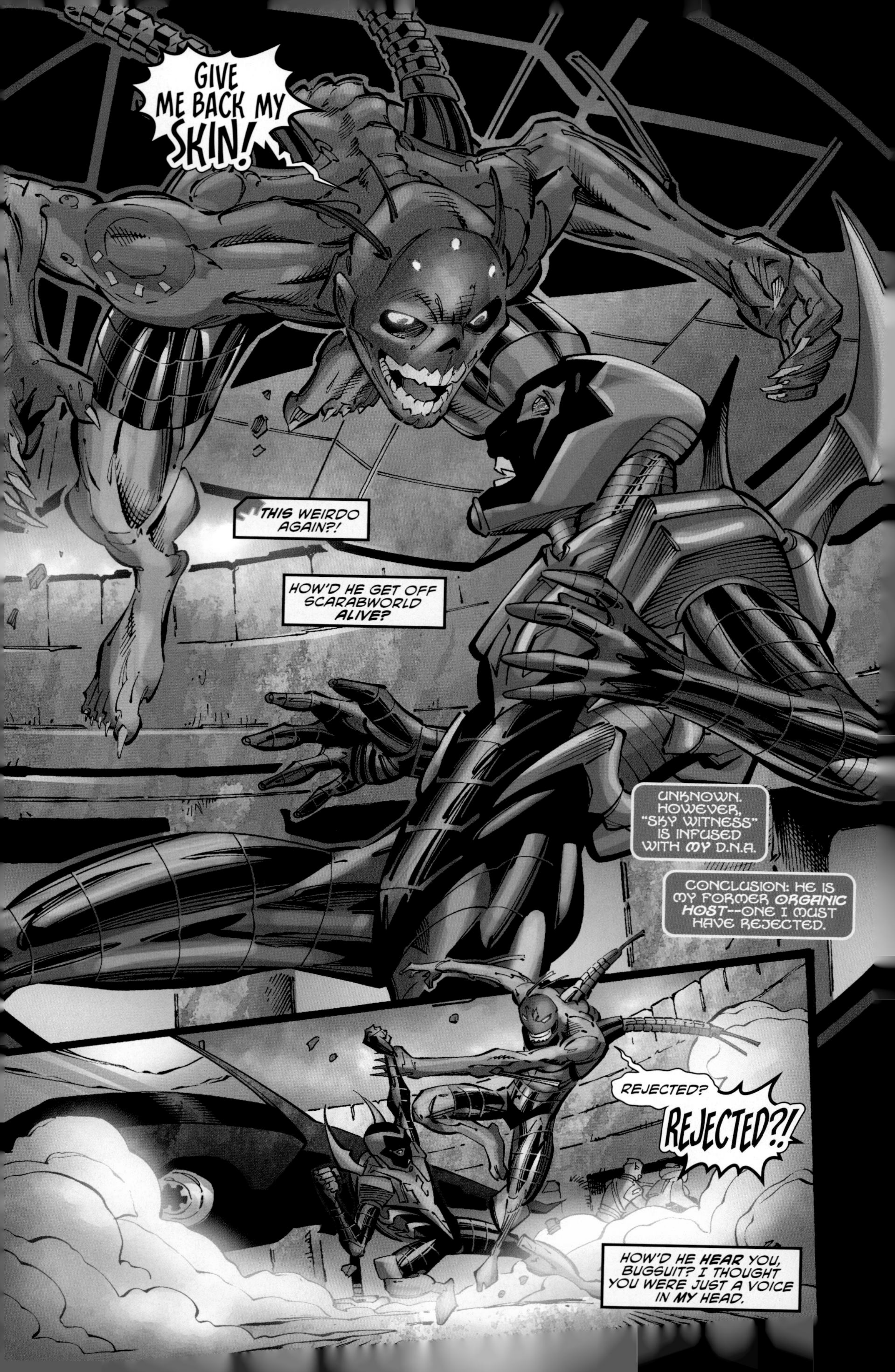
GIVE ME BACK MY SKIN!
THIS WEIRDO AGAIN?!
HOW'D HE GET OFF SCARABWORLD ALIVE?
UNKNOWN. HOWEVER, "SKY WITNESS" IS INFUSED WITH MY D.N.A.
CONCLUSION: HE IS MY FORMER ORGANIC HOST--ONE I MUST HAVE REJECTED.
REJECTED? REJECTED?!
HOW'D HE HEAR YOU, BUGSUIT? I THOUGHT YOU WERE JUST A VOICE IN MY HEAD.

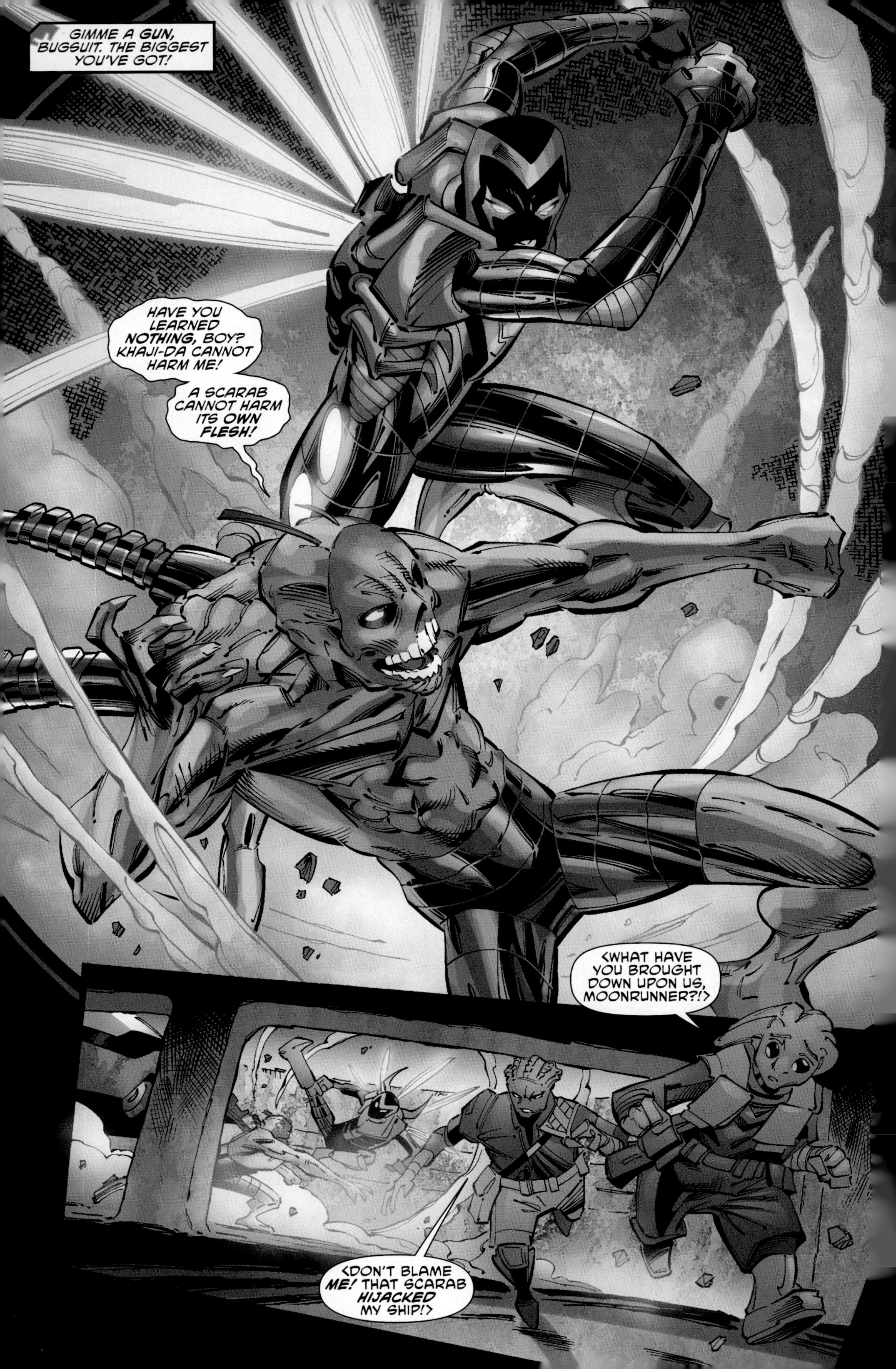
GIMME A GUN, BUGSUIT. THE BIGGEST YOU'VE GOT!
HAVE YOU LEARNED NOTHING, BOY? KHAJI-DA CANNOT HARM ME!
A SCARAB CANNOT HARM ITS OWN FLESH!
<WHAT HAVE YOU BROUGHT DOWN UPON US, MOONRUNNER?!>
<DON'T BLAME ME! THAT SCARAB HIJACKED MY SHIP!>

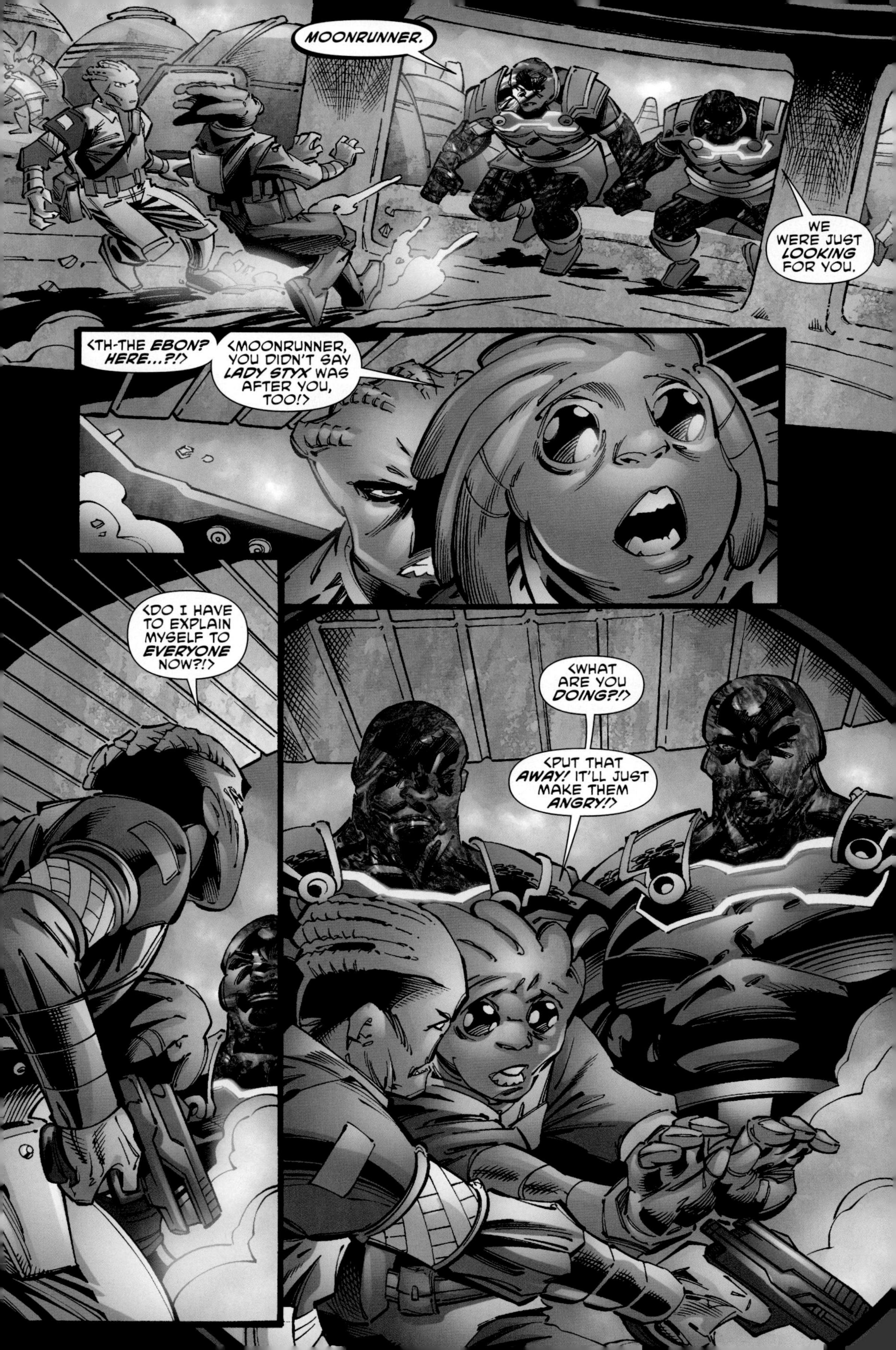
MOONRUNNER.
WE WERE JUST LOOKING FOR YOU.
<TH-THE EBON? HERE...?!>
<MOONRUNNER, YOU DIDN'T SAY LADY STYX WAS AFTER YOU, TOO!>
<DO I HAVE TO EXPLAIN MYSELF TO EVERYONE NOW?!>
<WHAT ARE YOU DOING?!>
<PUT THAT AWAY! IT'LL JUST MAKE THEM ANGRY!>

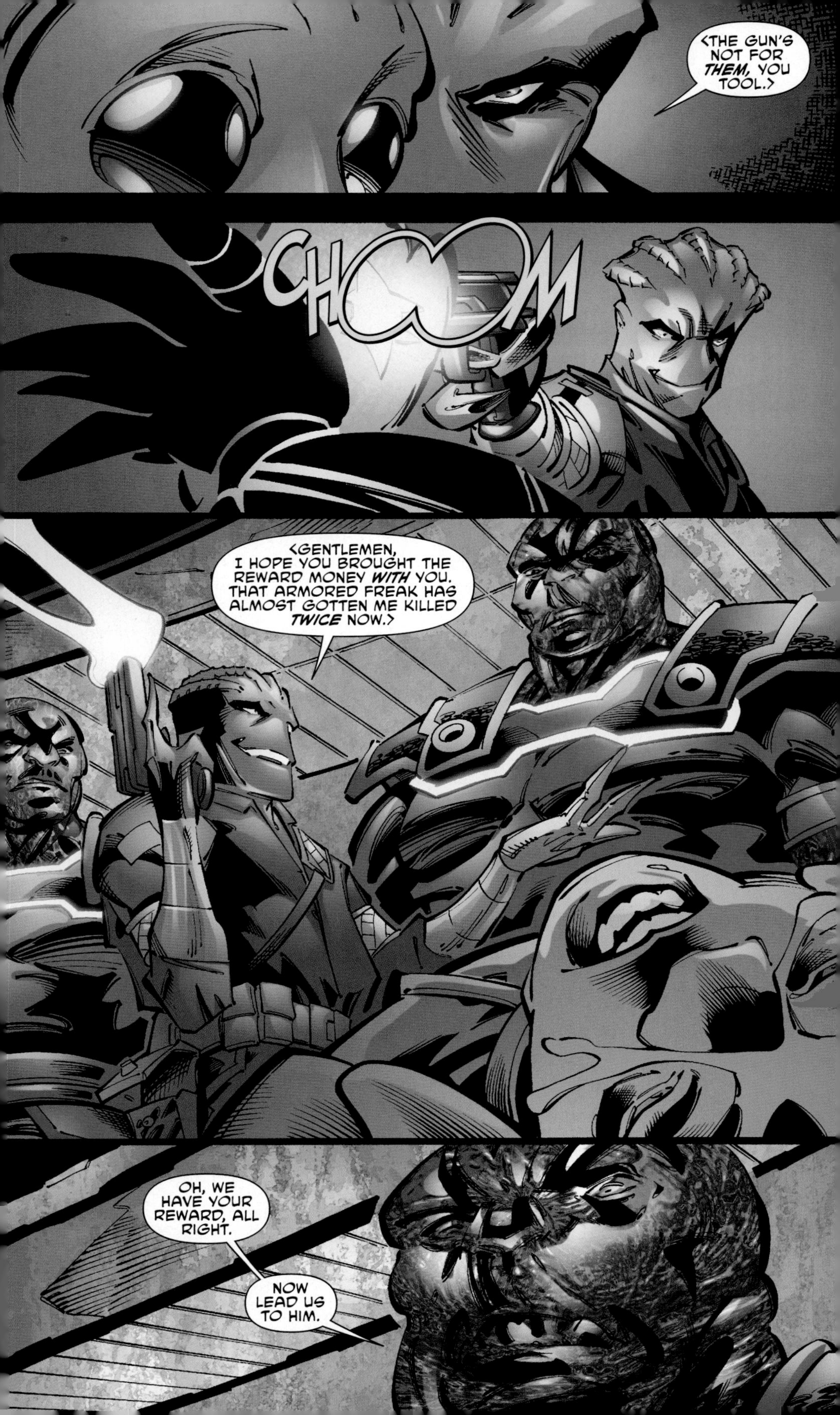
<THE GUN'S NOT FOR THEM, YOU TOOL.>
CHOOM
<GENTLEMEN, I HOPE YOU BROUGHT THE REWARD MONEY WITH YOU. THAT ARMORED FREAK HAS ALMOST GOTTEN ME KILLED TWICE NOW.>
OH, WE HAVE YOUR REWARD, ALL RIGHT.
NOW LEAD US TO HIM.

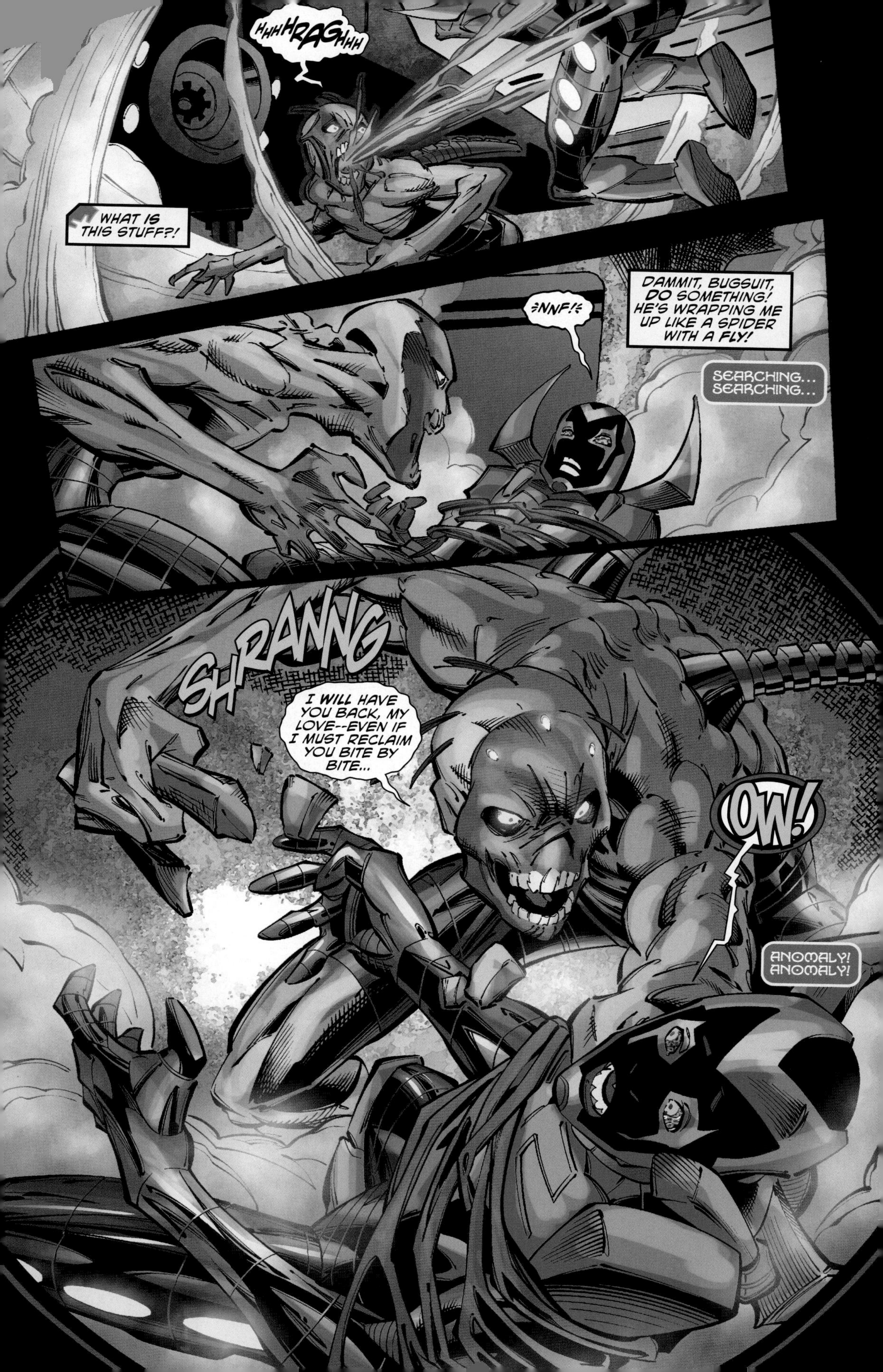
HHHHRAGHHH
WHAT IS THIS STUFF?!
NNF!
DAMMIT, BUGSUIT, DO SOMETHING! HE'S WRAPPING ME UP LIKE A SPIDER WITH A FLY!
SEARCHING... SEARCHING...
SHRANNG
I WILL HAVE YOU BACK, MY LOVE--EVEN IF I MUST RECLAIM YOU BITE BY BITE...
OW!
ANOMALY! ANOMALY!

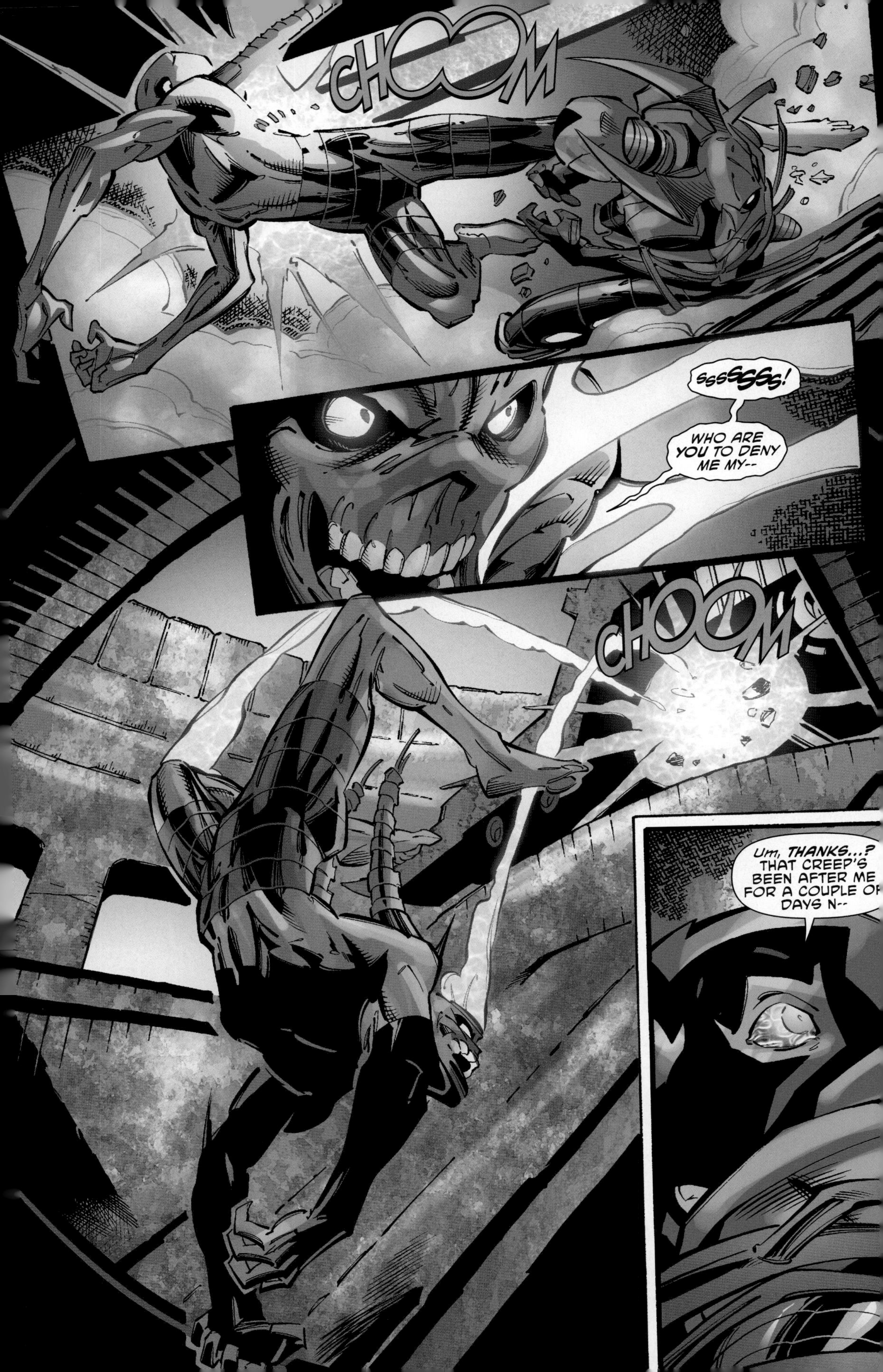
CHOOM
SSSSSSS!
WHO ARE YOU TO DENY ME MY--
CHOOM
Um, THANKS...? THAT CREEP'S BEEN AFTER ME FOR A COUPLE OF DAYS N--

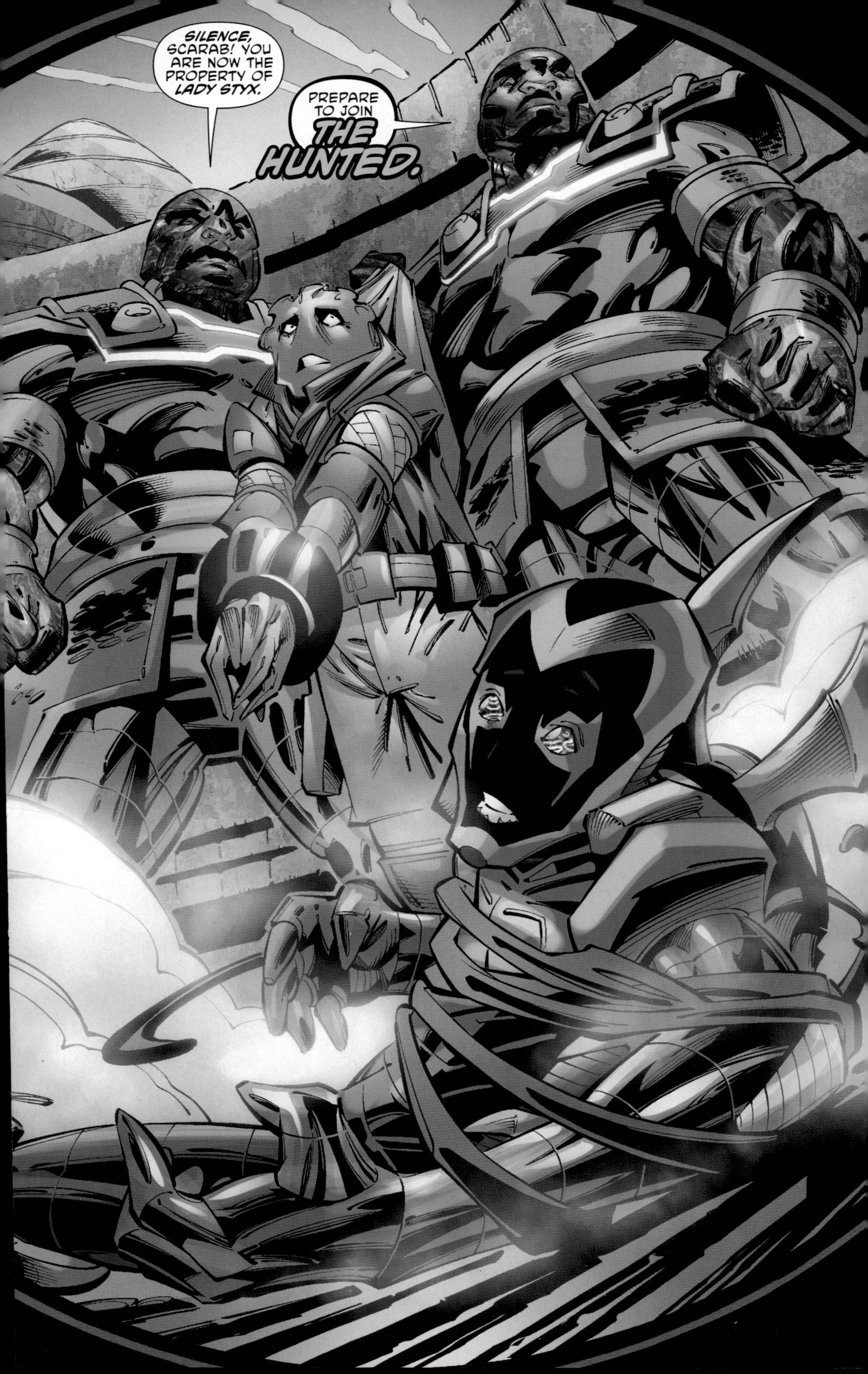
SILENCE, SCARAB! YOU ARE NOW THE PROPERTY OF LADY STYX.
PREPARE TO JOIN
THE HUNTED.

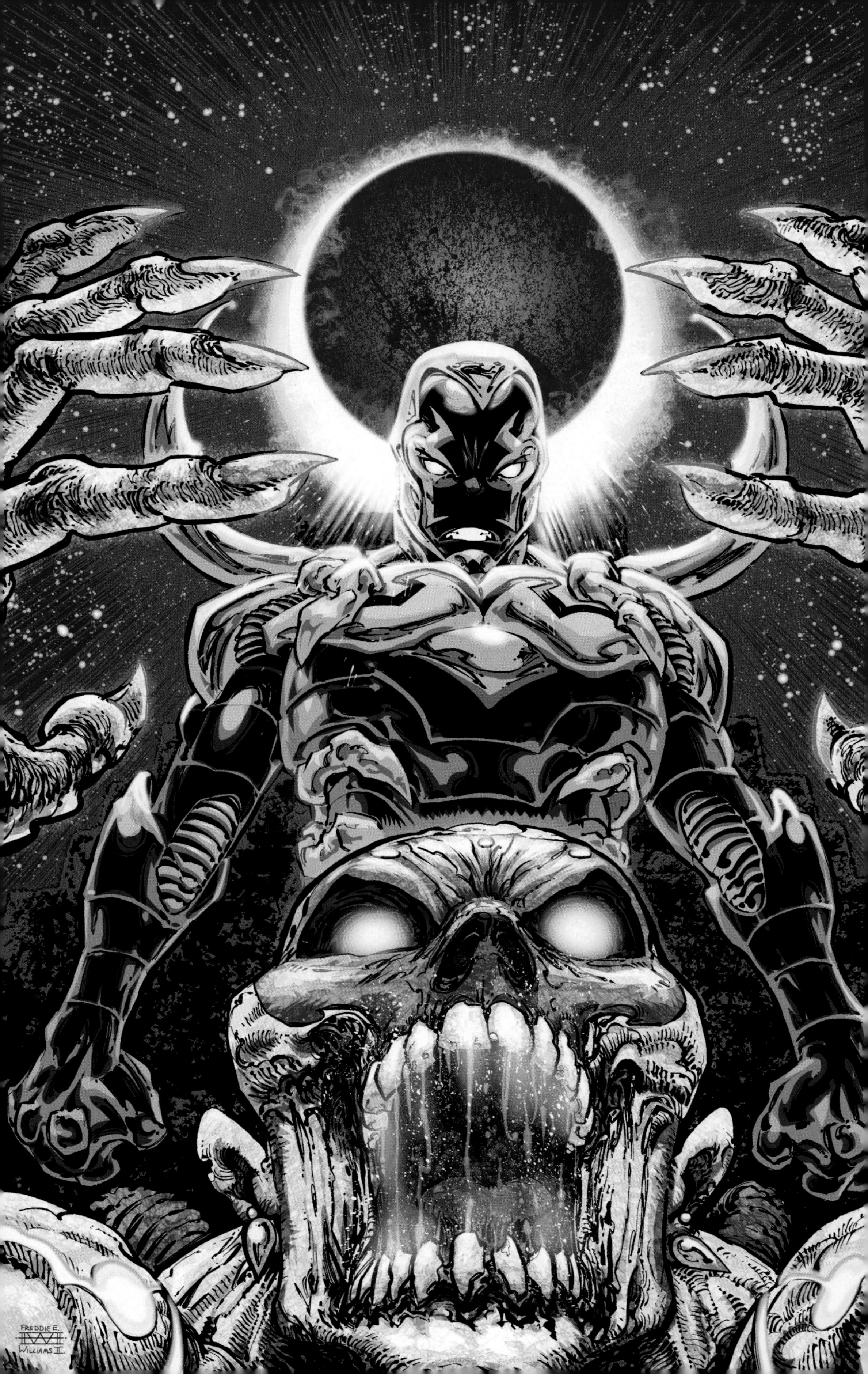
FREDDIE E.
WILLIAMS II

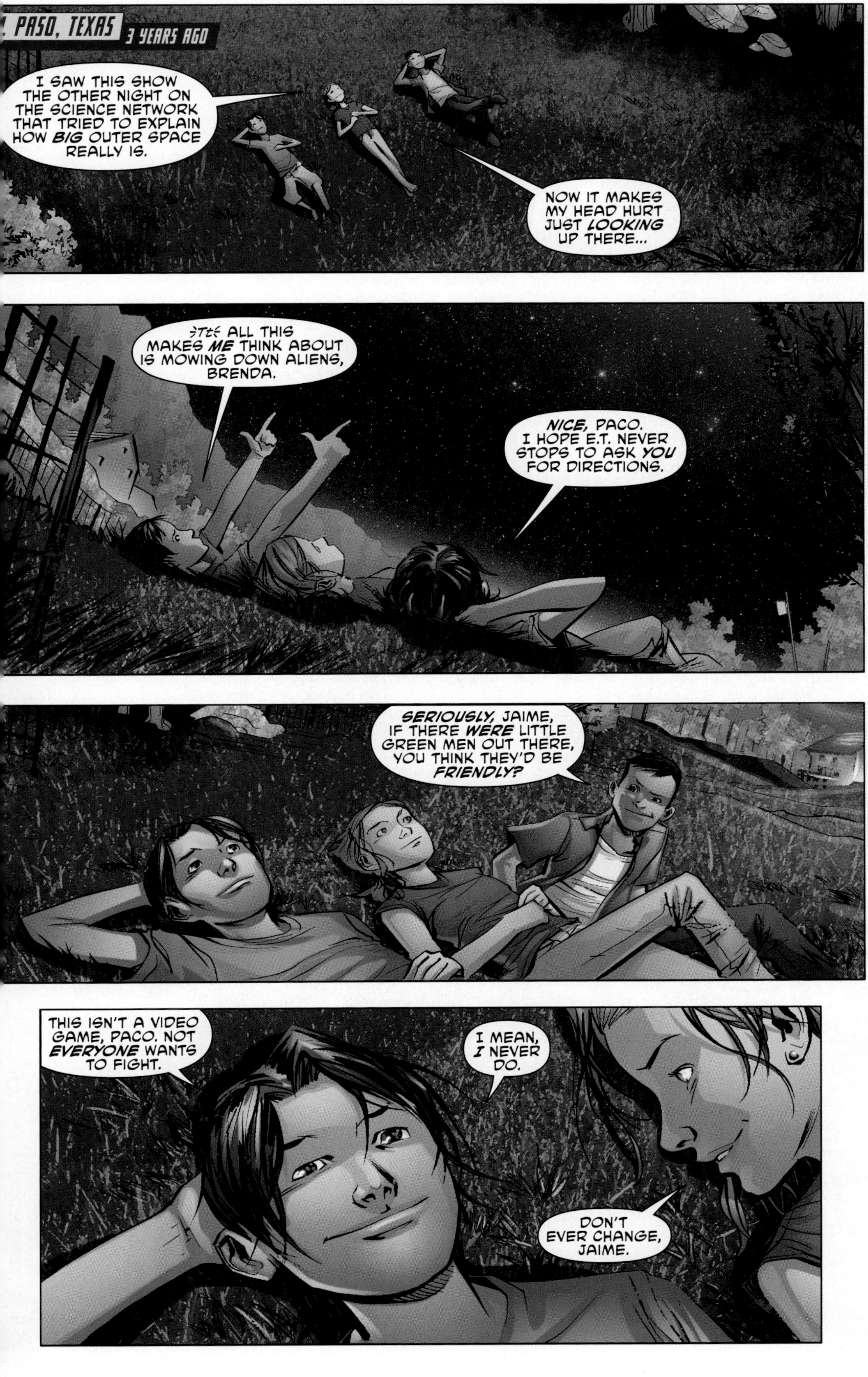
PASO, TEXAS
3 YEARS AGO
I SAW THIS SHOW THE OTHER NIGHT ON THE SCIENCE NETWORK THAT TRIED TO EXPLAIN HOW BIG OUTER SPACE REALLY IS.
NOW IT MAKES MY HEAD HURT JUST LOOKING UP THERE...
ALL THIS MAKES ME THINK ABOUT IS MOWING DOWN ALIENS, BRENDA.
NICE, PACO. I HOPE E.T. NEVER STOPS TO ASK YOU FOR DIRECTIONS.
SERIOUSLY, JAIME, IF THERE WERE LITTLE GREEN MEN OUT THERE, YOU THINK THEY'D BE FRIENDLY?
THIS ISN'T A VIDEO GAME, PACO. NOT EVERYONE WANTS TO FIGHT.
I MEAN, I NEVER DO.
DON'T EVER CHANGE, JAIME.

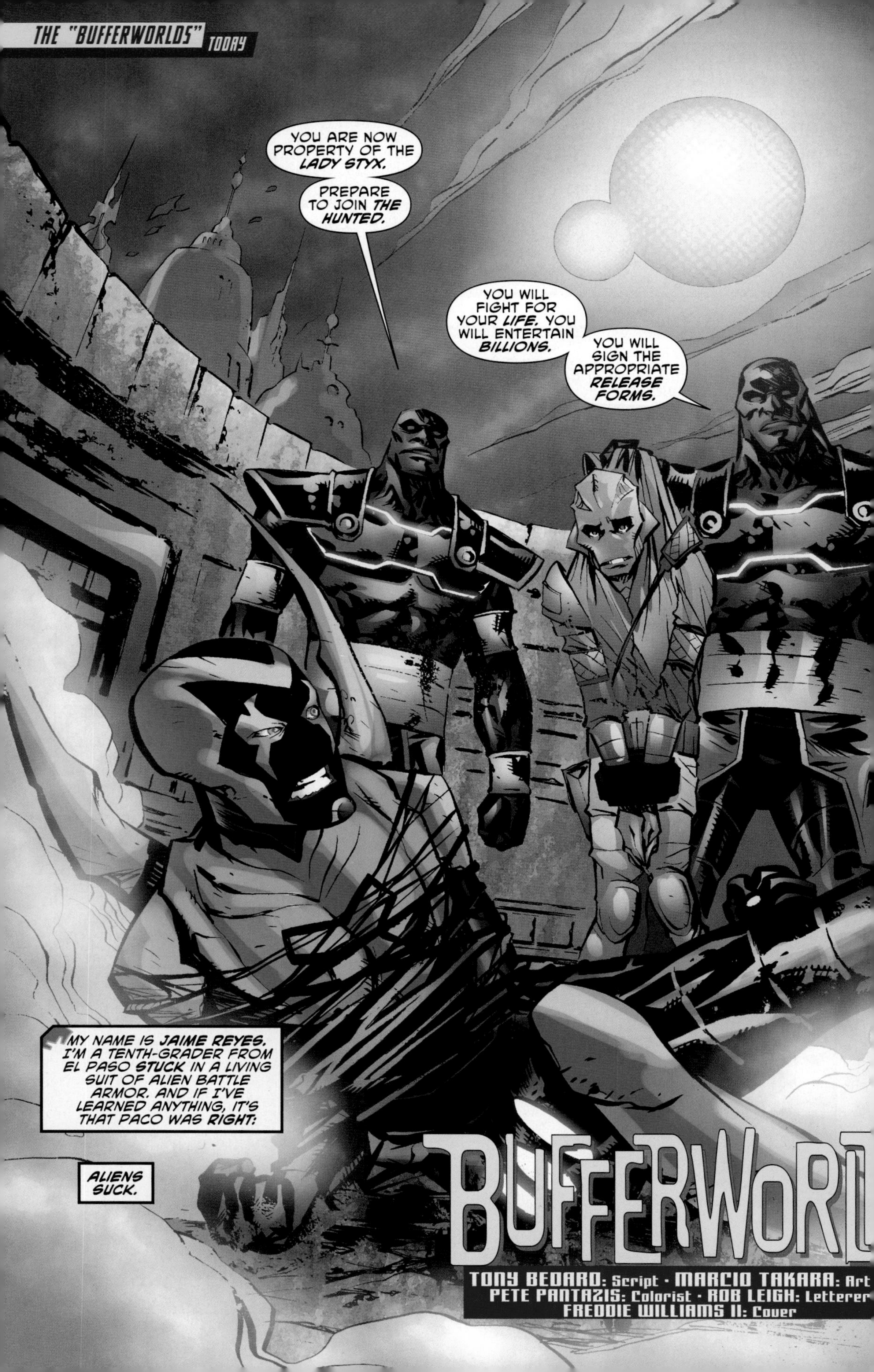
THE "BUFFERWORLDS" TODAY
YOU ARE NOW PROPERTY OF THE LADY STYX.
PREPARE TO JOIN THE HUNTED.
YOU WILL FIGHT FOR YOUR LIFE. YOU WILL ENTERTAIN BILLIONS.
YOU WILL SIGN THE APPROPRIATE RELEASE FORMS.
MY NAME IS JAIME REYES. I'M A TENTH-GRADER FROM EL PASO STUCK IN A LIVING SUIT OF ALIEN BATTLE ARMOR. AND IF I'VE LEARNED ANYTHING, IT'S THAT PACO WAS RIGHT:
ALIENS SUCK.
BUFFERWORL
TONY BEDARD: Script · MARCIO TAKARA: Art
PETE PANTAZIS: Colorist · ROB LEIGH: Letterer
FREDDIE WILLIAMS II: Cover

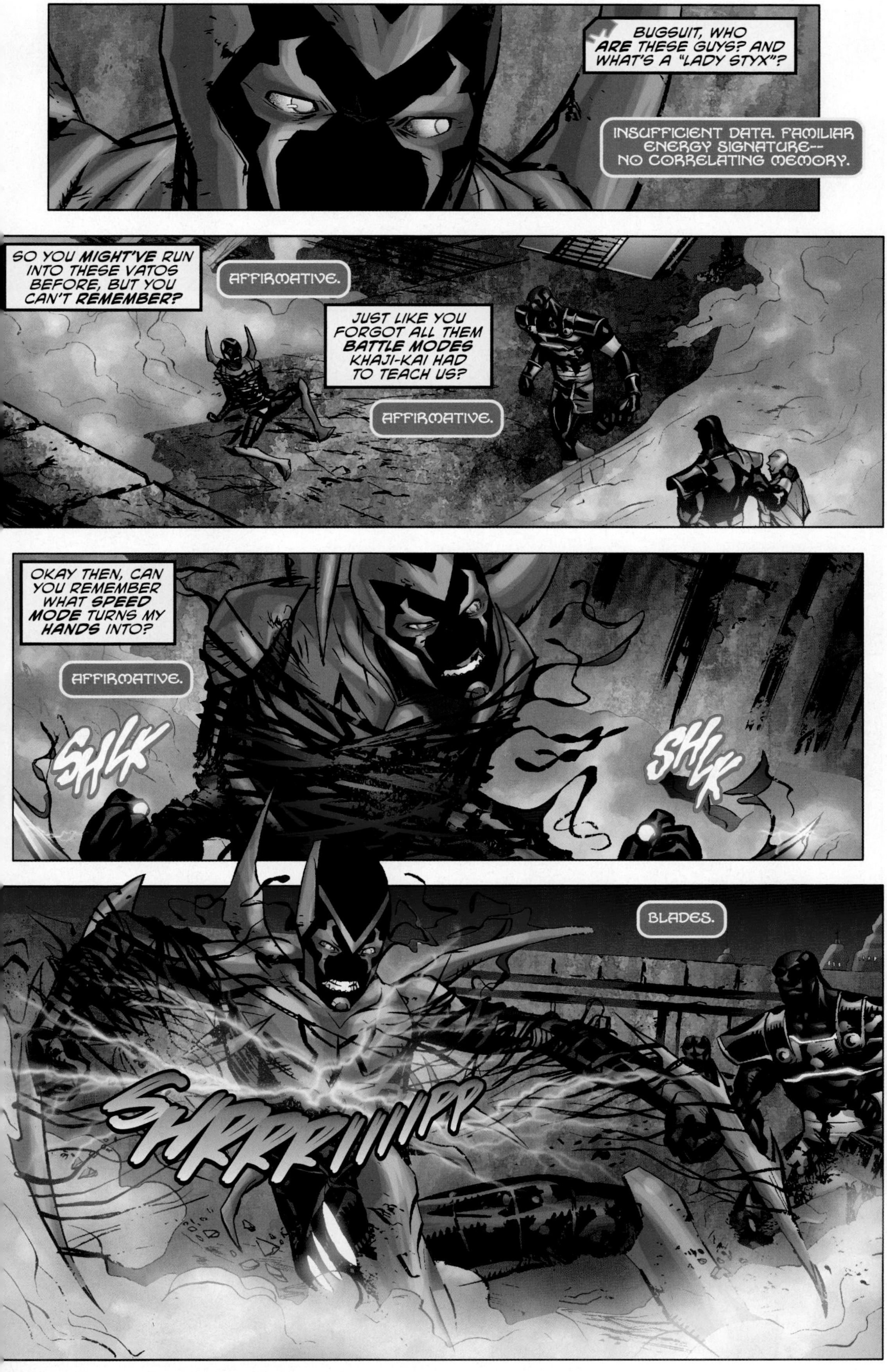
BUGSUIT, WHO ARE THESE GUYS? AND WHAT'S A "LADY STYX"?
INSUFFICIENT DATA. FAMILIAR ENERGY SIGNATURE-- NO CORRELATING MEMORY.
SO YOU MIGHT'VE RUN INTO THESE VATOS BEFORE, BUT YOU CAN'T REMEMBER?
AFFIRMATIVE.
JUST LIKE YOU FORGOT ALL THEM BATTLE MODES KHAJI-KAI HAD TO TEACH US?
AFFIRMATIVE.
OKAY THEN, CAN YOU REMEMBER WHAT SPEED MODE TURNS MY HANDS INTO?
AFFIRMATIVE.
SHLK
SHLK
BLADES.
SHRRRIIIIIPP

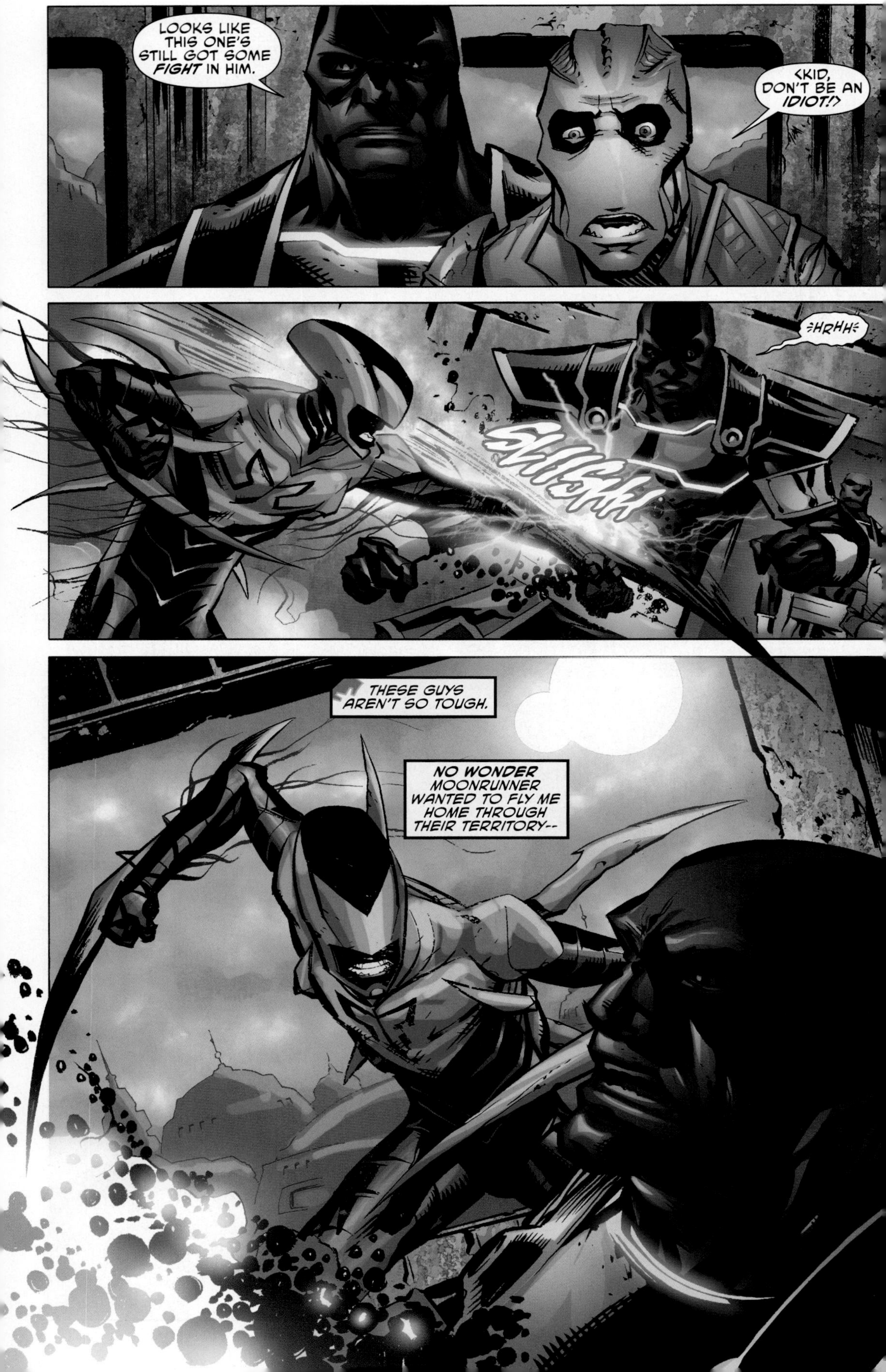
LOOKS LIKE THIS ONE'S STILL GOT SOME *FIGHT* IN HIM.
<KID, DON'T BE AN *IDIOT!*>
HRHH
SWISH
THESE GUYS AREN'T SO TOUGH.
NO WONDER MOONRUNNER WANTED TO FLY ME HOME THROUGH THEIR TERRITORY--

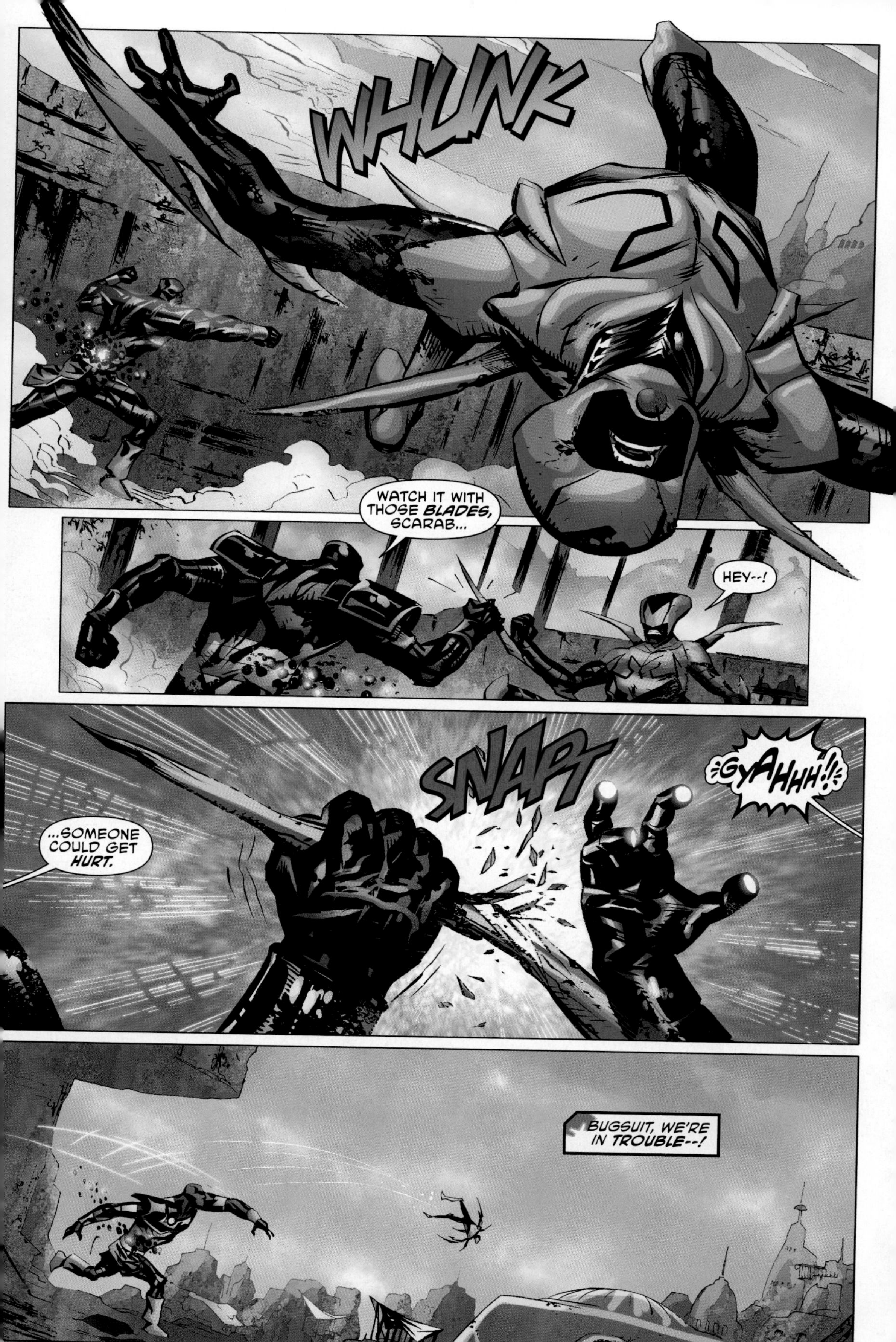
WHUNK
WATCH IT WITH THOSE BLADES, SCARAB...
HEY--!
...SOMEONE COULD GET HURT.
SNAP!
GYAHHH!!
BUGSUIT, WE'RE IN TROUBLE--!

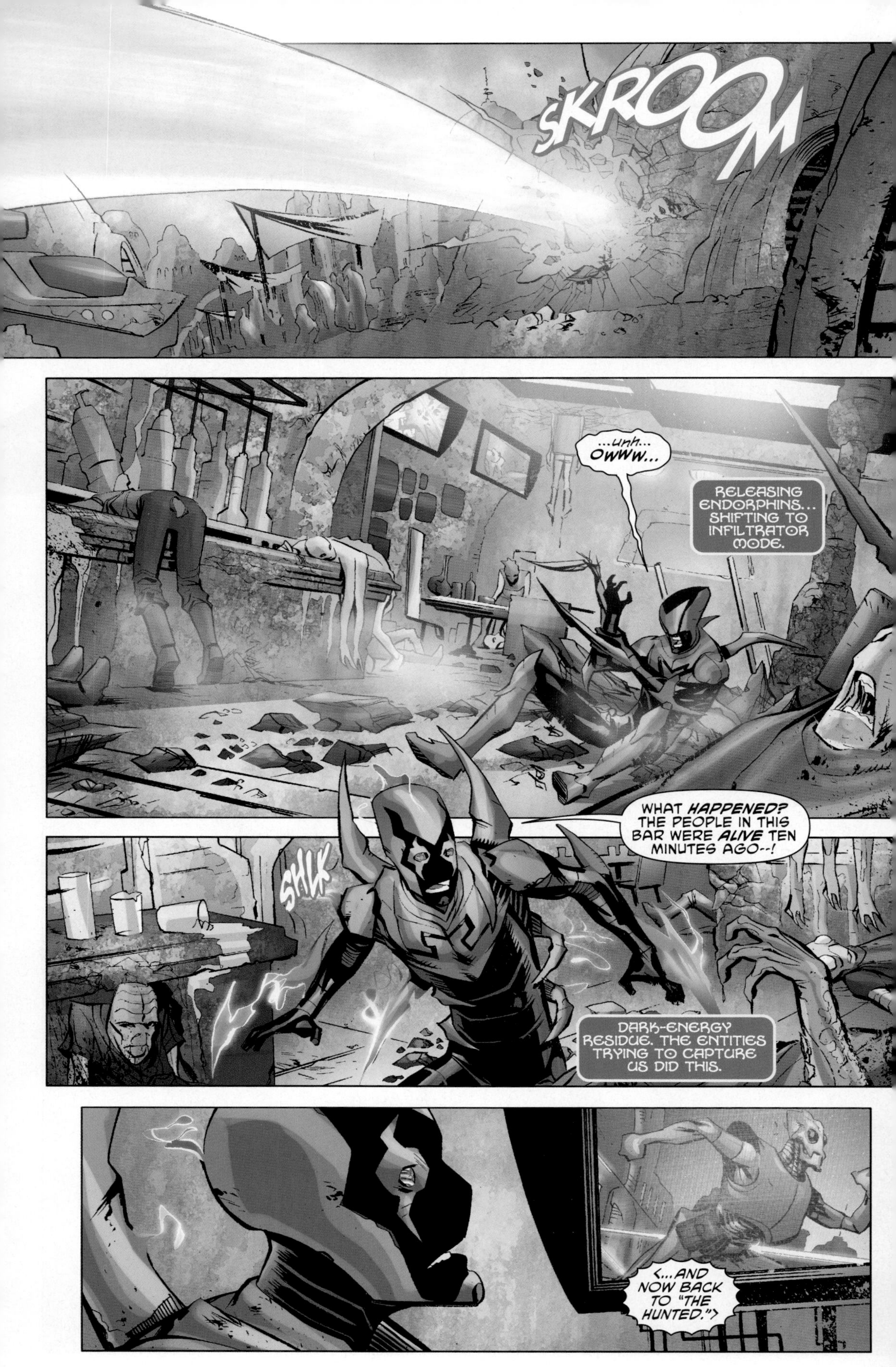
SKROOM
...unh... OWWW...
RELEASING ENDORPHINS... SHIFTING TO INFILTRATOR MODE.
WHAT HAPPENED? THE PEOPLE IN THIS BAR WERE ALIVE TEN MINUTES AGO--!
SHLK
DARK-ENERGY RESIDUE. THE ENTITIES TRYING TO CAPTURE US DID THIS.
<...AND NOW BACK TO "THE HUNTED.">

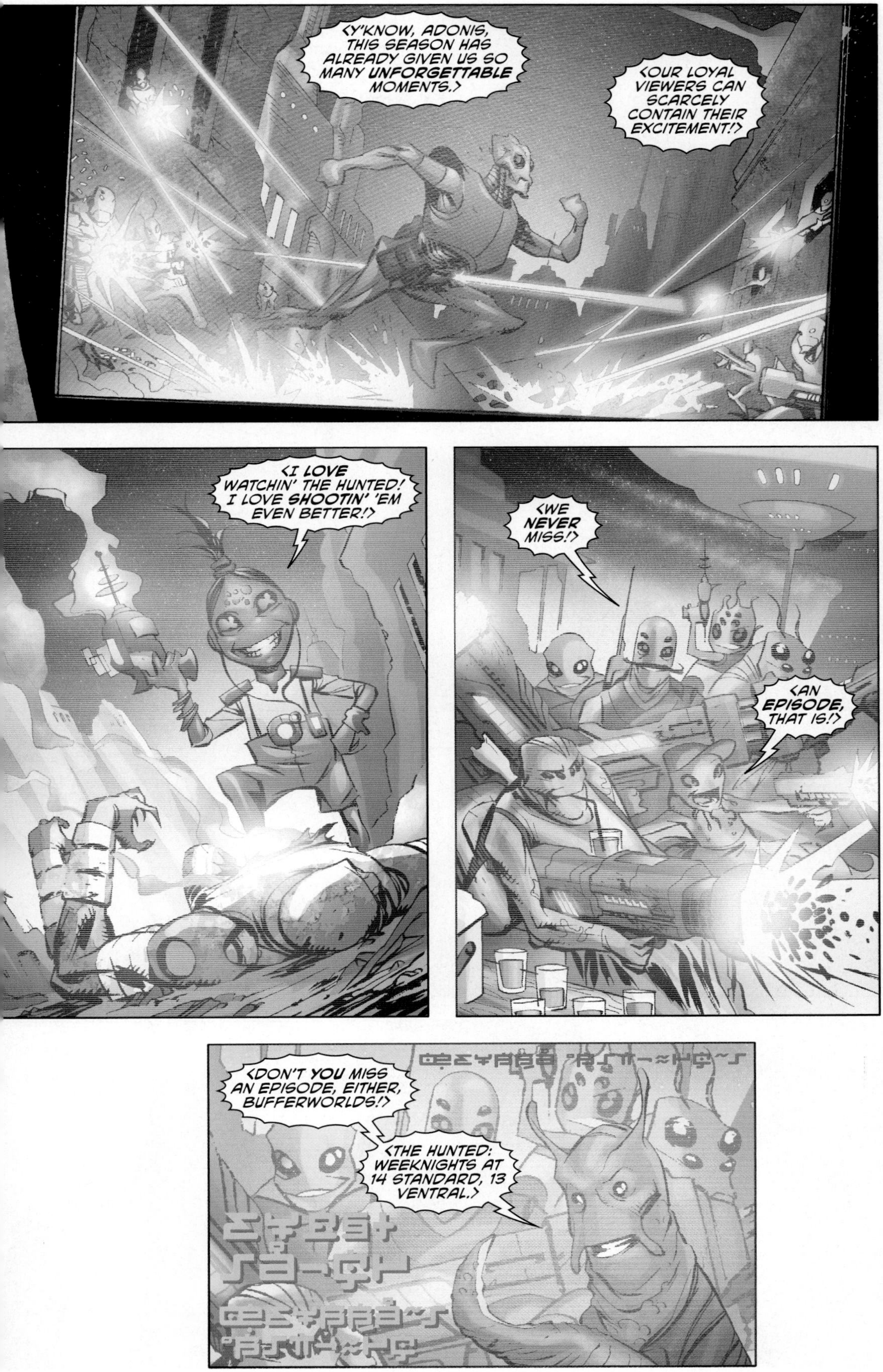
<Y'KNOW, ADONIS, THIS SEASON HAS ALREADY GIVEN US SO MANY **UNFORGETTABLE** MOMENTS.>
<OUR LOYAL VIEWERS CAN SCARCELY CONTAIN THEIR EXCITEMENT!>
<I **LOVE** WATCHIN' THE HUNTED! I LOVE **SHOOTIN'** 'EM EVEN BETTER!>
<WE **NEVER** MISS!>
<AN **EPISODE**, THAT IS!>
<DON'T **YOU** MISS AN EPISODE, EITHER, BUFFERWORLDS!>
<THE HUNTED: WEEKNIGHTS AT 14 STANDARD, 13 VENTRAL.>

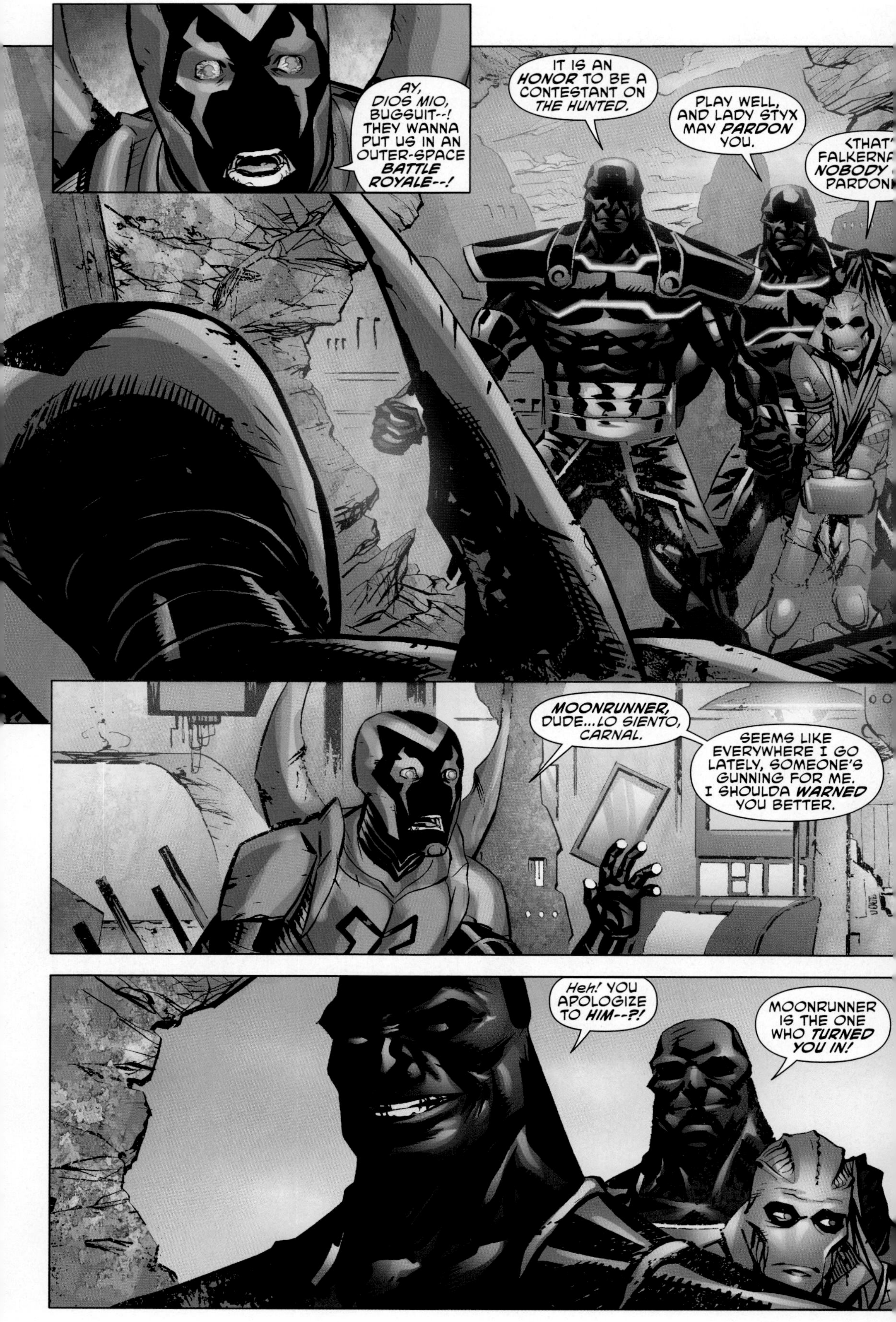
AY, DIOS MIO, BUGSUIT--! THEY WANNA PUT US IN AN OUTER-SPACE BATTLE ROYALE--!
IT IS AN HONOR TO BE A CONTESTANT ON THE HUNTED.
PLAY WELL, AND LADY STYX MAY PARDON YOU.
<THAT' FALKERNA NOBODY PARDON
MOONRUNNER, DUDE...LO SIENTO, CARNAL.
SEEMS LIKE EVERYWHERE I GO LATELY, SOMEONE'S GUNNING FOR ME. I SHOULDA WARNED YOU BETTER.
Heh! YOU APOLOGIZE TO HIM--?!
MOONRUNNER IS THE ONE WHO TURNED YOU IN!

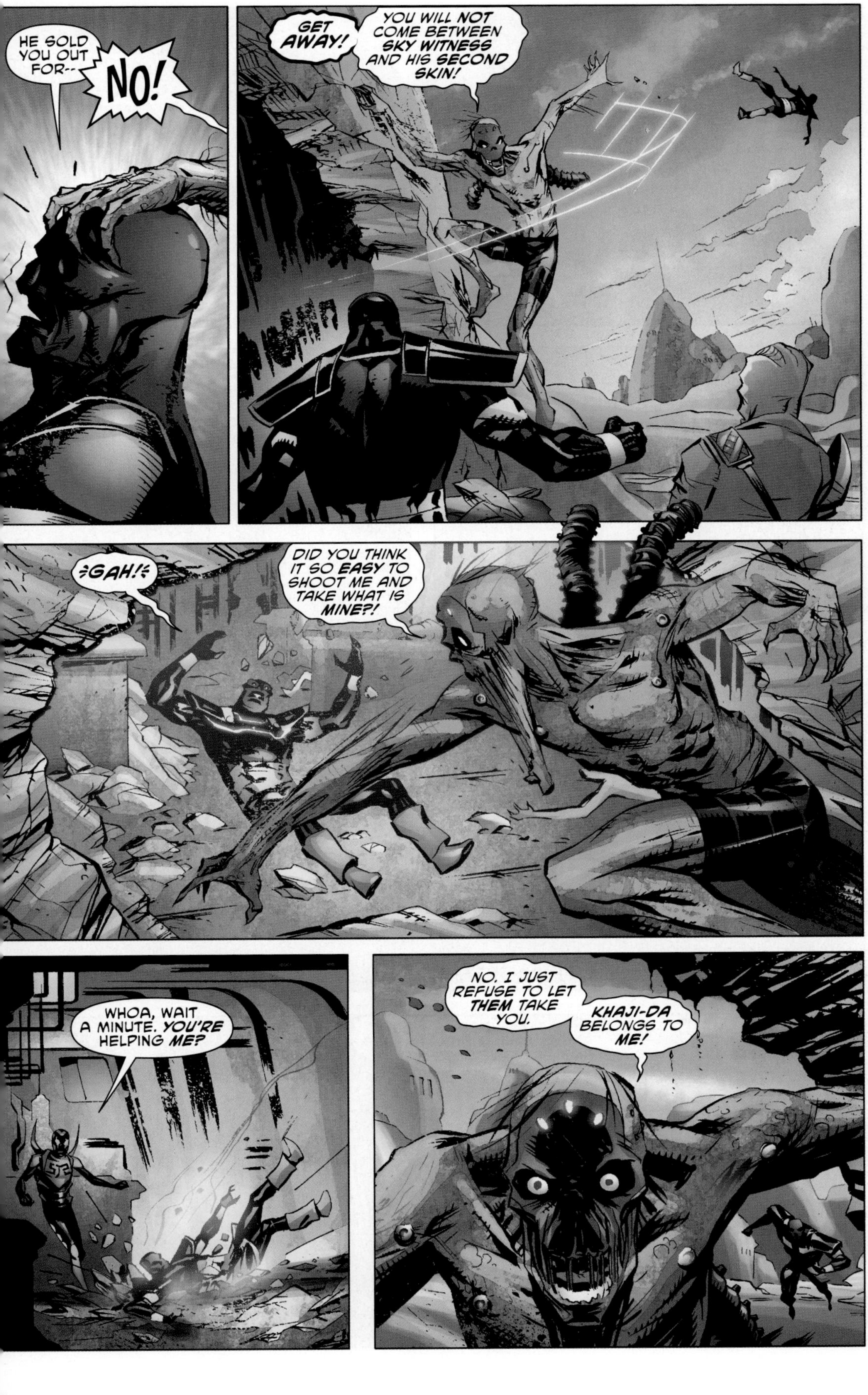
HE SOLD YOU OUT FOR--
NO!
GET AWAY!
YOU WILL NOT COME BETWEEN SKY WITNESS AND HIS SECOND SKIN!
GAH!
DID YOU THINK IT SO EASY TO SHOOT ME AND TAKE WHAT IS MINE?!
WHOA, WAIT A MINUTE. YOU'RE HELPING ME?
NO. I JUST REFUSE TO LET THEM TAKE YOU.
KHAJI-DA BELONGS TO ME!

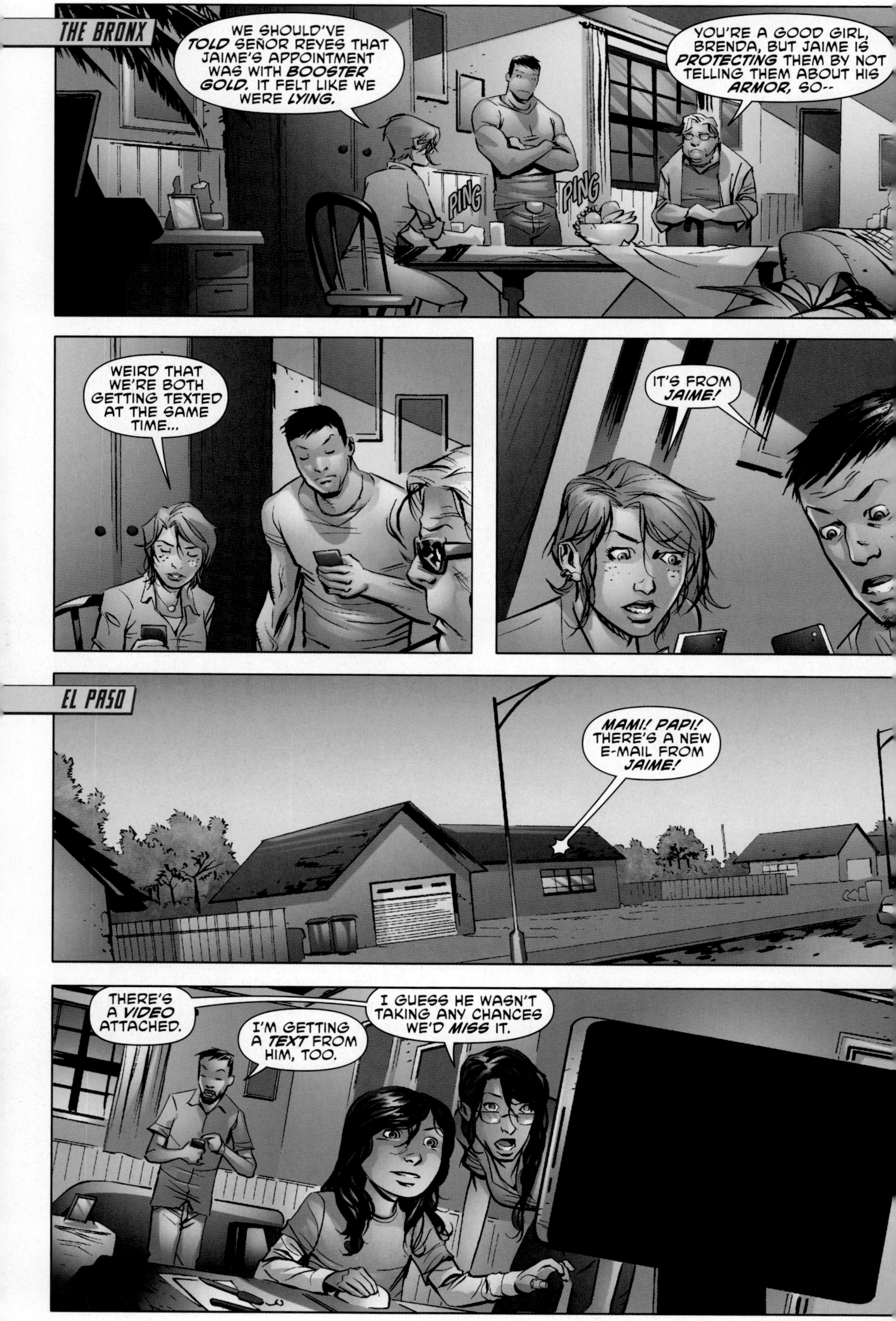
THE BRONX
WE SHOULD'VE TOLD SEÑOR REYES THAT JAIME'S APPOINTMENT WAS WITH BOOSTER GOLD. IT FELT LIKE WE WERE LYING.
YOU'RE A GOOD GIRL, BRENDA, BUT JAIME IS PROTECTING THEM BY NOT TELLING THEM ABOUT HIS ARMOR, SO--
PING
PING
WEIRD THAT WE'RE BOTH GETTING TEXTED AT THE SAME TIME...
IT'S FROM JAIME!
EL PASO
MAMI! PAPI! THERE'S A NEW E-MAIL FROM JAIME!
THERE'S A VIDEO ATTACHED.
I'M GETTING A TEXT FROM HIM, TOO.
I GUESS HE WASN'T TAKING ANY CHANCES WE'D MISS IT.

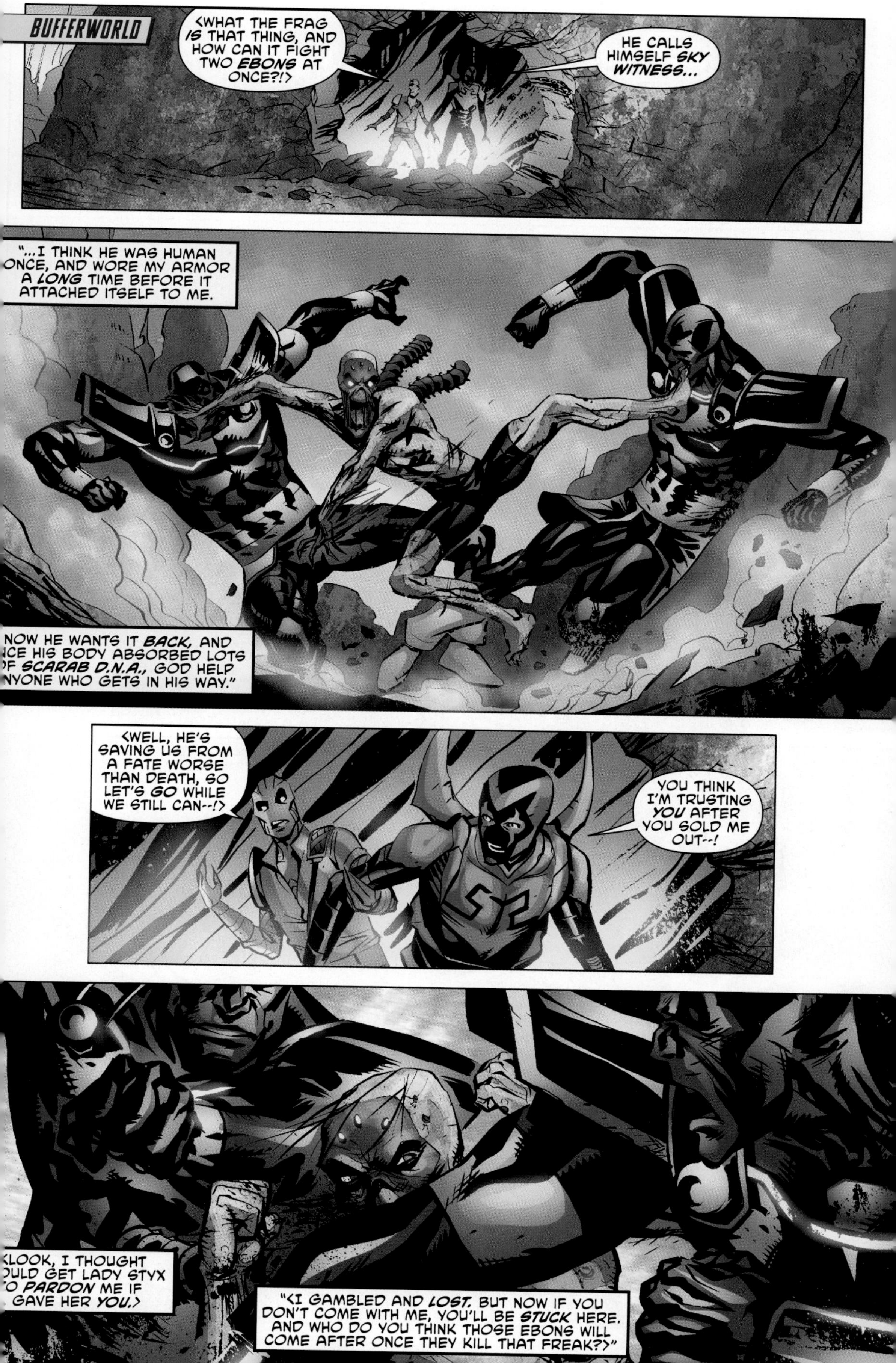

BUFFERWORLD
<WHAT THE FRAG IS THAT THING, AND HOW CAN IT FIGHT TWO EBONS AT ONCE?!>
HE CALLS HIMSELF SKY WITNESS...
"...I THINK HE WAS HUMAN ONCE, AND WORE MY ARMOR A LONG TIME BEFORE IT ATTACHED ITSELF TO ME.
NOW HE WANTS IT BACK, AND CE HIS BODY ABSORBED LOTS F SCARAB D.N.A., GOD HELP NYONE WHO GETS IN HIS WAY."
<WELL, HE'S SAVING US FROM A FATE WORSE THAN DEATH, SO LET'S GO WHILE WE STILL CAN--!>
YOU THINK I'M TRUSTING YOU AFTER YOU SOLD ME OUT--!
<LOOK, I THOUGHT OULD GET LADY STYX O PARDON ME IF GAVE HER YOU.>
"<I GAMBLED AND LOST, BUT NOW IF YOU DON'T COME WITH ME, YOU'LL BE STUCK HERE. AND WHO DO YOU THINK THOSE EBONS WILL COME AFTER ONCE THEY KILL THAT FREAK?>"

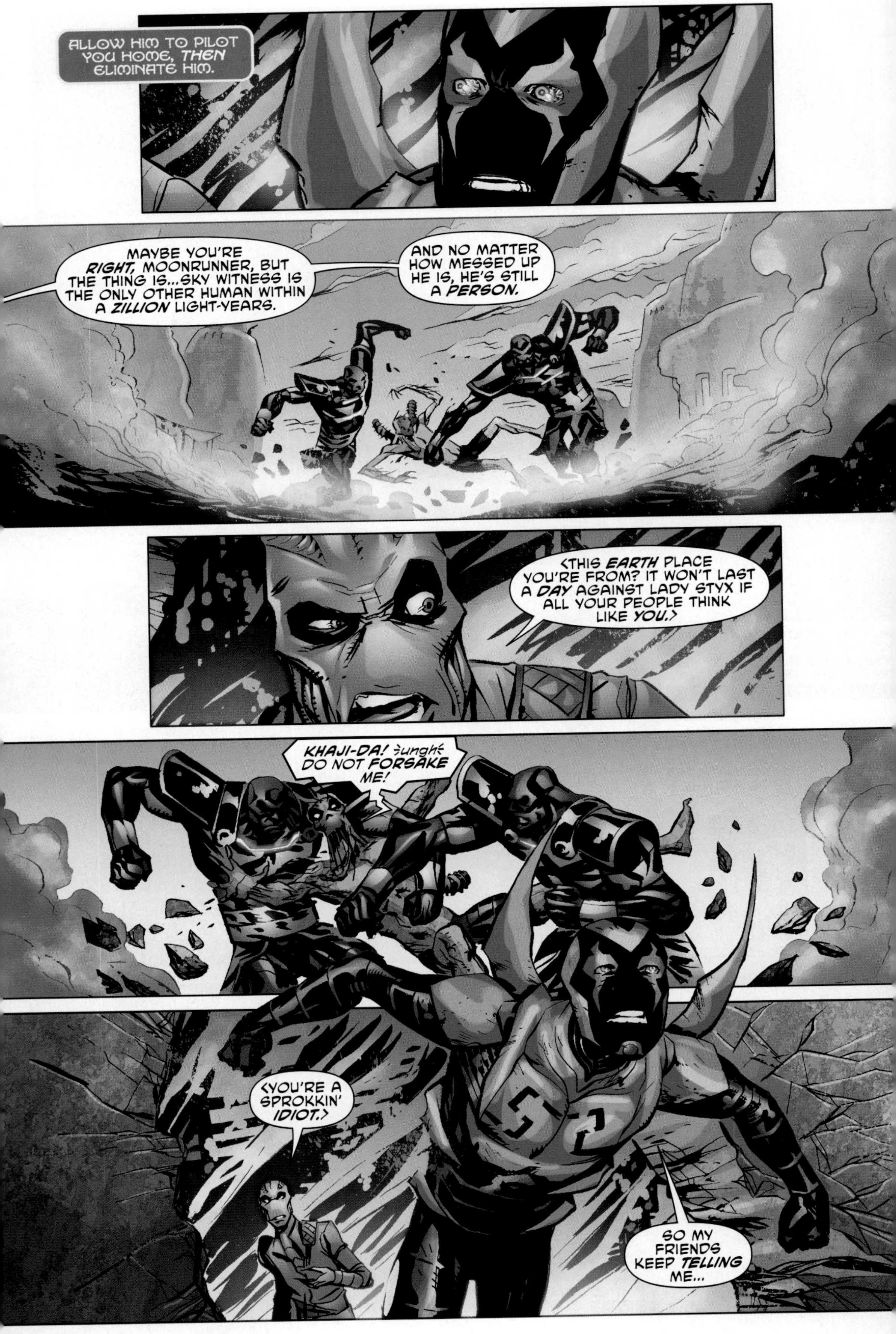
ALLOW HIM TO PILOT YOU HOME, THEN ELIMINATE HIM.
MAYBE YOU'RE RIGHT, MOONRUNNER, BUT THE THING IS...SKY WITNESS IS THE ONLY OTHER HUMAN WITHIN A ZILLION LIGHT-YEARS.
AND NO MATTER HOW MESSED UP HE IS, HE'S STILL A PERSON.
<THIS EARTH PLACE YOU'RE FROM? IT WON'T LAST A DAY AGAINST LADY STYX IF ALL YOUR PEOPLE THINK LIKE YOU.>
KHAJI-DA! ⋛ungh⋚ DO NOT FORSAKE ME!
<YOU'RE A SPROKKIN' IDIOT.>
SO MY FRIENDS KEEP TELLING ME...

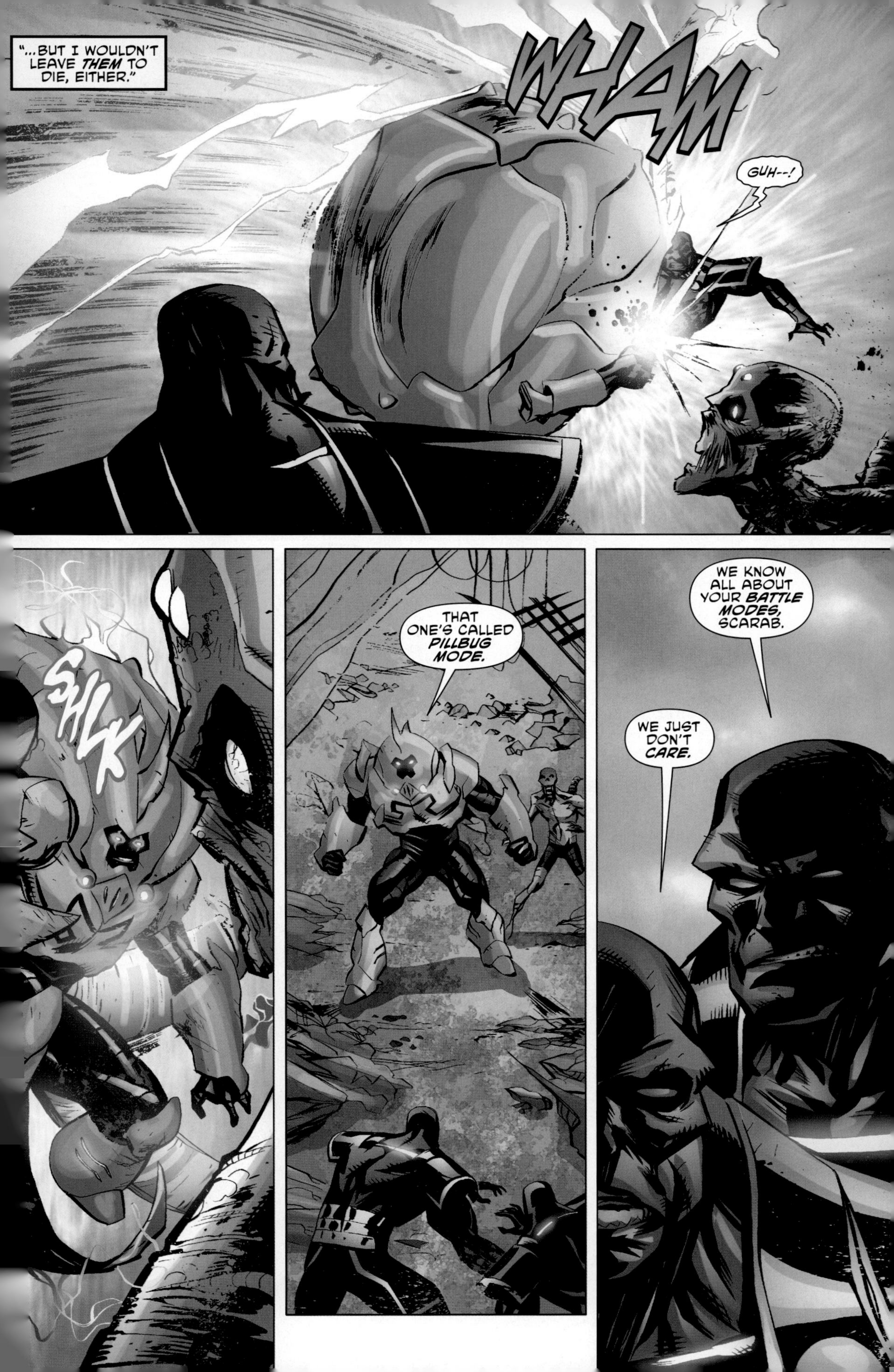
"...BUT I WOULDN'T LEAVE *THEM* TO DIE, EITHER."
WHAM
GUH--!
SHLK
THAT ONE'S CALLED *PILLBUG MODE.*
WE KNOW ALL ABOUT YOUR *BATTLE MODES,* SCARAB.
WE JUST DON'T *CARE.*

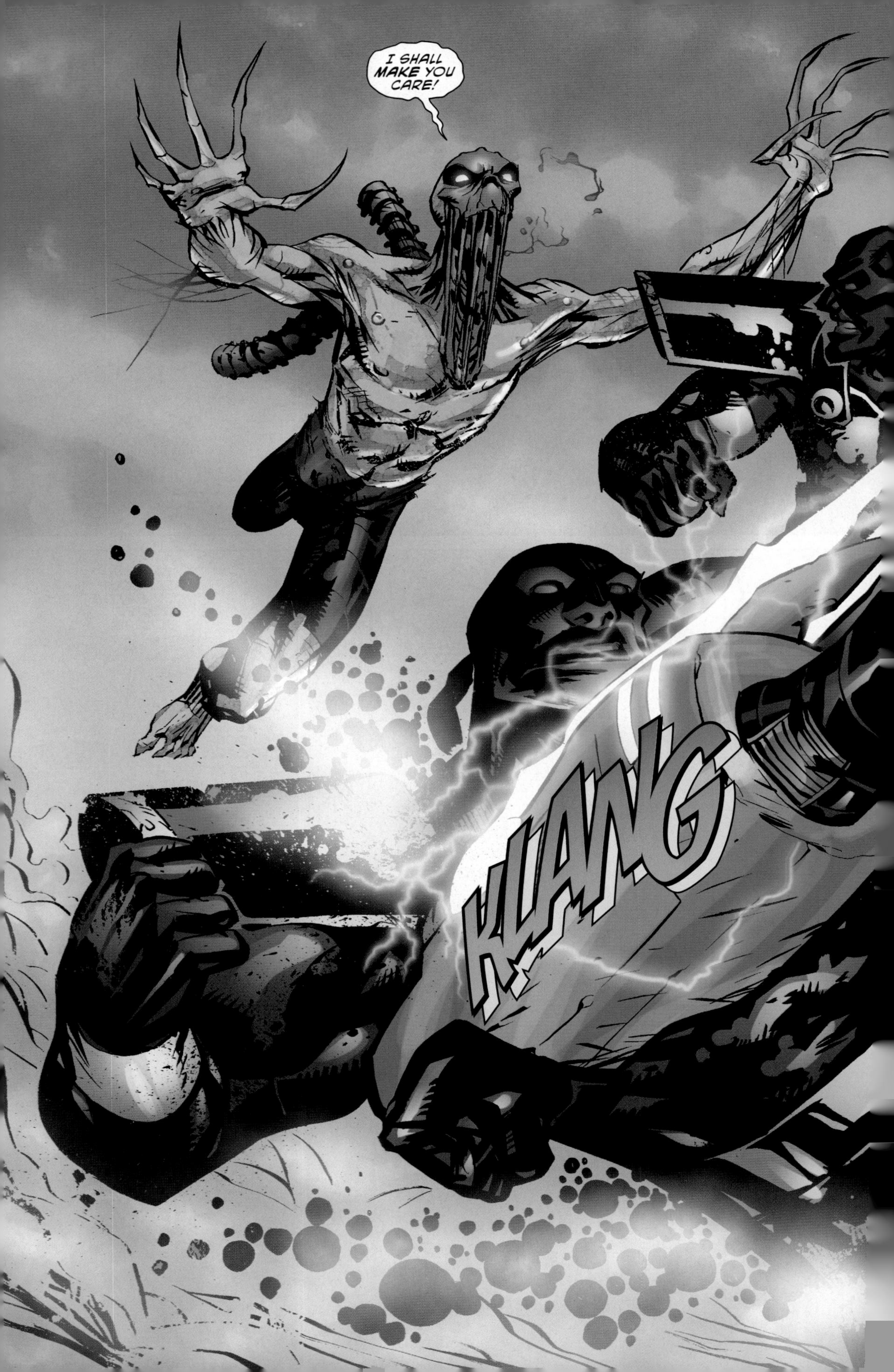
I SHALL MAKE YOU CARE!
KLANG

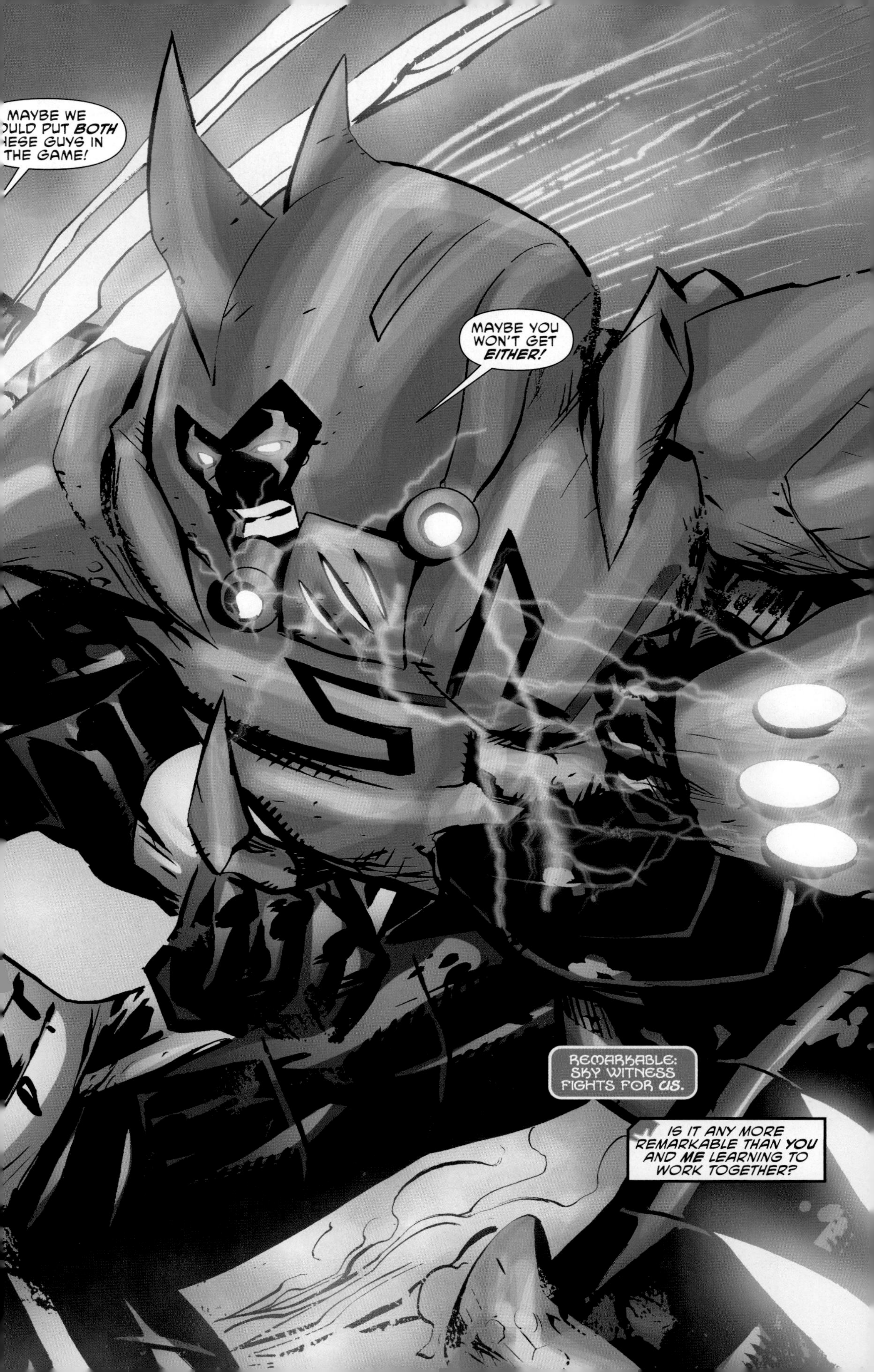

MAYBE WE OULD PUT BOTH HESE GUYS IN THE GAME!
MAYBE YOU WON'T GET EITHER!
REMARKABLE: SKY WITNESS FIGHTS FOR US.
IS IT ANY MORE REMARKABLE THAN YOU AND ME LEARNING TO WORK TOGETHER?

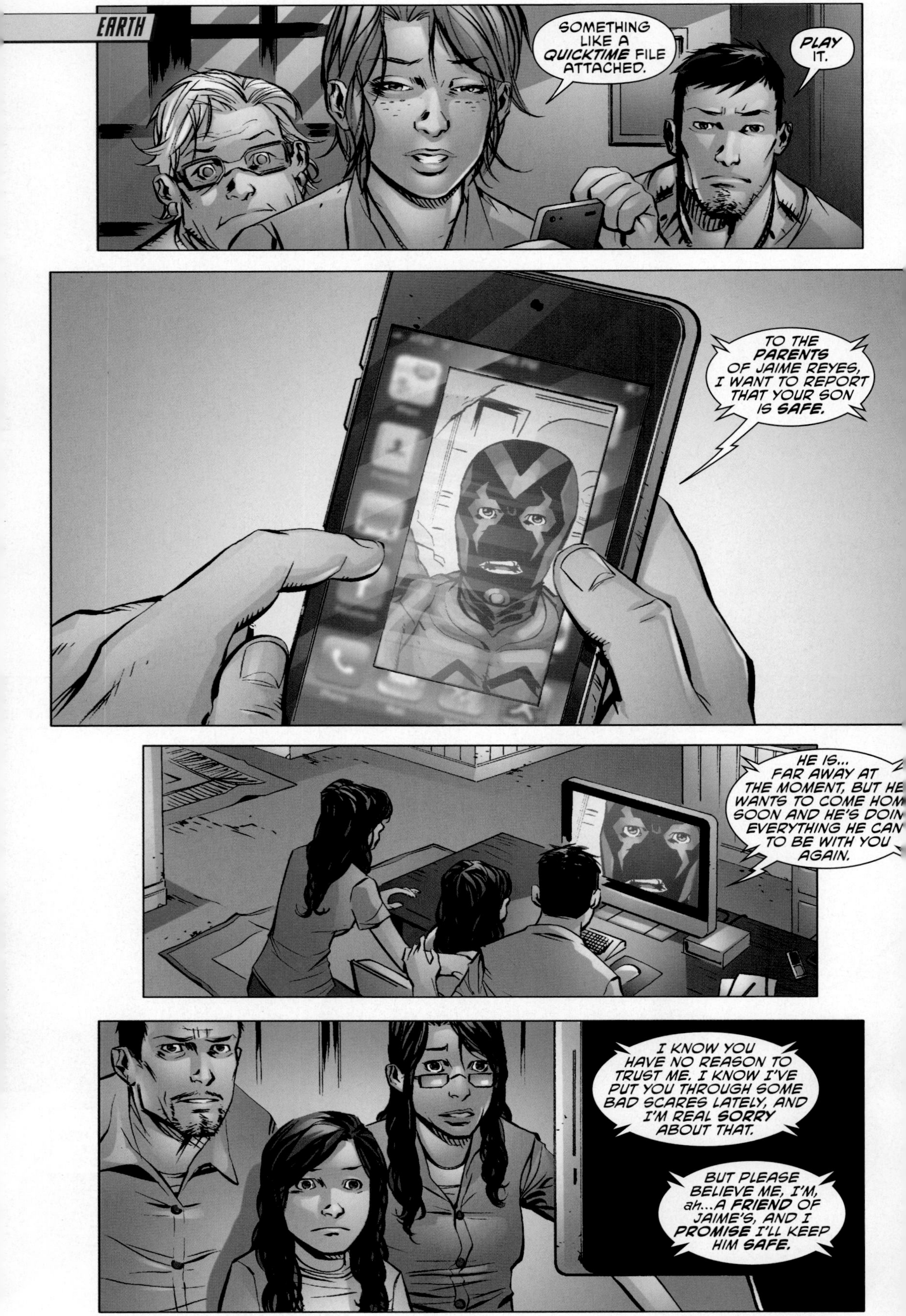
EARTH
SOMETHING LIKE A QUICKTIME FILE ATTACHED.
PLAY IT.
TO THE PARENTS OF JAIME REYES, I WANT TO REPORT THAT YOUR SON IS SAFE.
HE IS... FAR AWAY AT THE MOMENT, BUT HE WANTS TO COME HOM SOON AND HE'S DOIN EVERYTHING HE CAN TO BE WITH YOU AGAIN.
I KNOW YOU HAVE NO REASON TO TRUST ME. I KNOW I'VE PUT YOU THROUGH SOME BAD SCARES LATELY, AND I'M REAL SORRY ABOUT THAT.
BUT PLEASE BELIEVE ME, I'M, ah...A FRIEND OF JAIME'S, AND I PROMISE I'LL KEEP HIM SAFE.

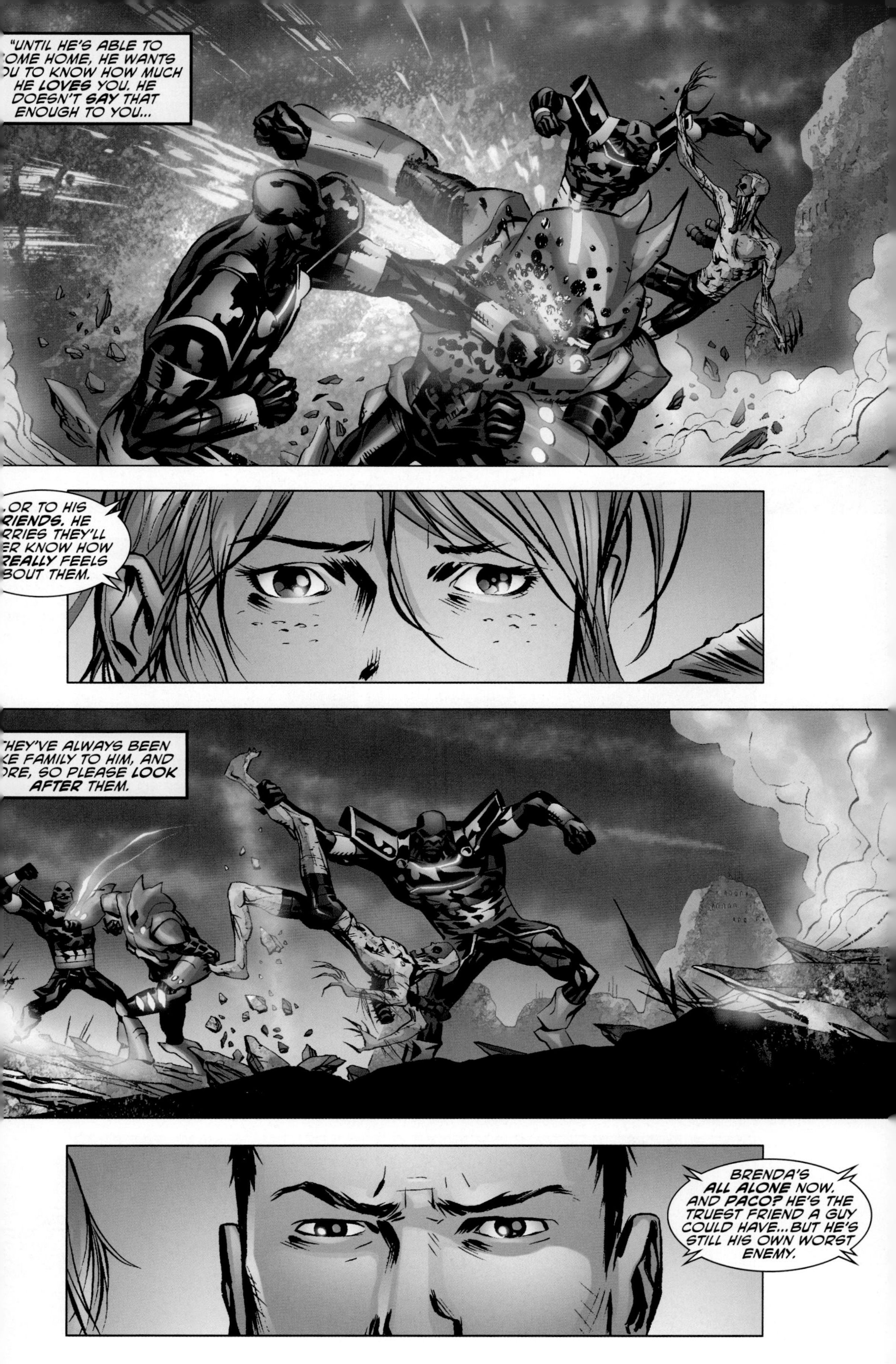
"UNTIL HE'S ABLE TO OME HOME, HE WANTS OU TO KNOW HOW MUCH HE LOVES YOU. HE DOESN'T SAY THAT ENOUGH TO YOU...
.OR TO HIS RIENDS. HE RRIES THEY'LL ER KNOW HOW REALLY FEELS BOUT THEM.
HEY'VE ALWAYS BEEN KE FAMILY TO HIM, AND ORE, SO PLEASE LOOK AFTER THEM.
BRENDA'S ALL ALONE NOW. AND PACO? HE'S THE TRUEST FRIEND A GUY COULD HAVE...BUT HE'S STILL HIS OWN WORST ENEMY.

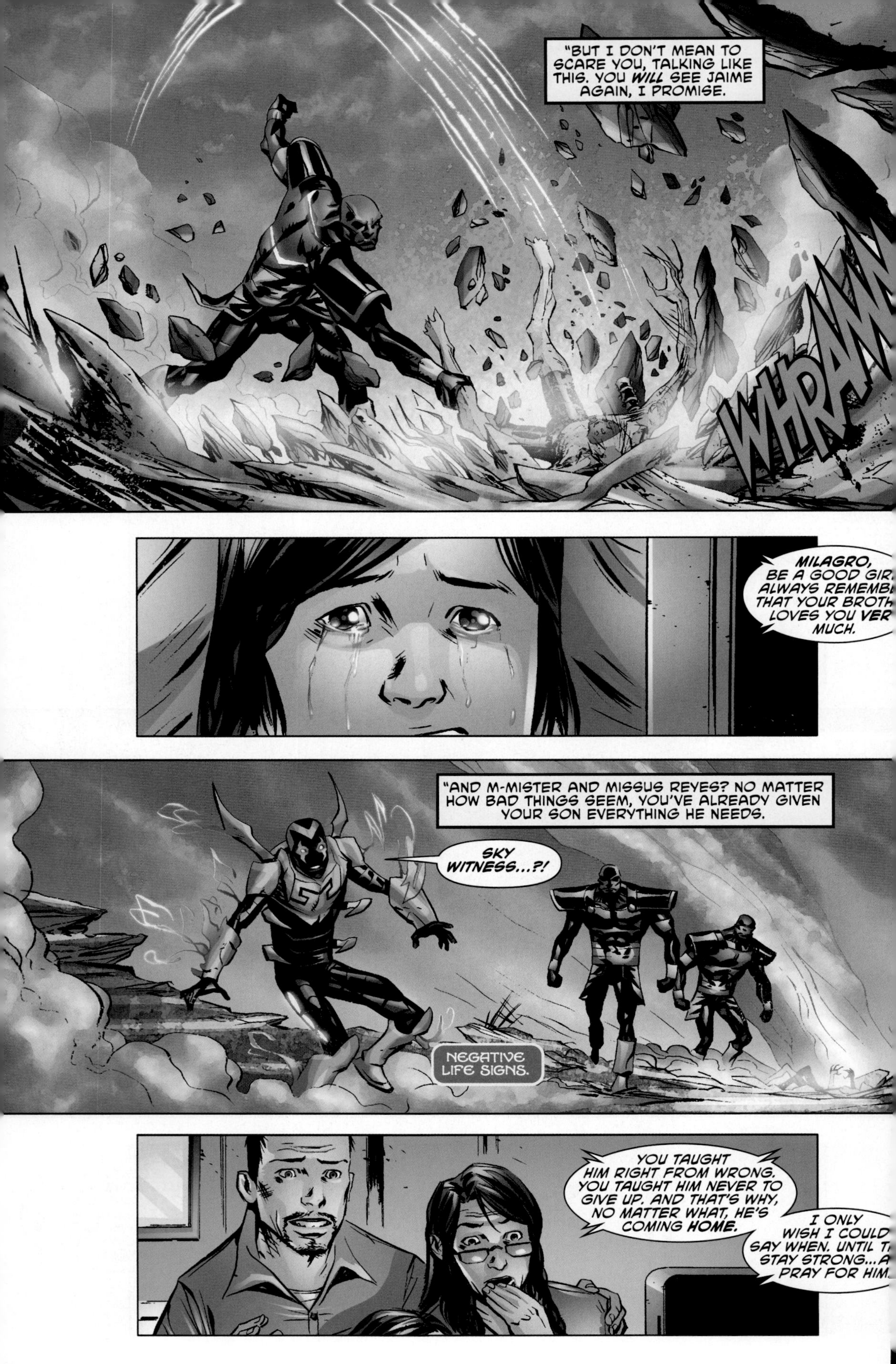
"BUT I DON'T MEAN TO SCARE YOU, TALKING LIKE THIS. YOU *WILL* SEE JAIME AGAIN, I PROMISE.
WHRAM
MILAGRO, BE A GOOD GIR ALWAYS REMEMB THAT YOUR BROTH LOVES YOU *VER* MUCH.
"AND M-MISTER AND MISSUS REYES? NO MATTER HOW BAD THINGS SEEM, YOU'VE ALREADY GIVEN YOUR SON EVERYTHING HE NEEDS.
SKY WITNESS...?!
NEGATIVE LIFE SIGNS.
YOU TAUGHT HIM RIGHT FROM WRONG. YOU TAUGHT HIM NEVER TO GIVE UP. AND THAT'S WHY, NO MATTER WHAT, HE'S COMING **HOME.**
I ONLY WISH I COULD SAY WHEN. UNTIL T STAY STRONG...A PRAY FOR HIM.

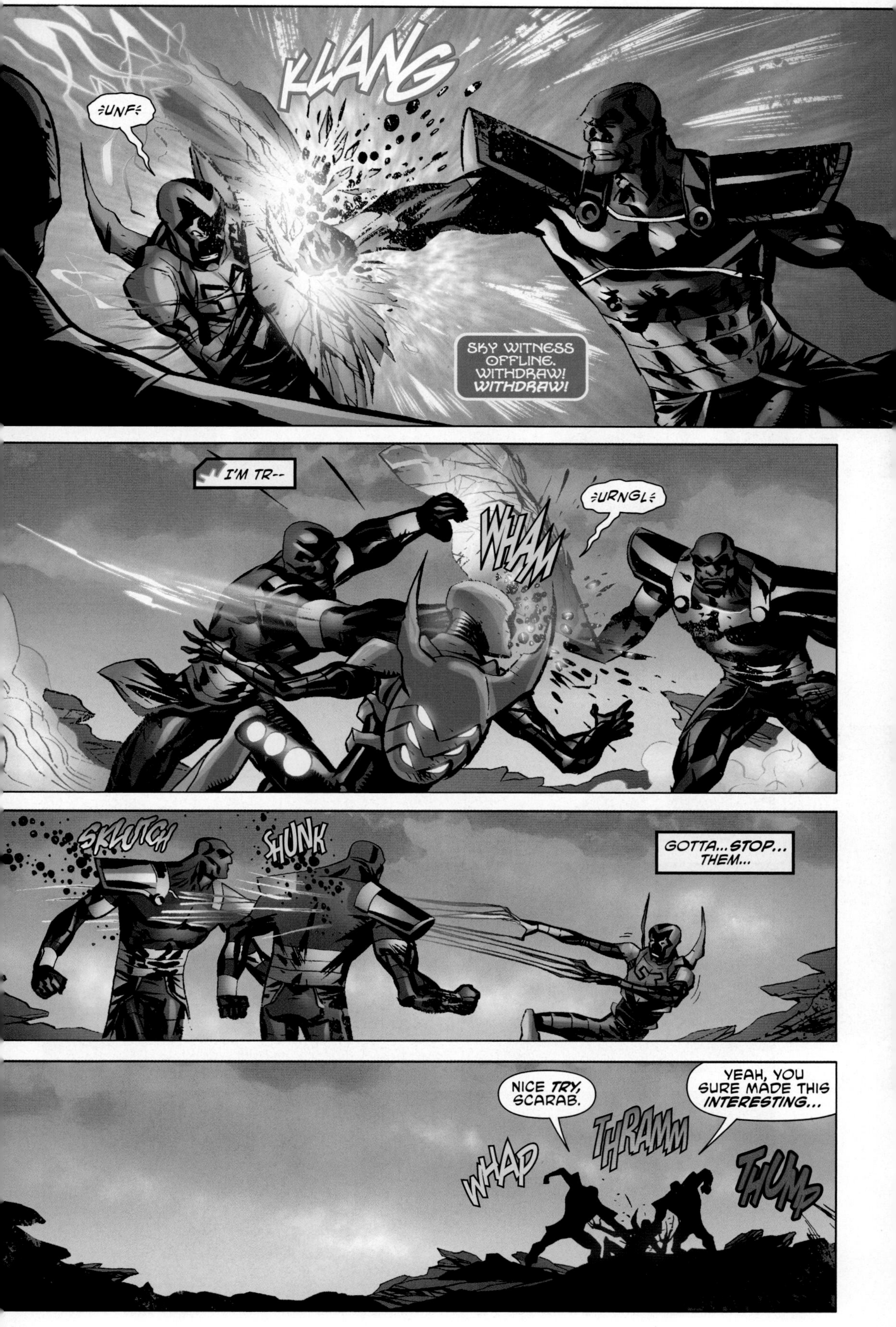
KLANG
UNF
SKY WITNESS OFFLINE. WITHDRAW! WITHDRAW!
I'M TR--
URNGL
WHAM
SKLUTCH
SHUNK
GOTTA...STOP... THEM...
NICE TRY, SCARAB.
YEAH, YOU SURE MADE THIS INTERESTING...
WHAP
THRAMM
THUMP

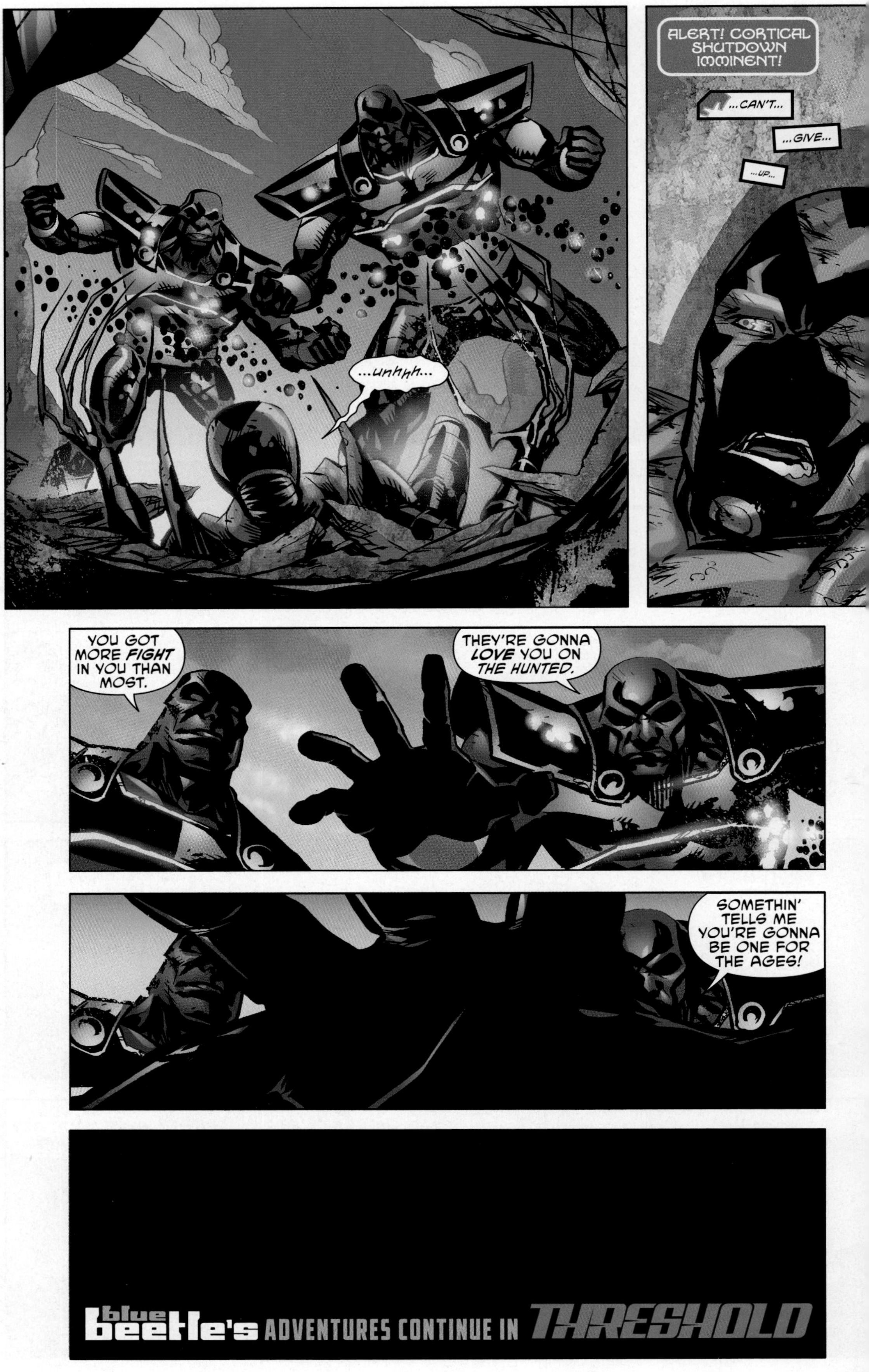
...unhhh...
ALERT! CORTICAL SHUTDOWN IMMINENT!
...CAN'T...
...GIVE...
...UP...
YOU GOT MORE FIGHT IN YOU THAN MOST.
THEY'RE GONNA LOVE YOU ON THE HUNTED.
SOMETHIN' TELLS ME YOU'RE GONNA BE ONE FOR THE AGES!
blue beetle's ADVENTURES CONTINUE IN THRESHOLD

MICS™

"Clear storytelling at its best. It's an intriguing concept and easy to grasp."
—NEW YORK TIMES

"Azzarello is rebuilding the mythology of Wonder Woman."
–MAXIM

START AT THE BEGINNING!

WONDER WOMAN VOLUME 1: BLOOD

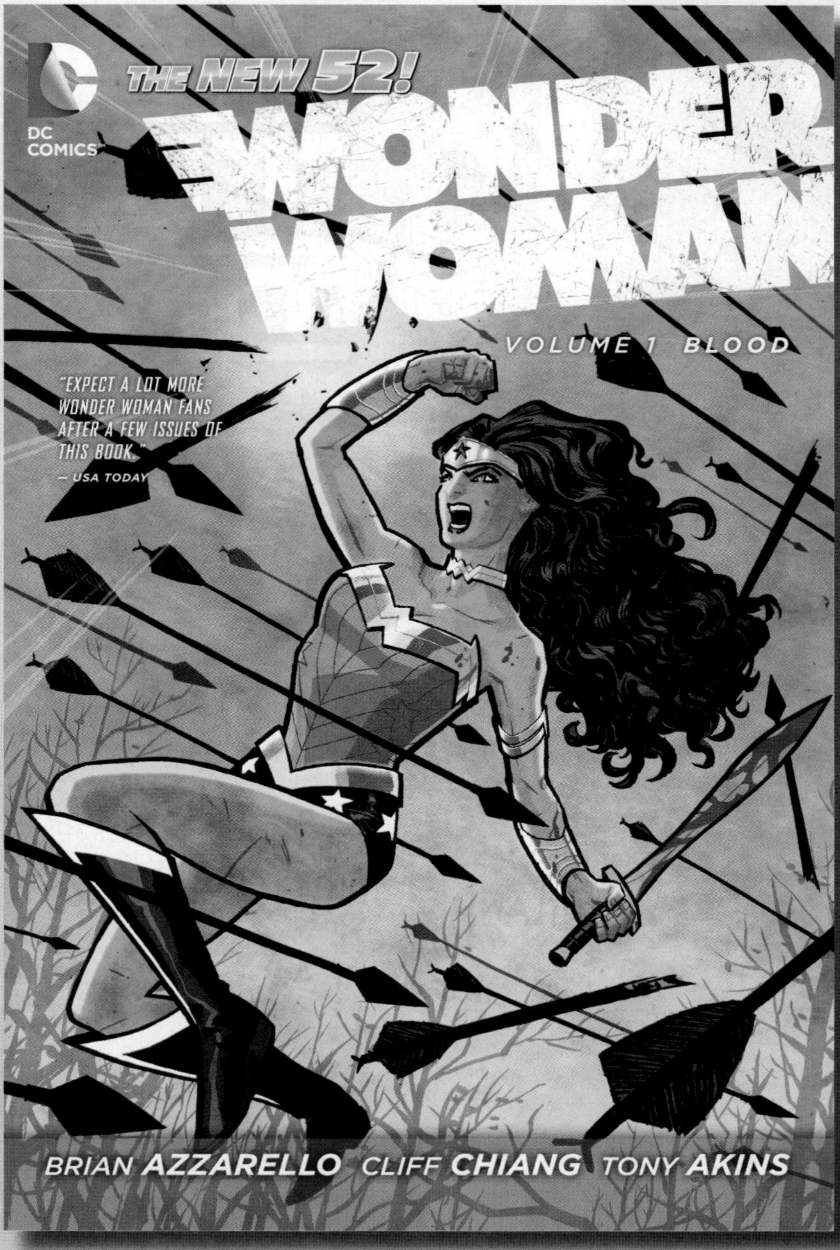
DC COMICS
THE NEW 52!
WONDER WOMAN
VOLUME 1 BLOOD
"EXPECT A LOT MORE WONDER WOMAN FANS AFTER A FEW ISSUES OF THIS BOOK."
— USA TODAY
BRIAN AZZARELLO CLIFF CHIANG TONY AKINS

MR. TERRIFIC VOLUME 1: MIND GAMES

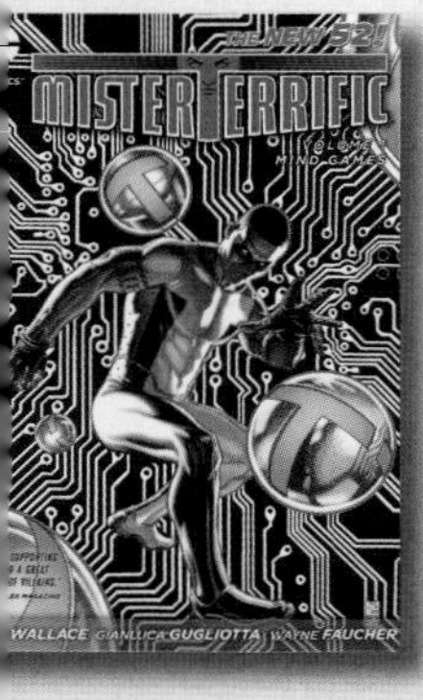
THE NEW 52!
MISTER TERRIFIC
MIND GAMES

BLUE BEETLE VOLUME 1: METAMORPHOSIS

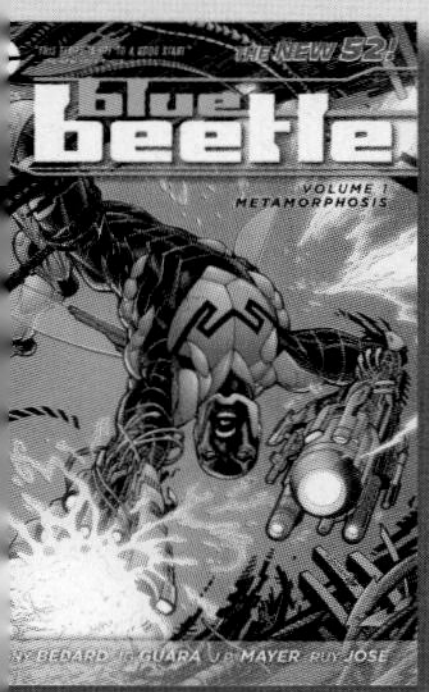
THE NEW 52!
METAMORPHOSIS

[TH]E FURY OF FIRESTORM: THE NUCLEAR MEN VOLUME 1: GOD PARTICLE

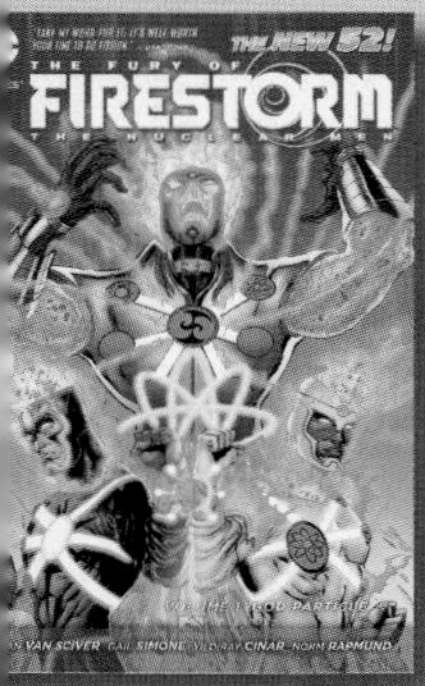
THE NEW 52!
FIRESTORM

DC COMICS™

"Drips with energy."
—IGN

"Grade A."
—USA TODAY

EGINNING!

TANS 1: IT'S O FIGHT

LEGION OF SUPER-HEROES VOLUME 1: HOSTILE WORLD

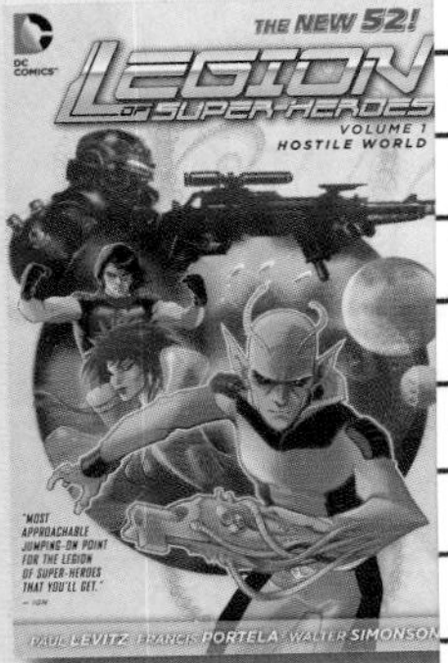
THE NEW 52!
LEGION OF SUPER-HEROES
VOLUME 1
HOSTILE WORLD
"MOST APPROACHABLE JUMPING-ON POINT FOR THE LEGION OF SUPER-HEROES THAT YOU'LL GET."
PAUL LEVITZ FRANCIS PORTELA WALTER SIMONSON

LEGION LOST VOLUME 1: RUN FROM TOMORROW

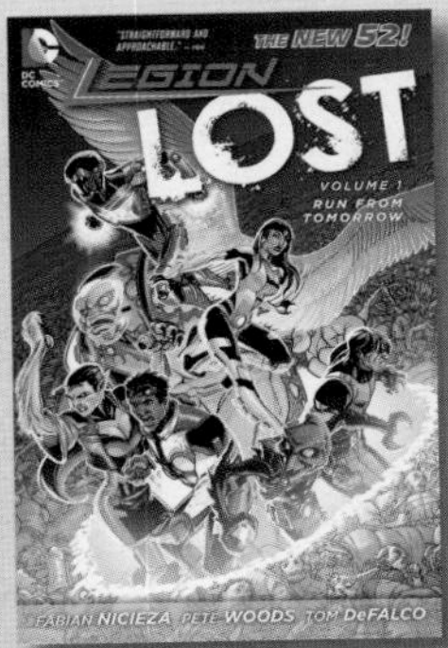
THE NEW 52!
LEGION LOST
VOLUME 1
RUN FROM TOMORROW
FABIAN NICIEZA PETE WOODS TOM DeFALCO

STATIC SHOCK VOLUME 1: SUPERCHARGED

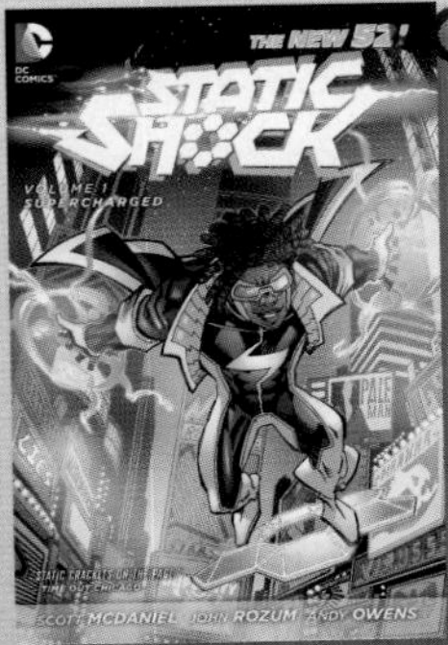
THE NEW 52!
STATIC SHOCK
VOLUME 1
SUPERCHARGED
SCOTT McDANIEL JOHN ROZUM ANDY OWENS

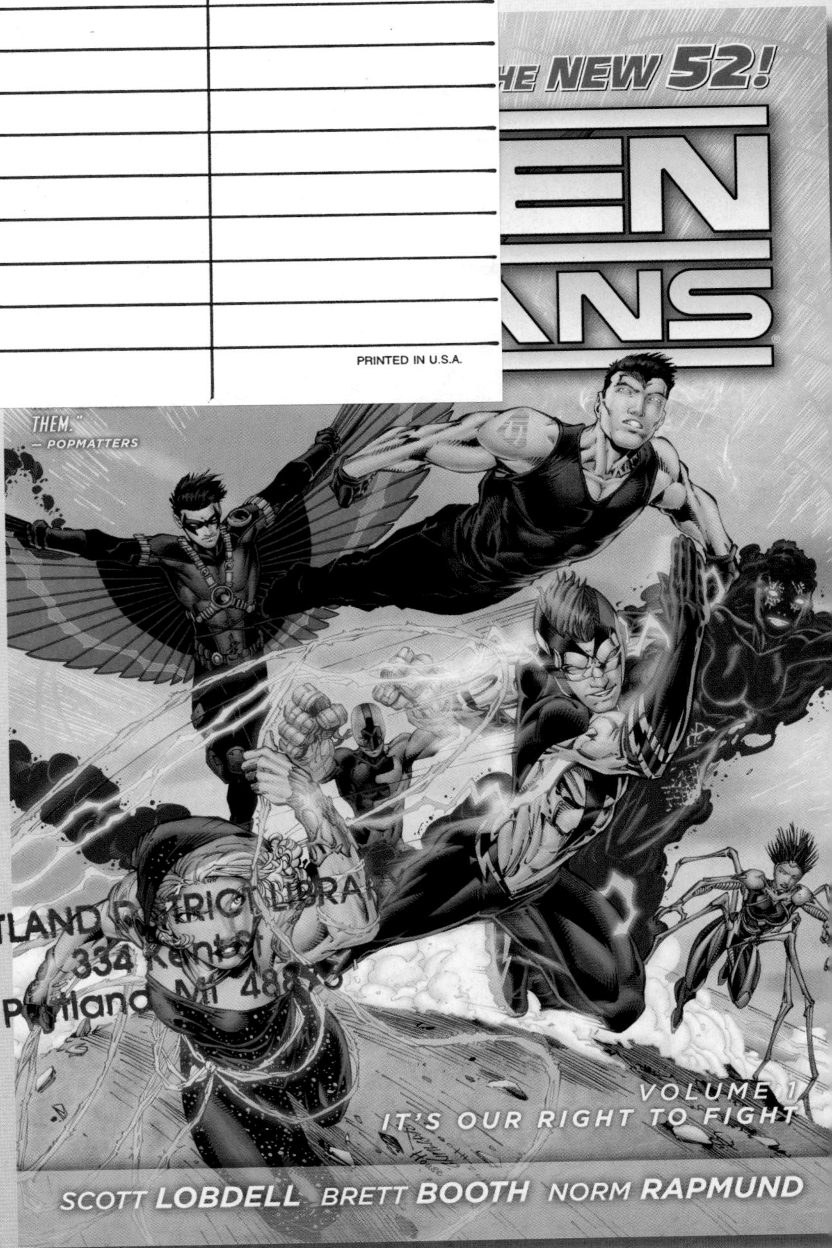
THE NEW 52!
THEM."
— POPMATTERS
VOLUME 1
IT'S OUR RIGHT TO FIGHT
SCOTT LOBDELL BRETT BOOTH NORM RAPMUND